Positive Child Guidance

SIXTH EDITION

Darla Ferris Miller

WADSWORTH
CENGAGE Learning

Australia • Brazil • Japan • Korea • Mexico • Singapore • Spain • United Kingdom • United States

WADSWORTH
CENGAGE Learning™

Positive Child Guidance, Sixth Edition
Darla Ferris Miller

Education Editor: Christopher Shortt

Developmental Editor: Shelley Murphy

Assistant Editor: Caitlin Cox

Editorial Assistant: Janice Bockelman

Media Editor: Ashley Cronin

Marketing Manager: Kara Parsons

Marketing Assistant: Andy Yap

Marketing Communications Manager:
  Martha Pfeiffer

Content Project Manager: Tanya Nigh

Creative Director: Rob Hugel

Art Director: Maria Epes

Print Buyer: Rebecca Cross

Rights Acquisitions Account Manager, Text:
  Mardell Glinski Schultz

Rights Acquisitions Account Manager, Image:
  John Hill

Production Service: Newgen

Copy Editor: Mary Ann Short

Cover Designer: Bartay Studio

Cover Image: © Al Satterwhite/
  Transtock/Corbis

Compositor: Newgen

For product information and technology assistance, contact us at
Cengage Learning Customer & Sales Support, 1-800-354-9706.

For permission to use material from this text or product,
submit all requests online at **www.cengage.com/permissions.**

Further permissions questions can be e-mailed to
permissionrequest@cengage.com.

Library of Congress Control Number: 2008942320
ISBN-13: 978-1-4354-1859-2
ISBN-10: 1-4354-1859-X

Wadsworth
10 Davis Drive
Belmont, CA 94002-3098
USA

Cengage Learning is a leading provider of customized learning solutions with office locations around the globe, including Singapore, the United Kingdom, Australia, Mexico, Brazil, and Japan. Locate your local office at **www.cengage .com/international.**

Cengage Learning products are represented in Canada by Nelson Education, Ltd.

To learn more about Wadsworth, visit **www.cengage.com/wadsworth.**

Purchase any of our products at your local college store or at our preferred online store **www.ichapters.com.**

Printed in Canada
1 2 3 4 5 6 7 13 12 11 10 09

Contents

Chapter 2 | Understanding Children's

Chapter **3** | Serving Culturally Diverse Children and Families 78

Chapter **4** | Understanding the Reasons for Problem Behavior 128

Chapter 5 | Guidelines for Effective Guidance 163

Chapter **6** | Planning the Developmentally Appropriate Prosocial Environment

Chapter **7** | Positive Communication 225

 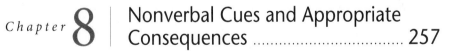

Chapter **8** | Nonverbal Cues and Appropriate
Consequences 257

Chapter **9** | Misguided Behaviors and Mistaken Goals 294

Chapter **10** | Taking a New Look at Children 321

Physical Conditions That Affect Behavior 368

Preface

As a brand-new teacher (two decades before Sue Bredekamp[1] turned the phrase "developmentally appropriate practice" into our guiding verse), I found myself beginning my work with children completely clueless about guidance. On my first day, a fellow teacher admonished me to start out from the beginning letting the children know who's the boss. "If they don't mind you, just grab them right here by the shoulder," she said as she demonstrated—her long, blood-red fingernails piercing into my shoulder. "You will have their full attention."

Well, she certainly had my full attention. Very soon, I experienced my first crisis. A little boy began hurling blobs of paint out the open window to see the interesting designs they made as they splattered on the sidewalk below. I thought, "Ah hah, I'm prepared for this." I marched up behind him and grabbed his shoulder, barking his name out in a stern tone of voice. While my stubby little nails were certainly no match for my coworker's shining red weapons, I did get the little boy's full attention.

I don't remember the boy's name, but I will never forget the look on his face as he whirled around, stunned, his pride hurt, embarrassed in front of his friends, and defensively pulling his shoulder away from me. An expected role for adults in the 1960s was to let children know, "I'm in charge, you are not, and the sooner you figure that out, the better off you are." But in the instant I looked at that child's face, I knew what I had done was destructive and wrong. I realized my well-intentioned fellow teacher was misguided and I needed to find a better way fast.

Another teacher I observed, in a different classroom setting, played such a passive role with children that her presence was almost ignored at times. Most of her guidance statements to children seemed to end with a question mark. She said she believed it was important for children to work out problems among themselves without adult intervention. What actually happened in her class was the most assertive children running roughshod over the less assertive children. Bullying was pretty routine. This teacher's occasional admonitions about sharing or not hurting others was met with blank stares at best and, at worst, rolled eyes, shoves, and that old chant, "You can't make me. You're not my mother." At that point, this teacher would usually just shake her head in frustration and helplessness and walk away.

At another time, in another school setting, I taught across the hall from a teacher whose favorite teaching tool was her yardstick—not an ordinary yardstick, but one

---

[1] For updated information on developmentally appropriate practice, see Bredekamp & Copple, 1997.

with the weight and heft of lumber you might use to build a barn, or at least it seemed that way to those of us who listened to her slam the yardstick down on her desk to get her children's attention. I can only imagine the stress her children felt. Every slam caused my classroom to stiffen and look toward the door; one little girl routinely started sucking her thumb each time we heard a smack, and our university student teacher dropped out, complaining that her nerves were frayed by the sound of the dreaded yardstick.

I'm sure the teacher with the yardstick imagined herself to be a really good teacher. She may have even felt pride that she could maintain absolute control of her classroom without having to so much as touch a child. She would probably have been horrified to know that her disciplinary method was probably just as destructive to the development of the children in her care as if she had actually spanked them.

I've been a classroom teacher (from infants and toddlers to middle school), a child care director, an early childhood professor, and a supervisor of elementary school student teachers. A lot has changed in my many years of watching teachers and children. But some things have not changed. Today, astonishingly, there are still early childhood educators who are out there in classrooms intimidating young children to keep them quiet, supposedly to help them learn better. And there are other parents and teachers out there who are turning their backs on troubling child interactions because they either don't want to get involved or don't know how to do it without becoming frustrated and angry.

Most adults who interact with children have good intentions and want only the best for children. Our shared quest, as early childhood educators, is to find authentic best practices that will really work for us on a day-to-day basis. Our genuine hope is to support children's development and enhance their lives. We all want to be successful. It is my sincere hope that this book will bring new levels of success to you and your students.

The guidance methods presented here are not my methods. I did not discover or invent them. What I have done is spend four decades observing, studying, working with, and learning about children and families. I've learned by studying people such as Piaget and Adler and Montessori—but I've also learned from coworkers like you who so generously share your ideas by presenting at conferences and writing journal articles. In this book I offer you my best effort at bringing together all the useful child guidance expertise, research, and wisdom that I can squeeze into these pages in a simplified, easy-to-read format.

Positive Child Guidance offers a broad and eclectic smorgasbord of guidance methods. Tactics are completely excluded, however, or described as unacceptable methods if their use does not clearly fit within the ideals of developmentally appropriate practice (DAP).

This book is based on the following three critically important assumptions:

- *Guidance methods must be flexible enough to accommodate children's individual differences in growth patterns.* Although predictable sequences of growth and change occur in children, individual growth rates, patterns of development, or other individual differences cause normal children to function at very different developmental levels physically, cognitively, socially, and emotionally.

- *Guidance strategies must be variable enough to be matched to individual children's interests, experiences, and emerging abilities, while challenging growth and stimulating new learning.* Each child is a unique person with an individual rate of growth, temperament, learning style, family background, and life experience.
- *Guidance methods must be referenced to the social and cultural settings in which the children live in order to ensure that guidance is meaningful, relevant, and respectful for the children and their families.* Children grow up in the context of families, neighborhoods, and communities.

Diana Baumrind's (1967) theory of parenting styles is presented in *Positive Child Guidance* as a point of reference for students to give them a typical continuum of adult guidance behavior—from the permissive "doormat" role to the authoritarian "sledgehammer" role. The role of the authoritative "guide" is presented as the assertive and caring, DAP alternative that is the ultimate goal to be achieved and maintained.

Philosophically, the book presents three major perspectives:

- **Maturationists**—Arnold Gessell advanced the maturationist belief that development is a biological process occurring automatically in predictable stages over time. This perspective provides useful guidance tools with the stern warning that taken too far it may be used as an excuse for *permissive,* "hands-off," or neglectful guidance.
- **Behaviorists**—Theorists such as John Watson, B. F. Skinner, and Albert Bandura contributed greatly to the environmentalist perspective of development that proposes the child's environment shapes learning and behavior. This perspective provides useful guidance tools for responding to very specific kinds of behavior problems. Its strategies are not developmentally appropriate, however, for responding to all guidance situations. In fact, use of behaviorist methods without children's active cooperation risks placing the adult in the manipulative and controlling *authoritarian* role.
- **Constructivists (Interactionists)**—Jean Piaget, Maria Montessori, and Lev Vygotsky helped develop the constructivists' view in which young children were seen as active participants in the learning process. Because active interaction with the environment and people are necessary for learning and development, constructivists believe that children are partners in their own learning. The constructivist philosophy is a natural match for the *authoritative* adult guidance role in the developmentally appropriate classroom.

Obviously, Positive Child Guidance *is heavily weighted to the constructivist perspective.*

New to This Edition

- A new chapter, "Understanding Children with Disabilities" (Chapter 12), which provides extensive information about children with disabilities, their guidance needs, the legal responsibilities of child care professionals regarding children with disabilities and special problems professionals are likely to encounter has been added.
- Because users have responded so positively to the bibliotherapy resources provided in *Positive Child Guidance,* extensive new children's book selections have been added to provide children's book recommendations related to culture, temperament, and disabilities.
- A new set of student activities have been added to the end of each chapter to engage students in applying their newly acquired skills.
- This new edition addresses sexual harassment as a topical issue that has caused some young children nationwide to be expelled inappropriately from elementary schools. It explains the correct definition of sexual harassment and why young children should not be accused of this adult offense.
- A helpful new section in Chapter 5 describes "prevention techniques" and "quick response techniques."

Features

- *Positive Child Guidance* develops critical thinking skills through the presentation of problem-solving strategies.
- *Positive Child Guidance* uses "Points to Remember" to review and clarify key items.
- Numerous photos and teaching captions appear throughout the book to add or to review important information. A problem-solving model is applied throughout the textbook, emphasizing clear and practical strategies for guiding behavior in infants, toddlers, and preschoolers. These strategies have been proven effective in existing children's programs.
- The child-centered approach views the teacher and caregiver as communicator, observer, supervisor, and facilitator. The objective is to build on the developmental needs of the children, providing them with freedom and safety, developmentally appropriate learning opportunities, and the tools needed to accept responsibility at their own level.
- Developmentally appropriate practices are emphasized throughout. This text recognizes that a child's resistance to limits may be developmentally appropriate as children take risks and challenge themselves. Included are suggestions for providing a child-centered environment that eliminates many behavior problems. When conflicts arise, the text describes strategies for validating children's feelings, encouraging children to negotiate, setting limits respectfully, and affirming children's positive behavior.

- Sample dialogues between caregivers and children are authentic and help prepare future caregivers for the problems and language of real children at different levels of development. These examples provide a realistic expectation of how children interact and give teachers a variety of responses to use in numerous situations while they are developing their own style of facilitating.
- Chapter 9, "Misguided Behaviors and Mistaken Goals," defines problem behavior, suggests possible causes, and offers alternatives for managing children who exhibit common problems. Included are ways to enlist parents' help in solving their children's behavior problems.
- An extensive art program reinforces learning with close to 200 illustrations and photographs of children and teachers in their daily routines.
- *Positive Child Guidance* is unique in that it contains a child prosocial behavior checklist, which allows parents and teachers to evaluate a child's current social and behavior development.
- The text is unique in that it includes a teacher prosocial guidance checklist, which allows teachers to evaluate themselves so they are in a better position to implement a prosocial guidance plan.
- The text is unique in that it includes a "A Short Quiz to Explore Cultural Beliefs," which allows teachers to contemplate their own cultural perceptions.
- *Positive Child Guidance* promotes eight prosocial behaviors: self-esteem, empathy, friendliness, generosity, helpfulness, self-control, cooperation, and respect.
- The text contains information on the "other-esteem conflict conversion" approach to help children resolve interpersonal conflicts.
- The text uses children's books and extension activities to promote positive behavior.
- *Positive Child Guidance* includes important new findings regarding research related to the brain and the emotions.
- The text covers ways teachers can use two-way communication (through books and photographs) to involve family members in a child's prosocial development at home.
- The book illustrates the important concepts in each chapter by listing videos, learning activities, and photographs of children engaged in activities with their teachers.
- There is a greater focus on the role of positive guidance in developing children with the self-discipline, self-reliance, and respect for others necessary to thrive in a global society.
- Extensive updated resources are featured at the end of each chapter and include related readings.
- This edition addresses new research findings, emerging social issues, and special challenges confronting contemporary families and early childhood professionals.

Ancillary Materials

Professional Enhancement Series

This booklet, which is part of the Early Childhood Education Professional Enhancement series, focuses on key topics of interest to future early childhood directors, teachers, and caregivers. Students will keep this informational supplement and use it for years to come in their early childhood practices.

Instructor's Manual

The Instructor's Manual contains resources designed to streamline and maximize the effectiveness of your course preparation. The contents include chapter outlines and summaries, review questions, discussion topics, helpful websites, test bank, and additional resources.
ISBN 1435418611

Companion Website

For the student: The book-specific website at academic.cengage.com/education/miller offers students access to a variety of useful resources such as Internet exercises, links to relevant websites, self-assessment quizzes for each chapter, flashcards, and various chapter study tools including objectives, overviews, notes, and more.

For the instructor: The instructor area of the book companion website at academic.cengage.com/education/miller offers access to password-protected resources such as an electronic version of the Instructor's Manual and Microsoft PowerPoint® slides.

PowerLecture

This one-stop digital library and presentation tool includes preassembled Microsoft PowerPoint lecture slides by Darla Miller. In addition to a full Instructor's Manual and Test Bank, PowerLecture also includes ExamView® testing software with all the test items from the printed Test Bank in electronic format, enabling you to create customized tests in print or online.
ISBN 143541862X

WebTutor Toolbox™

WebTutor Toolbox for WebCT™ or Blackboard® provides access to all the content of this text's rich book companion website from within your course management system. Robust communication tools—such as course calendar, asynchronous discussion, real-time chat, a whiteboard, and an integrated e-mail system—make it easy for your students to stay connected to the course.

Acknowledgments

Many of the beautiful photographs that appear on these pages were graciously provided by the families and staff of Montessori Country Day School of Houston. I especially appreciate the creative input I received for this edition from Margaret Ellison, owner/administrator of Montessori Country Day School, and three of her senior faculty who lead infant and toddler programs incorporating sign language to support early guidance. These talented early childhood professionals are Michelle Battistone, Lina Sendjar, and Marisole Sharp. They are three among many forward-thinking early care providers always seeking new strategies to better support children's natural stages of growth and development.

I also received encouragement, feedback, and inspiration from my husband Tommy and our two daughters, Michelle Denise and Cynde Allyson, all three of whom are professors. Michelle holds a doctorate in cognitive psychology from the University of California at Los Angeles and is an associate professor of psychology at Northern Arizona University. Cynde holds a master's degree in fine arts from the University of California at Irvine and is an associate professor at Chaffe Community College. My husband's graduate degree is from the University of California at Berkeley, and he holds an endowed chair at California State University, Fresno.

Christopher Shortt, Philip I. Mandel, Shelley Murphy, Caitlin Cox, and many other professionals at Cengage Wadsworth Learning have been of great assistance. Additionally, I sincerely thank the early childhood faculty who contributed to the readability, accuracy, and usefulness of this book by critiquing it and adding their own ideas and suggestions. These experts provided a remarkably perceptive level of insight, good judgment, and experience, pushing *Positive Child Guidance* to become a better and more useful text:

Tracy Bennett, M.S.
Vance-Granville Community College, Henderson, NC

Tamara B. Calhoun, M.S.
Schenectaday County Community College, Schenectady, NY

Joan Campbell, Ed.S.
Santa Fe Community College, Gainesville, FL

Jennifer Johnson, M.Ed.
Vance-Granville Community College, Henderson, NC

Michelle List, M.S.
Herkimer County Community College, Herkimer, NY

Dr. Paul W. Ogden provided invaluable help by contributing to the section "How Does American Sign Language Support Positive Child Guidance?" Dr. Ogden, who was born deaf, is a professor in and director of the Deaf Studies program in the Department of Communicative Disorders and Deaf Studies at California State University, Fresno. His publications include *The Silent Garden: Understanding Your Hearing Impaired Child; Chelsea: The Story of a Signal Dog; The Silent Garden: Raising Your Deaf Child;* and *El Jardin Silencioso: Criando a Su Hijo Sordo,* a Spanish translation of the first five chapters of *The New Silent Garden.*

Dedication

This book was inspired by and is dedicated to my parents, Evolee and Roy Ferris. "Papa Roy" did not live to see the book completed, but he had great interest in and enthusiasm for its writing. Because he grew up the youngest child of a troubled single parent during the Great Depression, he spent much of his adult life struggling to learn how to be a good parent and to let his children know that he loved them. When he read the beginning draft of the first edition of this book, his eyes got a bit misty, and he said, "You've said some important things in here. I'm really proud of you." Of course, no child ever outgrows the need to know she has made her parents proud.

As my husband, Tommy Miller, and I have reared our daughters, we, too, have struggled to learn how to be good parents and let our children know they are loved. We have three lovely granddaughters, Fiona, April, and Rosa, and a beautiful little grandson, Quinn. Today we feel awe as we watch our next generation learning and growing. Their parents are also learning and growing as they go step-by-step through the joyous, exhausting, scary, magical adventure of child rearing.

About the Author

Darla Ferris Miller holds a doctorate in early childhood education, Texas and Mississippi teaching credentials, and the American Montessori Society Preprimary Certification. She was a vice president, a division chair, and an associate professor at North Harris College. Dr. Miller has also served in a wide range of roles within the field of child care and development. She has been caregiver, early childhood teacher, center director, teacher trainer, and consultant, and she has worked with children from infancy to middle school. Dr. Miller's publications include:

Miller, D. F. (2004, Spring). Science for babies. *Montessori Life, 16*(2).

Miller, D. F. (2004, Winter). Early crusade planted seeds for NHC infant-and-toddler teacher education initiative. *Montessori Life, 16*(1).

Miller, D. F. (1993). *L'éducation des enfants une démarche positive.* (French translation of *Positive Child Guidance*). Ontario, Canada: Institut des Technologies Télématiques.

Miller, D. F. (1990). Room to grow: How to create quality early childhood environments. In L. Ard & M. Pitts (Eds.), *Room to grow: How to create quality early childhood environments.* Austin: Texas Association for the Education of Young Children.

Miller, D. F. (1989). *First steps toward cultural difference: Socialization in infant/toddler day care.* Washington, DC: Child Welfare League of America, Inc. (Continuously in print from 1989–2005 and was termed a Child Welfare League "classic" book.)

Introduction

Wadsworth/Cengage Learning

OBJECTIVES

After reading this chapter, you should be able to do the following:

- Identify contemporary practices in child guidance.
- Define developmentally appropriate practice.
- Recognize responsibility for healthy child growth and development.
- Know the purpose of child guidance.
- State the criteria for creating early childhood rules.
- Describe appropriate early environments.
- Become more introspective about the role of guidance in supporting families in today's society.

Overview

Parents and early childhood professionals worry about discipline: "How do I get kids to clean up after themselves?" "How can I keep toddlers from biting and pulling hair?" "What should I do when preschoolers call each other hurtful names?" "Am I being too strict?" "Am I being too lenient?" "How can I manage my own feelings of anger and frustration when children throw tantrums?"

Self-discipline and self-control do not automatically appear out of thin air. Competent, well-behaved children do not just happen. Dedication and skill on the part of parents and early educators help children reach their full potential. Effective guidance prevents

Every child represents a new beginning full of bright possibility.

Developmentally appropriate practice is

Appropriate for each child and relevant to the child's ability, needs, and interests

Collaborative with the child's family and respectful of the child's culture

Based on a practical and professional understanding of child development

■ Developmentally Appropriate Practice

developmentally appropriate practice
Early education and care that is carefully planned to match the diverse interests, abilities, and cultural needs of children at various ages and that is carried out with respect for and in cooperation with their families.

behavior problems, keeps children safe, safely channels emotional expression, and builds a solid foundation for children's future participation in society.

Child guidance is the very challenging process of establishing and maintaining responsible, productive, and cooperative behavior in children. Parents and early educators must devote a great deal of time, effort, and persistence to help children become considerate and self-disciplined members of society. *Knowledge of the natural stages of child development is the most powerful tool adults have to guide youngsters successfully through this process of maturing.* This book provides answers focused on **developmentally appropriate practice,** referred to as DAP.

This book has been written specifically for those adults who make an invaluable contribution to society by caring for and teaching the youngest and most vulnerable members of society—our children. The book is intended as a foundation for effective problem solving to guide adults as they strive to meet the developmental needs of children from infancy through early childhood. *Every child has unique needs. Consequently, no single guidance strategy will be appropriate for all children at all ages.* This book addresses typical characteristics and needs of children as they proceed through chronological and developmental stages. It provides a broad range of practical, effective, and flexible guidance strategies that are based on principles of straightforward communication and assertiveness. The underlying theme is that of respect for the dignity and human rights of the infant and young child.

Much writing in the area of child guidance has focused only on behaviorist learning theory, a view that all behavior can be explained as the result of externally reinforced (or rewarded) learning. This view assumes that, because a full understanding of the internal workings of the human mind is impossible, the process is therefore irrelevant. For too many people, discipline (or guidance) means giving rewards and punishments to control children's behavior. Far too many schools rely exclusively on competitiveness, grades, stickers, and time-outs to motivate and control children. A key problem with exclusive reliance on behavior modification—ignoring negative behaviors and reinforcing positive behaviors—is that it may be carried out in an aloof or manipulative manner.

Additionally, rewarding children for behaving a certain way raises several sticky issues. Because human beings of all ages are infinitely complex, the praise or prize that reinforces one child may embarrass, bore, or alienate another. *Doling out privileges and prizes may place an adult in the role of a stingy gift giver, rather than that of a democratic guide and role model, and may stimulate competition rather than cooperation among children.* Doling out attention and praise as reinforcement risks implying to children that compliance is a condition for affection and that only "good" children are loved. ·

Another problem that undermines the effectiveness of behavior modification as a *sole strategy* for guidance is the contemporary child's frequent exposure to many different adults and settings. Even intermittent reinforcement of a behavior through attention from children or other adults can undo an attempt by a teacher to eliminate that behavior by ignoring it. The behaviorist educator attempts to control the child's behavior by controlling the child's environment, a very helpful tool for guidance in specific situations but not a feasible overall plan for child guidance.

Strategies for **child guidance** *should not rely only on methods for external control but rather must interact with and extend the development of naturally unfolding internal mechanisms and motivations for self-control.* In this way, children can be encouraged to become independent and self-directed rather than dependent and other-directed. As they grow toward adolescence and adulthood, they will begin making more and more critical choices about what to do and how to behave.

Because imitation of modeling is a key avenue for early child learning, how adults cope with the stress and frustration of handling children's misbehaviors is critical. Children tend to do what we do rather than what we say to do. *The purpose of child guidance is to support and direct the growth of effective life skills rather than only to bring about the immediate control of annoying behaviors.*

Positive, persistent assertiveness is considerably more painstaking and time-consuming than bullying and intimidating children into compliance by scolding, screaming, or spanking. And it definitely requires a great deal more thought and effort than does giving up responsibility for children's behavior, allowing children to bully others, and assuming that maturation will somehow automatically bring discipline and self-control.

In child guidance—as in much of our instant, drive-through, disposable culture of expedience—taking the time to properly guide children has special value. In spite of the added skill and effort required to carry out **positive, assertive guidance,** its effect on a child's personal growth and on an early childhood setting make it worthwhile.

An early childhood program is a training ground in which very young people acquire and practice the skills needed for effective living. The personal characteristics and capabilities needed for survival in an autocracy or anarchy are very different from those needed for participation in a democracy. In an interdependent world, early child guidance should begin the development of self-respect; awareness of and consideration for the rights of others; and recognition that persons of all ages, colors, and creeds should be treated with equal dignity, although each may have very different roles and responsibilities.

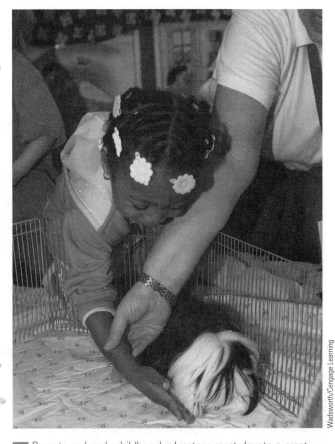

Parents and early childhood educators must devote a great deal of time, effort, and persistence over many years to help children become considerate, self-disciplined members of society.

Wadsworth/Cengage Learning

child guidance
Contrived methods for external control as well as interaction with and extension of the development of naturally unfolding internal mechanisms and motivations for self-control and self-discipline.

positive, assertive guidance
Guidance that bolsters self-esteem, nurtures cooperativeness, and models socially acceptable coping skills.

Positive assertive guidance creates a learning environment where children cooperate rather than compete. The child knows his work is valued because it is his.

The ultimate goal of child guidance is the child's development of responsibility, self-confidence, and self-control. Inner discipline, based on an intrinsic desire to be a cooperative community member, is more functional to adult life in a democracy than sole reliance on external discipline based on an artificially contrived desire to gain rewards and avoid punishments. Of course, there is no place in any democracy for laissez-faire anarchy in which people wantonly trample the rights of others in their quest for self-gratification.

This book outlines practical, workable steps for creating a cooperative, respectful community of children and adults. Behavior modification will be addressed, not as the foundation of child guidance, but as a single, carefully placed stone in a solid structure of active guidance. Maturation will be addressed, not as an excuse to relinquish responsibility for child behavior, but as a powerful tool for understanding and responding appropriately to various stages of child behavior. The method presented is one of assertive and respectful enforcement of cooperatively developed rules and persistent protection of individual rights.

Aggression, passivity, and manipulation are identified as hindrances to positive child guidance. They trigger negativity, even rebellion, in children, and they

Changing attitudes and expectations in society bring dramatic changes in contemporary childrearing practices.

set an example for behaviors that are hindrances to successful participation in democratic community life. *The role of the* ***adult****, in this book, is that of one who seeks not to gain control over children but rather to guide them effectively, while setting for them an immediate and tangible example of appropriate coping and assertive negotiation.*

In this model, the adult guards the safety and individual rights of children and stimulates their development of inner control by creating a functioning democratic community of children and adults. Positive child guidance means guiding children as firmly as necessary, as gently as possible, and always with respect.

adult
One who seeks not to gain control over children but rather to guide them effectively, while setting for them an immediate and tangible example of appropriate coping and assertive negotiation.

Child Rearing in Today's World

At dawn every weekday morning all across the country, from bustling cities to tiny rural communities, mothers and fathers struggle to begin another workday. In millions of homes and apartments, parents hurry to feed and dress babies and young children. Without a minute to spare, they grab diaper bags and satchels, buckle little ones into car seats, climb onto buses, or push strollers into elevators. They head for a variety of child care arrangements ranging from homes of relatives to registered family day homes to proprietary, religious, and government-funded child care centers; early childhood programs; and schools. Stress begins early for today's parents and children. The world is changing dramatically, but children still need protection, nurturance, love, and guidance. Whether mommy is a full-time homemaker or a business executive with an urgent 8 a.m. appointment makes little difference to a toddler who plops in the middle of the floor and cries because he doesn't want oatmeal for breakfast. Child guidance is a challenging task for any parent, but if parents work outside the home, managing their children's behavior may be more complicated, and they may rely a great deal on early childhood professionals to support their children's social and emotional development (Brazelton, 1985; Curran, 1985; Galinsky & Bond 2000; Bond et al., 1998).

Practical day-to-day responsibility for guiding the next generation is shifting from parents alone to parents, communities, and early childhood personnel working together. Today, there are fewer full-time homemakers caring for children and rapidly increasing numbers of exhausted **dual-earner couples, single parents,** grandparents, stepparents, and other arrangements of employed households juggling work while rearing young children (Capizzano & Main, 2005; AFL-CIO, 2004; Barnett & Rivers, 1998; Bond, Galinsky, & Swanberg, 1998; Daly, 1996; Francke, 1983; Hochschild, 1997; Thorpe & Daly, 1999; Yarrow, 1991). At the same time that **family structures** are changing, more and more research has surfaced highlighting the critical importance of early experiences for the long-term development of a child's personality, character, values, brain development, and social competence (Buysse at al., 2005; Capps et al., 2005; Adlam, 1977; Anyon, 1983; Banich, 1997; Bandura, 1977; Cook-Gumperz, 1973; Elman et al., 1997; Greenenough et al., 1993). Never before has there been such acute awareness of the influence early caregivers have on young lives, and never before has there been such need for people outside the family to assume major involvement in the process of child rearing (Kamerman & Gatenio,

dual-earner couples
Couples in which both partners are gainfully employed.

single parents
Mothers, fathers, grandparents, or guardians rearing children alone.

family structures
Various arrangements of people living together with children and possibly other generations of relatives.

2003; Loeb et al., 2004; Bronfenbrenner & Morris, 1998; Chugani, 1993; Galston, 1993; Hamburg, 1992).

Decades ago, babysitting provided a brief break from the real business of child rearing (which was most often handled by mothers). Having someone other than a family member look after the children represented only a brief interruption from day-to-day caregiving. It was assumed that any untrained but reasonably responsible teenager or adult could be relied on to sit with the baby or child for a short time just to ensure that the child was safe and that basic physical needs were met. Now, however, more than half of all babies and young children live in homes where the adults in the family work part- or full-time outside the home. Child care is not a brief interruption from routine caregiving but rather a major portion of it. Many children spend most of their waking hours in some form of child care by someone other than parents from as early as the first weeks of life (Blau, 1998; Skolnick, 1991; Hamburg, 1992; Howard & Toossi, 2001).

These changes place new pressures on parents and on early childhood professionals. Employed parents must face the stress of juggling family and career obligations. Fathers find that modern lifestyles present a new level of paternal involvement in caring for and managing young children. Early childhood educators find that more and more is expected of them by parents who depend on them to skillfully support wholesome growth and development in their children. Today, more households than ever are being shared by three or even four generations. Adult children often stay at home or return home, and the elderly live to such advanced ages that many families care for parents as well as children (Center for Policy Alternatives, 2002; Daly, 2000). Working parents' time and finances are often strained to the breaking point. In the United States, welfare reform pressures low-income single mothers to be employed, although their earnings may be meager and their child care costly (The Urban Institute, 2005).

Even parents who are full-time homemakers find that contemporary lifestyles bring new stresses and strains to child rearing. Many feel that their toddlers and preschoolers benefit from participating in professionally run early childhood programs, even if a parent is home full-time and child care is not linked to employment.

Why Is Parent and Professional Training in Child Guidance Important?

In today's world, many children do not spend the first years of their lives sheltered in cocoonlike home settings. They are up with the alarm clock; their days are structured and scheduled; they come in contact with adults other than their parents; and they must learn to get along with other young children in groups. Modern parents need help in developing skills for effectively guiding young children and preventing behavior problems. They may not have time to deal with a toddler throwing a tantrum and refusing to get dressed or a pouting preschooler who insists that everyone in the whole world hates her. Parents need support with child guidance so that behavior problems do not place additional strain on family-life structures that may already be stretched thin from the stresses of contemporary living (Schulman & Blank, 2004; Jenkins et al., 2005; Kamerman & Gatenio, 2003; Amato, 1997; Coontz, 1997; Cope-

> The teacher of little children is not merely giving lessons. She is helping to make a brain and nervous system, and this work which is going to determine all that comes after, requires a finer perception and a wider training and outlook than is needed by any other kind of teacher.
>
> *Margaret Mcmillan (1930)*

land & McGreedy, 1997; Salk, 1992; Stringer-Siebold et al., 1996).

Early childhood professionals need help in developing effective child guidance strategies so that they can truly meet the social and emotional needs of the children in their care, provide much needed support to family life, and assume a reasonable portion of the responsibility for teaching the next generation how to be responsible, cooperative, and competent citizens. Teachers and caregivers can never replace the important role of caring parents. Parents have an irreplaceable influence on their children's lives because of the emotional bonds that are a part of being a family. Although caregivers must never compete with or infringe on this special parent–child relationship, they can be a tremendous support to both children and their families. Parents are the first and most important teachers children will ever have.

Who Should Be Responsible for the Well-Being and Guidance of Children?

We are all responsible for the well-being and guidance of children. In past centuries, children were thought to be their parents' property. In western Europe only a century and a half ago, babies were not considered to be real persons. It was not even thought necessary to report their deaths (Aries, 1962). In a modern democracy, however, children are not viewed as property of their parents but rather as human beings with inalienable human rights. Governmental agencies hold responsibility for the welfare and guidance of young children because children are the future citizens of the country. Failure to address early needs costs government millions of tax dollars later in remedial education, indigent support, and crime (Focus Council on Early Childhood Education, 2004; Currie, 2005; Fox, Dunlap, & Buschbacher, 2000; Koplow, 2002; Rouse, Brooks-Gunn, & McLanahan, 2005; Schulman & Barnett, 2005; Schweinhart, 2004; Hernandez, 1997; Jackson, 1997; Lindjord, 1997; McAlister, 1997; White, 1995). Business and industry are responsible for the welfare of young children because they will be the workforce of the future, and competitiveness in world markets depends on the availability of competent, cooperative, responsible workers. Civic groups, churches, schools, and each of us are also responsible. Good citizenship obligates us to look toward the future well-being of humanity rather than to just our own personal interests. You can help your community build a brighter future by joining with other interested parents and professionals to support advocacy groups that inform and encourage better child care and education.

Throughout the country, there is growing recognition that investing efforts and resources to better the lives of children is not only humane but also very cost effective. Children are open to ideas and experiences. It is possible to bring about

Wadsworth/Cengage Learning

■ Every child, at every moment, is in the process of creating the adult he will become.

In the sweep of seven decades, the image conveyed is one of children, smaller than anyone else, lighter in physical weight and political clout, easily picked up and blown wherever the winds of economic, political, and social movements were heading.

Rochelle Beck (1973)

Sadly, Quality Child Care Is Not Available to All Families.

- Only 2 out of 10 child care centers in Philadelphia are able to provide quality care; the rest range from poor to mediocre. Poor children are less likely to participate in quality care programs (Improving School Readiness Project, 2001).

- The average percentage of family income spent on child care is 7.5 percent. Families with annual incomes of $18,000 or less tend to spend an average of 22.8 percent of their income on child care, whereas families with incomes of $54,000 or more tend to spend an average of 3.9 percent (National Association of Child Care Resource and Referral Agencies, 2004).

- In most states, families with annual incomes of $25,000 do not qualify for assistance with child care expenses (Schulman & Blank, 2004).

- Funding for child care has declined in recent years. Federal child care funding dropped from $4.817 billion in 2002 to $4.800 billion in 2005. During that time, funding from Temporary Assistance for Needy Families (TANF) for child care decreased from $3.96 billion in 2000 to $3.28 billion in 2004 (Administration on Children and Families, Child Care Bureau, 2005).

- As of early 2005, about 436,808 children nationwide were on the waiting list for subsidized child care.

Adapted from "National Fact Sheet 2007," Child Welfare League of America: Washington, DC, accessed online at http://www.cwla.org, February 16, 2008.

America's Children

- The racial and ethnic diversity of America's children continues to increase—Hispanic children are in the fastest growing group.

- Children are more likely to live in poverty.

- The death rate for children between ages 1 and 4 is the lowest ever.

- In 2003, 5 percent of children ages 4 to 17 were reported by a parent to have trouble with emotions, concentration, or behavior.

- Youth are more likely to commit or be a victim of a violent crime.

- In 2004, 68 percent of children from birth to age 17 lived with two married parents.

- Teenage girls who lived with both parents were less likely to become unmarried mothers than were those who lived with a single parent, and they were much less likely than were those who did not live with either parent.

- In 2002, 7 percent of births to married mothers were low birth weight, compared with 10 percent of births to unmarried mothers.

- Children who are born very premature remain at risk of psychological and psychiatric problems into adolescence, despite neonatal intensive care.

Federal Interagency Forum on Child and Family Statistics, 2005.

meaningful changes in their lives and to have real influence on their long-term development of values and character traits. Adults, in contrast, tend to be more rigidly set in their habits and potentials. If we are to continue to enjoy the benefits of living in a democracy, then we must begin by helping children learn personal responsibility and respect for others so that they will know how to function properly as adults (Administration for Children and Families, 2005).

Short-Term Objectives for Child Guidance

The short-term **objective** for child guidance is deceptively simple. Children will be helped to follow the same basic rules for decent and responsible behavior that are applicable to all persons living in a democracy. To accomplish this, we can use the following guidelines to determine the appropriateness of children's day-to-day behaviors and help them learn the difference between right and wrong:

objective
Immediate aim or purpose.

- Behavior must not infringe on the rights of others.
- Behavior must not present a clear risk of harm to oneself or others.
- Behavior must not unreasonably damage the environment, animals, objects, or materials in the environment.

To communicate these rules effectively, to translate them to the comprehension level of young children, they must be greatly oversimplified. By oversimplifying them, young children can be guided to make sense of what otherwise may seem to them to be an endless number of unrelated little rules. By lumping rules into three basic categories, young children can be helped to remember and understand the basic guidelines for appropriate behavior: be *kind,* be *safe,* and be *neat.* These ground rules can be stated as reminders before more specific and practical instructions are given. For example,

Be *kind!* Wait for your turn.
Be *safe!* Go down the slide feet first.
Be *neat!* Put your paper towel in the trash can.

These simple rules—be kind, be safe, be neat—are an appropriate place to start with toddlers. Gradually, however, children will need and be able to handle more complexity. You will need to determine when individual children are ready, of course, but at least by age five or six the rules should be phrased in this way:

(Be kind!) Respect the rights of others!
(Be safe!) Remember safety and health!
(Be neat!) Take care of the environment!

Wadsworth/Cengage Learning

"Be safe—sand is for digging, not for throwing. Sand hurts if it gets in your eyes."

Yes, five-year-olds can learn to say *environment* and know generally what it means. I remember one cute little boy whose family was from Alabama who had his own special pronunciation for *environment*. His mother came to class one day totally mystified and asked the teacher if she could see the "varmint." She told the puzzled teacher that her son talked often of cleaning the "varmint" and she just wanted to see what kind of varmint that they had.

By the time the children are five or six years old, we should talk about the concepts with them and then involve them in helping to decide how to word the rules so that everyone understands what the rules mean. At that age, they can help write and post the rules and develop relevant subrules that are related to these three main categories. For example, they could write down three subrules that would help people in the class remember to respect the rights of others, "Don't look in someone else's locker (cubbie) without asking," "Don't say you can't play kickball because you are a girl," and "Don't shove when you are waiting for the bus." Then you could help them decide how to rephrase their rules into positive do statements instead of negative don't statements. For example, "Ask before you look in someone else's locker (cubbie)."

Remember that the reason for these three basic categories—be kind, be safe, be neat—is to teach children the three basic foundations for social and behavioral rules and laws in democratic society. You can reword them, translate them, express them in sign language, or use your own special way to communicate these three ideas at each of children's developmental ages. Just don't lose the underlying concept. *We are trying to teach children to respect the rights of others, protect their bodies from unnecessary risk, and avoid unnecessary damage to the environment.* Whether a child is in the United States, Canada, Mexico, Korea, Africa, France, or anywhere else on the globe, these three rules are equally relevant.

Stating the guidelines for appropriate behavior is easy. Evaluating real behaviors in real children is a great deal more difficult, and it requires some critical thinking on the part of the adult. A very well-coordinated five-year-old is leaning back on two legs of his chair. Does this behavior infringe on the rights of others? (For example, is the walkway between tables blocked for other children?) Does this behavior risk an injury? (Could the child fall? If he fell, would he hit soft carpeting or a cement floor?) Does it appear that equipment could be damaged by this behavior? (How sturdy is the chair? Are breakable things nearby?) Personal judgment, practical experience, and knowledge of individual children and their capabilities will determine how different adults answer these questions and how they go about setting rules and enforcing discipline. I hope you will answer these questions with enough compassion to see every situation through children's eyes and enough courage to be true to your sense of fair play and good judgment.

What Are the Rights of Children?

Children Have a Right to Be Safe

Adults should be very conscientious about protecting every child's right not to be hit, kicked, bitten, or shoved. It is never okay to allow a child to be kicked because he did it first and "deserved to get a taste of his own medicine." It is never okay to bite a

Positive guidance helps children learn to maintain their environment independently.

toddler back "so that he will learn what biting feels like." A cliché that happens to be true is "Two wrongs do not make a right." The only thing that revenge really does is set the stage for more hurtful behavior. Adults should monitor children carefully and consistently so that aggression can be prevented or interrupted immediately when it does occur.

Children Have a Right to Avoid Unnecessary Discomfort

They have a right to eat lunch peacefully without an unnerving noise level caused by children around them screaming and yelling. They have a right to listen to a story without being squashed by others who are struggling to see the pictures. And they have a right to build sand castles without getting sand in their eyes because gleeful playmates are shoveling sand into the air just for the fun of it. Although all young children begin with a kind of thinking that limits them to a self-centered (or egocentric) view of the world, adults can help children begin to recognize that others have feelings. In time, children begin to get a sense of what it feels like to be someone else. A one-year-old may try to give his pacifier to an older child who is crying, or a preschooler may run to tell a teacher that his friend got pushed off the swing. Adults who are consistently sensitive to the comfort needs of children set an emotional tone in which children are much more inclined to be sensitive to each other.

Children Have a Right to Their Possessions

Adults sometimes impose very strange views of sharing onto children. In the adult world, government provides very precise laws related to possession and ownership. Law forbids others from tampering with one's possessions without permission. Even social customs follow the same rule. If I take a cart in a grocery store and begin doing my shopping, it would be extremely rude and surprising for another shopper to snatch that cart away and dump my groceries because she wanted "a turn" with the cart. I would greatly appreciate a store manager (authority figure) who intervened politely but assertively and redirected the offending shopper to other available carts. Oddly enough, a child in preschool who complains because another child grabbed the tricycle or snatched the container of crayons he was using is often not helped but instead chided for "tattling" and for "not sharing."

A child's personal possessions are his own, and no one—not even a parent or teacher, should tamper with them without asking the child or at least letting the child know that, for example, "I'm going to move your blocks over there." Objects that are available for shared use belong to the person using them at any given time (until, of course, that use infringes on the rights of others). In a home setting, if one child is watching television, another should not be allowed to march in and change channels without asking. In a group setting, a puzzle belongs to the child who chose to work with it, and no one else should be allowed to touch that puzzle without permission from the child who chose it first. Sharing is really sharing only if it is voluntary.

Children Have a Right to Fairness

Fairness is a concept that emerges slowly in children during the preschool and early elementary years. Even before that concept is well developed, however, children deserve fair treatment, and they need to observe role models of integrity and fairness. If one child is allowed to have a picture book during naptime, then it is unfair to deny that privilege to another child without some logical reason or explanation.

By the time children are around kindergarten age, they can sometimes be heard proclaiming loudly, "Hey, that's not fair." Although their logic is still rather limited and their actual concept of fairness may be hazy, they are likely to complain if the action of an adult or another child appears to them to be blatantly unequal or out of compliance with a rule. Sometimes, if an adult carries out a disciplinary action that appears arbitrary and capricious to a child, the child will immediately begin enforcing that action on other children, partly as revenge and partly in imitation of the adult. For example, a teacher angrily snaps at a child and yanks his lunch box out of his hand because it is not yet time for lunch. A few minutes later, the child mimics the adult's behavior and tone of voice, yanking away a smaller child's toy and snapping, "Gimme that, you baby!"

Wadsworth/Cengage Learning

This little girl has a right to explore her art materials without unnecessary interference from other children.

How Do We Tell the Difference between Enforcing Reasonable Safety Rules and Being Overprotective?

Just about every interesting activity or environment has some element of risk. Imagine for a moment trying to create an environment that has absolutely no possibility for any kind of accident. Unfortunately, a child can potentially misuse, fall off, throw, choke on, or bump into just about any kind of equipment or material that can be named. The only perfectly safe environment would probably be an empty room with padded walls and floor, and some child would undoubtedly find a way to get hurt there too. Of course, a padded cell would not offer many opportunities for exploration and skill development. So in an interesting, challenging environment, safety is always a matter of compromise. The difficulty for many teachers and parents seems to be in deciding what level of risk is acceptable and reasonable and what level is not.

Children feel a sense of pride and dignity when they succeed in mastering a difficult challenge that has a bit of risk involved. No baby ever learned to walk without risking a fall, and no child ever learned to jump off a step, climb a tree, roller skate, or ride a bicycle without risking a bump or bruise. Some pediatricians assume that children who make it through childhood without so much as a broken finger have been overprotected. The acceptability of risk must be weighed against the severity of possible outcomes. If the worst thing that could reasonably result is a 2-foot fall onto a thick gymnastic mat, then the risk seems very acceptable. If the child could possibly fall 10 feet onto brick pavement, then there is a clear risk of harm; that kind of accident could result in serious or permanent injury to the child.

Adults must be diligent about safety for young children. Environments in which young children play should be checked and double-checked routinely for hazardous equipment, toxic plants or substances, and dangerous but tempting situations. Then, but only then, can adults step back and allow children the latitude to negotiate challenges independently, under a watchful eye but without hovering control.

Why Should Children Be Involved in Maintaining and Protecting Their Environment?

To learn, children need the freedom to make mistakes, to know that it is really not so awful to break a glass or spill paint on a shirt. Most things can be restored or replaced. Stained clothes will soon be forgotten, but a child's first

Responsibility and independence develop when children learn to care for themselves and their environment.

Wadsworth/Cengage Learning

"Thank you for hanging up your backpack so nicely."

Wadsworth/Cengage Learning

painting may be treasured for many years, and the benefit of the experience of painting may stay with a child for life.

Although it is essential to keep a reasonable perspective about neatness, remember that responsibility, manners, and good citizenship require all of us to have respect for our surroundings. We all share the resources of this planet and have an obligation, therefore, to use them wisely and well. Early child guidance prepares children for good citizenship. When a child remembers to use one paper towel at a time and then throw it away, he is preparing for membership in adult society where everyone benefits if forests logged to make paper towels are replanted, water used in factories is cleaned before being dumped, and fish and game are taken according to lawful limits and seasons.

In the first years of life, children can gradually learn to take only what they need, use it with care, and then restore it (put it away) when they have finished using it. Toys, games, and learning materials should be arranged in an orderly manner on low shelves that are accessible to children. Even a very young child can learn to replace a puzzle if it has its own place on a shelf or in a puzzle rack. A stack of heavy puzzles crammed on a shelf makes it difficult or impossible for a child to easily take any but the top puzzle. Additionally, the number of learning materials available at any one time should match the capacity of the children. More is not always better.

Watch children carefully. Can they get materials from the shelf easily? Can they easily return the item to the correct spot? If they cannot, if the shelves are crowded or confusing, there is probably far too much available. Simplify the shelves and rotate in new materials as children tire of the old ones.

Adults must always set an example for care of the environment and must consistently assist children in learning that things are easier to find if they are always returned to the same spot.

Children should be stopped firmly but kindly when their behavior is damaging to the environment. While playing outdoors, children may innocently break limbs off shrubs, smash birds' eggs, or peel bark off trees. Teaching them about nature and the value of plants and animals assists them in building respect for living things and in accepting **responsibility** for their own actions. Indoors, children playfully smash riding toys into table legs and stuff tissues down the sink drain just to see what happens. These actions should immediately be interrupted in an understanding but matter-of-fact way. Children shown how tables are built, sanded smooth, and painted or how pipes bring water into and out of our homes will be more likely to understand and care for their environment.

responsibility
Individual accountability and answerability.

Long-Term Goals for Child Guidance

If children are to become responsible, they must learn to control their actions and impulses. Unfortunately, self-control is not an easy thing to teach. Children begin life without any self-control whatsoever, so our most critical long-term **goal** is to assist them in their journey to responsible adulthood by nurturing their mastery of self-control.

Children are not simply lumps of clay to be shaped by caregivers. They are born with individual potentials and personality traits. They are also, however, profoundly influenced by the people, experiences, and events they encounter, especially during the first years of their lives (Baillargeon, 1997; Begley, 1997; Begley & Springen, 1997; Berk, 1997; Bodrova & Leong, 1996; Eddowes & Ralph, 1998; Jackson, 1997; Stevenson & Lee, 1990). The effect of the environment on children, interestingly, is reciprocal. Children have tremendous impact on the behavior of the adults in their lives. Instead of being passively shaped by adults, children are actively involved in the experiences that influence their own development. Adults behave differently with different children. The actions and appearances of individual children trigger different emotions and reactions in individual adults.

Children are born with individual and distinctive behavioral patterns (Collins & Gunnar, 1990; Rutter, 1976; Santrock, 1997; Sroufe, 1996; Thomas & Chess, 1977; Thomas et al., 1970). These clusters of personality traits are referred to as **temperament.** The temperament of an infant or child has an influence on how adults will care for him. Also, the quality and style of the care that adults provide have a strong influence on that continually developing temperament. He affects his caregivers and they affect him; both change and are changed by their interactions. All these influences, both internal and external, ensure that no two people will ever be exactly the same. We must help children celebrate and appreciate their differences.

Furthermore, even if two children's behavior is similar, their gender, size, or appearance may trigger different adult reactions. A thin, frail infant girl may evoke more protective, nurturing behavior in adults than would a loud, robust infant boy who may evoke more roughhousing and active playfulness in caregivers. A child who appears defiant may be treated sternly, whereas a child who appears contrite may be treated indulgently after an identical incident. A cycle emerges in which the child begins to anticipate a certain kind of interaction with others so he behaves accordingly, actually triggering the expected interaction. What began as incidental action and reaction settles eventually into habit, attitude, and personality. The bottom line is, of course, that early experiences make a difference in children's lives.

goal
Overarching purpose or aspiration.

temperament
Clusters of personality traits with individual and distinctive behavioral patterns.

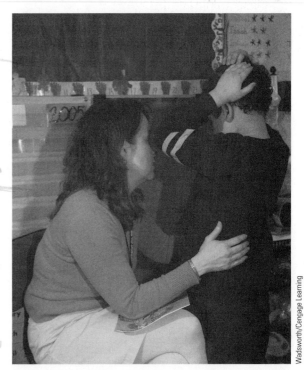

Children begin life without any self-control whatsoever, so our most critical long-term goal is to assist them in their journey to responsible adulthood by nurturing their mastery of self-control.

Wadsworth/Cengage Learning

We play a critical role in shaping children's future lives. Our long-term goal for guidance is our most important contribution: equipping children with the skills and attitudes they need for happy, responsible, and productive adult life. The early childhood setting, whether in the home or in a child care center, is a miniature community in which children develop and practice the rudimentary skills they will need to cope with the larger community they encounter as they go through school and then finally the big, wide world when they are grown. Child guidance builds a foundation on which everything else in the child's life is built, including social interaction with others, academic learning, and personal development. By their very nature, babies come into this world helpless, self-centered, and dependent. Guidance transforms them into full-fledged, functioning members of society.

The Nurturing Environment and Long-Term Development

High-quality early childhood settings look so simple that it is easy to underestimate the importance of the interactions there. An appropriate environment for young children is relaxed and playful. Children follow their own curiosity as they freely but respectfully explore objects, toys, and materials in the environment. They move about, chatter peacefully, laugh, and occasionally argue as they explore human social interactions and learn reasonable limits. A home where children are expected to be seen and not heard or a formal school setting with pupils sitting rigidly and silently following teacher instructions or listening to lectures is not an example of optimal early environments.

The rote memorization typical in lessons with workbooks, flash cards, and ditto sheets is definitely something many young children can master if coerced, pressured, and bribed. The abstract concepts this memorized jargon represent, however, are totally unrelated to young children's level of brain development and, therefore, rather meaningless for them. Even very young children can memorize and repeat chants and rhymes with long words, but they are unlikely to have a clue as to their meaning. If too much time is spent in such questionable ventures as rote memorization, the loss of time for more wholesome experiences can interfere with the really essential business of early childhood; that is, healthy development of the whole child, socially, emotionally, and physically. The foundation of early learning is exploring, practicing, constructing, pretending, and problem solving (Gestwicki, 1999; Gordon & Browne, 1996). Experience truly is the best teacher for young children (Dewey, 1959). For the child to reach full potential, early surroundings must support developmentally appropriate practice (DAP) experiences (NAEYC, 1993).

Wadsworth/Cengage Learning

Affection and attention foster the long-term development of children's potential to become competent, confident, cooperative people.

Positive Adult Role Models . . .

- Treat everyone with dignity and respect at all times.

- Rely on communication, persistence, and patience rather than on force.

- Respond assertively to misbehavior with both firmness and gentleness.

- Use problem-solving strategies to identify the causes of misbehavior.

- Plan and prepare appropriate activities, materials, and routines.

- Give unconditional affection and affirmation.

- Communicate in an honest, polite, and straightforward manner.

- Protect every child's individual rights.

- Celebrate differences.

- Really listen.

Matching early childhood settings to the natural stages of growth and development of infants, toddlers, and young children; involving their parents; and valuing their community and culture create the foundation for DAP. Detailed information about DAP can be obtained through the **National Association for the Education of Young Children** website (http://www.naeyc.org). (Further description of methods to set the stage for positive behavior by creating a developmentally appropriate early childhood environment is provided in Chapter 6.)

In family settings where parents have strong bonds of love for and attachment to their child, they will quite naturally respond to cries and smiles when that child needs attention or care. A healthy, well-developing baby or child gives many signals or cues to indicate needs. A sensitive, caring parent uses trial and error to discover what will work to stop the child's crying and to keep the child happy and comfortable. This same give-and-take can be the heart of group care. If we see child care as a tedious chore that can be made easier by ignoring the child's cries and refusing to become emotionally attached, then nature's way of ensuring healthy development is undone. Caregivers and teachers who do not find joy in working with children may well be advised to seek different careers.

National Association for the Education of Young Children (NAEYC)
A professional organization for early childhood educators dedicated to improving the well-being of all young children, with particular focus on the quality of educational and developmental services for all children from birth through age eight.

Children—Our Investment in the Future

In some child care situations where working conditions are stressful, pay is bottom of the barrel, training is inadequate, and staff turnover is never ending, teachers and caregivers may not be able to function consistently at a level that parents would want their children to emulate. Parents, early educators, and public policy makers are becoming acutely aware of the significance of early experience on long-term development. Too often, in past years, it has been assumed that child care need be little more

Wadsworth/Cengage Learning

▬▬Do adults in the child care center appear to genuinely enjoy and appreciate the individual qualities of each child in their care?

than a kindly but custodial parking lot for youngsters. Growing evidence from the study of human development indicates that the first years of life may be the most, rather than the least, critical years in a child's emotional, physical, and intellectual growth (National Association of Child Care Resource and Referral Agencies, 2006; Zigler et al., 2004; Webster-Stratton, 2000; Ackerman, 2006; Schweinhart, 2004; Carnegie Corporation of New York, 1994).

Child care centers, preschools, mother's-day-out programs, and other early childhood settings have the potential to help parents create a better future for children and for society in general. To have resources, support, and high expectations from communities, the child care profession must come to be viewed as an integral part of our educational system, as well as a necessary service to support the economic well-being of low-income families (Meyers & Jordan, 2006; Clampet-Lundquist et al., 2003; Scott, Gillespie, & Innes, 2003; Barnett & Ackerman, 2006; Adams & Rohacek, 2002; Galinsky & Bond, 2000; O'Donnell, 2006).

Because early experiences are so important to healthy development, child care outside the family takes on special significance. The first question parents should ask as they examine child care alternatives is "Are the adults in this setting warm, nurturing, and emotionally available to the children?" And because imitation and firsthand experience, rather than direct teaching, are the major avenues for learning in young children, the next crucial questions parents might ask are "Do I want my child to absorb the personality traits, communication styles, and problem-solving behaviors of the adults here?" and "Do these adult role models set an example for behavior that I value and want my child to imitate?"

Committing to Become the Child's Resource Team

Parents are children's first teachers—and they are children's teachers throughout childhood. We have only a brief opportunity to make a difference. If we are to reach our goals, we must partner with the people ultimately responsible for the children in our care—the parents. To be effective in guiding children, teachers and parents must work as a cooperative and cohesive team. Mother, father, or guardian, and teacher should communicate frequently and respectfully about the child's needs.

The key to creating an effective **parent–teacher resource team** is empowerment and communication. Parents are accustomed to being in charge of their children. It is very frustrating for them to be kept in the dark about their children's activities and progress. Many parents fear that they will be perceived as too intrusive. Other parents, especially those lacking in education, may feel intimidated by teachers. Additionally, some parents whose children are particularly challenging may avoid interacting with teachers for fear of hearing about their child's inappropriate behavior.

Teachers can open the channels of communication with all of these parents by treating them with respect. Teachers can show respect for each parent by conveying in everything they do that each child has strengths and is valued. They can empower parents by allowing them to have a meaningful voice in the child's education.

parent–teacher resource team
Teachers and parents working together as a cooperative, respectful, and cohesive team.

Handy Tips	
For Parents	**For Teachers**
• Read to children every day. • Read in front of children daily (set an example). • Talk often about how learning helps people. • Write frequent notes to teachers. • Take time to really listen to the child. • Sit on the floor; let the child lead play activity. • Give the child chores; ensure that the child succeeds. • Let the child make choices from three options. • Monitor and support play with peers.	• Convince parents that involvement is valuable. • Develop a simple parent involvement plan. • Know that intensive plans overwhelm. • Start a classroom newsletter to parents. • Take time to really listen to parents. • Use a folder to send work and notes home. • Teach parents how to be school volunteers. • Show parents how to make learning games. • Display children's work and invite parents to view it.

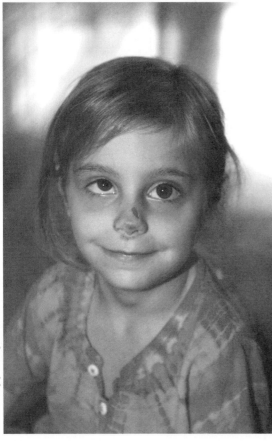

Teachers must convey to parents that the child entrusted to their care has strengths and is valued as a unique individual.

The parent–teacher resource team can brainstorm together what changes in the child's environment are needed from time to time. Will parents need to unplug the television at home to ensure more quality time? Will the teacher need to increase individual attention for a challenging child? How will the team communicate day-to-day changes in children's health and emotional well-being? How can the team nurture budding learning in a certain area? Or work on a negative habit pattern that has begun developing?

Critical Home–School Communication Issues

- Are daily, weekly, or monthly folders of student progress sent home for parent review, questions, and feedback?
- What is the procedure for daily communications? Is there an easy way for teacher and parent to communicate about the schedule, the child's needs, to request a conference, or to discuss a problem?
  - Is communication hurried, in front of the child, or limited to crisis situations?
- Are notes, letters, phone calls, newsletters, and other communications sent to parents frequently?
  - Are communications to parents easy to read? Are they simple, clear, and in the appropriate language?
  - What special arrangements are made for parents who have limited English, have reading problems, or have limited vision?
  - Is communication reciprocal? Are there frequent invitations for feedback from parents?
- Are conferences held with every parent at least once a year, with follow-ups as needed?
  - Are language translators available to assist families if needed?
- Do teachers always include parents as full participants in important school decisions?
  - Do teachers make sure parents know that they will be treated with dignity and respect regardless of their social, ethnic, or financial background?
  - Do teachers help parents recognize how important their involvement is to their child's educational success?
  - Do teachers help parents understand the school's educational philosophy— its programs and policies?
  - Do teachers enthusiastically work to recruit, train, and schedule parents as volunteers in school activities?

Wadsworth/Cengage Learning

- Do teachers see themselves as a support system for families?
  - Are teachers willing to tactfully provide help for families in the form of parenting and child-rearing skills?
  - Do teachers encourage families to become involved in learning activities at home?
  - Do teachers coordinate with businesses and community agencies to provide resources and coordinate services for families and children?

KEY TERMS

adult

child guidance

developmentally appropriate practice

dual-earner couples

family structures

goal

National Association for the Education of Young Children

objective

parent–teacher resource team

positive, assertive guidance

responsibility

single parents

temperament

POINTS TO REMEMBER

- Contemporary family life brings special stresses and strains to children and families.
- The basic rules for responsible human behavior are simple: respect the rights of others, take only reasonable risks, and protect and maintain the environment.
- Positive guidance is the process of proactively, assertively, and respectfully supporting the development of responsible, self-disciplined children.
- Caregivers should never worry about spoiling babies and toddlers. Attention and interaction helps babies develop to their full intellectual, physical, emotional, and social capacity.
- Ignoring infants' cries interferes with healthy development and undermines the foundation of trust that is critical to later development of self-control and self-discipline.
- To be effective in guiding children, teachers and parents must work as a cooperative, respectful, and cohesive team.
- Teachers should see themselves as a support system for families.

PRACTICAL APPLICATION

The Spoiled Child—Myth or Reality?

It is a glorious day at the park. Bright sunshine is radiating just enough warmth to balance a flag-snapping breeze. This sudden evidence of spring has drawn families and children outdoors like a magnet. Sitting on the grass alongside a large sandbox is a cluster of grown-ups who are laughing and talking as they watch their youngsters squealing and running or digging eagerly in the sand.

Al and Tamara's four-year-old son Joel makes gleeful whooping sounds as he chases his two-year-old brother Eddy with a wriggling bug he has found in the sand. Eddy screeches and dives onto his dad for protection as his mother beseeches Joel to "stop being so wild."

As he skids to a stop, Joel inadvertently smashes into a double stroller holding the Rodriguez twins. While Al escorts his boys back to their buckets and shovels, Tamara bends down with Elena Rodriguez to make sure the one-year-old twin girls are okay.

Several other parents have stopped talking and are watching attentively as Elena adjusts the little girls in their stroller and smoothes their crisp red dresses with identical embroidered collars.

Other mothers are amazed that the twins have not cried. Tamara takes one little girl by the hand and says, "Shall we get them out and let them play for a while?"

"Oh, no," says Elena, "They would get filthy. They know that they have to stay in the stroller." Al comments that his boys were never that "good." They would have pitched a fit to get out and get right in the middle of the dirt.

Several other parents chime in with awe-struck comments about how good the twins are. Elena responds, "I knew with twins and me working that they had better not get spoiled. In the child care center I use, they are very strict about not spoiling the kids. They only pick up the babies to change and feed them. The babies cried for a few days right at first, but now they're just no trouble at all."

The conversation about Elena's twins trails off as other parents scatter to chase after straying toddlers and to respond to their children's cries of "Watch me," "Push me in the swing again," and "Look at my sand castle." As Tamara rushes to Eddy to remind him not to eat sand, she feels a surge of envy for Elena and her "good" babies who are never any trouble.

DISCUSSION QUESTIONS

1. What do people really mean when they label babies either "spoiled" or "good?"
2. What appear to be Elena's priorities and values in caring for her children? What are her daughters learning about their role in the world? Why is that a problem?
3. Why do you think the staff in Elena's child care center were opposed to holding, rocking, and playing with babies? Does frequent holding and cuddling create a setting in which adults are "warm, nurturing, and emotionally available to the children"? Why is this important to children's development?
4. How do you feel about Al and Tamara's relationship with their children?
5. List, in order of importance, the 10 characteristics you personally value and admire most in a person (for example, kindness, sense of humor, energy, intelligence, enthusiasm, and so on). Are these the same characteristics you expect caregivers to model in their interactions with babies and young children? Describe a real situation in which you modeled the characteristic you most value in front of children.
6. List the 10 characteristics you like least in a person. Are these characteristics that you have seen caregivers demonstrate in their interactions with youngsters? Describe a real situation in which you modeled a characteristic you would not want children to imitate.
7. Al and Tamara have a different cultural background from Elena. Do you think their cultural background may have had an effect on their child-rearing style? How?

STUDENT ACTIVITY

1. Interact with one or more preschoolers, reminding them, "Be safe; take turns on the slide," "Be kind; use only words to tell John you are angry," or "Be neat; put your wrapper in the trash can."

   a. Practice until the phrases begin to come to you naturally.
   b. How do preschoolers react to rules?
   c. What have you learned?

2. Sit down with a group of children who are five years old or older. Using the ideas in this chapter, help the children develop their own list of classroom rules.
   a. Did they develop rules for respecting others?
   b. Did they develop rules for safety?
   c. Did they develop rules for protecting the environment?
   d. How do kindergarteners and school-agers react to rules?
   e. What did you learn?

3. Explore using "Be Safe, Be Kind, Be Neat" with one or more toddlers.
   a. Write down notes about your experience.
   b. Compare your notes with other students.
   c. How do toddlers react to rules?
   d. What have you learned?

RELATED READINGS

Contemporary Parenting

Aidman, A. (1997). *Television violence: Content, context, and consequences.* Champaign, IL: ERIC Clearinghouse on Elementary and Early Childhood Education.

Amato, P. R. (1997). Life-span adjustment of children to their parents' divorce. In E. N. Junn & C. Boyatzis (Eds.), *Annual editions: Child growth and development 97/98* (4th ed.). New York: McGraw-Hill. (Original work published in *The Future of Children,* Spring 1994).

Paul Amato provides information on children's adjustment to divorce, including their academic, social, and psychological well-being in childhood and as adults. Amato also describes how children's adjustment depends on many factors and explains that differences are generally small between children of divorce and children from intact families.

Barnett, R. C., & Rivers, C. (1998). *She works, he works: How two-income families are happy, healthy and thriving.* Cambridge: Harvard University Press.

Blankenhorn, D. (1997). Life without father. In K. M. Paciorek & J. H. Munro (Eds.), *Annual editions: Early childhood education 97/98* (18th ed.). New York: McGraw-Hill. (Original work published in *USA Weekend,* February 24–26, 1995).

The increase in divorce and in single-mother families has led to a situation that David Blankenhorn calls "disappearing dads." Children without two caring and supportive parents are at risk of future failure in a number of areas.

Bond, J. T., Galinsky, E., & Swanberg, J. E. (1998). *The 1997 national study of the changing workforce.* New York: The Families and Work Institute.

Bozett, F. W. (1987). *Gay and lesbian parents.* New York: Praeger.

Christian, L. G. (1997, May). Children and death. *Young Children, 52*(4), 76–80.

Cooksey, E. C., & Fondell, M. M. (1996). Spending time with his kids: Effects of family structure on fathers' and children's lives. *Journal of Marriage and the Family, 58*(3), 693–707.

Coontz, S. (1997). Where are the good old days? In K. M. Paciorek & J. H. Munro (Eds.), *Annual editions: Early childhood education 97/98* (18th ed.). New York: McGraw-Hill. (Original work published in *Modern Maturity,* May/June 1996).

Throughout our nation's history, families have always been in flux. Economic changes have resulted in increasing poverty, homelessness, and distress for young children.

Copeland, M. L., & McCreedy, B. S. (1997, January–February). Creating family-friendly policies: Are child care center policies in line with current family realities? *Child Care Information Exchange, 113,* 7–10, 12.

Council of Economic Advisors. (1999, May). *The parenting deficit: Council of Economic Advisors analyze the "time crunch."* Council of Economic Advisors, with commentary by Brian Robertson. Retrieved

March 21, 2006, from http://www.newecon.org/ParentingDeficitCEA-May99.html.

Crouson, R. L., & Boyd, W. L. (1993, February). Coordinated services for children: Designing arks for storms and seas unknown. *American Journal of Education, 101,* 141.

Daly, K. (1996). *Families and time: Keeping pace in a hurried culture.* Thousand Oaks, CA: Sage.

Denby, D. (1997). Buried alive. In E. N. Junn & C. Boyatzis (Eds.), *Annual editions: Child growth and development 97/98* (4th ed.). New York: McGraw-Hill. (Original work published in *The New Yorker,* July 15, 1996).

   In this essay, David Denby argues that "an avalanche of crud" from popular culture television, films, toys, and video and computer games buries today's youth. He offers insight into the impression this culture may leave on children's character and their views of reality.

deToledo, S., & Brown, D. E. (1995). *Grandparents as parents: A survival guide for raising a second family.* New York: Guilford.

   More than a million American grandparents today are the primary caregivers for their grandchildren. Most have found their lives altered, their finances spread thin, and their parenting techniques old-fashioned. They find themselves challenged by a new, different, and sometimes traumatized generation. The book is a useful resource for professionals who work with parenting grandparents, and a good reading recommendation for grandparents and family members who need some encouragement and advice.

Downey, D. B. (1994). The school performance of children from single-mother and single-father families: Economic or interpersonal deprivation? *Journal of Family Issues, 15*(1): 129–147.

Duis, S. S., Summers, M., & Summers, C. R. (1997, Spring). Parent versus child stress in diverse family types: An ecological approach. *Topics in Early Childhood Special Education, 17*(1), 53–73.

Ehrensaft, D. (1997). *Spoiling childhood: How well-meaning parents are giving children too much—but not what they need.* New York: Guilford.

   In this book, Dr. Ehrensaft discusses the difficulties and stresses that today's parents are creating
for themselves and their children. She describes the absurdities, frustrations, and possibilities of contemporary child rearing. She argues that parents today are all too often caught up in a guilt-driven pendulum swing between parenting too little and parenting too much. They are always in a hurry yet anxious for their children to succeed, aware of children's autonomy yet fearful of losing their love. Our culture has created a new kind of child, half miniature adult, half innocent cherub, whose new set of problems creates a divided sense of self and chronic anxiety.*

Elkind, D. (1981). *The hurried child.* Reading, MA: Addison-Wesley.

Elkind, D. (1997). School and family in the postmodern world. In E. N. Junn & C. Boyatzis (Eds.), *Annual editions: Child growth and development 97/98* (4th ed.). New York: McGraw-Hill. (Original work published in *Phi Delta Kappan,* September 1995).

   David Elkind describes how schools and education have undergone, in the postmodern era, major changes due to broader changes in the family and society. One such change is that schools now assume many parental functions.

Epstein, J. L. (1990). School and family connections: Theory, research, and implications for integrating sociologies of education and family. In D. G. Unger and M. B. Sussman (Eds.), *Families in community settings: Interdisciplinary perspectives* (99–126). New York: Haworth Press.

Frieman, B. B. (1993, September). Separation and divorce: Children want their teachers to know—meeting the emotional needs of preschool and primary school children. *Young Children, 48*(6), 58–63.

Galinsky, E. (2001, April). What children want from parents—and how teachers can help. *Educational Leadership, 58*(7), 24–28.

   Galinsky argues that the source of difficulty for modern families is not that many mothers work outside the home but that our society undervalues parenting. She identifies how schools can help parents manage their guilt and stress, value both working and stay-at-home roles, involve more fathers, and raise community awareness.

Gillis, J. (1996). *A world of their own making.* New York: Basic Books.

Helburn, S. W., & Bergmann, B. R. (2001). *America's child care problem: The way out.* New York: Palgrave.

This is a well-researched review of current problems associated with child care and a bold proposal for solutions.

Henderson, A. T. (1987). *The evidence continues to grow: Parent involvement improves student achievement.* Columbia, MD: National Committee for Citizens in Education.

Henderson, A. T., & Berla, N., Eds. (1994). *A new generation of evidence: The family is critical to student achievement.* Washington, DC: National Committee for Citizens in Education.

Hernandez, D. J. (1995, Winter). Changing demographics: Past and future demands for early childhood programs. *Future of Children, 5*(3), 145–160.

Hildebrand, V., Phenice, L. A., Gray, M. M., & Hines, R. P. (1996). *Knowing and serving diverse families.* Upper Saddle River, NJ: Merrill Education/Prentice Hall.

This book responds to the growing need for programs to work comfortably with all people and to help solve critical societal problems of relating to today's people at home and in the community, the nation, and the world. It examines both ethnic and structural diversity in families in the United States.

Hochschild, A. (1989). *The second shift.* New York: Avon Books.

Hochschild, A. R. (1997). *The time bind: When work becomes home and home becomes work.* New York: Henry Holt.

Howe, M. B. (2000). Improving child care and promoting accreditation: The military model. *Young Children, 50*(5), 61–63.

This article gives a brief history of factors leading to dramatic quality improvements in the military's child care system, how the military's child care system has promoted quality, and policies supporting its high accreditation rate.

Isenberg, J. P., & Jalongo, M. R., Eds. (1997). *Major trends and issues in early childhood education: Challenges, controversies, and insights.* New York: Teachers College Press.

Jackson, B. R. (1997, November). Creating a climate for healing in a violent society. *Young Children, 52*(7), 68–70.

Jacobs, J., & Gerson, K. (1998). Who are the overworked Americans? *Review of Social Economy, 4,* 442–459.

Kagan, S. L. (1997, May). Support systems for children, youths, families, and schools in inner-city situations. *Education and Urban Society, 29*(3), 277–295.

Kagan, S. L., & Neuman, M. J. (1997a, September). Highlights of the Quality 2000 Initiative: Not by chance. Public Policy Report. *Young Children, 52*(6), 54–62.

Kagan, S. L., & Neuman, M. J. (1997b). *Solving the quality problem: A vision for America's early care and education system. A final report of the Quality 2000 Initiative.* New Haven, CT: Yale University.

Lakey, J. (1997, May). Teachers and parents define diversity in an Oregon preschool cooperative—Democracy at work. *Young Children, 52*(4), 20–28.

Larson, R. W., Richards, M. H., & Perry-Jenkins, M. (1994). Divergent worlds: The daily emotional experience of mothers and fathers in the domestic and public spheres. *Journal of Personality and Social Psychology, 67,* 1034–1046.

Lee, S. (1993). Family structure effects on student outcomes. In B. Schneider & J. S. Coleman (Eds.), *Parents, their children, and schools.* Boulder, CO: Westview Press, 43–75.

Leland, J. (1997). Violence, reel to real. In E. N. Junn & C. Boyatzis (Eds.), *Annual editions: Child growth and development 97/98* (4th ed.). New York: McGraw-Hill. (Original work published in *Newsweek,* December 11, 1995).

John Leland looks at the debate on violence in film and television and challenges the research conclusion that there is a clear causal relationship between televised violence and real-life aggression. Leland critiques many of the famous studies on the topic, as well as discussing the recent controversy over the V-chip.

Lewin, K., Lippitt, R., & White, R. (1939). Patterns of aggressive behavior in experimentally created social climates. *Journal of Social Psychology, 10,* 271–299.

Three leadership styles—authoritarian, democratic, and laissez-faire (permissive)—were studied. Authoritarian leadership resulted in higher discontentment and aggression among the children but also in more work production. Children in the democratic *model showed less hostility, more enjoyment, and more independent self-direction in their work. The laissez-faire group accomplished relatively little and the children evidenced boredom.*

Lindjord, D. (1997, November–December). Child care: The continuing crisis for working families and child care teachers. *Journal of Early Education and Family Review, 5*(2), 6–7.

McAlister, B. G. (1997, Spring). Growing up in a violent world: The impact of family and community violence on young children and their families. *Topics in Early Childhood Special Education, 17*(1), 74–102.

McLanahan, S., & Sandefur, G. (1994). *Growing up with a single parent: What hurts, what helps.* Cambridge, MA: Harvard University Press.

McMath, J. S. (1997, March). Young children, national tragedy, and picture books. *Young Children, 52*(3), 82–84.

Mitchell, S. (1997). The next baby boom. In K. M. Paciorek & J. H. Munro (Eds.), *Annual editions: Early childhood education 97/98* (18th ed.). New York: McGraw-Hill. (Original work published in *American Demographics,* October 1995).

The nearly 76 million baby boomers born between 1946 and 1964 have produced 72 million children of their own, born from 1977 through 1993. This next generation of boomers is very different from the first. These new children and their families often do not have a father living at home. Parent lifestyles and responsibilities have changed tremendously.

Moore, W. E. (1963). *Man, time and society.* New York: Wiley.

Newman, S., Brazelton, T. B., Zigler, E., Sherman, L. W., Bratton, W., Sanders, J., & Christeson, W. (2000). *Fight crime: Invest in kids* (2nd ed.). Washington, DC: Fight Crime: Invest in Kids, Inc.

This book demonstrates how investing resources in quality early childhood care and development programs would yield such significant crime reductions and other benefits that government would have more money for Social Security, tax cuts, or any other purpose in the years ahead.

Nord, C. W., Brimhall, D., & West, J. (1997). *Fathers' involvement in their children's schools.* NCES, 98-091.

Washington, DC: U.S. Department of Education, National Center for Education Statistics. Retrieved January 20, 2008, from http://nces.ed.gov/pubs98/fathers/.

Nord, C. W., & West, J. (2001). *Fathers' and mothers' involvement in their children's schools by family type and resident status.* U.S. Department of Education, National Center for Education Statistics. Retrieved January 20, 2008, from http://nces.ed.gov/pubs2001/2001032.pdf.

Pallas, A. M., Natriello, G., & McDill, E. L. (1989). The changing nature of the disadvantaged population: Current dimensions and future trends. *Educational Researcher, 18*(5), 16–22.

Pleck, J. (1996). Paternal involvement: Levels, sources and consequences. In M. E. Lamb (Ed.), *The role of the father in child development.* New York: Wiley.

Roberts, P. (1997). Fathers' time. In E. N. Junn & C. Boyatzis (Eds.), *Annual editions: Child growth and development 97/98* (4th ed.). New York: McGraw-Hill. (Original work published in *Psychology Today,* May–June 1996).

Paul Roberts presents evidence on fathers' roles in the family, their influence on children's emotional and intellectual development, and their distinct interaction styles. Roberts also describes how fathers only recently have received attention from researchers, showing that they are no longer subservient in the parenting realm.

Scott-Jones, D. (1984). Family influences on cognitive development and school achievement. In E. W. Gordon (Ed.), *Review of Research in Education, 11.* Washington, DC: American Educational Research Association.

Seefeldt, C., & Glaper, A. (1998). *Continuing issues in early childhood education* (2nd ed.). Upper Saddle River, NJ: Merrill Education/Prentice Hall.

This book contains discussions, debates, disagreements, and disputes, with the expectation that these will lead the reader to explore and question various points of view.

Stengel, R. (1997). Fly till I die. In K. M. Paciorek & J. H. Munro (Eds.), *Annual editions: Early childhood education 97/98* (18th ed.). New York: McGraw-Hill. (Original work published in *Time,* April 22, 1996).

The shocking April 18, 1996, death in a plane crash of seven-year-old pilot Jessica Dubroff, her father, and a flight instructor led many people nationwide to question the parenting skills and knowledge of child development of her parents. Should there be a time when decisions made by families are questioned by the government? Just how much are young children today being pushed to achieve goals that may or may not be their goals?

Stoney, L. (1999, May). Looking into new mirrors: Lessons for early childhood finance and system building. Public policy report. *Young Children, 54*(3), 54–59.

This article reviews research on public policy in housing, health care, higher education, and transportation to evaluate how these policies can be applied to improve early childhood care quality and availability.

Stringer-Seibold, T., et al. (1996, Fall). Strengths and needs of divided families. Research Highlights. *Dimensions of Early Childhood, 24*(4), 22–29.

Stroud, J. E., Stroud J. C., & Staley L. M. (1997, Summer). Understanding and supporting adoptive families. *Early Childhood Education Journal, 24*(4), 229–34.

Swick, K. J. (1997, Spring). Strengthening homeless families and their young children. *Dimensions of Early Childhood, 25*(2), 29–34.

Thorpe, K., & Daly, K. (1999). Children, parents and time: The dialectics of control. In C.L. Shehan (Ed.), *Through the eyes of the child: Revisioning children as active agents of family life.* New York: JAI Press.

Zill, N., & Nord, C. W. (1994). *Running in place: How American families are faring in a changing economy and individualistic society.* Washington, DC: Child Trends.

The Online Companion™ to accompany the sixth edition of *Positive Child Guidance* is your link to additional guidance resources on the Internet. This supplement contains audio and visual materials; PowerPoint presentations; web activities with critical-thinking questions and practical-application assignments; and links to web resources. This additional content can be found at http://www.earlychilded.delmar.com.

Chapter 2

Understanding Children's Behavior

OBJECTIVES

After reading this chapter you should be able to do the following:

- Recognize typical ages and stages of early childhood.
- Identify developmental milestones that affect behavior.
- Identify relationships between maturation and guidance strategies.
- Outline changes over time in adult–child relationships.
- Trace the development of positive self-esteem.
- Reflect on your own ability to adapt to meet children's changing developmental needs.

Identifying individual levels of social, emotional, physical, and intellectual development is intended to assist us in creating developmentally appropriate activities for children. It must never be used to label or stereotype children.

Wadsworth/Cengage Learning

Typical Ages and Stages

The most important thing to remember when considering the typical ages and stages of childhood is that no child is completely typical. Every child is unique. Although typical or average patterns can be identified, children have individual patterns and rates of development that may be normal but not at all average. The only valid reason for comparing a child's rate of development to standard rates is to be alert to any consistent pattern of differences, or red flags, that may indicate a need for professional screening and possibly the need for therapeutic intervention.

Sometimes, by comparing a child's individual behaviors with typical behaviors, we can better understand the child, recognize that the child is only going through a normal phase, and anticipate phases that the child will soon be entering. Adults are often comforted to know that many children at a certain age behave the same way as the child with whom they are dealing. Babies shy away from strangers, toddlers become stubbornly assertive, preschoolers worry about who is or is not their best friend at any given moment, and school-agers reject everything that is not considered cool by their friends. Adults may or may not be relieved to learn that in some instances children outgrow worrisome behavior phases before parents and teachers figure out how to resolve them.

Typical behaviors tend to be consistently clustered together and in a sequential order, so a given child's nontypical behaviors might be those found typically in children at a different chronological age. A seven-year-old who is developmentally delayed may show a wide range of typical toddler behaviors. However, a gifted four-year-old who can already read may act a bit like a school-ager in some behaviors but very much like a preschooler in other behaviors. The value of assessing each child individually is to match guidance strategies to the individual child's developmental capabilities and needs and never to label or stereotype the child.

If, for example, a toddler is discovered trying to poke an object into an electrical outlet, the adult may look very concerned and say, "Ouch, that could hurt you. Come play with your toys." But the primary discipline strategy would be to change the environment to protect the toddler more effectively. A specially designed safety guard should be installed to prevent access to the outlet, or the child could be removed to a safer, better supervised, area.

A five-year-old who is discovered trying to insert an object into an outlet should be handled quite differently from a toddler. The adult must determine whether the child is curious, misinformed, or feeling rebellious. When the adult has a sense of why the behavior has occurred, he might firmly discuss the cause-and-effect dangers of playing with electrical outlets. He should then redirect the child's curiosity by helping the child explore the characteristics of electricity using a safe six-volt battery, wires, and a tiny flashlight bulb. The child's curiosity could be channeled into a whole new area of interest and knowledge by reading books about electricity. She can be taken outside to look at power lines, to talk about how workers protect themselves when they repair dangerous electrical wires, and to make pretend wires out of strings to attach to the child's playhouse.

The innate temperament of an individual child, the temperament of parents and early caregivers, the environmental setting, the culture, and even the child's role in the family all affect development. The important thing to remember is that every child is a unique human being.

Infants (Birth to 12 Months)

Babies are fascinating. Their big eyes and rounded contours are specially designed to turn grown men and women to mush (Alley, 1981). Babies are soft and warm and cuddly, but few parents are prepared for the powerful emotions that well up inside them when they, for the first time, have their own child. Some parents feel a jumble

How Does Guidance Change to Match Development?

Piaget's Stages	Appropriate Guidance
Sensorimotor—Birth to Age 2 • Development is largely nonverbal. • Motor control integrates with the senses. • Children develop the concept of object permanence and the ability to form mental representations.	• Provide responsive, affectionate caregiving. • Provide consistent, predictable routines. • Nurture the development of trust by responding promptly to the child's needs.
Preoperational—Ages 2 to 7 • Children's thought is egocentric—they cannot easily take the viewpoint of another. • Children develop an increasingly refined understanding of cause and effect. • They develop the ability to think symbolically and to use language skillfully.	• In a caring and consistent way, teach self-help skills such as self-feeding, toilet learning, and dressing. • Give children opportunities to make choices within reasonable limitations. • Provide a developmentally appropriate environment for the child to explore and challenge emerging skills. • As children grow, increase their responsibilities to match their abilities.
Concrete Operations—Ages 7 to 11 • Children learn the concept of two-way conversation. • They cannot reason abstractly or test hypotheses systematically, but they can think logically and see through obviously flawed thinking.	• Provide creative activities. • Give encouragement and deserved recognition to support the development of competence and self-esteem. • Use class meetings to solve problems. • Teach conflict-resolution skills. • Nurture each child to help her discover and develop her own special talents and abilities.
Formal Operations—Starts at Age 11 or 12 • Children begin to reason abstractly. • Thinking becomes issue focused and less egocentric. • Children can consider hypothetical possibilities. • Children begin to develop deductive reasoning, depending on educational opportunities and the child's willingness.	• Provide children support in developing a positive self-identity as their bodies begin to change and mature at different rates. • Provide support for the development of strong peer relationships and friendships. • Give children responsibility for tasks that genuinely contribute to the family, classroom, or community. • Stop any bullying and ensure routine use of conflict resolution.

Atherton, 2005; Donohue-Colletta, 1995; Schaefer & Digeronimo, 2000.

Erik Erikson's Psychosocial Stages of Human Development

Stage 1: Infants—Birth to 1 Year

Crisis: Trust versus mistrust

Description: Early in life, infants depend on others for food, care, and affection and must blindly trust caregivers to meet their needs.

Positive outcome: A *sense of hope*—if their needs are met consistently and responsively, infants will not only develop a secure attachment but learn to trust their environment.

Negative outcome: If not, infants will not trust people and things in their environment.

Stage 2: Toddlers—1 to 2 Years

Crisis: Independence versus doubt and shame

Description: Toddlers begin to develop self-help skills, self-feeding, potty learning, dressing, and so on, at this age. Their self-confidence in this stage hinges on their negotiation of this difficult new territory with caregivers.

Positive outcome: A *strong will*—if caregivers encourage the child's initiative and encourage her when she fails, she will develop confidence.

Negative outcome: If caregivers are overprotective, negative, or disapproving of her newfound independence, she may doubt her abilities or feel shame.

Stage 3: Preschoolers—2 to 6 Years

Crisis: Initiative versus guilt

Description: Children find a new sense of power and freedom as they develop the motor skills and the language skills they need to become fully engaged in the environment and the social interactions around them. They discover that with this power and freedom comes new adult pressure to control immature impulses and to follow rules.

Positive outcome: A *sense of purpose*—if parents are encouraging, positive, and consistent in guidance, children learn to accept rules without guilt.

Negative outcome: If not, children may develop a sense of guilt and may become clingy and dependent or rebellious and resistant.

Stage 4: Elementary and Middle School-Agers—6 to 12 Years

Crisis: Industry versus inferiority

Description: School is the critical factor of this stage. Children make a transition from the world of home into the world of community, school, and peers. Home is still important, but succeeding outside the home takes on new importance.

Positive outcome: A *feeling of competence*—if children learn that they can succeed, that others value their work, they develop a sense of competence.

Negative outcome: If not, they will develop a sense of inferiority and may start looking for negative ways to win status with peers.

Erikson, 1959.

Who can resist the soft, endearing face of a baby?

of emotions such as outrageous pride, a protectiveness as passionate as a tiger for her cubs, jealousy of any imagined competition for affection, overwhelming fatigue, fear of failure, and even grief over the loss of infancy as the child grows and matures so quickly.

Parenting is one of the most significant and challenging adventures adult human beings undertake (often with little or no preparation). If additional caregivers are involved in infant care, parents may be relieved of some stresses and strains, but other complex feelings or tensions may emerge. Many a mother has left her baby in a carefully chosen child care center for the first time only to sit in the parking lot, collapsed in tears on the steering wheel of her car.

Fathers, grandparents, even siblings also fret over the adequacy of anyone helping to care for the new baby. Jenny, a kindergartner in a child care center, talked her teacher into letting her go to the nursery where her two-month-old brother was newly enrolled. There, she held her baby brother's tiny hand through the bars of his crib for a long time as she carefully watched every move made by the nursery workers. The employees listened smilingly as the little girl pointed out to them, "You mustn't touch his head right up there where it's soft." Although Jenny was only five, she felt protective and concerned about her baby brother.

Do Infants Intentionally Respond by Crying?

Usually, the first kind of upsetting behavior adults must cope with in caring for infants are bouts of crying. A typical scenario is the adult trying all the usual problem-solving strategies: warming a bottle, changing a diaper, or rocking. Soon, the adult has done everything she knows to do, but the infant cries even more frantically. Some adults hear the infant's wails as a personal indictment of their competence, integrity, or authority: "How dare this baby accuse me of being a bad father (or mother, or caregiver)!" A howling baby can quickly fray the nerves of even the most patient and devoted adult.

A temptation for many of us is the tendency to project intentional motives on the baby for her crying. We say such things as "She's just crying because she knows I'm a pushover," "She always cries when I try to cook, because she thinks she should be the center of attention," or "She's only crying because she's mad at me. She was born with a fiery temper." These rationalizations may make us feel vindicated for angry or resentful feelings that surge through us as we try to deal with the screaming baby, but they are, nevertheless, inaccurate. Infants do not intentionally do much of anything. They simply react spontaneously and unconsciously to their environment.

Sadly, some adults with virtually no understanding of the processes of child development see infant crying as such a clear example of intentional "bad" behavior that they attempt to punish the infant for her crying. Child protective services workers and other social agents often deal with parents who begin shaking, hitting, and spanking babies in the first year of life—a terribly dangerous and inappropriate practice—in the mistaken belief that they are helping their babies learn to be "good."

Can Babies Misbehave on Purpose?

Regardless of many common misconceptions, in the first months of life, infants have no capacity for consciously intentional behavior. They are not able to think about or plan actions to get desired results. Until they have **object permanence** (the mental ability to envision persons, objects, or events that are not in sight), they cannot "think" or "know" that any action will bring about a desired result. They can react or respond only in a very unconscious way to internal feelings such as pain or hunger and to external **stimuli**—sensations the infant sees, feels, hears, tastes, or smells (Piaget, 1968).

Piaget believed that babies developed object permanence toward the end of the sensorimotor period (close to age two). New studies indicate that younger infants may develop object permanence but lack skills to act on that knowledge (Flavell et al., 2002).

object permanence
The knowledge that something hidden from view is not gone forever but rather is in another location at that time and likely to reappear.

stimuli
Something taken in through the senses that might incite activity or thought, something seen, smelled, heard, felt, or tasted; an incentive for action.

Infant Brain Development

- Brain development that takes place before age one is more rapid and extensive than previously realized.
- Early brain development is more vulnerable to environmental influence than was previously known.
- The influence of early environment on brain development is long lasting.
- The environment affects not only the number of brain cells and the number of connections among them but also the way these connections are "wired."
- There is increasing evidence of the negative impact of early stress on brain function (Gallagher, 2005; Gerhardt, 2004; Shonkoff & Phillips, 2000).

Even in toddlers, some behaviors that may seem intentional are actually **unconscious reactions** based on the child's having absorbed connections or relationships among day-to-day experiences. Unrelated objects, events, and sensations become connected. We might expect any nine-month-old to show curious interest in a brightly colored, shiny can. If the child immediately fusses and struggles for the can of soft drink she sees in her mother's hand, though, it is pretty clear her experience has led her to expect a sip whenever she sees a soft drink can.

unconscious reactions
Actions that are unplanned, devoid of forethought.

What Are Reflex Responses, and What Is Unconscious Conditioning?

In newborns, almost all actions are simple reflexes over which the child has no control. Infants blink, startle, grasp an object placed in the palm of the hand, and root toward a nipple, but not because they choose to do those things. They do them simply because their brains are designed to make certain behaviors happen automatically.

From the moment of birth, however, babies carefully study their environment, at first by staring and eventually by using all their senses. Babies gradually progress beyond reflex behavior. They begin to recognize and associate things they see, feel, hear, taste, and smell with other meaningful sensations or events. A hungry, breast-fed infant will become very agitated when she is held near her mother's breast. The feel, smell, and sight of the breast is closely associated with the memory of the sweet taste of milk. This is called **unconscious conditioning**.

What Is Classical Conditioning?

To a baby, hearing keys rattle means someone is leaving, being placed in a stroller means going for a walk, or hearing the rustle of plastic wrap means getting a cookie. This kind of learning is generally categorized as **classical conditioning**. Looking at a balloon does not normally make babies cry (seeing a balloon is an unconditioned stimuli). Loud noises, however, certainly do make them cry (crying in response to a loud bang is a naturally occurring stimulus–response connection). If a baby has been frightened and has cried on several occasions when balloons have popped, then the baby may begin to cry whenever she even sees a balloon. This is a conditioned stimulus–response connection.

Researchers have, for decades, attempted to document classical conditioning (pairing an unconditioned stimuli with a naturally occurring stimulus–response connection) in newborns. The best that has yet been documented is a rather rough kind of learning now called **pseudoconditioning.** Studying early responses is difficult because so little of the newborn's movement can really be classified as voluntary (Rosenblith & Sims-Knight, 1985; White, 1995). However, by the middle of the infant's first year, classical conditioning is clearly a part of the child's learning.

What Is Operant Conditioning?

Operant conditioning is quite different from classical conditioning. It occurs when the child's spontaneous actions (such as crying) are reinforced by pleasurable rewards (such as food). This type of conditioning has been studied and documented in infants from the first days and weeks of life (Sameroff & Cavanagh, 1979). Newborns automatically cry as a response to the discomfort of being hungry. Older babies and toddlers learn to whimper or make a "fake" crying sound to signal that they are hungry. In the classical conditioning example previously described, babies became excited by sensations that unconsciously reminded them of being fed. In operant conditioning, however, hungry babies learn to repeat whatever behaviors have in the past resulted in their being fed. For example, if a breast-fed infant is nursed whenever she roots and pulls at her mother's blouse, then that action (rooting and pulling) may become an unconscious but **learned behavior** that she repeats whenever she is hungry.

A baby first turns toward a nipple in response to an unconditioned rooting reflex. Then, over time, the pleasurable reward of warm milk stimulates more active and goal-oriented rooting. Eventually, the sight of the nipple, the feel of being placed in a nursing position, or other sensory cues (the smell of milk or the sound of a

unconscious conditioning
A response developed through the use of all the senses; an association of things seen, felt, heard, tasted, and smelled with other meaningful sensations or events.

classical conditioning
Teaching a new response triggered by a new stimulus by pairing it repeatedly with a stimulus for which there is a physiological reflex (sometimes called *Pavlovian conditioning*). This term derives from an experiment originally performed by Ivan Pavlov in which a bell was rung just as food was offered to a hungry dog. Soon the dog would salivate at the sound of the bell whether or not food was offered, demonstrating that the association had become learned.

pseudoconditioning
The pairing of an unconditioned stimuli with a naturally occurring stimulus–response connection.

operant conditioning
A kind of learning that occurs when a spontaneous behavior is either reinforced by a reward or discouraged by punishment. For example, mice who go through a maze the wrong way get a shock. If they go the right way, they get some cheese. So they eventually learn to go the right way every time.

voice) will trigger rooting and sucking. An adult who is unfamiliar with a specific baby may inadvertently cause her to become frustrated and cry simply by holding her, without feeding her, in a position that she associates with nursing.

What Is Metacognition?

Young infants need many repetitions of unfamiliar sensations, actions, and events to form associations. By the end of their first year, however, they have learned, through conditioning, to expect many specific responses to accompany certain actions and sensations (Papousek, 1967). This kind of learning is an unconscious process. Although unconscious, conditioned learning continues to take place throughout life, months and years will pass before a child will develop an ability to consciously and intentionally control her own behavior, a process we call **metacognition**.

When a child has developed metacognition, she will be able to think about her own thinking processes and develop strategies to help her manage her own behavior. Children between three and six years old are only beginning to develop metacognition. Janah, age four, was beginning to use her developing metacognition when she put glue into her mittens before she put them on because she was worried that she might lose them. School-age children have a much better developed ability to plan strategies. Babies and toddlers possess none of these skills; they just spontaneously react to the positive and negative sensations in their world.

How Do Babies Develop Control of Their Actions?

The first muscles babies can actively control are those around the face and head. A newborn can move her eyes to follow objects, she can suck effectively, and she can turn her head. Muscle development proceeds from head to toe and from the trunk to the extremities: **cephalocaudal** (top to bottom) and **proximodistal** (close to far). At first, infants are only able to control a few mouth, eye, and neck muscles.

Gradually, an infant expands body control downward into the trunk (she learns to turn over), outward through the arms to the hands (she learns to bat at objects and then to grasp them), and finally down the legs to the feet (she learns to crawl and then walk). Tiny muscles of the hands and fingers will not be fully developed for years (then she will finally be able to use her fingers to button her sweater, tie her shoelaces, and write her name).

Why Do Babies Cry?

In the child's first year of life, behaviors result almost exclusively from internal developmental characteristics along with gradually increasing conditioned learning. If a baby cries for a prolonged period, that behavior does not stem from manipulativeness, maliciousness, or any other kind of conscious intention but rather from internal discomfort, stress, or fatigue or from externally conditioned routines. Babies cannot be held responsible or blamed for their behavior. It is more realistic to think in terms

---

learned behavior
An action repeated because it produced a favorable response in the past. A behavior that is taught by the reinforcing response of another person. This develops in children in the preoperational stage of cognitive growth in Piaget's theory.

metacognition
The ability to reflect on or evaluate one's behavior or actions.

cephalocaudal
Development in a pattern from the head downward, toward the feet (head to toe).

proximodistal
Development in a direction from closest to the body's trunk to the farthest, such as controlling the muscles of the trunk, then the muscles down the arms, and finally the hands (close to far).

Babies naturally respond to such things as discomfort, hunger, boredom, and fear.

Wadsworth/Cengage Learning

habituated
The process of becoming accustomed to frequent repetition or pattern of behavior.

stress
The process of recognizing and responding to threat or danger.

of relieving the cause of a crying infant's unhappiness if the problem is internal or of changing adult routines or the environment if the problem is external.

Adults are the ones who establish routines and habits in infants through day-to-day basic care patterns. Infants become **habituated** (accustomed) to those patterns and object loudly when routines are abruptly broken. If an infant is accustomed to being in constant contact with her mother's body, she will cry pitifully when she is left unexpectedly in a playpen. If an infant is accustomed to quiet isolation, he may be terrified by sudden placement in a noisy, bustling child care center. Psychologists define **stress** as the process of recognizing and responding to threat or danger (Fleming, Baum, & Singer, 1984). While working directly with infants over the years in various child care facilities, I have on several occasions seen babies who seemed especially upset by a separation or by a stark upheaval in their care arrangements. In spite of attentive caregivers, the infants (ranging from three to nine months of age) appeared to slip from a long period of anguished, relentless crying into a period of quiet depression with only languid whimpering.

The infants withdrew from social contact, avoided eye contact, lost appetite, refused to play, slept too much or too little, and apparently as a result, appeared noticeably less healthy after a time. After various lengths of time (ranging from days to months), each of these babies eventually recovered spontaneously and became responsive, robust, and playful. Today, almost a decade later, even the one of these infants most severely affected gives every appearance of being a bright, healthy, and well-adjusted young girl. Nevertheless, stress should be considered in dealing with children of any age and avoided or eased whenever possible.

Careful planning of basic care and nurturing routines that can be maintained consistently will help protect the child from abrupt and upsetting changes. When changes in routines must occur, careful planning and gradual orientation should take place—especially before drastic upheavals in child care arrangements—to avoid subjecting babies to unnecessary stress (Gallagher, 2005; Trad, 1986, 1987, 1991, 1994; Provence & Lipton, 1967).

How Do Trauma and Chronic Stress Affect an Infant's Brain Development?

Constant exposure to stressful environments can dramatically change the way an infant or young child's brain develops, making the child more prone to emotional disturbances and less able to learn. Children exposed to severe, prolonged stress often develop learning disabilities and emotional and behavioral problems (for example, attention deficit disorder, anxiety, and depression). They also become more vulnerable to medical problems such as asthma, immune-system dysfunction, and heart disease (Poussant & Linn, 1997; Pransky, 1991; Prothrow-Stith & Quaday, 1995; Shore, 1997).

How Do Babies Develop Trust?

According to Eric Erikson (1959, 1963, 1982), trust developed in infancy is a primary foundation for development of the healthy emotional attitudes that must be built on throughout life. Basic care patterns offer our first opportunity to demonstrate our trustworthiness to an infant. Whenever the infant experiences internal distress, she automatically responds by crying. In time, through operant and classical conditioning, she can come to expect a dependable and pleasurable response from the adult caregivers in her life. This trust in the predictability of her environment and in the responsiveness of her primary caregivers helps the baby develop a sense that she is valued and that she can affect her surroundings, the first step toward the development of positive self-esteem.

Appropriate touch has a powerful calming and bonding effect for babies and young children (Mantagu, 1986). Infants need a great deal of physical contact. Not only does physical contact help them feel calm and organized but it is necessary for their growth and development. A pacifier, rocking or swinging motions, and cuddly toys calm the baby because they mimic the sensations she felt when nursing, being held, rocked, or cuddled. But these are just substitutes. What the baby needs most is authentic physical contact—holding, carrying, massaging, playing, hugging, and rocking.

appropriate touch
Suitable for the occasion and the person affected, nonexploitative, and having no concealed intention; physical contact that is casual, affectionate, reciprocal, and welcome, but never sexual or controlling.

What Is Learned Helplessness?

Babies who are caught in a flow of events that are unpredictable and clearly outside their control may develop an unfortunate style of response termed **learned helplessness** (Honig, 1986; Honig & Wittmer, 1997). Heartbreaking but very instructive studies of the Creche, a Romanian orphanage run by French nuns, helped researchers more fully understand the devastating impact of learned helplessness. Babies in this orphanage were adequately fed, clothed, and kept warm and dry, but the babies stayed in cribs with only uninteresting white crib bumpers and white ceilings to look at. There were few playthings and no structured activities. Caregivers were not aware that talking directly to and interacting with babies was necessary.

Because the babies were fed and changed on a schedule, there was no motivation for caregivers to respond to the babies' cries, so the babies soon learned that there was no use in crying. In effect, the children had no influence on their environment. Nothing that happened to them hinged on either spontaneous or learned actions on their part. They had no incentive to function in any way other than as passive objects in the environment, and in fact, their behavior was soon not much livelier than that of a potted plant. These babies did not learn to sit up until a year old or walk until four or five years old. By age six, their IQs were about 50, which is half the normal IQ and well into the range of serious mental retardation (Dennis, 1960, 1973).

learned helplessness
A person's inability to take action to make his or her life better, arising out of a sense of not being in control.

The Concept of Spoiling

A long-standing folk belief in some cultures is that responding quickly to babies and holding or playing with them will result in "spoiling" and will make the child excessively demanding and dependent. Sometimes caregivers are tempted to leave babies in cribs or playpens for the sake of convenience or to put them on a rigid schedule for feeding, changing, and sleeping, regardless of the child's day-to-day preferences. We know now that lots of holding, touching, talking, and playing with babies is critical for them to grow and learn properly, so do not ever hesitate to give positive attention.

Adults who care for babies should be down on the floor laughing, talking, singing, playing, and interacting with the babies, not sitting in rocking chairs watching television programs while babies are isolated and bored in cribs or playpens. Sometimes adults rationalize this inappropriate behavior by saying, "You shouldn't hold babies and play with them all the time. They'll turn into spoiled brats! It's better for them to learn to entertain themselves."

Obviously, the fundamental needs of an infant for the kind of care that will foster development of social, emotional, intellectual, and physical growth must take priority over questions of convenience for adults. Quality child care, like most other quality endeavors, involves a great deal of effort and hard work. Although overindulgence and overprotection do, indeed, undermine child guidance, lazy or haphazard care and teaching is never in the best interest of children (Bronson, 2001).

How Do I Answer Parents' Sleep Questions?

According to Sears and Sears (2001), infant night-waking has developmental benefits. Sleep researchers have discovered that babies sleep "smarter" than do adults. They theorize that light sleep helps the infant's brain develop because the brain doesn't rest during the active stages of rapid eye movement, or REM, sleep. In fact, blood flow to the brain nearly doubles during REM sleep.

During REM sleep the body increases its manufacture of nerve proteins, the building blocks of the brain. Learning is also thought to occur during the active stage of sleep. The brain may use this time to process information acquired while awake, storing what is beneficial to the individual and discarding what is not. Some sleep researchers believe that REM

Wadsworth/Cengage Learning

Giving babies lots of positive attention is critical for their growth and learning.

sleep acts to autostimulate the developing brain, providing beneficial imagery that promotes mental development. And we thought the baby was just fussy!

Parents often ask early childhood professionals about sharing their beds with their children (Okami et al., 2002; Lindsay, 2002). Bed sharing or cosleeping with a newborn supports breastfeeding. But great care must be taken. If parents choose to have a young infant sleep in their bed, they must be sure to do the following:

- The baby sleeps on his back (unless the doctor says otherwise).
- The baby does not come in contact with soft surfaces or loose covers.
- The sides or edges of the bed do not present entrapment possibilities.
- The bed is not also shared with other siblings.
- The adults do not smoke or use substances such as alcohol or drugs.

Parents also ask about having their preschoolers sleep with them or get in bed with them during the night. Studies show no evidence of any negative long-term results or problems related to responsible bed sharing or cosleeping by parents with their young children (Donohue-Carey, 2002; Sears, 2008; Hauck et al., 2003).

Which Is Best: Flexible Spontaneity or Predictable Routines?

Two opposing priorities for infants have been described so far in this chapter. The reader might well ask at this point, "Should I provide consistent, reliable routines or respond flexibly and spontaneously to cues from the baby?" On one hand, **external environment** (the infant's physical surroundings, daily routines, and patterns of interacting with others) is important because infants shape future expectations through day-to-day learning. On the other hand, an infant's **internal sensations** and needs are important as a basis for adult responses because that process stimulates the child to initiate self-directed behaviors and to assume responsibility for making things happen. Balancing these two opposing needs makes sense, but each individual teacher will develop and apply a personal educational philosophy (addressed in Chapter 10).

There is a third alternative, however. The "developmental interactionist" perspective describes an interweaving between external forces and internal processes. In terms of guiding young children, this process is called **positive child guidance,** the assertive but gentle nudge method. A caregiver can be very responsive to and respectful of **cues** (indications of interest or need) from a baby while gradually nudging the child toward routines that are appropriate and convenient for the adult.

A six-month-old may be allowed to follow her inner drives to explore the sensory qualities of her environment by feeling, squishing, pounding, and smelling her food as she tastes it. However, she can also be gently but persistently nudged over time to handle food in a more traditional manner, gradually to use eating utensils, and eventually, years later, to exhibit polite table manners.

In a domineering **authoritarian-style** setting, the baby would be forced to eat neatly with a spoon or not touch the food at all. In a **permissive-style** setting, where adults abdicate responsibility, they would shrug and passively accept the belief that

external environment
The physical surroundings or conditions around a child that influence his or her growth, development, and learning. A young child's environment can be described as everything the child sees, hears, touches, or experiences.

internal sensations
The physical feelings that are caused by one or more of the sense organs being stimulated. The feelings sensed by one's own body such as hunger or fear.

positive child guidance
Relying on the "developmental interactionist" perspective to create guidance that is primarily based on an interweaving between external forces and internal processes.

cues
Indications of interest or need.

authoritarian style
Interactive (or control) style relying on one-way communication, rigid rules, and punishment—"the sledgehammer."

permissive style
Interactive (or control) style relying on neglect, abdication of responsibility, or over-indulgence—"the doormat."

authoritative style
Interactive (or control) style relying on two-way communication, collaboratively developed rules, and positive guidance—"the guide."

children are hopelessly slovenly in their eating habits and nothing can be done about it. In a respectful **authoritative-style** setting, adults set very reasonable but slightly challenging expectations for the child based on needs, interests, and abilities. They assist the interaction between the child and her environment by allowing her freedom to explore, modeling appropriate behaviors for her, and encouraging her first clumsy attempts to master skills.

What Are Interaction Styles?

Interaction styles are sometimes referred to by researchers as styles, or modes, of control.

The Authoritarian Style

- "Do it because I said so."
- "I don't want to hear any more about it."
- "Do as you're told!"

Authoritarian adults tend to communicate in commands. Their one-way communication does not permit the child to air her concerns or express her opinions. The authoritarian adult relies on punishment, which may be harsh. Rules are rigid. There is no negotiation.

In this environment, children may become sullen, withdrawn, aggressive, quarrelsome, self-destructive, and unable to make responsible decisions. Both cognitive and social skills may lag developmentally (Baumrind, 1967).

The Permissive Style

- "Gee, I hope you're not going to fall off that eight-foot fence."
- "I'd rather pick up your clothes myself than listen to whining."
- "Here, darling, have more chocolates—unless you prefer ice cream."

Adults may be permissive in an indulgent, child-centered way, or they may be permissive in a negligent, uninvolved, adult-centered manner. Both forms of permissiveness hurt children. If children are left to their own devices, allowed to follow their own impulses without limits, and given no expectations, they can't learn positive social skills.

Children in a child-centered indulgent environment tend to become self-centered, bossy, dependent, destructive, and impulsive. They are more likely to have low levels of self-control and achievement.

Children treated in the negligent–permissive, uninvolved interaction style, however, are often harmed most of all. These children may develop very aggressive or destructive behavior patterns (Miller et al., 1993). These behavior patterns tend to persist over time, causing low academic achievement and dysfunctional, antisocial, hostile, or even delinquent behavior (Bullock & Dishion, 2003; Dishion & Bullock, 2002; Patterson et al., 1992; Lamborn et al., 1991).

The Authoritative Style

- "April, please stop."
- "When you shake the hamster cage, Fluffy feels frightened and his water spills."
- "Would you like to get fresh water for Fluffy so you can help him feel better?"

The authoritative style of interaction is characterized by respect, fairness, warmth, open communication, reasoning, consistency, and involvement (Baumrind, 1967). Adults give reasons for rules and are open to negotiation but never abdicate their final responsibility for making good decisions even when they have to say no. Children are given authentic and appropriate choices, are asked for opinions, and are genuinely heard.

Many positive character traits have been correlated with the authoritative style. These include independence, creativity, persistence, mature social skills, optimism, academic competence, original thinking, leadership skills, achievement motivation, self-control, and effective decision-making skills (Baumrind, 1993, 1995; Grolnick & Ryan, 1989; Steinberg et al., 1994; Raikes, 1996).

To learn more, read:

Baumrind, D. (1967). Child care practices anteceding three patterns of preschool behavior. *Genetic Psychology Monographs, 75,* 43–88.

What Do We Mean by Secure Attachment to Caregivers?

The attachment of babies to their adult caregivers is a critical part of their overall healthy social and emotional development. Early studies looked only at mother–infant relationships because that was the only interaction that was considered to be of any importance. Freud focused on the attachment of infants to the mother and theorized that the baby considered her a "love object" simply because she provided pleasurable sucking and warm milk. He believed that the process of weaning, whether it was too rigid or too lenient, set the emotional tone for all of the child's future relationships with people and institutions.

Erikson (1963) extended, revised, and updated Freud's theory. He believed that experiences in the first year of life established in infants a general point of view for perceiving the world, either the positive and accepting reaction of trust or the negative and rejecting reaction of mistrust. He theorized that not only interpersonal relations but also competence in learning to use objects was affected by the baby's relationship to the mother. Exploration is essential for skill development, but babies have the confidence to function competently in exploring the environment only when they have an adult who serves as a "secure base" from which to explore.

Konrad Lorenz (1966) discovered a kind of attachment in certain birds (ducks, chickens, and so on) that he called **imprinting.** The ducks he studied became attached to whatever, or whomever, they saw moving near them when they hatched. Baby ducks that attached to "Papa" Lorenz not only followed him around as they grew up but also tried to mate with his leg when they reached maturity. Ethologists

imprinting
A kind of early bonding in an animal's development that normally results in significant recognition ability and social attraction to members of its own species, especially to its mother.

Babies develop emotional bonds to the significant others in their lives.

(scientists who study behaviors in naturalistic surroundings) do not pretend that human beings behave simplistically and instinctively as ducks do, but they do theorize that some early experiences or attachments have long-term impact on human behavior.

Bowlby (1958) and Ainsworth (1973) studied the processes of human attachment as researchers experienced a dawning awareness that biologic mothers were not the only people who could develop important emotional relationships with infants. Writers began to use the word *parent* instead of *mother* when discussing attachment to reflect awareness of the effect of father–child relationships. Gradually, the term *caregiver* came into use to indicate awareness that babies could develop multiple loving attachments to grandparents, older siblings, and other consistent child care providers outside the family, as well as to adoptive and biologic parents.

Why Do Babies Cling?

It is essential that the process of early attachment be recognized by adults as a valuable occurrence in babies' early development rather than as an inconvenience to be avoided. Elise, a mother with a highly successful career, picked up her 11-month-old son from his child care center one afternoon. The little boy eagerly crawled to his mother and pulled up holding onto her legs. As he clutched at her skirt, clung to her legs, and whined to be picked up, Elise breathed a dismayed sigh, looked helplessly at the infant-room teacher, and said, "Look at him. He just clings to me. What am I doing wrong?"

Elise was not aware that her son was only showing the normal indications of healthy emotional ties to his mother, which Ainsworth called **secure attachment.** When babies brighten at the sight of a caregiver, visually follow that caregiver's movements, smile or vocalize to get attention, hold out their arms to be picked up, or cling to the caregiver, they are showing the typical signs of healthy attachment. Babies who turn or crawl away when a caregiver returns after an absence may be expressing the angry, rejected feelings that accompany a disrupted or poorly formed attachment. Babies who alternately cling and reject, or show a push–pull relationship with the caregiver, may not have built a really secure attachment to the caregiver. Developing secure attachments is an essential step in the growth of normal social and emotional skills.

The positive child guidance concept (assertive but patient nudging) applies well in the area of attachment. Caregivers can best assist infants' healthy social and emotional development by allowing and supporting closeness but also by gradually, as the child seems ready, nudging the child to move out on her own in exploring the environment. A newborn (or a baby in a new child care setting) may need to be held a great deal of the time at first, but gradually she can be enticed to spend increasing amounts

secure attachment
Healthy emotional ties to caregiver. Typical signs include brightening at the sight of caregiver, visually following caregiver's movements, smiling or vocalizing to get attention, holding out arms to be picked up, or clinging to the caregiver.

of time occupying herself by looking at or playing with interesting mobiles, toys, and other surroundings. By getting down on the floor to play with the baby, a caregiver can be readily available to serve as a "secure base" to facilitate the baby's moving out into more and more independent explorations of the surrounding environment.

Separation and Stranger Anxieties

Attachment to caregivers serves as a survival mechanism for the species because an infant's safety depends on staying close to a caregiver. Therefore, it follows logically that an infant would quite naturally resist being separated from the parent figure who provides comfort and security. Sometime between six months and a year, separation and stranger anxieties begin to appear in many children because of their newly developed cognitive adeptness in visually distinguishing between familiar and unfamiliar faces. Coincidentally, many parents first begin to rely on occasional or regular child care at about this same time. We adults are able to think and talk about child care arrangements. We may have studied a substitute caregiver's references or investigated carefully a center's license to provide care, but a baby has no way of comprehending all this.

When a baby looks up and sees that her daddy is not in sight, she feels the same way she would feel if she suddenly realized she was alone in the middle of a big department store. The swarms of strangers hovering around trying to be helpful would, at first, only be more frightening. Amazingly, it is not uncommon for parents or child care workers to be heard chiding a crying baby, "Hush! There is no reason for you to cry." If I were riding in an airplane that made an unexpected landing, or if I were pushed out kicking and screaming and left in a strange land with strangers who did not speak my language, I might cry, too, as I watched the plane carrying my family fly away. When the parent is out of sight, the child is unable to realize that daddy is not gone forever.

The more positive experiences a baby has had with meeting new people, the less uncomfortable she will feel when she separates from parents or encounters strangers. In time, the baby develops a concrete understanding that strangers can be relied on to provide care and that, after a while, parents reappear. Pushing the baby into frightening situations is not helpful, but avoiding encounters with strangers altogether is also counterproductive. Gently nudging the baby into pleasurable and trusting relationships with adults other than parents will assist her in developing confidence and an open, positive attitude toward the world.

How Do Babies Perceive Themselves and Their Surroundings?

In the first months of life, babies have not yet gained a mental conception of themselves as separate individuals. Their perception of their own existence is limited to what they see, feel, taste, smell, and hear. They unconsciously perceive their surroundings as if they were the center of the universe, and the people and objects around them were extensions of their own existence. They make no distinction between their own physical being and the surroundings they perceive through their senses.

Caregivers take on a very important role in this context. Caring for a baby means that they literally become a part of that baby's life. Adults facilitate and guide older children whose interests are focused on each other and on their own activities as much as or more than on adults. In the first year of life, however, infants focus an enormous quantity of their interest and energy on interacting with adult caregivers. They depend on adults for every aspect of physical care and safety, as well as for entertainment and affection. Their interest in peers is purely **egocentric** (centered on one's own needs and desires). A seven-month-old may crawl onto a younger baby and casually grasp a handful of hair to feel and taste, then look quite puzzled by the sudden loud, piercing noises emitted by the little friend.

By seeing adults rushing to rescue the younger baby and **modeling** (demonstrating) appropriate behavior—softly stroking the offended baby's head while saying to the offender, "Gentle, gentle. Be gentle"—babies can eventually **internalize** (adopt as their own) more appropriate ways of behaving. Because the baby identifies so closely with the adult caregiver, the baby will automatically mimic behaviors of that adult. Caregivers who respond harshly or aggressively reinforce inappropriate behaviors in babies by modeling loud or rough interactions.

Toddlers (12 Months to 3 Years)

Burton White (1975) called toddlers "a force to be reckoned with." Any parent, caregiver, or teacher who deals with toddlers probably knows exactly what he means. Young toddlers, the one-year-olds, are phenomenal human beings. For the first time in their lives, they have become upright bipeds like the rest of us. Also, for the first time, they do not depend on us to bring rattles or squeak toys to them for entertainment. They can walk through, wriggle under, or climb over any obstacle a grown-up can devise to get to the really interesting things that attract their curiosity. Although a young toddler can be an adorable timid rabbit one moment, sucking a thumb while peeking from behind a well-worn but snuggly piece of blanket, she can in an instant be raising the rafters and crumpled on the floor in a full-fledged tantrum.

Can Toddlers Control Their Feelings and Actions?

Young toddlers are totally transparent in their feelings. They are openly affectionate, easily delighted by attention, and full of wonder about their surroundings. They also become confused, frustrated, and overwhelmed by their newfound freedom. One moment they are amazingly grown-up and ready to take on the world; the next they regress to helpless clingy babies. Their needs are simple. They want food, comfort, affection, and approval and to learn about the huge, booming, wide world around them. As babies, they still respond to their sensations of need by crying for caregivers, but as growing children, they also begin responding to their own desires by literally moving out into the environment to get what they want.

They use senses (touch, sight, smell, taste, and hearing) to explore the physical attributes of their environment, and both small and large muscles to practice physi-

egocentric
Seeing oneself as the center of the universe, self-centered, selfish. This point of view is a perfectly normal developmental characteristic of babies and very young children.

modeling
Providing an example, being a role model. In positive child guidance, the adult is the primary role model.

internalize
The process of taking in experiences and absorbing learning, then making them part of one's own behavior or belief.

In each stage of child development . . . there is a central problem that has to be solved . . . if the child is to proceed with vigor and confidence to the next stage.

Erik H. Erikson (1971)

cal skills. They still do not consciously plan or think about their actions much. They just act. If the toddler feels hungry and the box of cereal in the grocery cart with her looks delicious, she may just rip it open and have a snack, then look hurt when her parents seemed shocked by her behavior.

How Does Awareness of Cause and Effect Develop?

Toddlers have made a huge cognitive leap since infancy in their ability to remember things and in their first crude ability to manipulate ideas mentally. Cause-and-effect relationships become a focal point for their learning. They are fascinated by light switches and will flip the light on and off many times, if they are allowed, alternately watching the switch and the light fixture and mentally connecting the cause-and-effect relationship between the two.

They also tirelessly explore cause-and-effect relationships in social interactions. The toddler will stick her little pointed index finger out to touch the electrical outlet (covered, of course, with a plastic safety cap) and look up at her caregiver or teacher expectantly as he patiently repeats for the hundredth time, "No, no. That's not for touching." Finally, the little girl will touch the outlet, shaking her head and repeating soberly, "No, no. No touch." She is preoccupied with connecting the cause-and-effect relationship between her action and the adult's words and has totally missed the point that he would rather she did not touch the outlet. With just a bit more time and patience, she will be satiated in her curiosity about the cause-and-effect connection, will be able to remember the connection each time she sees an electrical outlet, and will probably be quite willing to respect her caregiver or teacher's rule.

Toddlers Need to Explore Their Surroundings

Healthy, well-developing toddlers have a curiosity that is boundless. Their desire to explore at times overshadows all other needs. A toddler who is totally immersed in the miseries of teething will stop crying when her mother carries her to the refrigerator and opens the freezer to get her frozen teething ring. For the moment, her pain is forgotten as she watches the frosty air roll out of the freezer and feels the brisk difference in temperature from this strange part of her environment she has never explored before.

Toddlers learn to walk because their fascination with this form of locomotion outweighs their fear of falling or being hurt. They move out into the environment, away from the security of caregivers, because the exhilaration of discovery causes them to throw caution to the wind. Babies might stay in the comfort of their mother's arms forever if it were not for the powerfully motivating activator we call curiosity that drives toddlers out into the scary but exciting world. Baby birds are comfortable, secure, safe, and well fed in the nest. At some point, however, nature intends them to leap precariously into the air and to flap their little wings until they figure out how to fly—a frightening and exhilarating experience for babies, of course, but also a frightening and exhilarating experience for grown-up birds to watch.

Safety Is a Major Issue in Toddler Care

During toddlerhood, a child's motor development far outstrips her capacity to understand, remember, or abide by rules. Because she has not yet developed metacognition, she cannot look at a situation and then think about and plan for the potential consequences of her own behavior in that situation. Toddlers are still a bit unsteady in their walking, running, and climbing, and they are compelled to taste, feel, smell, and manipulate every interesting object or phenomenon they encounter. All this adds up to toddlers being in the most vulnerable period of their lives for accidents.

Unless toddlers are constantly and diligently supervised, they can inadvertently swallow objects and poisonous substances, fall off or bump into things, and touch things they should not touch despite warnings. If crying is the first major area of potential confrontation between infants and adults, then keeping toddlers from harming themselves or the environment is surely the second big area of stress and difficulty for parents and caregivers.

In past years, parents often bragged that their toddler was so well behaved that the most expensive, fragile, or even dangerous bric-a-brac could be left on the coffee table and the baby would never so much as touch it. They sometimes accomplished that feat by slapping the baby's hand or saying, "No!" sharply whenever the child attempted to touch the forbidden items. These adults believed that by teaching the baby to be still and not touch anything, they were helping her become well disciplined and polite.

Information about the processes of cognitive development, generated by research over the past few decades, has changed this old perception. A delightful poster that is very popular among child care workers pictures a young toddler standing forlornly in a playpen. The caption reads "What do you mean, 'Don't touch'? Touching is how I learn." To create a richly stimulating environment conducive to optimal development while protecting toddlers from unreasonable risk of harm, adults must set about childproofing all accessible areas of children's environments as soon as babies develop the motor skills to move about.

Have you ever heard a parent or child care worker say, "I don't intend to spend my life picking toys up off the floor. I let them have one or two toys and that's it"? Babies and toddlers scrutinize every sensory aspect of each object. How does it taste? How does it feel? How does it sound? And then they tire of it. They need a great deal of variety in textures, weights, colors, sounds and other properties in the objects they are allowed to explore. Two or three plastic squeak toys simply won't meet their need for exploration.

Wadsworth/Cengage Learning

This two-year-old is given a safe set of markers under close supervision. The marker lids are glued with durable marine glue into holes drilled into a solid wooden base. She is able to pull out the markers and then return them to the matched lid after use without the risk of mouthing or swallowing them. Toddlers can be guided in activities they can learn to do by themselves.

White (1975, 1995) theorized that the period from 10 months to three years is a critical period in a child's life for social, intellectual, and motor skill development. He also theorized that direct sensory exploration of the physical environment serves as a key requirement for optimal development. In his view, keeping toddlers in playpens or restricted in environments that are "hands off," excessively tidy, not child-proofed, or downright boring risks losing the child's most valuable opportunity for early learning.

Learning Environments for Toddlers

Toddlers thrive in settings that are made appropriate to their needs and abilities so that they can move about freely and safely, exploring and testing every aspect of their surroundings. Of course, they still need careful supervision, even in the most carefully planned environment, but they have a much more stimulating range for their play when swallowable objects, toxic plants and substances, sharp corners, and electrical cords are out of their reach.

Rather than struggling to force toddlers to behave safely and appropriately, adults should simply change the child's environment to make interaction in it safe and appropriate. As toddlers become older and more compliant, sometime around their third birthday, toys with parts small enough to be swallowed, blunt scissors, water-based marking pens with small caps, and other materials requiring special care can be introduced to children for independent use. Gradually, as children are developmentally ready, they can then be gently but firmly guided to understand and follow appropriate safety rules.

Can Toddlers Read Body Language?

From birth, children respond to facial expression, tone of voice, and body movement. Long before a child understands language, she will react to cues such as the nonoral body language, inflection, tone, and volume that are part of an adult's speech.

Betty Jo, the lively young mother of 12-month-old Jeremy, comes to pick up her son from the family day home where he is cared for during the day. She chats with other parents picking up their children as she zips Jeremy into his snowsuit. Jeremy makes a funny sound and his cheeks turn red as it dawns on Betty Jo that she will have to change his diaper.

Everyone downwind of Jeremy is, by this point, quite aware that the diaper is definitely more than just wet. As other parents chuckle, Betty Jo jokingly but energetically scolds Jeremy for being so rude after she has gone to all the trouble of bundling him up to go home. Although the little boy clearly does not understand all her words, he unmistakably interprets her fake scowl and sharp tone to mean that she is angry with him. He turns his face away from her and sobs. Betty Jo is quite startled by his reaction. Because he did not know how to talk, she assumed he would not have any idea what she was saying.

expressive language
Communication with others by oral or written language.

receptive language
Comprehension of written or spoken communication expressed by others.

The ability of very young children to make some sense of our feelings from our body language and tone of voice gives us an opportunity to communicate with them nonorally. Before children have mastered **expressive language** (the ability to speak), they have begun to develop **receptive language** (the ability to understand language). Therefore, if we are honest and sincere in the words we speak to babies and toddlers, our body language will quite naturally convey our feelings and attitudes to the child. If we speak to the child for the benefit of other adults, as if the child were not really present or listening, we may miss an important opportunity to build communication with the child.

From the very beginning adults can start speaking to babies as if they were (because they definitely are) worthwhile human beings. This has two important benefits for long-term child guidance. First, the child will learn early in life to pay attention to adults, because they seem to say what they mean and mean what they say. Second, adults have plenty of time to practice appropriate communication skills so that they will be prepared when the child really does have a command of language.

Using a kind facial expression and a caring tone of voice, an adult can speak reassuringly to a young toddler who resists going to sleep, "I know you would rather play with your toys, but it's time for a nap now. Would you like me to rock you for a minute before you lie down?" Even though the child will not understand all the words, she will sense the adult's caring attitude. She will also have an opportunity to hear language and associate it with objects and events in day-to-day living.

How Does Oral Communication Begin?

Toddlers seem to explode into language. At a child's first birthday, she may know only words such as "mama," "dada," and "baba," for bottle. Within a few months, the child may know many more single-word labels plus a number of holophrases (phrases made of words that are joined like Siamese twins and used as if they were inseparable single words). "Gofieys" may mean "Go to a fast food restaurant and get French fries." "Sousite" may mean "Let's go outside to play." The child soon learns to mix and match words or holophrases to create two-word sentences. Soon, the child's speech begins to sound like abbreviated telegrams, including key words but leaving less critical words out: "Paw Paw doggy big!" "No touch daddy gwas [glasses]." By age three, the child's speech begins to sound surprisingly like our own (with a few quirks here and there): "My daddy goed to work an he gots a big office."

The child's language changes each day as she adds new vocabulary and new levels of expression and understand-

Wadsworth/Cengage Learning

■■■ Important language development begins at birth. Even though we may hear only babbles and coos, the child's brain is taking in the language she hears, processing it and preparing her for the awesome transition she will make into speech.

ing. At birth, the child had no muscular control of her lips and tongue and no comprehension that language existed or had significance. In only three short years, she has learned how to create many different sounds with her lips, tongue, and vocal cords; amassed hundreds of words in her vocabulary; and grasped the basic syntax (structure) of her native language. Her language comprehension is complex but not at a conscious level. For example, she has simply absorbed an intuitive sense that the "s" sound on the end of a naming word means more than one, and that the "d" sound at the end of an action word means that the action has already happened. Remember that she will understand many words before she can say them.

What Kind of Language Experiences Are Good for Toddlers?

Infants and children of all ages need to hear the rich, lyrical words of adult conversational speech, as well as the musical word patterns in rhymes, songs, and jingles. These kinds of language experiences especially enrich and stimulate language learning in toddlers. For maximum comprehension, however, the child must hear language that is very close to her own level of development. This language should be at or slightly ahead of the child's own level. For example, in developing music appreciation, young children are allowed to hear a wide range of classical, folk, and pop music for enrichment, but for learning actual singing, they are introduced to extremely simple songs, such as "Here We Go 'Round the Mulberry Bush."

If a baby's language development is still limited to the cooing and babbling stage, the adult can effectively communicate through facial expression, tone of voice, and body language. If the child is using single words, the adult can best achieve communication through holophrases ("Allgone") or two-word sentences ("More milk?").

Toddlers may hear and comprehend only a few words in sentences that are above their comprehension. Often, they catch a few accentuated or familiar words from the beginning or from the end of the adult's speech. The toddler may innocently respond to the words "You . . . candy . . . mouth" from the adult's complicated sentence, "You need to make very sure you don't put that whole big piece of candy into your mouth." To maximize the toddler's comprehension of important communication, choose key words, speak slowly and clearly, and use facial expression and body gestures to emphasize your meaning.

We might use more elaborate enrichment language to say to a toddler, "I believe you need to have your shoelace tied. It could make you trip and fall down." But if a response is needed from the child, bend down, take the child's hand, deliberately establish eye contact, and then pat the floor expectantly as you articulate carefully, "Sit, please." We can then reinforce the child's cooperativeness the instant she looks as if she will comply by smiling warmly and saying, "Thank you!"

Stranger Anxiety

Toddlers show a wide range of reactions to strangers, depending on their own experiences and temperament. Some children go through a distinct phase in which they are terrified of strangers. When confronted by a stranger (or even a less familiar caregiver), many toddlers cling to their parent's or caregiver's clothing, hide their faces, and cry. Other children, especially those who have had broad exposure to many friendly adults since infancy, may show curiosity about new adults, attempt to make friends, and never give any indication of separation or stranger anxiety. To experience stranger anxiety, the child must be able to distinguish familiar from unfamiliar faces, which usually happens around six or seven months of age.

Separation Anxiety

Stranger anxiety is often coupled with separation anxiety, the distress children show when they cry on separation from a parent or primary caregiver. Separation anxiety can be seen at any time from infancy through preschool, but it is usually most pronounced in the second year of life.

How Can I Make Friends with a Shy Toddler?

To establish a relationship with a shy toddler, it is essential to understand and respect that child's discomfort in interacting with a new adult. Rather than directly approaching with a big smile and immediately attempting to touch or hold the child, avoid eye contact with the child at first.

Speak quietly and pleasantly with others around the child while moving a bit closer. If the child is standing or sitting on the floor, sit nearby to be at her eye level. Glance briefly in the child's direction occasionally to see if she is evidencing curiosity or stress at your presence. Smile, but avoid looking directly into the child's eyes until you are confident she feels comfortable with your presence.

After allowing the toddler plenty of time to stare at you, it may be helpful to touch the child's hand casually for a moment while glancing briefly in her direction with a smile. Eventually, she will probably indicate her willingness to make friends and allow eye contact. At this point, a diversion in the form of a game or toy may be a perfect way to cement the budding adult–child relationship. In a child care center, the teacher may be able, at this point, to interest the toddler in petting the class bunny rabbit, looking at

Wadsworth/Cengage Learning

▬ Separating from mother or father at the beginning of the day can be very stressful for the child, the parent, and the caregiver. The caregiver must plan strategies to ease the stress for everyone.

a book, or watching the teacher make a puppet tell jokes and eat pretend cookies. If no toys are available, sing a song, make up a rhyme, or talk about the child's clothing: "Look at those blue sneakers. You can run really fast in those." An effective diversion at this point will hold the child's interest but not require a great deal of sustained eye contact or active response from her.

Why Are Toddlers so Possessive?

Young toddlers may inadvertently callously step on each other to get what they want, take toys from each other, and scramble to grab food. Sometimes two-year-olds walk into their child care center in the morning, look suspiciously at their peers, tighten their grip on Dad's hand, and announce defiantly, "My daddy!" Very young children's behavior is not always civilized or polite because they do not yet have a well-developed ability to put themselves in the place of others. Some toddlers who have observed and experienced a great deal of **empathy** (understanding another's feelings) may show concern for others, but their way of expressing concern is still egocentric. For example, the toddler may try to give her pacifier or teddy bear to an adult who is crying.

> **empathy**
> The ability to understand or have concern for someone other than oneself, marked by identification with and understanding of another's situation, feelings, and motives.

There is little to say about toddlers and sharing except that it cannot be expected of them. Instead of attempting to coerce toddlers into behaving in a way that is developmentally incompatible, adults can rearrange the environment, change the routines, or increase their supervision to protect toddlers from inadvertent rough or rude treatment by their peers. In time, children develop the ability to recognize that other people have feelings and rights, and they develop the ability to imagine how others would feel if they were treated a certain way. Then it will be possible to teach them manners. Until then, setting a good example and tactfully but assertively protecting children's (and others') rights are all that adults can do. Having a wide variety of choices available to toddlers will ease this problem. It will also help to have multiples of the most popular objects such as shovels, balls, and dolls.

Why Do Some Toddlers Become so Attached to Security Blankets, Pacifiers, and Other Cuddlies?

Toddlers use various cuddlies to help them cope with being very little and very powerless in a big, fast, scary world. Some adults call toddlers' worn blankets, tattered stuffed animals, pacifiers, or whatever else they hold onto the child's "cuddlies." Child psychologists call them objects for "cyclical self-stimulation." Caregivers are sometimes tempted to just call them nuisances. Whatever they are called, when they are lost, they can cause the toddler's emotional world to come crashing down around her. As strongly as children are attached to these comfort items, they generally begin to lose interest in them by the time they turn three. Some preschoolers hang onto their cuddlies a while longer, but for many of them, their attachment at this point is more habit than emotional need.

In many primitive cultures, children stay in physical contact with their mothers' bodies much of the time during their first three years of life. In modern industrialized societies, children are separated from their mothers at birth to be placed in a hospital nursery, put to sleep in a separate bed (enclosed with bars) in a separate room at home, and buckled into high chairs and car seats. It is not surprising then that many babies improvise "caregiver replacements" to cling to for a while and to help them cope (nipple-shaped objects to suck and soft, warm, fuzzy, or silky objects to hold). The child's need for these objects should be respected, although she can be nudged gently to do without them for gradually increasing periods when they have become little more than habit.

Toddlers and children older than three should be helped to cope without having a pacifier or thumb "plugged in" for too much of their day. It is difficult for toddlers to practice language with their mouths immobilized. But it is equally important to allow infants plenty of sucking to develop the mouth, lip, and tongue muscles necessary for later speech. Because bottle-feeding requires less muscular effort and coordination to produce milk than breast-feeding, many babies benefit emotionally and physically from the availability of nonnutritive sucking. Pacifiers are healthier for teeth and thumbs and usually easier to wean children from than thumbs.

Although some authorities still encourage mothers to wean babies from breast or bottle at about 10 months of age, weaning in the first year of life will often cause the child to seek some form of replacement sucking or self-stimulation. We can take good advice from our grandmothers who have been saying for generations, "If you baby a baby when he's a baby, you won't have to baby him all the rest of his life."

Why Are Toddlers Stubborn One Minute, Then Clingy the Next?

Erikson (1982) focused on the development of autonomy (self-sufficiency) as the second step in his eight stages of **social growth** and **emotional** (affective) **growth.** After **trust** has been established in infancy, toddlers become immersed in the conflict between **autonomy** and **shame** and **doubt.** Toddlers are able for the first time to do many things that adults consider naughty or destructive. For the first time, adults begin to hold the child responsible for bodily elimination and controlling impulses. The child is torn between assertively resisting adult guidance and feeling fearful and ashamed for getting into trouble so often. She feels she can conquer the world with her new capabilities, but she is constantly getting into scrapes, making messes, and needing adult help and reassurance.

Adults can help toddlers through this period by being very supportive of the child's need to break away from infancy. To foster autonomy, we should not do anything for the toddler that she could be helped to do for herself. Toddlers can learn to peel their own bananas for a snack, pull up their own socks once the adult gets the sock started, and choose their own clothing from two or three appropriate choices. At home, they can be allowed to stand on a chair at the sink to wash unbreakable dishes (although mom or dad will undoubtedly have to rewash them later for sanitary reasons). They can even be given a small bucket with a little water, a squirt of liquid soap, and a small piece of sponge or rag to help wash the car or the windows. In

social growth
Learning to understand and function appropriately in one's social environment; learning how to effectively interact with others.

emotional growth
Developing and learning to manage the feelings that affect behavior and self-esteem.

trust
Sense of security; belief that one's needs will be met.

autonomy
A person's self-reliance, independence, and self-sufficiency. One's capacity to make decisions and act on them.

shame
A negative feeling or emotion of embarrassment, unworthiness, or disgrace.

doubt
A feeling of questioning, uncertainty, and hesitation.

early childhood programs, children can be provided small sponges for table wiping, small brooms for sweeping, and other utensils to help maintain the classroom.

Toddlers are interested in having the freedom and independence to be involved in the processes of grown-up activities. They are not at all interested in achieving specific end products to those processes and are confused and discouraged by adult concern over end products or results rather than processes. Adults usually do things the most expedient way to get the result that they want. Toddlers spend long periods in the process of dipping, pouring, and splashing dishes in soapy water, but lose interest before the dishes are actually rinsed and dried. Sensitive adults will foster the child's involvement in independent processes but wait until the child is older to expect results. They will redirect unacceptable behavior rather than make the child feel inadequate or naughty for following her curiosity and desire to attempt things she sees adults doing.

Are Toddlers Aware of Themselves?

When babies look in a mirror, they do not necessarily recognize that the image reflected there is their own. At some point in toddlerhood, they finally discover that the face in the mirror is theirs. If they see an unexpected smudge on the nose in the mirror, they touch their own nose to find out what is there. A younger child will touch only the mirror. Toddlers who are not yet aware of their own separate identity seem to think that they cannot be seen by anyone if their own eyes are closed. A toddler being reprimanded for misbehavior may cover her eyes, assuming (because of her egocentricity) that the adults will not be able to see her because she cannot see them.

Why Do Toddlers Get so Excited and Happy When They Imitate Each Other?

Toddlers who have just begun to get a sense of their separateness tend to be very "full of themselves." If a caregiver gathers two-year-olds around him for a snack, he will often discover that they are very entertained by each other. They giggle and poke each other, and inevitably one toddler will begin a gloriously spontaneous action like vigorously shaking her head until her hair stands out all around her head. In an instant, this action spreads into a **group contagion,** leaving the poor adult sitting rather foolishly, tray of snacks in hand, watching a band of toddlers laughing uproariously as they shake their heads (and perhaps wiggle their bodies and stamp their feet for good measure). The teacher should join in this moment of joy before focusing the children's attention back on snack.

As a toddler begins to recognize her existence as a separate person like the people she sees around her, she begins to develop a **concept** (or picture) of who she is based on feedback, primarily from the adults around her. Sometimes adults make casual comments that are very cutting, such as "You are as fat as a pig," "Why are you always so mean?" "I think you like to make me mad"—things we would probably hesitate to say to another adult. Sometimes these hurtful comments come from siblings or other children. Toddlers are very naive. They tend to believe what we tell

group contagion
Typical toddler group behavior in which one child's gleeful action, for example, foot stamping, head shaking, or squealing, is quickly imitated by the whole group of toddlers.

concept
An idea, understanding, or belief formed by organizing images or mental pictures from specific occurrences and experiences.

Competent Three-Year-Olds Are . . .
• self-confident and trusting
• intellectually inquisitive
• able to use language to communicate
• physically and mentally healthy
• able to relate well to others
• empathic toward others

them about themselves through our actions and words. As an older toddler's self-image begins to take shape, we can help her develop a healthy and confident view of herself by being very careful about what we say to her (and what we allow other children to say to her). "What a big girl you are." "Everybody makes mistakes sometime." "I really like your smile." "I didn't like the hitting, but I will always like you." The toddler's budding self-esteem will serve as a foundation for her growth as a confident, competent, cooperative, and productive human being.

Given consistently nurturing and responsive care, healthy babies develop a high level of "competence" by age three. Competent preschoolers are much more likely to be successful and well adjusted in school and throughout life (Carnegie Corporation of New York, 1994).

Preschoolers (3 to 5 Years)

Can Preschoolers Make Plans and Decisions?

Babies think about objects in terms of the way those objects actually feel, look, taste, smell, and sound. Toddlers have a new mental ability. They can conceive of objects both in terms of what they are perceptually and what they stand for symbolically. For example, a baby sees a block only as something to bite, hit, throw, or stack. A toddler can see the block as a toy that is meant for stacking. A toddler might recognize a key as something that makes the car go. She might recognize that the remote control is something that operates the television. As children become preschoolers, they are able to see a block as both a physical object and a pretend bar of soap to bathe a doll or a pretend car to zoom around the floor. The block can easily stand as an abstract symbol for something else in their imagination.

Preschoolers also become more consciously aware of their own interests and intentions. They look over the toys that are available to them and make intentional choices. Although toddlers function primarily by impulse, playing with whatever toy catches their eye for the moment, preschoolers are more inclined to select an activity very carefully and then stay with it longer, sometimes even coming back to play the same game day after day until they finally become bored with it.

Older preschoolers can verbalize what and how they want to play. For example, they may say, "Let's play like this is our house and you are the daddy and he is the baby and that box is the baby bed." They can become very frustrated or angry if things do not turn out the way they expect. Preschoolers often squabble over their conflicting perceptions of how their play should proceed: "I don't want to be the baby. I want to play Masters of the Universe!"

Adults can help preschoolers during this stage by focusing the children's attention on the probable consequences of their actions. Questions should never be used as oral battering rams, but adults can gently nudge cause-and-effect thinking by asking, "What might happen if someone ran out into the street without looking?" "Hmmm, I wonder what could happen if you paint without putting a smock on over your clothes?" "How would your friend feel if she never got a turn to be the pretend mommy?" Preschoolers are just beginning to be able to manipulate ideas in their heads and eventually can learn to weigh consequences and make appropriate decisions before acting.

Meeting Preschoolers' Needs for Communication

Because preschoolers have an increasing command of their native language, they benefit from talking about their own actions and events that have taken place or will take place in their lives. Before an event takes place, they can be helped to understand that event by parents or teachers talking about it in advance in very simple, concrete terms. Parents often try to shield preschoolers from adult concerns by not talking directly to their children about sensitive issues.

A three-year-old, whose parents often affectionately called her "our sweet baby girl," cried hysterically when an aunt said, "I hear there's going to be a new baby at your house." She had overheard her parents saying that they thought it best for her not to know yet that there was going to be a new baby. She knew, of course, that when they got a new car, the old car vanished, and when they got a new refrigerator, the old one was hauled away, and when she got new shoes, the old ones were dropped unceremoniously into the trash can. She could only guess what happened to little girls who she imagined were so naughty that their parents decided to get "a new one."

A four-year-old boy developed nightmares and bed-wetting after he heard family members crying and talking in somber but hushed tones about how his expectant mother had lost the baby she was carrying. His problem behaviors increased until a psychologist was consulted and discovered that the little boy had been nervously searching in closets and under beds to find the lost baby. He knew that those were places to look when you lost something. He worried that his parents might lose him too!

Communicating Successfully with Preschoolers

By talking to preschoolers in honest but simplified terms, we can help them understand and deal with events. We cannot take for granted that just because something is obvious to us it will be obvious to young children. There are many things about

Wadsworth/Cengage Learning

Expressing feelings through dramatic play can help preschoolers think through issues that worry or frighten them.

this world that preschoolers do not know yet. A caregiver can use very simple but clear sentences to say, "Marcus, your dad just called on the telephone. He will be late picking you up today. His car won't go so he has to get it fixed. It may be dark when he gets here, but it's okay. I will stay with you. We'll get some cheese and crackers and apple juice and play until he comes." Sometimes adults become so preoccupied with their own problems and plans that they forget to tell children what will happen to them.

Imitating through dramatic play can help children visualize an expected event. Talking through a puppet is a nonthreatening way to get a point across or model appropriate language and behavior. Helping a preschooler laugh at a puppet may dispel anxiety about such things as a parent being late, monsters living under the bed, or lightning that sounds really scary. Taking his aggressions out on the "pretend monster" puppet may help the preschooler feel less helpless and vulnerable. We can take a different opportunity another day to teach the child the importance of handling classroom toys carefully.

An adult can frequently prevent problems by anticipating and planning for them. Being especially careful not to communicate negative expectations, the adult could say, for example, "Shelley, your friend Jamie will be here soon. Sometimes when she is here it is hard for you to share your favorite toys. That makes Jamie feel sad. Would you like to choose the toys you want to share and put them in this cardboard box? We can take the toys you choose into the back yard, then Jamie will know which toys you want to share and play with." By helping the child positively think through this potential problem before it happens, the child may be able to consciously behave in such a way as to avoid the conflict before it erupts. When a child is angry and upset, it is unlikely that she will be able to listen to logic or behave rationally.

Teaching Preschoolers to Use Words to Express Their Feelings

Preschoolers can be guided firmly to use words to get a point across rather than relying on kicking, scratching, and hair pulling. They can be helped to practice appropriate words and allowed to express strong emotions, even anger, through their words. When a preschooler runs to tell parents or teachers about another child's action, instead of being chided for tattling, the child can be encouraged to talk to the other child: "Did you tell Kirin that it was your turn for the swing? Would you like me to go with you to talk to her?"

Adults sometimes try to squelch children's negative feelings. We say things to quiet children such as "Don't cry," "Don't make a fuss," "She didn't really mean to hit you." Maybe the other child really did mean to hit. A child deserves to express her feelings in an honest but respectful way: "I feel angry. I don't like it when you push me off the swing." Preschoolers especially need to be allowed to express their feelings. They can learn that it is okay to feel angry and it is okay to say so, but it is not okay to lash out by orally or physically hurting others.

Preschoolers can also be helped to verbalize their feelings by having adults **mirror** (reflect) those feelings. Young children may not realize that they are cranky because they are hot and tired or cold and hungry. Adults can put words to those feelings and assist preschoolers in learning to identify and express what they feel inside by saying, "Brrr, I feel cold! Look at the chill bumps on my arm. Are you cold? Let me feel how cold your hands are."

This mirroring of feelings is called **active listening** (repeating what you understood the child to mean). The adult refrains from lecturing, instructing, commanding, or telling (see Chapter 7 for more on active listening). Instead, she listens and sincerely reflects, or restates, what she thinks the child is feeling at the moment. In active listening (a useful communication tool for any age), the adult says things such as "It sounds as if you are really feeling angry with Tommy," "In other words, what you are saying is that you feel hurt and sad when you don't get to play," "You seem pretty frightened when the other children pretend to be monsters." The point of active listening is not to solve the child's problem for her but only to let her know that she has been heard and to give her a chance to talk about, think about, and confront her own feelings.

Democratic societies create laws allowing citizens to use physical force only as a last resort when other reasonable steps to defend themselves have failed. Law enforcement officials are empowered to use physical force—not to hurt, punish, or humiliate people—to protect people and property. In the child's world, this same principle should apply. Children prepare to participate as good citizens in society by learning the skills needed for peaceful conflict resolution. Adults should physically restrain a child only when absolutely necessary to prevent the child from hurting herself or others.

Does Stress Strain Your Patience with Children?

Perfectionism can be a stress trap for educators and parents. Children have bad days. Adults have bad days. In an environment that is basically nurturing and respectful, children learn to deal with occasional shortcomings in their teachers and parents. Adults must learn to cope with their own lapses in meeting the standards they have set for themselves. They must not shrug their shoulders and give up but admit and accept that they blew it and consciously take steps to do better tomorrow. It is helpful to say to the child, "I made a mistake. It's not okay to shout angry things at others. I was wrong. I'm going to really try to remember to talk calmly about problems so we can solve them the right way."

The need to always be in control can also be a stress trap. Teaching and learning is an interactive process. In the learning-centered environment, there is a great deal of give and take. Sensitive, responsive adults are willing to put aside planned activities

mirror
Reflect the feelings expressed by someone else—repeating what you understood someone to say (see active listening).

active listening
A form of attentive listening in which one concentrates on what is being said, then reflects the ideas back to the speaker to show an understanding of what the speaker is feeling and saying.

when they observe that children are simply not interested or ready for them. Nurturing adults offer choices within reasonable limits, allowing children to feel control in choosing their preferences. It is not a sign of failure or weakness for an adult to admit that he or she was wrong and the child was right in a given situation. Children who listen, question, and speak up for themselves are better suited to thrive in today's world than blindly obedient children who would never question authority.

People pleasing is another potential stress trap. Codependent people depend on other people's opinion of them for their own self-esteem. They have an impaired sense of their own worth and spend their lives trying to please others. Remember, you can't please everybody all the time. Work on defining and trusting your own philosophy and values. Learn to listen to your own conscience and trust yourself. Force yourself to use "I" messages (sentences starting with "I feel . . .") to express your feelings to others. Remember to take good care of yourself. You can't really nurture children if you allow yourself to become exhausted trying to please others. Take proactive steps to avoid physical, mental, and emotional exhaustion. (See Chapter 6, p. 214, for more about "I" messages, or statements.)

Self-doubt clouds judgment and increases stress. Avoid comparing yourself with others. Set your own standards and work every day to achieve them. Be a life-long learner. Open your mind and take advantage of books and other resources to expand your skills and confidence. Learn to trust your judgment. If you make mistakes, learn from them and move on. Don't be afraid to take reasonable risks. When others compliment your accomplishments, just say thank you rather than explaining that what you did was not really very good. It's okay to feel proud of your own achievements. It's most important that you feel good yourself about what you've done, not that others notice or approve of your accomplishment. Doubt and shame get in the way of being a responsive, nurturing caregiver.

To learn more, read:

Carlson, R. (1997). _Don't sweat the small stuff . . . and it's all small stuff: Simple ways to keep the little things from taking over your life._ New York: Hyperion.

Hull, R. (2002). _Drive yourself happy: A motor-vational maintenance manual for maneuvering through life._ Canada: Cypress House Nonfiction.

Moran, V. (2002). _Fit from within: 101 ways to change your body and your life._ New York: Contemporary Books/McGraw-Hill.

Reinhold, B. B. (1997). _Toxic work: How to overcome stress, overload, and burnout and revitalize your career._ New York: Dutton/Plume.

Thurman, C., Meier, P., Flournoy, R., Hawkins, D., & Minirth, F. B., Eds. (1997). _Beating burnout: Balanced living for busy people: How to beat burnout, before burnout beats you._ New York: Arrowood Press.

Websites:

American Institute of Stress, http://www.stress.org/
Centers for Disease Control and Prevention, http://www.cdc.gov/
Healthy People, http://www.healthypeople.gov/
Stress Busters, http://www.stressrelease.com/

Friendships Are Important to Preschoolers

Babies and toddlers are very curious about other children but are most concerned about the adults in their lives. Preschoolers, in contrast, begin to be interested in their relationships with other children. Throughout the rest of childhood, they will rely more and more on their friendships with peers and less and less on their attachment to adults. Between three and five, children need to learn how to be a friend and how to have friends, a very important kind of learning for the child's long-term social and emotional adjustment in life (Corsaro, 1981).

Friendship becomes an important part of the everyday lives of preschoolers.

This can be a very trying stage for adults. Children are elated when they feel liked by peers and emotionally crushed when they imagine that no other child in the whole world wants to play with them. Although some children quickly find a best friend or group of friends whom they get along with very well, other children experience a daily emotional roller coaster as they struggle to establish friendships and deal with peers who barter "I'll be your best friend if you give me your piece of chocolate cake." Paley (1992) suggests creating a class rule that requires inclusion: "You can't say you can't play."

Some preschoolers become very cliquish as they decide who is or is not a friend. They say things such as "You can't be our friend because you don't have a football shirt on," "We don't want you to play because you're a boy," "You draw scribble-scrabble so you can't color in our coloring book." Adults can feel frustrated trying to decide when or how to intervene in these troublesome and hurtful interactions. Children need proactive guidance, however, to learn to treat others the way they want to be treated. Cruelty cannot be tolerated.

How Do Preschoolers Learn to Accept Responsibility?

Erikson (1963) focused on the need of four- and five-year-olds to resolve the emotional conflict of initiative versus guilt. Preschoolers are struggling to become independent of adult caregivers and to find their own limits. Still, however, they want to please adults, and they feel guilty when they disappoint or anger parents and teachers. An excessive amount of guilt causes discomfort, which the child may relieve by withdrawing from any situation that involves a risk of failure or by adopting a rebellious tough guy facade and appearing to be immune to guilt.

To develop initiative, children must be encouraged to achieve independence from adults. Instead of doing things for preschoolers, adults must tactfully make it possible for the children to do things for themselves. Adults can simplify tasks and then teach simple skills such as how to refill the gerbil's water bottle, how to cut safely with a blunt knife, how to clip paper to an easel with clothespins, and how to get a jacket zipper started.

Allow Preschoolers to Do Things That Are Difficult

Preschoolers relish the opportunity to be in charge of their own environment. They make many mistakes and often forget to carry out tasks they have agreed to perform. Adults can respond best by remembering that the process of learning is much more important for preschoolers than the end products resulting from their efforts. Some adults become perfectionists about tasks and say, "It's easier for me to do it myself than to hassle with the kids trying to do it." It may be easier, but it definitely is not better for children who need encouragement and success in accepting and carrying out responsibilities.

With a great deal of practice, encouragement, and patient teaching (one tiny step at a time), preschoolers can learn to carry out fairly complex tasks responsibly and well. They will feel so confident about their accomplishments that they will eagerly show initiative (inner drive) in tackling new tasks or projects without having to be prodded or coerced every step of the way, as will a child who has fallen prey to feelings of guilt.

Helping Preschoolers Follow Rules

Preschoolers can understand simplistic guidelines, such as "Be kind! Wait until it's your turn to go down the slide." "Be safe! Stop at the gate so a grownup can walk with you across the street." "Be neat! Use a sponge to wipe up the tempera paint that has

Allowing preschoolers to care for pets helps them develop a sense of responsibility.

spilled." Preschoolers are **preoperational** (in Piaget's terms), so they perceive rules in a superficial way. They follow rules more to please adults than because they fully appreciate the relationship between actions and potential consequences. Preschoolers still must be supervised closely because they are not yet able to follow rules consistently. In their play, they make up rules on a whim and then break the rules they have made with total abandon when it no longer suits them.

They begin to make sense intuitively of adult expectations and anticipate what will or will not be allowed in various situations. They tell each other, "Oh! You're gonna get in trouble." They begin to enforce rules on each other, "You didn't flush. I'm gonna tell on you." Adults can redirect this sudden enthusiasm for rules by setting a good example in their own respectful enforcement of rules. If adults are punitive and critical and seem eager to catch wrongdoers, children will imitate that. If adults remind children of rules in an assertive but polite tone and then help them comply, children will imitate that as well.

Adults can maintain children's interest in rules by making very few rules but making sure that children know and respect the rules that are given. Rules always mean more to children if they played an active role in developing them and in deciding on logical consequences that should be enforced when the rules are broken. Overwhelming preschoolers with picky rules will alienate them and trivialize the whole idea of following rules. Children's perception of the value and importance of rules can be greatly enhanced when they are allowed to be part of the rule-making process. At group or circle time in a group setting, or in a family council meeting at home, children can be invited to think of new rules to solve simple problems such as pushing and shoving or taking other people's things without asking. Also, adults can help children by patiently explaining the reasons for rules rather than just saying, "It's a rule because I say so." Understanding the reasons for rules helps children develop moral values (see the section on moral development in Chapter 4).

Stating rules—"No one is allowed to climb on that fence!"—and then proceeding to ignore children who climb on the fence will convince children that grown-ups do not really mean the things they say and rules are not really to be followed. It is important to remember that following rules is not only to be kind, safe, and neat today but also to develop habits that will result in the child obeying laws as an adolescent and as an adult.

How Do Preschoolers Develop a Positive Sense of Self?

Although the child's self-esteem (or lack of it) has been developing unconsciously since birth, preschool-age children begin to develop a clear, conscious idea of who and what they are. Self-esteem and self-concept are two closely related concepts. **Self-concept** is one's idea or image of oneself. **Self-esteem** means that one's image of oneself includes a sense of being worthwhile and valuable. Children's ideas about themselves come from others around them, particularly from parents (Coopersmith, 1967; Cotton, 1984). As preschoolers become more adept at language, they also become more susceptible to the opinions of teachers, peers, and others outside the home.

Preschoolers become increasingly aware of their own identity in terms of larger groupings within society. The child may, for the first time, become aware of her

preoperational
The second stage of cognitive development in Jean Piaget's theory that begins with the achievement of object permanence. This stage is typified by imaginative play, egocentricity, the inability to take another person's point of view, and the belief that the number or amount is changed when objects are rearranged.

self-concept
Perception of oneself in terms of personal worth, life and school successes, and perceived social status.

self-esteem
Seeing oneself as a worthwhile individual.

Every individual preschooler can be helped to appreciate her own special talents.

ethnicity. Self-esteem can grow from pride in one's ethnic, regional, and religious heritage. Sadly, exposure to prejudice devastates self-esteem and generates a cycle of prejudice and low self-esteem. Low self-esteem is one of the root causes of prejudice in the first place (Musher-Eizenman et al., 2004; Van Ausdale & Feagin, 2001; Ramsey & Williams, 2003; Kivel, 2002; Derman-Sparks & Ramsey, 2005). Every child deserves to know that she is special but, of course, no more special than anyone else!

Preschoolers also become aware, for the first time, that their gender is fixed for life; girls will grow to be women and boys will grow to be men. Toddlers may distinguish between girls and boys or mommies and daddies, but they think they can turn into the opposite sex simply by wearing different clothing. Preschoolers identify with their own gender and may begin playing only with boys or only with girls.

Parents worry about their physically active daughters who prefer playing with the boys or their quiet, sensitive sons who prefer playing with the girls. Preschoolers worry about playing with toys that their friends consider to be "girl" toys or "boy" toys. Preschool teachers often worry about making sure boys feel okay about playing in the housekeeping center with dolls and dress-ups and girls feel okay about playing in the block center with trucks and cars so that all the children will have well-rounded educational experiences. Everyone worries, but children generally persist in play that reflects the real world as they know it. If they see daddy having a good time feeding the baby and cooking, little boys will probably play house more comfortably than if they have seen only women doing these things. The same is true for little girls who have seen their mothers repair a leaky pipe or wear a police officer's uniform.

Should Children Be Encouraged to Compete?

Another factor that affects preschoolers' development of self-concept and self-esteem is competitiveness. Preschoolers have become aware of themselves in comparison to others, so competitiveness reaches a peak during the preschool years (Stott & Ball, 1957). It can be very tempting for adults to exploit that tendency by saying things such as "Whoever can be the quietest at naptime will get a special treat," "The one who puts away toys the fastest will get to be first in line to go outside," "See if you can get dressed faster than your brother."

These challenges may strongly motivate some children to behave as the adult wishes, but the competition also stimulates friction rather than cooperation among children. Additionally, whenever there are winners, by definition, there will be losers. Winners may feel stressed and compulsive about continuing to win, and losers may feel more and more inadequate (Watson et al., 2003).

A more appropriate strategy to motivate desired behavior is to encourage children to work together as teams to accomplish tasks. Ideally, a classroom is a **community of learners** who share ideas, talk about and solve problems together, help each other, and cooperate as a team to clean up the classroom so that everyone can have more time for the next activity. In a true community of learners, children see themselves as valued members of an inclusive team.

community of learners
A group of individuals who share similar educational principles, who work toward common goals, whose activities are linked, and whose collaborative efforts create a synchronized energy in which the power of the group is more profound than that of any one individual. For children, a group that nurtures a sense of belonging among the children and adults in a program where children learn that all contribute to each other's learning.

Early School-Agers (5 to 8 Years)

Five- through eight-year-old children are very different from younger children, not only because of their gap-toothed smiles and taller bodies but also because their thinking and language skills are different.

Why Do Early School-Agers Ask so Many Questions?

As school-agers become more aware of the world around them, they want to know a simple answer to every puzzling phenomenon encountered. Preschoolers physically explore things that puzzle them, such as "Do rocks always sink in water?" "What's inside my toy car?" "How high will a swing go?" They ask simple, concrete questions about things around them, such as "What's this?" "What's that?" "What's your name?" Early school-agers question everything and often ask questions that are really hard to answer, for example, "Why can't I have pizza for breakfast?" "What if gravity stopped and everything flew off the earth?" "Why do things look small when they're far away?" "Why did Grandma die?" "What makes the car go?"

Early school-age children are less gullible than preschoolers. They are quick to see discrepancies in adult actions: "You said that nobody could eat or drink unless they sat down at the table. You're somebody and you're drinking coffee." Preschoolers believe just about anything you tell them, but early school-agers become more critical. For example, if you say, "You can't eat candy because it is not good for your teeth," a preschooler might protest and beg, but a school-ager will think about that

Early school-age children want simple answers to the questions that puzzle them.

explanation logically and answer with her own rationale, "Okay, then I'll brush my teeth after I eat the candy." After the early school-ager has asked a persistent series of logical why or why-not questions, parents and teachers often find themselves snapping with exasperation, "Because I said so!" Of course, this is the phrase we hated to hear as children and promised we would never say when we grew up.

Why Do They Get so Angry if They Do Not Always Win?

Early school-agers make observations and judgments about everything around them. Because of their immaturity, however, their judgment is limited to a simplistic, good-or-bad, win-or-lose view of the world. Naturally, they begin to compare themselves to others. Competition rears its ugly head as children struggle to best each other. They constantly fight over who likes whom best. Adults sometimes throw fuel onto this fire by encouraging competition. For example, teachers say, "Let's see who can be first to get their table clean," "The quietest person will get to go first," "I will put gold stars on the very best papers and put them on the bulletin board for parents' night." This tactic is tempting because early school-agers will practically trample each other to be first or best at anything. However, we should find ways instead to help children get along and cooperate more rather than less. Learning to be a **collaborative** team member is an important prosocial skill for children to learn during these years. In early childhood, competition should be focused on improving oneself, not on beating others.

According to Marilyn Watson (Watson et al., 2003, p. 198),

> The students who cannot control their emotions may find the threat of losing so overwhelming that they fail to keep their behavior organized; they may freeze or disintegrate into tears.
>
> . . . Competition in the classroom divides students and undermines bonds of care and respect. Students who lose feel inferior to and thus resent students who win. Students who win feel superior to and thus lose respect for those who lose.

Why Do They Call Each Other Names and Say Such Hurtful Things?

Early school-agers have gained skill in expressing themselves orally. They use more descriptive words to express their anger, frustration, or jealousy than do preschoolers. Preschoolers simply shove or hit someone who upsets them or bluster, "You're a

collaborative
Cooperative interaction of two or more people who are trying achieve a common goal.

pooh-pooh head an' I hate you." School-agers are more precise in their words, "Why do you act so bossy? You're not my mother." Their responses become more rational and logical. Angry words hurled at early school-agers can wound them deeply, though, so it is important to help them think about the effects their words have on others. Effectively expressing negative feelings in appropriate words is an important part of learning to communicate effectively, but hurtful or demeaning taunts or epithets must never be allowed.

How Can I Earn the Respect of School-Agers?

Early school-agers can be intimidating to adults. Young children who misbehave can be picked up and carried (kicking and screaming) away from a problem situation. School-agers are becoming too large. They can no longer be controlled by physical restraint. We must be able to rely on the child's inner control.

Parents who used spanking to control young children discover school-age children may be so emotionally immune to being hit that by this age they respond only with apathy. Or they may be so angered by being treated like a "baby" that an attempt to spank them could trigger outright defiance. Teachers and caregivers will encounter an occasional school-age child who has been subjected to a great deal of rough treatment in her life and has become aggressive, toughened, cynical, and very difficult to manage. Our best hope for breaking through this tough outer shell is

Wadsworth/Cengage Learning

School-agers begin to worry about their popularity among peers.

assertive rule enforcement tempered with unconditional affection and open, respectful communication.

The surest way out of this emotional trap is for the adult to break the cycle by finding some way to prove to each child that she is liked and respected by the adult. Then, and only then, can the adult begin to gain the children's respect and loyalty. External control methods do not work reliably for bright, capable, thinking children, who will feel they are being manipulated into doing things they do not want to do by someone who does not really like them.

Inner control depends completely on the child wanting to be a cooperative group member. If school-age children see the adult as someone who is absolutely fair, has a sense of humor, is reasonable, and who really cares about the needs and feelings of the children, they will be more willing to comply with that adult's wishes.

Why Do Early School-Agers Resist Going to Child Care?

Child care workers can especially be intimated by school-age children who have not yet developed inner control. Often, the youngest and least experienced workers are assigned to care for school-age children who attend the facility only during the early morning and late afternoon hours, summers, and holidays. After school, these children can be exhausted from long hours of sitting on hard desk chairs and feel pressured to meet adult expectations. During summers and holidays, they may envy friends who are at home or away on vacation. They may come into the child care setting with resentment for having to be in a "child care for babies." They may especially feel frustration over being expected to play quietly with blocks and puzzles they have outgrown in a room filled with all the trappings of a preschool.

In a typical scenario, school-age children begin to behave a bit wildly. Perhaps they start to throw pine cones at each other on the playground or stir their graham crackers into their milk, giggling and making a disgusting mush. Adults may respond in an abrasive and humorless attempt to stop this silly behavior. The children, feeling their oats, become sassy or perhaps stop the behaviors just long enough for the adult to turn her back for a moment. The angrier the adult becomes, the less compliant and cooperative the children will be. This situation can cause the adult to feel frighteningly out of control or helpless, a phenomenon that has an effect on older children similar to sharks smelling blood. Effective adults are able to model inner control, even in difficult situations.

Early school-age children will feel more cooperative about rules they have helped to create. Family council or class meetings provide an opportunity for school-age children to think about potential rules and to give their own opinions. If class meetings are run democratically, with real input from the children, then the children can begin to see rules not as inconveniences capriciously imposed by adults but as necessary protection for the rights and safety of all group members. Of course, it is critical that after-school programs are well planned, with opportunities for homework, sports, arts, music, dance, and interesting special projects. Bored children are not likely to exhibit self-control and self-discipline, no matter how caring the teachers are.

Why Do Early School-Agers Get so Upset about Fairness?

Early school-age children are able to see discrepancies in adult behaviors and so do not gullibly accept everything adults say the way that younger children do. "But that's not fair" seems to be the battle cry of early school-age children as they go about daily business. Even though they sometimes gleefully break rules themselves, they may become furious when it seems to them a rule is being enforced inconsistently: "But you didn't make Jerrod go back inside when he threw his book."

At this age, children's concrete operational perspective prohibits them from considering abstract extenuating circumstances that are important to adult decision makers. The school-age child may not see it as fair when a child who is new to a setting breaks the rules and is simply given an explanation of them, whereas a child who is expected to know the rules is given a stiff penalty for the same offense. Adults must constantly examine their own biases to determine whether there is any possibility that their treatment of the children is unequal.

Adults should be meticulous about not only their fairness but also their appearance of fairness. If a situation seems unfair to a child, the adult may assist the child's understanding by giving a concrete explanation for the action taken: "When you were younger, you needed many chances to remember rules. Now that you're seven, you know that throwing books is not allowed. Jerrod is only five now, but when he is seven he will have to stop playing, too, if he forgets the rule."

Why Do They Insist on Picking Their Own Clothes?

The early school years are an important period for children to develop their own identity. They develop a sense of personal identity by observing how others perceive them. They are especially sensitive to criticism or teasing about their appearance or clothing. Early school-agers also begin to worry about their status with other children. They assert their autonomy with parents by insisting on dressing like peers or role models.

Because physical development hinges on the active physical involvement of children in their environment by climbing, jumping, painting, gluing, and so on, parents and teachers can encourage (or require) clothing that is comfortable, washable, and not physically or socially restrictive. It is impossible to be ladylike in a frilly, short dress while climbing a jungle gym, and it is dangerous to climb the jungle gym in heavy, slick-soled cowboy boots. Whatever steps adults take, it is essential to remember how desperately children want to belong, to fit in, and to be viewed as special by their friends.

How Can We Help Early School-Agers Become Productive?

Erikson (1963) identified the emotional crisis for school-age children as one of **industry** (being productive) versus **inferiority** (feeling incapable). One of the enjoyable characteristics of school-age children is their ability to function independently. Young children need direction and help to do new things. School-age children have

industry
One's motivation to work constructively, to be diligent and productive.

inferiority
The feeling of being incapable, having a pervasive sense of inadequacy and experiencing a tendency toward self-diminishment.

the capacity to think of their own projects, to gather the needed materials, and then to work eagerly. They make miscalculations, messes, and mistakes, but they take great delight in having built their own crooked airplane or art object. Unfortunately, if they receive criticism instead of encouragement for their efforts and accomplishments, they may develop feelings of inferiority ("I'm no good," "Everything I try fails," "My ideas are stupid") and may be discouraged from trying new things.

Adults should not compare children's work to adult standards. One child's cookies may turn out tough and strangely shaped, but who cares? The purpose of the activity is for children to experience and learn from the process. The only importance of the activity outcome is that it makes children feel the pride of accomplishment.

How Can We Support the Early School-Age Child's Self-Esteem?

The big, wide world begins to have tremendous influence on the school-age child. Once she can read, whole new avenues of information are opened. She may see toothpaste ads on television and worry that her teeth have plaque monsters chomping away or see billboards about fire safety and worry that she will burn up in her bed at night. It is not unusual for school-age children to experience nightmares or develop irrational fears: "I'm not going to eat that chicken noodle soup because it has mushrooms, and they might be the poison kind that'll make you die."

We support early school-age children's self-esteem by listening respectfully to their concerns and helping them use their new reading and thinking skills to research topics that concern them. Instead of disputing their misperceptions of the world, we can help them discover on their own the facts of the situation. Instead of making them feel stupid, we empower them to learn about the world on their own. In the process, they discover that they are capable human beings.

Older School-Agers (9 to 12 Years)

Why Do Older School-Age Children Argue so Much?

concrete operational
In Jean Piaget's theory the third stage of cognitive development, which begins with the ability to analyze thoughts concerning a concrete idea (as opposed to an abstract idea).

As early school-agers become **concrete operational** (at about seven), they spend more time thinking about the things and events in their world. Preschoolers are just barely able to manage thinking through processes or mentally manipulating symbols that represent real objects or events, but by eight or nine, school-agers are usually able to manage manipulating thoughts about entire concrete processes. This enables them to mentally replay an event to evaluate it carefully and logically. Gradually, they begin to detect inconsistencies and gaps in logic. For example, an 11-year-old is likely to say, "Why do I have to wear my bicycle helmet? A lot more people have accidents riding in cars, and they don't have to wear helmets. Besides, if a car ran over my stomach, I'd be squashed anyway and a helmet wouldn't help." Most children will be adolescents or young adults before they can effectively manipulate abstract ideas and symbols, so they are not yet able to evaluate complex situations. Although

11- and 12-year-olds may look mature physically, emotionally and intellectually they still need a great deal of adult guidance and attention.

Older school-age children love to talk and listen to each other. Young children are more inclined to play together in a physically active way, using language as a supplement to running, jumping, climbing, and playing make-believe games. School-age children still enjoy active play but will sit under a tree or get on the telephone and talk excitedly for long periods about themselves, school events, and authority figures. They have discovered there really is no Santa Claus and are beginning to realize grown-ups are not omniscient deities but simply human beings who can make mistakes. When talking privately with a trusted friend or group of age-mates, school-agers may give an earful of complaints about parents, teachers, and siblings.

How Can I Get Older School-Agers to Trust and Respect Me?

Older school-age children can be delightful conversationalists. They will listen attentively and respond appropriately in conversations that hold their attention. They can also build new, more mature bonds of affection and loyalty to adults who are willing to listen to them and treat them fairly and respectfully. Older school-age children are especially sensitive to being "talked down to" by adults. School places new pressures on them. They are expected to assume a higher level of responsibility for their behavior and schoolwork. They will especially appreciate adults who really listen to their thoughts and feelings in an open-minded, nonjudgmental manner.

Why Do Older School-Agers Try so Hard to Be Popular?

School-age children have a powerful urge to belong to a peer group. They sometimes make up their own clubs or cliques with some semblance of rules and rituals, or even special taboos or requirements in clothing. Younger children may be oblivious to clothing, wearing whatever their parents buy for them, or they may have picky, but individual, tastes in clothing. School-age children become very concerned about wearing clothing that their friends approve of. Even first and second graders today seem to know the popular (and unpopular) brand names for blue jeans and sneakers, as well as for dolls and bicycles.

That mom, dad, or teacher prefers a certain style of clothing, shoes, or haircut may mean that the children automatically prefer something else. This tendency to dress for peers gradually increases but does not reach a climactic peak until adolescence. Perhaps some entrepreneur will ease the discomfort parents feel by selling buttons for children to wear that say "My parents are not responsible for the way I look, I dressed myself."

Wadsworth/Cengage Learning

As school-age children become adolescents, they often go through periods of moodiness and insecurity as they cope with their changing bodies and increasing need for peer acceptance.

Adults should first help children feel secure, valued, and accepted, because self-confidence and self-esteem assist children in resisting inappropriate peer pressure. Adults can also help children keep material possessions in a proper perspective by respecting the children's anxiety about peer approval but also by deemphasizing the value of objects. They can strengthen children's character by focusing attention on valuing people for their character rather than for their expensive clothing or toys.

Why Do Older School-Age Children Love Pranks and Jokes?

Older school-age children are becoming more adept at controlling their impulses. Although they may lapse from time to time into less mature behavior such as throwing a tantrum or pouting, they are finally able to wait for a while even though they are bored, hungry, or need to go to the bathroom. As they spend more time conforming to the social and behavioral expectations of authority figures and peers, they eagerly take advantage of opportunities where they feel safe being silly and whimsical. For example, when the teacher walks out of the room for a moment, a child might say, "Hey, wouldn't it be funny to pour this paint into the fish tank and then all the fish would turn purple?" Then, they laugh uproariously and (we hope) resist the urge to really do it. Preschool-age children are not quite as able to weigh consequences and resist temptations. For toddlers, thinking is doing. Preschoolers can barely resist following their impulses. As children move toward adolescence, they should be developing the ability to persist toward long-term goals. At this stage, they should not be so easily tempted by instant gratification that keeps them from accomplishing a specific task or project.

How Can We Support Older School-Agers' Self-Esteem?

As children leave early childhood and move toward adolescence, life becomes complicated and stressful. Their bodies seem to take on a life of their own, growing adult genitalia often far too quickly or far too slowly to suit the confused and disoriented owner of the body. We begin to see little children walking around in very adult-looking bodies, and suddenly we expect them to act like grown-ups.

Wadsworth/Cengage Learning

■■■ As older school-age children begin to grow into adolescents, it is critical for them to have opportunities to practice their prosocial skills in settings where they are really needed and appreciated. They can establish the lifelong habit of giving back to their community by organizing food drives, planning school projects, tutoring younger children, and participating in other beneficial activities.

Just as in toddlerhood when two-year-olds were torn between the security of infancy and the allure of childhood, preadolescents are likely to waver in their feelings about whether to be a little kid or a teenager. One minute the child is sitting on a curb crying over a skinned knee and the next she is choosing her favorite color of lipstick.

Adults must provide a great deal of support, affection, and patience during these years so that school-agers' self-esteem and confidence stay intact. Babies, toddlers, and preschoolers get many hugs because they are little and cute. Adolescents and adults get romantic hugs from the opposite sex. Older school-agers are at an awkward stage and, especially young boys, may be left out of shows of affection altogether. Everybody needs an appropriate (nonexploitative) hug now and then to feel valued and special, and there are many excellent ways other than hugs to express affection. A big smile, sincere recognition, and listening all let the child know we care (American Academy of Pediatrics, 1995; Charlesworth, 2004; Gartrell, 1997; Gronlund, 1997; Meece, 1997; Steinberg, 1995).

KEY TERMS

active listening
appropriate touch
authoritarian style
authoritative style
autonomy
cephalocaudal
classical conditioning
collaborative
community of learners
concept
concrete operational
cues
doubt
egocentric
emotional growth
empathy
expressive language
external environment
group contagion
habituated
imprinting
industry
inferiority
internal sensations

internalize
learned behavior
learned helplessness
metacognition
mirror
modeling
object permanence
operant conditioning
permissive style
positive child guidance
preoperational
proximodistal
pseudoconditioning
receptive language
secure attachment
self-concept
self-esteem
shame
social growth
stimuli
stress
trust
unconscious conditioning
unconscious reactions

POINTS TO REMEMBER

- Children have individual patterns and rates of development.
- Comparisons should never be used to label or stereotype a child.
- Trust developed in infancy is a primary foundation for the development of healthy emotional attitudes.
- *Spoiling* refers to overindulging and overprotecting children, shielding them from responsibility for their own behavior and rewarding inappropriate conduct.
- Toddlers strive to achieve autonomy.
- Preschoolers can be helped to express strong emotions or feelings of anger.

- Early school-age children develop an ability to replay events mentally to evaluate experiences carefully and logically.
- Older school-agers have a powerful urge to belong to a peer group and be well liked by friends.
- Authoritarian is the role of the "sledgehammer," rigid and demanding.
- Permissive is the role of the "doormat," overindulgent and sometimes neglectful.
- Authoritative is the role of the "guide," assertive, respectful, and consistent.

PRACTICAL APPLICATION

"I'm Never Gonna 'Vite You to My Birth'ay!"

Sarah and Lupita, both five-year-olds, have claimed a shady spot under a thick magnolia tree on the playground. It is their favorite place to play. They have staunchly defended their little territory against small bands of marauding playmates by insisting, "You can't play. We got here first. This is our house."

Although their teacher does not allow toys from home in the classroom, the students have been allowed to bring their dolls outside with them for their outdoor play period. Sarah has a well-worn Raggedy Ann doll and Lupita has a new, soft plastic baby doll, wrapped in a pink blanket, that looks just like a newborn baby.

They rocked their dolls to sleep and carefully placed them beside the trunk of the tree, and then they scurried around gathering leaves and sticks to outline a boundary for their playhouse. Sarah finds a large stick and announces that it is the door, "Nobody can come in unless they open this door. Tick tock. Now it's all locked up."

Robby, also five, has been watching and listening to the girls as he climbed and jumped off a climbing structure "fort" nearby. He cannot resist Sarah's challenge. "I

can too get in," he taunts as he dances around the line of leaves and sticks that is the pretend wall of the girls' playhouse. He pokes his foot over the line and darts just out of their reach as he sticks his tongue out, laughing and chanting, "Nanny, nanny, boo, boo!"

Sarah chases and yells at Robby, while Lupita furiously mends the pretend wall. Robby retreats to the top of the climbing structure insisting, "Uh-huh! I could get in there. It's not really your house."

Lupita plants her feet firmly in the grass and stares viciously at Robby, guarding hearth and home, while Sarah runs to tell on Robby.

Robby, of course, loses all interest in Lupita's mean look. He is perched behind a post at the top of the fort watching carefully to see what his teacher, Miss Gresham, will do next.

Miss Gresham bends down on one knee and listens intently as Sarah rants and raves about Robby's alleged offenses. Quietly, Miss Gresham says, "Did you tell Robby how you felt when he messed up your house? Would you like for me to come with you to talk to Robby?" Sarah takes Miss Gresham's hand and quickly leads the way back to the scene of the crime. Robby, meanwhile, is huddled on the fort hoping no one can see him. He forgets that Miss Gresham is tall enough to talk eye-to-eye with him at the highest part of the fort.

With a gentle and reassuring voice, Miss Gresham says, "Robby, let's talk with Lupita and Sarah. I think they're feeling very angry." Robby pauses for just a second, but Miss Gresham holds her hands out and says, "It's okay, Robby. Sometimes I make mistakes and people get mad at me, too." Robby leans off the fort and Miss Gresham lowers him to the ground. She looks right in his eyes and pats him as she says, "Thanks, Robby." Then she assumes the role of objective referee as the girls tell Robby, in no uncertain terms, "Don't you break our house no more!"

Robby's lip quivers and a big tear begins to slide down his grimy face as he pulls back his shoulders and announces, "You ain't my best friend and I ain't never gonna 'vite you to my birth'ay party!"

DISCUSSION QUESTIONS

1. Identify characteristics and behaviors of Lupita, Sarah, and Robby that are typical of five-year-olds.
2. List all the reasons you can think of for Robby's interference with the girls' play. Why were the girls so angry?
3. Do you agree with Miss Gresham's handling of the problem? Explain. What would you have done differently?
4. What might have happened if Miss Gresham had responded to Robby with an angry voice and negative punishment?

STUDENT ACTIVITY

1. Interview a first-time parent of an infant.
    a. Ask about the birth experience.
    b. What has surprised the parent most in caring for the baby?
    c. What parenting experiences have been most rewarding?
    d. What experiences have been most challenging for the new parent?
    e. Ask the parent to describe the baby's day-to-day routines.
2. Interview the parent of a toddler.
    a. Ask what has been done to childproof the home to allow safe exploration for the toddler.
    b. Ask whether the toddler has shown any signs of separation anxiety or stranger anxiety.
    c. Ask for examples. Has the toddler ever had a tantrum?
    d. If so, ask about the circumstances. Was the child tired? Hungry? Not feeling well?
3. Interview the parent of a preschooler.
    a. What are the child's favorite activities?
    b. How does the preschooler interact with peers?
    c. Ask about the preschooler's bedtime routine.
    d. Does the preschooler resist going to bed?
    e. Are there any strategies the parent uses to help get the child calmed down and into bed?
4. Interview the parent of a young school-age child.
    a. What are the child's favorite interests?
    b. How does the child interact with peers?
    c. How does this school-ager handle disagreements with peers?
    d. How is the child doing in school?
    e. How does this child handle frustrations in school?
    f. Does the parent have any concerns about particular behavior issues?
    g. How does the parent respond to them?

5. Interview the parent of an older school-age child.

    a. What are the child's favorite interests?

    b. How does the child interact with peers?

    c. How does this child handle disagreements with peers?

    d. How is the child doing in school?

    e. How does the child handle frustrations in school?

    f. Do the parents and the child have to negotiate about homework?

    g. When does the child do homework?

    h. Is homework a point of contention between the child and parents?

RELATED READINGS

Growth and Development

Baillargeon, R. (1997). How do infants learn about the physical world? In E. N. Junn & C. Boyatzis (Eds.), *Annual editions: Child growth and development 97/98* (4th ed.). New York: McGraw-Hill. (Original work published in *Current Directions in Psychological Science,* October 1994).

    On the basis of the pioneering work of Jean Piaget, researchers once assumed that infants lacked a sense of object permanence. Renee Baillargeon describes her well-known and ingenious research indicating that young infants do, in fact, possess more fundamental and elaborate knowledge about physical objects than once thought.

Bainer, C., & Hale, L. (2000). From diapers to underpants. *Young Children, 50*(4), 80–84.

    Two teachers offer guidance on readiness, parent communication, giving children a foundation of support and confidence, and preparing the environment to support toilet learning.

Banich, M. T. (1997). *Neuropsychology: The neural bases of mental function.* Boston: Houghton-Mifflin.

Begley, S. (1997). The IQ puzzle. In E. N. Junn & C. Boyatzis (Eds.), *Annual editions: Child growth and development 97/98* (4th ed.). New York: McGraw-Hill. (Original work published in *Newsweek,* May 6, 1996).

    Scores on intelligence tests have risen dramatically in many countries. Does this mean that children today are smarter than ever? Sharon Begley discusses the possible reasons for these gains—including the popularity of video games and cereal boxes with mazes and puzzles for children—and addresses the debate on whether IQ tests truly measure intelligence.

Begley, S. (1997). Your child's brain. In K. M. Paciorek & J. H. Munro (Eds.), *Annual editions: Early childhood education 97/98* (18th ed.). New York: McGraw-Hill. (Original work published in *Newsweek,* February 19, 1996).

    This article discusses recent research that suggests the human brain is sensitive to experiences very early in life, which influence brain development for skill in language, music, math, and other learning. Sharon Begley describes "learning windows" when children may be most influenced by environmental stimulation.

Behrman R. E., Ed. (1995). Long-term outcomes of early childhood programs. *Future of Children, 5*(3).

Berk, L. E. (1997). Vygotsky's theory: The importance of make-believe play. In E. N. Junn & C. Boyatzis (Eds.), *Annual editions: Child growth and development 97/98* (4th ed.). New York: McGraw-Hill. (Original work published in *Young Children,* November 1994).

    This article describes the view of Lev Vygotsky, a Russian psychologist who emphasizes the importance of pretend play as a forum for learning. In particular, children learn through guidance from parents and teachers, which creates a scaffold for experiences, allowing youngsters to take more responsibility as their skills increase.

Bornstein, M. H., & Lamb, M. (1992). *Development in infancy: An introduction* (3rd ed.). New York: McGraw-Hill.

    This overview of infant development is intended for experienced infant and child development profes-

sionals who want more information about research issues related to infant development.

Brazelton, T. B. (2001). *Su hijo: La referencia esencial.* Cambridge, MA: Perseus.

Brazelton, T. B. (2001). *The Children's Hospital guide to your child's health and development.* Cambridge, MA: Perseus.

Brazelton, T. B., & Greenspan, S. I. (2000). *What every child must have to grow, learn, and flourish.* Cambridge, MA: Perseus.

Brazelton, T. B., & Sparrow, J. D. (2001). *Touchpoints three to six: Your child's emotional and behavioral development.* Cambridge, MA: Perseus.

Bronfenbrenner, U., & Morris, P. A. (1998). The ecology of developmental processes. In W. Damon (Series Ed.) & R. M. Lerner (Vol. Ed.), *Handbook of child psychology: Vol. 1. Theoretical models of human development* (5th ed., 993–1027). New York: Wiley.

Campos, J. J., Bertenthal, B. I., & Kermoian, R. (1997). Early experience and emotional development: The emergence of wariness of heights. In E. N. Junn & C. Boyatzis (Eds.), *Annual editions: Child growth and development 97/98* (4th ed.). New York: McGraw-Hill. (Original work published in *Psychological Science,* January 1992).

How do we become afraid of heights? Are we born with the fear or do we learn it through life experiences? This article by prominent researchers describes careful experiments designed to determine whether babies are born with a fear of heights or if they acquire it only after learning to crawl and the experience of moving around in the world.

Caulfield, R. (1996, fall). Social and emotional development in the first two years. *Early Childhood Education Journal, 24*(1), 55–58.

Daniel, J. E. (1998). A modern mother's place is wherever her children are: Facilitating infant and toddler mothers' transitions in child care. *Young Children, 53*(6), 4–12.

Discusses the importance of supporting mother and child through the critical transition to out-of-home care. Identifies stressors that await mothers and ways providers can ease these stressors.

Eddowes, E. A., & Ralph, K. S. (1998). *Interactions for development and learning: Birth through eight years.* Upper Saddle River, NJ: Merrill Education/Prentice Hall.

This book emphasizes the importance of different types of interaction for supporting early development and learning. Research shows the importance of appropriate interactions between an adult and child, between a child and older and younger peers, or between a child and an object.

Elkind, D. (1996, May). Early childhood education: What should we expect? *Principal, 7*(55), 11–13.

French, L. (1996). "I told you all about it, so don't tell me you don't know . . ." *Young Children, 5*(2), 17–20.

A developmental psychologist and mother of young children discusses the development of the ability of two-year-olds to comprehend information from language alone. She also explains the negative effects of developmentally inappropriate teaching when inappropriate language expectations are made of children.

Gibbs, N. (1997). The EQ factor. In E. N. Junn & C. Boyatzis (Eds.), *Annual editions: Child growth and development 97/98* (4th ed.). New York: McGraw-Hill. (Original work published in *Time,* October 2, 1995).

Brain research suggests that emotions, not the traditional IQ rating, may be the true measure of human intelligence. This article examines this trend in the assessment of human ability to cope successfully with challenges.

Gowen, J. (1995). Research in review. The early development of symbolic play. *Young Children, 50*(3), 75–84.

This article reviews research on early development of symbolic play and ways its development can be promoted. Symbolic play is also called pretend play, fantasy play, dramatic play, or imaginative play.

Honig, A. (2000). Psychosexual development in infants and young children: Implications for caregivers. *Young Children, 55*(5), 70–77.

This article reminds teachers that young children's sexual curiosity and activity are perfectly natural, and gives tips for promoting healthy psychosexual development. Discusses anatomical differences, Freudian stages, sexual identity, and play choices.

Howard, V., Williams, B. F., Port, P. D., & Lepper, C. (1997). Very young children with special needs:

A formative approach for the 21st century. In E. N. Junn & C. Boyatzis (Eds.), *Annual editions: Child growth and development 97/98* (4th ed.). New York: McGraw-Hill.

Using a formative, holistic, family-centered approach, this essay provides comprehensive coverage of normal childhood development—from birth to age six—and a description of more than 50 of the most common medical conditions that early childhood educators should understand before working with families and professionals in other fields.

Hunter, T. (2000). Knowing things before we know them. *Young Children, 55*(4), 85.

This article explores stages of learning and addresses key factors in designing a lively environment focused on child learning.

Kantrowitz, B., & Wingert, P. (1997). How kids learn. In E. N. Junn & C. Boyatzis (Eds.), *Annual editions: Child growth and development 97/98* (4th ed.). New York: McGraw-Hill. (Original work published in *Newsweek*, April 17, 1989).

Between the ages of five and eight, children absorb an enormous amount of information. New research indicates that learning is best facilitated when active hands-on exploration, cooperation, and problem solving are emphasized over more traditional forms of passive rote learning of information. Implications for teachers and parents are discussed.

Leong, D., & Bodrova, E. (1996). *Tools of the mind: A Vygotskian approach to early childhood education.* Upper Saddle River, NJ: Merrill Education/Prentice Hall.

The authors' objective is to enable future teachers to arm young children with the mental tools necessary for learning. The authors view mental tools as a cycle in which ideas are (1) learned from others, (2) modified and changed, and (3) passed back and on to others.

Marose, N. R. (1997, November). Successful toilet learning: At a child's pace. *Young Children, 52*(7), 81.

An early childhood professional discusses practical tips for supporting toilet training when the child is ready.

Nash, J. M. (1997, February 3). Fertile minds: From birth, a baby's brain cells proliferate wildly, making connections that may shape a lifetime of experience. *Time, 149*(5), 48–56.

Newberger, J. J. (1997, May). New brain development research: A wonderful window of opportunity to build public support for early childhood education! *Young Children, 52*(4), 4–9.

Novick, R. (2002). Learning to read the heart: Nurturing emotional literacy. *Young Children, 57*(3), 84–89.

The author argues that social and emotional school readiness is critical to successful kindergarten transition, early child success, and later adult accomplishment.

Peterson, R. W. (1994, April). School readiness considered from a neuro-cognitive perspective. *Early Education and Development, 5*(2), 120–140.

Powlishta, K. K. (1995). Research in review. Gender segregation among children: Understanding the "cootie phenomenon." *Young Children, 50*(4), 61–69.

This article reviews research into gender segregation (the preference for same-sex playmates among children). The author focuses on why it occurs, its consequences, and its implications.

Raikes, H. (1996). A secure base for babies: Applying attachment concepts to the infant care setting. *Young Children, 51*(5), 59–67.

This article explains the basic principles of attachment theory and shows how these principles can be used in infant programs.

Reinsberg, J. (1999). Understanding young children's behavior. *Young Children, 54*(4), 54–57.

This article guides parents and caregivers in identifying underlying causes that might explain children's behavioral actions, adopting reflective rather than reactive approaches to achieve more positive outcomes, and establishing environments that support and nurture children.

Rushton, S. P. (2001). Applying brain research to create developmentally appropriate learning environments. *Young Children, 56*(5), 76–82.

This article argues that brain research confirms the validity of developmentally appropriate practice and the relevance of child-centered constructivist ideas of Dewey, Piaget, and Vygotsky.

Sameroff, A., & McDonough, S. C. (1997). Educational implications of developmental transitions: Revisiting the 5- to 7-year shift. In K. M. Paciorek & J. H. Munro (Eds.), *Annual editions: Early childhood education 97/98* (18th ed.). New York: McGraw-Hill. (Original work published in *Phi Delta Kappan*, November 1994).

The ages between five and seven mark an important milestone in the lives of young children. Educators who have a clear understanding of child development are able to assist children as they make a smooth transition into the primary grades. The onset of this developmental shift depends on the environment, culture, and previous school experiences and the child's unique characteristics.

Schiller, P. (1997, September–October). Brain development research: Support and challenges. *Child Care Information Exchange, 117,* 6–10.

Sroufe, L. A. (1996). *Child development: Its nature and course.* New York: McGraw-Hill.

This book gives information on gender socialization; emotional development; prenatal effects drugs; genetic research; postnatal development; brain growth; infant intelligence, assessment, bilingualism, early roots of morality, and cross-cultural education; and mixed-gender social relationships.

Thorne, B. (1997). Girls and boys together but mostly apart. In E. N. Junn & C. Boyatzis (Eds.), *Annual editions: Child growth and development 97/98* (4th ed.). New York: McGraw-Hill. (Original work published in *GenderPlay: Girls and Boys in School,* Rutgers University Press, 1993).

Gender segregation—boys playing with boys, girls with girls—is very common during the elementary school years. How might this affect boys' and girls' social and interpersonal development? Barrie Thorne describes how not only peers but teachers as well contribute to gender segregation.

U.S. Department of Education. (1997, Spring). What new research on the brain tells us about our youngest children: Summary on the White House Conference on Early Childhood. *Dimensions of Early Childhood, 25*(2).

Books for Overwhelmed Parents

Granju, K. A. (1999). *Attachment parenting: Instinctive care for your baby and young child.* New York: Atria.

La Leche League International (2004). *The womanly art of breastfeeding.* La Leche League International, New York: Plume Books.

Sears, W., & Sears, M. (2002). *The attachment parenting book.* New York: Little, Brown.

Sears, W., & Sears, M. (2003). *The baby book: Everything you need to know about your baby from birth to age two.* New York: Little, Brown.

The Online Companion™ to accompany the sixth edition of *Positive Child Guidance* is your link to additional guidance resources on the Internet. This supplement contains audio and visual materials; PowerPoint presentations; web activities with critical-thinking questions and practical-application assignments; and links to web resources. This additional content can be found at http://www.earlychilded.delmar.com.

Chapter 3

Serving Culturally Diverse Children and Families

OBJECTIVES

After reading this chapter, you should be able to do the following:

- Define culture.
- Recognize cultural differences that affect child guidance.
- Appreciate the importance of culture in positive child guidance.
- Identify and eliminate prejudice, bias, and ethnocentricity in yourself and your community.
- Identify early signs of discrimination in young children to nip it in the bud.
- State the criteria for selecting multi-cultural items for the early childhood environment.
- Be aware of and respect cultural differences among children and parents.
- Reflect on your own cultural affinity.
- Reflect on your own sensitivity to cultural differences.

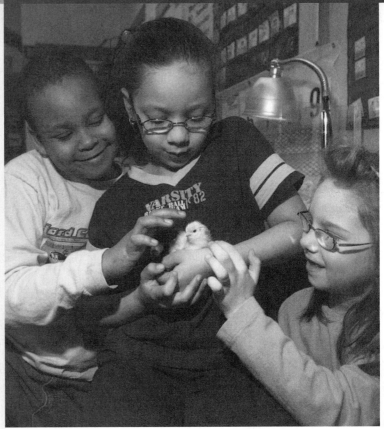

Wadsworth/Cengage Learning

Children from diverse cultural backgrounds bring rich cultural qualities to the classroom.

Cultural Influences on Child Guidance

The ideas that many Americans and Canadians take for granted about the nature of infancy and childhood are different from those held by others in different places in the world and at different times in history. Other Americans and Canadians, some who may be first-generation immigrants, hold dramatically different perspectives. By carefully examining our own beliefs and assumptions about children, we can recognize and put into perspective biases and miscommunications that interfere with our ultimate goal of effective child guidance.

Child care practices have been strikingly different over time for various economic classes. A long period of protected childhood has largely been a luxury of the middle and upper classes, and views of infancy have fluctuated according to cultural and class settings (Bremner, 1974; Cole, 1950; Froebel, 1887; Glubok, 1969; McGraw, 1941; Osborn, 1980; Rousseau, 1893; Ulich, 1954). Much of what is written about child rearing, infant care, and early child care curriculum is sometimes thought to present a generic, "culture-free" model for quality care. That assumes, of course, that all parents hold a similar idea about what kind of care is good and right for babies and young children. To the contrary, there is growing evidence that strategies for guiding young children have cultural significance and vary according to the parents' cultural backgrounds. Parents have diverse ideas about what is and is not appropriate for guiding and disciplining children (Ball & Pence, 1999; Loeb et al., 2004).

People from different cultural and economic backgrounds frequently hold starkly contrasting views about what proper child care really is. Methods of caring for and educating young children routinely used by families in one community may shock and repel families in another community, and vice versa. A mother in one cultural setting may be astonished that a mother in another setting still allows her two-year-old to nurse at the breast, whereas the nursing mother may be horrified that the first mother allows her two-year-old to eat candy and drink soda. In some settings, people expect infants to be taken everywhere the parents go. They think that is good for babies. In other settings, people think it is best for infants to be left safely at home in their cribs with a babysitter.

Routines considered very desirable by one parent may be seen as inane by another. Guidance strategies believed essential or healthy to growth by some early educators may be considered inhumane or manipulative by others. Some people believe misbehaving children should be spanked. Some people believe children should be made to sit in a chair for a few minutes for punishment. Some people do not like either of those two ideas. Beliefs can vary dramatically between two parents.

What some consider essential experiences for effective early learning, others consider utter nonsense. Some people think infants can be made to learn at an accelerated pace by being shown flashcards of letters and numbers. Others think no child of any age should be subjected to flashcards. Social workers, early educators, and child care professionals have often felt the tension among these opposing views, and they have sometimes been snagged unknowingly by their own culturally biased inflexibility.

Cultural perceptions of desirable and appropriate care for children reflect the perceptions and beliefs of a person at a given time and place in history. The socialization of a new generation reflects the goals, philosophies, and values of the parent

Wadsworth/Cengage Learning

Parents around the world have different ideas about how best to care for and nurture babies. Some carry their babies on their bodies most of the time; some use swings and bouncy chairs. Some sleep with their babies in a family bed; some use a crib in a separate room. Some bottle-feed; some breast-feed. Many parents feel passionately that their way of caring is best.

culture
The traditional beliefs and patterns of behavior that are passed down from parents to children by a society; beliefs, customs, practices, and social behavior of any particular cluster of people whose shared beliefs and practices identify the particular nation, religion, ability, gender, race, or group to which they belong.

cultural pluralism
The peaceful coexistence of numerous distinct ethnic, religious, or cultural groups within one community or society.

cultural bias
Unfair preference for or dislike of something or someone based on culture.

pluralistic culture
(See cultural pluralism.)

generation related to their specific social and economic circumstances. In other words, **culture** plays a key role in defining acceptable methods for dealing with children. **Cultural bias** is inescapable. To create an environment that is supportive and a **pluralistic culture**, however, cultural differences must be understood, accepted, and respected. We live in a world where cultures are no longer isolated. Cultures move easily around the world. Communication is instant and becoming available to almost everyone. There is no room for intolerance of cultural diversity. Immigrants have a right to keep their own distinctive cultural roots and uniqueness. Each of us has a right to celebrate our own heritage. But we must also sometimes make compromises when strong evidence emerges indicating that a culturally based tradition is harmful or ineffective in reaching desired goals (Tomasello et al., 1993).

People used to believe that applying leaches to suck blood out of people cured many diseases. Bloodletting was discovered to be harmful, but then leaches and maggots were found to be helpful in a few specific medical situations (if the patients can be convinced to cooperate!). In many parts of the world, it has been believed that eating the heart of a lion confers bravery and aids in recovery from such conditions such as depression, bad mood, and nervousness. Obviously, there isn't much research on the effectiveness of ground-up rhinoceros horn on relieving anxiety. There is, however, a great deal of research telling us that antidepressant medications relieve the symptoms of depression. We must be tolerant of other's choices, but when we want to work together to achieve the same goal, compromise is the magic word.

In one country culturally committed to medical products from wild animals but facing world pressures for protecting the remaining endangered wild animals, a creative zookeeper worked out a compromise. He raised funds for the zoo by selling elephant urine, snake skin, hair shed by lions, dung from tigers and bears, and anything else the predators left behind. The animals weren't harmed and local citizens had their important physical substances from predators at the top of the food chain. Everyone compromised and everyone won.

All of us have a lot to gain by adapting our cultural beliefs to include information on practices and artifacts that have proved effective and then using that information in achieving a goal. We can all work toward that goal, regardless of our cultural heritage, by respectfully communicating and agreeing on our mutual goal and then working together to find an acceptable compromise.

Cultural crises happen every day in child care centers. For example, a teacher might say, "Mrs. Quiroga, I noticed that you seemed surprised when I mentioned that children, both boys and girls, are encouraged to wear T-shirts, jeans, sneakers, and other such play clothes to school. Did you have a question about that?" Mrs. Quiroga's cultural background may cause her to place an especially high value in dressing her children well. She expected her daughter to wear a neatly ironed, frilly dress to preschool each day. To Mrs. Quiroga, the picture of her daughter, Lupita, wearing a paint-smeared T-shirt and dust-covered jeans, with sand in her hair, evokes an all-too-real image of poverty, not the picture-perfect image of developmentally appropriate practice (DAP).

Empirical research tells us that play is extremely important to children's social and emotional development, their growth and learning (McClelland et al., 2000;

Raver, 2002; Raver & Zigler, 1997; Emde et al., 2003; Warren et al., 2000; Favez, 2006). Communication will be needed to help Mrs. Quiroga understand why her daughter will benefit by being dressed appropriately to paint, play in the sand, crawl around on the floor, use messy substances such as glue, and generally get dirty and have fun. The conference may have several different types of conclusions. If the teachers agree to respect Mrs. Quiroga's preference that Lupita wear dresses, Lupita will miss out on many important activities or risk ruining her dresses. If Mrs. Quiroga agrees to dress Lupita casually, she may feel disrespected. If, as a parent–teacher resource team, they decide together that Lupita will bring a second set of clothes to school for Lupita to change into for play, the goal will be accomplished and Mrs. Quiroga will feel empowered because her needs have been respected. She will also understand more about why it is so important to Lupita's learning and development for her to paint and play with messy materials.

Of course, there is always the chance that Mrs. Quiroga will not understand, will not want to change her cultural viewpoint. She might want Lupita in clean, starched, frilly dresses every day and want to find her spotlessly clean at the end of the day—an impossible task for a DAP learning environment. Your task as an early childhood professional in that case is to continue to communicate as caringly, respectfully, and honestly as you can about what DAP is and what you are trying to accomplish during the day. Patience, persistence, and compromise offer the best chance to work through this obstacle.

Janet Gonzalez-Mena (2008) describes a marvelous compromise reached by parents and child care professionals in one center. African American parents often express frustration about their children coming home with heads full of sand. Parents whose young children have fine, straight hair have it easy when it comes to brushing and washing out sand. Parents whose children have dense, curly hair (especially if it needs certain kinds of hair products to be manageable) find it grueling to get the sand out each night. Many complain that the sand actually cuts the hair. These parents know playing in the sandbox is important, but they also would like to have a clean, presentable child. In one child care center, this long-standing friction was resolved by a particularly clever solution. Shower caps were made available to the children whenever they played on the playground.

Forming effective helping relationships between families and early childhood professionals hinges on recognizing and working through differences in backgrounds, personality characteristics, child-rearing perspectives, cultural beliefs, and role expectations (Bruns & Corso, 2001; Dinnebeil & Rule, 1994; Kalyanpor & Harry, 1999; Kochanek & Buka, 1998; Lynch & Hanson, 1998). Families are more likely to develop effective working relationships with professionals they trust (Dinnebeil & Rule, 1994). Of course, trust is essential to cooperative, effective collaboration between families and educators as they strive to provide positive guidance.

Cultural sensitivity does not include relying on stereotypes about what different groups like and dislike. Differences among people inside a cultural group can be as great as differences between cultural groups (Lynch & Hanson, 1998). Every person should be seen and related to as a unique individual. Some people expect a formal relationship with early education professionals (Schwartz, 1995). Others expect an

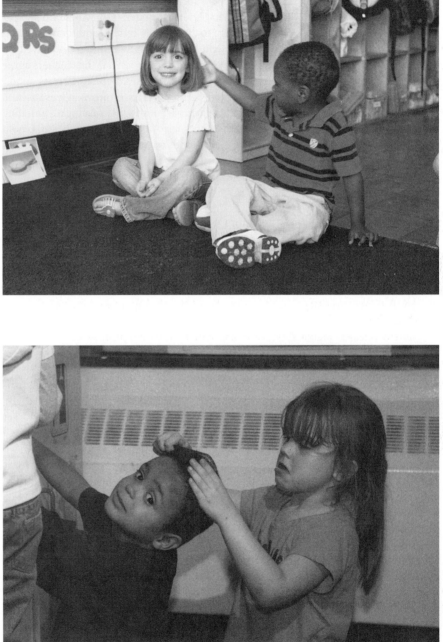

Wadsworth/Cengage Learning

Wadsworth/Cengage Learning

If young children have the opportunity to play and learn in the presence of diverse children and adults, they learn to accept cultural and ethnic differences as a natural part of their world. The children in these photographs are quite comfortably exploring their hair differences as a simple and natural part of their play.

informal friendly relationship (Gonzalez-Alvarez, 1998). If early educators domi-nate interactions, the family may feel uncomfortable and may not be willing to talk about their needs and concerns (Dennis & Giangreco, 1996; Gudykunst et al., 1996). Domineering teacher styles may be particularly offensive to families from traditional Hispanic, Native American, and Asian backgrounds (Gonzalez-Alvarez, 1998; Joe & Malach, 1998; Schwarz, 1995; Bruns & Corso, 2001). Resourcefulness in finding com-munity resources and skill in using interpreters are becoming more and more impor-tant for early education professionals. Communicating successfully with diverse fam-ilies often requires finding community volunteers, family members, or professionals fluent in the families' primary language to answer questions and resolve problems (Ohtake, Santos, & Fowler, 2000). Being a sensitive, respectful listener opens the door to understanding the needs and expectations of persons from other cultures.

How Do Young Children Learn about Their Role in the World?

From birth to school age, children develop basic assumptions about how the world works and what their role is in that world. Children glean different sets of perceptions from different settings. Following are some typical examples of the way adults treat children in early childhood programs. Decide whether you think these are cultural differ-ences, teaching-style differences, or a combination of both.

Concept: If children's early childhood environment is rigid and they are herded through the day with no allowance for individual choice, they learn that the world is impassive and individual needs and interests do not matter.

Scenario: Children are all required to sit at a long table. They are told and shown exactly how to glue precut pieces of a Santa Claus face onto a paper plate. If a child does this differently than the adult intends, the adult makes the child do it over or the adult does it herself and puts the child's name on it.

Concept: If, in contrast, the environment is flexible and geared to individual needs, choices, and responsibilities, children learn that the world is malleable and that with persistence and effort they can affect the world around them.

Scenario: Winter holiday craft materials such as paper plates, glue, glitter, cotton balls, and bits of colored construction paper are made available in the art center. Children are not shown an adult model to copy but rather are encour-aged to use their own imaginations to create Christmas, Hanukkah, or other seasonal decorations. When done the children responsibly clean up the mate-rials each used. Unique differences in the finished products are recognized and honored, and all are displayed with pride.

Concept: If early authority figures are aloof from the children and control them by issuing frequent imperative commands ("Be quiet," "Sit up straight," "Stand in line," "Don't talk"), children develop a perception of authority figures as omnipotent powers to be obeyed without question, enemies to be rebelled against, obstacles to be avoided, or irrelevant annoyances to be ignored.

(Continued)

How Do Young Children Learn about Their Role in the World? (Continued)

Scenario: The adult attempts to maintain total control by having children do everything in unison—they must all sit and wait passively while the adult has children come up to the front of the class one by one to point out letters of the alphabet or say numbers. Children must all line up to wash hands and use the toilet at the same time. Even if their food becomes stone cold, no child is allowed to eat lunch until all are given the signal to begin together. Children may even be required to stand in straight lines on the playground and do calisthenics for exercise (rather than running and playing freely). The adult imagines that no learning is taking place unless she is in charge and the children are quiet, controlled, and attentive.

Concept: If caring adults are warm, responsive, and assertive, children develop a perception of authority figures as dependable and resourceful allies who protect and help.

Scenario: The adult structures the environment and the schedule to encourage children to function independently and individually as well as part of a cohesive group. Children choose learning materials from learning centers and work at their own pace during large, uninterrupted blocks of time. They generally use the restroom according to their own body needs rather than according to group routines. Transitions from one activity to the next are flexible rather than abrupt. If a child finishes lunch earlier than others, she can throw away her trash, sponge off her area of the table, and then curl up and look at picture books until it is time for nap.

Concept: If adults treat children as underlings with few rights and are careless, degrading, or threatening in their treatment of children, children learn to treat others with rudeness and aggression and fail to develop self-respect.

Scenario: Adults often talk to each other as if the children weren't even present, sometimes laughing at or making fun of individual children. Adults order children around without saying please or thank you. Punishment is meted out according to the adults' moods and whims rather than being based on fair and consistent rules. The adults act as if they are above rules.

Concept: If early caregivers stereotype children by gender, ethnicity, or other characteristics, children internalize the belief they are limited in what they can achieve.

Scenario: Adults select only boys to act out the role of the fire marshal in a skit, totally ignoring girls who have their hands raised. Picture books are used that show only one ethnic, cultural, regional, or economic background. Adults take it for granted that all children celebrate Christmas and Easter. A particularly tall three-year-old is expected to behave more responsibly than a particularly tiny five-year-old. Children are singled out and treated differently according to how they look, how they dress, or what their parents do for a living.

Concept: If early caregivers see all children as unique individuals who can be helped to reach their own special potential, children develop high expectations for themselves and the self-esteem needed to master challenges they set for themselves.

Scenario: Children are all seen as unique and valuable individuals. Books, puppets, and dolls are multicultural. Children are helped to appreciate various cultures through food, music, and holiday celebrations that expose them to many perspectives. Adults respect and help the children learn about religious and ethnic differences in children and their families. Girls and boys are expected to participate fully in all activities, and girls are especially encouraged to be competent and confident.

Concept: If the early environment is overly adult centered and adult controlled, the child develops a sense of the world as a place she has no control over.

Scenario: The adult stands over children, telling them exactly what to do and what will result from each action. Adults see free play at recess as fun but a waste of valuable time. Adults believe that children have little capacity for or interest in learning and so must be taught directly through adult-controlled and educationally preplanned initiatives.

Concept: If early curriculum is individualized and discovery oriented, children come to see learning as something actively sought after and knowledge as something one can create. Their learning is spurred by intrinsic curiosity rather than by pressure from parents and teachers.

Scenario: Early childhood professionals use developmentally appropriate teaching methods. They create an environment that entices the young child to explore, discover, and learn to love learning.

Concept: If early role models limit their oral communication primarily to criticism and commands, children, who are in the most formative period of their lives for language development, may be discouraged in the development of a level of vocabulary, grammar, and expression that is necessary for later school success.

Scenario: Adults use worn out clichés, sarcastic overstatements, and meaningless threats. They say things such as "Move, or you're really going to get it!" "Shut up and sit down!" "Hush, I don't want to hear your voice!" "Everybody freeze this instant." "You'd better straighten up and get your act together." These imperative commands do not require any thinking, only blind obedience.

Concept: If early role models are articulate, accurate, and expressive in their oral communication with children, and if they are responsive and supportive of children's attempts to express themselves, children can blossom in their development of linguistically elaborate communication skills, which form the basis for all later academic learning.

Scenario: Adults use meaningful statements of cause and effect, descriptions of actual events or consequences, and expressions of honest feelings. The adult's words are relevant to the actual situation. Children are expected to think, understand, predict, and evaluate actions and reactions. Children are exposed to a descriptive and elaborate vocabulary through the adult expressions. Adults say things such as "If you stand up at the top of the slide, you may fall down." "If you hurt Genevieve, she may not want to play with you next time." "People have to wash their hands after they use the toilet to keep from spreading germs." "You must walk slowly and quietly here in the library because other

(Continued)

How Do Young Children Learn about Their Role in the World? *(Continued)*

people are trying to read." "I feel really sad when I see all the blooms pulled off our pretty petunia."

Concept: If adults treat children with respect and concern for their comfort, dignity, and basic human rights, then children learn to expect politeness and civility in their dealings with others and they learn to function with confidence and self-esteem.

Scenario: Adults behave as if children are the focal point of the environment and adults are facilitators or helpers. Adults are careful not to talk about children in a critical or humiliating way. Adults maintain a role of clear adult leadership while treating children with dignity and respect. All discipline is based on fair, consistent rules, and adults also show respect for class rules. If children are not allowed to eat, adults do not walk around in front of them drinking coffee and eating a doughnut. If an adult has to stand in a chair to change a light bulb, she explains why it was necessary for her to break a class rule about standing on furniture.

Preparing Children for the Realities of an Adult World

From earliest childhood, children take in information about the roles and relationships of people and things in their environment. Consciously or unconsciously, adults are teaching children indirect lessons as a part of every interaction they have with children.

A frustrated father at a gas station vending machine has patiently explained to his toddler over and over that the machine is broken, and he has no more money so he cannot get candies for her. After the little girl falls on the floor kicking and screaming for the candies, the father finds an attendant and insists that the machine be opened so his daughter can have the candy she wants. The tiny girl has learned two important lessons: one, sometimes authority figures do not tell the whole truth, and, two, if you make enough fuss, people sometimes find a way to get you what you want.

A second child in another family may be harshly punished for even asking for candy. She may be learning that the world is hard and unyielding and that she has little control over what happens to her in her surroundings. A third child who asks for candy may be told no and given a reason for the action, but allowed to choose between appropriate alternatives—an apple, a carton of milk, or a banana. She may be learning that, although she doesn't always get every whim indulged, she does have influence on the world around her. She is learning that it is okay to have desires and it is okay to express desires, but it is essential to cooperate to achieve goals.

On one hand, we adults could rationalize any kind of harsh or careless behavior with children by explaining that we are preparing children for the "real" world. On the other hand, we could attempt to prepare children for what we believe would be a better world. Research into a phenomenon called self-fulfilling prophecy indicates that the expectation that something will occur increases the chances that it will occur (Rosenthal & Jacobson, 1968).

If children, therefore, grow up expecting to be treated with respect and fairness, they may behave in a way that evokes that treatment. If children grow up expecting to be treated harshly and unfairly, their behavior may trigger that response from others. The self-fulfilling-prophecy effect may also occur because we are attracted to people and situations that match those of our childhood. An abused child may feel familiar and comfortable with the idea that someone who says she loves you can also beat and hurt you "for your own good." That child may consequently grow up and marry an abusing spouse. People tend to be drawn toward what is familiar and repelled by what seems strange and unfamiliar.

We can best prepare children for life in the "real world" by modeling and teaching caring, respectful behavior. By using DAP to guide children, we help them develop the skills and knowledge they need for future success in a diverse global society.

When Does Cultural Learning Begin?

Learning is important and possible for human beings at all stages, from birth to death. However, during the earliest years of life, people are in a particularly fertile period for learning (Baillargeon, 1997; Begley, 1997a; Berk, 1997; Berndt, 1997; Boyatzis, 1997; Bruner, 1978a, 1978b; French, 1996; Hildebrand, 1997; Leong & Bodrova, 1996). In the first half dozen years of children's lives, they absorb the cultural beliefs and values of their parents and early caregivers. As they grow older, they begin to take in cultural perceptions more and more from external sources such as other children, books, television, movies, records, role

The concept of *self-fulfilling prophecy* tells us that if we expect a child to be well behaved, bright, and successful, we increase the chance that he will be.

Wadsworth/Cengage Learning

models, and folk heroes. Because child care by caregivers other than parents plays an important role in the development of most children today, we must look carefully at the kind of social and emotional nurturance child care settings provide children.

Parental Expectations Related to Social and Economic Settings

A basic survival mechanism for the species is the process through which adults recreate for children miniature communities that reflect and represent the adults' perceptions of the larger adult community. For example, if parents perceive that their own successful participation in the society hinges on being obedient and taking orders or taking control and giving orders, then they will expect their children to be exposed to imperative commands. If, in comparison, parents perceive that giving and taking orders are inappropriate in their own adult dealings, then they will probably feel more comfortable with their children being allowed to negotiate and make compromises rather than being told what to do (Miller, 1986).

Parents who endure long hours of crushing boredom in repetitive jobs may see nothing wrong with their children being pressured early in life to sit still for long periods without complaining or resisting. These adults may also be very tolerant of rowdy "cutting loose" behavior when it is the children's free playtime, because work and play are totally separate and unrelated in the adults' lives. If extreme financial limitations in a community cause parents to depend on cohesion, cooperation, and frequent help from their relatives and neighbors for their very survival, then it is likely that they will expect their children at an early age to accept major responsibility for chores such as tending farm animals, cooking, cleaning, or taking caring of younger children. If these parents are expected in their jobs to follow set procedures and are not encouraged to think or evaluate, then it is natural that they will expect rote memorization rather than creative thinking to be the core of their children's learning. If parents perceive that the world is full of hard knocks, unfair practices, and personal insults, then they may unconsciously toughen their children for survival by exposing them early to a world that is harsh and not always fair or logical. The children learn early that they will not always get whatever they want when they want it (Cook-Gumperz, 1973).

At the opposite extreme, parents with abundant financial resources and stimulating jobs live in a very different world and thus expect a very different environment for their children. Their work may be creative and self-directed. Their hobbies may also be creative and self-directed and require as much concentration and effort as their work, so there is not a clear distinction between work and play for them. These parents probably expect a creative environment for their children in which children can initiate their own self-fulfilling activities through innovative thinking and active involvement. Children are expected to master challenges simply for the fun of it.

Because comfort and individuality are priorities in this cultural viewpoint, a young child would probably not be expected to care for younger siblings; that would be someone else's responsibility. Parents may expect their children's desires to be met quickly and fully. Parents would unconsciously condition children to be prepared for a world in which they will expect to be treated fairly and respectfully (perhaps even preferentially) and to get what they want much of the time. Our culture includes many variations of adult life other than the two extremes described here. Parents, caregivers, and teachers approach their work with children from many different cultural perspectives. One cultural perspective is not necessarily any better than any other. It is clear, however, that early experiences prepare children to fit into existing cultural settings (Beaty, 1997; Cárdenas, 1995; Clark, DeWolf, & Clark, 1992; Denby, 1997; Derman-Sparks & the A.B.C. Task Force, 1989; Flynn, 1996; Gaetano, Williams, & Volk, 1998; Gonzales-Mena, 1998a, 1998b; Gordon & Browne, 1996; Krogh, 1995; National Association for the Education of Young Children, 1993; Phillips, 1988).

Unfortunately, preparation for one cultural setting may make it difficult for a child to function in a totally different cultural setting (Lubeck, 1985). The child conditioned to obedience and rote memorization may be very confused and overwhelmed if she, as an adult, finds herself in a situation that requires initiative, innovation, and creative problem solving. And a child who has been conditioned to a pliable world where she always immediately has her needs met may be cruelly unprepared for adversity in a tough, unfair "real world" situation. Ideally, all children from all settings could have enough multicultural exposure to various perceptions of the world that they could learn the skills to function in any setting and not be limited to only one strata in the diverse cultural rainbow available. The day is long gone when children could be reared to stay for life in the cultural community of their birth, living there their entire lives and dying without ever having ventured out into the larger world to deal with people whose perceptions are quite different (Gough, 1993; Harrison et al., 1990; Howard, 1993; Majors & Billson, 1992; McLoyd, 1990; Stevenson, Chen, & Uttal, 1990). Children can be helped to appreciate differences by learning more about how all people are the *same,* regardless of color, clothes, language, size, food preferences, or special needs.

Respecting Families' Religious Beliefs and Customs

Public early childhood programs are required by law to provide an environment free from harassment or intimidation directed at any person's race, color, religion, national origin, sex, age, or disability. Any form of harassment or intimidation is not tolerated. Most private facilities also strive to prevent discrimination simply because it is the right thing to do, as well as an effective and professional business practice. Failure to prevent discrimination could result in a devastating lawsuit, a lost reputation, and a failed business. It can also damage children's self-esteem and impair their ability to function in a diverse society.

Unless parents are informed that a program is religious, teachers should focus on supporting multicultural learning by offering diverse learning experiences in an environment of tolerance and respect that is free of partiality for any one particular religious view. Teachers, however, should allow children to express their own beliefs and traditions. There is a stark difference between children freely expressing their own beliefs and teachers instructing children in one set of beliefs without parents' prior knowledge and consent. Allowing a child the freedom to pray, for example, is very appropriate. Instructing children how to pray without parental knowledge or approval would not be appropriate and might be construed as a form of discrimination or disrespect.

Developmentally appropriate programs teach tolerance and respect for individual beliefs and customs. Every family's individual religious and cultural perspectives are to be respected. Some cultures prohibit foods common in other cultures, some religions forbid the celebration of birthdays, and some Native American families are offended by Thanksgiving because it commemorates the coming of European people to North America (which they believe harmed their culture and their people). Every family is unique, and as far as the developmentally appropriate early childhood program is concerned, every family's beliefs and customs are special to that family. By internalizing tolerance and respect for others, children learn an important life skill. They develop the ability to see things from someone else's point of view, a crucial social and cognitive developmental milestone.

In recent years, even Halloween has become a point of controversy for early childhood professionals. Parents can hold strong opinions about Halloween for a number of reasons. They may love Halloween, object to it for religious reasons, see gruesome costumes as offensive, fear dangers associated with trick-or-treating, or simply dislike commercialism directed at children. Teachers worry about managing behavior in classrooms filled with children focused on candy and costumes. Teachers also may worry because toddlers and younger preschoolers are usually terrified by masks (and sometimes by costumes) because they can't yet fully distinguish between real and pretend.

Developmentally appropriate programs can provide neutral alternatives to celebrations that concern some parents. For example, the traditional Halloween party in a classroom could be replaced by a fall costume event or harvest festival geared to the cognitive and social skills developed through role-playing. Teachers can further support children's creative expression by allowing the children to create their own costumes with grocery sacks, construction paper, tape, and markers; and their own masks with face-painting. Children express their individual cultural ideas and traditions within established ground rules.

Whenever possible, appropriate materials and activities can be brought into the classroom to help the children explore diverse cultural traditions. Developmentally appropriate programs avoid endorsing traditions tied to religious beliefs without prior knowledge and consent of all the parents. Teachers must trust parents to decide what religious beliefs are right for their child. Teachers should stay focused on ground rules that are based on the core values of democracy: *be safe* (don't unreasonably cause harm to oneself or others), *be kind* (respect the rights, beliefs, and possessions of others), and *be neat* (don't unreasonably damage shared property or the natural environment).

Understanding Cultural Differences

Cultural differences affect the way a person perceives or thinks about things. Almost every aspect of human existence is affected by culture to some extent. Culture defines for us what is right and what is wrong, our values, our day-to-day behavior, our relationships with others, and our perception of our own worth. Religion, ethnic customs, political affiliations, gender roles, social rituals, food preparation, literature, art, and music all express cultural uniqueness and serve to pass cultural traditions from one generation to the next. **Cultural pluralism** is essential to a democracy. If the concept of cultural pluralism is made an integral part of the first years of children's lives, they may be better able, as they grow up, to avoid being pulled into struggles with racial hatred, prejudice, or the stereotyping of individuals based on gender, religion, ethnic origin, age, or handicapping conditions.

Honoring cultural differences involves recognition and **respect.** Although few people openly admit to prejudice, most of us consciously or unconsciously lump people together to some extent: boys are aggressive, the French are romantic, and overweight people are jolly and good hearted. Some generalizations are patently untrue, and others revolve around some kernel of truth—but all generalizations have

respect
The process of showing regard for the rights and needs of another. To display polite expressions of consideration for another.

exceptions. There are boys who are gentle and non-aggressive, French lovers who are clods, and over-weight people who are crabby and mean.

Respect means being given the opportunity to be seen as a unique individual rather than as a stereotypical caricature of some larger group. Underneath all the cultural and physical differences, we are all just people. We all put on our pants the same way: one leg at a time. We all want food, comfort, security, fulfillment, and most of all, the sense of belonging that comes with being loved and respected.

It is possible to urge children to better behavior and more functional habits while clearly letting them know that we accept and respect them as they are. Sometimes adults label children by saying things like "Vanessa, you are being so bad. Look how good Jeremy is." This sets an example for stereotyping people whose appearance or behavior is different. We can say instead, "Vanessa, hitting hurts. Use words instead of hitting, please." This way, an unacceptable behavior can be identified without lumping Vanessa into the category of "bad people."

By age three, children can recognize and identify different skin colors (Katz, 1981; Landreth & Johnson, 1953; Morland, 1972; Parrillo, 1985; Werner & Evans, 1971). They are very sensitive to subtle non-oral as well as oral indications from adults about the

■ To provide a multicultural and nonsexist environment for young children, adults should consider a variety of possible ways to expose children to diverse cultures. Here, a child is playing with pretend tacos and tortillas (traditional Mexican foods) in the housekeeping center.

Wadsworth/Cengage Learning

meaning and importance of differences in people. Adults may unconsciously solicitously respond to people who are of similar ethnic and religious backgrounds while inadvertently snubbing those whose background is different.

Ethnicity and religion are not the only characteristics that generate prejudice. Some of us have difficulty showing warmth and respect for children whose parents behave in a way that is foreign to us, live a lifestyle we disapprove of, or are unappealing to us because of hygiene or style of dress. Some of us are obvious in our preference of girls over boys or boys over girls. We make comments such as "The boys can go first because all the girls want to do is talk" or "You boys go on and find something to do. The girls just want to play by themselves without you causing trouble."

To provide a multicultural and nonsexist environment for young children, adults must consider all aspects of cultural exposure such as foods, books, toys, songs, rhymes, television shows, language, and clothing. Children can be helped to know and understand traditions of their own heritage as well as to know and honor the traditions of other cultures. They can be given dolls that are male and female as well as black, white, and brown. They can be exposed to books, songs, and art that show girls tackling adventurous challenges and boys expressing feelings. Dollhouse furniture can be combined with blocks and men's dress-up clothing can be

Take Time to Think before You Judge Others

What to Consider

- Do you find yourself having negative thoughts or feelings about a child or parent?
- Does the parent have values, expectations, or communication styles different from your own? Does the child dress, speak, or behave in a way that seems unfamiliar or offensive to you? Examine your discomfort as objectively as you can. Could the differences be due to cultural backgrounds?
- Ask whether the family members being served understand and relate to the values, assumptions, and philosophy of the early childhood program or school. Through parent meetings and one-on-one discussions, explore how parent views are the same as or different from those of the early childhood professionals. Listen, ask questions, and make a conscious effort to better understand their perspective. Someone's point of view being different does not necessarily mean it is wrong.
- Are you proactive in providing an antibias learning environment? Are you setting a good example for the children of tolerance and respect for others? Do you give respectful "I" messages to coworkers? Parents? Children? Are you diligent about putting into practice the principles of active listening? Are you willing to really listen to others and understand how things seem to them from their perspective? Do you validate others' perspective, showing them that you understand and respect their view, even if you hold different views?
- Have you taken steps to evaluate the effectiveness of your program's cultural sensitivity? Have children of different backgrounds had difficulty fitting in? Have parents from different backgrounds tended to remove their

What to Do

- Respect the uniqueness of each family system. Value every child and parent.
- Remember that a family's cultural differences may relate to their race, ethnicity, religion, nationality, regional heritage, age, wealth, poverty, disability, gender preferences of parents, and many other factors. Individual perspectives evolve out of life experiences, upbringing, social status, and education.
- Create a warm, respectful, collaborative relationship with families. Encourage parents to talk about their dreams for their child. Involve parents in school activities. Learn about different cultures. Make the curriculum culturally relevant by including books, activities, songs, and field trips intended to expand multicultural awareness. Find creative ways to use DAP to achieve the goals parents have for their children.
- Don't tell parents what is wrong with their views. Validate their values, prior experiences, and cultural knowledge. Use active listening, actively involve parents in the program, and always treat them with respect. Build on individual children's strengths. Consciously identify their strengths and allow them opportunities for recognition and leadership that draw on their individual strengths. Help other children learn to understand and appreciate cultural differences. Never allow hurtful teasing or bullying.
- Take advantage of professional development for staff concerning multicultural curriculum development and cultural differences in kinship roles, beliefs, values, and communication styles. Read books and professional journals related to cultural sensitivity and multicultural

children from the program at a higher rate than other families? (The National Association for the Education of Young Children [NAEYC; http://www.naeyc .org] provides information on effective early childhood evaluation tools and techniques.)

teaching. Attend workshops, college classes, and discussion groups to expand knowledge and skill in this area. Observe highly regarded programs and respected early childhood professionals. Take notes, ask questions, and most importantly, have an open mind.

mixed with dishes and doll beds. Young children should not be exposed to television unless the commercials have been removed and the content has been carefully reviewed.

Young children can be exposed to terms such as *police officer, mail carrier,* and *repairperson* rather than *policeman, mailman,* and *repairman.* Teachers, doctors, nurses, and secretaries can be referred to as "he or she" rather than in the stereotypical way that implies all doctors are men and all secretaries are women. Children can learn nursery rhymes and songs in Spanish or Swahili as well as in English. Foods can be offered that sensitize children to regional and national dishes, ways of preparing foods, and food-related traditions and rituals.

The Antibias Curriculum

The purpose of multicultural, nonsexist, and antidiscrimination exposure for children is not to force children into any specific mold but rather to enhance their respect for others who are different and to empower them to be whatever they have the talent and motivation to become. By fully appreciating differences in others and by recognizing that different does not necessarily mean inferior, children may become stronger in their own beliefs and traditions and more resistant to peer pressure for conformity.

Children who have disgust for or fear of differences in others may be cruel in their treatment of children with disabilities, unusual appearance, or different ethnicity. They may also be vulnerable in adolescence to popular peers who insist that anyone is a nerd who does not conform to group standards by smoking, drinking, taking drugs, participating in premarital sex, or driving at illegal speeds. Sometimes it takes a great deal of courage to be different and to know that being different is okay (Teaching Tolerance Project, 1997; Trawick-Smith, 1997).

Wadsworth/Cengage Learning

We celebrate our cultural and physical differences and remember that, underneath the skin, we are all very much the same.

Understanding the Dynamic Nature of Culture

Culture is often defined as the traditional beliefs and patterns of behavior that are passed on from parents to children by a society. But culture also represents the beliefs and patterns of behavior passed on from parents to children by members of smaller groups of people within the larger society who are part of social, religious, ethnic, or other groups.

Children are capable of learning to function in more than one cultural context. By creating an environment of unconditional acceptance of different cultures in early childhood programs, children can learn to accept, respect, and function across cultures without giving up their appreciation for their own culture.

The word *culture,* coming from the Latin root "colere" (to occupy, cultivate, or cherish), refers to the patterns of activity in our lives that give our lives meaning and importance. Symbols (such as those found in spoken and written language) are usually recognized only within a specific cultural context (Chinese is understood in China, French in France). Culture gives us the capacity to communicate our experiences and express our needs within communities. This capacity to use symbols to express culture is considered a defining feature of human beings.

What Is Ordinary Culture?

When we think about culture, we should first think about the systems of shared beliefs, values, customs, behaviors, and objects that the members of individual communities use to cope with their world and with one another, and that they pass down from generation to generation of children through parenting and direct teaching. Some people wrongly think culture only means opera, Renaissance paintings, and ballet. Certainly those are a limited part of Western society's culture, but there is a great deal more to culture.

Raymond Williams (2001), an early pioneer in the field of cultural studies, argued that culture was "ordinary." He forced an important shift in researchers' thinking about culture. He wrestled the term *culture* away from the "high culture" that was clearly restricted to the rich and powerful members of society, and broadened the term *culture* to encompass the lived, day-to-day experience of everyday people like you and me.

Does Everyone Have Culture?

Some traits of human life are transmitted genetically—an infant's desire for food, for example, is triggered by physiological factors within the genetic code. My desire specifically for tortillas and queso fresco with salsa for lunch, however, can't be explained genetically. That is a learned cultural response to hunger. Children learn culture at home, at school, in the community—and even from television—whether we intend for them to learn culture from those particular places or not. That is culture's essential feature—everyone, everywhere is exposed to culture. All socially interacting humans have culture.

Children accept some lessons of culture and keep them throughout life. They reject others and replace them with new ways. Parents and teachers don't always have control over which lessons about culture will be kept and which will eventually be rejected. We do know that the more the child feels valued and respected by parents and teachers during childhood, the more likely he will be to follow parents' and teachers' rules and keep their values as he grows up (Garces, Thomas, & Currie, 2002).

The process through which culture is passed down from one generation to the next is called **enculturation**. It is the process of learning about culture by observing, imitating, practicing, and being taught. Enculturation teaches a child the accepted norms and values as well as the language and skills he needs to become an accepted member of his community.

As part of cultural learning, children pick up **body language** (the gestures, facial expressions, and body postures that people use to communicate along with or instead of speech). Body language, like spoken language, can mean different things in different cultures. For example, winking one eye to indicate a shared secret is an example of body language in North America, but this gesture does not mean the same thing in every country or community. For example, in Japan a wink doesn't mean anything but in India a wink would be interpreted as a rude, sexual gesture. Body language is learned and changes over time as part of a culture. Differences in body language can cause confusion, miscommunication, and embarrassment. The best antidote is to be alert to signs that someone is uncomfortable and ask questions. For example, "You looked surprised when I winked. I hope I didn't offend you. In my cultural background, a wink means you and I share a secret. In your cultural background, does a wink mean something different? You have helped me a lot by sharing information with me I didn't know about your culture."

A special concern for young children is their coping with a sudden immersion into an alien culture. Young children tend to adapt much more quickly and easily to an unknown environment than do adults and adolescents, and they definitely learn foreign languages more easily. They can still, however, experience **culture shock** (a feeling of confusion, alienation, and depression that occurs during initial immersion in a new culture). Until the new culture becomes familiar and comfortable, it is quite customary for children to feel homesick.

If they are learning a new language, they will most likely have difficulty communicating and probably make frequent, embarrassing, and humiliating oral mistakes. This is usually compounded by feelings of melancholy, fear, and frustration. These feelings can be emotionally stressful. Culture shock usually eases rapidly as the surroundings become more familiar, so long as the new setting is warm and supportive. We need to pay special attention to make sure the environment is welcoming and encouraging for the child coming from a different culture.

Understanding Children and Families in the Context of Their Communities

Uri Bronfenbrenner, a cofounder of the national Head Start program, is widely regarded as one of the world's leading scholars in developmental psychology, childrearing, and **human ecology**—the interdisciplinary field he created. Bronfenbrenner

enculturation
The process whereby an established culture teaches an individual its accepted norms and values, so that the individual can become an accepted member of that culture. It is the process of passing the culture down to the child through teaching, learning, and guiding at a given time in a given place.

body language
The gestures, facial expressions, and body postures that people use to communicate along with or instead of speech.

culture shock
A feeling of confusion, alienation, and depression that can result from the psychological stress that typically occurs during a person's initial immersion in a new culture.

human ecology
The theory that people don't develop in isolation but in relation to their family, home, school, community, and society. Each of these constantly changing multi-level environments, as well as the interactions among these environments, is key to a human being's development.

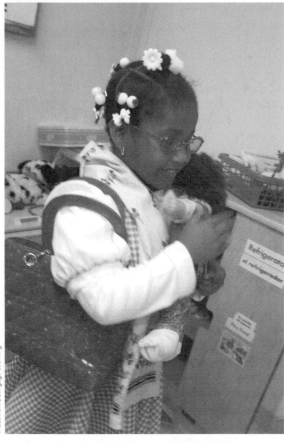

We can best understand each child by looking at her in the context of her family and her cultural community.

cultural context
The situation or circumstance in which a particular cultural event, action, behavior, or imagery occurs. Actions, events, and behaviors can have different meanings, depending on their cultural context.

(1979, 1988, & 1993; Bronfenbrenner & Morris, 1998) taught us that a child's development is best understood within the social and **cultural context** of that child's family and community. In today's globally competitive world, it seems that the more we learn about the conditions that are needed to nurture babies' development and young children's competence and character, the more we see those exact conditions being eroded. Far too many parents of babies and young children today are routinely battered by time crunches and exhausted by work-induced stress. Certainly, families need help and support from early childhood professionals, now more than ever.

How Did Bronfenbrenner Suggest Visualizing a Person's Inner Self?

Bronfenbrenner (1979) and Moen and colleagues (1995) advised professionals working with children and families to take an ecological perspective. Bronfenbrenner's groundbreaking work combined components of sociology with developmental psychology, creating a new way of approaching and supporting children and families. He realized that the relationships between human beings and their communities were "mutually shaping." He described the individual person's interactive experience as "a set of **nested structures,** each inside the next, like a set of Russian dolls" (Bronfenbrenner, 1979, p. 22). To really understand a child's or parent's inner nature, one has to see within, beyond, across, and through these complex nesting structures. One has to see how the parents, their workplace, the community, the society, the school, and even the economy all interact and affect the children.

Imagine that I use Bronfenbrenner's image of the Russian nesting dolls to help me relate to Ca Nguyen, the mother of a new child in my school. As I talk to her, get to know her, and observe her in different situations, I begin to visualize the tough, assertive businesswoman on the outside, but inside I observe a mother whose confidence can easily be shaken but who wants to do the very best for her child. Inside that, I notice a generous, encouraging neighbor who translates for and helps many members of her community, and very importantly, at the center, I envision the remnants of a young child who lost both parents to the horrors of war several decades ago.

Of course Ca Nguyen is far more complicated than my simple imaginings can construct, and I may be totally incorrect, but by making these observations and taking the time to learn about her and imagine her life from her perspective, I begin to feel empathetic toward Ca Nguyen. Empathy creates warmth, helps broaden trust,

Wadsworth/Cengage Learning

and invites further communication. I can now see Ca Nguyen as a complex person, with multifaceted layers in her identity. Importantly, once someone is truly perceived as a complex human being, the person can no longer be stereotyped as a one-dimensional cartoon character.

What Is Unconditional Acceptance?

Cultural knowledge about a child's family and community especially supports child guidance. To effectively guide a child over time, we need to know and understand that child. The strategies for guidance described in this book can, of course, be used in a pinch to assist a child you don't know at all or don't know very well. But to make a real difference in a child's life, you need to have a relationship with that child. The child needs **unconditional acceptance** from you. The child must come to know that you unconditionally accept her as a worthwhile human being. Bronfenbrenner (1994, pp. 118–119) said it best:

> The person must be someone "with whom the child develops a strong, mutual, irrational emotional attachment, and who is committed to the child's well-being and development. . . . What is meant by "an irrational emotional attachment?" There is a simple answer: "Somebody's got to be crazy about that kid, and vice versa!" But what does "crazy" mean? It means that the adult in question regards this particular child as somehow special—especially wonderful, especially precious—even though objectively the adult may well know that this is not the case.

By learning about the cultural, family, and community context of the children in your care, you are better able to serve children and families. It is impossible to unconditionally accept someone if you don't even know them. By learning about the cultural experiences and expectations of a child's family, you can express unconditional acceptance for that child and her family and take the first important steps toward open communication with her parents.

You don't need a memorized list of typical behaviors for every racial, ethnic, regional, disability, gender, or other potential culturally based grouping known to humankind. If you had that, it would be far too easy to pigeonhole people into stereotypes rather than getting to know them as individuals anyway. (A stereotype is still a stereotype, even if it is positive instead of negative.) You just need the skills of a good observer, an open heart, an open mind, and the willingness to take the time to get to know someone. Most people love to tell you about themselves. Most people respond well to genuine interest and respect. Use eye contact. Learn the parent's name and use it regularly. Unless urgent matters dictate otherwise, greet parents and chat for a moment in a friendly way before you launch into things you need them to do or

To see the individual child, we must look across, around, and through the nested structure made up of community, family, and individual within a culture.

nested structures
An individual's interactive experience; that is, how the parents, their workplace, the community, the society, the school, and even the economy all interact and affect the children.

unconditional acceptance
The process of accepting someone as a worthwhile human being; recognition and appreciation without any strings attached.

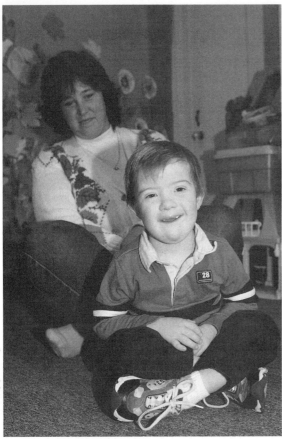

■ Every child deserves to know he is unconditionally accepted, and that somebody is "crazy about him."

personal interaction
Reciprocal social activity that should express genuine interest and respect for the other individual.

questions you need to ask. Remember to have a **personal interaction**. Treat this parent as a valuable and worthwhile person you are happy to see.

What Is Ethical Responsibility?

When we accept responsibility for the care and education of a baby or a child, we implicitly promise to follow our profession's **ethics** and look beyond that child's runny nose, messy hair, disability, or country of origin to see a precious creation, full of hope and wonder. Only people who are able to approach *all* children with open hearts—people who are ready to give unconditional acceptance to *all* families regardless of creed or color—should enter into this important occupation.

It isn't enough just to unconditionally accept the child; you must also unconditionally accept the child's family. Unconditional acceptance does not mean that you think someone is perfect. A parent may have problems and may even be a very difficult person to get to know. The question is, can you get beyond those feelings and unconditionally accept that person as a worthwhile human being? If you cannot find a way to respect that parent, you may not be able to be fully effective in working with and guiding that parent's child.

Every parent who loves his or her child deserves child care by someone who can respect him or her as a parent. If a parent is unfit, is abusive or neglectful, then authorities should be contacted for intervention. If you can't find a way to respect a parent who is neither abusive nor neglectful, then you must decide whether prejudice is preventing you from accepting that adult as a worthwhile human being. And you must carefully try to see the situation from that parent's perspective. Use Bronfenbrenner's advice and try to see the parent as if she were made up of many complicated layers. Put yourself in her place and try to think through what those layers of culture and experience feel like. Does that parent love her child in her own way? Why can't I accept her? What are my issues?

Prejudice, Racism, and Discrimination

The home, community, and school are all interconnected, and all have a powerful influence on a developing child. We can't afford to ignore any part of that triangle of influence. For example, even a child in a loving, supportive family within a strong, healthy community can be affected by **prejudice** from the larger society or school.

> ### NAEYC Code of Ethical Conduct
>
> - Appreciate childhood as a unique and valuable stage of the human life cycle.
>
> - Base our work on knowledge of how children develop and learn to appreciate and support the bond between the child and family.
>
> - Recognize that children are best understood and supported in the context of family, culture, community, and society.
>
> - Respect the dignity, worth, and uniqueness of each individual (child, family member, and colleague).
>
> - Respect diversity in children, families, and colleagues.
>
> - Recognize that children and adults achieve their full potential in the context of relationships that are based on trust and respect (NAEYC, 2005, p. 1).
>
> Specifically, ethics compels us to do the following:
>
> ### Early Childhood Ethical Standards
>
> - Early childhood professionals will hold paramount the welfare of the children and families whom they serve—never, ever participating in practices that are disrespectful, degrading, dangerous, exploitative, intimidating, or physically harmful to children or their families.
>
> - Early childhood professionals will not discriminate regardless of race, gender, religion, economic status, values, national origin, or disability.
>
> - Early childhood professionals will strive to maintain objectivity, integrity, and competence in fulfilling the mission, vision, and values of DAP and each professional's program.
>
> - Early childhood professionals will continually seek knowledge and skills that will update and enhance their understanding of issues affecting the children and families they serve.
>
> - Early childhood professionals will take action to report any practice or situation that endangers the health or safety of children so that the circumstances can be appropriately resolved.
>
> - Early childhood professionals will respect the privacy of children and families.

The Code of Ethical Conduct is an NAEYC position statement. Copyright © NAEYC. Used with permission.

Children can be developmentally harmed by such influences as **racism, sexism, negative stereotyping,** and **discrimination.** Culture plays a powerful role in developing all children. Our knowledge of culture can help sensitize us and ensure that we make children's experiences multicultural and supportive of their developing self-image.

The hard-core avenues for encountering prejudice are usually familiar to all of us in American society—hate-filled racial prejudice, religious intolerance, gay bashing, needless barriers for persons with disabilities, and gender stereotypes that

ethics
The ideals and the shared conceptions of professional responsibility that reflect the aspirations of a group of practitioners and affirm their commitment to the core values of their field. The basic principles that are intended to guide their conduct and assist them in resolving dilemmas encountered in their field.

prejudice
As the name implies, prejudice is the process of prejudging someone. Racial prejudice comprises negative attitudes, beliefs, and rigid stereotypes against an ethnic group that are resistant to change despite contradictory evidence.

racism
Founded on a belief that race is a major determinant of human characteristics and causes the superiority of some races over others. Racism is a combination of racial prejudice and discrimination. Racism uses the inflexible assumption that group differences are biologically determined and therefore inherently unchangeable. Racism does not exist in a vacuum but rather is enacted and reinforced through social, cultural, and institutional practices that endorse the hierarchical power of one racial group over another.

sexism
Historically, sexism has been male-driven and accompanied by a belief in male superiority.

negative stereotyping
To categorize individuals in a group according to an oversimplified, standardized (usually racist or sexist) image or idea that ignores the unique characteristics of the individual.

discrimination
Participation in harmful actions toward others because of their membership in a particular group; the behavioral manifestation of negative prejudice.

ethnocentrism
The deeply felt belief (possibly unconsciously held) that one's own culture is superior to all others. Being unyielding in attachment to one's own way of life and condescending and intolerant toward other cultures. Alien cultural practices are often viewed as being not just different but as silly, weird, evil, or unnatural.

cultural adaptation
The process of human societies making cultural changes to better accommodate diverse environments across the globe. Slowly evolving adaptations may have neutral or even maladaptive effects in a rapidly changing cultural environment.

stop women from reaching their goals. Persons from other countries around the world have also had to cope with varying levels of prejudice—from countries where discrimination is minimal to countries where horrific bloodbaths have taken place in the name of ethnic cleansing.

We may not be as familiar with the term **ethnocentrism** as we are with some of the other terms related to prejudice. Ethnocentrism is very often an unconsciously held assumption that one's own culture is superior to all others. It is the sort of belief that has not been consciously examined or really thought about logically. It is just an unconscious presumption that shows up in the holder's everyday attitudes. Typically, ethnocentric people shun outright prejudice, but their subtle discrimination slips through the cracks as they give evidence of being condescending toward other cultures.

People who are ethnocentric often claim to be open-minded, but may see cultural traits that are different from their own as meaningless, sinful, comical, or just plain peculiar. For example, they may mention to a friend that it's just weird to wear a burka (an all-enveloping cloak worn by some Muslim women) to an American grocery store, without even thinking about what that burka means to the woman wearing it. They may make jokes about and casually mimic word mispronunciations by an immigrant without really wondering how it feels to struggle in a country where you are trying to learn a second language as an adult. We each need to watch ourselves carefully for ethnocentrism. Some vestiges of it lurk in each of us, ready to leap out if we don't continually reexamine our cultural assumptions.

Where Did Prejudice Come From?

Destructive cultural behaviors such as prejudice didn't come from thin air. They weren't just thought up one day by a group of evil villains who wanted to create harm in the world. They slowly evolved over many centuries as a primitive **cultural adaptation,** long before cars, telephones, and jets ever came along. Culture is the critical element that has helped human societies survive in stunningly dissimilar locations across the globe—from frozen wastelands to burning deserts, from tropical forests to asphalt jungles of high-rise buildings and multilane freeways.

Sometimes, though, adaptations that worked in the ancestral environment in which they evolved don't necessarily work later in a totally different cultural environment. Perhaps some tiny, ancient, primitive tribe, frightened that its very survival depended on making sure everyone stick together and avoid other tribes, was the first to start negative stereotyping and prejudice. Slowly evolved cultural adaptations such as prejudice, however, can have terribly dysfunctional behavioral effects in today's rapidly changing cultural environment. *Prejudice hurts children and families and works against our economic interest as a global society. We have to make it stop.*

When Does Discrimination Begin in Children?

Three- and four-year-old children begin telling other children they can't play because "you don't have the right kind of sneakers," "you are a girl," or "you aren't wearing a Cinderella ring like we are." Young children don't know better, but it hurts, and it is a rudimentary form of discrimination. That's when you need to use Vivian Paley's (1992) class rule, "You can't say you can't play." It fits in our basic rules category "Be kind." Discrimination may or may not be based on prejudice, although when children interact without adequate adult supervision, discrimination may sometimes escalate into prejudice. Research shows that prejudice leads to hatred.

In fact, research suggests that prejudice and discrimination feed on and enhance each other (Frederickson & Knobel, 1980). Allport (1954) and Milner (1983) wrote about the negative and unreasonable thinking strategies that are characteristic in prejudiced people. Allport refers to these attitudes as "faulty and inflexible," and Milner describes them as "irrational." This inflexibility leads prejudiced individuals to refuse to change their prejudices even when they are faced with contradictory information. Discrimination occurs when hurtful actions are inflicted on others simply because of their association with a particular group. As we work with children using DAP, our learning methods will specifically help children develop flexible thinking strategies. They will have the capacity as adults to think logically about issues and make rational choices.

What Are Other Early Signs of Prejudice in Young Children?

Another early indication of prejudgment we need to watch for and squelch is any sign that children are being **stigmatized** (labeled and excluded) on the basis of some unusual physical characteristic or item of clothing—such as wearing orthopedic shoes, being extraordinarily tall, or wearing a yarmulke (a traditional Jewish head covering). Teachers must take whatever steps are necessary to ensure that finger-pointing, teasing, and name-calling don't happen, and that all children find their niche. Exposing children to excellent multicultural books about others with a wide range of differences is essential for developing empathy in youngsters. You will find a huge selection of delightful children's books in the Online Companion™ that are ideal for helping the children in your care learn to respect and value a wide range of cultural and ethnic identities. (See the end of this chapter to learn how to access the online resources.)

Sometimes children target other children to bully and stigmatize simply because they are looking for a scapegoat. An insecure child trying to justify her own failures or trying to impress her social group may try **scapegoating** a weaker child to enhance her social status among her peers. But as Katz's (1981) research shows, children are frequently ambivalent about the persons they try to stigmatize. That ambivalence often leads children to exaggerate either their negative or positive responses. One exaggerated negative response may be expressed as hatred. It disconcerts us to see such strong negative emotions in young children.

To avoid a spiraling negative effect on child guidance for all the children involved, it is essential to identify and stop scapegoating immediately. Teachers must help the insecure child who was tempted to scapegoat find socially appropriate ways to impress her friends and become more self-confident. Research shows that children with strong self-acceptance are less likely to become prejudiced against

stigmatized
Labeled as socially undesirable on the basis of some specific characteristic, damaging the stigmatized person's self-esteem and excluding him or her socially.

scapegoating
Putting blame on another by someone who wants to cause harm or is unwilling to take responsibility for his or her own actions.

others. Prejudiced individuals tend to have low self-acceptance (Taylor, 2000; Fishbein, 2002).

Helping children get along socially in a multicultural group is very important. The development of prejudice and discrimination in young children is tied to the development of a **group identity**, as well as **self-identity**. The psychological literature suggests that a group identity emerges between the ages of three and four and increases for at least several years after that. Just sticking diverse children into a classroom next to each other does not necessarily have any benefit, especially if the children always pair off into racial and ethnic groups for work, lunch, and playtime. Research does strongly indicate, however, that positive, cooperative, successful social and work interactions among diverse groups of children reduce prejudice in the long term (Taylor, 2000; Fishbein, 2002).

What Is Multicultural Education?

Multicultural education should be approached not as a subject area but as an ever-present thread woven throughout all curriculum areas and throughout each and every day. Early childhood professionals should recognize that children learn to value diversity not just through a multicultural curriculum but also from the attitudes and behaviors that are revealed to them each day as a part of their daily activities and as part of the attitudes of the adults around them. Recognizing this, adults must carefully evaluate their own behavior, as well as the total classroom environment.

An important way that cultural diversity is represented in the classroom is through the images that are present in the environment. Books, pictures, and other items representing children or family members should show people of different ethnicities, genders, and ages. Music, art, and literature should be selected to reflect ethnic and cultural diversity and should reflect the lives of children with disabilities and girls in heroic and exciting roles. Children should hear songs from around the world and learn about food, clothing, and toys typical of other cultures. Teachers must ensure that a multicultural approach does not occur in isolation but continues in the year-round curriculum.

How Can We Teach Young Children to Resist Bias?

Between the ages of two and five, children become aware of their general identity, their gender, and some of the ways they are the same and different from others. Depending on their environment, by the age of five they may already be intensely aware of their race or only vaguely conscious of their cultural identity. This is a time in their lives when children are particularly vulnerable to absorb both positive and negative attitudes and **bias** (unfair dislike) from those around them. It is, therefore, a critical time to help children form strong, positive self-images and learn to get along with and respect people who are different from themselves.

If we want children to feel good about themselves and to respect others, we must learn how to help them resist the biases and prejudices that are still far too prevalent in our society. Bias harms children and damages their development. To develop

group identity
A young child constructs group identity primarily by internalizing whatever that child's family considers important in defining who is "like us." Creating a strong and positive group identity is essential for young children who happen to be part of a cultural grouping that has been devalued or stigmatized by the larger society.

self-identity
The set of characteristics that a person recognizes as belonging uniquely to himself or herself and constituting his or her own individuality.

bias
One's own set of beliefs, values, perceptions, and assumptions that develop from one's upbringing, past experience, and personal philosophy of life; bias can include an unfair preference for or dislike of something or someone.

What Parents and Teachers Can Do to Help Children Resist Bias

- Recognize that because we live in a society where many biases exist, we must counteract them—or else we will support them through our silence.

- At home or at school, give children messages that deliberately contrast stereotypes by providing books, dolls, toys, wall decorations, TV programs, and records that show:
  - men and women in nontraditional roles
  - people of color in leadership positions
  - people with disabilities doing activities familiar to children
  - various types of families and family activities

- Show no bias in the friends, doctors, teachers, and other service providers that you choose, or in the stores where you shop. Remember what you do is as important as what you say.

- Make it a firm rule that a person's appearance is never an acceptable reason for teasing or rejecting them. Immediately step in if you hear or see your child behave in such a way.

- Talk positively about each child's physical characteristics and cultural heritage. And, help children learn the differences between feelings of superiority and those of self-esteem and pride in their own heritage.

- Provide opportunities for children to interact with other children who are racially and culturally different from themselves and with people who have various disabilities.

- Respectfully listen to and answer children's questions about themselves and others. Don't ignore, change the subject, or in any way make the child think she is bad for asking such a question.

- Teach children how to challenge biases about who they are. Give them tools to confront those who act biased against them.

- Use accurate and fair images in contrast to stereotypes and encourage children to talk about the differences. Help them to think critically about what they see in books, movies, greeting cards, comics, and on TV.

- Let children know that unjust things can be changed. Encourage children to challenge bias and involve children in taking action on issues relevant to their lives.

- Building a healthy self-identity is a process that continues all our lives. Help children get a head start by teaching them to resist bias and to value the differences between people as much as the similarities.

NAEYC, 1997. "Early Years Are Learning Years: Teaching Young Children to Resist Bias." Washington, DC. Retrieved February 24, 2008, from http://www.naeyc.org/ece/1997/10.asp. Used by permission.

healthy self-esteem, children must learn how to interact positively and effectively across cultures.

Young children often ask embarrassing questions, often at exactly the wrong moment: "Why can't I ride in a big chair with wheels like that man?" "Why does that pink boy have little spots on his nose?" "Why is that lady so fat?" "Why doesn't that little girl

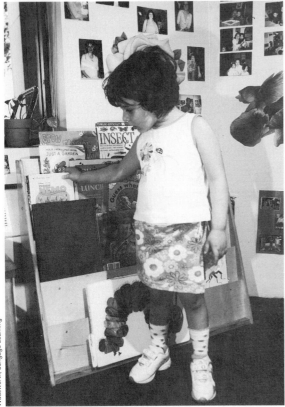

Wadsworth/Cengage Learning

■■■ Multicultural books are a critical part of a developmentally appropriate environment.

media
Materials that convey information and cultural expression. Media can bring data by paper (books), film (videos), plastic (CDs), electronic wires, etc.

have any lip?" As part of the enculturation process we must help children learn about not staring, about remembering that *everyone* has feelings and deserves to be treated with respect even if they look different. Of course, we should honestly and discreetly (so we don't embarrass the person who has been pointed out) answer children's questions to remove any mystique and help children see people who seem different as individuals with feelings similar to theirs.

How Can I Spot Bias, Stereotypes, and Myths about Underrepresented Groups in Books and Other Media?

No matter how hard we try, in our society today young children inevitably will be exposed to some racist and sexist attitudes. If these are pervasive, however, they can distort children's perceptions until stereotypes and myths about underrepresented groups and women begin to be accepted as their reality. We not only want to expose children to an unbiased environment as they begin to develop the skills to think logically, around the age of four or five, but we also need to help them learn how to identify bias. If a child can be shown how to detect racism and sexism in a book, for example, the child can generalize that skill to wider areas.

The following 10 guidelines (adapted from the Council on Interracial Books for Children, 1998) are offered as a starting point for learning to spot bias in books and other **media.**

- *Check the illustrations*—Look for stereotypes. Are underrepresented-group faces depicted as genuine individuals with distinctive features? Do underrepresented-group characters play subservient and passive roles or leadership and action roles? Are males the active doers and females the inactive observers?
- *Check the story line*—In friendships between white children and children of color, is it the child of color who does most of the understanding and forgiving? Is a problem that is faced by a person of color resolved through the benevolent intervention of a white person? Are the achievements of girls and women owing to their own initiative and intelligence or to their good looks or their relationship with boys or men?
- *Look at the lifestyles*—If a nonwhite group is depicted as *different,* are negative value judgments implied? If the illustrations and text attempt to depict another culture, do they go beyond oversimplifications and offer genuine insights into another lifestyle?

- *Weigh the relationships between people*—Do white characters in the story possess the power, take the leadership, and make the important decisions? Do people of color and females function in essentially supporting roles?
- *Note the heroes*—Are there minority heroes, female heroes, and heroes with disabilities? When underrepresented-group heroes do appear, are they admired only because what they have done has benefited white people?
- *Consider the effects on a child's self-image*—Are norms established that limit the child's aspirations and self-concepts? What effect can it have on African American children to be continually bombarded with images of the color white as the ultimate in beauty, cleanliness, virtue, and so on, and the color black as evil, dirty, menacing, and so on? Does the book counteract or reinforce this positive association with the color white and negative association with black? What about a girl's self-esteem if she is not fair skinned and slim?
- *Consider the author's or illustrator's background*—If a story deals with a multicultural theme, what qualifies the author or illustrator to deal with the subject?
- *Check out the author's perspective*—Children's books in the past have traditionally come from white, middle-class authors, with one result being that a single ethnocentric perspective has dominated children's literature in the United States.
- *Watch for loaded words*—A word is loaded when it has insulting overtones. Examples of loaded adjectives (usually racist) are *savage, primitive, conniving, lazy, superstitious, treacherous, wily, crafty, inscrutable, docile,* and *backward.* Look for sexist language and adjectives that exclude or ridicule women. Look for use of the male pronoun to refer to both males and females. Although the generic use of *man* was accepted in the past, it is recognized today as sexist. The following examples show how sexist language can be avoided: *ancestors* instead of *forefathers; community* instead of *brotherhood; firefighters* instead of *firemen; manufactured* instead of *manmade;* the *human family* instead of the *family of man.*
- *Look at the copyright date*—Not until the early 1970s did the children's book world begin to even remotely reflect the realities of a multiracial society or the concerns of feminists. The copyright dates, therefore, can be a clue as to how likely the book is to be overtly racist or sexist, although a recent copyright date is no guarantee of a book's relevance or sensitivity.

What Things Should I Know so I Can Be More Considerate to People from Other Cultures?

It would be great to have a simple list of cultural dos and don'ts to memorize that would protect you from ever offending a parent or coworker of a different background. Unfortunately, life just isn't that simple.

It's great to learn all you can about the cultural ways of other groups. However, individuals are unique and there is enormous diversity within cultures. Always attributing common characteristics to specific cultural groups tends to create stereo-types—and we certainly don't need any more stereotypes.

There are trends or cultural traits common to some—but not all—families of similar cultural backgrounds. African American and Native American families, for example, tend to place a high cultural value on kinship bonds. They are more likely to rely heavily on extended family members and friends for such things as child care, financial assistance, advice, and emotional support (Dykeman et al., 1996; Lum, 1992; Tower, 1996). It is not unusual for aunts, grandparents, friends, or even siblings to be the primary care providers for children.

Latin American, Asian, and Pacific Island families also rely strongly on the extended family. Asian, Pacific Island, and Native American families may rely on a strict family hierarchy to make decisions. Decisions within Latin American families may be made primarily by the father because of the respect given in his culture to his familial position and the responsibility he bears. Shame is frequently used in Asian families as a strategy for disciplining children and should not be misunderstood by non-Asians as emotional abuse (Tower, 1996). Obviously, people from all cultural backgrounds can learn new, more effective methods for guiding children.

Religion is important to members of many cultures. Catholicism, the predominant religion for Latin Americans, is an important source of support and comfort (Rose & Meezan, 1996). Native Americans have great respect for grandparents. The religions of Asians and Pacific Islanders vary greatly, but there is often a common belief that lives are controlled by fate. Grandparents sometimes hold the final authority in child-rearing decisions (Tower, 1996). Native Americans have strong respect for nature and believe they must live in harmony with the earth. Native American children tend to grow up believing they should always control their emotions (Lum, 1992; Tower, 1996).

How Can I Help Parents from Other Cultures Feel More Comfortable?

The following cultural tips are often given to teachers to advise them on how to behave politely and courteously and help them avoid embarrassing situations. By all means, try these tips. No one ever complained about too much courtesy. But remember, these bits of information may or may not always apply in real life to every complicated human being you encounter. You still need to get to know the unique individuals you meet to determine what their cultural expectations and needs really are.

- The Vietnamese gesture for beckoning someone is made by extending the arm with the fingers pointing down and wiggling the fingers.

Body language differs greatly from culture to culture, and misunderstandings and embarrassment can result when gestures are misinterpreted. For example, the thumb-to-index-finger gesture used in the United States to signal "okay" is considered vulgar in Mexico, but in Japan it is a sign for money. The American gesture used to beckon people (palm up with fingers moving) is considered rude by Vietnamese people because that gesture in their culture is used only to beckon animals. To be safe, it is usually best to avoid using an upward palm to beckon anyone from another culture. Also avoid pointing with your index finger. Those gestures are considered rude in many parts of the world where they opt for other gestures such as summoning with the palm down and more subtle pointing with the chin or a wave of the palm.

- Don't touch a Hispanic child on the head while discussing his or her negative behavior with parents.

You shouldn't be discussing guidance issues in a child's presence, but if you must, don't pat a Hispanic child on the head during the discussion with parents or you might offend the parents.

- Some African American children are expected not to look adults in the eye when they are being reprimanded.

Of course, it's *never* positive guidance to demand that any child look you in the eye while you are scolding him or her. But if a child is African American and is culturally unaccustomed to looking adults in the eye during even positive interactions, gradual, optimistic encouragement in that direction may help her become more comfortable and successful in multicultural settings.

- In many parts of the world—for example, Asia, eastern Europe, the Middle East, and Thailand—it is considered rude to show the soles of the feet or shoes to others.

You should avoid crossing your legs in such a way that you expose the soles of your shoes to others in a culturally mixed setting. That's a little thing that may make a big difference.

- Use two hands when taking anything from or passing anything to an Asian person, including your business card; using one hand can be interpreted as a sign of disrespect for the receiver. Many Asians will shake hands with both hands as well.

Why not take the diaper bag with both hands just to show a little extra politeness and respect? And why not present their child's artwork with two hands instead of one?

- When developing a relationship with someone from another culture, take your time. A Chinese proverb states, "Never talk business before the third cup of tea."

Americans often launch into business with less regard for relationship building than for speed and efficiency. This can be confusing and upsetting to people whose culture places more emphasis on politeness than on rushing through a business transaction in an impersonal way just to get the job done quickly. Early childhood professionals can certainly stand to slow down a bit to make their interactions with families more personal.

- In many cultures, elders hold a position of great respect and leadership in the family.

Remember that grandparents and great-grandparents accompanying families may be highly respected by the child's family. Just because that older person is not actively participating in the conversation doesn't mean that she should be treated as an invisible being. Bring in a translator when possible and if needed. But most importantly, recognize and show respect for elders.

- The left hand is considered unclean in many Middle Eastern cultures.

Unless members of the Arab culture are handling something considered unclean, they prefer to use the right hand. Moreover, they avoid gesturing with the left hand. In Arab communities, people tend to stand very close to the person they're talking to. The thumbs-up sign, which means "good job" in the United States, is an offensive gesture throughout the Arab world, so be sure to avoid it.

Will These Tips Keep Me from Ever Culturally Offending Anyone?

Sorry, but no. Our problem is that the world is a very, very big place. In today's urban settings, there are infinite combinations of cultural backgrounds that can come together. You would need a list the size of an encyclopedia to memorize all the possible ways you might culturally offend or confuse someone from another background.

In addition to languages and ethnic cultures different from your own, you are likely to encounter deaf culture; parents and children with disability differences; religious differences; social and economic differences; differences in family structures;

◼◼ Our world is a very big place. Children can begin to learn early in life about the cultural diversity around the world.

gay, lesbian, bisexual, and transgendered parents and adoptive parents; a wide variety of family structure differences; and unfamiliar child-rearing customs unique to different parts of the country (Lum, 1992).

The only really reliable tool is not a memorized bag of tricks but honest, forthright *caring*—being very attentive to make sure parents are comfortable. It is okay to say to a parent (in a genuine, nonthreatening way) something such as "I am not familiar with your culture, but I want to make sure that the way we care for and teach your child is respectful of your culture." "Please help us do a better job by telling us the things we need to know about your child's special needs." "This is how we usually handle lunch. Are you comfortable with this?" "How can we be more supportive of you and your child?"

Childhood professionals must use active listening and careful observation of parents' body language to see whether the parents are uncomfortable, offended, or shocked by something. Childhood professionals must be sensitive to and look for these feelings, and they must encourage conversation. People are often hesitant to express feelings, and they are especially hesitant when those feelings are related to cultural differences. But feelings should be addressed so potential problems can be resolved in a way that is acceptable for all involved.

What Can I Do to Help Children from Other Cultures Feel More Comfortable?

Cultural differences can cause painful adjustments and misunderstandings regardless of the age of the person making the adjustment. Children can suffer from feelings of stress, fear, embarrassment, and failure because they are unable to communicate with the people around them. They desperately want to fit into their school environment, but it is difficult to adjust to a new set of values and behaviors in a new culture.

Changes in customs, climate, and foods can also be confusing. If a child is a recent refugee, she may be emotionally struggling to deal with the impact war and death has had on her family. If the child is old enough to be aware of punctuality, privacy, and appropriate public behavior, she may be confused by differing ideas about them. She may be totally confused about what is expected for girls and boys and what kind of relationship she is expected to have with her teacher.

Bronfenbrenner (1979) suggests that the transition to a new setting is improved when the following conditions are met:
- there are supportive linkages between settings
- a child's entry into a new setting is made in the company of someone the child knows and trusts
- there is open communication between settings that includes the family
- the mode of between-setting communication is personal

In *Transitions to School*, Bronfenbrenner (1995) describes effective practices:
- parent involvement
- preparation of children for the transition

(Continued)

- clear goals and objectives agreed on by all parties involved
- a shared commitment to the successful transitions of young children
- shared decision making among home, preschool, school, and community representatives
- cultural sensitivity
- specific assignments of roles and responsibilities among all parties, including interagency agreements
- specific timelines for transition activities

Child care providers can help this new child and children like her feel welcomed and at home in the early childhood program by taking some important steps. First and foremost—children's names are integral to their identity in any culture, so it is important to learn to pronounce names correctly. Or if the child is deaf, learn to sign the child's name correctly. Ask the parents whether you need to know anything special to use the child's name correctly. For example, in the Vietnamese culture, the surname is first, followed by the middle name, and the given name is last. If a specific name is challenging, tape record the parent saying the name and play it for yourself and staff until you can reproduce the name properly. Remember, the sounds our ears didn't hear when we were babies are almost impossible for our brains to detect now, so we have to work very hard at this task. Do what babies do—listen to that sound over and over again.

Teachers should never Anglicize names to make them easier to pronounce or give the children nicknames. The children's and their families' names may have been the only authentic cultural possession they had left when they arrived in this country. They will appreciate any efforts to safeguard their given names. Make it one of your goals to ensure that all children in your class (from toddlers on up) learn everyone's name in the class. There are many games and songs that lend themselves to name awareness in a classroom. Having artwork on the walls at the children's eye level with their printed names, calling names out loud for activities, and telling stories that incorporate the children's names are only a few of hundreds of things teachers can do to raise the children's awareness of names in the classroom.

An awkward situation may occur in which the teacher encounters a child whose name does not transfer well into English. If, for example, the child's name has a pronunciation that is beautiful in his own language but a bit too simi-

Wadsworth/Cengage Learning

Having children's names posted to designate the day's jobs helps children focus on and identify their own and other children's names.

Welcome Children with Limited English

1. Take the new child around and personally introduce him to other children, or have designated children do this.

2. Give the new child special class responsibilities so she feels she is a part of the class.

3. Set a good example for the class of cultural acceptance and respect.

4. Provide contextualized, authentic learning.

5. Let the new child silently observe if he at first feels uncomfortable participating.

6. Partner the new child with a compatible learning cohort.

7. Never pressure a new child to speak; when she does speak, don't overcorrect.

8. Learn some words and phrases in the child's native language; use these with the new child and teach them to the other children.

9. Simplify your English as needed and speak slowly in a clear, normal tone.

10. Repetitive stories, songs, and rhymes allow the new child to practice the rhythms and patterns of language in addition to learning new vocabulary.

11. Role-playing invites the new child to explore lifelike situations so she can have fun practicing the language structures needed for conversation. She can role-play settings in a grocery store or a doctor's office or pretend to make a call to the fire department.

12. Teach the new child the vocabulary and skills he needs to know to participate in group activities and on the playground.

13. Remember, "Students who feel their culture is valued and understood by the school and the larger community tend to do better in school than those who feel it is rejected" (Ashworth, 1992, p. 14).

---

lar to a profane or obscene word in English, then that might warrant talking with the parents to see whether they want to think about a nickname. In that case, the parents should decide on a culturally appropriate nickname. If the parents treasure the child's name and want to keep it, that's fine. Then it is the teacher's responsibility to ensure that no child ever teases him about his name on the teacher's watch. The teacher, of course, will also want to do everything possible to instill enough pride in him about his wonderful, proud name that future teasing won't distress him.

How Can I Learn to Be More Culturally Sensitive?

Before we can be effective in working with children and families, it is essential to examine our own racial and cultural attitudes and values. It is possible to be culturally sensitive to children and families only if we are honestly aware of our own racial and cultural point of view (Davis & Proctor, 1989).

A Short Quiz to Explore Cultural Beliefs

Family (check only the statements you agree with most strongly)

☐ I usually place family priorities before my career.

☐ I believe that children should be sheltered.

☐ Women's most important role is in the home.

☐ I usually ask my family to make sacrifices for my career.

☐ I believe that children should be independent.

☐ Women's most important role is in society.

Education

☐ I believe that education should stick to the basics—memorization of reading, writing, and arithmetic facts.

☐ I believe that education should take an analytic approach to problem solving and there should be an emphasis on practical application.

Religion

☐ I believe in fate: "As God wills."

☐ I believe that I decide my fate.

Status

☐ I believe that title and position are more important than money in the eyes of society.

☐ I believe that money is the main status measure and is a reward for achievement.

Personal Sensitivity

☐ I have difficulty separating work and personal relationships.

☐ I am bothered when people around me have differences of opinion.

☐ I sometimes go to extremes to avoid confrontation.

☐ I separate work from my emotions and my personal relationships.

☐ I think sensitivity at work can be a sign of weakness.

☐ I often don't get subtle hints when people don't come right out and say what they mean.

Personal Appearance

☐ I believe that dress and grooming are extremely important status symbols.

☐ I believe appearance is not as important as performance.

Manners

☐ I was brought up to use Old World manners and etiquette.

☐ I believe others see courtesy and manners as an indication you're from a good family.

☐ I usually like to be informal to make life simpler and get things done faster.

☐ I always prefer getting down to the point rather than sitting around making chit chat.

Adapted from Kras, 1995.

The purpose of the cultural-belief quiz is to focus your attention on your own cultural point of view. When you listen to others, remember that they may not share your views, and they may not necessarily be wrong simply because they have a different point of view.

Sometimes it is enough to recognize that we see the world through different eyes. This knowledge will help us keep our humility as we share information about strategies for effective child guidance with parents who may be trying hard to be open-minded.

Each section of statements in the culture quiz has an even number of statements for you to choose from. If the answers you selected were mostly in the top half of the section, your responses were somewhat similar to respondents from Mexico in a study. If the answers you selected were mostly in the bottom half of the boxes, your responses were somewhat similar to respondents from the United States and Canada in that same study (Kras, 1995). None of the answers are right or wrong except in your own heart and mind—which should be respected, just as should the beliefs of others.

We may come together and agree on rules for how people must behave at work and at school, but we can't make up rules for what someone else has to believe. We each believe what we believe, and we don't have to change that, but we can modify our actions (insofar as we consider it ethically and morally appropriate) to honor the rights and needs of others. If you discuss the results of this quiz with your classmates, you may discover interesting differences among classmates with similar backgrounds as well as differences between students with different backgrounds. Each individual is indeed unique!

Cultural Differences

How Does Culture Affect Adults' Styles of Interaction?

Adults' styles of interaction (sometimes called *styles of control*)—*authoritative, authoritarian,* and *permissive*—are strongly affected by their cultural backgrounds. People tend to replicate the guidance style of their own parents. People can, however, learn more effective guidance styles that they consciously decide to adopt. To make the change, they will need to believe that the new methods will work and will fit into their cultural lifestyle.

People don't accept new guidance styles simply because someone tells them to. They have to believe that new guidance strategies will be meaningful in the context of their own lived experiences and in terms of their own cultural perspectives. They have to really understand how a new guidance method will help children, or it just won't function in any authentic way that empowers families and strengthens classrooms. This book explains the process of understanding how and why authoritative, respectful guidance will prepare children to be competent, stress resistant, and prepared to cope with change in the multicultural global economy of today.

How Does Culture Affect a Person's Learning Approach?

People from different cultures approach learning differently. People from some cultures approach education and educators almost with a feeling of reverence. Learning and knowledge is something that you accept humbly. A professor, a teacher, a parent, or a wise elder from the community should be consulted if you want to *receive knowledge*. The learner could not possibly be presumed to create knowledge. As we know, throughout history a great deal of knowledge has been passed down to younger generations by wise elder generations.

Some cultures approach learning in a radically different way. Just because something has been traditionally thought to be true doesn't convince people in these cultural settings that it is really true. If they want to know something, they may form a focus group or a think tank. They don't ask only wise elders, they do research. They always like to confirm things for themselves. They believe that learning is something anyone can construct. At the rate information is changing in our world, I wonder if our great-grandchildren will have to be issued textbooks (electronic, of course) marked with time stamps, like my carton of yogurt—best if used before May 30, 2036.

DAP teaches us that children really do have to learn how to *construct knowledge* or they will be left in the lurch as they grow up in this fast-moving technological world. I would hope, though, that when you encounter cultural reverence for education among any of the children and families you serve, you will try to spread its cultural beauty and importance among all the children in your class. I will never forget a small two-year-old boy from a Middle Eastern country I taught years ago. I was invited to his home for dinner. To my astonishment, his parents had placed my framed photograph, like a shrine, on his bedside table. My husband, a journalism professor, particularly enjoyed occasional e-mails he received from one of his adult international students that always began "Dear Honored Sir." Wouldn't it be lovely if American society revered education *and* supported constructivist educational methods?

How Does Culture Affect Social Role Expectations?

A particularly interesting cultural difference that is often overlooked is that of individuals' social role expectations. Members of some cultures focus on **cohesive interaction.** Their cultural background has prepared them to think in terms of kinship.

cohesive interaction
Reciprocal teamwork; sticking together to carry out tight-knit group activity.

They tend to gravitate toward group or team-oriented goals. Children who grow up in cohesive interaction cultural settings often have responsibility caring for other children in the family. They grow up with a strong sense that the community of kinship can be depended on to meet their emotional and physical needs and are often extremely attached to their community of origin.

In contrast, children growing up in a cultural context where social role expectations tend toward **individual development** and **fulfillment** operate very differently. There is more likely to be a strong nuclear family bond than a wide kinship bond. The family is more likely to rely on itself and less likely to ask for help from others outside the nuclear family. Although they may do volunteer work or give to charity, they are much less likely to know what the needs of their neighbors are or to be available to help them. The parents are more likely to move from region to region to achieve higher-paying work. The children are more involved in individual, self-fulfilling work and play and much less likely to have the responsibility of caring for a sibling.

At preschool, the child from a cohesive interaction background would likely look for a group of children with which to actively engage in play. The child from an individual development background might be interested in a dinosaur puzzle and sit down alone or with another child to try to figure out how to put it together. A cultural challenge for early childhood educators is to help each of these children learn some of the cultural skills of the other child without squashing the unique abilities of either child.

During my research for *First Steps Toward Cultural Difference* (1989), I observed remarkable displays of caretaking by very young children. I saw African American preschoolers (mostly girls but occasionally even boys) from low-income families look up from their play, notice that a toddler needed something, and instantly drop what they were doing to assist. I did not tend to see that same behavior in privileged, predominantly white children.

Our goal in a developmentally appropriate program would be to help children who are comfortable with cohesive kinship find and build a strong, cohesive kinship at school and then gradually learn that it is okay occasionally to stretch out and experience individual fulfillment all alone. Our goal with the child who is comfortable with individual development and fulfillment is to support that process, but also to help her learn to function as part of a team. We need her to experience and succeed in more situations where she has to push aside her own needs for the needs of

In some cultural settings, young children are accustomed to interacting in lively kinship groups, toward group goals.

Wadsworth/Cengage Learning

individual development
A particular person, distinct from others in a group, changes, advances, or progresses to a more advanced state.

fulfillment
Completely developing one's abilities and interests; a feeling of pleasure because you are getting what you want from life.

In some cultures, young children are accustomed to working alone on independent projects for self-fulfillment.

visceral
Proceeding more from instinct than logical thinking. Characterized by or showing emotion.

differentiated
Made apparent or categorized differences between two or more things.

the group. Being in a multicultural environment will help both of these children have the role models they need to achieve better cultural balance and the ability to function across cultures.

How Does Culture Shape Our Use of Language?

Language is a key factor in culture. Obviously, cultures use different languages, but even when different cultural groups use the same language, they are likely to use it differently. In other words, you may both be speaking English, but culture may cause you to use the language in very different ways to express yourself. We know that different regions have their own accents and regional words, but even beyond that, culture shapes the thinking behind the use of words and how those words are constructed into meaningful communication.

To focus on important cultural linguistic code differences, I have divided language usage differences into two groups. I call these two groups **visceral** (intuitive) usage and **differentiated** (categorized) usage. You can see these differences if you examine speech closely (Miller, 1989). For example, if you watch two three-year-olds digging in the garden, you might overhear the following conversation:

Josie: "Hey, I got bait! You find any bait yet?"

Tim: "That's a worm. I feed worms to my box turtle, but he also eats frogs and bugs."

Josie: "This my bait . . . don't you go feeding it to your turtle. I'm going fishing, and I'm gonna catch a whale that will eat your turtle."

If you think what you have just heard sounds like meaningless, trivial conversation, you'd miss some very important insight into Josie and Tim and the way enculturation has structured their use of language. The two children were delighted to find earthworms, but their oral reactions were different. When Josie sees the worms, she intuitively lights up and remembers fishing with her grandfather. She intuitively knows the feel of the moist wiggly worms, the smell of the fish they caught, the sounds of the water splashing against the dock, and the wonder she felt exploring the worms and seeing fish come lurching out of the water and being yanked to the deck by what looked to her like a long string. No one in her family has ever spent a lot of time specifically naming or labeling objects for her to learn, so the designation *worm* doesn't leap to her mind today. What does come to her mind is the label she heard in *context* when she was exposed to worms on fishing trips—"bait." Bait has no dry, memorized mental connection; Josie learned it in the context of richly lived social and emotional experiences.

Tim may or may not have known what bait was, but his thinking style clearly tends toward categorization. He immediately thought of worms as part of the category of foods that his turtle ate—worms, frogs, and bugs. If you asked Tim to name three different kinds of worms, he might be able to think of earthworms, gummy worm candy, and the cartoon worm on *SpongeBob SquarePants*. Josie might have needed a moment to comprehend the connection between the worms in her hands and Tim's grouping that included candy and cartoons. Her brain is not culturally attuned to his perspective. Of course, his brain is not culturally attuned to her perspective either. She energetically and dramatically role-plays an imagined fishing trip in which she catches a giant whale that eats his turtle. He cries and is very bewildered.

Tim's brain has been prepared through his infant and toddler language enculturation to unconsciously differentiate categories. His parents did frequently and routinely point out objects to him, label them, and point out connections, "See . . . the elephant has a long trunk, but the giraffe has a long neck." Tim's cultural background prepares him to be an exceptional test taker. (It helps him that tests have been traditionally written and produced by persons of Tim's cultural background.)

How Does Culture Shape Our Intellectual Approach?

Unfortunately, some teachers and parents may leap to the mistaken assumption that Tim is brighter than Josie. What they don't realize is that there are many kinds of intelligence, and Josie has different capacities and potentials from Tim. By no means should she be considered in any way lesser than Tim. The world needs all sorts of people with all sorts of unique skills and abilities. Howard Gardner (1983) explained that his view of personal intelligence was based on **emotional** (intrapersonal) **intelligence** and *interpersonal* **social intelligence.** Carolyn Saarni (1990) described emotional competence as including eight interrelated emotional and social skills.

Lev Vygotsky, a Russian psychologist who emphasized the importance of pretend play as a forum for learning, was concerned with social learning, now often called **authentic learning** (learning positioned in a context). He believed that all higher cognitive functions have their origins in social relations. As we know, schools from our own childhoods all too often cut off social interactions between students ("Be quiet and look at your own work!") and sometimes even interactions with the real world ("Don't look out the window! Your eyes should be on the chalkboard.") Contemporary academic strategies have brought new success to schools through innovations such as manipulative learning materials, collaborative learning, block scheduling, and peer tutoring, which have given children the opportunity to share in the social construction of learning and meaning (Spielberger, 2004). These strategies also make learning more fair and relevant to children with differing cultural backgrounds.

Earlier theories of knowledge stressed its absolute, permanent quality. Recent theories put more and more emphasis on the continual development or evolution

emotional intelligence
The level of one's self-awareness, mood management, self-motivation, empathy, and understanding of one's inner feelings.

social intelligence
An individual's fund of knowledge about the social world and ability to act wisely in human relations, to get along with others, and to interact with skill and ease in social matters.

authentic learning
A family of research efforts that explain cognition in terms of the relationship between learners and the properties of specific environments. The emphasis of research on authentic learning (or "situated cognition" as it is often called) is to study complex learning, problem solving, and thinking in a realistic environment.

of knowledge, its dynamic, changing interaction with the world and its subjects, and its relativity, or situation dependence. The whole trend moves from a static, passive view of knowledge toward a more and more adaptive and active one. Although many of the critical skills required in the high-performance workplace have not changed, the pace of knowledge advancement requires constant updating of knowledge and skills.

Education no longer ends at graduation. Some experts have estimated that the shelf life of a technical degree today is less than five years. Viewing a college education as the mastery of a body of knowledge or a complete preparation for a lifetime career has become outmoded. Today, quality education teaches students the underlying critical-thinking skills they need to become successful lifelong learners. Our role with young children today is to start them on the road toward becoming effective, multicultural, lifelong learners.

Historically, the focus was on assessing children's intelligence through such instruments as the Wechsler Intelligence Test, or IQ (intelligence quotient) test. **Intelligence** was defined as "the aggregate or global capacity of the individual to act purposefully, to think rationally, and to deal effectively with his environment" (Wechsler, 1958, p. 7). Wechsler was aware that there were other noncognitive factors such as affective, personal, and social factors that were going untested, but nobody knew how to test those other qualities. IQ by itself has proved not to

intelligence
The aggregate or global capacity of a person to act purposefully, think rationally, and deal effectively with his or her environment.

Components of Emotional–Social Intelligence

Intrapersonal
To have an ability to be aware of oneself, to understand one's strengths and weaknesses, and to express one's feelings and thoughts nondestructively.

Interpersonal
To have the ability to be aware of others' emotions, feelings, and needs and to establish and maintain constructive and mutually satisfying relationships. This means to be able to effectively manage personal, social, and environmental change by realistically coping with the immediate situation, solving problems, and making decisions.

Stress Management
To have the emotional resilience and coping strategies to deal effectively with stressful environments, and to be able to regulate impulses, especially outbursts and irrational behavior.

Adaptability
To have the ability to be flexible in changing situations and make appropriate changes to thinking and behavior and find solutions to problems in keeping with the environment.

General Mood
This is an overall assessment of one's sense of well-being.

Adapted from Bar-On, 2005.

be a very good predictor of long-term life or job performance. Meanwhile, societal pressures for social justice and equal treatment have brought enormous pressure on researchers to develop intelligence assessments that are not distorted by cultural bias.

Peter Salovey and John Mayer studied the social and emotional aspects of intelligence and first coined the term "emotional intelligence" in 1990. Their work was then popularized by Daniel Goleman with his book *Emotional Intelligence* in 1995. Other researchers have gone on to develop instruments to assess emotional intelligence such as Reuben Bar-On (1997).

Emotional–social intelligence refers to the personal and social skills that lead to improved performance in the workplace and better social functioning; these skills are a necessary prerequisite for social competency. The Bar-On model of EQ, emotional–social intelligence quotient, is a set of interconnected emotional and social competencies, skills, and facilitators that determine how effectively we can understand and express ourselves, understand others, relate with others, and cope with daily demands (Bar-On, 2000, 2005).

Research has expanded rapidly in this field. Brain research began to include exploring the brain circuitry that controls emotional awareness (Lane, 2000), as well as other emotional and social functions (Bar-On, 2005; Lane & McRae, 2004). Findings from these studies have begun to provide physical evidence of the anatomical brain-circuitry process that takes place during social and emotional attentiveness (Matthews et al., 2002, 2003; Zeidner et al., 2001).

> Darkness cannot drive out darkness; only light can do that. Hate cannot drive out hate; only love can do that.
>
> *Martin Luther King Jr., "Loving your enemies," sermon delivered at Dexter Avenue Baptist Church, Montgomery, Alabama, November 17, 1957.*

How Can We Expand Children's Emotional–Social Intelligence?

Quality educational programs make a difference in children's EQ. Early childhood professionals can help children begin to understand their emotions. They can help children learn to be in charge of expressing their emotions appropriately, and they can help children to learn socially intelligent behavior through positive child guidance. Such strategies as these have been shown to increase self-awareness and reduce stress (Bar-On, 2005).

As shown earlier in this chapter, increased self-awareness and more well-developed interpersonal skills help individuals decrease prejudice and increase cooperation among diverse cultures. By working effectively with young children in developmentally appropriate programs, we can help make the world a better place.

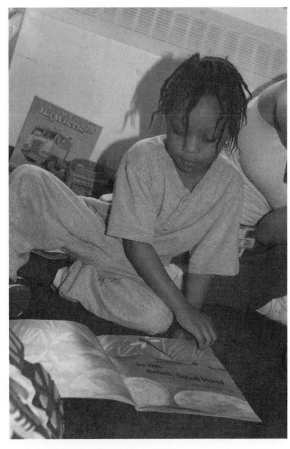

Teach tolerance through the wonderful world of multicultural children's books.

KEY TERMS

authentic learning
bias
body language
cohesive interaction
cultural adaptation
cultural bias
cultural context
cultural pluralism
culture
culture shock
differentiated
discrimination
emotional intelligence
enculturation
ethics
ethnocentrism
fulfillment
group identity

human ecology
individual development
intelligence
media
negative stereotyping
nested structures
personal interaction
pluralistic culture
prejudice
racism
respect
scapegoating
self-identity
sexism
social intelligence
stigmatized
unconditional acceptance
visceral

POINTS TO REMEMBER

- Culture is the beliefs and patterns of behavior that are passed on from parents to children.
- A child's development is best understood within the social and cultural context of that child's family and community.
- Unconditional acceptance of a child and her family is the first important step toward open communication.
- It is ethically wrong for early childhood professionals to discriminate based on race, gender, religion, economic status, values, national origin, or disability.

- People who are ethnocentric often claim to be open-minded but may see culture traits that are different from their own as meaningless or peculiar.
- Multicultural education is not a subject area, but an ever-present thread woven throughout all curriculum areas and throughout each and every day.
- Prejudice harms children and damages their development.
- Cultural differences can cause painful adjustments and misunderstandings regardless of the age of the person making the adjustment.

PRACTICAL APPLICATION

Boba Rebear and Salty Green Paper

The day Ying Ying started preschool he was only three and very scared. He didn't know a single word of English. He needed open-heart surgery and his doctors urgently needed him to attend preschool to learn some English before the surgery. But poor Ying Ying didn't like the doctors, the hospital, or the preschool, so he cried—oh, how he howled, endlessly it seemed.

The teachers tried patiently to interest him in the soft white bunny in the science center, the wonderful block center, even the food preparation center, but he just sobbed and watched suspiciously.

After several days, at circle time, it was Malika's turn to lead the group in a song. Well, Malika was an amazing child, a beautiful, confident African American child who loved the spotlight. Of course, she picked her cultural folk favorite, a jazzed-up rhyming version of "The Three Bears," which she preceded to lead with un-inhibited charm, energy, and talent:

Once upon a *time* in a little log *cabin*

Lived the three little bears—CHA, CHA, CHA.

One was the papa, *one* was the mama

And *one* was the *wee* bear—CHA, CHA, CHA.

One day they went a *walking* in the cool woods
   a *talkin'*

And along came a *girl,* a girl with long *hair*.

Her name was *Goldilocks* and upon the door she
   knocked,

But no one was *there;* no, no one was *there*.

So she *walked* right in and she had herself a *chair,*

Cause she didn't care, the *girl* with long hair.

Then *home, home, home* came the three bears.

Someone's been sitting in *my* chair, said the
   papa bear.

Someone's been sitting in *my* chair said the
   mama bear.

Hey Boba *Rebear,* said the little *wee* bear,

Someone has broken my *chair*—CRASH.

Goldilocks she *woke* up, she *broke* up the party,

And she *beat* it out of there; she *beat* it out of there,

And *that* is the story of the three little bears

Boba *Re*, Boba *Re*, Boba *Ra Ra Ra!*

Of course the whole class responded with delight as the classroom rocked with this bebop chant. Ying Ying's sobs were completely drowned out by the ruckus. As things died down, it dawned on the teachers that Ying Ying wasn't crying anymore. He was standing there looking amazed and actually grinning. Malika yelled out, "Hey, Ying Ying likes it. He isn't crying. Let's do it again."

Apparently, Ying Ying's Chinese cultural background had not prepared him for a roomful of children cheerfully boogieing down to a jazzy version of the three bears. The teachers let Malika lead the class in the rhyme again. This time Ying Ying shook with laughter. The children enthusiastically "Boba Reed" and "Boba Rood" with every jazzy bone in their bodies. Well, that is when Ying Ying fell in love with Malika.

Malika took Ying Ying under her wing and he became her constant shadow. Soon he had mastered her cocky walk and learned to speak English, making sure to pronounce his words just like Malika. He was her buddy.

One day when Ying Ying's mother, Mrs. Sung, came to pick him up from school, Malika was at his side. Mrs. Sung opened her purse and gave Ying Ying a small rectangle of crinkly green tissue. Ying Ying instantly and eagerly popped it into his mouth.

Malika shrieked, "Teacher! Teacher! Ying Ying's mama fed him green paper!" Mrs. Sung said, "Here, Malika, let me show you. In my country this is a great treat for children. It is made out of seaweed and it tastes salty. Would you like to taste?"

Nothing in Malika's cultural background prepared her for eating crinkly green paper. The teacher and Mrs. Sung talked with Ying Ying and Malika and decided to wrap some laver (dried, edible seaweed) for Malika to take home to show her parents.

At home that evening, Malika's parents loved the idea of her trying the laver. They even tasted it too. Malika loved the taste of the laver so much that she suggested Mrs. Sung bring enough of it one day for all the children at preschool to have a taste of "green paper."

Malika and Ying Ying came from totally different cultural backgrounds, but with the help of supportive teachers and parents they learned to appreciate, respect, and value each other's cultural background.

DISCUSSION QUESTIONS

1. Why was Ying Ying so taken with the Three Bears poem?
2. Can you think of anything the teachers could do to support the budding friendship of Ying Ying and Malika?
3. What would have happened if Malika had been sent away from the circle for yelling out?
4. What would have happened if the teacher had insisted that the children calm down, sit with their legs "criss-cross" and sing "nicely" with an inside voice.
5. What is the most effective way for teachers to respond when an exciting, joyous group activity suddenly crosses over into an overstimulated and out-of-control activity?

a. Talk to the children about how and why their behavior is inappropriate.
b. Begin an even more active activity like dancing to fast music.
c. End the activity and take the children outdoors.
d. Use exaggerated, very dramatic facial and body gestures to silently pantomime movements for the children to imitate.
e. List other possibilities.
6. What could the teachers do to help the children learn about and appreciate the cultural backgrounds of other children in the class?

STUDENT ACTIVITY

1. Discuss how prejudice or intolerance has affected your own life or the life of someone you know personally.
2. What do children gain from learning to respect other people's diversity?
3. What are some things that can happen when children are stigmatized?
4. What is tolerance? (List examples of ways children can practice tolerance in the classroom.)
5. What is prejudice? (List examples of how prejudice harms children's development.)

6. How might you respond to a parent who demonstrates obvious prejudice in front of the children?
7. List specific things that a classroom teacher can do to create an environment that encourages respect for all persons.
8. What do you think the United States and the world in general gain or lose from not respecting diversity?

RELATED READINGS

Antibias Issues

Anti-Defamation League (ADL). (2000). *Close the book on hate: 101 ways to combat prejudice.* New York, NY: Barnes & Noble. Retrieved February 17, 2006, from http://www.adl.org.

Aronson, E., & Patnoe, S. (1997). *The Jigsaw classroom: Building cooperation in the classroom.* New York: Addison Wesley Longman.

Banks, J. A. (2001). *Cultural diversity and education: Foundations, curriculum, and teaching.* Boston: Allyn & Bacon.

Banks, J. A., & Banks, C. A. M., Eds. (2003). *Multicultural education: Issues and perspectives.* New York: Wiley.

Bisson, J. (1997). *Celebrate! An anti-bias guide to enjoying the holidays in early childhood programs.* St. Paul, MN: Redleaf Press.

Bullard, S. (1996). *Teaching tolerance.* New York: Doubleday.

Byrnes, D. A., & Kiger, G., Eds. (1996). *Common bonds: Anti-bias teaching in a diverse society.* Wheaton, MD: Association for Childhood Education International.

Compton-Lilly, C. (2004). *Confronting racism, poverty, and power: Classroom strategies to change the world.* Portsmouth, NH: Heinemann.

Cortés, C. E. (2000). *The children are watching: How the media teach about diversity.* New York: Teachers College Press.

Davidson, F. H., & Davidson, M. (1994). *Changing childhood prejudice: The caring work of the schools.* Westport, CT: Bergin & Garvey.

Delpit, L., & Dowdy, J. K., Eds. (2002). *The skin that we speak: Thoughts on language and culture in the classroom.* New York: New Press.

Derman-Sparks, L. (1989). *Anti-bias curriculum: Tools for empowering young children.* Washington, DC: National Association for the Education of Young Children.

Derman-Sparks, L. (1999). *Teaching/learning anti-racism.* New York: Teacher College Press.

Dumas, L. (1992). *Talking with your child about a troubled world.* New York: Fawcett.

Franklin, V. P. (2001). *Learning while black: Creating educational excellence for African American children.* Baltimore, MD: Johns Hopkins University Press.

Gay, G. (2000). *Culturally responsive teaching: Theory, research, and practice.* New York: Teachers College Press.

Hall, N. S. (1998). *Creative resources for the anti-bias classroom.* Clifton Park, NY: Thomson Delmar Learning.

Hall, N. S. (1999). *Creative resources for the anti-bias classroom.* Clifton Park, NY: Thomson Delmar Learning.

Hall, N. S., & Rhomberg, V. (1995). *The affective curriculum: Teaching the anti-bias approach to young children.* Clifton Park, NY: Thomson Delmar Learning.

Howard, G. R. (1999). *We can't teach what we don't know: White teachers, multiracial schools.* New York: Teachers Press.

Kirshbaum, M. (1994). *Family context and disability culture reframing: Through the looking glass. The Family Psychologist.* Retrieved from http://lookingglass .org (five-page brochure).

Klug, B. J., & Whitfield, P. T. (2002). *Widening the circle. Culturally relevant pedagogy for American Indian children.* New York: Routledge Falmer.

Ladson-Billings, G. (1994). The dreamkeepers: Successful teachers of African American children. Hoboken, NJ: Jossey-Bass.

Lee, E., Ed. (2002). *Beyond heroes and holidays: A practical guide to K–12 anti-racist, multicultural education and staff development.* Washington, DC: Teaching for Change.

Marshall, P. L. (2002). *Cultural diversity in our schools.* Belmont, CA: Wadsworth/Thomson Delmar Learning.

Nieto, S. (1999). *The light in their eyes: Creating multicultural learning communities.* New York: Teachers College Press.

Nieto, S. (2000). *Affirming diversity: The sociopolitical context of multicultural education.* New York: Longman.

Ostrow, J. (1995). *A room with a different view: First through third graders build community and create curriculum.* York, ME: Stenhouse Publishers.

Paley, V. G. (1992). *You can't say you can't play.* Cambridge, MA: Harvard University Press.

Paley, V. G. (1995). *Kwanzaa and me: A teacher's story.* Cambridge, MA: Harvard University Press.

Ramsey, P. G., Williams, L. R., & Vold, E. B. (2002). *Multicultural education: A source book.* New York, NY: Routledge Falmer.

Salend, S. J. (2001). *Creating inclusive classrooms: Effecting and reflective practices.* Upper Saddle River, NJ: Merrill.

Segal, J., & Simkins, J. (1996). *Helping children with ill or disabled parents: A guide for parents and professionals.* London: Jessica Kingsley Publishers.

Sparks, L. D. (1991). *Anti-bias curriculum: Tools for empowering young children.* Washington, DC: NAEYC.

Stephan, W. G. (1999). *Reducing prejudice and stereotyping in schools.* New York: Teachers College Press.

Stern-LaRosa, C., & Bettmann, E. H. (2000). *Hate hurts: How children learn and unlearn prejudice.* New York: Scholastic.

Thompson, G. L. (2004). *Through ebony eyes: What teachers need to know but are afraid to ask about African American students.* Hoboken, NJ: Jossey-Bass.

Van Ausdale, D., & Feagin, J. R. (2001). *The first R: How children learn race and racism.* Lanham, MD: Rowman & Littlefield.

Wates, M. (2002). *Supporting disabled adults in their parenting role.* London: Joseph Rowntree Foundation.

Wright, M. (2000). *I'm chocolate, you're vanilla: Raising healthy Black and biracial children in a race-conscious world.* Hoboken, NJ: Jossey-Bass.

York, S. (2003). *Roots and wings: Affirming culture in early childhood programs.* St. Paul, MN: Redleaf Press.

Cultural Differences

Back, L. (1996). *New ethnicities and urban culture: Racisms and multiculture in young lives.* London: UCL Press.

Befu, H. (1986). The social and cultural background of child development in Japan and the United States. In H. Stevenson, H. Azuma, & K. Hakuta (Eds.), *Child development and education in Japan* (13–27). New York: W. H. Freeman.

Bhatti, G. (1999). *Asian children at home and at school.* London: Routledge.

Bronfenbrenner, U. (1958). Socialization and social class through time and space. In E. E. Maccoby, R. M. Newcomb, & E. L. Harley (Eds.), *Readings in social psychology* (400–425). New York: Holt, Rinehart, & Winston.

Bull, T. (1998). *On the edge of deaf culture: An annotated bibliography of hearing children/deaf parents.* Alexandria, VA: Deaf Family Research Press.

Burts, D. C., Hart, C. H., Charlesworth, R., & Kirk, L. (1990). A comparison of stress behaviors observed in kindergarten children in classrooms with developmentally appropriate versus developmentally inappropriate instructional practices. *Early Childhood Research Quarterly, 5*(3), 407–423.

Chao, R. K. (1995). Chinese and European American cultural models of the self reflected in mothers' childrearing beliefs. *Ethos, 23,* 328–354.

Chavajay, P., & Rogoff, B. (1999). Cultural variation in management of attention by children and their caregivers. *Developmental Psychology, 35,* 1079–1090.

Cohen, A. (1955). *Delinquent boys: The culture of the gang.* Chicago: Free Press.

Cote, L. R., & Bornstein, M. H. (2000). Social and didactic parenting behaviors and beliefs among Japanese American and South American mothers of infants. *Infancy, 1,* 363–374.

DeLoache, J. S., & Gottlieb, A., Eds. (2000). *A world of babies: Imagined childcare guides for seven societies.* New York: Cambridge University Press.

Dickinson, D. K. (2002). Shifting images of developmentally appropriate practice as seen through different lenses. *Educational Researcher, 31*(1), 26–32.

Feinman, G. M., & Manzanilla, L., Eds. (2000). *Cultural evolution: Contemporary viewpoints.* New York: Kluwer Academic/Plenum.

Garcia Coll, C. T., & Pachter, L. M. (2002). Ethnic and minority parenting. In M. H. Bornstein (Ed.), *Handbook of parenting* (vol. 4, 1–20). Mahwah, NJ: Erlbaum.

Gay, G. (2000). *Culturally responsive teaching.* New York: Teachers College Press.

Gutiérrez, K. (2002). Studying cultural practices in urban learning communities. *Human Development, 45*(4), 312–321.

Harkness, S., & Super, C. (1995). Culture and parenting. In M. H. Bornstein (Ed.), *Handbook of parenting, Vol. 2: Biology and ecology of parenting* (211–234). Hillsdale, NJ: Erlbaum.

Hirsch, E. D. (1987). *Cultural literacy: What every American needs to know.* Boston, MA: Houghton Mifflin.

Kagitcibasi, C. (1996). *Family and human development across cultures: A view from the other side.* Mahwah, NJ: Erlbaum.

Keller, H. (2003). Socialization for competence: Cultural models of infancy. *Human Development, 46,* 288–311.

Levine, R. A., Levine, S. E., & Schnell, B. (2001). "Improve the women": Mass schooling, female literacy, and worldwide social change. *Harvard Educational Review, 71*(1): 1–50.

Leyendecker, B., Harwood, R. L., Lamb, M. E., & Schoelmerich, A. (2002). Mothers' socialization goals and evaluations of desirable and undesirable everyday situations in two diverse cultural groups. *International Journal of Behavioral Development, 26,* 248–258.

Matusov, E. L., Bell, N., & Rogoff, B. (2002). Schooling as cultural process: Working together and guidance by children from schools differing in collaborative practices. In R. V. Kail & H. W. Reese (Eds.), *Advances in child development and behavior* (vol. 29). Spanish Fork, UT: Academic Press.

Melamed, B. G. (2002). Parenting the ill child. In M. H. Bornstein (Ed.), *Handbook of parenting* (vol. 5, 329–348). Mahwah, NJ: Erlbaum.

Miller, A. M., & Harwood, L. R. (2001). Long term socialization goals and the construction of infants' social networks among middleclass Anglo and Puerto Rican mothers. *International Journal of Behavioral Development, 25,* 450–457.

Miller, D. F. (1989). *First steps toward cultural difference: Socialization in infant/toddler day care.* Washington, DC: Child Welfare League of America.

Reagan, T. (2000). *Non-western educational traditions: Alternative approaches to educational thought and practice.* Matwah, NJ: Erlbaum.

Rogoff, B. (2003). *The cultural nature of human development.* New York: Oxford University Press.

Rogoff, B., Mistry, J. J., Göncü, A., & Mosier, C. (1993). Guided participation in cultural activity by toddlers and caregivers. *Monographs of the Society for Research in Child Development, 58* (7, serial no. 236).

Shapiro, A. H. (1999). *Everybody belongs: Changing negative attitudes toward classmates with disabilities.* New York: Garland Publishing.

Sheldon, A. (1997). Talking power: Girls, gender, enculturation and discourse. In R. Wodak (Ed.), *Gender and discourse* (225–244). London: Sage.

Tatum, B. D. (1999). Why are all the black kids sitting together in the cafeteria? And other conversations about race. New York: Basic Books.

Wang, Q., Leichtman, M. D., & Davies, K. I. (2000). Sharing memories and telling stories: American and Chinese mothers and their 3-year-olds. *Memory, 8,* 159–177.

Williams, R. (2001). Culture is ordinary. In J. Higgins (Ed.), *The Raymond Williams reader* (10–24). Oxford, UK: Blackwell.

Yovsi, R. D., & Keller, H. (2003). Breastfeeding: An adaptive process. *Ethos, 31, 1.*

Emotional–Social Intelligence

Bar-On, R. (2000). Emotional and social intelligence: Insights from the Emotional Quotient Inventory (EQ-i). In R. Bar-On & J. D. A. Parker (Eds.), *Handbook of emotional intelligence.* San Francisco, CA: Jossey-Bass.

Bar-On, R. (2005). The Bar-On model of emotional-social intelligence. In P. Fernández-Berrocal & N. Extremera (Guest Eds.), Special issue on emotional intelligence. *Psicothema, 17.*

Brackett, M. A., & Mayer, J. D. (2003). Convergent, discriminant, and incremental validity of competing measures of emotional intelligence. *Personality and Social Psychology Bulletin, 29*(9), 1147–1158.

Brackett, M. A., & Salovey, P. (2004). Measuring emotional intelligence with the Mayer-Salovey-Caruso Emotional Intelligence Test (MSCEIT). In G. Geher (Ed.), *Measuring emotional intelligence: Common ground and controversy.* Hauppauge, NY: Nova Science.

Gardner, H. (1983). *Frames of mind.* New York: Basic Books.

Lane, R. D. (2000). Levels of emotional awareness: Neurological, psychological and social perspectives. In R. Bar-On & J. D. A. Parker (Eds.), *Handbook of emotional intelligence.* San Francisco, CA: Jossey-Bass.

Lane, R. D., & McRae, K. (2004). Neural substrates of conscious emotional experience: A cognitive-neuroscientific perspective. In M. Beauregard (Ed.), *Consciousness, emotional self-regulation and the brain* (87–122). Amsterdam: Benjamins.

Mayer, J. D., & Salovey, P. (1997). What is emotional intelligence? In P. Salovey & D. Sluyter (Eds.),

Emotional development and emotional intelligence: Implications for educators (3–31). New York: Basic Books.

Mayer, J. D., Salovey, P., & Caruso, D. (2000). Models of emotional intelligence. In R. J. Sternberg (Ed.), *Handbook of intelligence.* Cambridge, UK: Cambridge University Press.

Saarni, C. (1990). Emotional competence: How emotions and relationships become integrated. In R. A. Thompson (Ed.), *Socioemotional development.* Nebraska symposium on motivation (vol. 36, 115–182). Lincoln: University of Nebraska Press.

Spielberger, C., Ed. (2004). *Encyclopedia of Applied Psychology.* Academic Press.

Parenting Guides

Armstrong, T. (2000). *In their own way: Discovering and encouraging your child's multiple intelligences.* East Rutherford, NJ: Putman.

Arnow, J. (1995). *Teaching peace: How to raise children to live in harmony—without fear, without prejudice, without violence.* New York: Perigee.

Black, C. (2003). *Straight talk from Claudia Black: What recovering parents should tell their kids about drugs and alcohol.* Center City, MN: Hazelden Publishing & Educational Services.

Bloom, B. & Seljeskog, E. L. (1988). *A parent's guide to spina bifida.* Minneapolis: University of Minnesota.

Briar-Lawson, K., Lawson, H. A., Rooney, B. J., Hansen, V., White, L. G., Radina, M. E. & Herzog, K. L. (1998). *From parent involvement to parent empowerment and family support: A guide for community leaders.* University Heights, OH: Institute for Educational Renewal.

Bullard, S. (2002). *Teaching tolerance: Raising open-minded, empathetic children.* New York: Doubleday.

Comer, J. P., & Poussaint, A. F. (1992). *Raising black children: Two leading psychiatrists confront the educational, social and emotional problems facing black children.* New York: Plume.

Connel, M., & Bunch, M. (2000). *Beyond the limits: Mothers caring for children with disabilities.* North York, Ontario, Canada: Roeher Institute.

Freed, J., & Parsons, L. (1997). *Right-brained children in a left-brained world: Unlocking the potential of your ADD child.* New York: Simon & Schuster.

Freeman, J. M., Vining, E. P. G., & Pillas, D. J. (1990). *Seizures and epilepsy in childhood: A guide for parents.* Baltimore, MD: John Hopkins University Press.

Gardere, J. R. (2002). *Smart parenting for African Americans: Helping your kids thrive in a difficult world.* New York: Citadel Press.

Gottman, J., Declaire, J., & Goleman, D. (1998). *Raising an emotionally intelligent child.* New York: Simon & Schuster.

Haerle, T. (1992). *Children with Tourette syndrome: A parent's guide.* Rockville, MD: Woodbine House.

Hamaguchi, P. M. (1995). *Childhood speech, language and listening problems: What every parent should know.* Toronto: Wiley.

Harris, S. L. (1994). *Siblings of children with autism: A guide for families.* Bethesda, MD: Woodbine House.

Holmes, R. M. (1995). *How young children perceive race.* Thousand Oaks, CA: Sage.

Kirby, A. (1999). *Dyspraxia: The hidden handicap: A parents' guide from pre-school to adulthood.* London: Souvenir Press (Educational and Academic).

Kranowitz, C. S. (1998). *The out-of-sync child: Recognizing and coping with sensory integration dysfunction.* New York: Skylight Press.

Lash, M. (1991). *When your child is seriously injured: The emotional impact on families.* Boston: Tufts University, New England Medical Center.

Lindenmann, S., & Lindenmann, J. E. (1988). *Growing up proud: A parent's guide to the psychological care of children with disabilities.* New York: Warner Communications.

Lutkenhoff, M. (1999). *Children with spina bifida: A parents' guide.* Bethesda, MD: Woodbine House.

Mannheim, K. (1956). *Essays on the sociology of culture.* London: Routledge & Kegan Paul.

Mathias, B., & French, M. A. (1996). *40 ways to raise a nonracist child.* New York: HarperPerennial.

Medwid, D., & Weston, D. C. (1995). *Kid-friendly parenting with deaf and hard of hearing children.* Washington, DC: Gallaudet University Press.

Reddy, M. T., Ed. (1996). *Everyday acts against racism: Raising children in a multiracial world.* Seattle, WA: Seal Press.

Steinberg, G., & Hall, B. (2000). *Inside transracial adoption: Strength based, culture sensitizing parenting strategies for inter country or domestic adoptive families that don't match.* Indianapolis, IN: Perspectives Press.

Vazquez, C. I. (2005). *Parenting with pride Latino style: How to help your child cherish your cultural values and succeed in today's world.* New York: HarperCollins. (Also available in Spanish.)

The Online Companion™ to accompany the sixth edition of *Positive Child Guidance* is your link to additional guidance resources on the Internet. This supplement contains audio and visual materials; PowerPoint presentations; web activities with critical-thinking questions and practical-application assignments; and links to web resources. This additional content can be found at http://www.earlychilded.delmar.com.

Chapter 4

Understanding the Reasons for Problem Behavior

OBJECTIVES

After reading this chapter, you should be able to do the following:

- Define characteristics of inappropriate behavior.
- Articulate subjective perceptions of behavior.
- Recognize children's behavioral limitations according to normal stages of moral development.
- List underlying causes of problem behavior.
- Examine causes of misbehavior.
- Prevent misbehavior by correcting its cause.
- Reflect on your own temperament.

Wadsworth/Cengage Learning

Maturity and practice are needed for children to learn what adults expect of them.

Defining Problem Behavior

Through a process called **socialization** babies begin to learn what parents and others expect of them. Infants have no comprehension of proper or improper behavior. Early on, they would have no ability to inhibit their impulses even if they knew what was expected. Gradually over the first few years of life, however, children develop self-control and learn how to get along with others and how to follow the accepted rules of their family and community. Before self-control develops, children are totally impulsive in following their feelings and desires. They act like children (of course), making mistakes, acting on impulse, and stubbornly resisting external control, actions we consider to be problem behaviors. Chapter 1 identified three specific categories of problem behavior and recommended interrupting or redirecting any child behavior that

- infringed on the rights of others (be kind)
- presented a clear risk of harm to the child or anyone else (be safe)
- resulted in the mishandling of objects or living things (be neat)

Those three guidelines were used for defining basic ground rules for children: Be kind! Be safe! Be neat! Next, we need to ask ourselves why children might behave in an unkind, unsafe, or careless manner. **Misbehavior, problem behavior,** and **inappropriate behavior** are used interchangeably, and all three terms tend to be misinterpreted as meaning naughtiness and mischief. Many inappropriate behaviors, however, are not at all mischievous in intent. A child may not even realize that adults will consider a particular behavior naughty. Positive child guidance requires that adults gauge their reaction to misbehaviors by looking at the child's level of understanding, the severity and frequency of the behavior, and possible underlying causes.

A baby who has innocently climbed on top of a coffee table must be dealt with differently than a five-year-old who knowingly uses the couch as if it were a trampoline, although both must be redirected because the behaviors present a clear risk of harm to the children and involve the mishandling of objects in the environment. To get positive results, we must have reasonable expectations for children at various ages and recognize whether they can really be expected to control their actions in particularly difficult or tempting situations.

In many cases, it is far more effective to change the situation than to try to stop a child's behavior. By removing the baby from the coffee table and taking him to a safe piece of play equipment designed for climbing, we can change an inappropriate behavior to an appropriate behavior (even though the child may not yet recognize any difference in the two situations). We assume that the five-year-old knows the difference between a living room sofa and a trampoline, so our emphasis is on giving the child a clear understanding of pertinent facts, choices, and consequences. For example, we might say, "The couch is not for jumping. If you want to jump, you may jump outside on the soft grass." If the action continues, we should give the child our close, undivided attention at eye level and add in an assertive but sincere tone, "I know jumping on the couch is fun, but it could break the couch, or you could fall on something hard or sharp in here. If you jump on the couch again, you will not be allowed to play in the living room for the rest of the afternoon." Most importantly, we have to follow through and see that what we say will happen actually happens.

Assessing the appropriateness of any individual child's behavior requires us to step into his shoes and

socialization
The process by which children learn acceptable behavior.

misbehavior
Inappropriate, troublesome, and sometimes unsafe behavior.

problem behavior
Difficult and troubling behavior that requires planning and problem solving to resolve.

inappropriate behavior
Behavior that is out of place, immature, unproductive, or socially inept.

Wadsworth/Cengage Learning

■ We sometimes fail to see the world from the child's point of view.

see the world from his perspective and requires accurate insight and wise judgment. We are prone, sometimes quickly and flippantly, to label actions that are inconvenient, annoying, or embarrassing to us at the moment as misbehavior, regardless of reasons the child might have for behaving in such a manner.

Children are confused when they do not expect a negative reaction from us and when they cannot make sense of our logic in requiring different behaviors in different situations. They are bewildered when a behavior is praised in one setting but reprimanded in a situation they do not recognize as being very different. Mrs. Perez was exasperated with three of her toddlers, who persisted in climbing up on the picnic table in the toddler playground. She had not realized that the wood of the picnic table looked exactly like the wood of the climbing structure nearby. Although the adults could clearly see the differences between a climbing structure "fort" and a picnic table, a closer look would reveal that both objects are just boards nailed together. Young children's inexperience and naivete are just two of the many reasons they behave in ways that adults perceive as naughty.

What Do We Mean by Functional and Dysfunctional Behaviors?

dysfunctional
Inappropriate or self-destructive behavior not serving any positive or productive function in a child's life.

functional
Appropriate actions or behaviors that serve some productive or positive function in a child's activities and patterns of interactions.

When children evidence a compulsive and chronic pattern of inappropriate or self-destructive behavior, the behavior can be termed **dysfunctional.** In contrast, **functional** behaviors are appropriate actions that serve some productive or positive function in a child's life. Functional behaviors help a child get his needs met. Dysfunctional behaviors produce a negative reaction that may be opposite to the outcome desired by a child. The child's strategies for coping and for interacting with others do not work, causing the child increasing stress and unhappiness and creating a vicious cycle. A lonely child lacking in social skills may relentlessly tease other children to get their attention, but the teasing is dysfunctional because it does not attract friends; instead it causes the child to be disliked. Consequently, the child becomes more isolated and lonely, and even more trapped in the existing cycle of dysfunctional behavior.

The Adult-Centered Definition of Misbehavior

Adult-centered definitions of misbehavior focus on the effect a child's behavior has on the adult. Individual actions are evaluated according to the seriousness of their effect on things the adult cares about, as well as the adult's emotional state or mood. If a child spills his juice in the grass during a picnic, the adult may hardly notice because nothing has to be cleaned up. If the same child spills juice on the kitchen floor, the adult may be annoyed and may reprimand the child. If, however, the spill is grape juice on brand-new, light-colored dining room carpeting, the adult may be very angry and punish or spank the child.

The child learns that his behaviors are not always met with a consistent or predictable adult reaction. Children may learn that they can get away with inappropriate behaviors when their caregiver is in a relaxed and playful mood. They may also perceive that nothing they do makes any difference when the adult is in a bad mood. They may believe that they will get in trouble regardless of what they do or do not do. (Remember the definition of learned helplessness? We never want children to think they have no control over their circumstances, that things just happen to them randomly.)

Because adult-centered definitions of misbehavior focus only on the adult's needs and desires, desirable behaviors are perceived to be actions that are convenient and desirable to the adult. Being quiet, staying out of the way, and performing on cue the role of a cute (but undemanding) little kid may be seen as the hallmarks of a good child. Crying, squealing with joy, being frightened, or being a chatterbox may be perceived as naughty misbehaviors if they are annoying, embarrassing, or inconvenient for the adult.

The Child-Centered Definition of Misbehavior

[handwritten annotations: ability level, motives long-term well being; violates others; unsafe, damage]

In contrast, a child-centered definition of misbehavior focuses on the ability level, motives, and long-term well-being of the child in evaluating the appropriateness or inappropriateness of actions. If an action is wrong or inappropriate, it is judged to be wrong because it infringes on the rights of others, is unsafe, or is unnecessarily damaging to the environment, not because the action is a bother or because the adult happens to be in an intolerant mood. Defining behaviors this way brings about consistency and a sense of fairness. Children learn to be responsible for the consequences of their own actions. They learn that there is a direct relationship between their actions and the reaction they receive from authority figures. (Remember, no learned helplessness, please.)

By taking into consideration the ages and developmental stages of children, adults can recognize that exploring, or getting into things, is normal and beneficial learning behavior for a baby or toddler, not misbehavior. It is the adult's responsibility to childproof the environment so that everything accessible to the baby is safe and appropriate. If the baby gets into something inappropriate, the baby is simply moved to an area that is safe for exploration.

Children who are allowed to become actively involved in daily processes will undoubtedly make mistakes more often than children who are encouraged to stand by passively while things are done for them. Allowing young children to help with food preparation, for example, may be messy and time-consuming. It is quicker and easier for the adult to complete such tasks alone, but the confidence and

Wadsworth/Cengage Learning

■ Children explore the physical limitations of their world because they want to learn, not because they want to be naughty.

skill development children gain from such experiences are well worth the extra effort. Dropping an egg or inadvertently spilling flour are not seen as mischief from the child-centered perspective but rather as important opportunities for children to learn responsibility and independence. Instead of being scolded for making a mess, the child is taught how to accomplish daily tasks successfully and how to clean up after himself.

Stages of Moral Development in Young Children

A critical priority for parents, schools, communities, and even entire countries is the moral development of their children and future citizens. Morality is the ability to distinguish right from wrong and to act accordingly. Moral development is the process by which human beings learn to monitor their own actions and to decide whether a tempting behavior is a good or a bad thing to do and then to inhibit inappropriate impulses. In other words, morally developed people are able to stop themselves from doing things they know are wrong.

Although the guidance children receive early in life is essential to their moral development, moral behavior is not exclusively a concern of early childhood. Adults who are quick to respond harshly to a young child's misbehavior may forget their own difficulty in inhibiting the inappropriate impulses they have in their own daily lives. Even adults with well-developed morals experience difficulty resisting the temptation to gossip, smoke cigarettes, indulge in foods that are bad for them, or tell fibs to get out of tight spots. Remember that one of the key avenues for early childhood learning is imitation. It is essential for adult caregivers in their day-to-day actions to consciously set the best possible example of integrity and strong moral character (Grusec et al., 1979; Toner et al., 1978; Toner & Potts, 1981).

As children observe adult behaviors and experience the cause-and-effect sequences that are a part of interacting with others, they internalize (adopt as their own) the character attributes and ethical standards of the important role models in their lives. Attachment, love, and respect for an adult trigger the child's internalization of that adult's values. When a child has internalized the standards of his adult role models, he begins to experience the emotional component of morality, or **moral affect** (the feelings associated with a guilty or clear conscience). Having moral affect means that when he behaves in a way that he knows to be wrong, he has feelings of guilt and shame. When he behaves properly, he feels pride. Moral affect serves as an internal regulator that guides a child or adult toward appropriate behavior and away from misbehavior.

Feelings of guilt play a role in regulating moral behavior, but it is not helpful to push guilt on a child by saying such things as "Aren't you ashamed of yourself, you naughty boy?" Forcing guilt on a young child may actually harden him emotionally and delay his development of moral affect. Conscience that comes from inside us is always more meaningful than guilt imposed on us by someone else. Two specific child-rearing practices are known to help children internalize values and prosocial moral judgment:

moral affect
The ability to feel guilt or shame—feelings associated with a guilty or clear conscience indicate whether behavior was appropriate and guide one to choose appropriate or desired behaviors.

- nurturing and affectionate adult guidance
- consistency in explaining reasons for rules and expectations

Adults help children develop moral behavior by being loving and gentle and by putting into words the rationales for imperatives. Instead of just saying, for example, "Don't touch that!" they say, "Please use a different crayon because that one belongs to someone else" (Eisenberg-Berg, 1979).

Another important component of moral development is **moral reasoning.** The way children think about right and wrong changes dramatically as their intellectual capacity matures (Piaget, 1952). Children younger than seven tend to focus on the concrete consequences of actions rather than on the abstract motivations or intentions behind them. As they get older and their moral capacity increases, they are better able to take into consideration complicated rationales for various actions (Ferguson & Rule, 1982).

moral reasoning
The thinking processes that guide people in deciding what is or is not moral behavior.

> We must see childhood as a stage of life, not just the anteroom to life.
>
> *David Elkind (1981)*

Components of Moral Development

Berkowitz and Grych (1998) described four components of moral development: empathy, conscience, altruism, and moral reasoning.

Empathy

To develop empathy in young children, talk frequently with them about behavior and feelings. Talk about the consequences of their positive and negative actions on others. Help children identify and talk about how others' actions affect them. Empathy has been identified by Kagan (1984) as one of the "core moral emotions." Damon (1988) considers it "one of morality's primary emotional supports" (p. 14) and argues that, "because morality is fundamentally concerned with one's obligations to others, it cannot be developed solely through introspection and recognition of one's inner feelings. . . . Children must learn to become attuned not only to their own emotional reactions but also to those of others" (p. 128).

Conscience

A powerful influence on children's moral development is something researchers call **induction.** Induction is the process of stimulating children's understanding of the reasons for choosing one behavior over another by thinking about the effect that behavior will have on another person. When children disobey, adults have the opportunity to teach children what is right and wrong and, more importantly, *why* certain behaviors are preferable to others. This rather simple process is a powerful force for shaping children's moral development because it helps children internalize standards for moral behavior. As Lickona (1983, p. 22) points out, children "need to see us lead good lives, but they also need to know why we do it. Children develop a conscience best in an environment of mutual respect, empathy, and affection." Parents and early

induction
The process of inducing a state, feeling, or idea. Here we are inviting the child to think through the cause–effect sequence to understand better why certain behaviors hurt others, are unsafe, or damage the environment.

childhood professionals can support conscience development by making sure children know that they are willing to listen, really care about the children's feelings, and respect the children's individual needs and interests (Hoffman & Saltzstein, 1967; Kochanska & Aksan, 1995; Kochanska, 1997; Allinsmith & Greening, 1955).

Altruism

To support the development of altruism (generosity with no motive of personal gain), consistently use an authoritative guidance style (Baumrind, 1971). Regularly talk with children about the differences between right and wrong (Zahn-Waxler et al., 1979). Oliner and Oliner (1988) found that altruistic adults were motivated by "values learned from their parents which prompted and sustained their involvement" (p. 143).

Moral Reasoning

Authoritative guidance, especially with its focus on open, supportive communication, most effectively nurtures children's moral-reasoning development. Parents' promotion of induction, expression of nurturance and support, use of limit-setting, modeling of sociomoral behavior, and reliance on democratic open discussion and conflict-resolution style are positively related to the foundation of morality (Baumrind 1967, 1980; Hoffman & Saltzstein, 1967).

How Do Young Children Learn Right from Wrong?

Sarah, a four-year-old, was told that Jimmy broke four plates and three glasses while trying to help, and Annie broke one cookie jar lid while trying to steal cookies. She insisted that Jimmy was naughtier and deserved more punishment than Annie. Sarah has focused on the idea that breaking a lot of dishes is worse than breaking one dish. The child is not yet able to think about all aspects of the dilemmas presented or to consider such things as motive. Piaget (1952) studied children's sense of right and wrong through a series of interviews in which he confronted children of various ages with moral problems such as the one in the preceding description. He found that young children's responses contrasted sharply with the responses of older children. The moral reasoning of young children tends to be simplistic and limited to enforcing the letter of the law (or rule) rather than interpreting the spirit, or intent, of the law.

Kohlberg (1969, 1976) described the stages through which human beings develop moral reasoning. He describes three levels and six stages.

Kohlberg's Theory of Moral Development (Birth to Nine Years)
Level One—Preconventional Morality

- Stage One: The child obeys rules only to avoid punishment and to gain rewards. For example, a toddler examining an electric outlet may reach for it, then look up at the adult while saying, "No, no. No touch." The toddler will probably resist the urge to touch the outlet only if the adult appears attentive and ready to enforce the rule (or if the child has unfortunately discovered the pain of an electric shock).

- Stage Two: The child bargains to have her needs met. Prosocial behaviors are intended to bring about favors from others. For example, "If you let me ride the tricycle, I'll be your best friend."

Level Two—Conventional Morality (Nine Years to Young Adulthood)

- Stage Three: There is an emphasis on gaining approval by being "nice" or "good"—the focus is on getting positive attention from authority figures. For example, when an adult tells one child to taste just a bite of green beans, another child nearby may hurriedly stuff her mouth full of beans, saying, "See me? I'm eating my vegetables!"

Young children lack the self-control necessary to consistently control their impulses.

- Stage Four: The focus is on law and order. At this stage, the child is concerned that everyone do his duty and follow the letter of the law. It is okay to break a rule only if everyone else is doing it. For example, school-age children become very indignant when rules are broken. They may resent that a child suffering from diabetes is given a candy bar by the teacher. Never mind that the child is ill; it is just not right. Adults sometimes rely on conventional morality when they say, "I can't let you do this, or I would have to let everyone do it." They are assuming that "a rule is a rule," and there could never be a moral reason to deviate from the rule or make an exception.

Level Three—Postconventional Morality (Adulthood)

- Stage Five: At this stage, correct behavior is defined in terms of individual rights according to widely held moral beliefs of society. For example, a teacher at this level would recognize that the urgent health need of a child with diabetes is more important than the usual fair and reasonable rules about candy at school. Protecting the health of a child is more valued in this situation than following a rule.
- Stage Six: Individuals decide whether a behavior is moral on the basis of a personal decision of conscience in accordance with personal ethical principles that are logical, consistent, and universal. For example, a child care center director might risk the solvency of her business by testifying in accordance with her conscience in a child abuse case against a powerful and popular community member.

A New Perspective on Moral Development

Carol Gilligan brought an important, new approach to studying moral development. She started as a research assistant for Lawrence Kohlberg, but after studying his theories, became critical of his work because he studied only privileged white men and boys. She believed his stage theory of moral development represented a male perspective, which more highly valued individual rights and rules than would a woman's point of view. She thought females were more likely to value caring in human relationships and that Kohlberg's theories were skewed by gender bias.

Gilligan carried out her own studies and found that women were taught to care for other people and to expect others to care for them. She helped to form a new psychology for women by listening to women and girls and rethinking the meaning of self and selfishness. She outlined three stages of moral development progressing from selfish to social, or conventional, morality and finally to postconventional, or principled, morality (Gilligan, 1982).

Gilligan found that the male approach to morality assumes that individuals have certain basic rights and that you must respect the rights of others, thus morality imposes restrictions on what you can do. The female approach to morality assumes that people have responsibility toward others, so morality is an imperative to care for others. Gilligan summarizes this by saying that male morality assumes a **justice orientation** and female morality assumes a **responsibility orientation.**

She believed that girls and women needed to learn to tend to their own interests and to the interests of others. She found that women and girls were often hesitant to judge others because they were more likely to see the complexities of interpersonal relationships. Gilligan noticed that boys were more likely to argue through a dispute so that they could finish a game, but girls were more likely to simply stop and choose to do something different to keep from arguing and hurting each others' feelings.

Some scientists have criticized Gilligan's research methods, just as she criticized Kohlberg. But Kohlberg did change his research methods so that he included more diversity in his research subjects in his later studies. Gilligan opened the door to a wide range of gender studies that are ongoing and open our minds daily to the individual needs of girls and boys (Kimmel, 2004, 2000; Ruble & Martin, 1998; Sheldon, 1990).

One distinct characteristic of more advanced levels of moral reasoning is the ability to consider motivation and intention when evaluating the outcome of a behavior. Young children rarely achieve this, but adult caregivers must achieve this if they wish to be effective in positive child guidance. Adults who blindly enforce rules just because rules are rules, regardless of circumstances, motives, or effects on individual children, are also functioning at a low level of moral development. Adults who enforce rules only when it is convenient or in their own best interest to do so are also functioning at a very low level of moral behavior. Morally mature adults focus on the intents and motives of children, not on the outcomes of their behaviors. If, for example, Alicia tries to knock someone off the jungle gym but no one gets hurt, and Albert is being silly and accidentally knocks someone off who is hurt badly, the morally mature adult will recognize that Alicia's behavior was more inappropriate than Albert's.

justice orientation
Perspective in which integrity tends to be the dominant moral compass for making autonomous, independent, and *self-oriented* ethical and principled decisions.

responsibility orientation
Perspective in which sensitivity to others, loyalty, responsibility, self-sacrifice, and peacemaking reflect *interpersonal* involvement and caring and ethical and moral decision making.

Methods to Support Children's Moral Development

Berkowitz and Grych (1998) identified four key methods to support children's moral development. They urged parents and teachers to provide nurturing and support, set limits, model appropriate behavior, and teach democratic decision making and discussion.

Provide Nurturing and Support

Authoritative guidance supports the development of morality (Baumrind, 1980). Baumrind's research showed that authoritative guidance fosters social sensitivity, self-awareness, and respect for rules and authority (Baumrind, 1978; Damon, 1988). Authoritative child guidance provides a perfect balance of nurturing and limit-setting, and it is both gentle and firm. This style of guidance is very different from authoritarian disciplinary interactions with children, which tend to be more negative and sometimes antagonistic or combative (Berkowitz & Gibbs, 1983). Warm, responsive guidance communicates to children that they are valued and appreciated. As children learn they are worthy of such treatment, their self-esteem blossoms. They also learn that people in general deserve respectful treatment and that it is wrong to hurt others. Authoritative adults routinely discuss moral issues with children in a respectful and emotionally supportive way (Powers, 1982; Walker & Taylor, 1991).

Set Limits

An important part of authoritative parenting is something called **demandingness.** Effective demandingness requires three major ingredients.

demandingness
Requiring certain behaviors from children. Having high expectations for children that are reasonable and supported with encouragement and optimism.

1. Adults must set high but realistic goals. Children whose parents have low expectations for them develop low expectations for themselves. Children whose parents set unreasonably high expectations for them become overstressed, frustrated, or angry and may develop a sense of inadequacy.
2. Adults must help children achieve reasonable expectations by carefully supporting, encouraging, and monitoring progress.
3. Adults must provide consistent follow-up to evaluate whether children achieve the goals. Children recognize when expectations will be forgotten if they stall long enough. High but reasonable standards that are consistently and caringly enforced will help the child develop self-control and self-esteem.

Model Appropriate Behavior

How we live our lives in front of children, how we treat others, and how we handle our own frustrations and problems all shape children's behavior (Lickona, 1983, p. 20). Children observe the adults in their lives and imitate their behavior. Adults can model respect and compassion toward others, or they can model behavior that is harmful and abusive by belittling, coercing, or physically dominating others (Grych & Fincham, 1990, 1993). Even if children do not directly imitate the specific behaviors they observe, their beliefs and attitudes about how to treat other people may well be shaped by these experiences. The fact that these lessons are unintended makes them no less powerful. Adults who model prosocial behaviors teach their children to treat others with respect (Damon, 1988).

Teach Democratic Decision Making and Discussion

Teach children to rely on group processes—negotiation, consensus, compromise, and discussion—to solve problems. Decisions and rules developed this way are more likely to be just, and participating in the process helps children learn the skills necessary to function in a democracy (Power, Higgins, & Kohlberg, 1989). Using democratic processes produces compliance, moral reasoning development, conscience, high self-esteem, and altruism in children (Lickona, 1983). Children begin to develop a "fairness" approach.

To learn more, read:

Berkowitz, M. W. (1997). The complete moral person: Anatomy and formation. In J. M. DuBois (Ed.), *Moral issues in psychology: Personalist contributions to selected problems* (11–42). Lanham, MD: University Press of America.

Berkowitz, M. W., & Grych, J. H. (1998). Fostering goodness: Teaching parents to facilitate children's moral development. *Journal of Moral Education, 27*(3), 371–391. Retrieved February 25, 2006, from http://parenthood.library.wisc.edu/.

Colby, A., & Damon, W. (1992). *Some do care: Contemporary lives of moral commitment.* New York: Free Press.

Temperament

What Is Temperament?

Temperament theory attempts to identify and explain inborn traits that organize a person's approach to the world. Why does an event motivate one person but cause another person in the same situation agonizing stress? Knowing temperament patterns helps us identify children's core needs and helps identify potential talents we may assist them in developing. Temperament traits are considered instrumental in the development of a person's distinct personality. The traits that make up temperament have a profound effect on a child's style of interacting with people and things in his environment. From infancy, the traits help shape a child's distinctive approach to learning about the world around him.

The study of temperament dates back more than 25 centuries. People have struggled to understand how people can be so different—even siblings who grow up side by side. In 450 BC, Hippocrates described four dispositions he called temperaments:

- *Choleric*—Easily aroused and sensitive
- *Phlegmatic*—Coolly detached and impassive

- *Melancholic*—Very serious, dour, and downcast
- *Sanguine*—Impulsive, excitable, and reactive

During the Middle Ages, astrologers theorized that temperaments were influenced by spirits—nymphs, sylphs, gnomes, and salamanders. Most 20th-century psychologists began to think that human beings were similar in their potential, and individual differences were due primarily to chance or conditioning (Berens, 2000; Kagan et al., 1998).

A major breakthrough in the study of temperament came in 1942 with the emergence of the Myers–Briggs Type Indicator (MBTI), an assessment that could identify and score distinct differences in adult temperament. Although it has been revised over the years, this test is still widely used today to provide insight for people from adolescence through adulthood.

Isabel Myers and Katharine Briggs based their theory of temperament on the systematic classification of personality types originally created by Carl Jung. Myers and Briggs believed that temperament differences shaped the way people thought, especially in the way they made judgments. Myers and Briggs identified **perceiving** as the process of becoming aware of things, people, occurrences, and ideas. They defined **judging** as the process of using *perceptions* to create conclusions. They believed that, together, perception and judgment governed most of a person's outward behavior (Berens, 2000; Kagan, 1998).

perceiving
Becoming aware of, by direct use of senses; noticing; or understanding in one's own mind.

judging
The process of using perceptions to create conclusions.

Wadsworth/Cengage Learning

■ Any group of children presents a range of temperaments—contemplative, sensitive, animated, fretful, resilient, anxious, and myriad others.

In the 1980s, David Keirsey refined these theories. He distinguished four patterns—Sensing Judger, Sensing Perceiver, Intuitive Feeler, and Intuitive Thinker. The assessments of these four categories examine pairs of opposing characteristics. For example, perceiving and judging measure whether a person tends to perceive information neutrally or to quickly form opinions. Thinking and feeling measures whether a person tends to allow her head or her heart to rule in making decisions. Keirsey believed these four patterns describe the basic human temperament—the way human personality interacts with the environment (Keirsey, 1998):

- *Sensing Judger* (SJ)—Thrives in stable and predictable environments, with clear reporting hierarchies and a high level of responsibility
- *Sensing Perceiver* (SP)—Prefers jobs with a great deal of variety and change, where each day offers a new challenge
- *Intuitive Feeler* (NF)—Enjoys work that is personally meaningful and rewarding, with a positive influence on other people
- *Intuitive Thinker* (NT)—Prefers work environments full of high intellectual pursuits and new technologies

Human beings are complex, and experts have devised many different ways to look at and understand our inner workings. One temperament assessment designates 16 personality types. Another focuses on the qualities of introvert versus extrovert. In reality, my multifaceted personality can't be reduced to a neat, easy-to-read category on a chart, and neither can yours—but a chart might help me discover some useful things about myself.

Using assessment testing to learn more about your own temperament type can help you notice things you didn't realize about yourself, including what you need in your surroundings to be truly satisfied. Knowledge about your own temperament can also pinpoint for you why you may have more success in guiding one child than another.

How Do Infants Show Differences in Temperament?

Mary Rothbart developed a Measurement of Temperament in Infancy that assessed areas of infant temperament such as activity level, soothability, fear, distress when faced with limitations, smiling and laughing, and length of time paying attention to single objects (Rothbart & Derryberry, 1981; Rothbart et al., 2000).

Here is a summary of Rothbart's assessment list:

- *Activity Level*—Constantly moves arms and legs, squirms
- *Distress to Limitations*—Fusses, cries, or shows distress when in a confining position, being cared for, or unable to perform a desired action
- *Approach*—Approaches objects quickly, shows excitement and positive anticipation of pleasurable activities
- *Fear*—Startles and becomes upset at sudden changes, novel objects, or new people; inhibited approach to novelty
- *Duration of Orienting*—Pays attention to or interacts with a single object for long periods

- *Smiling and Laughter*—Smiles and laughs easily in caregiving and play situations
- *Vocal Reactivity*—Frequently vocalizes (cooing, babbling, and making early attempts at words) during daily activities
- *Sadness*—Experiences low moods or lowered moods because of discomfort, because an object is lost, or because of an inability to perform a desired action
- *Perceptual Sensitivity*—Detects slight, low-intensity stimuli from the external environment
- *High-Intensity Pleasure*—Enjoys high-intensity stimulus (finds pleasure in varying rate, complexity, novelty, and incongruity)
- *Low-Intensity Pleasure*—Prefers low-intensity stimulus (may be upset by too much variation in rate, complexity, novelty, and incongruity)
- *Cuddliness*—Enjoys being held by a caregiver and molds body to caregiver's
- *Soothability*—Reduces fussing, crying, or distress when the caregiver uses soothing techniques
- *Falling Reactivity or Rate of Recovery from Distress*—Recovers quickly from distress or excitement; falls asleep easily

Rothbart's inventory is useful in helping identify differences in babies' temperaments so we can better address their needs. The better we know the children in our care, the better we can meet their individual needs and guide their behavior.

What Has Jerome Kagan's Research Taught Us about Temperament?

Jerome Kagan (2004), a retired professor emeritus at Harvard and considered one of the top psychologists of the 20th century, has devised an interesting test. Present a four-month-old baby with a series of colorful new toys—ones she's never seen before—one after another, for 20 seconds each. Does she stare calmly and wait for more toys or start crying madly and shaking her arms and legs? If the baby finds this experience extremely distressing, Kagan found she was at higher risk for developing anxiety over social interactions as she grows older.

Kagan also found that although the baby who calmly accepts more toys was more likely to experience a future of relaxed and comfortable social interactions, she was at slightly more risk for getting into trouble later because she may be unfazed by warnings from parents and teachers.

Kagan and associates (1999) carried out their study of temperament by dangling toys in front of

Wadsworth/Cengage Learning

Jerome Kagan studied temperament by studying the reaction of four-month-old babies. Researchers presented the babies with a series of colorful new toys—ones they had never seen before—one after another, for 20 seconds at a time. If a baby became extremely upset by this activity, they discovered that she was more likely to have social anxiety later in her life.

500 babies. Twenty percent of the babies showed distressed "crying and vigorous pumping of the legs and arms, sometimes with arching of the back" on at least 40 percent of the trials. These were described as high reactive. Forty percent showed little motion or emotion and were described as low reactive. The remaining babies' reactions fell somewhere in the middle.

Many of the children from the original test were given follow-up tests at 2, 4, and 7 years of age. Then 237 of these children, at some point between the ages of 10 and 12, were given a full battery of brain scans, heart-rate analyses, and body-temperature readings, both at rest and during moments of stress (such as when they were asked without warning to give a speech).

Kagan's key finding was that about 20 percent of the children who had been labeled high reactives as infants still did not like things that were new and strange as they grew older. They gave off biologic signals indicating they were stressed when they were confronted with unexpected situations. The quality that had been labeled high reactive when they were infants was now manifested in these children as shyness.

Kagan found that the third of the children who had been labeled low reactives as infants remained calm and relaxed in the face of strange situations as they grew older. The study also established that as they grew up many infants drifted away from the extreme and toward more moderate temperaments—a sign of the importance of parents and the children's environment, Kagan explained. Only a few infants, 5 percent in each category, switched to the opposite extreme in temperament as they grew up.

How Can We Support the Spirited Child?

In her book *Raising Your Spirited Child,* Mary Sheedy Kurcinka (1991) identifies five temperament traits that children she described as spirited often have in common. Compared with the typical child, these children are more intense, persistent, sensitive, perceptive, and slow to adapt to new situations. Also, according to Kurcinka, many but not all spirited children also may seem irregular in their day-to-day patterns, exceptionally energetic, cautious in new surroundings, and unusually serious.

Here are some typical characteristics of challenging children and some suggestions:

Intensity

- Laughs and cries loudly
- May shriek so loudly in play that it is almost overwhelming for parents and teachers
- Can become extremely upset
- Is physically passionate and dramatic
- Is very easily frustrated
- May take toys from others
- Can experience emotional meltdown at the drop of a hat
- May be prone to fiery name-calling or swearing
- Can create earsplitting disturbances when he doesn't get his own way

To Bring Down the Volume

- Pay close attention to the child's cues.
- Intervene before the child's intensity builds too high.
- Change the scene.
- Learn what kinds of things sent her intensity spiraling so they can be prevented.
- Learn what kinds of things effectively calm her so those activities can be made available.
- Put on soothing background music.
- Initiate a relaxing physical activity (for example, walk, jump rope, climb, swing, rock a doll).
- Introduce a pleasurable project that takes concentration (for example, put together a puzzle, paint a box, feed the rabbit, cut strawberries for snack).
- Provide some relaxing one-on-one attention to get the child talking about her feelings.
- Find and tap into the child's natural sense of humor (for example, invite all the children to show their funniest face, ask who can jump like a bunny, or pretend you are confused about something the children know the answer to: "Hey, why doesn't this shoe fit my foot?" "Ha, ha, ha! That's Jimmy's shoe, not yours!").

Persistence

- Has a really hard time taking no for an answer
- Because he is so sure he is right, he may argue to his last breath, "But why not? Huh? Why not?"
- Has a one-track mind; once she is committed to an activity or project it is extremely difficult to get her to move on to anything else
- Often has his own mental plan of how everything should be (for example, he can become distraught when his mental plan doesn't match reality: "I expected my peanut butter sandwich in triangles, but you cut it in squares.")
- Wants to do everything independently and persists in spite of obvious difficulties

To Avoid Power Struggles

- Remember that persistence is a positive virtue; honor every child's uniqueness.
- Pick your battles wisely, prioritize expectations, and stay focused.
- Try to find acceptable ways to make no into yes through appropriate compromise (for example, "It would not be safe for you to do that, but what if we did this instead? How would that be?").
- Frequently talk with the spirited child to ask about her plans and expectations so she won't be surprised.
- Help the child find stopping points by giving a five-minute warning before clean-up time, a reminder that playtime will be over in three minutes, and a heads-up that as soon as the book is finished it will be time for a nap.

- Allow flexibility in scheduling so that children who need longer periods with the same learning project can be protected and encouraged in their concentration.
- Don't allow external interruptions to interfere with the child's natural patterns of persistence (for example, turn off the television, radio, and phone during mealtimes, homework, chore time).
- Stay focused on basic ground rules—be safe, be kind, be neat.
- Kurcinka (1991) suggests breaking the standoff of a tug-of-war by asking the child to "give you five" (that is, give you five alternative ideas so together you can choose one on which you both agree). For a very young child or a child with a disability, you may offer to help the child think of the five alternatives.

Sensitivity

- Probably becomes overstimulated by parties, crowds, shopping malls, and amusement parks
- May have food likes and dislikes, perhaps taking pickiness to the extreme
- Often overreacts to smells, sounds, lights, and textures in the environment
- May be overly sensitive to the moods of others around her
- Can become disproportionately annoyed by seams in his underwear or tags in his shirts

Wadsworth/Cengage Learning

■■■ To avoid a power struggle, make sure to go to the child and give him a personal heads-up that play time will be over in five minutes. You might give him another warning at three minutes. Then, when time is up, ease the anticipated problem by making a game out of the parking the tricycles. "The fire trucks are lining up in the firehouse. RRRRRRRRRRR!" Talk about the following activity. If this transition is often a problem, schedule the following activity to be one the child especially likes, such as a snack or painting.

To Boost Coping

- Talk with the child to help her describe and label the sensations she feels.
- Model appropriate oral expression of feelings in "I" messages when you are feeling frustrated, tired, or annoyed.
- Affirm the legitimacy of the child's feelings (that is, feelings are not right or wrong, they are just feelings).
- Try to eliminate or avoid triggers that irritate the sensitive child.
- Change the environment to reduce triggers that can't be avoided.
- Let the child practice coping with triggers that can't be changed—when he is ready and at his own pace.

Perceptiveness

- Is very easily distracted
- Finds it hard to focus with other things going on
- Because of scattered concentration, often loses things
- Forgets what he was doing because something else catches his attention
- High levels of curiosity and attentiveness force him to notice every detail
- Becomes exhausted when he does become absorbed in long periods of uninterrupted concentration

To Channel Focus

- Modify the environment to reduce distractions.
- Get down at eye level and make eye contact when you give instructions.
- Give simple, one-step instructions and follow-up to ensure she doesn't become distracted.
- If telling her doesn't work, show her (demonstrate for her) what you expect.

intervention plan & case study info.

Adaptability

- Has a hard time coping with changes in environment, routine, schedule, food, and important people
- May dig heels in and refuse to comply with adult requests, becoming negative even when it doesn't make sense (for example, "Do you want some ice cream?" "No!!")
- Can seem obstinate, bossy, and stubborn at times
- May be quick to irritation and slow to get over being angry

To Alleviate Stress

- Plan flexible classroom scheduling that eliminates nonessential transitions by allowing children to move from learning center to learning center at their own pace.
- Talk with the child ahead of time about plans and give him time warnings before transitions.
- Role-play and rehearse changes and new activities in advance.
- Give him adequate time and encouragement to deal with the process of stopping and moving through a transition to a new activity.

mighty minutes songs

Wadsworth/Cengage Learning

Even within the same family, siblings can show dramatic differences in temperament.

- Acknowledge his feelings and encourage him to express himself in words.
- Sometimes it helps to sit down and start the new activity with the child to help him adapt to the new activity with less stress.

Think about and evaluate your own intensity, persistence, sensitivity, perceptiveness, and ability to adapt to new situations. Temperament may have a hereditary component from one or both parents. What happens if a spirited adult is matched with a spirited child? What happens if an easy-going adult is matched with a spirited child? A spirited adult with an easy-going child?

Understanding a child's temperament as well as your own can help you avoid pitfalls and develop discipline strategies that match individual children in specific situations. You can gain insight into why a child behaves the way she does in certain circumstances. You might also begin to understand why certain child behaviors intensely irritate and exasperate you.

Knowing what to expect gives you power over situations. Instead of being surprised and taken off guard, thinking the child's behavior is intended personally to annoy you, you can step back and remember why the child is behaving the way she is.

Remember, if we can forecast a child's looming breakdown, we can plan for it and, perhaps, even avoid it. Knowing more about what makes a child tick emotionally enables us to help the child learn the skills she needs to get along successfully in the world.

Underlying Causes of Problem Behavior

Lying on a couch and watching cartoons for hours on end is not a desirable use of a child's time. To redirect the behavior, an adult may need to think through any potential reasons the child is not involved in healthier, more active play. Is the child reinforced for being quiet and passive? Does the adult respond negatively to active play that is sometimes messy or noisy? Are interesting toys and challenging play equipment accessible to the child? Does the child need someone with whom to play? Adults must always take into account possible reasons for undesirable behavior to have a chance at changing the situation and preventing the behavior from happening. In child guidance, as in health care, the best cure is always prevention.

Inappropriate Expectations

Sometimes, children's misbehavior is the direct result of inappropriate expectations on the part of adults. We expect children to be able to do things that they are not capable of doing.

Helena and Ray are sitting in the pediatrician's waiting room with their 18-month-old son, Billy. The little boy is dressed in his very best clothes and wearing shiny black shoes and a tiny bow tie. He is sitting on his dad's knee looking like a fashion model for baby clothes. Billy sits silently for a while, then looks around at the room and at his mom and dad, who are preoccupied in their discussion of the questions they want to ask Billy's doctor.

After a few more minutes of sitting, Billy points to a large aquarium with huge tropical fish swimming around and says, "Yook!" (his word for *look*). After a few seconds, he gestures insistently and looks at his mother, repeating, "Yook, wha' dis?" (What's this?). Helena straightens Billy's tie and says, "Yes, they're fish. Shhh, be still now. You'll get your clothes all messed up."

Billy stares at the aquarium a few seconds longer, then scrambles to get down off his dad's lap. His dad pulls him back in his lap and says firmly, "Those aren't for you to touch. You need to stay here and sit still. If you get down, you'll break something for sure." Billy begins to whine and rub his eyes with his fist, periodically struggling to get down from his dad's lap. His mother pulls a bottle out of her diaper bag and offers it to Billy, but he throws the bottle on the floor and begins kicking and crying loudly.

As the nurse comes in to announce that the doctor is ready to see Billy, Helena and Ray seem to be at their wit's end. With great frustration in her voice, Helena says, "Why does he act like this? What are you supposed to do when they get like this? He's just impossible to deal with sometimes."

Little can be done to resolve the situation at this point except to remove Billy from the setting and wait for him to wind down. A great deal, however, could have been done to prevent the situation. If Helena and Ray had known in advance more about what to expect from a toddler, they might have anticipated that he really could not sit still for 30 minutes to an hour.

Perhaps they could have brought one of his favorite toys or books with them, or they could have distracted him by playing peek-a-boo or by allowing him to scribble on a notepad from his mother's purse. Or perhaps his dad could have followed up on his interest in the aquarium by supervising him closely and talking with him about the fish as he looked at and touched the aquarium.

Misunderstanding Expectations

Sometimes, children misunderstand what is expected of them.

Miss Jean, a preschool teacher, was dismayed to discover that her preschoolers had left the bathroom in a mess. Water was all over the floor and paper towels were everywhere except in the trash can. She turned to three-year-old Misha and said, "I'm going to go get a mop. Can you please put all of the paper towels into the trash can where they belong?"

When Miss Jean returned with her mop, she found poor little Misha struggling to pull clean paper towels out of the dispenser and stuffing them by the handfuls into the trash can. In a pitiful voice, Misha said, "It too much, Teacher. It too much paper towels."

(Continued)

Luckily, Miss Jean recognized that although the outcome of Misha's behavior was not the desired one, her intentions were good. Misha simply took her teacher's instructions literally when she said, "Put all the paper towels into the trash can." Miss Jean had not specified "wet paper towels on the floor."

Miss Jean thanked Misha warmly for trying to help and then proceeded to say matter-of-factly, "Let's put the wet, dirty paper towels in the trash can. The dry ones are good for us to use next time we wash."

If Miss Jean had scolded Misha or snapped, "Now look what you've done, you silly thing," Misha might not have been so eager to cooperate the next time someone asked her to help. Instead, she would have felt shamed for her good intentions, hard work, and inability to read the adult's mind.

Immature Self-Control

Sometimes, it seems that children really want to abide by an adult's request, but somehow they just cannot seem to manage the self-control needed to accomplish what the adult expects.

Eloise provides child care for four children in her licensed family day home. She is committed to being an early childhood educator, not just a babysitter. To help her children learn about science and nature, she has bought a baby guinea pig.

The guinea pig caused a flurry of excitement on Monday morning as the children arrived for the day. Eloise sat by the cage with the two toddlers on her lap and talked with the two preschool-age children about the new pet. While the guinea pig ran around in circles making high squealing sounds, the boys decided that he should be named Squeaky.

Eloise explained that Squeaky would be frightened if people made too much noise or shook his cage. She also explained that, although Squeaky was very gentle, he might be confused if he saw a finger sticking into his cage and try to nibble on it. The children talked excitedly about Squeaky and tried to keep their hands behind their backs or in their pockets so they would not forget about shaking the cage or sticking their fingers through the bars.

Eloise stepped into the bathroom to help one of the toddlers. Suddenly she heard a commotion with shrieks and squeals. The children had gotten a bit too excited and had accidentally tipped the cage off the table. Squeaky was running around squealing, the children were running around shrieking, the toddlers had started crying, and water and guinea pig food were spilled everywhere.

Eloise quickly captured the terrified guinea pig and then, gently stroking the shaking Squeaky, said in a calm voice, "Listen boys and girls, can you hear the little sound Squeaky is making? He's very scared. Let's sing a quiet lullaby to Squeaky so he won't be frightened." Softly, the older children joined Eloise in singing "Rock-a-Bye Baby" to little Squeaky. The toddlers watched wide-eyed. When everyone was calm and quiet, Eloise put Squeaky back into his cage and said, "We'll put Squeaky's cage in the storage room for a while so he can rest. After naptime, we'll get him out and watch him again."

Eloise realized that the children had not maliciously intended to harm or frighten Squeaky; they were so excited that they could not manage the necessary self-control to deal with the situation successfully. Eloise felt confident that with enough time, patience, and practice, the children could eventually develop the self-control they needed to watch the guinea pig properly. She also knew that until that time, she needed to remove Squeaky, except during the times that she was able to supervise the children very closely as they watched him. Eloise recognized that reprimanding or punishing the children for their lack of self-control was not appropriate or helpful, because the children, at that point, were not yet capable of behaving in a more mature or controlled way. Instead, she helped them identify with Squeaky's feelings and needs so they could understand why they needed to watch without touching. She also knew that it was better to change the environment temporarily rather than trying to change the children's behavior.

Children's innate desire to explore every possibility around them stretches their learning, but also stretches adult patience.

Gleeful Abandon, Group Contagion

Close your eyes for a minute and try to remember the exhilarated sensations you felt as a young child at a terrific birthday party, in a basement full of laughing cousins at a big family celebration, or maybe at a school Halloween carnival. Can you remember you and your friends or siblings going a little berserk? You knew you would get a stern lecture from your parents later, but it just felt so good you could not stop yourself. Whenever we have come to the end of our rope with gleeful, goofy children, it may help for us to pause for a second and remember those magical moments in our own childhoods. I know I would love to feel that way again—totally uninhibited and free.

Tuesday mornings are always lively at the Elm Street Public Library. The sleepy little library comes to life as neighborhood children troop in for the children's story hour.

Mrs. Asaad, the children's librarian, spends hours choosing just the right books and practicing reading them to make sure her program is interesting and fun for the children. One Tuesday morning, Mrs. Asaad helped a very young group of children get seated on the floor and ready for story time. She began singing a song about three little ducks.

One of the preschoolers folded his hands under his armpits (to make duck wings) and helped her with the "quack, quack, quack" part of the song. The other preschoolers caught on and began wagging their arms and quacking too. The first quacking preschooler

(Continued)

began giggling and falling over on the floor. Of course, all the other preschoolers imitated by giggling and falling down and kicking their feet in the air.

Mrs. Asaad finished her song and good-naturedly helped Chris, the preschooler who appeared to be the leader of the gang, to sit up. "Are you ready to hear a story about a little duck named Ping?" she asked. Chris vigorously nodded his head and shouted yes. Of course all of the other preschooler began vigorously nodding their heads too.

Mrs. Asaad, with great suspense in her voice, began the story. "Once upon a time in a faraway land, there was a little duck named Ping." All of the children leaned forward to hear every word. When Mrs. Asaad, however, got to the very exciting part of the story where Ping gets into mischief, the preschoolers were overcome with their enthusiasm. Several began stamping their feet on the floor and Chris let out a squeal. As the other preschoolers joined in the squealing, Chris began shaking his head so vigorously that his hair stood out all around his head.

Mrs. Asaad stood helplessly watching the preschoolers, seemingly possessed by this gleeful group contagion of head shaking and foot stamping. Suddenly, it dawned on Mrs. Asaad that the preschoolers were more interested in the social presence of the other children than they were in her planned story. She laid down the book and stood up, saying, "Who can stretch high toward the sky? Great! Now, who can stamp your feet? Terrific! Let's sing 'Head and Shoulders, Knees and Toes.'"

Mrs. Asaad was very insightful to recognize that the preschoolers' rowdy behavior was not a personal affront to her. Chris and the others were not naughty but just immensely happy. They were thrilled to be in a group of children at an exciting event and did not have a clue about the life of a duck from a faraway land. Singing and moving as a group met their needs at this particular time, not hearing good literature.

Boredom

Boredom is one of the most predictable causes of misbehavior.

Neighborhood Nursery School was closed for the day, but staff members' children hung around, waiting for their parents' staff meeting to end. The nursery school staff took pride in their professionalism and high standards, and to reach their goals for quality, the staff met every Thursday afternoon after nursery school closed to discuss concerns.

Because most of the staff members were also parents, their own children had no alternative but to wait around while the parents met. Staff members took turns bringing a snack for the "staff kids" and attending to their needs and disagreements during meeting times, but it was clear that the staff kids dreaded the long Thursday afternoons. In early December, a meeting went on for hours as the staff planned special Christmas events. The staff kids had eaten their snack, colored pictures, and gone through stacks of puzzles and books. Shelley, five, and Jasmine, four and a half, were terribly bored and beginning to get a little silly. They were going through familiar books, making up ridiculous things for the characters to say, and then laughing uproariously at themselves.

Next, they decided that they were Harriet the Spy, so they sneaked around under tables and behind furniture, trying to get a peek at the adults without being seen, and then retreating to the restroom to roll on the floor in laughter. The spies decided that the next time they made a foray into enemy territory (the staff meeting room) they would attack the grown-ups' coffee table. Ever so slowly, Shelley crept under the refreshment table while Jasmine crouched excitedly in the hall, watching with both hands clasped over her mouth to stifle her giggles. While the adults talked on, a little hand slowly made its way up to the box of sugar cubes by the coffee pot and a strange sound—a muffled giggly sort of chortle—burst from Jasmine in the hall. The adults droned on, not noticing a thing.

The little hand (now grasping a whole handful of sugar cubes) slowly made its way back down the table. Unfortunately, it snagged the cord to the coffee pot on its way, and abruptly, the whole great adventurous fantasy came crashing down around little Shelley.

While Jasmine watched from the hall in horror, Shelley huddled under the table, her hands full of sugar cubes, surrounded by a dented coffee pot and huge puddles and rivulets of coffee. Her face flushed with embarrassment as the room full of astonished adults rushed toward her. Her mother looked the most shocked of all. Shelley was the kind of child no one ever expected to misbehave. Fortunately, no one was injured in this mishap. The adults' assumption that their children would behave appropriately without supervision, however, might just as easily have resulted in a real disaster.

Boredom, especially when coupled with lax supervision, is an open invitation to errant behavior (as well as to some extraordinary bursts of "creativity"). Diligent supvervision is essential to positive child guidance. Attentive adults can identify the first indications of boredom and take steps to correct it.

Fatigue and Discomfort

If we do not feel well, we may have difficulty behaving appropriately.

Wadsworth/Cengage Learning

Boredom and fatigue have a definite effect on children's behavior.

The Jacobsons had spent a wonderful day at the zoo. They had left home before sunrise and had driven several hours to a large city nearby to expose their four children to the wonders of a first-class zoo. The youngsters, three boys and a girl, ranged in age from 15 months to eight years. They had enjoyed a near-perfect day. The weather was great, the orangutan had hung upside down and delighted the children with wonderful ape tricks, and Allison, the toddler, had learned to say "monkey" and "bird" and make lots of new animal sounds. By the end of the day, the car trip home seemed particularly long and tedious. Al drove, and his wife, Regina, and the kids fell asleep shortly before the family reached home.

As they pulled into the driveway and everyone woke up, it was clear that the children were hungry, crabby, and generally exhausted. Al said, "I think I'll make pancakes for supper. That won't take long at all." Regina got the children bathed and dressed for bed, and everyone sat down to big fluffy pancakes, applesauce, and bacon, usually one of the kids' favorite meals.

Regina collapsed into a chair as Al lifted Allison (in her cute little footy pajamas and thick overnight diaper) into her high chair. He began to cut her pancake. Suddenly, Allison began to whine, shake her head, and push the high-chair tray. Al said, "What's wrong? Didn't you want me to cut up your pancake?" Allison stiffened and struggled, getting louder and louder. Al said, "Here, I'll trade pancakes. Mine isn't cut up." Allison took a swipe at the pancake and it landed on her brother William, causing him to start crying.

Al tried to calm William as Regina lifted Allison out of the high chair and said, "Honey, I know you're tired. We're all tired, but you may not throw food." Allison stiffened, struggled, and screamed even louder. Over her screams, Al and Regina racked their brains to figure out what to do. Nothing they tried seemed to help, and every effort just seemed to make matters worse. They finally decided that the only thing to do was to put Allison in her crib for the night. She sobbed herself to sleep, finally making the little rhythmic gasping sounds children make after they have cried hard.

After the boys were fed and asleep, Al and Regina puzzled over Allison's tantrum but could not decide whether this was a new stage or just the result of her being over-stimulated and exhausted from the busy day.

The next morning, Regina leaned over Allison's crib to say good morning. Allison was all smiles while her mother unsnapped her pajama bottoms and pulled off her diaper. Then Regina stopped. She discovered to her dismay that a little plastic toy dinosaur had somehow gotten stuck down in Allison's diaper, poking sharply into her skin. Allison had a bright red spot where it was stuck. Regina removed the offending toy. "Why," she asked herself, "didn't I think to check her diaper last night?"

Fatigue or anything that causes discomfort can cause children (and adults) to lose control and act aggressively, defy rules, or behave inappropriately. Being hungry, cold, hot, sick, or hurt are all reasons for children to be cranky and uncooperative. Very young children usually do not even realize that the source of their misery is a waistband that is painfully tight, a sock thread twisted around a toe, or scratchy sand in a wet diaper. Even older children sometimes become negative without recognizing that they just do not feel good. We need to remember that what appears on the surface is not always the whole story.

Desire for Recognition

Being ignored hurts at any age.

At three, Kelley was the middle child. His big sister, Kathryn, brought home papers from her elementary school teacher saying how smart and good she was. She also had lots of girlfriends who came and knocked on the door asking to play with her almost every day. Whenever Kelley tried to play with Kathryn and her friends, they would tell him to go away, and Kathryn would yell, "Mother, make Kelley go away and leave us alone!"

Kelley's baby brother, Nick, in comparison, always seemed to be in mommy's arms, getting fed, or burped, or bathed, or rocked. When Kelley asked his mother to read him a book or push him on the swing, she said, "Kelley, please go play with your toys. The baby's crying, and I can't play with you right now." Kelley thought his mother did not love him any more, only that stupid baby (and Kathryn with all her important homework and prissy friends).

Kelley wet his pants. His mother said, "Kelley! You're such a big boy. You know how to go to the potty." Kelley sneaked a bottle and climbed into baby Nick's crib. He pretended to be a baby and drank the bottle even though it tasted pretty nasty. His mother said, "Kelley! What are you doing in there? This crib isn't built for a big boy like you. It's for the baby. Look, your shoes have gotten the sheets all dirty."

Kelley pushed an old lawn chair against a tree and climbed up into the tree. Even though it was very scary, he climbed higher and higher until he could not climb any farther. Then he started to cry. Kelley's mother ran outside when she heard Kelley crying. "Oh, my soul!" she yelled, "Kelley, how in the world did you get up there?" She called Kelley's dad, and it took two hours and the help of several neighbors to get Kelley safely out of the tree. When his dad got him to the lowest branch, he handed Kelley down to his mother. She hugged him so hard he could hardly breathe, but he did not mind. He was just glad to be out of that tree.

Kelley's dad sat down on the grass. He was still panting and sweating from all the climbing and worrying. He motioned for Kelley to come sit on his lap. "Son," he said, "your mother and I love you. You're the only Kelley we have. We can't ever get another boy just like you. Kathryn is special and Baby Nick is special, but Kathryn can't ride on my shoulders and Baby Nick can't sing all the words to 'I've Been Working on the Railroad.' You are the only one who can do those things."

He gave Kelley a playful squeeze and said, "Did you think we could put a penny in a gumball machine and out would roll another Kelley just exactly like you? That I could just go down to the grocery store and put a shiny new penny in there and, POP, out would come a new Kelley? No siree! We couldn't get a new Kelley that way. You're the only one exactly like you in the whole world."

Kelley sat in his dad's lap, encircled by his dad's strong arms, his face snuggled so close to his dad's chest that he could hear the sound of his dad's big heart thumping, the deep voice, and rumbly laughter. Kelley imagined brightly colored gumballs with his face on them rolling out of a grocery store gumball machine. He took a deep breath and grinned.

Feeling ignored is far more painful and frightening for young children than being in trouble and having everyone angry or upset. All human beings need to feel a sense of belonging, to feel that they are wanted and needed. If a child feels unwanted or left out, he may not be able to cooperate and follow rules.

Discouragement

Becoming overwhelmed by discouragement can cause anyone to feel depressed and angry.

Fiona's family moved to a new neighborhood. In her old school, she had already started second grade and had really liked the teacher there. She got good marks on her schoolwork, and the teacher often let her help other children when her own work was finished. The teacher had praised Fiona for her careful block printing and often put Fiona's papers on the bulletin board for all to see. In her new school, however, Fiona did not think the new teacher, Miss Crane, was very happy to have her in class. On the first day she attended the new school, Miss Crane acted annoyed, and Fiona heard her complain bitterly to another teacher about having to take a student from a different school district in the middle of the year. When Fiona began carefully printing her name in the new workbook Miss Crane gave her, Miss Crane snapped, "Young lady, in this school, second graders do not print! We write in cursive."

Fiona hung her head and stared at her feet, wondering what cursive was. She knew she had heard her mother say many times that she did not like cursing at all. Miss Crane gave Fiona a little workbook filled with grown-up writing and pale blue straight and dotted lines. She said, "I don't have time to teach you everything I've already gone over with the rest of the class. Just go through this workbook and write the words on each page like the ones in the examples. I don't ever want to see you doing printing in this class again. Do you understand?"

Fiona sat at the back of the room by herself, feeling terribly dejected but struggling to copy the weirdly shaped letters in the workbook. Finally, it began to make sense to her that some of the words were made of familiar letters. The letters were just hooked together in a long string like beads on a necklace. She printed the letters she knew and then connected them to make them look like the examples.

Miss Crane did not like Fiona's work at all. "This is not how you write in cursive! Can't you see how the other children are writing?" Fiona was too embarrassed to look around. She hoped none of the other children were staring at her.

Fiona became very quiet at home. She did not bubble with stories about her day. She stopped looking forward to school and began to have stomachaches almost every morning. She begged her mother to let her stay home. She also seemed unusually irritable and often had angry fights with her sisters and brothers. At school, Fiona went to the pencil sharpener every time she thought Miss Crane was looking or walking in her direction. With so much sharpening, the pencil lead was always too pointed so it snapped every time she nervously pressed down on the paper. She erased until she finally wore holes in the sheets of paper in her workbook, which began to look like Swiss cheese and made her work look even more awful. Miss Crane became exasperated with Fiona and began to wonder whether Fiona was a slow learner or just a difficult, uncooperative little girl.

Actually, Fiona was not sick, slow, or difficult, but she was very, very discouraged. Her self-esteem had slipped, leaving her vulnerable and disorganized, and not at all able to do competent schoolwork, make friends, or live up to the teacher's expectations. Being harshly criticized and subjected to put-downs makes it harder, not easier, for a child to accomplish difficult tasks.

Frustration

No matter how old or how young, we all risk losing control when we hit a certain level of frustration.

Wadsworth/Cengage Learning

▬▬ Feelings of discouragement cause children to be less, rather than more, cooperative.

Benny was two years old. Hardly a day went by without his mother, Virginia, pointing out to someone that he was a "typical terrible two." He vacillated between acting like a baby and trying to act like a grown-up. He whined, "Me do it," whenever his mother tried to tie his shoes. When Virginia became exasperated with him over the shoelaces, she said, "Okay, you tie them." Of course Benny did not know how to tie them, but he stubbornly worked for 15 minutes, twisting the laces into a scrambled mass of knots.

Virginia said, "Now look what you've done. I told you that you didn't know how to tie them. Be still so I can get these knots out and tie them right." Benny kicked and fought hard to keep his mother from touching his shoes. She finally spanked him to make him let go of his shoes so she could tie them.

Even though Virginia was a single mother with a demanding job and classes two nights a week, she kept her apartment perfectly clean and went to garage sales and resale shops on weekends to see to it that Benny had all the toys and clothes a toddler could need. Every day, he was dropped at his child care center looking freshly scrubbed and starched, with every hair in place.

When Virginia got Benny home on the weekday evenings that she did not have to go to class, she always had a lot of work facing her. She usually put Benny on the floor and told him to play with his basket of toys while she cooked, cleaned, and studied. Most often, Benny abandoned the toys and followed his mother around getting into her schoolbooks or the kitchen cabinets and making messes. When her patience with him wore thin, she would smack his hand and say, "No," or give him a firm swat on the bottom.

Tension built in their little household between the busy, frazzled mother and the clingy, insistent toddler. At his child care center, Benny began biting other children when they refused to give him a toy or let him have a turn on the tricycle. Even being made to sit on the "thinking chair" for a time-out by his teachers seemed to have absolutely no effect on stopping his biting. In fact, it seemed to make him more stubborn and agitated.

(Continued)

One day, Benny had been in trouble several times, so he was sitting by himself playing with a jack-in-the-box. He cranked the tiny handle and listened to the tune as it played "around and around the cobbler's bench the monkey chased the weasel . . ." until out popped the little clown.

Benny watched attentively, then tried to push the little clown back into the box to close the lid so that he could do it again. He pushed the little clown's head down into the box and mashed hard on the lid, but the toy clown's two little flat, plastic hands were sticking out and the lid would not close. Benny pushed on the lid as hard as he could, but his hand slipped and the little clown popped back out.

Benny glared at the uncooperative toy clown then bent down and bit the little clown's hand. Benny bit so long and hard that his whole body shook with the effort, and he left a clear imprint of his teeth on the plastic hand.

Much of Benny's aggression probably stemmed from the stress and pressure he was encountering in his daily life. His mother, Virginia, had a lot of frustration building up in her as she tried to survive financially and emotionally as a single parent, a working mother of a toddler, and as a student. She felt frustrated in her efforts to be a perfect mother while also trying to deal with her own personal and social needs. Benny "caught" some of her stress like a contagious illness. He did not know why he felt so tense and stubborn all the time, and he did not know how to make the feelings go away.

Stress is a very real crisis for many children and families today. Children can absorb stress unknowingly from their parents and caregivers or develop stress symptoms directly from their own lifestyles. Today there are children who, from earliest childhood, spend their days going from classroom to tutoring to individual lessons to social events, virtually every day from dawn to dusk. Whatever the cause of stress, its symptoms often include inappropriate behavior (along with health, appetite, and concentration problems).

Rebellion

Under repressive enough circumstances, even the most docile of us might be inclined to rebel.

Coach Sam, a tall, muscular 19-year-old, had just been hired as the gymnastics instructor in a large, inner-city community center that provided afterschool care for 6- through 12-year-olds. His childhood dreams of reaching the Olympics had been dashed by a troublesome back injury, so he found himself teaching gymnastics to small children, something he had never particularly wanted to do.

He decided that to create discipline in his class he would start from the very beginning with his class by being very tough and demanding. He assembled his group of first, second, and third graders on the floor and, towering in front of them with his hands on his hips, announced in a booming voice, "If you talk without my permission, you're out of here. If you don't pay attention and follow my instructions, you're out of here. And if you even think about being lazy or careless, you're history. Is that understood?" The children chorused back in unison, "Yes, Coach."

At first the children seemed very intimidated by Coach Sam and did everything he said. They were serious and attentive and jumped when he said jump. Gradually, their obedience became more and more strained. Coach Sam never praised the children's accomplishments other than to make a curt comment such as, "Well, finally you're paying attention." He was, however, very quick to mete out caustic criticism such as "If that's the best you can do, just go sit by the wall. You're not worth me wasting my time." These comments hurt, and the children grew to dislike Coach Sam intensely.

The children wondered why Coach Sam so frequently threatened to kick them out of class but never followed through on the threat. They did not know that he lacked the authority to expel students from class. They did, however, begin to recognize that most of his threats were empty gestures. In his annoyance and frustration, Coach Sam became colder and more demanding with the children. They became more callous and uncooperative with him. Coach Sam regularly punished children by making them sit by a wall for long periods. They found ways to use this sitting time to create more mischief and disruption for Coach Sam. They expressed their dislike of him and his tactics by causing him endless frustration and interruption.

Coach Sam was filled with feelings of rage and helplessness. He knew he would be fired instantly if he struck any of the children, but he was overwhelmed with the urge to show them he had control over them. If he could not use physical force to control them, then he simply did not know how to maintain discipline and order. Coach Sam did not know that positive discipline can best be achieved by establishing an atmosphere of fairness, trust, honesty, and mutual respect, not by trying to create fear and submission.

The stage is set for rebellion when the following conditions exist:

- Children feel anger and contempt rather than affection and respect for the authority figures in their lives who set and enforce rules.
- A situation exists in which it is overly difficult for children to abide by specific rules or live up to expectations.
- Children realize that rules are just hollow threats that will not be consistently or fairly enforced.
- Children are discouraged to such an extent and feel they are in so much trouble that they think nothing else they do can make things any worse for them.

These conditions trigger rebellion in not only young children but also, in a more general way, adult populations in society at large, where it takes the form of defiance of law and order. Alienation, discouragement, and outrage at inequity are feelings not limited to adults but, on a much smaller scale, also tempt children to defy authority in spite of the risk of punishment (Crockenberg, 1997; Edwards, 1997; Fields & Boesser, 1998; Gallo, 1997; Gartrell, 1997; Katz & McClellan, 1997; Leach, 1996; McCloskey, 1997).

Frustration triggers misbehavior. Feeling cornered and threatened can trigger rebelliousness.

Wadsworth/Cengage Learning

KEY TERMS

demandingness
dysfunctional
functional
inappropriate behavior
induction
judging
justice orientation

misbehavior
moral affect
moral reasoning
perceiving
problem behavior
responsibility orientation
socialization

POINTS TO REMEMBER

- Positive child guidance focuses on the child's ability level, the severity and intent of the behavior, and possible reasons for the behavior. (Remember the authoritative style.)
- Adult-centered definitions of misbehavior focus on the effect a child's behavior has on the adult.
- Child-centered definitions of misbehavior focus on the ability level, motives, and long-term well-being of the child in evaluating the appropriateness or inappropriateness of actions.

- Spirited children need special support and understanding.
- Moral reasoning is the thinking that guides children in deciding what is right or wrong.
- High but reasonable standards that are consistently and caringly enforced will develop self-control, altruism, and self-esteem in children.
- Harsh punishment can trigger fear or rebellion (Remember the authoritarian style.)

PRACTICAL APPLICATION

Is a "Really Good Spanking" Really Good?

Edna and Wilbert stopped at a neighborhood fast-food restaurant for a quick hamburger on Saturday afternoon. The place was buzzing with activity, and children of all ages were everywhere.

Edna and Wilbert had no children of their own, but they watched in amazement as many different types of adults talked to, played with, and reprimanded children.

Wilbert was especially curious about one harried woman who seemed to be in charge of a half-dozen youngsters. One of the children, a six-year-old, shook salt into her hand, licked it, then laughed as she brushed her salty hands over the children near her. They shrieked with laughter as they dodged the salt, throwing napkins to defend themselves. The woman looked sternly at them and threatened to make them sit in the car if they did not settle down.

Wilbert leaned over and whispered to Edna, "What those children need is a really good spanking!"

DISCUSSION QUESTIONS

1. What could be some possible reasons the children Wilbert was watching were behaving the way they were?
2. Why do you suppose Wilbert believed spanking would be helpful?
3. What do you think would be the most effective and appropriate thing for the woman to do in the preceding situation?

STUDENT ACTIVITY

1. To be authoritative, you must set high but realistic goals for children.
   a. Think of a troubling behavior problem in a child of a specific age.
   b. Figure out potential reasons for the behavior.
   c. Decide how to go about setting a goal for improved behavior.
   d. Create a hypothetical plan to guide the child and support any behavior improvements.
   e. Decide on a plan for tracking and evaluating progress toward the goal.
2. Authoritative adults must help children achieve high and realistic goals by carefully supporting, encouraging, and monitoring progress. Interact with one or more preschoolers.
   a. Determine a guidance goal for a preschooler that is optimistic and realistic.
   b. Use positive guidance techniques to gently nudge the child toward the guidance goal.
   c. How have you encouraged the child in making small steps toward the goal?
3. Authoritative adults must provide consistent follow-up to evaluate whether children achieve goals.
   a. How have you made sure to provide consistent follow-up? Give examples.

   b. After a period of time, assess to see whether the preschooler has made progress toward the goal.
   c. Do you still believe the goal you set is appropriate (both optimistic and realistic)?
4. If you were a teacher, what would be the most effective way to collaborate with parents to work toward child behavior goals?
   a. Tell parents what they are doing is wrong and you know what is best for their child.
   b. Talk to the parent in front of the child while the parent is rushing to leave for work in the morning.
   c. Meet with parents at a convenient time away from the child to discuss the child's behavior and work together to decide what goals are appropriate.
   d. Make it a point to really listen to what the parent has to say about the child.
   e. Show respect for the parents and ask for their input in thinking through the problem and agreeing on *developmentally appropriate* methods to respond.
   f. Other possibilities (list them).

RELATED READINGS

Morality

Berkowitz, M. W., & Grych, J. H. (1998). Fostering goodness: Teaching parents to facilitate children's moral development. *Journal of Moral Education, 27*(3), 371–391. Retrieved February 25, 2006, from http://parenthood.library.wisc.edu/.

DeVries, R., & Zan, B. (1994). *Moral classrooms, moral children: Creating a constructivist atmosphere in early education.* New York: Teachers College Press.

Eisenberg, N., & Mussen, P. H. (1989). *The roots of prosocial behavior in children.* New York: Cambridge University Press.

Gilligan, C. (1977). In a different voice: Women's conceptions of self and of morality. *Harvard Educational Review, 47,* 481–517.

Gilligan, C., & Attanucci, J. (1988). Two moral orientations. In C. Gilligan, J. V. Ward, & J. M. Taylor (Eds.), *Mapping the moral domain* (73–86). Cambridge, MA: Harvard University Press.

Kohlberg, L. (1976). Moral stages and moralization: The cognitive-developmental approach. In T. Lickona (Ed.), *Moral development and behavior: Theory, research, and social issues* (31–53). New York: Holt, Rinehart & Winston.

Kohlberg, L. (1984). *Essays on moral development: Vol. 2. The psychology of moral development: The*

■ Children can learn about behavior issues by reading books.

nature and validity of moral stages. San Francisco: Harper & Row.

Lickona, T. (1983). *Raising good children*. New York: Bantam Books.

Lickona, T. (1991). *Education for character: How our schools can teach respect and responsibility*. New York: Bantam.

Piaget, J. (1965). *The moral judgment of the child.* (M. Gabain, Trans.). New York: Free Press.

Sizer, T. R., & Sizer, N. F. (1999). *The students are watching: Schools and the moral contract*. Boston, MA: Beacon Press.

Sroufe, A. (1995). *Emotional development: The organization of emotional life in the early years*. New York: Cambridge University Press.

Nurturing At-Risk Children

Anderson, C. A., Berkowitz, L., Donnerstein, E., Huesmann, R. L., Johnson, J., Linz, D., et al. (2003). The influence of media violence on youth. *Psychological Science in the Public Interest, 4,* 81–110.

Barker, M., & Petley, J., Eds. (2001). *Ill effects: The media/violence debate* (2nd ed.). London: Routledge.

Freedman, J. I. (2002). *Media violence and its effect on aggression: Assessing the scientific evidence.* Toronto: University of Toronto Press.

Gentile, D., Ed. (2003). *Media violence and children: A complete guide for parents and professionals.* Westport, CT: Praeger.

Guralnick, M. J. (2000). An agenda for change in early childhood inclusion. *Journal of Early Intervention, 23*(4), 213–222.

Kim, Q. S. (2004, September 8). Playing games: Toymakers launch video game consoles aimed at preschoolers. *The Wall Street Journal,* B1.

Kranowitz, C. S., & Wylie, T. J. (2003). *The out-of-sync child has fun: Activities for kids with sensory integration dysfunction.* New York: Perigee.

Levine, M. (2002). *The myth of laziness.* New York: Simon & Shuster.

Levine, M. (2003). *A mind at a time.* New York: Simon & Shuster.

McWilliam, R. A. (2000). Recommended practices in interdisciplinary models. In S. Sandall, M. E. McLean, & B. J. Smith (Eds.), *DEC recommended practices in early intervention/early childhood special education* (47–54). Longmont, CO: Sopris West.

Odom, S. L. (2000). Reschool inclusion: What we know and where we go from here. *Topics in Early Childhood Special Education, 20*(1), 20–27.

Torr, J. D., Ed. (2001). *Violence in the media.* San Diego, CA: Greenhaven Press.

Turnbull, A. P., Pereira, L., & Blue-Banning, M. J. (2000). Teachers as friendship facilitators. *Teaching Exceptional Children, 32*(5), 66–70.

Villani, S. (2001, April). Impact of media on children and adolescents: A 10-year review of the research. *Journal of the American Academy of Child & Adolescent Psychiatry, 40*(4), 392–401.

Temperament

Aron, E. N. (2002). *The highly sensitive child.* New York: Broadway Press.

Ausubel, D. (1968). *Educational psychology: A cognitive view.* New York: Holt, Rinehart, & Winston.

Bates, J. E. (1980). The concept of difficult temperament. *Merrill-Palmer Quarterly, 26,* 299–319.

Bates, J. E. (1987). Temperament in infancy. In J. Osofsky (Ed.), *Handbook of infant development* (2nd ed.). New York: Wiley.

Bates, J. E. (1989). Concepts and measures of temperament. In G. A. Kohnstamm, J. E. Bates, & M. K. Rothbart (Eds.), *Temperament in childhood*. Chichester, UK: Wiley.

Berens, L. V. (2000). *Understanding yourself and others: An introduction to temperament—2.0*. Huntington Beach, CA: Telos Publications.

Berens, L. V., Ernst, L. K., Robb, J. E., & Smith, M. A. (2003). *The guide for facilitating the self-discovery process for identifying temperament*. Huntington Beach, CA: Telos Publications.

Berens, L. V., Ernst, L. K., & Smith, M. A. (2000). *The guide for facilitating the self-discovery process using the TRI methodology*. Huntington Beach, CA: Temperament Research Institute.

Berens, L. V., & Nardi, D. (1999). *The sixteen personality types, descriptions for self-discovery*. Huntington Beach, CA: Telos Publications.

Bloom, B., Englehart, M., Furst, E., Hill, W., & Krathwohl, D. (1956). *Taxonomy of educational objectives, handbook I: The cognitive domain*. New York: Longmans Green.

Budd, L. (1991). *Living with the active, alert child*. New York: Prentice Hall.

Carducci, B. (2003). *The shyness breakthrough: A no-stress plan to help your shy child warm up, open up, and join the fun*. Emmaus, PA: Rodale.

Carey, W. B. (1997). *Understanding your child's temperament*. New York: Macmillan.

Carey, W. B., Jablow, M. M., & Children's Hospital of Philadelphia (Corp. Author) (1998). *Understanding your child's temperament*. New York: Macmillan.

Chess, S., & Thomas, A. (1986). *Temperament in clinical practice*. New York: Guilford Press.

Chess, S., & Thomas, A. (1989). *Know your child: An authoritative guide for today's parents*. New York: Basic Books.

Davidson, R. J. (2002). Anxiety and affective style: Role of prefrontal cortex and amygdala. *Biologica Psychiatry, 51*, 68–80.

Fackler, A. (2003). Understanding your toddler's unique temperament. Boise, ID: Healthwise.

Gunnar, M. R. (1994). Psychoendocrine studies of temperament and stress in early childhood: Expanding current models. In J. E. Bates & T. D. Wachs (Eds.), *Temperament: Individual differences at the interface of biology and behavior* (175–198). Washington, DC: APA Books.

Hepburn, S. L. (2003). Clinical implications of temperamental characteristics in young children with developmental disabilities. *Infants and Young Children, 16*, 59–76.

Kagan, J. (1998). Temperament. In W. Damon (Ed.), *Handbook of child psychology* (Vol. 3, 177–209). New York: Wiley.

Kagan, J., & Herschkowitz, N. (2005). *A young mind in a growing brain*. Mahwah, NJ: Erlbaum.

Kagan, J., Reznick, J. S., & Snidman, N. (1988). Biological bases of childhood shyness. *Science, 240*, 167–171.

Kagan, J., & Snidman, N. (2004). *The long shadow of temperament*. Cambridge, MA: Harvard University Press.

Kagan, J., Snidman, N., Arcus, D., & Reznick, J. S. (1998). *Galen's prophecy: Temperament in human nature*. Boulder, CO: Basic Books.

Kagan, J., Snidman, N., Zentner, M., & Peterson, E. (1999). Infant temperament and anxious symptoms in school age children. *Development and Psychopathology, 11*, 209–224.

Keirsey, D. (1998). *Please understand me II: Temperament, character, intelligence*. Del Mar, CA: Prometheus Nemesis.

Kochanska, G. (1993). Toward a synthesis of parental socialization and child temperament in early development of conscience. *Child Development, 64*, 325–347.

Kurcinka, M. S. (1991). *Raising your spirited child: A guide for parents whose child is more intense, sensitive, perceptive, persistent, energetic*. New York: Harper Perennial.

Lemery, K. S., Goldsmith, H. H., Klinnert, M. D., & Mrazek, D. A. (1999). Developmental models of infant and childhood temperament. *Developmental Psychology, 35*, 189–204.

Lerner, C., & Dombro, A. L. (2000). *Learning and growing together: Understanding and supporting your child's development*. Washington, DC: Zero to Three.

Neville, H., & Johnson, D. C. (1997). *Temperament tools: Working with your child's inborn traits.* Seattle, WA: Parenting Press.

Quenk, N. L. (1999). Essentials of Myers-Briggs Type Indicator Assessment (Essentials of Psychological Assessment Series). New York: Wiley.

Rapee, R. M. (2002). The development and modification of temperamental risk for anxiety disorders: Prevention of lifetime of anxiety? *Biological Psychiatry, 52,* 947–957.

Rothbart, M. K., Ahadi, S. A., & Evans, D. E. (2000). Temperament and personality: Origins and outcomes. *Journal of Personality and Social Psychology, 78,* 122–135.

Rothbart, M. K., Ahadi, S. A., & Hershey, K. L. (1994). Temperament and social behavior in childhood. *Merrill-Palmer Quarterly, 40,* 21–39.

Rothbart, M. K., Ahadi, S. A., Hershey, K. L., & Fisher, P. (2001). Investigations of temperament at three to seven years: The Children's Behavior Questionnaire. *Child Development, 72,* 1394–1408.

Rothbart, M. K., & Derryberry, D. (1981). Development of individual differences in temperament. In M. E. Lamb & A. L. Brown (Eds.), *Advances in developmental psychology* (vol. 1, 37–86). Hillsdale, NJ: Erlbaum.

Rothbart, M. K., Derryberry, D., & Hershey, K. (2000). Stability of temperament in childhood: Laboratory infant assessment to parent report at seven years. In V. J. Molfese & D. L. Molfese (Eds.), *Temperament and personality development across the life span* (85–119). Hillsdale, NJ: Erlbaum.

Rothbart, M. K., Ellis, L. K., Rueda, M. R., & Posner, M. I. (2003). Developing mechanisms of conflict resolution. *Journal of Personality, 71,* 1113–1143.

Rothbart, M. K., & Rueda, M. R. (2005). The development of effortful control. In U. Mayr, E. Awh, & S. Keele (Eds.), *Developing individuality in the human brain: A tribute to Michael I. Posner* (167–188). Washington, DC: American Psychological Association.

Schmidt, L. A., & Fox, N. A. (2002). Individual differences in childhood shyness: origins, malleability, and developmental course. In D. Cervone & W. Mischel (Eds.), *Advances in personality science* (83–105). New York: Guilford Publishers.

Schwartz, C. E., Wright, C. I., Shin, L. M., Kagan, J., & Rauch, S. L. (2003). Inhibited and uninhibited infants "grow up": Adult amygdalar response to novelty. *Science, 300,* 1952–1953.

Shick, L. (1998). *Understanding temperament: Strategies for creating family harmony.* Seattle, WA: Parenting Press.

Stein, M. (1998). *Jung's map of the soul: An introduction.* Chicago: Open Court.

Turecki, S. (1989). *The difficult child.* New York: Bantam Books.

Wood, J. J., McLeond, B. D., Sigman, M., Hwang, W., & Chu, B.C. (2003). Parenting and childhood anxiety: theory, empirical findings, and future directions. *Journal of Child Psychology and Psychiatry, 44,* 134–151.

The Online Companion™ to accompany the sixth edition of *Positive Child Guidance* is your link to additional guidance resources on the Internet. This supplement contains audio and visual materials; PowerPoint presentations; web activities with critical-thinking questions and practical-application assignments; and links to web resources. This additional content can be found at http://www.earlychilded.delmar.com.

Chapter 5

Guidelines for Effective Guidance

Wadsworth/Cengage Learning

OBJECTIVES

After reading this chapter, you should be able to do the following:

- Develop specific strategies for effective guidance.
- Formulate guidelines for responding to inappropriate behaviors.
- Identify methods to shape positive behavior.
- Specify techniques for assertive redirection and follow-up.
- Contemplate your own strategies for remaining calm and objective during guidance interactions.

Ignore Mildly Annoying Behavior That Is neither Harmful nor Unfair

Children are not helped by intrusive and overwhelming attempts to change too much of their behavior at one time. Adults do well to focus guidance actions on urgent priorities while overlooking mildly annoying behaviors that are neither harmful nor unfair to others. In dealing with a child who has behaved aggressively but who also bites her fingernails and rocks her chair back and forth, an adult should initially focus attention only on the aggression. A mental note could be made to address the other problems in a more subtle

Healthy, well-developing children are naturally lively and full of energy.

and indirect manner at a later time, well after the aggression has been resolved. We adults tend to overwhelm children with too many demands, especially when we are angry and upset. If a child has an unusual number of behavior problems, a medical professional may be able to identify a common cause and recommend possible solutions.

Focus Attention Elsewhere

When a child does something that is mildly annoying or embarrassing (but not unacceptable), simply focusing the child's attention elsewhere may resolve the problem. A baby who is banging a spoon on a metal high-chair tray in a restaurant may be distracted by a parent who plays peek-a-boo or dangles a softer, quieter toy. A thumb-sucking toddler may be distracted from the sucking by being given an interesting toy to explore. A curious preschooler may be distracted from handling items on shelves in the grocery store by being allowed to help push the grocery cart or to help arrange foods in the basket as they are selected.

replaces
Substitutes one action for another when both cannot be done at the same time, so that an undesired behavior must be given up or suspended for the new action to take place.

Discreetly Redirect Slightly Inappropriate Behavior to More Positive Substitute Behavior

Slightly annoying behaviors can also be redirected by involving the child in an activity that **replaces** the undesirable behavior. For example, a child who is picking at her nose can be directed to use a tissue to blow her nose. Without ever even mentioning the nose picking, the adult can explain how using a tissue, throwing away the tissue, and then washing hands may keep others from catching a cold.

To redirect slightly inappropriate behaviors, we can identify activities that involve the part, or parts, of the child's body currently used in the undesirable action, then an alternative action involving those body parts can be substituted. For example, a child who is using her hands to feel the blossoms of a neighbor's delicate and expensive garden plants could be shown how to put her hands behind her back or in her pockets while she leans over to smell the wonderful fragrance of the gardenias. She could also be redirected to use her hands to gather interesting leaves and acorns from the ground.

This helps the child know that it is okay to explore and enjoy nature, but not okay to damage another person's property. Snapping, "Don't touch those plants!" discourages curiosity, a key factor in the child's long-term ability to develop intellectually. Of course, standing by passively while your child damages a neighbor's prized gardenias would be rude and disrespectful.

Wadsworth/Cengage Learning

"Here is a tissue. After you blow your nose, I will help you wash your hands."

Assist the Child in Recognizing the General Effects of Positive Behaviors

Another method for gently redirecting minor misbehaviors involves focusing the child's attention on the positive outcome of more desirable behaviors. The adult gives information to the child. The adult might say, "If you put your glass of milk on the top corner of your place mat, it will be safely out of your way until you want to drink it." A teacher might say, "If you erase mistakes slowly and lightly, your paper will look very nice." A toddler can be told "I like to hear 'thank you.' Oh, how nice! Brett remembered to say 'thank you.'"

Immediately Interrupt Behavior That Is Harmful or Unfair

Children rely on adults to enforce rules and protect individual rights. Children will be willing to follow rules only if they come to believe that the rules are meaningful. Consistency and fairness in the enforcement of rules help children learn to trust authority figures. Behaviors that are harmful or unfair must be interrupted immediately by a responsible adult.

Adults do not help children become cooperative and respectful by passively watching them fight, saying, "They'll just have to learn to stand up for themselves. When Jimmy has had enough of Gerald hitting him, he'll learn to hit back." We also fail to help children when we say, "Don't come tell me that someone hit you. I don't want to hear about it!" Children can be helped to resolve their own disagreements, but they must know that adults will reliably stop unacceptable, hurtful behavior.

What Do I Do about Biting?

Biting is a worrisome issue for parents and teachers of toddlers. In the case of biting, the inappropriate behavior dramatically affects a child other than the biter. Not only does the teacher have to worry about how to deal with responding to the biter, the teacher also has to contact the parents of the bitten child to inform them of the bite. The parents of the child who has been bitten will undoubtedly feel concerned; perhaps they will feel frustrated; maybe (if this has happened before) they will feel angry.

A very disturbing trend has been for child care centers to solve the problem by expelling the biting toddler

Children will be willing to play by the rules only if they come to believe that rules are meaningful.

from the child care center. This is a shocking way to dismiss this problem: it leaves a family with no child care and a toddler with a behavior problem unsolved. Yale researcher Walter Gilliam (2004) studied preschool expulsions and found that pre-K students are expelled at a rate more than three times that of children in grades K–12. He found that black children were getting expelled at alarming rates and that boys were expelled 4.5 times more often than girls.

Biting is an inappropriate behavior that affects a significant number of toddlers, particularly those who are having a hard time communicating orally. This book offers many positive guidance strategies that can be used to address this behavior.

- Communicate—Use eye contact at eye level, use the child's name, and use appropriate touch while saying, "Gentle, be gentle!"
- Role-play with a doll—"Ouch! Be gentle, Dolly! No biting! Biting hurts!"
- Use sign language—Signing may be especially helpful in offering alternative methods for communication.
- Supervise adequately—Ensure that proper ratios of adult supervision are maintained and developmentally appropriate practice is in place and consistently used!

Take Time to Think before You Respond to Biting

What to Look For

- Does the biting seem to be a reflexive response rather than an aggressive act?

  Babies younger than one year have limited self-awareness and almost no conscious control over their behavior. A baby beginning to cut teeth may bite unexpectedly while breast-feeding. An older baby may bite when emotionally overwhelmed with discomfort, excitement, fatigue, or fright. In fact, an older baby involved in an overly exciting game of peek-a-boo may be laughing wildly one moment then suddenly bite anything or anyone who is handy the next moment.

- What were the circumstances surrounding and just before the biting?

  Toddlers in the second and third year of life have begun to gain some control over their behavior, but they have limited oral skills and may feel powerless and overwhelmed when they are frustrated, angry, in pain, or

What to Do

- Be calm, firm, and consistent.

  Establish eye contact at eye level, make gentle physical contact with the child, and calmly but urgently say, "No biting. Biting hurts." Then immediately redirect the child's attention to a different activity. Gently stroke the bitten child or adult while soothingly saying, "Gentle . . . be gentle." If needed, carry the biter to a different location and engage her in a totally different activity. Trying to have a baby or young toddler sit in time-out makes absolutely no sense, but an abrupt change in location and activity will interrupt the behavior and reinforce a growing sense in the child that biting is not okay and will not be tolerated. (Remember, biting a child back is never okay!)

- Prevention is the key.

  Focus your energy on preventing that first bite by providing close supervision and by removing sources of frustration and stress. Biting is con-

frightened. It is almost inevitable that toddlers discover the sheer power of a bite: toddler teeth can make even a big strong grown-up flinch and howl. No wonder it is so tempting for toddlers to latch onto this tactic for self-expression. Kicking and screaming may be ignored, but a bite is sure to get immediate attention from just about anyone.

Remember that babies and toddlers are just beginning to develop the ability to think about an action (biting) then consciously choose *not* to do it. Learning takes time, consistency, and patience. In the initial stages of learning, a baby or toddler may bite, then immediately look up, shake her head, and say, "No, no!"

• Has the biting become chronic?

Although most older babies and toddlers bite someone at some time or other, chronic biting is a different matter. A preschool-age child who still bites is a source of serious concern. Biting is painful, it can be a source of infection, and adults and other children must be protected.

Ask yourself the following questions:

• Are the child's physical needs met? Is she getting adequate sleep, nutrition, and health care?
• Are there other indications that the child may be experiencing emotional or health problems?
• Are there reasons the child might be feeling overwhelmed and helpless?
• Is the child developing as generally expected for her age?
• Has the child been exposed to violence or aggression in the community, the family, or child care?
• Does the child feel unconditionally loved and accepted by the adults in her life?
• Is the child abused?

tagious. A toddler who gets bitten is highly likely to try out this new tactic on others. Biting spreads in a toddler classroom faster than a runny nose in January. Diligent supervision and developmentally appropriate care will help adults prevent biting outbreaks. Be sure children are getting plenty of rest, a calm environment, and plenty of emotional nurturing.

Boredom is a major source of stress for babies and toddlers, so ensure a safe, accessible environment with interesting things to explore and challenge budding motor skills. Babies and toddlers need things to climb over, under, and around; things to empty, fill, and carry around; things to stack, knock down, and bang together; and safe substances for exploring unfamiliar sounds, sights, smells, tastes, and textures.

• Convene a "summit meeting" of parents and caregivers.

Bring the adults together, not to blame anyone, but to brainstorm the problem and collaborate in problem solving. Usually it's not a single problem leading to chronic biting but a cluster of irritants interfering with the child's ability to develop self-control.

Typically, child care staff blames the family, the family blames the child care staff, and everyone blames the child. Successful resolution is most likely, however, when the adults resist the temptation to point fingers, and all commit themselves to systematically identifying and removing possible causes of the misbehavior. The simple act of meeting regularly and cooperatively to discuss progress and strategies has an almost magical effect on chronic misbehavior. Medical experts and counselors who specialize in evaluating and treating developmental problems can be a tremendous asset to families and teachers. Don't hesitate to call on them.

Intervene as Firmly as Necessary but as Gently as Possible

When we find it necessary to stop an unacceptable behavior, we should always proceed as firmly as necessary to stop the unacceptable action, but as gently as possible to remind the child that he is accepted and respected as a person, even if his behavior must be ended.

As Miss Melanie firmly pries a toddler's clenched fingers one by one out of another screaming toddler's hair, she says with a tone of urgent concern (not anger) in her voice, "Ouch! Pulling hurts. No pulling. Touch gently, please!" After the toddlers are safely separated, she softly strokes each toddler's hair saying, "Gentle, be gentle. Please touch hair gently." Miss Melanie has interrupted a harmful behavior as firmly as necessary but as gently as possible.

Roger grabs a little car from his friend Chris and runs away. Chris yells and starts to cry. Mr. Reese follows Roger (persistently but without chasing him), saying in a deeply concerned tone, "Stop, please. Roger, I need you to stop so we can talk about Chris's car." When Roger finally pauses for a second, Mr. Reese says, "Thank you for waiting. Let's sit down and talk about Chris's car. You like Chris's car, don't you? It's really a neat car, isn't it?" Mr. Reese does not immediately attempt to snatch the car away from Roger. He patiently asks, "What should you do if you want to see someone else's toy? Should you ask, 'May I play with your car?'" Roger hangs his head and says, "But if I ask him, he might say no." Mr. Reese answers, "You're right. He might say yes or he might say no. Would you like for me to come with you so you can ask? If he says no, I will help you find a different toy to play with. Remember, taking things without asking is not allowed, so when you choose a toy, no one will be allowed to take your toy away without asking you first, right?"

Roger's unfair action has been stopped, firmly but gently, and Roger has had a chance to learn a very important lesson. Although rules sometimes stop him from doing what he wants to do, they also ensure that his own rights are protected.

Maintain Objectivity

Marilyn's three-year-old daughter, Stephanie, waited patiently (although she was becoming very bored) while her mother shopped for new towels in a department store. Stephanie caught sight of a little boy about her age shopping with his mother on the other side of a large pillow display. Stephanie peeked around the edge of the pile of pillows to get a better look at the little boy. He grinned at her. Embarrassed, she quickly scrambled back behind the pillow display. Unfortunately, in her haste, she dislodged the display, and an avalanche of pillows piled down on top of her.

Two salespersons rushed over (looking very annoyed), and several other shoppers stared at the mess. Marilyn was startled and horrified to see what Stephanie had done. She grabbed Stephanie by the arm and marched her off to the ladies' lounge to have a "few words."

Marilyn did not manage to stay objective about her daughter's behavior. She took her own feelings of embarrassment out on Stephanie. She could have been more helpful to Stephanie if she had been able to maintain a more objective and less emotional perspective.

We can greatly assist the development of self-control in children by staying focused on the reality of a situation rather than on adult feelings that are not relevant to the child's problem, such as preconceived notions and biased attitudes that do not relate directly to what the child has done. Marilyn's guidance will be more effective if she can push aside her feelings of humiliation (and apprehension that complete strangers will think she is a bad mother). Marilyn should focus on the objective reality of the situation: Stephanie had been trying to wait patiently, she did not intentionally do anything wrong, and she was obviously feeling upset and embarrassed already.

Positive child guidance is a teaching process. As in any educational process, powerful emotions such as anger, disgust, or the threat of harm damage rather than assist the process of learning. People, children included, are better able to concentrate and absorb information when they are reasonably calm and relaxed. A terrified child may remember vividly the look of daggers in a parent's eyes, but completely forget the whole point of the reprimand and not be able to recall what behavior caused the problem in the first place.

Even a child who has misbehaved deserves reassurance that he is still loved.

It is perfectly normal and healthy for us to feel waves of sheer fury now and again. Because of our size and power, however, it is appropriate for us to release most of those feelings of frustration and rage away from young children by jogging, punching and kneading bread dough, or by pounding out melodies on a piano. It is not fair nor helpful to blast powerful and scary expressions of anger at children. We can be honest without being overpowering.

Remove the Child from a Problem Situation

Removing a child from the scene of a conflict allows a cooling-off period for the adult and child, removes whatever temptation the child is having difficulty with (out of sight, out of mind), and ensures that a gawking or giggling audience is not watching and triggering further misbehavior. Although compromise should never be considered during the heat of a full-blown tantrum, compromise after the child has gained control may serve as an effective role model for the child to imitate as she learns to talk rather than scream to get what she wants.

Occasionally, adults have no choice but to pick up a young child who may be kicking and screaming and haul the child (as gently as possible but as firmly as necessary) away from the scene of a conflict. A preschooler who is having a tantrum in a grocery store because she cannot have the candy bar she wants should probably be escorted or, if necessary, picked up and carried out of the store. She can be helped to understand that she has two, and only two, choices: she can sit and cry for a long, long time in the car with her patient but assertive father, or she can return to the grocery store and continue the shopping trip, accepting the fact that there will be no candy bar.

If the father, through consistent oral and nonoral communication, convinces his daughter that he will not become angry or argumentative, and that he will also absolutely not back down, the little girl will soon recognize the futility of a long, dramatic, exhausting fit of crying. She will learn that that sort of thing simply does not work.

When she seems ready to throw in the towel, recognizing that she cannot bully or manipulate her father, she should be given an opportunity to save face. At this point, restraint, tactfulness, empathy, and perhaps an appropriate compromise (letting her choose a nutritious snack to take home) would keep the situation from having a winner and a loser. The little girl's future cooperativeness will hinge on her feeling confident that she can be cooperative without losing her dignity and autonomy and without having her past mistakes thrown in her face.

Questions about Sex-Related Issues

Sex-related issues often need to be dealt with early in childhood. Questions do come up about activities related to children's genital areas. Toddlers or preschoolers may rub their genital areas to fall asleep at naptime. Preschoolers or school-agers may show curiosity about each other's genitalia. Children may demonstrate totally unexpected behavior. Parents and teachers are sometimes at a loss as to how to respond, how firmly to respond, or even whether they should respond. With society's grave concerns about sexual abuse ever present, we must be extremely alert to authentic signs of abuse.

Take Time to Think before Reacting to Genital Touching

What to Look For
- Does the behavior appear to be simple, childlike curiosity?

  Toddlers or preschoolers take a moment in the bathroom to compare, touch, explore, or talk about their genitals. A preschooler whose mother is breast-feeding pulls off her shirt to "breast-feed" the doll in the housekeeping center.

What to Do
- Take care not to overreact.

  These behaviors are perfectly normal expressions of healthy curiosity. Sometimes, it is appropriate to acknowledge the differences and take advantage of a teachable moment. For example, say, "Yes, boys and girls have different bodies, but everybody's special. Girls grow up to be women, and boys grow up to be men." If necessary, the behavior can be gently and matter-of-factly redirected to a different activity.

- Does the behavior appear to be cyclical self-stimulation?

  Like thumb sucking, nail-biting, and hair-twisting, masturbation may become a child's stress reduction habit. A young child rubs her genitals when extremely tired or upset or simply as a habit when falling asleep.

- Does the behavior appear to be nonsensical silliness or intended to shock adults or entertain other children?

  Preschoolers stuff bark mulch in their underwear and waddle around the playground giggling and chanting, "We got big butts!" Children taunt each other with bathroom insults such as "I saw your wee-wee" or "You're a pooh-pooh diaper baby."

- Does the behavior appear to be oddly unchildlike? Does it seem to be a childish imitation of adult sexual behavior?

  You find two preschoolers hiding behind a bush with one on top of the other imitating adult sexual activity. A child playing dolls invents a pretend scenario that involves graphic sexual behavior or language.

- Gently redirect the behavior.

  If the child is an infant or toddler, there is little to do but ignore the behavior and focus your energy on removing sources of stress. Be sure the child is getting plenty of rest, a calm environment, and enough emotional nurturing. If the child is a preschooler, be more proactive in helping the child replace the habit with a more socially acceptable substitute behavior. For example, "Would you like to hold this teddy bear when you fall asleep to help you remember not to rub your bottom?" "You must go into the bathroom when you need to touch your bottom."

- Be understanding, firm, and consistent.

  Follow the basic guidelines for handling any misbehavior. For example, say, "Bark mulch is not for putting in your underwear." Taunting should always be stopped. Say, "Be kind, use kind words. Mean words hurt. If you feel angry, tell your friend why you feel angry. Tell him, 'I feel angry when you take my blocks.'" Remember that overly shocked reactions from adults or laughter from other children can tempt a child to repeat the behavior to get attention.

- Take an honest look at the big picture.

  Have you noticed any other warning signs that the child is being molested or sexually abused? Does it seem likely that the child has been exposed to pornography or sexual behavior at home, at school, or by other children? Is the child significantly delayed in social or emotional development? Does the child appear to be unhappy and withdrawn much of the time? Is the child seriously aggressive or rebellious? If the answer to any of these questions is yes, immediately seek advice from a counselor, child protective services professional, or other expert.

What Is Sexual Harassment?

sexual harassment
Unwelcome attention given for sexual gratification; for personal sexual stimulation; or to antagonize, bully, and dehumanize another person by using sexually related activity.

Sexual harassment is unwelcome attention of a sexual nature. It includes a range of behavior from disruptive annoyances to serious abuses and even forced sexual activity. Sexual harassment is not only morally wrong but *illegal*.

There have been a few highly publicized cases of young children being expelled from kindergarten or elementary school for "sexual harassment" because they hugged a teacher inappropriately or pinched another child on the bottom. Fortunately, these bizarre situations have been rare.

Young children before puberty are by definition incapable of sexually harassing anyone. They *are* capable of bullying, misbehaving, and behaving in a socially inappropriate manner. And they *can* be molested or sexually harmed by an adolescent or adult. So we should always be alert to those concerns. But if a child is not yet physiologically, hormonally, or psychologically capable of sex, touching another child's genitals *is not of a sexual nature*. It may be from curiosity. It may be in imitation of inappropriate things the young child has seen. It may simply be silly play. But whatever it is—*it is not sexual harassment*.

It may be appropriate for a third grader who has pinched his teacher on the bottom to face consequences for his action. (See the discussion about logical and natural consequences, page 183.) It would be essential to find out why a child this age is behaving inappropriately so we can help him change his behavior.

Perhaps this child was acting out as class clown because of an unmet need for attention from the teacher or from other children. Perhaps he was imitating something he has seen. Pinching a teacher on the bottom clearly is not appropriate, but children make mistakes. That's why we supervise them. They are immature. They are children!

Donnie is an energetic five-year-old in a university lab school preschool. His practice student today is Chiquitha, a university sophomore. She is giving him a lesson in geometric shapes. "Donnie," she says, "This is a square. Can you look around the room and find anything that is shaped like this?" Donnie looks around and points to a window. "Good job, Donnie. That window is shaped like a square. This is a circle. Can you find something that looks like a circle?"

Donnie looks around the room for a long time. Then he brightens, grabs both of Chiquitha's breasts with his hands and, with earnest sincerity, says, "Your brezez is round." Chiquitha is stunned. She quickly moves Donnie's hands. "Uhhh, yes, ummm, round, umm . . . let's put this away, and you can go build with the blocks now."

age-typical behavior
Behavior that is characteristic to specific developmental stages, thus it is typically seen in children of a certain age.

Chiquitha rushes out to the director, completely distraught and a little angry, to report that Donnie has grabbed her breasts. The director explains that Donnie's behavior is perfectly normal **age-typical behavior.** She praises Chiquitha for tactfully redirecting Donnie when it occurred. The director explains that Donnie's behavior should be ignored. If the behavior persists, however, it should be discreetly redirected. Focusing on the behavior might reinforce it and could cause it to be inappropriately repeated.

The director also explains that Donnie's family has a new baby who is breast-feeding. Donnie has been very interested in the process and has asked his mother lots of questions about how the baby gets milk from her breasts. Donnie's behavior was not *of a sexual nature*. He was simply being a typical inquisitive child, innocently learning about his world.

Assertively Shape Positive Behavior

When a child must be subjected to an unpleasant occurrence, the situation should be discussed squarely and honestly to give the child a chance to cooperate voluntarily. The situation should not, however, be allowed to stall or become a stalemate if the child refuses to cooperate. When medicine must be applied to a scrape on an unwilling child's knee, the adult must quickly and matter-of-factly explain what must be done, then get the unpleasant task over with. The longer discussion, whining, and arguing are tolerated, the more unpleasant and stressful the task of applying medicine will become.

Separation is a good example of a necessary but unpleasant occurrence in the lives of toddlers. Before a separation, parents must be given all the time they want to visit with their child and express affection. A parent should not be rushed but should clearly indicate to the caregiver when she is ready to leave (and willing to actually walk out the door). At this decisive moment of separation, a skilled caregiver will firmly but lovingly state, "Mommy needs to leave now. You may give mommy a hug and wave bye-bye through the window, or if you need, I can hold you while mommy leaves." If the child is clearly not willing to hug mommy and wave good-bye, then the parent and caregiver can move quickly and assertively to get the separation over with, even if the child resists loudly and has to be held.

The caregiver can express empathy, "Yes, you love your mommy. You miss her when she leaves. Sometimes I miss my mommy too. Did you know I have a mommy? Let's go see the dolls. Would you like to feed a bottle to our baby doll? Which baby doll do you want?" Shape positive behavior by making sure that it happens. Adults can often help children avoid situations in which they may experience failure by quickly and decisively making the right thing happen and then rapidly moving on to happier activities, all this without giving an appearance of frustration, anger, guilt, or disgust with the child's inability to actively cooperate or comply.

Children's negative feelings should be acknowledged and accepted, but they do not necessarily need to be dwelled on for a lengthy period (Claxton & Carr, 2004).

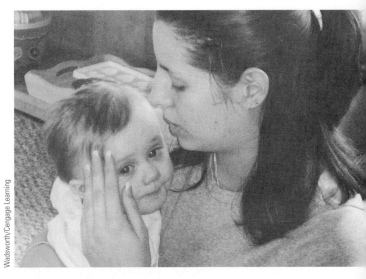

Wadsworth/Cengage Learning

■ Infants and toddlers in child care need a calm, consistent routine for separating from parents in the morning—waving bye-bye, finding a favorite toy or activity, or being held and talked to by a caregiver.

Teach Ground Rules

Children need to know exactly what is expected of them. Simple, consistently enforced guidelines help children learn to respect and abide by rules. Children, however, must have adult help to understand and remember ground rules. Following are several ways adults can actively teach children about rules (Clewett, 1988).

Role-Play

Give children a chance to act out, or practice, the correct following of rules. For preschoolers, switch roles so that the child can see and experience an appropriate response. Pretend to be the child and allow the child to pretend to be the adult, or pretend to be the child's troublesome friend; for example, "I will pretend to be Bert. Let's pretend I just pulled your hair. Can you point your finger at me, make a frown, and say, 'Don't pull my hair. That hurts!'?" Role-play can also be supported with puppets and appropriate children's literature (bibliotherapy).

Repetition

Children need many opportunities to hear a rule repeated before knowledge of that rule has fully reached the child's long-term memory bank. Any adult who has experienced an electrical power failure but mindlessly continued attempting to turn on appliances and lights knows that having knowledge of a thing does not necessarily bring about an immediate change in habitual behaviors. We have to remind ourselves over and over, "Oh, yes, I can't listen to the radio. . . . Oh, the electric can opener won't work. . . . Oh, the clock is not right." Children need and deserve patient reminders of rules and expectations so they will be encouraged to change their habit patterns.

Discussion

Rules have a great deal more meaning for children when they really understand reasons for the rules. Adults should remove from their vocabulary that age-old phrase "because I said so," which so often has been used as a blanket explanation for all rules and regulations issued by adults. Positive guidance requires that adults explain things to children simply and honestly; for example, "You must use the blunt knife instead of the sharp knife. I don't want you to get cut." "You may not open the gate without permission because the street is busy and dangerous." "You must wash your hands with soap and water before you eat. Your hands are dirty, and you could get sick from getting germs in your mouth." Children feel ownership when they are allowed to help create classroom rules.

Clarify Expectations

If we want children to follow our instructions, we must make sure they really understand what we intend for them to do. Adults often speak in vague, general terms. They say things such as, "Be good," "Be nice," "Act like a big girl." What children need are simple but specific statements of our expectations. For example, we might say such things as the following:

- "Sit down, please. Make sure your bottom is in the chair and your feet are on the floor."
- "Please hold your milk with both hands."
- "Please wait at the bottom of the slide until the person in front of you has gone down the slide. Then you may climb up and have your turn."
- "Please use a soft, slow voice to talk to me about your sister. I can't understand whining and screaming."

Additionally, adults sometimes assume that children automatically know how objects are intended to be used. Instead, children older than three need to be told specifically what various objects are for. Babies and toddlers put bowls on their heads, try to eat decorative plastic fruit, and attempt to pull T-shirts on like underpants. (That's why they're so much fun to be around.) Gentle guidance helps them toward the proper use of objects, but they also need a great deal of freedom to explore safe objects thoroughly, using all their senses and muscles to discover their world. If a baby or toddler stands up in a chair that could fall, she should tactfully be redirected to a safer place to climb or else the chair should be removed. A child older than three, however, can be told, "Please remember, a chair is for your seat, not your feet."

Children older than three can be taught the difference between toys, tools, and weapons; for example, "A toy is something you can play with, a tool is something useful to help you do something, and a weapon is intended to hurt someone. At school we use toys and tools but not weapons." A ball can be used as a toy to play catch, or it can be used as a tool to knock a kite out of a tree, but it must not be used as a weapon to hit someone in the face. A fork should only be used as a tool to pick up food, not as a toy to wave around or as a weapon to poke at another child. School-age children are especially capable of comprehending and identifying categories of objects and will spontaneously point out to one another, "That pencil is a tool. It's for writing. You mustn't use it like a toy or a weapon!"

Maintain Consistency

For children to behave appropriately, there must be consistency, with a reasonable level of flexibility, in the adult's expectations and enforcement of rules. Discipline should not be enforced based on the adult's mood or coincidental circumstances. For example, it would be inconsistent to

"Be kind. Please remember to use words instead of hitting. Tell Andy you don't want him to push you off the slide anymore."

Wadsworth/Cengage Learning

indicate to a young child (through our actions), "You can walk around the house eating and dropping crumbs, except when I am too tired and crabby to clean up after you or when we have company." There should be a consistent rule either that eating takes place at the table or that eating at various places in the house is allowed as long as family members clean up after themselves.

Older children, who have a clear understanding and acceptance of specific rules, can deal with occasional exceptions to those rules. They can understand that family members are expected to eat in the kitchen, even though breakfast in bed is a perfect Mother's Day surprise, and a pizza around the coffee table might be a perfect treat for a slumber party. Toddlers and young preschoolers, in contrast, do not have a full grasp of rules. They view the world in very literal black-and-white terms. An action either is or is not allowed. They become very frustrated and confused and tend to ignore a rule altogether if it seems to them to be inconsistently enforced. For example, little ones should never be allowed, even once, to ride in a car without being properly buckled into an appropriate car seat. If they believe there is absolutely no chance the car will move unless they are belted into a car seat, they will accept the car seat as a fact of life rather than something to be negotiated through whining and resisting.

To be consistent, adults should make very sure that a child's behavior is not laughed at on one occasion and reprimanded on another. Bathroom terms that brought giggles at home may not be nearly so funny at church or synagogue or when announced loudly at a family gathering. The toddler with spaghetti in his hair may be adorable the first time, but if he receives a great deal of attention (laughter, photographs, calling the neighbors to come see), he may be inclined to frequently repeat the behavior, which will not be nearly so entertaining to harried parents the second, third, or fourth time. In the early childhood setting, consistency, with reasonable flexibility, is essential.

> Marty, a toddler teacher, tried to teach her 18-month-olds not to climb on the low, redwood picnic table on their playground. Toddlers who climbed on the foot-high plank table were removed and placed on a foot-high, redwood plank deck nearby for a time-out. Marty knew that decks were to walk on and tables were not. To the toddlers, however, the rule about climbing seemed inconsistent. Both structures looked about the same. They were being removed from one low redwood structure and placed on the other, for a time-out, as a negative consequence. Being on the second structure was intended to teach them not to get on the first structure. Of course, the toddlers were never able to make sense of Marty's rule, so they simply ignored it. And time-out for toddlers is utter nonsense to begin with.

Adapt Objects, Events, and Attitudes to Remove Possible Causes of Problem Behavior

In many situations it is easier to change the circumstances surrounding the child than it is to change the child. Additionally, it is almost always more nurturing and less stressful for everyone involved if adults focus on setting the stage for proper behavior rather than on reprimanding children after they have behaved improperly. For example, if children are running in the classroom, it will be better and easier to change the room arrangement to make running difficult than to end-lessly remind children to walk. If toddlers persist in spill-ing their milk, they can be given smaller cups with only an ounce of milk at a time. That way, if they do have a spill, very little milk is wasted and very little effort is needed to clean it up. Children have to make mistakes to learn.

Rather than yelling to get the attention of rowdy chil-dren, an adult can use a dramatic whisper. Children will almost always pay more attention to a wide-eyed, dramatic whisper than to a rude, bellowing voice.

If children in a preschool program consistently be-come tired and irritable on field trips, then perhaps field trips can be rescheduled to a different time of day or for a shorter period. Or perhaps trips can be made less often but to more carefully chosen locations. When confronted with troublesome behavior problems, we should ask ourselves, "Instead of trying to change the child, is there any way I can reasonably change the child's environmental surround-ings or my own actions or attitudes to ease the problem?"

"Those are round and look a lot like our throwing balls don't they? But they are hard. They can hurt, so they're not for throwing. Let's be safe. I'll help you find a ball that is soft and good for throwing."

Offer Assistance and Encouragement

Children thrive on positive attention. They usually become very compliant when adults say, "How can I help you re-member this rule?" "What can we do to make it easier for you to get to bed on time?" "Let's practice the words you should say when you feel angry." Positive guidance means that adults work diligently to help children behave appro-priately not just to punish children for behaving inappropriately.

Give Undivided Attention

Children immediately recognize whether an adult is serious enough about what she is saying to stop and see that a request is followed. Even toddlers and preschoolers know that instructions do not mean much when they are given by an adult casually glancing back across her shoulder, making an offhanded comment across a room, "Come on now, put those toys away." In contrast, children sense that instructions mean a great deal when the adult stops what she is doing, walks over to the child, bends down to eye level, gently touches the child's shoulder, looks directly into the child's eyes, and says in a gentle but firm tone, "Sherrie, I need you to stop now and put the blocks away." A half hour of nagging and threatening from across the room will not have the impact of a gentle touch and one quiet statement made eye to eye and using the child's name.

Undivided attention has a powerful effect on children. In positive child guidance, attention focused directly on children will be assertive, be positive, and build self-esteem rather than be negative, angry, and destructive of pride and confidence. The following four actions can be carried out in a positive way to show children that they have our undivided attention and that we really care about their behavior:

Eye Contact

Move close and try to establish eye contact. A shy child or a child who has experienced eye contact as part of threatening, angry interactions will feel compelled to look away. Do not force the child to look you in the eye, but rather attempt to win the child's trust by associating eye contact with positive, loving interactions. If the child does look you in the eye, sincerely commend him, "Thank you for listening so well."

Body Positioned at Child's Level

Bend down to the child's eye level. Staring down your nose at a child tempts the child to look away and may also seem cold, threatening, or belittling to the child.

Appropriate Touch

Gently placing a hand on a child's shoulder or arm, or lightly holding one or both of the child's hands, helps focus attention. If the child is sitting on the floor, gently touching a foot or knee will obtain the child's attention and communicate caring concern. Appropriate touching is never grabby or forced. Follow the child's signals. Children usually make it very clear whether they find the adult's touch aversive or comforting.

Use of Child's Name

Using a child's given name or accepted nickname is more personal and appropriate than are general terms of endearment such as "sweety" or "honey." Adults in early care and education settings must learn every child's name very quickly to be effective. Sadly, some young children hear their names yelled so often as a reprimand that they fail to respond as we would expect when their name is used in a positive context. They do not recognize their name as a symbol for who they are, but only as a negative word that means they are in trouble.

Redirect Inappropriate Behavior Firmly and Respectfully

When a child's inappropriate behavior must be stopped, cooperation can be gained and resentment avoided by offering the child an acceptable alternative activity. A child who is pouring milk back and forth from cup to bowl during a meal may be told, "You may not play with your food. After lunch (or after nap), I will show you a good place for pouring." The child could then be directed at an appropriate time to pour, squirt, dribble, and splash to her heart's content with dishes and toys at a sink,

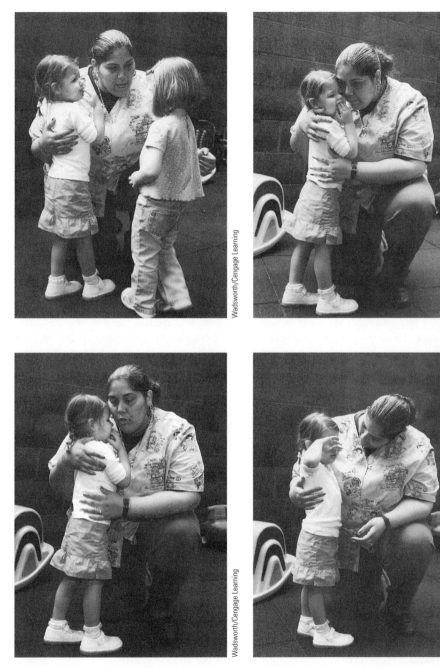

The nurturing adult listens to and reflects the child's feelings, then helps her resolve her problems in a fair way. Children's negative feelings should be acknowledged but not dwelled on.

bathtub, commercial water table, outdoor wading pool, or plastic basin placed within her reach with an inch or two of water.

When children feel angry, they hit, kick, pinch, and scratch. These typical aggressive behaviors must be stopped. The child's anger should, however, be given an appropriate outlet. When a child is told, "Hitting hurts; no hitting is allowed," the adult should also add, "Use words. Tell Jessica you don't like it when she steps on your fingers. Show Jessica your fingers and tell her how much they hurt."

Common sense and knowledge of the basic principles of child development will guide the effective use of **redirection** (interrupting an inappropriate activity and involving the child in a more appropriate choice). The idea is to replace misbehavior with a desired behavior so that the focus is on what the child should do rather than on what the child should not do. It is important, however, to ensure that the replacement activity does not become a reward for inappropriate behavior. Operant conditioning is the process of reinforcing or strengthening a behavior by rewarding it with a pleasurable response.

redirection
The process of offering a substitute focus to distract the child from a current undesirable one. For example, a child may be offered a developmentally appropriate water play activity to refocus his or her inappropriate interest in pouring milk from a cup onto the floor.

prevention techniques
A specific procedure or special type of action taken to make it difficult or impossible for someone to do a certain thing or for a certain type of thing to happen.

quick response techniques
A specific procedure or special type of action done swiftly in reaction to a situation.

Miss Kimberly, a toddler caregiver in a child care center, was concerned about the biting that was happening almost daily in her room. She thought that perhaps the toddlers were biting because their gums were uncomfortable with teething and they needed strong oral stimulation. She decided to offer hard crackers for the toddlers to bite as a substitute for biting each other. Within a few days, she discovered, to her dismay, that the toddlers were attacking and biting each other whenever they felt hungry for crackers. They had become conditioned to expect crackers in response to biting.

Miss Kimberly decided to resolve the biting problem with both **prevention techniques** and **quick response techniques**. She added interesting new activities and materials, moved snack time to an earlier part of the day, and increased her supervision efforts. She vowed to respond quickly, caringly, and firmly to any threat of biting. Her efforts worked.

Prevention Techniques

- Plan carefully to ensure developmentally appropriate activities and environments.
- Create calm, stress-free surroundings.
- Closely observe children to forestall problems that need to be prevented.
- Expect children to behave appropriately.
- Maintain a warm, friendly, optimistic attitude—smile!
- Express requests to children in positive rather than negative statements.
- Sincerely recognize (rather than praise) children's accomplishments.
- Keep your expectations realistic.

- Keep the big picture in mind—don't get caught up in things that don't really matter.

- Allow children to express their opinions.

- Listen to children.

Quick Response Techniques

- Make eye contact.

  - Position yourself so that you can establish eye contact with a child who seems to be having trouble.

  - Facial expressions should be caring rather than annoyed.

- Make physical contact.

  - Avert trouble by sticking close to a child who seems to be having problems.

  - Sit down next to the child and place an arm on his shoulder or make other appropriate contact.

  - Be calm and firm rather than menacing.

- Offer assistance.

  - Ask, "May I help you?"

  - Intervene, taking the child's hand gently and saying, "You seem to be having a problem. Would you like to tell me about it?"

  - "I'm sorry Raul, but you seem to have forgotten our rules. Please sit here so we can talk about this. Thank you."

- Give choices and consequences.

  - "Hussein, first you may help me tape these pages back in the picture book, then we'll find another activity for you. When you are ready to read books again, let me know and I'll show you how to turn the pages really carefully, okay?"

  - "Emma, you may have two choices. You may swing safely or pick out a different activity."

  - "Bettina, you have lost your chance to use the sand table this morning. Come with me. Let's find another fun activity for you. I feel sure you'll be able to remember the rules next time."

- Remove the child from the problem and help him express feelings.

  - Physically remove a child from the situation that has triggered an outburst so that he can begin to calm down.

  - If the child has been aggressive, find ways to help him verbalize his feelings. "I understand that you feel really angry, but hitting is not acceptable."

  - Acknowledge the child's feelings while clarifying boundaries. "What are some other things you could do when you feel angry with Zackary? What are some words you could say to him? You could say, 'I feel . . .'"

Wadsworth/Cengage Learning

■■ Sincerely acknowledge appropriate behavior. "Thank you for turning the pages so gently and carefully."

Clearly Express Appropriate Feelings

Although it is appropriate for adults to be honest in their expression of feelings to children, an adult's expression of anger can be too overwhelming for a young child to handle. Rage has no place in positive child guidance. When confronted by a large, snarling, furious grown-up, a young child has two possibilities: recoil in fear and try to stay out of the grown-up's way, or fight back by being rebellious and insubordinate. Neither of those options helps the child become a more confident, competent, and cooperative person. Children who are frequently shamed develop a general sense of guilt and unworthiness.

Rather than focus on feelings of anger, the adult can identify the underlying feelings that caused the anger. We can ask, "Am I feeling angry because I was startled, disappointed, worried, frightened, or frustrated?" Instead of saying, "I am furious with you," we can say, "I felt really frightened when I didn't know where you were. I was afraid you were hurt or lost. I was so upset I felt like crying." Following are several other examples of appropriate oral expressions of adult feelings that give the child information but do not directly attack anyone.

- *Surprise, Disbelief* "I can't believe this beautiful plant has had its leaves torn off. Plants can die if their leaves are harmed."
- *Sadness, Disappointment* "I feel very sad when I find books with the pages torn out. Books are beautiful and fun to read, but they aren't of any use when they are ripped apart."
- *Concern, Worry* "I feel worried when I see you scratching your mosquito bite. Scratching may cause it to become infected and sore. Let's cover it with a bandage."
- *Apprehension, Fear* "I feel very frightened when I see you climbing on the top rail of the fort. You must stay off the rails or else choose a different place to play on the playground."
- *Distress, Frustration* "I feel very frustrated when I find the door has been left open. We can't keep our house warm and comfortable inside when a door is left open. Please check the door each time you go out to make sure it's properly closed."

Explain the Potential Consequences of Unacceptable Behavior

Children older than three are usually perfectly capable of mentally connecting the cause-and-effect relationship between their conscious actions and potential consequences. If simple, polite, assertive statements of rules and expectations do not bring about an appropriate response from children, then it is time to discuss potential consequences. Explaining potential consequences is not the same as bribing, intimidating, or giving idle threats. It is intended to inform the child, to give an honest, sincere warning of an impending consequence. It is not intended to manipulate, coerce, or trick the child into behaving a certain way, but rather to give the child honest, reasonable choices such as, "If you do this, this will happen. If you do that, that will happen." We should give children only reasonable choices that we know we will be comfortable carrying out. It is not acceptable to say, for example, "If you don't come with me this instant, I will leave you here in the store by yourself." This is an idle threat of an illegal action that leaves parents and teachers only two options: lose credibility or neglect the child. Both of these are unacceptable.

The cliché that "you can lead a horse to water, but you can't make him drink" fits children quite well. We can offer a well-balanced meal to a young child, but we cannot presume to force the child to eat it if she chooses not to. What we can do is say, "You may eat your vegetables and meat if you feel hungry. If you are not hungry enough to eat your dinner, then you may wait until breakfast to eat. I will put your plate in the refrigerator in case you change your mind." This statement is assertive, confident, and reasonable, but not threatening or punishing. It is merely a recognition that the child has choices about her own body, and the adult has choices and responsibilities about what foods are healthy and appropriate to offer.

Provide Persistent Follow-Up

A motto to be emblazoned in the memory of all adults who deal with children is "Say what you mean, and mean what you say." Support positive guidance by allowing natural consequences to run their course when the results are reasonable and safe. There is no magic wand or bag of tricks in positive child guidance, only persistence, persistence, persistence. Adults who persevere in firm, assertive, respectful, and caring discipline will surely see positive results in the children they care for and teach. Children may be very persistent in their patterns of misbehavior. We, as adults, however, must be even more persistent in our supervision and follow-up.

The consistency of small but persistent nudges toward appropriate behavior is far more effective than erratic and inconsistent explosions of anger, harsh punishments, or intimidating threats. A gentle, rippling stream etches deep patterns in solid rock. Pounding on rocks with sledge hammers changes the shape of the rocks but risks a lot of damage in the process.

Emphasize Unconditional Caring and Affection

Unconditional caring, the giving of affection without any strings attached, is the foundation on which good discipline is built. Unconditional caring lets children know that they do not have to perform or achieve or submit to be loved and respected. We may disagree with things they do and work hard to change them, but we will still love and care for the child. Adults should create an environment that tells children orally and nonorally that they are valued (Clarke, 1978; Bardige & Segal,

The nurturing adult resolves conflicts assertively but respectfully.

2005; Honig, 2000; Patterson & Hidore, 1997; Ciaramicoli & Ketcham, 2000).

Maintain and Express Confidence That a Problem Will Be Resolved

Guiding children can be frustrating and distressing at times. We look at our children and shake our heads, wondering whether they will ever gain self-control and self-discipline. We must, however, firmly maintain and express confidence that specific problems will be resolved and our children will learn to behave appropriately, at least most of the time. Our confidence will strengthen children and convince them that control over their own behavior is a reachable goal.

Protect Children's Dignity and Privacy

When positive but assertive disciplinary measures are necessary, children should be afforded the dignity of being talked to in private. They are humiliated by being corrected in front of their friends, or even in front of other adults. Adults should refrain from discussing, in front of a child, all the careless, immature, and improper things the child might have done. Adults should refrain from talking and laughing about the child's past mistakes. And most of all, adults should treat children the way they themselves like to be treated: with dignity and respect.

Be Willing to Start Over to Forgive and Forget

In positive child guidance, adults should do the best they know how to do and then never look back. Worrying about the past, carrying grudges, or keeping mental lists of past misdeeds all undermine positive child guidance. For young children, every day is a new day. No matter what happened yesterday, today can be a good, successful day. When children know that adults are willing to forgive and forget, they will be more compliant and more willing to admit it when they know they are wrong. Forgiveness encourages honesty in children and motivates them to try harder to meet adult expectations.

KEY TERMS

age-typical behavior
prevention techniques
quick response techniques

redirection
replaces
sexual harassment

POINTS TO REMEMBER

- Consistency and fairness in the enforcement of rules help children learn to trust authority figures.
- Behaviors that are harmful or unfair must be interrupted immediately by a responsible adult.
- Children's negative feelings should be acknowledged and accepted but not dwelled on.
- The enforcement of discipline should never hinge on the adult's mood or coincidental circumstances.
- It is usually easier to change the circumstances surrounding the child than it is to change the child.

- Attention focused directly on children should be assertive, be positive, and build self-esteem.
- To show children they have our undivided attention, we give eye contact, position our body at the child's level, give appropriate touch, and use the child's name.
- Children are indeed full-fledged human beings and as such should be treated with the respect we give to and expect from other people we admire and care deeply about.

PRACTICAL APPLICATION

Will and the Cream Cheese Won Ton

Renee and Tom are loving and assertive parents. They have taught their children to respect the rights of others.

One evening, the entire household is aflutter with excitement because the children's grandparents have arrived for a short visit. Because Renee and Tom both worked, Renee had picked the children up from child care and Tom had picked up Chinese food for dinner from a favorite restaurant. Tom made sure to include an order of cream cheese won tons; the children were not too wild about Chinese food, but they especially loved the restaurant's specialty: cream cheese won tons.

Everyone sat around the table chatting and enjoying dinner. Will, who is five, perched on his knees in the big dining chair so he could see better. He listened attentively to every word of conversation as he slowly nibbled at the food on his plate.

As the adults finished eating, they pushed back their plates and continued to sit at the table, laughing and talking, catching up on family news and funny stories about the children and all their great adventures and escapades. Tom leaned back in his chair, stretched out his long legs, and draped an arm across the back of Will's chair. As he laughed and talked, he

happened to glance at Will's almost empty plate. He noticed one last cream cheese won ton pushed to the back of the plate. Absentmindedly, he picked up a fork, stabbed the won ton, and popped it into his mouth.

The instant Tom swallowed the won ton, he saw a stricken look fall across Will's face, and he knew he had made a big mistake. Will leaned close to his dad's ear and whispered intently, "Dad, we have to go to a lonely place and talk." Quietly, Tom got up from the table and followed Will to the bathroom. Tom sat down on the side of the bathtub while Will ceremoniously closed the bathroom door and then, with big tears sliding down his cheeks, said, "Dad, you're not supposed to take other people's things without asking. That was the only cream cheese won ton left, and I was saving it for last. You did a wrong thing."

Tom lifted Will into his lap, and they hugged each other long and hard. Tom said, "You're right, son. I did do a wrong thing and I apologize."

Tom didn't know whether to laugh or cry, but his heart was filled with pride that his son had been able to stand up for his rights and also had made a special effort to spare his dad's dignity by asking to talk in a "lonely place."

DISCUSSION QUESTIONS

1. Why do you suppose Tom ate Will's won ton? Have you ever inadvertently hurt a child's feelings? How did the child respond?

2. How do you think Will learned to resolve problems the way he did? Why do you think he asked for a lonely place to talk with his father?

3. How would it make you feel if a child responded to you the way Will responded to his father? How do you imagine Will's father felt? What do you suppose he was thinking during his conversation with Will?

STUDENT ACTIVITY

1. Tyler is two years old. He sucks his thumb. What is the most effective way to respond?
   a. Ignore the behavior or discreetly redirect it. Consider changes in the child's surroundings that may be helpful.
   b. Immediately disrupt the behavior and follow up assertively to determine the cause and change the behavior.

2. Cyndie is six. She has become enraged with her best friend, AnnaBelle, and is scratching her face. What is the most effective way to respond?
   a. Ignore the behavior or discreetly redirect it. Consider changes in the child's surroundings that may be helpful.
   b. Immediately disrupt the behavior and follow up assertively to determine the cause and change the behavior.

3. Arturo is nine. He is an extremely picky eater. At dinner, he refuses to eat his vegetables. What is the most effective way to respond?
   a. Ignore the behavior or discreetly redirect it. Consider changes in the child's surroundings that may be helpful.
   b. Immediately disrupt the behavior and follow up assertively to determine the cause and change the behavior.

4. Megan is four. She frequently has tantrums. Today, she didn't want to take a nap, so she is scream-ing and kicking the wall. She has almost kicked a hole in the wall. What is the most effective way to respond?
   a. Ignore the behavior or discreetly redirect it. Consider changes in the child's surroundings that may be helpful.
   b. Immediately disrupt the behavior and follow up assertively to determine the cause and change the behavior.

5. Hong is twelve. He doesn't know anyone is looking, and he is going through a girl's purse. What is the most effective way to respond?
   a. Ignore the behavior or discreetly redirect it. Consider changes in the child's surroundings that may be helpful.
   b. Immediately disrupt the behavior and follow up assertively to determine the cause and change the behavior.

6. Denny is six months old. He is rubbing his mashed bananas on his face and in his hair. What is the most effective way to respond?
   a. Ignore the behavior or discreetly redirect it. Consider changes in the child's surroundings that may be helpful.
   b. Immediately disrupt the behavior and follow up assertively to determine the cause and change the behavior.

RELATED READINGS

Helping Children Cope with Anger

Brooks, R., & Goldstein, S. (2001). *Raising resilient children: Fostering strength, hope and optimism in your child.* New York: McGraw-Hill.

Crawford, V., & Silver, L. B., Eds. (2001). *Embracing the monster: Overcoming the challenges of hidden disabilities.* Baltimore, MD: Paul H. Brookes.

Fabes, R. A., & Eisenberg, N. (1992). Young children's coping with interpersonal anger. *Child Development, 63*(1), 116–128.

Flynn, C. (1996). Regional differences in spanking experiences and attitudes: A comparison of northeastern and southern college students. *Journal of Family Violence, 11*(1), 59–80.

Gallo, N. (1997). Why spanking takes the spunk out of kids. In E. N. Junn & C. Boyatzis (Eds.), *Annual editions: Child growth and development 97/98* (4th ed.). New York: McGraw-Hill. (Original work published in *Child,* March/April 1989.)

Greeme, R. W. (2001). *The explosive child.* New York: HarperCollins. (A condensed audiotape of the first edition is also available.)

Harris, B. (2003). *When your kids push your buttons: And what you can do about it.* New York: Ballantine Books.

Hennessy, K. D., Rabideau, G. J., Cicchetti, D., & Cummings, E. M. (1994). Responses of physically abused and nonabused children to different forms on interadult anger. *Child Development, 65*(3), 815–828.

Hyman, I. A. (1997). *The case against spanking: How to discipline your child without hitting.* Hoboken, NJ: Jossey-Bass Psychology Series.

The author documents the long-term negative effects of spanking—how it brutalizes kids and creates violent adults—and gives commonsense advice on alternative methods for dealing with such everyday situations as what to do when your toddler becomes fussy in the grocery store or how to react if your child runs into the street.

Jalongo, M. (1986). Using crisis-oriented books with young children. In J. B. McCracken (Ed.), *Reducing stress in young children's lives* (41–46). Washington, DC: NAEYC.

Kurcinka, M. S. (1991). *Raising your spirited child.* New York: HarperCollins.

Kurcinka, M. S. (2001). *Kids, parents and power struggles.* New York: HarperCollins.

Ladd, R. E., Ed. (1996). *Children's rights revisioned: Philosophical readings.* Belmont, CA: Wadsworth.

Leach, P. (1998) *The physical punishment of children: Some input from recent research.* London, UK: NSPCC.

Levin, J., & Shanken-Kaye, J. M. (2002). *From disrupter to achiever.* Dubuque, IA, Canada: Kendall/Hunt Publishing.

Lewis, M., & Michalson, L. (1983). *Children's emotions and moods.* New York: Plenum.

Lewis, M., & Saarni, C. (1985). Culture and emotions. In M. Lewis & C. Saarni (Eds.), *The socialization of emotions* (1–17). New York: Plenum.

Miller, P., & Sperry, L. (1987). The socialization of anger and aggression. *Merrill-Palmer Quarterly, 33*(1), 1–31.

Ruben, D. (1996, September). Should you spank? *Parenting,* 136–141.

Russel, J. A. (1989). Culture, scripts, and children's understanding of emotion. In C. Saarni & P. L. Harris (Eds.), *Children's understanding of emotion* (293–318). Cambridge, UK: Cambridge University Press.

Saifer, S. (1996, Winter). Dealing with hitting and aggression in the classroom. *NHSA Journal, 15*(1), 37–39.

Samalin, N., & Whitney, C. (1995, May). What's wrong with spanking? *Parents, 70*(5), 35–36.

Straus, M. (1995). *Beating the devil out of them: Corporal punishment in American families.* New York: Lexington Books.

Whitehousse, E., & Pudney, W. (1996). *A volcano in my tummy: Helping children to handle anger, a resource book for parents, caregivers and teachers.* Gabriola Island, BC, Canada: New Society Publishers.

Zeman, J., & Shipman, K. (1996). Children's expression of negative affect: Reasons and method. *Development Psychology, 32*(5), 842–850.

Sexual Harassment

Biter, J. F. (2000). Classrooms and courtrooms: Facing sexual harassment in K–12 schools. *CHOICE: Current Reviews for Academic Libraries,* April, *37*(8), 1522.

Fried, S., and Fried, P. (1996). *Bullies and victims: Helping your child through the schoolyard battlefield.* New York: M. Evans.

Goleman, D. (1995). *Emotional intelligence.* New York, NY: Bantam.

McNamara, B., & McNamara, F. (1997). *Keys to dealing with bullies.* Hauppauge, NY: Barron's.

Miller, S. (1996). Youth and guns. In S. Miller, J. Brodine, & T. Miller (Eds.), *Safe by design* (423–430). Seattle, WA: Committee for Children.

Olweus, D. (1993). *Bullying at school.* Cambridge, MA: Blackwell.

Sexual harassment at an early age: New cases are changing the rules for schools. (1993, July/August). *The Harvard Education Letter, 4*(4).

Stein, N. (1993). It happens here, too: Sexual harassment and child sexual abuse in elementary and secondary school. In S. K. Biklen & D. Pollard (Eds.), *Gender and Education.* Chicago: National Society for the Study of Education.

The Online Companion™ to accompany the sixth edition of *Positive Child Guidance* is your link to additional guidance resources on the Internet. This supplement contains audio and visual materials; PowerPoint presentations; web activities with critical-thinking questions and practical-application assignments; and links to web resources. This additional content can be found at http://www.earlychilded.delmar.com.

Chapter 6

Planning the Developmentally Appropriate Prosocial Environment

Wadsworth/Cengage Learning

Prosocial Behavior

Prosocial behavior benefits others and demonstrates the presence of a social conscience. **Antisocial** behavior harms others and indicates a disregard for the rights and needs of others. The concept of prosocial behavior focuses on three critical elements of a child's beneficial, or helping, interactions with others: cooperation, empathy, and altruism.

A well-designed, developmentally appropriate practice (DAP) environment makes it easy for children to interact with learning materials independently and successfully. Busy, successful children are less likely to behave inappropriately.

prosocial
Behavior that improves the welfare of others or has a generally positive effect on persons with whom one comes in contact.

antisocial
Behavior that detracts from the welfare of others or has a generally negative effect on persons with whom one comes in contact. Antisocial personality behaviors are typically marked by lack of ethical restraint, lack of moral control, impulsiveness, and an inability to experience feelings of guilt.

Three Key Elements of Prosocial Behavior

- Cooperation—working with others unselfishly toward a common goal
- Empathy—putting oneself into others' shoes, to understand what they feel, to have insight into their thoughts and actions
- Altruism—behaving generously, acting in a way that benefits others with no motive of personal gain. Because patterns of natural human growth and development teach us that young children always begin life locked into egocentrism, we know that prosocial behavior is not an inborn trait, but a slowly learned way of acting that wins approval and affection from others.

Young children are not likely to postpone immediate gratification to work cooperatively with others toward a common goal. They do not start life with a capacity to recognize that others have feelings and needs similar to their own. And, of course, they do not come into the world equipped with the logical, cause-and-effect thinking skills necessary to understand that generously giving a valued object or favor today may bring affection and loyalty from a friend tomorrow (Peterson, 1983). Children adopt prosocial behaviors only after much experience and practice in an environment that demonstrates and nurtures positive social interaction (Holmes-Lonergan, 2003).

Setting the Stage for Appropriate Behavior

We give subtle messages to children about how we expect them to behave by the surroundings we plan for them. We can prevent many behavior problems before they ever begin by careful planning, by understanding children's developmental needs, and by creating a perfect match between their needs and the settings around them.

How Can the Physical Environment Support Prosocial Behavior?

Parents need to adapt home environments to make them safe, childproof, and interesting for children of various ages. Periodically, as children grow, parents must reexamine their children's bedrooms, playrooms, and play yards to see that the space matches the child's growing skills and interests. Children can gradually deal responsibly with and reliably use and put away more complicated equipment and furnishings.

Adults planning living space for groups of children also have a challenging task facing them. The well-planned early childhood environment is orderly but not rigid, clean but not sterile, and interesting but not overstimulating. In other words, it is carefully balanced. The only way to be sure that it is properly balanced is to watch the children who live, play, and work there, to see whether the environment seems overwhelming, boring, frustrating, or just right.

How Will I Recognize an Ineffective Child Care Environment?

Some early childhood settings have an atmosphere that seems halfway between a festival and a flea market. Almost every square inch of the walls is plastered with pictures, posters, signs, crafts, and notices. Things dangle from the ceiling like a swarm of butterflies, and furniture and toys form a wall-to-wall obstacle course on the floor. Walls and furniture are painted in taxicab yellow, stoplight red, and iridescent lime green. Special rugs are purchased with bright, busy, dizzying patterns of letters, numbers, and game boards to "stimulate learning."

This kind of environment invites loud, wild, unbridled activity. Children will probably feel comfortable running, leaping off tables, and bellowing across the room. Adults will probably have great difficulty guiding children into quiet concentration on a puzzle or book or teaching children to use soft "inside voices" rather than screaming and yelling. If the environment has long open pathways or open circular pathways around furniture, these **traffic patterns** may invite children to run amok rather than settle down with the learning materials. If children must cross through learning centers as they move through the room, they may disrupt other children. If there is a long, open pathway, toddlers and preschoolers will be tempted to run. An uninterrupted circular pathway around furniture or walls seems to capture the imagination of toddlers. They will run repeatedly in a circle, surprised each time that they came back to the same place. (This has learning value for toddlers, so you'll just have to decide when and where you can support it safely.)

Children may initially have great fun in this environment but will likely become bored, tired, and overwhelmed eventually. Because the adults are likely to have difficulty coping with the children's level of intensity, they may become irritable and restrictive, falling into negative power struggles with the children.

Other early childhood settings have an atmosphere somewhat like a dentist's waiting room. They may be stark white, lacking in any color. The sparse furnishings have an eerie appearance as if they have never been touched by human hands. Insipid elevator music may be piped in softly, and any toys or books seem to be on display rather than intended for actual use (they may actually be arranged out of the children's reach). The adults seem most anxious that the children "don't mess anything up." Painting, water play, and messy clay are out of the question. Everything the children do may be regimented into rigidly controlled activities that the whole class does together.

Little about this environment invites children to explore freely. Children become passive recipients of the experiences adults provide, and they are pressured to sit still,

In the DAP environment, furniture and learning equipment are used to clearly define learning centers such as the block center, housekeeping center, art center, reading center, science center, and manipulative center.

Wadsworth/Cengage Learning

traffic patterns
The most obvious routes children will take as they move around the classroom.

How Can I Promote Prosocial Behavior?

- **Model prosocial behavior.**

    Take advantage of children's natural tendency to imitate. Be considerate of others and set an example for kindness, generosity, and calm negotiation of problems.

- **Help children see the effects of their behavior.**

    Help the child determine how to make amends for the damage he has done. Also, when it seems appropriate, encourage role-playing. Just telling a child he hurt someone's feelings may not get through to him. Role-play may give him the opportunity to really identify with that person's thoughts and feelings.

- **Encourage individual responsibility.**

    At a young age, children can gain a sense of competency by pouring their own milk from a small pitcher, picking up their own toys, and putting on their own shoes. Having kids take on responsibilities, no matter what age, will give them a sense of pride and independence.

- **Help children learn social skills and strategies.**

    Interacting with and being accepted by peers is an essential part of early development. Preschool children benefit developmentally from being involved in quality early childhood programs. If that is not available, adult supervised play such as in casual neighborhood playgroups and with other children in the park can help children develop the social skills they must have.

- **Teach conflict resolution and negotiation skills.**

    Even children as young as three can use **conflict-resolution** skills to resolve problems. Initially, the adult must help the children calmly talk through possible compromises and alternatives. In the event the conflict cannot be resolved, the toy or object being fought over should be removed and the preschoolers redirected to other activities.

Adapted from Landy, 2002.

conflict resolution
A problem-solving strategy to help two disagreeing parties dissipate their frustration and bring their opposing views to a common solution. The method requires active listening and respectful, nonjudgmental communication.

be quiet, and not touch anything without permission. The children may at first be subdued, restrained, even intimidated by their surroundings, but they will become bored, restless, and eventually, either rebellious or submissive.

How Will I Recognize a DAP Environment?

Developmentally appropriate early childhood settings are warm and homey. Focal points of interest are at various places in the environment (displays of children's artwork, holiday decorations, or decorative touches), but they are not overwhelming. Ceilings, walls, and floors are muted, neutral tones so that the visual emphasis is on the learning equipment and the children's art masterpieces. Instead of seeing chaos when you look into the classroom, your eye should automatically go to the colors and shapes of the learning materials and equipment and the children's artwork.

Developmentally appropriate environments are well organized, interesting, and visually focused on the learning materials.

Materials are arranged neatly on child-size shelves so that children can easily put their own work away.

In the case of learning materials, more is not always better—sometimes less is better. *A hundred two-dimensional items* pasted on the wall that are hardly noticed by the children have minimal learning value and detract from the environment. *One three-dimensional item* has authentic learning value when it is introduced individually to the child and has interesting sensory qualities (for example, texture, color, smell) and the child is allowed to explore and interact with it freely.

Even babies and toddlers can begin to learn that their learning materials go back on a shelf. (Toy boxes are not appropriate.)

The DAP environment includes soft, warm, cozy areas that remind children of home.

The DAP environment is well lighted with plenty of sunny windows. Acoustical ceiling tiles or other materials are used to soften the sound level. Furniture and equipment are arranged to break the floor space into clearly defined learning centers to discourage running; to encourage focused attention on learning materials such as books, puzzles, and blocks; and to allow easy supervision.

DAP teachers look carefully at classroom traffic patterns. They ask themselves the following questions:

- At busy times, how do children move around the room?
- Where do clusters of children collect?
- Are there any specific problem areas?
- What changes in the room will discourage running?

Messy activities such as food preparation, clay projects, water play, and painting are regularly available for children two and older, and they are carefully structured to be used successfully and independently by the children. A preschooler who wants to finger paint knows that a chart posted at her eye level shows, in picture symbols, each step of the process she will follow:

1. Put on apron.
2. Use clothespins to hold paper.
3. Paint with hands.
4. Use sponge to clean area.
5. Wash hands.
6. Dry hands.
7. Hang up apron.
8. Put picture on drying rack.

Not only is the child having a creative expression experience, she is also learning to deal with symbols, to follow a sequence of tasks in a specific order, and to be responsible for herself. These are all important skills for children to master over time if they are to become successful in school and in life. The child may not follow all the tasks in the same order every time, but she is exposed to the idea of symbols, instructions, and independent responsibility.

If the child gets into trouble with the finger paint and has a mess she can't handle, she may either leave it or ask an adult for help. The adult's role is to supportively help the child work through problem solving. A more experienced child might be called on to help with the process. "Let's see. What do you think we should do first? What about this apron on the floor? Where should it go? Should we get sponges to wipe off the counter? Great idea! Would you like for me to help?"

In a developmentally appropriate preschool classroom, painting may be routinely set up with a day's supply of paper available to be fastened with clothespins onto a child-size easel. Just an ounce or two of fairly thick paint in a couple of nontip containers with short, fat paintbrushes makes the activity almost goof proof for a young child wanting to paint all by herself. A clothesline or drying rack at the child's height is ready nearby for placing wet paintings to dry.

Plan for appropriate behavior by limiting quantities. It may be tempting to put paint, glue, and Play-Doh out for children in the container they came in, but that is a mistake. Maria Montessori developed a concept that can be very helpful in preventing inappropriate behavior. She called her idea the **control of error** (Montessori & Hunt, 1989). She believed that children would rather correct themselves than depend on an adult to do it for them. She believed that making mistakes was a perfectly

control of error
A teaching strategy originally developed by Maria Montessori and also known as self-correction. Materials are designed to provide instant feedback to the child if he has made a mistake, or they are designed to make it impossible to make a mistake. This puts control in the hands of the learner and protects the child's self-esteem and self-motivation.

natural part of learning and that developing self-correction skills helped children develop confidence and decision-making skills.

If I put a large, economy-size bottle of glue on the child's shelf, the child is likely to squirt glue until the bottle is empty. Young children are more focused on the process than on the end product. The child may not even notice that the glue is pouring off the edge of the table and dripping onto her shoe. She has been enthralled with the sight, smell, and process of squeezing and watching the white glue oozing out of the tip of the bottle. If I intervene, she is bound to feel a letdown from the pleasure of her activity. No matter how tolerant I am, I am bound not to be too thrilled about a bottle's worth of glue on the table, her shoes, and the floor. Yikes!

On the other hand, if I place one ounce of glue in a collection of tiny glue bottles and put two on the shelf at a time, I have created control of error. If the child uses too much glue, she runs out of glue. No adult has to intervene to tell her she has made a mistake. She hasn't made a mistake. She can simply report that the glue is empty and more glue is needed. Instead of putting out 100 sheets of paper, put out 10 at a time and invite children to report when more paper is needed.

A tiny pitcher of milk, water, or juice should hold only a small quantity. An adult will have to fill it up frequently, but that is fine. If a child spills the pitcher, little is lost and it is manageable for the child to clean it up independently. If children are making their own snacks, be sure to put out small, manageable quantities, and ask the children to let you know when they are ready for more.

Classroom pets such as hamsters and fish, plants to water and enjoy, and many other opportunities provide occasions for children to be involved in real-life activities such as preparing food and cleaning up. Adults should structure independent pet

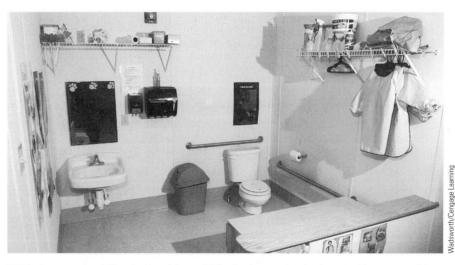

Bathrooms should be designed for a child's size, be spotlessly clean, and have everything the child needs within reach. The area is designed specifically for child independence, so adult supplies must be well out of children's reach.

Areas for children's personal items, often called cubbies, should be safe (no sharp edges), at the child's eye level, accessible, and easy for the child to use independently.

feeding so that no more food is available to children on the shelf on a given day than would be appropriate for that specific fish, bird, or animal. All activities are geared to meet the children's ability levels and to enhance independence. Food preparation for toddlers, for example, may consist of simply removing the peel from cut sections of bananas or washing apples.

Whether a DAP environment is designed for infants, toddlers, preschoolers, or school-age children, children's individual levels of development and interests are taken into consideration. Toddlers cannot function properly in environments that are arranged with hazardous and inappropriate furniture and toys, even though that same equipment may be perfectly suited to preschoolers. Infants and toddlers need unstructured toys and materials for sensory exploration and safe motor skill practice.

School-age children will be bored and offended if they are placed in a room filled with preschool blocks, picture books, and baby dolls. They too need a space suited to their special needs and interests. In afterschool care settings, children need a clubhouse environment with games, music, and quiet places to study. Outdoors, they need a soccer field, a basketball hoop, and elementary-school-size swings and slides.

> The lessons are individual, and brevity must be one of the chief characteristics.
>
> *Maria Montessori (Montessori & Hunt, 1989)*

What Effect Does the DAP Environment Have on Child Guidance?

In DAP environments, behavior problems are minimized because children are challenged and their needs are met. They are busy and excited about their accomplishments. At the beginning of the year, adults often have to simplify an environment to

The well-planned environment includes a wide range of interesting materials that are carefully matched to the ages and needs of the children.

ensure that children can manage independently and successfully. Gradually, as the children develop new skills, adults add new materials and increase the complexity of the environment so that it continually challenges the children. Adults are constantly searching for materials that match children's skills perfectly, somewhere right in the middle, between materials that are so simple that they are boring and materials that are so complex they are overwhelming. Adults in the DAP environment allow children to carry out play activities individually or in small groups of their own choosing rather than marching them all lockstep to do the same activities at the same time as a large group.

School-age children spend much of their time in discovery learning. They don't spend all their time sitting in desks listening to and reciting for a lecturing teacher. Large group activities for preschoolers are limited to short periods for sharing, singing, and hearing stories. Group activities are avoided for infants and toddlers, although adults often sit on the floor and read or sing to any babies or toddlers who cluster around them.

The adult constantly looks for ways to increase the children's independence and mastery of their environment. He has taught the children how to spread their jackets on the floor, stand with feet near the collar or hood, stick hands in the armholes, and then flip the jackets over their heads. Like magic, they know how to put their own coats on without help. He has used color-coding to help children know where things go. Everything in a yellow container goes in the art center, which is marked with yellow tape; everything red goes in the science center, which is marked with red tape.

In some areas he has taped pictures of toys and games on shelves to remind children where to put things away. Children are allowed to rearrange the playhouse furniture and get out all the dishes and toys out in the housekeeping center as long as they remember to be good citizens and put it back when they are finished. The children know that the environment is their space. They feel pride and self-confidence. They know the adult is their ally, not their enemy. To set the stage for positive child guidance, ensure that the environment follows DAP:

- Arrange shelves and furniture to identify the learning centers.
- Route children's traffic patterns so that children don't interrupt each other.
- Make sure that teachers can observe every part of the room without any obstruction.
- Separate noisy areas from quiet ones (for example, reading area and puzzles on one side of the room, blocks and housekeeping center on the other).
- Place learning centers near necessary resources (for example, water source, door).
- Display materials at a height easily accessible to children.
- Ensure that materials can be seen easily by children and are visually appealing.
- Place no materials on top or in front of other materials; space them out so they are not too close to each other.
- Provide only two or three duplicates of a few highly sought after types of learning materials (crayons, markers, tricycles, dolls, swings); emphasis should be on variety, not duplication.
- Color code, label, or use picture icons so children can put the materials away without help.
- Ensure that the environment reflects authentic, diverse life experiences.
- Change the environment to reflect the changing interests and abilities of the children over time.

How Do Schedules Support Positive Behavior?

Schedules are terribly important to planning a DAP environment. Young children adamantly resist being hurried, and they can barely tolerate standing around and waiting. They have their own pace. Adults are well advised to respect the individual pace of babies and young children. You may be wondering, "Okay, at home with my own baby I can be flexible and follow her schedule. But at school, I have too many preschoolers to do that. How can I possibly adapt to all their needs? Some zip around at a million miles an hour. Some move like a snail, studying every detail as they go."

Child-directed activity is an essential part of DAP scheduling. Different children definitely have different paces, but by scheduling large blocks of time for child-directed activities, children are able to work and play at their own pace. One child may take only three seconds to paint a paper plate turkey to her satisfaction, another child may want to spend 20 minutes painting it just the way he wants, and a third may not want to paint one at all. Children appreciate having a blocks of time devoted to child-directed activity. Having regularly scheduled blocks of child-directed

child-directed
Learning activity instigated by the child's natural curiosity and desire to learn rather than by the adult's direction, manipulation, or coercion.

activity gives children secure, predictable scheduling patterns while allowing enough time to meet an individual child's needs.

If children are forced into a rigidly scheduled lock-step group activity, the fast child will be bored and tempted to get into mischief as he waits for others to finish. The slow child will be forced to stop the activity before he has fully benefited from the learning value of the activity. He may also feel frustrated and irritated because he was unable to finish a project he cared about. Individualized, self-paced, child-directed learning is DAP—it supports authentic learning, strengthens self-esteem, and enables positive guidance.

The following is typical of a developmentally appropriate preschool child care schedule. It includes large blocks of time to allow children the flexibility to select materials of interest to them and to work at their own pace.

6:30–9:30—Breakfast and Learning Activity Center Time
Children arrive at the center and go to the appropriate classroom. Learning centers are open for play, and breakfast is available until 9:00.

9:30–10:00—Circle Time
Children and teachers sit together at circle time to sing, read books, tell stories, discuss the past day's events, talk about special materials or projects that will be available in the classroom that day, and discuss who will be selected for jobs such as feeding the turtle and passing out napkins.

10:00–11:00—Learning Activity Center Time
Center time features developmentally appropriate small group activities, most child-initiated but some teacher-assisted. Center time provides an opportunity for cooperative and independent learning within a developmentally supportive structure. Centers may include such areas as housekeeping, dramatic play, art, blocks, science and nature, reading, writing, math, sensory recognition, and music.

11:00–12:00—Outdoor Play
Children need an outdoor play area in which to develop their gross and fine motor skills. They need to learn to negotiate with others, work out conflicts, and explore the world around them.

12:00–1:30—Lunch
1:30–3:00—Rest Time
3:00–3:30—Snack
3:30–4:30—Outdoor Time
4:30–6:30—Learning Activity Center Time
The final two hours—during which most children are picked up by their parents or guardians—are usually a flexible time that includes learning activity center time, music, dancing, and dramatic play.

Parents too should pay close attention to scheduling activities at home to set the stage for positive child guidance. Planning to take a young child shopping in the late afternoon when she is likely to be tired and irritable is less likely to be successful than a trip planned midmorning, for example. Allowing a school-age child to begin watching a television show and then abruptly intervening to say that it is bedtime shows poor planning.

Bill and Irene both work. They hate getting their three children up in the morning. Because evenings are so hectic, the children often do not get to bed until 9:30 or 10:00 p.m. Of course they are cranky and out of sorts when their parents try to wake them at the crack of dawn. Bill and Irene are so rushed in the morning that they wait until the last possible moment to get the kids up. Then there is a mad rush to get them dressed and fed. Almost always, there is conflict with one or more of the balky, groggy children.

For a happier family life, Bill and Irene will have to reschedule evening activities to make sure they and the children have adequate rest. They will also have to wake the children earlier, rather than as late as possible, so the children have time to wake up and plenty of time to eat and dress. Rushing a sleepy child is almost guaranteed to create an unmanageable child.

Transitions are those difficult changeovers between activities, when children may balk at moving from one thing to the next. Special attention must be paid to transition periods to hold children's attention, to keep them on task if cleanup is needed, and to gently nudge them to the next activity. Excellent planning, organization, and an upbeat, optimistic attitude can go a long way to help ease children through transitions.

Some children have far more trouble than others with transitions. Bright children become especially engrossed in their activities and may have a particularly difficult time tearing themselves away from whatever they are doing at the moment. A parent may confide, "I can't get her to stop playing with her toys to get in the bath, then once she is in the bath, I can't get her out of the bath. I finally get her in bed to read her a goodnight story and she cries for me to read more books. Help!"

These children seem to live every moment of their lives to the fullest. They are eager to learn and wonderfully self-directed, but during a transition they need special support to avoid excessive dawdling, resistance, tears, or even a tantrum.

transitions
Phase in daily activities in which a child must give up or leave one activity and begin another activity. These difficult phases between activities may cause children to balk at moving from one thing to the next. Additionally, the confusion and stress of the changeover may trigger misbehavior.

How Can I Improve Transition Times?

For calm transitions . . .

- Give advance notice: "Five minutes till clean-up!"

- Make transitions predictable and timely.

- Keep transitions unrushed and peaceful.

- Consider individual children's needs: "Johar, let's put your name on that puzzle so you can finish it after naptime."

- Eliminate boring waiting times: "While we are waiting for the other children to wash their hands, let's sing a song."

Adapted from Feldman & Jones, 1995.

The Nurturing Social Environment

Adults who hope to stimulate prosocial behavior in young children must first establish a nurturing social environment, a setting in which children feel safe enough and comfortable enough to be cooperative, empathetic, and altruistic. Children who worry about being hurt, feel stressed to perform beyond their capability, or feel pushed into competition with playmates will probably have little interest in prosocial behavior. Children who are afraid that their own needs will not be met may not be able to be generous with others. Children may behave in a prosocial manner in one setting but not in another; day-to-day behavior depends to a great extent on the surroundings (Hartshorne & May, 1928; Berk, 2001; Carr et al., 2002; Charney, 1997, 2002; Katz & McClellan, 1997).

How Relaxed, Playful Environments Encourage Prosocial Behavior

Early childhood is a special time in life. The young of other mammals (puppies, kittens, colts, and so on) frolic and play as they develop the skills they need to survive in adulthood. Adults of various species go about the serious work of providing food, shelter, and protection while the young chase around, pouncing on bugs, climbing trees, rolling in the grass, and having pretend fights. Their gleeful freedom enables them to coordinate muscles and practice skills.

Young human beings also need a protected period of childhood in which to play and explore. If children are forced into somber, little-adult behavior, they may turn sour and critical. Instead of taking pleasure in their friends' playful antics, they may feel compelled to report, or tattle, to adults about even the most trivial misdeed of another child. Children should feel free to complain to adults when personal rights have been violated and to report misbehavior to authorities (adults) when rules have been broken or hazardous behavior is taking place. That kind of telling-on is sincere and should never be labeled tattling. Frivolous or malicious telling, however, is a different matter. The child who obsessively tells, hoping to get peers in trouble, may expect adults to stamp out or punish every silly or childish behavior and to reward him for telling, for being little Mr. Goody-Goody. This behavior is inappropriate and should be addressed.

A child who persists in telling on others for no good reason will seem antisocial to playmates who have been told on. The child who tattles, however, will probably have inferred from adult criticisms of childish behavior that it is not okay to be a child, to be one of the gang. This child may feel aloof and apart from other children: he may actually view himself as a little adult. These feelings hinder the development of friendships that lead to wholesome cooperative play and to optimal social and emotional development, so we need to let the child know that it is definitely okay to be a silly kid sometimes. Children can be helped to refrain from tattling on other children when they are taught to help a friend who made a mistake. "Yes, Shelley, I see that James forgot to take his turn. How can we help him remember?"

A relaxed, playful atmosphere for babies and young children helps them develop tolerance and a sense of humor. Exposure to adults who are tolerant of others and do not take themselves too seriously greatly aids children in developing the ability to feel empathy for others. Adults sometimes forget to step into children's shoes to imagine what they feel and see things from their perspective.

Adults consider sitting back, staring into space, and doing nothing an indulgent luxury. Children consider this sitting and doing nothing an aversive punishment. Adults have a slower, quieter rhythm and pace than do children and may feel annoyed by children's squealing, wriggling, wrestling, and running. Intolerant adults force children to function within the adult's comfort zone for noise and movement. In contrast, when young children sense the generosity of adults who kindly tolerate and gently redirect the bustling chaos of active, noisy children, then the children in turn learn to demonstrate generosity and tolerance for others.

The nurturing social environment is relaxed and playful.

Instead of expressing exasperation, Allen, a young daddy, sits down and has a good laugh when his toddler walks in wearing underwear on his head rather than on his bottom. Mrs. Farrel, a long-time member of Weight Watchers, grins and takes it as a sincere compliment when little Jennifer says, "I think you're beautiful. You're the prettiest fat lady in the whole world." Miss Cindy laughs good-naturedly with her school-agers after the gruesome spider that has startled her turns out to be nothing more than a plastic Halloween party favor.

We might be tempted to take normal childish behaviors more seriously than necessary or even become angry and punitive with the children described earlier. In a relaxed, playful atmosphere, however, children can learn discipline, but they can also learn that it is okay to be generous and forgiving (Mussen & Eisenberg-Berg, 1977; Wilcox-Herzog & Ward, 2004; Webster-Stratton, 2000). Children learn that it is okay to make mistakes because parents, teachers, and caregivers are allies, not enemies. It is okay to be playful and silly at times because others can let down their barriers and share in a good laugh.

Clearly, there is a boundary between silliness and genuine misbehavior, between playfulness and antisocial activity. Playfulness is neither hurtful nor mean spirited; maliciousness is both. Silly behavior that is not totally appropriate can be dealt with patiently and with a sense of humor, even though it may need to be firmly redirected at some point if it begins to interfere with necessary routines or to annoy others.

Wadsworth/Cengage Learning

An overwhelming need of early childhood is the need for interesting, authentic, and challenging activities. This little girl is completely engrossed in replaying a very important event in her culture. She creates a birthday cake out of Play-Doh while singing "Happy Birthday" to herself. Then she blows out the pretend candles. She may want to come back to this activity many times.

Creating a Cooperative Setting

When adults say things such as "See if you can put your lunch box away before anyone else" or "Whoever is quietest can be first in line," children are encouraged to be competitive rather than cooperative. We are often tempted to use competitive challenges because they work so much more powerfully and effectively than does nagging or threatening, and they seem less negative. Remember, even if something works well to achieve short-term goals, it may not necessarily achieve the long-term goals we seek. In the long run, getting children's coats on quickly or getting trash picked up without a second reminder is not nearly as important as fostering cooperative and caring relationships among children who will someday be adult citizens.

By urging children to win at the expense of others, we may be establishing patterns of greediness and a lack of regard for the feelings of others. It is far more helpful to redirect children's natural competitive urges into competition with their own best records: "I wonder if you can build these blocks even higher than you did yesterday?" or "Deonicia, you are so quiet and still. You must be ready for lunch. Would you like to be our leader today?"

Developmentally Appropriate Activities, Materials, and Routines

Bored children become irritable and mischievous. Children who are pushed beyond their limits into irrelevant memorization or tedious busy work may become antagonistic and rebellious. Unhappy children are more likely to behave in antisocial ways. When adults hold unrealistic expectations for children, stressful, even angry, relations erupt. This friction becomes contagious, and soon, interactions among the children themselves are tinged with irritability and annoyance. This is quite obviously not a situation in which children can learn and practice prosocial behavior.

The secret to a cooperative, caring, and generous atmosphere among young children lies in our meeting children's basic needs: social, emotional, physical, and intellectual. An overwhelming need of early childhood is the need for fascinating, authentic, and challenging activities. John Dewey, Maria Montessori, Jean Piaget, and other experts have shown us that children love to learn. These experts have made it clear that children learn easily through spontaneous as well as guided play experiences. Children find fulfillment in activities that are developmentally appropriate (Worth & Grollman, 2003; Hatch, 2005; Helm, 2004; Rim-Kaufman et al., 2005; Sanders, 2002; Zigler et al., 2004).

Children become deeply involved in their play and are amazingly relaxed and compliant when their need for fulfilling activity is met. This kind of productive, fulfilling activity is defined as DAP (Dunn & Kontos, 1997).

Why Is Consistency Important?

Teachers, parents, and child care providers quite often are trapped by the idea that if something does not work the first time, then it will never work. Children eventually change a behavior when they finally comprehend and remember that the action will quickly and consistently be stopped or redirected. A caregiver who decides that preschoolers should learn to scrape their plates independently after lunch may feel exasperated when the children mistakenly throw their plates and utensils away on their first try. A kindergarten teacher may throw up his hands in frustration after disastrously introducing finger painting for the first time to rowdy five-year-olds who leave school looking like splotchy rainbows. And any adult who has ever dealt with toddlers knows that the point does not get across the first hundred times one-year-olds are told that sticks and leaves should not go in their mouth.

Children learn positive ways of interacting with others when we can be consistent and persistent (not angry and impatient). We can avoid a great deal of irritation by recognizing that it takes time for children to absorb new skills and habits. Our task is to structure a consistent and predictable environment for children where they are allowed adequate periods to develop new skills introduced in tiny, bite-size bits.

Activities Should Be . . .

- Relevant: match the child's capabilities and interests.
- Active: encourage movement.
- Sensorial: appeal to the five senses.

To Support Positive Behavior . . .

- Get to know children personally and respond to their individual capabilities, interests, and preferences.
- Plan room arrangements that minimize frustration, congestion, and confusion for children.
- Prepare and arrange interesting toys and activities that relate to all areas of children's development: social, emotional, and physical, as well as intellectual.
- Establish routines that allow uninterrupted blocks of time for spontaneous, self-directed play in a carefully planned environment.
- Make arrangements for hands-on exploration of real objects to be a natural and integral part of learning activities.
- Allow children to express their own individuality by making their own choices within clearly defined limits, by saying, for example, "Would you rather paint or play with clay?" "Would you rather have orange juice or milk?" "Would you rather wear a skirt or blue jeans?"

- Greatly limit situations in which children are forced to sit still, to wait for something to happen, or to stand in line (toddlers are especially unable to cope with these situations).

We adults are prone to set absurd goals. We focus our attention on children's behavior in fits and starts. We ignore messiness for months or years, then suddenly insist on neatness: this minute!

Three-year-old Fernando had always traipsed around the house after his bath in a big, soft bath towel. When he was ready to get dressed, he had a habit of dropping the damp towel in a heap on his bedroom floor. Freshly scrubbed little boys wrapped in towels are so endearing that his parents had always quietly tolerated his towel-dropping ritual. One day, however, his poor mom reached the end of her patience and yelled, "Fernando, get this wet towel into the bathroom, and I mean step on it!" After she cooled off a bit, she peeked into the bathroom to check on Fernando. There he stood in the middle of the bathroom, crying pitifully but standing obediently on the towel.

How Can I Support Cooperativeness?

We live in an instant society. When we feel a child is old enough to behave in a certain way, we want that behavior instantly. One popular paperback book confidently tells parents that children can be toilet trained in a day. In reality, children cannot master toilet training in a day, a week, or even a month. A two-year-old may go from diapers to dry pants literally overnight, but this only happens after the child has mastered hundreds of little prerequisite skills. The toddler must gradually learn how to recognize body sensations, communicate needs, inhibit sudden impulses, consciously manipulate the muscles that control elimination, and even balance on top of a big scary bowl of water, all this just to please grown-ups. Many children will be three or older before they have gained reliable control over bowel and bladder.

Consistent, Predictable Routines Help a Child Ease Comfortably into Learning New Skills

For months, toilet training may consist only of talking about the potty, looking at it, exploring it, and sitting for a second or two on it, just as a playful part of a diaper-changing routine. It may be months before the child's consistent, predictable routines expand to include actually using the potty. The important thing is that the child keeps moving in the right direction. Someday, nobody will remember or care how fast or slow the learning was.

Be patient with potty learning.

Wadsworth/Cengage Learning

Children are quite naturally inclined to resist when they are confronted with a sudden, unexpected demand that they change a long-standing behavior. Likewise, some of us adults put up quite a fuss when we were first told that we ought to wear seat belts in cars. We argued, "But it feels weird . . . but I'm not accustomed to it . . . but I don't want to change." A toddler who has never had a worry in the world about when or where to relieve himself might well feel those same feelings when we insist that he ought to keep his pants dry by urinating in a toilet. Consistency and predictability in our expectations for children help them accept and gradually adapt to our standards. Children do not instantly develop an ability to take turns or to resist greedily grabbing a toy. Slowly and persistently, however, we can nudge children into behaving in a more responsible and prosocial manner.

The Nurturing Adult

One might jump to the erroneous conclusion that a nurturing parent, teacher, or caregiver is one who is either a saint or a pushover. The word *nurture*, however, means to train, to educate, or to nourish. The truly nurturing adult is simply an honest, emotionally healthy person who has learned how to be both assertive and caring at the same time.

How Can I Be More Nurturing and Patient?

Teaching children in a way that nourishes them does not mean pointing out every flaw, criticizing every imperfection, and punishing every lapse in judgment. In fact, the first step toward positively shaping children's behavior is simply setting a good example; that is, modeling appropriate behavior. Unbeknownst to us, many of children's most upsetting misbehaviors are little more than instant replays of our own behavior in a context we do not expect. They imitate our own practice of hitting when we want to communicate our displeasure. We hit children and then we tell them not to hit others. Consider, for example, the classic irony of an adult saying, "If you don't stop hitting your brother, I'm going to spank you."

What about Spanking?

The experts tell us that spanking is an inappropriate and ineffective method for disciplining children. We know that hurting children is never acceptable in DAP. Slapping, pinching, biting, and shaking children are dangerous and clearly unacceptable ways for adults to guide children in any situation. **Shaken baby syndrome** is a devastating, dangerous, potentially fatal condition caused by shaking a baby or young child in anger.

A big reason for not ever using physical punishment with young children is that you never have to worry about becoming angry when you are meting out physical punishment and accidentally going too far. That parent who has a toddler gripped by the arm and just means to give him a swat on the bottom forgets that she is angry and her adrenalin is pumping. She knows he is wearing a thick diaper and she means

shaken baby syndrome (SBS)
A particularly devastating type of child abuse that is caused by forcefully shaking a baby or young child. It can cause brain damage, blindness, learning impairment, and death.

for him to feel the swat. What she doesn't realize is that when she whacks his bottom, his neck receives a strong whiplash effect that could be dangerous to his neck and brain, given his disproportionately large head and small body.

Very few adults are actually cruel and set about to injure children. Far too many adults get frustrated and angry and accidentally go too far. Opening the door invites the problem. Graziano and colleagues (1996) found that 85 percent of parents surveyed felt moderate to high anger, remorse, and agitation while administering corporal punishment to their children. Most say they would rather not spank if they had an alternative in which they believed. This contradicts the common warning to parents to refrain from spanking in anger.

In almost all states, spanking other people's children in school and child care settings is against the law. Striking a child in a child care or school setting could ruin your career, your reputation, and your financial future (lawsuits do happen).

That doesn't mean that parents who spank don't love their children. Lots of children who are spanked manage to grow up to be kind, bright, healthy, and responsible. That number undoubtedly includes many readers of this book. Generations of our parents and grandparents had great faith in a phrase some of us heard growing up, "I'll blister you till you can't sit down and then you'll remember not to touch other people's things" or ". . . and then you'll learn to be nice to your brother" or ". . . and then you'll remember not to run out in the street again." Sure enough, fear and pain turned out to be pretty good deterrents. But some of us may also remember a few problems and resentments along the way as we grew up.

The powerful controlling effect of spanking lies in its ability to frighten and intimidate a child. Although corporal punishment may seem to work quite well at first, when children are small and easily intimidated, it models aggressive behavior and accustoms children to being controlled by external physical force. After a child has been spanked on many occasions, he becomes so accustomed to the way it feels that it no longer has the same effect. It may make him furious, but it probably will not scare him. This creates a difficult situation for everyone as children grow bigger and stronger. In any case, eventually the child will be too large to control physically.

Experienced teachers know they must pay special attention to the child who seems well controlled by a strict authoritarian mother or father who spanks often. Unfortunately, quite often, as soon as the parent's back is turned, this child is out of control. Typically, the child will severely test the teachers' patience as they begin using their authoritative guidance strategies. The child is expecting to be spanked, to be controlled externally. When she isn't punished, she feels compelled to see how far out of control she can go before something bad happens to her. She will test this process many, many times before she begins to trust the teachers. With trust, support, and caring, assertive role models, she will finally begin the process of learning how to control her impulses and choices *internally*.

The point of this book is not that one spank will ruin a child's life. It is that relying on hitting children to control them interferes with their development of inner control. Spanking is simply not as effective for winning a child's cooperation as guiding the child with positive assertive methods. Spanking and yelling at children increase stress for children and raise many other negative concerns if we are truly committed to providing a healthy environment where children can grow and learn to their highest potential.

What's Wrong with Spanking?
- Angry actions and words hurt children, making them feel threatened and devalued.
- Spanking can cause children to overreact with pent-up feelings of anger, hostility, or fear.
- Spanking threatens to damage the important bond of trust between the adult and the child.
- By modeling physical aggression, the adult shows the child that it is proper to hurt others when they wrong us.
- Children who are spanked show more aggressive behavior toward peers and more retaliatory anger than do children disciplined with positive methods.
- Because spanking doesn't usually work, it is all too easy to lose emotional control and unintentionally hurt a child emotionally or physically.
- There is ample evidence that physical abuse leads to poor self-esteem, long-term school and work failure, drug abuse, and involvement in crime (Child Welfare League of America, 2005; Hyman, 1997; Larzelere, 1986).

Why Do People Spank?
- People don't really know what else to do when a child misbehaves.
- People are unable to control their own anger and frustration.
- Most parents don't want to hurt their children, but unusual stress can make even a gentle parent occasionally lose control.
- Violence in the media tends to desensitize parents to aggressive behavior—hitting, slapping, using angry words with a child.
- Drug or alcohol use causes a loss of judgment.
- Issues such as poverty, workplace problems, marital stress, or being a single parent become overwhelming and cause a loss of emotional control.
- A parent's family, religious, or cultural teachings may favor spanking, and the parent hasn't considered potential problems that result from spanking (Marshall, 2002; National Center for Children in Poverty, 2004; Douglas & Finkelhor, 2005).

If a child is overly loud and boisterous, we may focus on being particularly soft voiced and calm. If a child is angry and unyielding, we can model patience and forgiveness. If a child is aggressive and hurtful, we can demonstrate gentleness and kindness. Being nurturing must not be used as an excuse to ignore behaviors that must be stopped. Our own prosocial behavior will be a good example for the child as we assertively protect property and personal rights by interrupting and redirecting unacceptable behavior. Additionally, we can make a mental note to find future opportunities, after a conflict situation has been resolved, to continue modeling desired behaviors such as calmness, forgiveness, and gentleness. This focus on assertive but nonaggressive guidance is particularly noteworthy, because many adults rely on angry and aggressive methods of discipline. In the late 1960s, 94 percent of the U.S. adult population approved of spanking a child. More recent studies show a decrease to 68 percent in 1994 (Straus & Mathur, 1996). Studies over the past 20 to 30 years generally show 70 to 90 percent of parents believing it is sometimes "necessary to discipline children with a good, hard spanking." In terms of actual practice, studies generally show corporal punishment (especially spanking) to be widely used, with some 90 percent of parents or children reporting having used or received, respectively, corporal punishment at least once (Pitzer, 1997; Day et al., 1998; Straus, 2001; Simons et al., 1994). Although corporal punishment tends to result in immediate child compliance, it also increases aggression, slows moral internalization, and risks mental health (Gershoff, 2002).

Ask These Questions about Annoying Behaviors

- What specific aspects of the behavior are particularly annoying to me?
- Is there any way that I might have been inadvertently setting an example for that behavior?
- What positive behavior could be modeled and reinforced to replace the undesired behavior?
- How can I model appropriate behaviors so the child will be sure to notice and respond?

> Mrs. Young cares for one-year-olds in a mother's-day-out program. When a toddler bites, she does whatever she has to—as firmly as necessary but as gently as possible—to stop the biting and to get the bitten child free from the biter. In a deeply concerned (but not angry) voice, she tells the biter assertively, "No biting, biting hurts." She then takes great pains to model touching the bitten child gently. Mrs. Young delicately strokes the bitten child's arm, saying in a soothing voice, "Gentle. Be gentle." Often, the biter will imitate her and touch the other child, and then she responds, "That was so gentle. Thank you." Slowly, the toddlers begin to absorb the gentleness they see in Mrs. Young's actions every day.

How Does a Nurturing Adult Respond to Aggression?

When the children are older, Mrs. Young will begin emphasizing another concept: using words rather than aggression to express anger. Because she uses the word *no* very sparingly and only when she really intends for an action to stop, the children learn through observation that it is a powerful and important word. We will not hear Mrs. Young snapping at a child, "Don't you dare say no to me!" She allows children to express their thoughts and feelings orally.

By being positive and assertive rather than negative and confrontational with children, Mrs. Young does not overuse the word *no* herself. Consequently, she does not hear the word *no* from toddlers very often. When she does, however, she acknowledges the balky child's feelings, even if the child cannot reasonably be allowed to have his own way. She says, "I know you don't want to wash your hands right now, but you must have clean hands to be allowed to eat." Furthermore, she actually coaches her toddlers in the skill of saying no. She prompts them, "Can you tell Marcus no? Say, 'No, Marcus. My cracker. Mine.'" In time, children learn by direct teaching as well as by imitation to use words rather than aggression to express their feelings of anger.

Can Children Learn Appropriate Behavior through Imitation?

Although babies and toddlers are able to mimic only bits and pieces of behaviors they observe, even these first attempts at imitation are critically important to their development. Preschoolers imitate entire sequences of behavior. Preschoolers are in a particularly sensitive period of their lives for imitation. As they mime adult actions in their play, we get to see them reenact their world as they perceive it (Mussen & Eisenberg-Berg, 1977; Gladwell, 2000; Mayes & Cohen, 2001). These glimpses into their world range from the delightfully funny to the downright alarming. Children's imitative play discloses their innocent misconceptions of the adult world, as well as the fears and pains they sometimes feel.

School-age children also imitate, but they are more selective in choosing role models. They are constantly (but unconsciously) absorbing subtle behavior characteristics from those around them. But they are not likely to mimic the behaviors of adults or children they do not like. They will make conscious attempts, however, to talk, dress, and act like those they admire (Bandura, 1977). Adults can enhance positive imitative learning by becoming a respected and admired member of the child's immediate world rather than an aloof and distant authority figure.

Imitation is an important and logical tool for teaching prosocial behavior. Adults waste a great opportunity to influence children if they do not become particularly aware of their own actions and attitudes as well as those communicated by such cultural media as television (Aidman, 1997; Bandura, 1977; Cairns, 1979; Gerbner & Gross, 1980; Lefkowitz & Tesiny, 1980; Leland, 1997; Parke & Slaby, 1983; Gladwell, 2000; Mayes & Cohen, 2001; Gowen & Nebrig, 2002). If children spend long periods

Rather than focus all our attention on correcting children's behavior, we must take a cold, hard look at ourselves and correct some of our own flaws. (Illustration by Gregory Nemec. Used with permission.)

Nurturing adults serve as good role models by showing the same kind of self-control, compassion, tolerance, and love of learning that they hope for in their children.

watching television, they are bound to internalize the language and behavior they see there. The nurturing adult will closely monitor and limit programs to avoid overexposure to violent, irresponsible behaviors.

Rather than focus all our attention on correcting children's behaviors, we must take a cold, hard look at ourselves and correct some of our own flaws. Even if we are unsuccessful in weeding out all of our personal quirks and imperfections, we will certainly become more sensitive to the child's dilemma of truly wanting to stop an undesirable behavior but not being able to accomplish it. If our goal is to develop children's self-discipline and self-control, then we had best see how much of those admirable characteristics we are able to muster so we can show children (rather than just tell them) how people should behave.

Am I a Positive Role Model?

- Can children easily observe cooperation, empathy, and altruism in my day-to-day actions?
- Are my values evidenced clearly in the environment I provide for children?
- What kinds of books do I read to them?
- What kinds of toys, movies, and television shows do I make available?

How Can I Be More Attentive to Children's Individual Needs?

Nurturing adults respond to children's individual needs. Parents generally have no difficulty in seeing their own children as individuals. Family intimacy and shared history throughout a child's life make it likely that there is at least awareness of (if not respect for) individual differences. A key problem for parents may be accepting individual differences among their children and resisting the temptation to compare them to one another. A parent may say, "I'm sure that Ramona will love taking piano lessons just like her older brother did," while knowing full well that little Ramona would much rather do wheelies on a bicycle than learn to play the piano.

In a group setting, sadly, young children may be seen as tiny cogs in a very large machine. Babies' diapers may be changed not when they become wet or soiled, but at routinely scheduled times. Eating, playing, and sleeping may take place as scheduled for whole groups rather than in response to children's individual feelings of hunger, playfulness, or fatigue. A child may not be hungry for breakfast on a given day or may be ready for a nap before naptime. It is easy for a child to feel overlooked in a group. Although routines are essential to sanity and survival for group caregivers, nurturing adults will find ways to be sensitive and make allowances for children's individual needs.

A nurturing adult will not be callous to children sleeping facedown on uncovered plastic mats in sweaty August heat or make little ones nap with their shoes on because taking shoes off and putting them back on is too much bother. The nurturing adult would not be inclined to toss snack crackers unceremoniously onto a bare table without even the dignity of a napkin or paper plate. A nurturing adult will really care about the comfort and feelings of individual children. Even if every individual child's need cannot reasonably be met this instant, the nurturing adult will express awareness of and concern for children's individual circumstances. For example, "I know you are very hungry. As soon as we can get everyone's hands washed, you will have some lunch. I promise." Showing attentiveness to children's individual needs is an excellent way to demonstrate cooperative behavior for them.

Adults should become actively involved in the child's world so they will not be seen as cold, aloof authority figures. Come close, establish eye contact at the child's eye level, use appropriate touch, and call the child by name.

The No-Lose Method of Conflict Resolution

Often, children and adults become locked in a struggle over who will be in control. These power struggles become win–lose situations in which the only way the adults get their needs met is for children to submit to control, and the only way for children to get their needs met is for adults to submit to control. This tug-of-war pits adults and children against each other. Typically, this results in misbehavior patterns becoming well established. Antagonism between adults and children can also begin to interfere with the pleasurable, nurturing interactions that strengthen self-esteem and are a critical part of daily life for children. Adults find themselves chronically annoyed with children, and children become more and more resistant and noncompliant.

What Is Conflict Resolution?

The no-lose method of conflict resolution is a strategy for avoiding power struggles, and for adults and children working together to solve problems positively and cooperatively. There are six steps to use in resolving conflicts (Dinkmeyer & McKay, 1982; Gordon, 1970; Vance & Weaver, 2002).

What Is Conflict Resolution?

Teach Children to Follow Basic Ground Rules

- Use "I" statements (or "I" messages; start sentences with "I feel, I need, I want . . .").
- Own the problem rather than blame (avoid "You" sentences).
- Recognize and respect feelings.
- Don't interrupt.
- Be kind (no name-calling, ridicule, or sarcasm).
- Stick to the topic.

Conflict-Resolution Steps

1. *Listen*

- You talk—I listen.
- I tell you what I heard.
- We agree about what you said.
- I talk—you listen.
- You tell me what you heard.
- We agree about what I said.

2. *Agree*

- We agree that we've figured out the problem.

3. *Think*

- We both come up with solutions (the adult may need to add suggestions).

4. *Choose*

- We compromise; we choose a solution.

5. *Solve*

- We act on our decision; we solve the problem.

6. *Evaluate*

- Talk about what worked and what might work better next time.

What to Do When No Solution Can Be Found

- Agree to disagree.
- Walk away from the source of disagreement and find other activities.
- Try to negotiate again at another time.

Adapted from Coleman, 2004; Carlsson-Paige & Levin, 1998; Kreider, 1984.

Conflict-Resolution Example

1. Listen—Use reflective listening to clarify feelings. (*You talk—I listen; I tell you what you said.*)

Teacher: "Michonda, you seem really angry and in a bad mood."

Michonda: "I hate Amy!"

2. Agree—Determine the problem. (*We agree that we've figured out the problem.*)

Teacher: "Michonda, are you feeling angry because Amy pulled on your swing?"

Michonda: "Yes. She keeps pulling on me, and she won't leave me alone."

3. Think—Evaluate the probable consequences of possible solutions. (*We both think up solutions.*)

Teacher: "What are some things you could do to solve this problem?"

Michonda: "I could run away from her."

Teacher: "Do you think that will work?"

Michonda: "I don't think so. She would probably just start chasing me."

Teacher: "Hmmm . . . what if you ask Amy why she's bothering you?"

4. Choose—Choose the best possible solution. (*We agree on a solution.*)

Michonda: "Okay, but what if she won't listen to me?"

Teacher: "Would you like for me to come with you?"

Michonda: "Yes."

5. Solve—Carry out the solution. (*You solve the problem.*)

Michonda: "Why are you being so mean to me and making me mad?"

Amy: "Because you won't play with me. You just keep swinging all the time. I don't like swinging anymore."

Michonda: "Well, I don't want to dig in the sandbox all the time."

Amy: "Will you play with me if we play like we're dinosaurs in the jungle?"

Michonda: "Okay . . . but can I be *Tyrannosaurus rex* this time?"

Amy: "Sure! I'll be a flying dinosaur with big sharp claws . . . okay?"

6. Evaluate—Evaluate how well the solution worked.

Teacher: "Michonda and Amy, I'm happy to see you playing and having fun together. You must feel proud that you were able to solve your problem all by yourselves."

For more on effective communication see Chapter 7.

How Can I Provide Affirmation, Affection, and Acceptance?

Affirmation, affection, and acceptance assure a child that he is wanted and appreciated. Unconditional positive regard is the process through which affirmation, affection, and acceptance are conveyed. In contrast, conditional affection is attention given to a child only when he pleases the adult. Conditional affection carries the hidden

Even very young children can begin to learn the process of conflict resolution. In the beginning, an adult will need to provide the words. As the children become familiar with the process, they will be able to provide their own words.

Wadsworth/Cengage Learning

message "I will love you only if you are good." Unconditional positive regard lets children know they are liked simply for who they are, not for how they perform at any given time. Children absorb the message "You are a loved, worthwhile individual even if you sometimes make mistakes." According to Clarke (1978), for children to develop healthy self-esteem, they must absorb the following clear messages from the words and actions of their caregivers:

- Affirmations for being

  "You have a right to be here."

  "I'm glad you are who you are."

  "It's okay for you to have needs."

- Affirmations for becoming independent

  "You don't have to do tricks (be cute, sick, sad, mad, or scared) to get attention."

  "It's okay to be curious and try new things on your own."

- Affirmations for learning to think

  "You can stand up for the things you believe even if there is some risk involved."

  "You can own the consequences of your own actions; others don't have to rescue you."

  "It's okay to make mistakes as long as you accept responsibility for making amends."

- Affirmations for developing an individual identity

  "You can express your own thoughts and feelings without fear of rejection."

  "It's okay to disagree."

  "You can trust your own judgment."

Sometimes the preceding messages of affirmation can be orally expressed to children. They can also be conveyed to children in day-to-day actions throughout children's lives. Affirmation is communicated to a baby by his caregiver's facial expression during such routines as diaper changing. If he looks up and sees disgust or annoyance in the caregiver's face, he will sense that it is not okay to be a baby and to need a dirty diaper changed. If he sees a relaxed smile, he will know that he is welcome and his needs are okay. If a preschooler accidentally tramples a flower bed while trying to pull weeds like his daddy, he will sense affirmation as his dad patiently acknowledges the child's good intentions and teaches him how to weed the garden without trampling it.

Nurturing adults are not afraid to show affection to children (Hoffman, 1979). Smiles, warm hugs, and sincere interest in a child's world let him know that he is the recipient of unconditional positive regard. Appropriate affection should never be intrusive, overwhelming, or one sided but rather respectful and reciprocal. A basic human need is for a sense of belonging. We human beings are essentially social creatures. We cannot really be happy or functional without a secure feeling that we have a place in the social order around us. The most desirable social position is one in which we feel admiration, acceptance, and approval from the important people around us.

If that situation cannot be found, people (children as well as grown-ups) may substitute negative relationships to find recognition and acceptance. People assume leadership by becoming gang members, achieve recognition by defying rules, and hold others' attention by shocking, frightening, or angering them. The very last thing children (or anyone else) will settle for is being ignored and left out. Only the most emotionally disabled members of society retreat into and accept a life of total social isolation.

To stimulate prosocial behavior, the nurturing adult will be generous in making sure children know that they are accepted and approved. Instead of focusing only on children's unacceptable behaviors, the nurturing adult makes a point of noticing and commenting on positive behaviors, thanking the child for remembering to wipe his feet, commenting on the lovely colors in his crayon drawing, and listening with interest to his excited but rambling account of a weekend camping trip. The nurturing adult is careful to separate clearly the difference between bad actions and bad people: "I don't like hitting, but I like you very much. You are a good person. You can learn to use words rather than hitting." In spite of inevitable disciplinary intervention from time to time, the nurtured child always knows he is a good and worthwhile human being (Brady et al., 2003).

Children should never be forced to apologize, but a sincere apology is always welcome.

How Can I Provide Positive Recognition and Encouragement?

On special occasions, children want and deserve recognition and encouragement just as we do in our own personal and professional lives. An occasional, sincere pat on the back can trigger a surge of motivation in us (Mussen & Eisenberg-Berg, 1977). Too much praise, however, can be burdensome, causing us to feel pressured to live up to unrealistic standards. We either awkwardly stammer thank you, or worse, become addicted to praise, needing more and more every day to maintain our self-esteem (Landy, 2002; Fox, Dunlap, & Cushing, 2002).

Recognition and encouragement are more moderate alternatives to an over-abundance of gushy or insincere praise. Often, we praise a child by stating a value judgment such as "Oh, what a good boy you are!" Unfortunately, by implying that cleaning up makes him good, we hint that if he does not continue the action in the future, he might become bad. (Young children tend to think in simplistic terms: if you are not good, then you must be bad.)

Recognizing and encouraging are different from praising. To recognize and encourage a child, we might say, "I noticed that you wiped the table with a sponge. The table is clean and beautiful. Thanks!" The recognition is very specific (tells exactly what the child did) and encourages the child by letting him know that we appreciate the action. He is not labeled good or bad, just sincerely acknowledged for a job well done. The nurturing adult says thank you very frequently to children. When children do the right thing, it is not appropriate or helpful to dredge up old problems, saying, for example, "Why didn't you do this yesterday?" or "Well, now that you have done this, you can do everything else I've been telling you to do." Children who are overwhelmed with criticism become very defeatist. They think, "Why should I even try? Everything I do just gets me into more trouble." The child will feel more encouraged if he is allowed to bask in every little bit of success before tactfully being guided by a nurturing adult to complete other unfinished tasks.

Praise focuses a child's attention on gaining external rewards. Recognition and encouragement focus the child's attention on internal rewards, feelings of accomplishment, pride, and self-worth. Internal rewards build the child's capacity for self-control and self-direction.

Am I Willing to Enforce Rules Even if It Would Be Easier to Look the Other Way?

The nurturing adult is able to be both assertive and caring at the same time.

> Mr. Leone really enjoys children. He is tenderhearted and kind but has trouble being assertive. When Jenny runs to him complaining, "Anna pulled my hair and broke my new crayons," Mr. Leone shrugs and says, "I'm sure it was just an accident." When children throw food during lunch, Mr. Leone pretends not to notice but tries to distract the ringleaders by talking loudly about the weather, "Listen, I think I hear thunder. Do you hear that?" Mr. Leone is kind, but he is definitely not assertive.

Lackadaisical permissiveness cultivates antisocial and aggressive behavior in children (Sears, Maccoby, & Lewin, 1957; Steinberg et al., 1994; Lamborn et al., 1991; Miller et al., 1993; Patterson et al., 1992).

Children Want and Need Rules

A truly nurturing adult earns children's respect by being firm and fair in a way that reminds children that a sturdy protective wall of reasonable limits surrounds them and keeps them safe. (They also need to know, of course, that this "wall" of rules can and will be broken in specific situations where it becomes a hindrance rather than a help to the children.) What they do not need is anger and retaliation. Anger is frightening to people generally because it can cause them to lose control of their actions. Children especially feel vulnerable because they have not developed the self-control to stop themselves from going too far when they are angry and out of control. Children feel nurtured and safe when they know they can trust a strong adult to stop them before they behave aggressively or destructively. They also want to know with certainty that their safety and rights will be protected if someone else loses control. The nurturing adult is not hesitant to enforce appropriate rules fairly and firmly. Remember that the permissive role does not serve children's developmental needs. Children need a consistent authoritative guide.

Am I Willing to Protect Individual Rights?

Mary Beth is the mother of two young children, a five-year-old boy, Trey, and a three-year-old girl, Betsy. Betsy adores her big brother and attempts to follow every step he takes. Sometimes, when Trey is alone, he seems proud of Betsy's attention and plays with her for hours, but when he has friends his own age to play with, he chases Betsy away and tells her to leave him alone. One day, while Mary Beth is waxing the kitchen floor, she hears a loud altercation in the backyard. Betsy is crying because Trey and his chums will not let her play with them and are taunting her by chanting, "Betsy is a tagalong! Betsy is a tagalong!"

Because Mary Beth's mind is on the waxy yellow buildup in her kitchen, she is tempted for a moment to order Trey to entertain his little sister and stop the silly nonsense with his friends. Luckily, however, she stops to assess the individual rights of everyone involved in the situation. As a parent, she has a right to do her housework without interruption, but of course, she also has an obligation to care for her children (she thinks children are considerably more important than waxy yellow buildup). Trey has an obligation to treat his sister with kindness and to help out by entertaining her from time to time, but he also has a right to lead his own life and to play with his own friends. Betsy has a right not to be called names, but she also has an obligation to respect her brother's privacy and to learn to play alone sometimes.

After Mary Beth patiently listens to complaints from all sides, she says, "Trey, Betsy feels hurt when you call her names. You have a right to play with your friends, but name-calling can't be allowed. Let's make a compromise. Please push Betsy on the swing for a few minutes so that I can finish my work in the kitchen, then I will bring Betsy in the house, and you and your friends can have the backyard to yourselves until your friends go home. Betsy, you may play with Trey for a few minutes, then you and I will go inside and I will show you how to give your dolls a bath."

Because Mary Beth is a nurturing parent, she is able and willing to make an extra effort to see that everyone's rights are protected and that everyone behaves responsibly. She does not do only what seems expedient or convenient at the moment, but tries hard to create an environment of fairness and mutual respect for the rights of others.

KEY TERMS

antisocial

child-directed

conflict resolution

control of error

egocentrism

prosocial

shaken baby syndrome

traffic patterns

transitions

POINTS TO REMEMBER

- Prosocial behavior is conduct in which a person cooperates with, cares about, and helps others.
- To develop prosocial behavior, children must interact with peers in a nurturing social environment.
- Children who are afraid that their own needs will not be met will not be able to be generous with others.
- Encouraging children to compete with each other reduces cooperativeness.
- The nurturing adult is an honest, emotionally healthy person who is both assertive and caring.

- Modeling is an important and logical tool for teaching prosocial behavior.
- Affirmation, affection, and acceptance assure a child that she is wanted and appreciated.
- Unconditional positive regard is the process of conveying affirmation, affection, and acceptance.
- Recognition and encouragement are appropriate alternatives to an overabundance of gushy or insincere praise.

PRACTICAL APPLICATION

William and the Nature Walk

Brenda's three-year-olds were ready to go outside. Several days of heavy autumn rains had kept them indoors in the child care center, so today's clear sky and bright sun were a welcome invitation to break away from usual morning routines and release some pent-up energy.

Brenda and her assistant teacher, Theresa, decided that playing on the playground was out of the question because there were still big puddles in the sandbox and under the swings. "A nature walk," Theresa suggested, "would be perfect. There are lots of pretty fall leaves, and we could walk to the park to collect acorns and leaves for our science center."

The children excitedly prepared for their walk. Each child chose a buddy to hold hands with, and the pairs of young children danced and wriggled with anticipation as Brenda and Theresa helped them get into a straight line on the sidewalk.

"Remember," said Brenda, "we need to hold hands with our partners and walk very carefully on the sidewalk until we get to the park." Before they had gone even a few feet, however, William, who had just turned three, saw a bright yellow leaf and, dropping his partner's hand, bent down to pick it up. Louisa, the older three-year-old directly behind William, immediately tumbled on top of him.

Brenda helped William and Louisa up, and then, kneeling at eye level to William and gently taking his hand, said politely but firmly, "Excuse me, William, you must wait until we get to the park before looking for leaves. Remember, be safe! Hold hands with your partner." She then gave William a little pat on the shoulder and a smile as she announced, "Okay, is this train ready to go again? Let's chug, chug, chug down the railroad track! Whooo, whoo! Ding, ding, ding!"

Within minutes, William was again distracted and stooped to pick up an irresistibly bright red leaf, and poor little Louisa was sprawled on top of him just like before. This time, however, she quickly scrambled to her feet, took William's hand and said in a confident voice, "Exsqueeze me, Weeyum! When you do dat, I faw down!" (Excuse me, William! When you do that, I fall down!)

DISCUSSION QUESTIONS

1. Why do you think Louisa was able to use words to express her frustration with William rather than biting or hitting him?
2. How should Brenda respond to the interaction between William and Louisa? Should she do anything further to correct William's behavior? Should she attempt to reinforce Louisa for remembering to use words?
3. What should Brenda and Theresa do if William continues to disrupt the nature walk? Can you think of anything preventive that could be done to stop the problem and avoid difficulty on future walks?
4. Are these children learning prosocial behavior? How?
5. Did Brenda and Theresa seem playful, consistent, assertive, and sensitive to the children's basic needs? Did it appear that developmentally appropriate activities and routines were being carried out?

STUDENT ACTIVITY

1. Practice using "I" statements to express feelings in day-to-day situations. (Start sentences with "I feel, I need, I want . . .")
2. Role-play a conflict resolution using the six steps:
   a. You talk—I listen.
   b. I tell you what I heard.
   c. I talk—you listen.
   d. You tell me what you heard.
   e. We both think up solutions (the adult may need to add suggestions).
   f. We solve the problem together.
3. Help a young child learn to use "I" messages to express her feelings.
4. Help two young children work through a conflict resolution by taking them through each of the six steps. Make sure that they follow the basic ground rules for respectful conflict resolution.
   a. Use "I" statements (start sentences with "I feel, I need, I want . . .").
   b. Own the problem rather than giving blame (avoid "You" sentences).
   c. Recognize and respect feelings.
   d. Don't interrupt.
   e. Be kind (no name-calling, ridicule, or sarcasm).
   f. Stick to the topic.

RELATED READINGS

Supporting Prosocial Behavior

Bredekamp, S., & Copple, C., Eds. (1997). *Developmentally appropriate practice in early childhood programs* (rev. ed). Washington, DC: National Association for the Education of Young Children.

Chenfeld, M. B. (2000). Get the elephant out of the room! We're finished with the Es! *Young Children, 55*(6), 20–22.

   This article offers tips for energizing the classroom by building curriculum on unexpected opportunities for learning and supporting children's self-motivation through spontaneous discovery learning.

Child Welfare League of America. (2005). *National Fact Sheet 2005*. New York: Author. Retrieved January 18, 2005, from http://www.cwla.org/advocacy/national factsheet05.htm.

Chung, A. (2000, July). *After-school programs: Keeping children safe and smart* (Free booklet from the U.S. Department of Education). This document was prepared under contract ED-00-PO-1711 to the U.S. Department of Education. Jessup, MD: Editorial Publications Center. Retrieved from http://www.ed.gov/pubs/afterschool/afterschool.pdf.

   This booklet discusses the importance of safe and enriching afterschool learning opportunities for children and youth. It explains what works in after-school programs and provides resources and examples of communities with strong afterschool programs. To access copies online, go to http://www.ed.gov/ and click on Publications. To order paper copies, write to ED Pubs, U.S. Department of Education, P.O. Box 1398, Jessup, MD 20794-1398. Fax request to 1-301-470-1244. Send e-mail requests to edpubs@edpubs.ed.gov. Or call toll-free 1-877-433-7827 (1-877-4-ED-PUBS). To use a telecommunication device for the deaf (TDD or TTY), call 1-877-576-7724. This report is available in alternative formats (Braille, large print, audio tape, or computer diskette). Call the Alternate Format Center at 1-202-205-8113.

Couture, L. A. (2001). Corporal Punishment: Society's Remaining Acceptable Violence. Condensed essay based on unpublished master's thesis *Evidence against the Efficacy of Corporal Punishment*. Retrieved June 9, 2008, from http://www.childadvocate.org/.

Dale, S. (1993, Winter). Spanking as an addiction. *Mothering, 69*, 31–35.

Douglas, E. M., & Finkelhor, D. (2005). *Child maltreatment fatalities fact sheet*. Durham, NH: Crimes Against Children Research Center.

Driscoll, A. (1995). *Cases in early childhood education: Stories of programs and practices*. Needham Heights, MA: Allyn & Bacon.

This book provides case studies showing developmentally appropriate practice and reflective teaching methods. It gives examples of a variety of practices seen in a range of settings. The "snapshots" provide examples of typical situations in early childhood settings and examples of developmentally appropriate practice with the day-to-day problems and issues that happen in "real classrooms."

Edwards, C. P., Gandini, L., & Forman, G. E., Eds. (1998). *The hundred languages of children: The Reggio Emilia approach—Advanced reflections* (2nd ed.). Westport, CT: Ablex Publishing.

The Hundred Languages of Children gives a comprehensive overview of the schools of Reggio Emilia, Italy. Notable differences in the Reggio Emilia curriculum include basing the curriculum on projects that grow out of the teachers' observations of students, emphasizing collaborative relationships, and documenting processes for evaluation and planning.

Flynn, C. (1996). Regional differences in spanking experiences and attitudes: A comparison of northeastern and southern college students. *Journal of Family Violence, 11*(1), 59–80.

Gestwicki, C. (1999). *Developmentally appropriate practice* (2nd ed.). Clifton Park, NY: Thomson Delmar Learning.

This book is designed to assist teachers in implementing the widely recognized philosophy of developmentally appropriate practice. The text is organized into "environments" for each developmental stage to help focus on specific appropriate responses and to nurture overall development.

Gordon, A., & Browne, K. W. (2004). *Beginnings and beyond* (6th ed.). Clifton Park, NY: Thomson Delmar Learning.

This book offers comprehensive approaches to the curriculum, education, developmentally appropriate practice, and other hot topics in early education.

Gronlund, G. (2001). Rigorous academics in preschool and kindergarten? Yes! Let me tell you how. *Young Children, 56*(2), 42–43.

By understanding the nature of early learning, teachers integrate traditional academic goals and objectives into spontaneous play activities to help children create learning geared to their own interests and abilities.

Hewitt, K. (2001). Blocks as a tool for learning: A historical and contemporary perspective. *Young Children, 56*(1), 6–13.

This article reviews the importance of block play and construction to the historical context of early childhood philosophies in Europe and the United States including Friedrich Froebel, Maria Montessori, Caroline Pratt, and Patty Smith Hill.

Honig, A. S., & Wittmer, D. S. (1997). Helping children become more prosocial: Ideas for classrooms. In K. M. Paciorek & J. H. Munro (Eds.), *Annual editions: Early childhood education 97/98* (18th ed.). New York: McGraw-Hill. (Original work published in *Young Children*, January 1996).

Teachers can promote positive social development by emphasizing cooperation and conflict resolution *as they guide behavior. Families should be involved in programming to encourage social interaction with special needs children.*

Howell, J., & Corbey-Scullen, L. (1997). Out of the housekeeping corner and onto the stage-extending dramatic play. *Young Children, 52*(6), 82–88.

This article describes methods for extending dramatic play into a classroom play project to better support children's development.

Hurwitz, S. C. (2001). The teacher who would be Vivian. *Young Children, 56*(5), 89–91.

This article reviews Vivian Paley's ideas on children's language practice, writing, and problem-solving through play, storytelling, and play-acting, and emphasizes the importance of teachers' having effective listening skills.

Hyman, I. A. (1997). *The case against spanking: How to discipline your child without hitting.* San Francisco, CA: Jossey-Bass.

Jensen, B. J., & Bullard, J. A. (2002). The mud center: Recapturing childhood. *Young Children, 57*(3), 16–19.

This article describes an inexpensive, child-friendly outdoor mud "kitchen" stocked with cooking utensils, measuring implements, found items, and buckets of dirt and water to create an engaging dramatic play area that promotes children's cooperation, communication, responsibility, and learning.

Katz, L. G. (1999, December). *Curriculum disputes in early childhood education.* ERIC digest. Champaign, IL: ERIC Clearinghouse on Elementary and Early Childhood Education. (ERIC Document No. ED436298).

This article compares instructivist and constructivist approaches to early childhood education, and suggests that attention to children's intellectual development may inadvertently be overlooked by both sides.

Larzelere, R. E. (1986). Moderate spanking: Model or deterrent of children's aggression in the family? *Journal of Family Violence, 1*(1), 27–36.

Lawhon, T., & Lawhon, D. C. (2000, Winter). Promoting social skills in young children. *Early Childhood Education Journal, 28*(2), 105–110.

This article points out how social relationships can be improved through the child's efforts and those of supportive teachers, parents, and caregivers. Presents two observation checklists: one for children's behaviors and another for adult self-assessments.

Lewin, K., Lippitt, R., & White, R. (1939). Patterns of aggressive behavior in experimentally created social climates. *Journal of Social Psychology,* 271–299.

Three leadership styles—authoritarian, democratic, and laissez-faire (permissive)—were studied and typical outcomes identified. Findings support the value of democratic child guidance in lieu of authoritarian or permissive styles.

Mahany, B. (1997). Mrs. Paley's lessons. In K. M. Paciorek & J. H. Munro (Eds.), *Annual editions: Early childhood education 97/98* (18th ed.). New York: McGraw-Hill. (Original work published in *Chicago Tribune,* June 25, 1995).

Vivian Paley was a kindergarten teacher at the University of Chicago Lab School for 24 years. She has deep respect for young children and considers the kindergarten classroom an important place for social development. Paley regards teaching as a moral act.

Marshall, M. J. (2002). *Why spanking doesn't work: Stopping this bad habit and getting the upper hand on effective discipline.* Springville, UT: Bonneville Books.

Montessori, M., & Chattin-McNichols, J. (1995). *The absorbent mind* (reprint ed.). New York: Henry Holt.

Dr. Montessori gives an in-depth look at the workings of young children's minds. She describes how spontaneous activities of children are often misunderstood by adults as mischief or needless "fooling around" when the actions are actually "the work" of being children. She argues that young children are driven to explore and learn about their world.

Moran, M. J., & Jarvis, J. (2001). Helping young children develop higher order thinking. *Young Children, 56*(5), 31–35.

Strategies for supporting the process of learning, helping children build confidence, social skills, and problem solving.

Parents and Teachers against Violence in Education (PTAVE). (2002). Project NoSpank. Alamo, CA: author. Retrieved February 21, 2006, from http://www.nospank.net/.

Ratcliff, N. (2001). Use the environment to prevent discipline problems and support learning. *Young Children, 56*(5), 84–88.

    This article explores strategies for planning an effective classroom environment to minimize crowding, deal with inadequate space, monitor problem areas, create calm, structure appropriate activities, establish routines, and plan transitions.

Slaby, R. G., Roedell, W. C., Arezzo, D., & Hendrix, K. (1995). *Early violence prevention: Tools for teachers of young children*. Washington, DC: NAEYC.

Stork, S., & Engel, S. (1999, Winter). So, what is constructivist teaching? A rubric for teacher evaluation. *Dimensions of Early Childhood, 27*(1), 20–27.

    This article gives an overview of constructivist theory and practice, along with an assessment tool to help teachers broaden their teaching skills.

Strassberg, Z., Dodge, K. A., Pettit, G. S., & Bates, J. E. (1994). Spanking in families and subsequent aggressive behavior toward peers by kindergarten students. *Development and Psychopathology, 6,* 445–461.

Straus, M. A. (1994). *Beating the devil out of them: Corporal punishment in American families*. San Francisco: New Lexington Press.

Straus, M. A., & Gelles, R. J., Eds. (1990). *Physical violence in American families: Risk factors and adaptations to violence in 8,145 families*. New Brunswick, NJ: Transactions.

Straus, M. A., Sugarman, D. B., & Giles-Sims, J. (1997). Corporal punishment by parents and subsequent antisocial behavior in children. *Archives of Pediatrics and Adolescent Medicine, 155,* 761–767.

Yen, S., & Ispa, J. M. (2000, March). Children's temperament and behavior in Montessori and constructivist early childhood programs. *Early Education and Development, 11*(2), 171–186.

The Online Companion™ to accompany the sixth edition of *Positive Child Guidance* is your link to additional guidance resources on the Internet. This supplement contains audio and visual materials; PowerPoint presentations; web activities with critical-thinking questions and practical-application assignments; and links to web resources. This additional content can be found at http://www.earlychilded.delmar.com.

Chapter 7

Positive Communication

Wadsworth/Cengage Learning

OBJECTIVES

After reading this chapter, you should be able to do the following:

- Identify effective listening strategies.
- Address feelings and emotions underlying communication.
- Recognize the rationale for positive statements of instruction.
- List the characteristics of assertive communication.
- List the characteristics of nonproductive communication.
- Discuss strategies for positive confrontation.
- Reflect on your own success in using "I" messages in daily life.

Building a Foundation for Positive Communication

Positive communication is like a dance filled with expressive and responsive give-and-take. Children begin this interactive dance early in life, but effective communication skills are acquired gradually over many years. Children can best learn to communicate effectively by imitating and interacting with adults who model well—that is, setting an example for children and participating with them in both conversational roles: speaking and listening, and leading and following.

Effective guidance depends on positive communication.

When Does Communication Begin?

auditory physiology
The physical makeup of the ear that enables hearing. Sounds are channeled through the external auditory canal to the tympanic membrane (eardrum) and the middle ear (ossicles), and then through the auditory nerve to the brain for interpretation of what has been heard. Auditory perception encompasses the ability to understand what has been heard.

The development of communication begins before birth when the fetus hears the muffled tones of her mother's voice. The **auditory physiology** of infants is relatively well developed at birth. Immediately after birth, the infant may turn toward or startle at sounds and may even be able to distinguish the mother's voice from that of another female (DeCasper & Fifer, 1980). Although newborns have not yet developed any concept of language, they respond attentively to the sounds of speech (Begley, 1997a; Eisenberg, 1976; Kuhl, 1981; White, 1995; Gallagher, 2005).

One-day-old infants move their bodies in rhythm to the sounds of a caregiver's speech (Condon & Sander, 1974). One-month-olds are able to discriminate between certain vowel sounds (Trehub, 1973). In time, babies learn to mimic bits and pieces of adult communication such as inflection, intonation, facial expression, and timing, as well as the give and take of dialogue (Yoshinaga-Itano, 2004).

How Can Adults Assist the Development of Early Communication Skills in Infants?

From the time children are infants, adults should both lead and follow in communication with them. An adult may lead by talking to an infant in a way that is sensitive to the baby's mood and attention span. An infant will participate in this interaction by watching and responding as the adult speaks, and then, when the interaction becomes too intense and tiring, by looking away, grimacing, or yawning to signal fatigue and the need for a time out (Brazelton et al., 1974; Field, 1982; Shore, 1997; Stern, 1974; White, 1995).

A sensitive adult will follow the baby's lead by being quiet until after the baby rests for a few seconds, then look back indicating that she is ready to interact again. The adult may also follow the infant by waiting for the infant to make some sound, then repeat the baby's gurgling, cooing, or babbling. This form of baby talk (or "parentese"), in which the baby leads, is very useful for helping babies get a sense of conversational give and take long before they are able to say or understand any words (Bruner, 1978a, 1978b).

When adults pace their interactions with infants so that a specific infant behavior elicits a predictable adult response, infants begin to learn that their environment is controllable and predictable, which increases their motivation for involvement in surroundings and stimulates learning. Infants who sense they are powerless over interactions may become distressed, irritable, or passive and withdrawn (Watson, 1973).

Older babies learn to look back and forth between an object and a caregiver, grunting, pointing, or reaching to indicate a desire for the object (Harding &

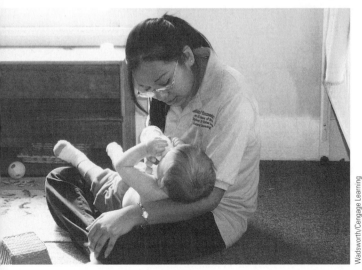

Wadsworth/Cengage Learning

▬▬The beginnings of communication take place in infancy.

Golinkoff, 1979). This effort to communicate reflects the child's dawning ability to bring about a desired action by communicating with adults. Well-developing toddlers grasp the essential elements of conversation: meaningful words, intonation, inflection, facial expression, gesture, and give-and-take. It may be impossible, however, to make much sense of what the toddler is trying to say. An adult who is tactful will find ways to avoid repeated requests that the toddler repeat herself.

A positive and supportive response to children's early attempts at speech will encourage continued effort (Hess & Shipman, 1967). Excessive correcting or prodding discourages further practice. Even after two-year-olds have mastered many of the words and phrases of the language, they will need a bit of gentle prompting to carry on a dialogue. Adults can help by asking simple questions (for example, "Is this your big teddy bear? What is your teddy bear's name?") to maintain the child's active participation in a conversation (Honig & Wittmer, 1997; Kaye, 1982).

What Are Typical Characteristics of Early Communication?

Usually, toddlers seem oblivious to the notion that one should speak only when a listener is present. One- and two-year-olds sometimes carry on animated self-talk while engaging in solitary play (Weiss & Lillywhite, 1976). In fact, toddlers may stare blankly and silently when urged to talk, then jabber freely later when alone or with a very trusted caregiver. Toddlers who are new to a group care setting may attend for weeks or months before trying to communicate orally with a nursery school teacher, even though parents report they talk a great deal at home with family members.

Three- and four-year-olds gain the vocabulary needed to understand and express many ideas and feelings, and they become more concerned that there is an audience present for conversations. A preschooler who thinks an adult is not listening may move directly into the adult's line of vision or may even try to hold the adult's face to keep that person from looking away. It is not uncommon, however, for two preschoolers to be looking straight at each other, chatting excitedly at the same time without either of them seeming to notice that neither is listening. Preschoolers also talk to inanimate objects such as stuffed animals and television characters without seeming to be bothered that these objects are not very responsive listeners.

School-age children become more refined in their communication. They finally recognize that communicators must take turns listening and speaking for anyone to be heard. Their growing vocabulary and maturity increase their capacity. Toddlers and younger preschoolers tend to be physical in their expression of feelings. Anger may be expressed by biting or hitting and affection by bear hugs and moist kisses. In contrast, school-agers use words more expertly to express affection or to lash out when they feel angry. They tend to use insults, threats, or name-calling to express anger and oral promises of friendship to show affection. Although school-agers are no longer as sensitive to adult modeling as younger children (who seem to absorb everything they see) school-agers emulate role models, and thus will be influenced by, adults and children they admire (Bandura, 1977).

Through daily experience and practice, children learn to listen to others and to express their own feelings and ideas.

Why Positive, Mutual Communication Is Important for Child Guidance

As children develop and their communication style changes from stage to stage, adults must recognize and adapt to the various limitations of children to guide them toward effective communication. The achievement of effective child guidance really hinges on the achievement of mutual communication. The ultimate goal of positive discipline is not just to control or manipulate children externally but rather to stimulate inner control based on responsibility and respect for the rights of others. This inner control depends on an understanding of the needs and expectations of oneself and others gained through open, honest dialogue.

Preparing children to function as adults in a democratic political system requires that children become competent communicators. In an autocracy, citizens can blindly and ignorantly follow leaders without ever discussing or questioning commands. For a democracy to work, citizens must accept responsibility to grasp and take a stand on various issues. These goals are achieved by communication: listening, reading, discussing, and so forth.

The most effective tools for children to learn communication skills are modeling and practicing. Children learn effective skills as they watch, listen to, and interact with consistent adults who set a good example. Children are able to make those skills a part of their repertoire by practicing again and again the words and interactions they have observed. Therefore, adults who care for and teach children need well-developed communication skills. These skills help them to

- understand and interpret children's needs accurately
- clearly express expectations to children
- teach effective communication to children by modeling

Adults often complain that children do not listen. The view presented here proposes that children be taught effective communication skills through exposure to capable models and by participation in appropriate interactions.

Effective Listening

Randall pulls his chair up to the table close to his teacher, and spreads out a large sheet of drawing paper and an assortment of crayons. He says, "Hi, Miss Katie. I'm gonna color me a big picture." Miss Katie glances at him and smiles briefly, saying, "Uh-huh, that's nice." Miss Katie's attention is focused on a group of children playing across the room. She does not seem to notice Randall as he repeats, "Look, Miss Katie, look here!"

Finally, Randall tugs at her sleeve and says, "Look at this. I'm drawing great big mountains. My daddy took me camping, and I found lots of rocks. Wanna see my real mountain rocks?"

Randall jumps up from his chair and begins emptying his pockets onto the drawing paper. Miss Katie suddenly sees his small pile of rocks and pebbles. She says in a stern voice, "Randall! What is all this? Get these dirty rocks off here. Go throw them in the trash. You can't color with rocks all over your paper."

Randall stammers "but, but . . . ," as tears fill his eyes. Miss Katie insists, "Randall, would you quit making such a fuss, and just do what I said."

Randall hangs his head and drags his feet as he slowly shuffles across the room to the trash can. One by one he ceremoniously drops his pebbles, his "real mountain rocks," into the trash. Miss Katie did not listen.

How Attentive Listening Can Nurture the Child's Developing Sense of Self

The greatest need children have is for attention, recognition, and a sense of belonging. If a child is routinely ignored, she may begin to feel invisible. Much that is called misbehavior is simply an attempt by a child to become visible one way or another. A child who does not feel a sense of belonging may gradually become alienated, rebellious, or withdrawn.

The surer a child is that she is an accepted member of a group, the more confident and cooperative that child will be. Adults can indicate their recognition and acceptance of a child by listening well. Attentive listening includes

- maintaining eye contact
- giving relevant nonoral gestures such as nodding, smiling, and appropriate touch
- giving relevant oral responses to draw out and encourage the child to continue
- waiting patiently for the child to complete what she is saying, without rushing the child or trying to finish the child's sentences

This polite, attentive listening not only gives children the confident feeling that what they have to say is important enough for the adult to listen but also teaches children by modeling how they should listen to others. Also, careful listening will help the adult hear, interpret, and respond accurately to children's needs (Close, 2002; Egan, 2002; Griffin, 1997; Pearson & Nelson, 1994; Tannen, 1990).

Three Basic Human Needs Underlying Requests for Help

Gazda and colleagues (2006) define three needs at the heart of communications that indicate a desire for some kind of response or help. Adults and children have the same basic human urge to get their social, emotional, intellectual, and physical needs met. Young children (and sometimes older children and adults) function at an unconscious level in which they react to a vague feeling of need without recognizing or understanding that need. There are an infinite number of complicated ways that people of all ages approach others to get help, but at the bottom of all that complexity are three simple human needs. These three needs are expressed as requests for

- action or information (for example, "Please do . . ." or "Please tell me . . .")
- understanding and attention (for example, "Please listen to and show concern for me.")
- inappropriate interaction (for example, "Please let me cling, whine, complain, undermine, and so on.")

Time, effort, and practice are required to become skilled at recognizing the underlying needs hidden in everyday communications. A question such as "Where is my mommy?" may be a simple request for information, or it may be an emotion-packed request for understanding and attention by a child who knows very well where mommy is. A major source of miscommunication is the tendency of persons in the helping role to jump to the wrong conclusion and respond in a way that does not meet the real need of the person requesting help. Listening carefully and waiting attentively for the child to find words to express herself encourage the child to practice speaking. Impatience can discourage the child and delay language development.

Are These Listening and Helping Strategies Appropriate Only for Use with Young Children?

The following sections will give strategies for identifying and responding to expressed needs. These strategies are not intended as gimmicks or as a bag of tricks to manipulate children's behavior but as a respectful and effective way of communicating with children and adults. As has been previously stressed, children learn by seeing adult modeling. Children will quickly recognize an adult who is snide and sarcastic with other adults but artificially sweet or patronizing with children. Parents and early childhood professionals set the emotional tone for children's interactions and personal relationships. The communication method presented here can be most effective only if it is applied to adult-to-adult, adult-to-child, and child-to-child interactions. We can't say, "Do as I say and not as I do."

The phrase "children are people too" has become such a cliché that the significance of its meaning has been lost. But children really are people who deserve the same recognition of their dignity and human rights as anyone else. Children's perceptions are different, their logic and experience are limited, and their needs, roles, and responsibilities are not the same as those of adults, but they can definitely feel the sting of humiliation and the pain of rejection. Most adults can remember in vivid detail some painful experience that occurred early in their childhoods. Yet we often act as if children's feelings do not really merit much consideration. Every baby or child is, in fact, the very same person who will some day be a teacher, senator, artist, or carpenter. The events of that person's early childhood will be an integral part of her character and personality, whether these events are consciously remembered or not.

Wadsworth/Cengage Learning

▬▬Tell me and I forget; show me and I remember; involve me and I understand (Chinese proverb).

Children learn as if by **osmosis.** They absorb information simply by living day to day in an environment. Effective listening is not only a learning objective for children but also a necessary component of children's daily lives, to be used directly with children as well as among the various adults who interact with children. For example, an ancient proverb says Tell me and I forget; show me and I remember; involve me and I understand.

Children learn to listen well by experiencing respectful listening as a regular part of daily life. Simply telling children to listen is not enough.

osmosis
A gradual, often unconscious mental process of assimilating ideas or absorbing information that resembles the tendency of fluids to gradually flow through an absorbent material.

Appropriate Responses to Requests for Action or Information

Joey, an 18-month-old, sits on a small stool, rocking and crying. "Beah, beah, ma beah," he sobs. Miss Rosario squats beside him and gently coaxes him to show her what he wants. Joey quickly leads her to the bathroom. He stretches his arm toward a high shelf where diaper bags are kept. Urgently, he opens and closes his hand pleading, "Beah, beah!"

Miss Rosario takes his diaper bag from the shelf. Immediately she sees that Joey's fuzzy white teddy bear is inside. She says, "Oh, you want your bear. Is that right, Joey, bear?"

Joey nods and says, "Ma beah." He hugs his bear and toddles away dragging it by one leg.

Even though Miss Rosario could not understand Joey's words, she recognized that Joey was requesting action from her. People who work with young children spend a great deal of time responding to requests for action or information. Some requests are straightforward and simple to understand: "Is it time for snack yet?" or "Tie my shoe, please." Other requests, such as Joey's request for his bear, are difficult to interpret.

Requests may also be hidden or masked. What sounds like a simple statement may really be intended as a request for action. "I can't sleep," may really mean, "Come sit by me and read me a story." A comment may really mask a request for information. "Latecia's mama is too fat" may really mean, "Latecia told me there is a baby in her mama's tummy, and I am very frightened and confused." Because children do not have fully developed communication skills, adults must accept additional responsibility for keeping the channels of communication open and clear.

Five-year-old Malika is standing on the playground beside her teacher, Mrs. Johnson. She sees a caterpillar crawling toward her and starts to shriek. Mrs. Johnson bends down and gently allows the fuzzy caterpillar to crawl onto a leaf she is holding. Malika screams, "It's gonna kill you! Is it gonna kill you?"

Mrs. Johnson says, "No, Malika. This little caterpillar has a very tiny mouth and no teeth and no poison. He likes to eat leaves. When he gets very fat, he will wrap himself in a cocoon that is like a little blanket. While he is inside, he will change into a beautiful butterfly. Then, after a long time, that beautiful butterfly will come out of the cocoon and fly away." Mrs. Johnson helps Malika make a suitable home for the caterpillar in a large jar. Later, at circle time, she reads the book *The Very Hungry Caterpillar.*

Mrs. Johnson has redirected Malika's fear of bugs to curiosity about science and nature. Mrs. Johnson recognized that underneath Malika's shrieking and screaming was a need for information. Mrs. Johnson responded to a hidden request for information.

After a birthday party, four-year-old Seth sees that his mother is wrapping leftover cake. He says, "Mommy, I want more cake, please." His mother says, "No, Seth. No more cake." Seth begs, "Please, I'm hungry. I want more cake."

Seth's mother bends down to Seth's eye level and takes his hand gently. In a sympathetic voice, she says, "Seth, I understand that you really want more cake. That cake tasted great, didn't it? But a lot of cake is not good for you. I love you and I want you to have a healthy body and healthy teeth, so I have to say no. No more cake."

Seth pulls his hand away, bouncing up and down, whining and flapping his arms like an angry old hen (the preschooler's dance of frustration and impending tantrum). Seth's mother does not flinch a muscle. She bends back down, and in a very calm tone she says, "It's okay to feel angry. Sometimes I feel angry, too. Sometimes I get so angry I feel like crying. Sometimes I feel so bad that I just need a hug."

Without looking at her face, Seth climbs into his mother's arms and gets a long hug. Suddenly, he brightens and says, "How 'bout apples. They make you get strong teeth like Superman." His mom smiles and replies, "You know, Seth, that sounds like a great idea." Seth's mother clearly understood her son's request for action, but she also knew that providing what he wanted was not in his best interest.

Seth's mother loved him enough to say no to his request and enough to accept an appropriate compromise. Adults are ultimately responsible for the health, safety, and welfare of children in their care. Complying with potentially harmful or unfair requests hurts children and, eventually, damages adult–child trust and respect.

Sometimes, adults are tempted to comply with questionable requests to avoid conflict or in a misguided attempt to win the child's affection. Seth's mother not only stood firm in making the decision that is in Seth's best interest but also taught her son a valuable lesson.

Her gentle strength has shown Seth an example of self-discipline, doing the right thing even though it would be easier to give in and avoid a fuss. Through her calm, patient persistence, even when he threatens a tantrum, she serves as a positive role model for Seth. Seth can learn positive coping skills, to stay calm, and to persist in finding a solution when he feels upset. (Some adults inadvertently reinforce children's tantrums by pitching tantrums of their own.) And most importantly, her sensitive understanding of his feelings helps him know that he is loved and respected, even while a limit is being enforced.

In this case Seth didn't have a tantrum, but if he had, that would have been okay. Most young children need to have a certain number of tantrums to discover that tantrums don't really work. The best thing a parent can do during a tantrum is to stay calm and assure the child that he will feel calm soon and that everything is okay.

Appropriate Responses to Requests for Understanding and Attention

Some requests may appear on the surface to be requests for action or information, but they are not. The real need at the core of this type of communication is for someone to listen and show interest.

Learning to communicate effectively is an important part of daily life.

Mr. Wilke watches as his kindergartners work and play in various learning centers. Angelica, a shy five-year-old, is alone in the art center. As Mr. Wilke walks past, she calls out, "Mr. Wilke, I need some help." He smiles and perches his tall frame on the little chair beside her. Angelica hands him her paper and plastic scissors and says, "Help me cut, I don't know how to."

Mr. Wilke has always made careful observations and kept records of his students' levels of skill with learning center materials. He feels sure that Angelica does know how to use scissors. He looks at the situation and mentally rules out possibilities such as broken scissors or thick paper that is too difficult. He decides that Angelica may not really be seeking action (cutting for her) or information (teaching her how to cut), but instead, seeking understanding and attention.

Mr. Wilke knows it will not help Angelica to embarrass her by confronting her in a harsh way. He also knows that he does not want to reinforce her perception that she can get the attention she needs by feigning incompetence. He says, "Sometimes

(Continued)

Very young children will gradually learn to express their angry feelings in words rather than action.

Wadsworth/Cengage Learning

cutting seems really hard, doesn't it?" He gently pats her shoulder and adds, "Would you like for me to sit beside you while you try cutting this yellow paper?" Angelica eagerly cuts her jagged paper while Mr. Wilke watches attentively. After a few minutes, as he gets up to leave, he says, "Angelica, you must really feel proud that you cut that out all by yourself."

Mr. Wilke was correct in his assumption that Angelica was really requesting understanding and attention. Seeking attention is not a perverse behavior that must always be extinguished in children. Human beings are primarily social beings; we all need attention from others to thrive. The goal with young children is not to stop attention-getting behaviors but to teach children how to get an appropriate amount of attention in a socially acceptable manner. If Mr. Wilke observed that Angelica continued in a pattern of pretending ineptness to get attention (see "How Should Caregivers Respond to Requests for Dependency or Inappropriate Interaction?" p. 237), it might become necessary for Mr. Wilke, privately and tactfully, to confront her behavior by saying, "Angelica, you seem to need some attention. It's okay to need attention. Please say, 'Mr. Wilke, I feel lonely. I need some attention.' That will help me know exactly what you need."

In an environment in which needs are respected, children come to know that it is okay to have needs and feelings. Sometimes adults inadvertently give children the impression that their needs or emotions make adults angry. This problem often occurs when the adults are having a difficult time getting their own emotional needs met.

A particularly helpful strategy for dealing with feelings and needs honestly and respectfully is active listening (also referred to as mirroring, reflective listening, empathetic listening, or responsive listening). In active listening, the listener refrains from lecturing, advising, or informing. She simply listens and reflects the feelings she perceives from seeing and hearing the other person. This gives the listener plenty of time to really hear the other person, to let the other person know her feelings and needs are important and respected, and to think of ways to help the person resolve the problem (Aitken & Shedletsky, 1995; Carkhuff, 1994; Cronen, 1995, 2001; Egan, 2002, 2006; Socha & Stamp, 1995; Verderber & Verderber, 1998).

Jenny, who directs an infant and toddler child care program, treats the teaching and caring staff with the same respect and dignity she expects them to extend to the babies. She knows that even infants and toddlers are unconsciously absorbing the behaviors around them. She also knows that caring for little ones can be incredibly stressful.

Fred, a four-month-old whose mother has just returned to work after her maternity leave, is crying. He has attended the child care program for only a few days and has cried most of the time. Kate, his primary caregiver, has tried everything she knows to calm him. She has walked him, patted him, and rocked him, and she is now at the end of her patience.

Kate storms into the director's office and demands, "What is that child's problem? Nothing I do works. What am I supposed to do?" Luckily, Jenny realizes that Kate is not really seeking action or information. What Kate needs most is understanding, so Jenny offers her a chair and closes the door for privacy. Instead of focusing on solving baby Fred's problem, Jenny focuses on hearing and understanding Kate's feelings. In a caring voice, Jenny says, "Kate, you seem really frustrated."

"You bet I am," replies Kate, "I don't think I can deal with his crying another minute. I don't even know if I ought to work with children. I am really at my wit's end."

Wisely, Jenny refrains from making judgments, giving information, or taking action. Gazda and colleagues (2006) note that rushing to give someone a quick solution is "cheap and dirty" advice, because the helper has not had a chance to learn all the facts. If problems were so easy to solve that an "off the top of the head" solution was adequate, one would wonder why the person suffering with the problem had not already thought of it.

Instead of rushing to tell Kate why she has a problem or how to solve it, Jenny simply mirrors to Kate (through active listening) what she hears Kate saying.

She responds with nonjudgmental active (or reflective) listening statements that begin with phrases such as

"What I'm hearing you say is . . ."

"In other words, you are saying that . . ."

"It sounds as if you feel . . ."

Jenny says, "Kate, it sounds like what you're saying is that you're feeling so frustrated that you're afraid you've lost your patience. You seem to be wondering if you're really cut out to work with children." A calmness settles over Kate as she realizes that she is not being judged or told what to do, but that her director is really listening and understanding what she is saying. She thinks for a moment and says, "I guess I'm just having a bad day. I really do love working with babies. It's just that Fred keeps screaming no matter what I do."

(Continued)

Sometimes all that is needed is a little understanding and attention.

Wadsworth/Cengage Learning

Jenny leans close and touches Kate's arm. "You know, it sounds as if you feel inadequate because you can't stop Fred's crying. I think Fred is lucky to have someone like you to care so much and try so hard to comfort him."

Streams of tears spill down Kate's face. She feels enough trust to let go of her feelings and let everything out that has been bottled inside her. Now that her own needs for understanding and attention have been met, she can return to her nursery classroom and try again to meet Fred's needs for understanding and attention.

Even though Fred did not see or hear the adult interaction (and would have been too young to make sense of it if he had), he undoubtedly sensed the tension and frustration in Kate's voice and body language when she was upset. He will feel and benefit from the calmer, more accepting attitude Kate will have when she returns to care for him. By sensing the patience and understanding of his caregiver, Fred will begin learning the coping skills he will need to develop confidence and self-esteem as he grows older.

Active (Reflective) Listening Requires Open-Ended Questions

What are open-ended questions?

- Questions that require a more complex answer than a simple yes or no.
- Open-ended questions do not begin with accusatory "detective" questions such as, "Why did you . . . ?" "Who did it first . . . ?"

Here are some examples of open-ended questions:

- "How would you like things to be different between you and Sophie?"
- "When you are tired of playing, what are some different ways you could let Zack know?"
- "How does fighting with José make you feel?"
- "When Michaela has the swing, what things could you say to let her know you want a turn?"

[handwritten margin note: maybe on quiz essay]

How Should Caregivers Respond to Requests for Dependency or Inappropriate Interaction?

Adults who care for young children often have difficulty knowing where understanding ends and dependency begins. A child begs, "Hold me," "Put my coat on for me," or "Help me finish my puzzle." Many adults struggle to know what is right for the child. Is holding, helping, and nurturing meeting the child's needs or reinforcing a pattern of dependency?

Under usual circumstances, as soon as children are able, they spontaneously break away from various levels of dependence on adults. Toddlers stubbornly resist the hovering care that was necessary to their survival as infants. Adolescents rebel against the close parental attachment that protected them in early childhood. For most children, achieving independence is the motivating force behind the process of growing up. But this force does not always move steadily forward. Even highly competent, well-developing children regress from time to time and need the security of someone big to depend on. A bit of babying, on infrequent occasions, does little harm to well-developing children. This regression only seems to recharge their energy and desire for independence. But for chronically dependent children, coddling undermines self-esteem and destroys initiative.

In certain situations, children learn to be helpless (Altenor et al., 1977; Finkelstein & Ramey, 1977). Some adults have difficulty accepting change and may fail to recognize a child's emerging capabilities. Other adults may inadvertently interfere with children's efforts at learning to function independently because they don't understand the process and importance of the development of autonomy.

Children's first efforts to do things by themselves are often messy and fraught with mistakes. Babies learning to feed themselves splatter, smear, and spill food. Toddlers learning to dress themselves put both feet in the same leg hole of their training pants. Preschoolers learning to tie their own shoes create nightmarish knots in their shoelaces. And school-agers learning gardening walk on the seedlings they have just planted. Little mishaps such as these are a necessary part of learning by experience. In a demanding, perfectionist, or punitive atmosphere where a child begins to fear making mistakes, she may learn to avoid risk by becoming passive, by not attempting anything that requires initiative or involves the chance of failure.

Children who have learned to be helpless and dependent (learned helplessness) need special guidance and support to break away from patterns of dependency. Children sometimes express requests for dependency through such actions as persistent whining, clinging, or regularly demanding special favors such as being first in line, sitting in the teacher's lap, or being carried. Indulging these inappropriate requests is not helpful for children.

Solicitations for dependence should be redirected in a way that encourages more appropriate behavior. An infant who whines for help after one halfhearted attempt at reaching a toy needs to be encouraged to try again rather than having the toy handed over. A preschooler who whines, feigns exhaustion, and begs for help putting blocks away may respond to a game, such as "I'll close my eyes. You tell me when to open them, and I'll count how many blocks are on the shelf." Or a kindergartner who follows the teacher, clinging and asking for help, may need to be given some important responsibility such as helping a younger child.

In some cases, redirection is not enough. It may be necessary to clearly communicate unwillingness to participate in interactions that indulge or solicit inappropriate dependency, spread gossip, reinforce inordinate complaining, or involve actions that turn adults or children against one another. Gazda and colleagues (2006) tell us that if we support inappropriate behavior, even by remaining silent, we may not only lose our opportunity to be helpful but also inadvertently become a model for negative or hurtful behavior.

Gazda further adds that this rule is easier to preach than to practice because it is necessary to end the inappropriate interaction without offending the person

Wadsworth/Cengage Learning

Wadsworth/Cengage Learning

■■■ Babies and toddlers feeding themselves is a messy but critically important factor in their beginning to develop a sense of autonomy.

initiating it. Offending a child or other adult damages trust, closes off communication, and projects an image of haughtiness. The recommended response is a polite but firm refusal to be part of the inappropriateness accompanied by a straightforward, warm, and respectful indication of caring about the person as an individual (Gazda et al., 2006).

Tactfulness, fairness, and warmth ease the sting of a refusal to participate in an inappropriate interaction. For example, Mr. Hernandez arrives one afternoon and prepares to teach his afterschool gymnastics class. Sarah and Cynthia, twin third graders, eagerly volunteer to help spread mats. As Sarah and Cynthia help, they confide to Mr. Hernandez how much they dislike James, one of the least popular boys in the gymnastics class.

Sarah says, "Ugh! We can't stand James. He's fatter than an elephant." Cynthia chimes in, "Have you ever listened when he laughs? He sort of snorts and makes some weird sound." They giggle uproariously.

Mr. Hernandez values the positive relationship he has with Sarah and Cynthia and does not wish to embarrass them, but he also knows that to smile and say nothing would be tacit approval of their remarks about James. That would be hurtful to James and would fail to guide Sarah and Cynthia toward more appropriate behavior.

Mr. Hernandez carefully chooses his words then bends down, touching each girl lightly on the shoulder. He says gently, "I don't feel good talking about James." Then his tone brightens and he deftly changes the subject, "But, you know what, I surely do like all this great help. How about this balance beam, girls? Do you think you both can get at that end and help me move it? Thanks."

Mr. Hernandez has not been judgmental or critical. He has simply and politely declined to participate by focusing on his own feelings. The girls probably felt a moment of embarrassment, but they also knew their teacher accepted and cared about them. As a result of this encounter, the girls may become more thoughtful about ridiculing others, not because of an external fear of punishment or chastisement, but from a growing internal sense of right and wrong bolstered by a strong and admired role model in the person of Mr. Hernandez.

Are Listening and Helping Strategies Relevant to the Care of Babies and Toddlers?

The complexity of words and sentences must always be adjusted to the level of maturity of the listener. However, the integrity and content of a message need not be diluted. Physical actions, facial expression, intonation, and gestures convey a sense of your message, even to an infant.

Mrs. Wang, who cares for infants in her church's mother's-day-out program, hears 11-month-old Kyle crying. He is banging on a low cabinet door that is locked with a child-guard latch. Mrs. Wang perceives the baby's cry is a request for action. Kyle wants the cabinet door opened. Mrs. Wang tries to distract him with several toys, but he continues to cry and pull at the door.

Mrs. Wang picks Kyle up, kicking and screaming, and carries him to her big rocking chair. She rocks and pats Kyle as she says in a caring voice, "I really understand that you want to explore that cabinet, but the things in there could hurt you. I can't let you play there because I like you and I want to keep you safe." As Kyle begins to calm down, Mrs. Wang carries him around the nursery showing him alternative areas to explore and continuing to talk to him.

Kyle does not understand her words but he definitely can sense her warmth and empathy, and he can sense the firmness of the limit she has set. He may test the limit many more times, but Mrs. Wang's warmth will communicate to him that he is still accepted as a person. Her consistency will communicate to him that limits are sometimes a part of life. She recognizes that babies explore bounds because they have a limited capacity to understand or remember rules and because they learn through trial and error. She will refuse Kyle's demands that she open the locked cabinet, but his actions will not change her feelings about him.

Additionally, by talking to Kyle, Mrs. Wang is able to focus her own thoughts and feelings on the situation. She, as well as Kyle, needs to hear the words she has said. By expressing in words the reasons she is doing what she is doing, she feels reassured that she is doing the right thing. Also, by putting her feelings into words, she is able to make sure her facial expression and body language are consistent with the message she wants to convey to Kyle.

Mrs. Wang, knowing that Kyle could not really understand her words, might have said instead, "Listen, I'm tired of fooling with you. Are you just trying to bug me?" However, it is nearly impossible to say these words in a sincere, warm, and

Babies and toddlers pay close attention to an adult's face and tone of voice, even if they do not understand the words that are spoken.

caring way. Mrs. Wang's face and tone would probably have conveyed sarcasm, impatience, and blame to Kyle. In an unconscious way, he would have absorbed these negative feelings and reflected them in his behavior. Also, words such as *fooling* and *bug* are ambiguous words that do not help Kyle learn language. Luckily for Kyle, Mrs. Wang would not think of behaving rudely to him any more than she would be rude to anyone else she respected and liked as a person.

Addressing Underlying Feelings

Most people who work with children would agree that child care and early childhood education are emotionally draining occupations. Young children ride an emotional roller coaster. They can go from laughter to tears in the blink of an eye. Responsive adults who are closely involved in the lives of young children are pulled along in the wave of emotions from the elation of a new discovery to the heartbreak of a best friend who says, "I hate you."

Children's emotions are real. Before six months, infants are capable of only three undifferentiated emotions: pleasure, wariness, and rage. By nine months, the baby has a dramatically increased range of emotional responses. By age three, children have virtually the entire panorama of human emotions (Sroufe, 1979).

An important part of early childhood learning is the child's gradually developing awareness of feelings and the child's growing ability to express those feelings. Very young children react unconsciously. A toddler may whine and act out in an aggressive way without realizing that she is feeling hunger, discomfort, fatigue, and so on. Adults play an important role in identifying, labeling, and explaining children's feelings to them. Adults also give children important feedback about certain behaviors by expressing relevant adult feelings (Dinwiddie, 1994, 1997; Kottler, 2000; Knapp & Vangelisti, 1992).

When and How Should Adults Express Their Feelings to Children?

Discretion must be used in expressing adult feelings. Young children can be overwhelmed if adults unload too much on them or if the expression is too intense. Simple, clear statements of feelings limited to relevant situations are most helpful. Following is a fill-in-the-blank statement, called an "I" message, that is very helpful for stating feelings appropriately and in a nonthreatening way (Gordon, 1970):

When _____ happens, I feel _____ because
_____.

This statement does not contain the word *you*. Statements such as "You make me angry" or "You are hurting my ears with your yelling" may induce an unnecessary feeling of guilt in the child by suggesting blame. Positive discipline should bring about responsibility rather than guilt. It is more helpful to say simply and sincerely, "When there is loud screaming, I feel uncomfortable because the noise hurts my ears. I need for you to use a soft voice." "Biting makes me feel really upset because biting hurts and biting is dangerous. It is okay to bite crackers and apples, but it is never okay to bite people."

If adults consistently use assertive yet controlled words to express strong feelings, then children will eventually imitate by using words instead of physical attacks to express their own anger and frustration. A child will also feel more compliant when the adult's anger is focused on the action rather than on the child.

Additionally, adults can clarify and express positive feelings using the same sample sentence. For example, "When I see you share a special toy, I feel proud because I know you are learning how to get along." (In positive contexts, the word *you* does not suggest blame.) "When the sun is shining, I feel elated because we can go outside and enjoy the grass and trees." "When I discovered that you had put every single block away all by yourself, I felt like jumping up and down because I was so happy and proud."

Positive and negative expressions of feelings can have a powerful effect on a child's behavior, but only when the person expressing those feelings is admired and

Attempting to identify the child's feelings focuses our attention on the underlying causes of inappropriate behavior.

liked by the child. Neither adults nor children are particularly concerned about the feelings of someone who is not liked or respected. In fact, knowing that a disliked adult's ears hurt with loud noise would stimulate screaming from some children who may purposely intend to inflict pain or to manipulate the adult to get attention.

How Can Children Be Helped to Understand Their Feelings?

In the previous section on requests for understanding and attention, nonjudgmental active (or reflective) listening was described. This kind of listening and responding can assist children in identifying, labeling, and understanding their feelings. A major difference here is that, often, the child's feelings must be inferred from her behavior.

Carolyn is a child care professional teaching and caring for a group of four-year-olds. As her children leave the playground and come inside for a snack, she says, "Ummm, I feel hungry. Do you feel hungry, Clay?" Clay agrees, and the children expand on Carolyn's expression of hunger: "I am as hungry as a tiger." "I'm so hungry I could eat this whole building." "I'm so hungry I could eat the whole world!"

The children giggle about eating the whole world as they find their seats at the table. Clay rushes to sit by his best friend Misha, but Ellen has already taken the chair. Clay stamps his foot and complains loudly as he shakes the back of the chair he wants. The child in the chair stubbornly holds on.

Carolyn quickly comes to intervene in the brewing fight. She kneels down at eye level to Clay and says, "You feel angry because someone took the chair you wanted. Can you use words to tell Ellen how you feel?"

Clay shouts, "I want that chair. Gimme it, now!" Ellen grips the chair tighter and ignores him. Carolyn turns to Ellen and says, "Ellen, can you tell Clay how you feel?" Ellen looks at the floor and shakes her head no. Carolyn asks her, "Would you like me to tell Clay how you feel?" Ellen vigorously nods yes.

Carolyn says, "Clay, Ellen is feeling very upset because you are shaking her chair and yelling at her. She got here first and she doesn't want you to take her chair away." Clay begins to shake the chair again, so Carolyn firmly removes his hands from the chair. Then, restraining his hands, but with concern and empathy in her voice, Carolyn says, "Clay, I know you feel really frustrated, but you have two choices. You may choose another chair and have a snack, or you may come out in the hall and talk with me until you feel better. What do you choose?"

From experience, Clay knows Carolyn is gentle and caring, but he also knows that she always means what she says. He does not relish the idea of throwing a tantrum that will only succeed in delaying his snack.

Carolyn sees a look of indecision on his face and quickly says, "Look, Clay. There is an empty chair right at the end of the table by Joey. Would you like to sit there?" Clay decides that Joey would not be so bad to sit by after all and shuffles along to take a seat. Carolyn smiles and pats his shoulder.

Positive Instructions versus Negative Commands

A key factor in positive communication is focusing on identifying and stating desired behaviors rather than focusing on inappropriate behaviors. Children and adults tend to respond more cooperatively to positive requests than they do to negative admonitions. For example, a parent would probably feel more responsive to a request from a child care worker that was worded as "Please check to see that Kelly has enough diapers for the day," rather than, "You never bring enough diapers for Kelly." The difference in children's responses to negative and positive commands is stark.

Additionally, toddlers are so limited in their comprehension of language that they tend to hear and respond only to key words in sentences. If an adult tells a toddler, "I do not want you to touch this cake," the toddler may actually hear, "Do . . . want . . . touch . . . cake." And, of course, because the toddler wants to touch the cake, she probably will. The adult could bring about better communication by designating a desired activity to replace touching the cake. The adult could provide paper and crayons at a location away from the cake and say, "Please color on this big piece of paper," which the toddler may accurately interpret as "Color . . . big . . . paper."

Toddlers and young preschoolers have difficulty hearing and interpreting every word of sentences, and also have difficulty thinking about a behavior, then inhibiting that behavior. Thinking and doing are almost inseparable at this stage of development. For example, if an adult says firmly, "No spitting," to a young child who has not even yet thought of spitting, she may comprehend both words but, as she thinks about not spitting, it is almost inevitable that the child will act out the spitting. The statement, "Don't wet your pants," causes the child to have a

Wadsworth/Cengage Learning

"Chew your food first, then talk."

mental image of wetting pants, which may trigger urination. The statement "It is time to use the potty" evokes a mental image of sitting on the toilet, which is desired.

Following is a list of typical negative commands and alternative positive commands.

Negative Commands	Positive Requests
Don't run in the hall.	Walk slowly, please.
Don't spill your milk.	Use both hands, please.
Quit poking at Jimmy.	Hands in your lap now.
Shut up.	Please listen quietly.
Stop interrupting me.	It is my turn to talk now.
Don't talk with a full mouth.	Swallow first, then talk.
Quit shoving in line.	Walk carefully, please.
Stop yelling my name.	Please say my name softly.

Negative commands are strongly entrenched as habit patterns for many of us. Time, commitment, motivation, and persistence are needed to break any habit pattern, and communication habits are no exception. Many adults find that as they try to improve their communication style, they first begin to hear themselves using ineffective phrases but cannot seem to stop using them. A toddler, standing in a puddle with an innocent and surprised look, saying, "Go potty," is taking the first tentative step toward changing a habit pattern. An adult who feels guilty about yelling "shut up" to a child may be taking the first step toward consciously controlling and changing an ineffective communication strategy.

Characteristics of Assertive Communication

Communication is always intended to convey a message, just as a radio transmitter is intended to transmit a radio program. For the music of a radio program to be heard, the waves sent from the transmitter have to match the receiver equipment of the radio. The communication transmitted from an adult must match the mental and emotional equipment of the child or the message will not be received.

Children, and adults as well, will close off communication that is incomprehensible, threatening, vague, or rude, just as they would tune out or turn off a radio with unpleasant static. Although you may sometimes feel justified in lecturing or lashing out, there is no value in conveying a message if the message is rejected. Our goal is to have messages accepted and acted on.

Key Factors in Assertive Communication

Simplicity Is the First Rule for Assertive Communication

Although babies, toddlers, and young children need plenty of opportunities to hear the rhythm and flow of complex adult language, assertive statements need to be short and to the point. Decide what needs to be said and say it in as few words as possible. Oral clutter gets in the way of stating a desired action.

The younger the child, the more essential simplicity becomes. Toddlers need simple two- or three-word sentences, such as "Sit, please" or (if a child has already bitten) "No biting. Biting hurts." Preschoolers need only slightly longer sentences, such as "Apples are for eating, not for throwing," "Please hold your glass with two hands," or "A chair is for your seat, not your feet."

Honesty Is Essential for Assertive Communication

Children quickly identify adults who do not really mean what they say. Empty threats are counterproductive. They teach children only that adults cannot be relied on to do what they say, no matter how many times they insist that "this time I really mean it!" It is never acceptable to lie to children or to trick them into compliance. They should be told honestly when a parent is leaving, even if that causes tears. Feeling sad is a natural and healthy response; feeling tricked is not.

Directness Helps Communicators Get Right to the Point

Rambling, hinting, and insinuating are of little value to adult listeners and are totally lost on children. Instead of saying, "The art area is getting pretty sloppy, children," say, "Please pick up all of the scrap paper and put it in the trash can. Thank you. Now get a sponge and wipe the table." Instead of saying, "Let's keep it down now," say, "Please walk softly and speak quietly." Words used with children should be literal words with clearly definable meanings. A phrase such as "You two cut it out now" should be reserved for occasions when scissors and paper are involved.

Tact Keeps Channels of Communication Open

Gushing sweetness is usually not any more palatable to young children than it is to adults, but tactfulness and sincerity are greatly appreciated. It is tactful to say, "Your glass may tip off the table. Please push it back away from the edge. Thank you." It is not tactful to say, "Stop being so careless with your glass of milk." It is overly patronizing to say, "Here, sweetheart, let's push our little glass back so we don't spill it, okay, honey?" Children can be given affection and kindness without being drowned in cloying sweetness.

Concreteness Makes Communication Clear

Abstractions such as *good* and *bad* can be very confusing to children. The statement that lying is bad, for example, may cause a child to think she is a bad person. It is more concrete to say, "If you lie, other people may not trust you. They may learn not to believe things you say." With younger children, concreteness is expressed through actions. It is not concrete to tell a toddler, "Be nice to your friends." A toddler or preschooler has no real concept of the word *nice*. It is a vague, value-laden term for which no two adults have exactly the same definition. A toddler or preschooler would not know precisely what to do to be nice. It is concrete to repeat "Touch softly" while demonstrating stroking the friend's arm gently. The toddler can see and comprehend exactly what action is expected.

Respect Is an Integral Part of Assertive Communication

It is impossible to have open, honest communication with someone for whom one has disgust and disdain. In a democracy, a garbage collector deserves as much respect as the president, even though each has distinctly different roles and responsibilities. Similarly, the person and human rights of a newborn are as deserving of respect as they are for any other member of society. Respect for children is expressed by recognizing and protecting their dignity and rights. A police officer may stop a citizen and issue a citation that makes the citizen feel very unhappy, but the officer has no right to hurt, humiliate, or threaten the citizen. Respectful adults assertively enforce fair rules without name-calling, teasing, embarrassing, hurting, or bullying. A respectful adult confronts children privately and focuses on improving behaviors rather than on punishing children.

Optimism Boosts Cooperation by Sharing Hope

A child trying to cope with an assertive adult needs to know that the adult really believes she can succeed. Confrontation is softened and made more acceptable by reassurance that problems can indeed be solved. After confronting Jennifer, you might say, "Jennifer, everyone makes mistakes. Our mistakes help us learn. Perhaps tomorrow you can help by reminding the younger children how important it is not to run out of the gate without permission."

Flexibility Is Necessary to Distinguish Assertiveness from Stubbornness

No matter how firm your intention to carry out a plan of action, the possibility always exists that additional information could indicate the need for a change in plans. Young children need consistency to make sense of what is expected of them, but that need is not contradictory with their need for flexibility. (The trick is finding the right balance.) Effective, assertive guidance requires that adults provide as much consistency as possible but also as much flexibility as needed to make discipline humane and reasonable.

Adults must constantly seek a balance between firm, predictable limits and the flexibility to listen, adapt, and compromise appropriately. For example, an adult might firmly refuse to talk about or compromise a stated rule while a child is having a tantrum or behaving very inappropriately. Later, however, when the child is calm and able to explain logically her problem with the rule, the adult might decide that justice is best served by bending or eliminating the rule. With a very young child, the adult may rely on direct observations rather than on oral discussions to determine if a rule is fair and reasonable.

Confidence Projects Assurance That What Is Said Is Really Meant

Children are especially sensitive to nonoral signals, or cues from facial expression, intonation, body positioning, and the use of hands and feet. Adults who do not really believe children will do what is asked of them project an air of uncertainty and weakness. A clear-eyed look of confidence greatly increases the probability of compliance from children as well as from listeners of any other age. Fidgeting, speaking in a weak or shrill voice, and avoiding eye contact hint to the child that compliance is not really expected.

When adults say sarcastic things such as "Well, let's see if you can keep from being a little monster as usual, running around and tearing everything up while we wait for the doctor," children know immediately that they are expected to behave badly. In contrast, a confident adult might say firmly but caringly, "Here is a book to look at quietly while we wait. We must sit very still. People are not allowed to be rowdy and noisy in a doctor's office." This indicates assurance that the adult believes the child can and will behave appropriately.

Persistence Makes Assertive Communication Work

Punishing, threatening, and intimidating get quick results on the surface but undermine discipline in the long run. Assertive communication does not always bring about an immediate solution, but persistence over time makes it an effective and lasting technique for solving problems. Adults are sometimes tempted to surrender to children's demands when first efforts at communication do not bring about an immediate resolution. A generous amount of persistence, however, will reap important benefits by letting children know that we really mean what we say. A child may stubbornly reject a rule on a whim, but if we persist in letting her know we expect the rule to be followed, she will almost surely comply eventually. As with the tortoise and the hare in their fabled contest, slow and steady wins the race.

Empathy May Seem Out of Context with Assertiveness but Is Essential

Sympathy means feeling sorry for others; empathy means walking in their shoes, understanding what they feel. Assertiveness without empathy is hollow and insincere. Assertiveness with empathy is strength and love rolled into one. A little person with grimy hands, a runny nose, and a knack for creating havoc does not always trigger feelings of warmth and empathy in parents and caregivers. Nonetheless, effective communication requires sincere understanding and caring. Empathy is expressed to listeners, from infancy to adulthood, primarily through the eyes and face, but all other oral and nonoral cues can also express empathy (or the lack of it).

For example, adults can begin reprimands by making an initial positive statement of some kind to show empathy. An adult might take a child by the hand and

When we truly understand a child's feelings, we can more accurately identify possible reasons for her inappropriate behavior.

say, "I know you just want to play with the kitty, but chasing him and pulling his tail really frightens him. Would you like to feed him to show him you're his friend?"

How Can I Be a Guide and Not an Authoritarian?

- Listen carefully.
- Avoid giving directives to solve children's problems: "Do this and your problem will be solved."
- Minimize use of statements such as "I'm the expert" and "I always know what is best for you."
- Ask, "How can I be helpful?"
- Remind 8- to 12-year-old children that they will make the final choices and decisions in their lives as they get older, regardless of what others say or do. They must learn to be in charge of their own bodies and their own minds.

Characteristics of Nonproductive Communication

Adults use many different communication styles. Of course, some styles are more effective than others. The least effective styles usually deal only superficially with the content of the communication and fail completely to address the feelings or emotions of the persons sharing in the communication. It is most important that adults avoid the communication pitfalls that inhibit dialogue and alienate children (or others of any age).

Gazda and colleagues (2006) list nine stereotypes of ineffective communication styles.

1. Florist—avoids issues through flowery euphemisms
2. Detective—skirts issues by persistently prying with questions
3. Magician—vaporizes problems with the wave of a wand
4. Drill sergeant—avoids conflict by barking orders
5. Foreman—clouds issues by the use of compulsive busyness
6. Hangman—induces guilt to avoid confronting problems
7. Guru—covers over issues by giving a cliché for every occasion
8. Swami—obscures issues by predicting dismal outcomes
9. Sign painter—dismisses problems by tacking labels on them

Although two-dimensional stereotypes do not reflect the complex facets of real people, they are helpful for identifying characteristics real people display from time to time. One stereotype may be the predominant way an individual responds, but others might recognize a little bit of each stereotype in their behavior occasionally.

The purpose of these stereotypes is not to label children or adults but to better recognize and understand ineffective communication styles.

How Do These Stereotypes Show Up as Problems?

Florists do not see any problems. If a child communicates that she has been hurt by another child, the florist ever so sweetly croons, "Why, Suzy, I'm sure he didn't mean to hurt you!" If a tearful child sobs, "I hate my mommy," the florist teacher just smiles knowingly and says, "Of course you don't hate your mommy. Children don't hate their mommies." The florist loses many opportunities to communicate by tossing garlands of optimism rather than by confronting and exploring problems.

Detectives want answers: "Why did you do that?" "Who did it first?" "Did I tell you not to do that?" "What do you think you're going to do now?" The listener is not only dazed by the battery of questions but also tempted to lie or to give whatever answers the detective seems to want.

Magicians dismiss issues conveniently. If a child says, "Someone pushed me off the swing," the magician says with flourish, "Yes, but playtime is over now so it really doesn't matter, does it?" If a father expresses concern that his baby's pacifier is lost, the magician responds, "That's okay. Sarah really doesn't need a pacifier. She'll scream for an hour or two then forget all about it."

Drill sergeants do not have time to communicate; they are too busy barking orders. The drill sergeant nursery school teacher hears a heated argument in the block center. Instead of encouraging communication, she says, "Get these blocks picked up off the floor. Kaleb, tuck in your shirt. Samantha, you wouldn't have these problems if you'd pay attention and mind your own business."

Foremen keep everyone so busy they cannot think about problems. A mother confides to her child's kindergarten teacher that her husband has left her and she has lost her job. She is worried that her son, Joshua, is being affected by her stress and depression. The foreman teacher responds, "You need to get out of the house and stop feeling sorry for yourself. Take an art class. Volunteer at the hospital. Throw a party." The mother leaves feeling even more guilty and overwhelmed.

Hangmen dish out blame. The hangman's favorite phrase is "Well, I'm not surprised. You know, it's your own fault." When Jamey asks his hangman preschool teacher, Miss Judy, for help printing his name, she says, "If you had paid attention last week, you would already know how to do this." When the director asks Miss Judy for help with a new child who is crying for his mother, Miss Judy says, "Of course he's crying. What do you expect? Did you see the way his mother let him manipulate her? She's to blame for this."

Gurus have a mental storehouse of meaningless clichés to scatter like rose petals over problems. A mother asks her toddler's nursery teacher whether she thinks speech therapy is needed for the child. The guru teacher answers brightly, "Well, a stitch in time saves nine!" A nine-year-old boy asks his guru dad why countries have scary things such as nuclear bombs and is told "An ounce of prevention is worth a pound of cure." A four-year-old cries, "Nobody likes me. I don't have any friends." Her guru teacher responds, "Well, you have to be a friend to have a friend." The guru's pat answers end dialogue rather than stimulate insight and understanding of problems.

Swamis are not exactly a comfort in time of need. A swami is always prepared to predict all the terrible and hopeless things that will probably happen as a result of the listener's actions. When a three-year-old runs into the house crying because she has a splinter in her finger, her swami mother says, "I told you not to play on that seesaw. Now you're going to get an infection and I'm going to be stuck with a big doctor bill. Look at this, your fingernail will probably turn black and fall off." And of course, there is the classic swami response, "Johnny, when you fall out of that tree and break both your legs, don't come running to me."

Sign painters make quick work of problems by assigning labels. A nursery school teacher complains to her coworker that she is having difficulty with one of her toddlers having temper tantrums. The sign painter coworker shrugs his shoulders and says, "I don't know of anything you can do about terrible twos. They're just that way." In a parent conference with child care staff, a single mother asks, "What is happening to my son? He seems to be trying to hurt everyone and everything around him." A sign painter teacher pats her on the shoulder and says, "Hey, all hyperactive kids do that." Meaningful communication is hindered by sign painters. There seems to be hardly any reason to discuss a problem after a label has been stamped on it with such finality.

If These Stereotypical Communication Styles Are Ineffective, What Will Work?

In each of the preceding stereotypes, the communicator avoids, dismisses, evades, or thwarts feelings. An effective, assertive communicator addresses feelings with kindness, respect, and honesty. Often, it seems easiest to do whatever is expedient to stop a child's crying, end a dispute, or make a parent or coworker feel better. Unfortunately, when feelings are pushed under the rug, they can fester into even more unmanageable feelings.

Managing the Positive Confrontation

When confronting a problem issue, first use active listening to allow the child or adult to identify, explore, and express feelings related to the situation. Advice should not be tossed out lightly. Instead, persons being helped can be guided to recognize the choices they have and the possible outcomes of those choices. Only then can a person be assisted in solving her problem. Adults must assume responsibility for solving their own problems before real help can be given. Imposing unwanted help on another adult is almost always counterproductive. Helping children is another matter. If a child does not show motivation to solve a problem, parents and caregivers must assume that responsibility for the child. The child should be assisted as firmly as necessary but as gently as possible in confronting and solving problems (Gudykunst, 1995; O'Brien & Kollock, 1997; Tannen, 2002).

When Is Confrontation Appropriate?

Albert is waiting excitedly for his dad to pick him up from his child care center. He and his buddy, Joshua, have been planning to ask whether they can spend the night together. As they dig in the sand, they giggle and scheme about the fun they will have watching television and eating grape popsicles.

Finally, Albert sees his dad. Both boys run to the gate and watch as Albert's dad parks his car. Before his dad is even inside the gate, Albert is talking so fast that his dad cannot understand him. Albert's dad hoists him into the air saying, "How's my big boy?" Albert excitedly says, "Daddy, can Joshua spend the night? Can he? Huh? Can he?"

Albert's dad takes both boys by the hand, and as they walk up the sidewalk, he says quietly, "No, son, I have some paperwork I need to do tonight. This is not a good day. I will be happy to call Joshua's parents, though, and arrange for him to stay over one night next week." Albert pulls his hand away and starts to cry. His dad bends down and says, "You really had your heart set on having Joshua spend the night, didn't you?" Albert nods yes through his tears. His dad continues, "You feel sad and angry because next week seems a long time away." Albert nods again.

His dad hugs him and says, "It's okay to cry. Even grown people cry sometimes. I bet Joshua feels pretty bad, too." Albert stops rubbing his eyes and looks at Joshua. Albert throws his arms around his dad's neck for one last round of begging, "Pleeeeease, Daddy, I promise we won't bother you." His dad's expression remains calm and empathetic. He says, "Albert, it is okay to ask, and it is okay to cry and feel sad, but the answer won't change. Joshua can't spend the night tonight."

Albert's next tactic is pouting, but his dad remains calm and firm as he gathers Albert's belongings and prepares to leave. As his dad buckles him into his seat belt, Albert plants a wet kiss on his cheek and says, "I love you, Daddy." His dad grins and says, "I love you, too, son."

Albert's dad successfully avoided the stereotypes described previously. He did not delay confrontation by saying, "We'll talk about it later." He did not avoid confrontation by giving in to something he knew he would regret. He did not squelch confrontation by saying, "I don't want to hear another word about this. Hush right now or I won't let Joshua stay with you next week either." He did not try to force Albert to like the decision by arguing with him, and he did not try to make Albert agree with him and stop being mad.

Instead, Albert's father confronted Albert simply, directly, and immediately but with a great deal of empathy and respect. He listened, made what he believed was a fair decision, allowed Albert to express his feelings, and then recognized and reflected those feelings. In the end, Albert probably felt very secure in knowing his dad was a strong authority figure to be relied on rather than a weakling to be manipulated or a tyrant to be dreaded.

How Confrontations with Children Can Be Made Positive and Assertive

Anger undermines assertive confrontation. An adult who becomes enraged with a child should forget about child guidance and do only what is necessary to protect the child's safety and well-being for the moment. She could ask for assistance from another adult who is calm, leave the baby screaming in the crib and do deep breathing and relaxation exercises, or say to an older child, "I feel angry now. I will talk to you when I feel calm."

Confrontation should be delayed until the adult feels in control and is able to muster some level of empathy. Hurtful confrontations attack children in an angry, punitive way. Effective, assertive confrontations guide, protect, and nurture children; they do not intimidate them.

An angry adult may find it helpful to think about and answer the following questions:

- Why do I feel the way I feel?
- What did I feel before I felt anger? Was it frustration? Fear? Embarrassment?
- Am I afraid to say no to this child?
- Am I tired, hungry, not feeling well?
- How would I feel right now if I were the child?
- Are my expectations reasonable?

Adults who lack assertiveness are usually afraid to use the following three phrases in their daily speech: "I want," "I need," and "I feel." Parents and other caregivers often try so hard to keep children happy that they suppress their own wants, needs, and feelings. Then, instead of being appreciated as long-suffering martyrs, they are taken advantage of, and eventually they explode in anger and resentment. They are rarely appreciated. The more they try to give, the more children and other adults expect of them. As they learn to take an assertive stand, they discover that they are less angry, more appreciated, and a great deal happier.

How Attention Can Be Kept Focused on Confronting the Issues at Hand

The stereotypical communication styles previously presented were described as adult characteristics; however, these same evasion tactics are often used by children. (Remember, children learn from modeling by adults.) Children who have imitated parents and caregivers with poor or manipulative communication styles are especially prone to using those styles to evade issues.

Children evade confrontations by persistently asking questions, by issuing bossy little commands, and by giving cliché responses, such as "Everyone else's mother lets them stay up as long as they want." Children not only learn roles directly by imitating them but also create roles as mirror-image opposites of those to which they are exposed. The child of a drill sergeant parent may learn to behave as a magician: "Get that trash picked up off the floor!" "What trash? I don't see any trash. Where? That's not trash. That's my cans I'm saving."

The more adept adults become in direct, assertive communication, the more successful they will be in keeping children's attention focused on confronting and resolving problem issues. Children will not need to evade issues when they trust adults to confront issues in a gentle but firm and fair manner. For many children and adults, the thought of a confrontation triggers terror, because their primary experiences with confrontation have been frightening interactions filled with rage, their own rage as well as the rage of powerful, threatening adults.

Confrontation, without anger, is an essential and healthy part of social interaction (Hall, 1997; Lickona, 1991; Pearce & Pearce, 2000, 2001).

We can tell a great deal from body language. What do you suppose these two children may be feeling?

How Children Can Be Taught Responsibility

Responsibility cannot be taught through lectures. Responsibility can be shown through example, it can be nurtured and reinforced, and, most importantly, it can be learned firsthand by dealing with the consequences of one's own actions. Adults often feel compelled to prevent children from experiencing consequences: "You have to eat this! You might get hungry later." They rescue children: "You were careless and left your doll in the rain. Now I'll have to buy you another." The child feels only the adult's annoyance. She is not allowed to feel the natural consequences of behaviors.

It is better for the child to have support and warmth from adults as she feels and owns the sting of unpleasant consequences from poor decisions. Adults must prevent dangerous or damaging consequences. A child cannot learn firsthand the consequences of such things as running out into a busy street or never brushing teeth. However, exploring and discussing possible consequences should be a part of confrontations.

Rather than lecturing children about consequences, adults should make simple statements ("If you throw food, you will have to leave the table.") and ask simple questions ("What do you think could happen if you stood on the edge of the balcony?"). Children can be regularly encouraged to explore potential consequences. Children who have a habit of considering and weighing consequences are well on their way to becoming responsible and self-directed.

KEY TERMS

auditory physiology   osmosis

POINTS TO REMEMBER

- Adults influence children by setting a good example for them and by encouraging them to practice appropriate communication skills.
- Responsive, active listening is essential to child guidance, but dependency and inappropriate interaction must be firmly and respectfully redirected.
- Feelings and emotions must be considered in order to provide appropriate responses to behaviors.

- Adults can assist children in developing responsibility by encouraging children to talk about and think about the potential consequences of their behavior.
- "I" messages begin with terms such as "I need . . . ," "I feel . . . ," or "I am concerned." "I" messages are not accusatory.

PRACTICAL APPLICATION

"I'll Leave You Here Forever"

Marlene pauses in the shopping mall waiting for her two-year-old to catch up with her. Her four-month-old, who is asleep on her shoulder, is beginning to feel very heavy. "Crystal," she calls to her two-year-old, "Please come on. We need to get home."

Crystal stalls as she climbs on and off benches and stops to look at other shoppers. Her mother loses patience, "Crystal! You come here now or you're going to be sorry." Crystal ignores her.

Marlene walks quickly back to Crystal and, taking her firmly by the wrist says, "Let's go." Crystal responds with the rubbery-legs strategy toddlers use when they rebel. Her legs go limp as she slumps to the floor; her mother clutches her wrist as her body dangles from it and she whines, "Don't want go home."

Marlene realizes that she cannot safely carry her baby and Crystal both out of the shopping mall. In exasperation, she snaps, "That's it, I'm leaving. If you won't come, then I'll just leave you here forever. Good-bye!"

She turns and begins to walk briskly out of the mall. She hears Crystal howling and running to catch up with her.

DISCUSSION QUESTIONS

1. What would you have done in Marlene's place? Why?
2. What has Crystal really learned from the interaction?
3. Could anything have been done to prevent Marlene's predicament?

4. Role-play the scene using positive, assertive communication and confrontation, then compare possible outcomes.

STUDENT ACTIVITY

1. Practice active (reflective) listening in day-to-day interactions.
2. Identify interactions you have had in which another person asked you for information or action without any underlying emotional needs or messages.
   a. What did you do?
   b. Give examples.
3. Identify interactions you have had in which another person talked to you, but you sensed that what the person really was asking for was understanding and involvement.
   a. How did you respond?
   b. Did you use active listening?
   c. Give examples.
4. Identify interactions you have had in which another person talked to you, but you sensed

that the person was seeking an inappropriate interaction.
   a. How did you respond?
   b. Was the interaction inappropriate because the person was overly clinging and dependent?
   c. Was it inappropriate because it was gossip or some kind of negative undermining communication?
   d. Was it inappropriate because it was racist, sexist, or demeaning to some person or group?
   e. Did you clearly communicate your refusal to participate in the interaction, but in a kind, caring manner that did not come across as arrogant?
   f. Give examples.

RELATED READINGS

Effective Communication

Covey, S. R. (1998). *The 7 habits of highly effective families: Building a beautiful family culture in a turbulent world.* New York: St. Martin's Press.

   Sharing insightful experiences from his own life and from the lives of other families, Covey gives practical advice on solving common family dilemmas.

Devine, M., & Olmstead, P. J. (1991). *Babytalk: The art of communicating with infants and toddlers.* Cambridge, MA: Perseus.

Diffily, D., & Morrison, K. (1996). *Family-friendly communication for early childhood programs.* Washington, DC: National Association for the Education of Young Children.

Edwards, C., Gandini, L., & Forman, G. (1993). *The hundred languages of children.* Norwood, NJ: Ablex.

French, L. (1996, January). "I told you all about it, so don't tell me you don't know": Two-year-olds and learning through language. *Young Children, 51*(2), 17–20.

Friedman, E. H. (1990). *Friedman's fables.* New York: Guilford.

   Teaching by parable has an old and honorable tradition. Ed Friedman, rabbi and family therapist, writes stories that are funny, but also profound, even shocking, as they present lessons of family life in a slyly modern, hard-nosed reevaluation of the wisdom of the ages. Dr. Friedman presents stories to show that neither insight, nor encouragement, nor intimidation can in themselves motivate an unmotivated person to change. These provocative tales playfully demonstrate that new ideas, new questions, and imagination, more than accepted wisdom, provide each of us with the keys to overcoming stubborn emotional barriers and facilitating real change, both in ourselves and others.

Mahoney, G., & Neville-Smith, A. (1996, Summer). The effects of directive communications on children's interactive engagement: Implications for language intervention. *Topics in Early Childhood Special Education, 16*(2), 236–250.

Swick, K. J., et al. (1997, Summer). On board early: Building strong family-school relations. *Early Childhood Education Journal, 24*(4), 269–273.

Turnbull, A. P., & Turnbull, H. R. (1997). *Families, professionals and exceptionality: A special partnership* (3rd ed.). Upper Saddle River, NJ: Merrill Education/Prentice Hall.

Collaboration means sharing resources and creating a context that empowers families and professionals alike. The book presents comprehensive, data-based, and conceptually consistent approaches for families and professionals to collaborate for empowerment.

White, M. (2002). Teachers on teaching. A lesson on listening. *Young Children, 57*(3), 43.

The author argues that young children be allowed to mull over ideas and construct theories of their own. By listening to the children and following their lead, teachers can encourage investigation and support learning.

The Online Companion™ to accompany the sixth edition of *Positive Child Guidance* is your link to additional guidance resources on the Internet. This supplement contains audio and visual materials; PowerPoint presentations; web activities with critical-thinking questions and practical-application assignments; and links to web resources. This additional content can be found at http://www.earlychilded.delmar.com.

Chapter 8

Nonverbal Cues and Appropriate Consequences

OBJECTIVES

After reading this chapter, you should be able to do the following:

- Create a setting that supports positive child guidance.
- Focus on the role of nonverbal communication and body language in assisting positive behavior.
- Define logical and natural consequences, and understand their importance in guidance.
- Identify reasonable and effective circumstances for the use of external reinforcement.
- Become more introspective about your role as mediator, and think about ongoing strategies for improvement.

Wadsworth/Cengage Learning

Nonverbal Cues and Body Language

The environment gives messages to children about what we expect from them, and our own physical postures, movements, and gestures communicate a great deal of information to them. We may not even be aware of the body language signals we send out, which the children receive and to which they react.

Positive, assertive guidance strengthens children's confidence and self-esteem.

What Is the Significance of Nonverbal Cues for Young Children?

nonverbal communication
Communicating ideas without the use of speech through such cues as gesture, tone of voice, facial expression, or body posture.

Before verbal language is well developed, young children rely heavily on **nonverbal communication** in their interactions with others. Infants pay attention to the touch, facial expressions, and sounds of their caregivers to interpret the adults' moods and expectations. Even a six-month-old baby can recognize clear differences between the meanings of a frowning parent with his hands firmly on his hips and a smiling parent with his arms stretched toward the baby. Rather than interpreting the meaning of a caregiver's words or sentences, very young children focus all their attention on sense perception. They pay attention to things they can actually see, hear, feel, taste, or smell.

As children reach preschool age, they gradually pay more attention to the actual words in adults' speech, but they are still very sensitive to nonverbal cues. (Drumming my fingers on the table may be my cue, or signal, that I am feeling annoyed.)

Why Should Nonverbal Cues Be Consistent with Verbal Communication?

Adults must take nonverbal expressions into consideration whenever they attempt to communicate with children. A typical situation in which children receive conflicting messages between verbal and nonverbal cues occurs when children are brought to an early childhood setting for the first time. Typically, a parent will say, "You'll have a lot of fun playing with other children, and I will be back later to pick you up. It's okay now, go ahead with your teacher." The words are full of confidence and optimism. The adult, who focuses only on the words, may not notice that she is tense, strained, and anxious in appearance.

The adult's facial expression is one of uncertainty, her voice sounds uncharacteristically high, and her hands are wringing and twisting nervously. Instead of leaving quickly, she hangs near the child while insisting that the child "act like a big boy and go play." The parent says she is going, but she looks as if she is staying.

Of course, the child pays more attention to the nonverbal cues than he does to the spoken words. He will sense that his parent is frightened and unsure about leaving him, so he will probably feel frightened and unsure about being left. He will probably resist being left with a great deal of volume and energy. If, in contrast, he senses that his parent is confident and optimistic, he may feel a bit uncomfortable at first, but he is likely

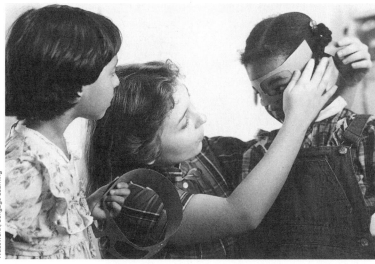

Wadsworth/Cengage Learning

Children pay close attention to the nonverbal signals adults give as part of their communication.

to adjust more quickly and easily to the separation. He absorbs the confidence of his parent as she smiles and says in a relaxed tone of voice, "I know you will have a great time today," and then leaves.

> Elena, a preschool teacher in a child care center, took her youngsters outside to play early one summer morning to avoid the midday heat and humidity. As the children played happily, Elena looked up and noticed swarms of hungry mosquitoes circling in clusters near the eaves of the building.
>
> She stood silently with her arms tightly folded across her chest, staring at the buzzing dive bombers and wondering what she should do. Should she take the children back inside? Should she spray the children with repellent? She felt a tug at her skirt. Willie, a three-year-old who had been riding around Elena on a tricycle and watching her carefully, blurted out in a sad voice, "Miss Elena, how come you're mad at me?" Willie had read Elena's body language and sensed tension and frustration. Because he was a normally developing preoperational child, he naturally (and egocentrically) assumed that he was the cause of Elena's unhappiness.

Elena had not realized the effect her nonverbal body language could have on the children around her. Because the vocabulary and language comprehension of young children are so limited, their understanding of their environment hinges on their ability to be very alert to nonverbal cues from those around them.

Focus Attention at the Child's Eye Level

If an adult stands across the room from a child and casually looks over a shoulder, saying, "Letecia, don't touch those scissors; you'll cut yourself," Letecia will probably interpret that the adult is not too concerned about the danger of the scissors and will probably not enforce the command. It is likely that Letecia will continue to touch the scissors while watching the adult carefully for stronger or more direct cues about the scissors.

If the adult stops what he is doing and bends down to the child's eye level, holding out a hand for the scissors, and says, "Please give me the scissors. These are too sharp. They could cut you. We'll find you a plastic pair," the adult's assertive nonverbal communication matches his verbal communication. Letecia is likely to perceive that the adult is serious and is willing to follow through to see that the sharp scissors are removed.

As Letecia decides whether to comply with the command she has been given, she will read the adult's facial expression (is there a playful twinkle in the eye or a look of concerned resolve?), tone of voice (is there a weak tone of uncertainty or a tone of absolute confidence?), and hand gestures (are hand motions assertive or physically threatening?). If the adult's nonverbal cues are too playful or casual, Letecia will assume that she really does not have to comply. If they are too threatening and intrusive, Letecia will be likely to bristle and resist the command. If they are assertive, caring, confident, and no-nonsense, Letecia may decide that it is a good idea to comply quickly and willingly.

Helping Children Independently Resolve Problems

A primary goal for early childhood development is the growth of personal responsibility and independence in children. Learning how to behave appropriately requires self-control, which is closely related to responsibility and independence. To become socially competent, children need to learn to **negotiate** so they can successfully resolve on their own at least some of their problems (Winslade & Monk, 2000).

Children often come to adults begging to be rescued from various unhappy situations. Sometimes the child's grievance is legitimate. Children have a right to call on someone bigger, stronger, and with more authority when their rights have been violated, just as I have a right to request legal help if my rights have been violated. (See the discussion of conflict resolution in Chapter 6, page 192.)

If I call a police officer for help because my purse has been stolen, I will feel very resentful if the officer responds by saying things like the following:

- "Don't tattle!"
- "Don't be so stingy. The thief probably needs the money more than you do anyway."
- "You got what you deserved. You shouldn't have been carrying a purse that would tempt people anyway."
- "Well, did you tell the purse snatcher you didn't like that?"

We are a tiny bit embarrassed by some of our most frequently used expressions when we step back and compare them with what we expect from children. There are times when we must intervene as the authority figure to ensure that rights are protected.

Nevertheless, there are also occasions when the child should not be rescued by an adult. To foster independence, children should be helped to do as much for themselves as they can reasonably be expected to handle successfully. Common sense will tell us that we should firmly nudge children into assuming responsibility for resolving any manageable problems they encounter. Skill and practice will help us know when to help and when to nudge children firmly toward independence.

What Is Bibliotherapy?

Bibliotherapy can be fun, relaxing, and educational as well as therapeutic. Although only some children experience

negotiate
The process of settling disputes through interactive verbal exchanges rather than by physical force.

bibliotherapy
The use of literature by children or adults to aid them in processing specific problems (depression, anxiety, stress, frustration, and so on). Many libraries have listings of bibliotherapy selections categorized by concerns (divorce, death and dying, new baby, stepparenting, and so on).

Wadsworth/Cengage Learning

Children have a right to ask for adult help when their rights are infringed on.

events that are life-changing and traumatic, all children experience events that worry or confuse them. Adults can use reading to help children come to grips with issues that create emotional turmoil for them. Reading can also be used to raise awareness about the rights and needs of others and can be very effective in preventing and resolving behavior problems.

Choose books that are appropriate: Books should match children's ability level, capture their imagination, and be relevant to their cultural experiences.

Create an emotionally supportive environment: Children need to feel completely safe to ask questions and express thoughts freely, even if the topic is a sensitive one. Sometimes, reading a story about someone else makes it possible for a child to talk about painful or frightening concerns.

Encourage creative problem solving: Adults should encourage children to talk about how the characters in the book might be feeling and how they deal with their experiences. Ask children things such as "What would you do if you were that little girl?" "How would you solve her problem?" "What are some different things she could have done?" "What lesson did she learn?" (For recommendations of children's books that address values and feelings, see the list at the end of Chapter 9, Appendix A, and the Online Companion at http://www.earlychilded.delmar.com.)

Help Children Learn to Use Words to Express Themselves to Each Other

Toddlers scream, hit, shove, and bite primarily because they lack the verbal ability to express themselves otherwise. They are transparent and physical in letting another child or adult know they feel angry. We may regret the onset of name-calling in children older than three, but we are very likely to see a decrease in physical aggression as oral communication skills are mastered. Preschoolers discover they can cause a peer to dissolve in tears just by calling her a "weenie baby" or by tauntingly chanting nonsense words such as "Nanny, nanny, boo, boo! Nanny, nanny, boo, boo!"

In positive child guidance, children are taught ways to communicate feelings honestly and assertively without having to resort to verbal aggression. Following is a list of adult statements that facilitate child-to-child communication:

- "Jarrod, please say, 'Excuse me, Christie, I need to get past.' Christie doesn't like to be shoved."
- "Alva, use words. Tell Erin you feel very angry when she grabs your crayons without asking. Would you like for me to help you tell her?"

Bibliotherapy offers a wonderful opportunity for a child to work through a social or emotional problem by learning how a book character works through that same problem.

Wadsworth/Cengage Learning

- "Erin, Alva feels really mad when you grab her crayons. Can you ask for a crayon? Can you say, 'Please, may I have a crayon?'"
- "Jerusha, thank you for saying, 'Excuse me, this chair is mine.'"
- "Adam and Beth, you need to sit here on the step and talk until you both feel better."
- "Beth, your friend Adam says you scratched his face. Adam, Beth says you wadded up her drawing and threw it in the wastebasket. Adam, you're upset because your face really hurts."
- "Beth, you're sad because you really wanted to take that picture home to your mother."
- "Can either of you think of some way to make your friend feel better?"
- "That's a great idea, Adam, you could get the drawing out of the trash can and try to smooth it out."
- "Yes, Beth, I think Adam would really like a wet paper towel to hold on his scratched cheek."

By giving children help in what to say to playmates when trouble breaks out, we encourage them to use appropriate words rather than inappropriate physical or verbal aggression. It is okay (even desirable) for children to express strong emotions. We should never push children into being so "nice" that they hold their emotions inside. Our goal is to channel their emotional expression into words that inform rather than words that hurt.

Should We Force Children to Apologize?

It seems very odd that we tell children, "Be honest; always tell the truth," and then proceed to order them to "tell so-and-so you're sorry" (never even wondering if they actually feel sorry). No child should be encouraged to say he feels something that he really does not feel. It is more appropriate to simply point out how the other child feels. He may spontaneously give some indication of remorse or regret if he really feels it.

If a child appears to be sorry for something he has done, it may be helpful to say, "Would you like to tell Ricky that you're sorry about what happened?" "Would you like me to tell him for you?" It is even more important for us to find some way to help the child make amends to Ricky. He will feel good about himself if he has a chance to make things right. We discourage children terribly when we imply to them, "You have made such a mess of things that there is no way you can undo what you've done."

If a child wants to make amends, she can learn to ask the offended child, "Is there something I can do to make things right?" The adult may need to intervene at first to help the children brainstorm appropriate ways to make amends.

Ways Children Can Make Amends

- Get a damp paper towel for a friend to place on his bumped knee.
- Bring the friend a bandage.

- Share a toy.
- Give a hug.
- Pick up the blocks that were knocked over.
- Ask whether the friend would like to sit at your table.
- Draw a picture.
- Make a homemade card that says "Be my friend."
- Sit by the friend until he feels better.
- Say, "I'm sorry," if it is really sincere.

How Can We Recognize and Encourage Internal Control?

Graciela quietly moved from cot to cot in the darkened child care room as restless four-year-olds settled in for naptime. Several of the children could always be counted on to fall sound asleep almost before she got the light off. Most took 10 or 15 minutes to wind down and fall asleep. Then, of course, there were the really challenging three who squirmed and fidgeted and tried everything in the book to keep themselves awake.

Graciela never knew if she would eventually get them to sleep or not. She especially worried about Brett because his parents had complained that he was so exhausted when they picked him up from child care that they were not able to spend enough quality time with him in the evenings.

Brett was lying on his stomach with his chin resting on one hand and the other hand twisting a loose thread hanging from his blanket. Graciela moved quietly to his side. She sat down cross-legged on the floor beside him and gently stroked his back. She bent close to him and whispered, "Brett, thanks for being so quiet and still. You were so quiet, I couldn't hear a single sound."

Brett grinned and felt very good about himself.

Nurturing adults should always be alert to opportunities for recognizing and reinforcing little indications that a child is making progress in controlling impulses and resisting tempting but inappropriate behaviors.

How Does American Sign Language Support Positive Child Guidance?

There are many reasons today's parents and early educators should be taking a hard look at adding American Sign Language (ASL) to their list of routine child guidance skills. A wider public knowledge of sign language would not only help bring deaf children and their family members into the mainstream but also allow babies and toddlers to use their hands to express their needs much earlier than they can use spoken words. The discovery that babies and toddlers can learn to understand signing has sparked a sign language educational crusade by parents and early educators who find it extremely valuable (Acredolo et al., 2002; Briant, 2004; Daniels, M., 2001; Goodwyn et al., 2000; Glazer, 2001; Jaworski, 2000; Snoddon, 2000).

A particularly important guidance reason for using sign language with toddlers and young preschoolers is that it is often easier for very young children to move their hands when they are angry or excited than to think up words. We often tell them, "Use your words," but in their excitement, their words don't come. Unfortunately their hands are still free for grabbing and hitting. By instilling the habit of sign language, young children will have something urgent to do with their hands, something easy and memorized, something that we hope will take the place of the hitting and pushing.

Can Sign Language Help Bridge Communication Barriers When English Is Not the Primary Language?

For decades, special education teachers have been using sign language to enhance their communication with children who have autism or other kinds of special needs that challenge oral interactions. Now we realize that sign language coupled with oral language heightens the impact of communication for well-developing young children too.

In classrooms today, where diversity so often brings multiple languages not only among the children but also parents and teachers, sign language may be the best hope to open up communication. Simple ASL signs can be used while speaking Japanese, Spanish, English, or any other language. It can help transition children from one language to another. And it can help adults communicate better with each another.

You may be groaning, "Oh, no, I can't learn another language!" But you might be surprised. In fact, you might not know it but you've been using some ASL signs already. For example, everybody knows that saying "shhhh" with a blank face to a three-year-old won't have as much impact as holding your index finger up in front of your lips and motioning with raised eyebrows and a very expressive face. If you have ever raised your index finger to your lips like that, then you have spoken your first ASL word. Now all you have to do is learn a few more signs.

What Are Some Basic ASL Guidance Phrases I Need to Learn?

ASL is a unique language. Like any individual language, it has its own grammar and it does not translate word for word into English or any other language. For example, sign language does not have a sign for the word be. Obviously, the ASL phrases that follow are not literal translations, but they do give a clear sense of the meaning intended. In sign language, facial expression and body language are critical to the overall communication of your message. Always try to convey a consistent, animated, but simple message with your face and body.

Careful 1

Careful 2

▰▰ Careful, step 1. *You can use this to say, "Be careful" (instead of "Be safe").* Show concern on your face. Use your thumbs to hold down your pinky and ring fingers on both hands so that each hand has its index and middle fingers sticking up like little rabbit ears. (In sign language this is called a "K" hand.)

▰▰ Careful, step 2. Place your right "K" hand on top of your left "K" hand and hold them together, moving them up and away from your body in a small circle a couple of times.

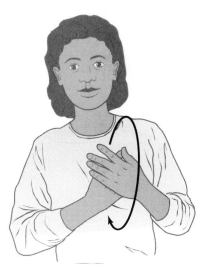

Kind 1

Kind 2

▰▰ Kind, step 1. Place both hands 4 inches in front of your heart and then roll your hands over each other as they move down and away from your heart. Show kindness in your facial expression.

▰▰ Kind, step 2.

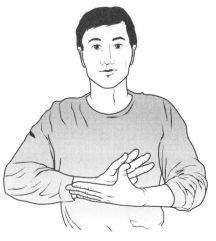

Clean 1

Clean 2

Clean, step 1. *You can use this to say, "Be clean" (instead of "Be neat").* Use your right hand to quickly wipe your upturned left hand, from wrist to fingertips.

Clean, step 2.

Stop 1

Stop 2

Stop, step 1. Combine "stop," "please," and "walk" signs to teach children the phrase, "Stop, please, and walk away!" Children can use this handy phrase instead of hitting or fighting when another child makes them angry.

Stop, step 2. Hold out your left hand, palm upward, and sharply slice down on your left palm with the little finger edge of your open, stiff right hand. Your hands will be at right angles.

Please 1

Please 2

■ Please, step 1. Make a counterclockwise circle with your right hand flat over your heart.

■ Please, step 2.

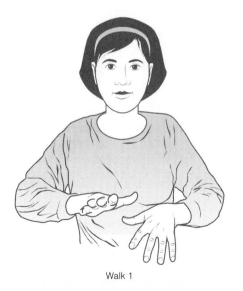

Walk 1

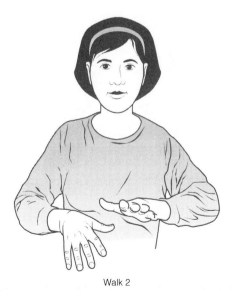

Walk 2

■ Walk, step 1. Hold your palms flat and facing down, hands in front of you and move them up and down as if they were little feet in the process of walking.

■ Walk, step 2.

Bite 1

Bite 2

 Bite, step 1. *Combine the signs for "bite" and "hurt" to create the especially useful phrase for toddlers "Biting hurts!"* Place your left hand in front of you flat and palm down, elbow out to your left.

Bite, step 2. Cup your right hand to represent your mouth, with your fingernails serving as little teeth, and chomp down on your left hand. Use your face to show biting at the same time.

Hurt 1

Hurt 2

Hurt, step 1. Close your fists in front of you with both index fingers pointed straight toward each other.

 Hurt, step 2. Bring the tips of your index fingers toward each other twice using a jabbing movement. Two jabs indicate "Ouch, that hurts!" Use a single jab to indicate "That can hurt you."

Thank you 1

Thank you 2

▰▰▰ Thank you, step 1. Touch your lips with the fingertips of one or both flat hands, then move the hands forward until the palms are facing up (almost like blowing a kiss).

▰▰▰ Thank you, step 2.

What 1

What 2

▰▰▰ What? step 1. Turn both hands palms up in front of you and about a foot apart, with your fingers spread out and relaxed. Hold your elbows close to your body.

▰▰▰ What? step 2. Your facial expression is very important, so furrow your brow quizzically as you move your hands horizontally outward and back a couple of times.

Quiet 1

Quiet 2

▇▇▇ Quiet, step 1. ASL uses the same time-honored index finger in front of the lips that parents and early educators have always used. (Remember to add appropriate facial expressions such as raised eyebrows and an expectant look.)

▇▇▇ Quiet, step 2.

Listen 1

Listen 2

▇▇▇ Listen, step 1. Place your slightly cupped hand behind your ear to say "listen" in sign language.

▇▇▇ Listen, step 2.

Look 1

▬▬ Look, step 1. Use your thumb of your right hand to hold down your pinky and your ring finger so that your index and ring fingers stick up like rabbit ears, palm forward (remember the "K" hand).

Look 2

▬▬ Look, step 2. Touch your index finger lightly to your cheekbone and then point your rabbit-ear fingers toward the object you want someone to look at.

Think 1

▬▬ Think, step 1. Move the tip of your index finger in a small circle in front of your forehead while furrowing your brow to show that you are thinking.

Think 2

▬▬ Think, step 2. Firmly touch your forehead to ask the listener to think.

Put away 1

■ Put away, step 1. Raise your left palm and hold it facing right, as an imaginary shelf.

Put away 2

■ Put away, step 2. Use your right hand to grasp imaginary objects and touch them to the left palm. Repeat several times.

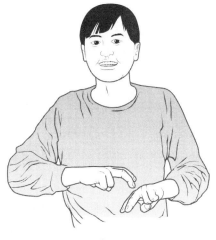

Sit 1

■ Sit, step 1. Begin by making rabbit ears with both hands. Hold the index finger and middle finger of the left hand straight out in front of you to represent the chair.

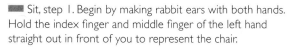

Sit 2

■ Sit, step 2. Bend your right index and middle fingers to indicate tiny legs then place them on the little finger chair. This sign is both a noun and a verb. If you mean "sit down," you place your fingers down once and stop. If you mean "chair," you tap them twice.

All gone 1

All gone 2

▰▰ All gone, step 1. Hold out your hand, palm up, and blow something invisible off your palm. (Note: ASL has many different ways to say "all gone.")

▰▰ All gone, step 2.

Gentle 1

Gentle 2

▰▰ Gentle, step 1. Hold out both hands in front of you and a few inches apart, palms up, and fingers spread apart. Gently pull hands down while bringing the fingers and thumbs of each hand tightly together. Repeat.

▰▰ Gentle, step 2.

Eat 1

Eat 2

▬▬ Eat, step 1. Squeeze the tips of all your fingers of your right hand together with your thumb and bring them to your lips as if bringing food to your mouth.

▬▬ Eat, step 2.

Drink 1

Drink 2

▬▬ Drink, step 1. Hold an invisible glass in your cupped right hand. Make a short arc, bringing your hand to your mouth so your thumb touches your lip.

▬▬ Drink, step 2.

Danger 1

■■ Danger, step 1. Show extreme concern on your face. Hold your left fist across your chest, palm toward your body, as if to protect yourself.

Danger 2

■■ Danger, step 2. Sharply bring the right thumb of your right fist over the top part of your left hand two or three times.

Logical and Natural Consequences

Children learn skills and information through active involvement in their day-to-day environment. They learn by watching others, by being told things, and most importantly, by experiencing life. In life, actions are often followed by logical or natural consequences. If I forget to water my potted plant, it will probably die (a natural consequence). If I am regularly late to work, I may lose my job (a logical consequence). No one is trying to hurt or annoy me. These consequences are merely the way the world works. Through them, I learn that I must behave in certain ways if I want to avoid undesired results and achieve desired goals.

Natural Consequences

A natural consequence occurs when a child is allowed to learn from a situation without any intervention from adults. This guidance technique is based on the idea that learning appropriate behavior should come from direct experience whenever possible (Dreikurs & Grey, 1968).

For example, if you don't eat your lunch you may become hungry before snack time. If you don't put your artwork into your cubby, you may not be able to find it when you are ready to go home. If you leave your cup of milk on the edge of the table, you may knock it off. Adults must refrain from saying, "I told you so." If the child deals with being covered in milk, copes with the frustration of her lost artwork, and feels her empty, growling stomach, she will soon make the connection between her behavior and natural consequences. Adults can provide tactful, positive information. "If you place your cup here, it probably won't spill." "If you put your coat on the coat hook, you will know where it is."

Obviously, natural consequences cannot be allowed any time they present a significant safety risk, infringe on the rights of others, or threaten unreasonable damage to the environment. (Be safe! Be kind! Be neat!)

Experience is a great teacher, but adults must be careful not to intervene after the negative consequence has occurred. Nagging, lecturing, or punishing the child risks destroying the natural learning that takes place and, even worse, may start a power struggle.

Logical Consequences

logical consequence
An outcome that results from a situation where adults determine and control the conclusion.

natural consequence
An outcome that results from a situation without any external intervention to change or control the conclusion.

Logical consequences are appropriate when natural consequences cannot be used because they might present a significant safety risk, infringe on the rights of others, or threaten unreasonable damage to the environment.

Whereas **natural consequences** involve guidance situations that are allowed to take place without any intervention from adults, logical consequences involve guidance situations in which the adults determine and control the consequences. The successful outcome with these consequences depends on how logically connected a given consequence is to a specific behavior (Dreikurs & Grey, 1968).

For example, the logical consequence of tearing the pages out of a picture book might be having to carefully tape the pages back into the book. The logical consequence for throwing blocks in the block area may be losing the privilege of playing there for one hour. The logical consequence of coloring on the wall instead of the paper is having to scrub off the marks.

Again, nagging and lecturing will ruin the lesson. The child should be allowed to learn freely from the experience. Patience rules the day here. Don't be shocked if the young child is so taken by the experience of sponging up his spilled milk that he purposely spills more so that he can continue to wipe up spilled milk.

Remember, it is the exciting process of learning that young children find so fulfilling. If the child's interest continues, you will need to redirect this budding interest in sponging and water play to materials more appropriate than the cup of milk at the table and the spilled milk on the floor.

A small basin with a limited amount of slightly soapy water and a child-size scrub brush might be just the thing to extend this child's exploration of how people clean floors. After he has scrubbed to his heart's content, he should be shown how to empty the basin, use a sponge to soak up excess water on the floor, wring out the sponge into the basin, and empty the basin again.

Always observe children to try to understand the motives for their behavior. By understanding what children are trying to do, you will be able to find creative ways to redirect inconvenient or unsafe behavior into legitimate and meaningful learning experiences.

Your everyday guidance responses, not nagging or lecturing but allowing children to make connections between their behavior and the natural or logical consequences of their actions, helps them see you as their ally rather than a stubborn obstacle who stops them from doing things they want to do.

But remember, relying on natural and logical consequences does not give any adult the right to ignore or allow child behaviors that present a significant safety risk, infringe on the rights of others, or threaten unreasonable damage to the environment. It is your responsibility to intervene in these situations to set an example of how we live in a democratic society that respects and protects the rights of all its citizens.

Should Children Be Rescued from the Consequences of Their Actions?

Sometimes, when we see a child feeling disappointed or sad, we may be tempted to interfere and rescue him from the consequences of his actions. It is not, however, a useful practice for us to rescue children from the logical and natural results of their actions and choices so long as the consequences are reasonable and safe. We would never risk a child being run over as a natural consequence of running into the street or allow a child to go hungry as a logical consequence of spilling food.

> Tina, age seven, arrived home after a family outing to a downtown restaurant and exclaimed, "Oh, no! I left my purse in the restaurant!" Her dad fumed and sputtered, "Tina, why are you so careless? It'll take me a half hour to drive back downtown, and by then the purse will probably have been stolen. You'd lose your head if it wasn't tied down." After yelling at Tina for 20 minutes while she sniffled and made excuses for her behavior, he called the restaurant and drove back downtown alone to search for the purse.

Even though Tina's dad reprimanded her loudly and angrily, in actuality he **rescued** her from any responsibility for her forgetfulness. (He absorbed the consequences for her.) He was the one who made the telephone call, drove all the way back to the restaurant, and did the searching. Tina had nothing to do but feel miserable and stupid. Tina's dad would have used natural consequences if he had said the following:

> Tina, I'm sure you feel awful about losing your purse. Can you think of anything we could do to find it? Would you like me to help you look up the telephone number of the restaurant? Would you like me to drive you back to the restaurant so you can look for it? I don't know if we'll find it or not. Purses left in public places often get stolen.

Tina's dad would have used logical consequences if he had said,

> Tina, it isn't fair for me to have to drive all the way back to town. Next time we go to the theater, you will have to leave your purse at home. When you're a little older, you can try again. Perhaps by then it won't be so hard for you to remember your things.

By helping Tina find ways to solve her problem (rather than solving it for her), Tina's father guides her to focus on her forgetfulness as the problem, not her father's

rescued
A situation in which one has been removed from experiencing the logical consequence of an inappropriate behavior. Typically, a child acted improperly without any negative results because an adult intervened to extricate the child from a precarious situation the child has created.

anger. She realizes that her discomfort results from the natural or logical consequences of her forgetfulness, not from someone trying to punish or embarrass her. She will become responsible when she learns to remember her possessions because it is frustrating and inconvenient to lose them, not to please her father. If Tina learns to behave appropriately only as a way to please her father, she may be tempted to behave inappropriately just to annoy him when she is angry with him or feeling rebellious.

What Is the Difference between Punishment and Guidance?

Punishment is negative. It is intended to hurt, humiliate, or retaliate (pay a child back for something he has done). The purpose of guidance, in contrast, is to teach children (assertively and respectfully) to behave appropriately. Discipline is a part of positive child guidance; punishment is not. Following are examples of punishment versus discipline as used with a preschooler.

Punishment

"Don't you dare touch that cake. Get away from here and go play. If I catch you fooling around with it, you're really gonna get it!"

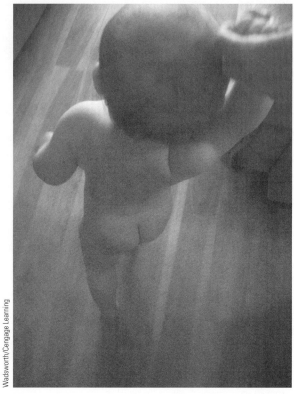

A child's body is not designed for hitting or shaking.

"I saw you touch that cake. Get in the time-out chair and stay until I say you can get up. Everyone's going to see you sitting in the 'naughty' chair and know that you were being bad."

"I'd better not see you get up from the time-out chair! If I see you try to get up, I'll make you stay twice as long."

Punishment is used to bully or coerce children into behaving the way we want them to behave. Some of the ways adults punish children are by

- spanking, slapping, arm-yanking, and shaking
- biting, hair-pulling, or pinching (so he will know how it feels)
- withdrawing affection, ignoring the child, avoiding eye contact, and not speaking
- humiliating the child, putting him in a position to be ridiculed
- endlessly lecturing, nagging, or harping on problems that are in the past (they are done, the child cannot undo them)
- forcing the child to sit or stay somewhere for a set period, regardless of whether the child is sincerely remorseful and ready to make amends
- arbitrarily taking away privileges, and forbidding activities that the child particularly enjoys (especially privileges that are totally unrelated to the child's offense)

What NAEYC Says about Time-Out

In 1997 the National Association for the Education of Young Children (NAEYC) produced a strong statement about use of time-outs in an article, "Time out for 'Time-Out.'" It is posted on their website, and they freely grant reproduction rights to anyone who gives credit to NAEYC, so the document can legally be copied and given to coworkers and families. Here is the first paragraph in NAEYC's document giving serious cautions about the use of time-out:

> The purpose of discipline for young children is to teach coping skills and discourage inappropriate behavior. "Time-out" is not a first choice, but a last resort technique for a child who is harming another or in danger of harming herself. Used infrequently and for very brief periods (no longer than two or three minutes), time-out may give a child the opportunity to calm down and cool off after a frustrating situation. Used often or inappropriately, time-out may not only be ineffectual—it may be damaging to the child. (Available at http://www.naeyc.org/ece/1996/15.asp)

What Head Start Says about Time-Out

On April 29, 2004, Windy Hill, associate commissioner of the Head Start Bureau, wrote an open letter about time-out to Head Start personnel and posted it on the Internet for all to see. She said she was not trying to encourage or discourage the use of time-out, but just wanted to clarify what time-out is in the context of appropriate guidance. Here is part of what Ms. Hill said:

> Appropriate use of time-out by a trained adult provides for a very brief and adult-supervised separation from an ongoing group activity and social interaction. The approach must not be used in a punitive manner, but rather to provide an opportunity for a positive integration of the child into the social activity with the support and guidance needed to participate in that activity more successfully. (More about time-out is available at http://www.vanderbilt.edu/csefel/briefs/wwb14.html.)

Think Twice before You Give a Time-Out

Time-out should be used rarely (if at all) in a developmentally appropriate program. There are many, many other guidance strategies described in this text that can be used with less risk of misuse or harm. Many forward-thinking developmentally appropriate early childhood programs have decided to use a wide range of positive guidance strategies that don't include time-out (Betz, 1994; Crosser, 2002; Gartrell, 2001, 2002).

Time-out is *not* appropriate if

- it is used routinely or often
- it is used as a logical (or, more accurately, illogical) consequence
- if children spend more than two or three minutes there
- it is used for children younger than three
- a special chair or area is designated for time-out

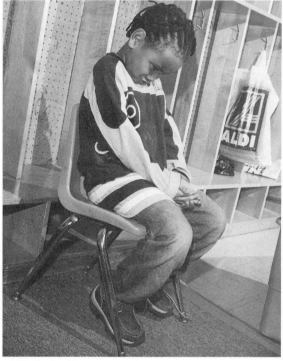

Wadsworth/Cengage Learning

■■■Time-out is no longer considered a positive, supportive guidance strategy that should routinely be used in developmentally appropriate programs.

time-away
Removing a child from an overwhelming situation to provide a supportive cooling off time with an adult present.

Use "Time-Away" rather than Time-Out

Time-away is a very different thing from time-out. Time-away is appropriate even for toddlers. Time-away is simply removing a child from an overwhelming situation to provide a supportive cooling off time. Time-away gives time for a child to be *with an adult* and aside from the group after he has lost control. A preschooler may need to cry, express anger, talk, think about what happened, regroup, and gain composure. When he has determined how to make amends and prevent further loss of control, he will be ready to return to the group without a loss of face. A toddler needs to be removed from the source of stress and given calming support for as long as needed and then redirected to an appealing activity.

The purpose of time-away is not to provide a logical consequence or to remove stimulation to avoid giving positive reinforcement. It has to do only with giving the child much needed privacy and time to wind down a tantrum, to save face, to be reminded that she is valued, and to be reminded that she must make amends for harm she has done.

The length of a time-away is for as long as it takes the child to become calm. The adult stays with the child. Some children (including toddlers) want and need to be held, hugged, or patted. Many despise being touched. Some have to be kept from harming themselves and the environment until they calm down—remember to be as gentle as possible but as firm as necessary. The adult should speak soothingly and reassuringly throughout this ordeal. Be alert to the child's movements. You may have to stay calm, firm, and caring while you are protecting yourself from being pinched or bitten. The child needs assurance that you are calm and in control and that you will not allow yourself or the child to be harmed.

When the out-of-control preschooler finally gains control, he usually has warm feelings for the adult who has so patiently helped him through this difficult time. The child is usually eager at this point to make amends for whatever he did wrong so he can return to his play.

The child learns that his angry outburst didn't get his needs met. It didn't send the adult into a tailspin (which can be emotionally rewarding to an angry child). No one gave in to the shrieking and hitting. In fact, nothing much happened. The child was just removed from the group so he could cry until he was finished.

The angry outburst was anticlimactic because it didn't create any real impact except patient support and a quiet reminder about how to appropriately get needs met: "Remember to use your words next time. . . . Say, 'Please don't touch my blocks,' instead of kicking and screaming." This support helps children gradually develop the skills they need to better control their impulses.

Positive guidance is used to nurture and shape children's behavior. Following are some of the ways adults can discipline children using positive guidance:

- Change the surroundings to remove the likelihood or temptation for misbehavior.
- Focus the child's attention on logical and natural consequences that will, or may, follow a specific behavior.
- Express concern for the child's feelings, but refusing to rescue the child from reasonable and safe consequences that are natural or logical results of his behavior.
- Carefully supervise the child to prompt or cue appropriate behavior and remind the child of rules.
- Firmly but respectfully redirect the child's behavior away from inappropriate actions and substituting more appropriate activities.
- Decisively stop or interrupt any behavior that is clearly dangerous.
- Physically remove a very young child from a conflict or during a tantrum (even if the child is kicking and screaming) when it is necessary to protect the child and the environment.
- Let an older child know that you refuse to join in the tantrum but that you will be glad to talk when he is ready to speak calmly and respectfully.
- Assure the child that he is loved and valued; let him know that you accept and respect his negative feelings, even if you must stop his negative action (it is okay to feel angry but not okay to hurt others).

How to Tell the Difference between Punishment and Guidance

Punishment	Guidance
lowers self-esteem	builds self-esteem
humiliates	strengthens character
degrades	respects
hurts (physically or emotionally)	heals
angers	gives hope
frustrates	models coping skills
thwarts efforts	enables efforts
embarrasses	gives confidence
discourages	encourages
belittles	enhances self-image
socially isolates	facilitates trust
emotionally abandons	gives emotional support
denies affection	is loving and caring

Even very young children can be guided to clean up after themselves, as much as their skills allow.

At this point, you might respond by saying, "Those lists are lovely, but when little Elroy draws on my freshly painted walls with his crayon, I'm furious. I don't care about enhancing his self-image, I just want to wring his little neck!" Actually, Elroy's infuriating behavior gives us an excellent opportunity to put our preaching into practice. We can show Elroy, through our own behavior, that feeling angry is natural and normal but that hurting, humiliating, or belittling others is not okay. Socially accepted rules for appropriate behavior do not apply only to children; they apply to all of us.

Having Elroy tediously scrub the crayon marks off the wall and taking the crayons away until he can be more carefully supervised are both assertive and effective disciplinary methods. They are a part of positive child guidance, but only if the adult's attitude is optimistic and assertive rather than mean spirited and punitive. Our attitude toward Elroy should be one of helping him succeed in behaving more appropriately in the future, not making him miserable by punishing him for his bad deed.

How Can I Be Firm without Seeming Angry?

To be firm and fair in guiding children, deeds must be seen as separate from the person who did them. In other words, what a child has done may have been dishonest, but that does not mean the child is now a dishonest person. Because children are prone to become what we tell them they are (remember that prophecies are often self-fulfilling), we must be very careful about what we tell children they are. It is helpful to tell a child, "Pouring water on a cat is a thoughtless and unkind thing to do. You are a kind and thoughtful boy, but even kind, thoughtful boys make mistakes. The important thing is to do better next time."

Phrases that are not helpful do little more than stereotype children in negative roles (naughty, bad, stupid, lazy). Helpful phrases give children very specific information about what is expected, without labeling the child in a negative way. Children always appreciate being reminded, "I'm very upset with what you did, but I'm not angry with you. I still love you a whole lot, even when you make mistakes."

Avoid Overindulging and Overprotecting Children

Caring adults know how to say no. The idea of positive child guidance is sometimes interpreted to mean that adults are slaves to children, that adults must somehow keep things happy, glowing, and idyllic for children at all times. This could not be

Helpful and Not Helpful Phrases

Helpful	Not Helpful
"Spitting at people is not allowed!"	"You are a naughty boy!"
"You seem angry with your brother."	"Why are you so bad?"
"What will happen if you spill the paint?"	"Don't act like a dummy."
"After your room is clean, then you may go outside to play."	"You lazy thing! Look at your room."
"Be kind. Be gentle. Biting hurts."	"You'll never make it through school."

delay gratification
The process of putting off something desired until a later time. This skill can be learned gradually during early childhood by children who develop a strong sense of trust that their essential needs will be met.

further from the truth. We have an obligation to be fair, caring, and available, but we are not responsible to make sure that children are completely happy at every moment of their lives.

Caring for and guiding children is physically demanding, emotionally draining, and intellectually taxing work, and growing up is not an easy task for the children either. Adults and children will sometimes be at cross-purposes, so there are bound to be conflicts. Overindulgence and overprotection (sometimes referred to as spoiling) are not a part of positive child guidance. Not being firm enough is just as damaging as being too firm.

One mother says, "But I have to give Lindy ice cream while I'm preparing dinner. If I don't, she screams and holds her breath until she turns blue. I have no choice!" Of course Lindy's mother has a choice. She is the only one tall enough to reach the freezer!

Lindy's mother needs reassurance that it is perfectly okay for Lindy to cry. Lindy feels frustrated, and crying is her way of expressing herself. When Lindy was a helpless newborn, her mother needed to respond quickly to her cries of hunger to instill in her a sense of trust. Now Lindy is older. She can **delay gratification** of her needs being met. In fact, she must learn how to delay gratification if she is ever to develop responsibility and self-control.

Her mother needs to feel more relaxed about Lindy's breath holding. Babies and toddlers often forget to breathe for a few seconds when they are very stunned or hurt. Parents often hear the loud thump of their toddler falling, then a moment of silence, and then loud, howling cries. The toddler isn't holding her breath to be manipulative; that's just how her body works. If, however, a great deal of attention is paid to that pause in her breathing, the child might eventually learn to hold her breath just for dramatic

"I am still a good person even if I sometimes break a rule."

Wadsworth/Cengage Learning

apnea
A breathing abnormality
marked by momentary delays
in breathing.

effect. Unless Lindy is suffering from a disorder such as **apnea,** the worst that will happen is that Lindy will succeed in causing herself to faint, at which time breathing will automatically resume.

The most effective way for Lindy's mother to deal with the child's behavior is to assertively and caringly acknowledge that wanting ice cream is okay but that no ice cream will be served until after dinner. The mother could tell Lindy, "I know you wish you could have ice cream. It's all right to cry. Sometimes I cry when I'm mad or upset. You may cry as long as you need to. If you need to cry for a long, long time, then you must cry in your room so that you don't hurt other people's ears."

After Lindy has finished crying (remember, no child ever cried forever), her mother can redirect Lindy's hunger (present a compromise) by offering peanut butter crackers or apple slices. Or if she senses that even bringing up the subject of hunger would cause another scene, she may wait and offer a nutritious treat the next time she anticipates a problem, before Lindy even has a chance to mention ice cream. She can also choose not to purchase ice cream for a while to reduce Lindy's temptation (as well as her own temptation to give in). Whatever she does, she must not give in to Lindy's tantrum and reinforce her inappropriate behavior by rewarding it with ice cream.

Giving in to Lindy's demand—while yelling, complaining, or making her feel guilty—is inappropriately overindulgent and very confusing. Lindy may not learn that the word *no* really means *no,* or she may come to view herself as an unlovable and spoiled brat, thinking badly of herself but not really knowing how to behave differently.

Help Children Learn to Make Choices within Limits

Children need freedom within clear limits. Freedom without limits is not really freedom. Instead, it is chaotic and dangerous. Jesse's parents have tried to give him complete freedom.

> Jesse rules the family with the total abandon of a dictator. Whatever is being served for breakfast is not what he wants. Even if he is asked in advance for his breakfast order, he goes through several changes of mind. His parents meekly pour out bowls of cereal and make waffles or throw away waffles and make oatmeal.
>
> Whatever clothes Jesse's mother has chosen for him to wear are almost never to his liking either. He stamps down the hall like a little emperor and stuffs the clean clothing into the laundry hamper. His mother meekly offers alternative selections of clothes she hopes he will like. Sometimes Jesse goes to school wearing clothes that are totally inappropriate for the weather or the setting.

His parents wonder why he is so demanding. They are proud of their beautiful little boy, and they want so much for him to love them that they fail to use good judgment. They also hate to confront him and risk an ugly scene. They do not realize it, but what Jesse really wants and needs is strong, loving parents who are willing and able to help him grow up. Secretly, Jesse realizes he is acting like a baby.

Jesse did not become a dictator overnight, and he will not be able to change into a reasonable and polite person overnight. With time and patience, however, Jesse can learn to make choices within clearly defined, reasonable limits. Jesse can be given a choice between eggs and cereal, between the red shirt and the blue shirt, and he can be allowed to deal with the natural and logical consequences of refusing to accept the limits he has been given.

His parents can explain, "Jesse, if you're not hungry enough to eat the corn flakes you asked for, then you're obviously not very hungry for breakfast." "You may take 10 minutes to choose what you want to wear from these clothes. If you are not able to choose, then I will choose for you." "If you stuff clean clothes in the laundry hamper, you will have to help with the extra laundry by sorting and folding clothes instead of watching television."

To enforce freedom of choice within reasonable limits, Jesse's parents will have to make a commitment to confront Jesse with love and persistence. Of course, in the long run, Jesse will be a happier, friendlier, more likable person.

External Reinforcement

Developing children's inner control and motivation for behaving acceptably have been addressed throughout this text. Previous sections have emphasized the concept that children must want to behave well, that they must assume responsibility for their actions. Positive child guidance is not a gimmicky strategy to manipulate children into behaving according to our specifications, but instead a process of guiding children to become competent, confident, and cooperative human beings who behave well, not to win favors, but because behaving well is the right thing to do.

Now, however, it is time to look at the opposite side of the coin: techniques for refining external control. Some behaviors do not come from internal motivation. They are unconscious habits that are very resistant to even the most sincere desire for change. We know from our own experiences that wanting to quit smoking, lose weight, or exercise regularly is not always enough to make those things happen. I can want desperately to lose weight, but if I am unconsciously conditioned to open the refrigerator every time I pass it, I may be my own worst enemy.

Jeremy tells his mother that he does not want to practice the piano each day (as his piano teacher has asked him to do). Consequently, his mother delves into Jeremy's inner motivations. She talks with him about his hope to become a famous musician and his feelings of pride when he masters difficult pieces of music. If Jeremy really has an inner desire to play the piano, and the lack of practicing is simply a matter of establishing new habits, then giving him a cute little sticker as a reward each day that he practices may work wonders. If he does not practice because he lacks inner motivation, then stickers will be a waste of time. In fact, they may be worse than a waste of time. Jeremy may base his decision not to practice on the fact that he is giving up only a little sticker that really is not very valuable anyway. Also, if Jeremy is coerced into practicing to get a reward, he may respond to future reminders of things he is supposed to do by saying, "What will you give me if I do it?"

In contrast, when Jeremy decides to train his pet chicken to "play the piano" for a county fair, he does not waste any time telling the hen how proud she will feel; he just drops a pellet of corn into her dish each time she inadvertently steps on the keyboard of the toy piano he has placed on the floor of her cage. Before long, Jeremy's chicken clucks loudly and pounds on the piano keyboard every time she sees him.

My placing coins in a candy vending machine every day may be every bit as mindless as the chicken's stepping on the toy piano keyboard to get pellets of corn. I may need to change my external surroundings to break my habit cycle. Perhaps I could walk a different route so that I do not pass the vending machines, think of a reward to give myself if I resist candy bars for a whole week, or even bring nutritious, low-calorie snacks with me as a substitute when I am tempted to eat candy. We can assist children in breaking undesirable habits in exactly the same way.

External Conditions That Support Appropriate Behavior

> Stephanie runs up to her mother when her mother arrives to pick her up from her child care center. Stephanie has a handful of drawings, and she is dancing around her mother squealing, "Mommy, look what I made! Look what I made!" Stephanie's mother is busy chatting with other mothers, so she ignores Stephanie. Finally, Stephanie throws the drawings down on the ground and yells, "I hate you, Mommy!" Instantly, her mother bends down and says (in an irritated tone), "Stephanie, what do you want?"

Stephanie has learned a lesson that her mother did not intend to teach her: When you want your mother's attention, be hateful and destructive because you will get attention faster than by just asking for attention.

Children generally do whatever they need to do to get their needs met. Many unconscious habits are formed simply because they work. We need to analyze our daily procedures very carefully to identify how children get the things they want and need in the environment.

Does the child who pushes and shoves the hardest always get to be first in line? Does whining and arguing always succeed in extending bedtime or television viewing time? Does pitching a fit mean the child does not have to buckle his seat belt? Does the child who misbehaves the most during story time get almost all of the adult's eye contact, verbal contact, physical contact, and name recognition? Remember, even negative attention is preferable to being ignored.

intermittent reinforcer
A stimulus or reward given after some, but not all, occurrences of a particular behavior. The intermittency tends to increase the specific behavior that is reinforced.

We also need to consider the powerful effect of **intermittent reinforcer.** People who gamble do not need to get a reward every time they put money in a slot machine. They will keep feeding money to "one-armed bandits" for hours just to get a chance at one really big payoff. Children, likewise, can pester for hours on the chance that a disgusted adult will finally give in and reward their inappropriate behavior with the desired privilege or response. Without realizing it, we may reinforce and reward dysfunctional and annoying behaviors daily. By consciously looking at what a child gets out of various behaviors and changing our own behaviors, we may take big steps in preventing or resolving many frustrating misbehavior patterns.

What Is Behavior Modification and How Should It Be Used?

To use **behavior modification,** the adult follows a highly structured process:

- *Observe* a child's present behavior.
- *Identify* a desired future behavior.
- *Break* the distance between the two behaviors into tiny steps.
- *Systematically* **reinforce** each small step as the child moves closer to the desired behavior.

Behaviorists see learning as a process of piecing together a chain, one link at a time. The process is external to the child, because the adult chooses the skill to be learned and then rewards that behavior in the child.

behavior modification
A specific method for changing a child's behavior by rewarding new and desirable behaviors and making undesirable behaviors less attractive to the child, often by simply ignoring them.

Elinor is a beautiful little girl who is a victim of autism. She cannot speak, and she constantly flutters around the room flapping her arms and making small grunting sounds. Pleading with her to stop these behaviors would only confuse her, making her so anxious that the behaviors would probably increase. Using behavior modification, however, would be an effective and caring way to shape her behavior into more socially accepted patterns.

Elinor's teacher, Thomas, simply ignores the flapping and watches carefully for the instant that Elinor stops to look at something. Immediately, Thomas gives Elinor a tiny paper cup of Cheerios, her favorite cereal, and says, "Good job, Elinor." Over a period of months, very quietly and unobtrusively, Thomas has conditioned Elinor to focus more of her attention on the toys and books in the classroom and to spend a great deal less time flapping and grunting. Very importantly, Thomas ignored Elinor's undesirable behavior but he never ignored or withdrew affection from Elinor herself.

Thomas' next task is to gradually wean Elinor off the cereal and replace that reinforcement with shiny plastic coins he calls tokens. He hopes that eventually Elinor will comprehend that if she collects a certain number of tokens she can trade them in for a special treat, privilege, or snack.

Children with developmental delays, learning deficits, and language disabilities may lack the ability to discuss or reflect on their inner motivations. Behavior modification may truly be a godsend for guiding these children.

Behavior modification can be used very successfully with well developing, even gifted, children. It is, however, essential to enlist the bright child's voluntary and active cooperation. Adults and children who are capable of examining their own motives and those of others will feel coerced if they realize that their behavior has been manipulated without their knowledge. If I, for example, suddenly realize that someone has rigged the candy vending machine to steal my quarters so I will stop buying candy and lose weight, I will feel furious. I may stubbornly eat even more candy just to assert my autonomy.

Behavior modification works most effectively with mentally capable children when adults are straightforward about their plan. An adult might say, "Ginger, let's make a little booklet to help you remember to go to the bathroom on time. I will set the timer for one hour, and each time it rings, if your pants are still dry, you may paste a special sticker in your book. Do you think that would help you remember? Would you like to try it?"

Obviously, the sticker booklet will help only if Ginger is wetting her pants because she has a habit of delaying visits to the bathroom. A young toddler will not suddenly be able to master toilet training just to get stickers if she does not yet understand the signals her body is giving her or how to control those sensations. The strategy also will not work if Ginger has inner motivation problems (such as needing to be a baby to compete for attention with a new baby in her family). If, however, Ginger really wants to stop wetting her pants and she just needs a little boost to break a bad habit, she is likely to cooperate fully and feel very proud of herself when she succeeds. The sticker tokens will give her just the boost she needs to be successful.

Why Behavior Modification Does Not Work All the Time

Behavior modification is a useful tool when used appropriately. A primary concern, however, is that ignoring inappropriate behavior may become an excuse to give up responsibility for children's unacceptable behavior. Tactfully overlooking certain inappropriate behaviors may be helpful in some situations, and reinforcement has a tremendous effect on habit patterns. There is a risk, however, that if used inappropriately, behaviorist tactics can become manipulative and aloof. Ignoring a child's behavior can become punitive and hurtful when the adult is working *on* the child rather than *with* the child.

As adults, we have a responsibility not to passively stand by when a child is labeled as bad or wild, but to actively involve ourselves in making it easy for children to behave properly and very, very difficult for them to behave improperly. We may not always succeed, but we can give our most persistent and energetic effort. Then, at least, a child with behavioral problems will know we care very much about him and that we will not give up on him, no matter what he does.

Parents and educators are becoming more and more aware that punishment and threats are not effective. Punishment, even if it is disguised as "consequences," often triggers immediate compliance but tends to increase aggression and damage the crucial bond between adult and child. In their efforts to avoid punishments, teachers and parents turn to the use of stickers and stars as praise and awards and to privileges to induce children to master skills and obey adults (Kohn, 1990, 1993, 1994; Fantuzzo et al., 1991). Rewards can result in temporary compliance from children but are no more effective than punishments at helping children become self-directed learners or caring, cooperative, responsible people (DeVries & Zan, 1994).

In short, good values have to be grown from the inside out. Attempts to short-circuit this process by dangling rewards in front of children are at best ineffective and at worst counterproductive. Children are likely to become enthusiastic, lifelong learners as a result of being provided with an engaging curriculum; a safe, caring community in which to discover and create; and a significant degree of choice about what (and how and why) they are learning. Rewards—including negative ones such as punishments—are unnecessary when these things are present and are ultimately destructive in any case (Kohn, 1994).

Child guidance programs and commercial classroom management "kits" that rely on external rewards should be avoided by any early educator or parent who values moral development more than mindless obedience and wants children to become responsible for their own behavior. Moral reasoning develops best in a caring environment where children learn by relying on problem solving, collaboration, and cooperation to resolve social predicaments (DeVries & Zan, 1994; Solomon et al., 1992). Behavior modification has a role in early education for limited, targeted, and strategic use such as with children with severe developmental delays or to help break a mindless habit. It can't, however, help children construct knowledge and build solid, moral internal values.

KEY TERMS

apnea

behavior modification

bibliotherapy

delay gratification

intermittent reinforcer

logical consequence

natural consequence

negotiate

nonverbal communication

reinforce

rescued

time-away

POINTS TO REMEMBER

- We can prevent many behavior problems before they ever begin simply by careful planning, by understanding children's developmental needs, and by creating a match between their needs and the environment.
- Our physical postures, movements, and gestures communicate a great deal of information to children.
- If nonverbal cues are too threatening and intrusive, children bristle and resist commands.
- If requests are assertive, caring, confident, and respectful, children are more likely to comply quickly and willingly.

- Toddlers behave aggressively because they lack the ability to express themselves verbally.
- Insisting that children apologize, whether or not they feel regret, is neither an honest nor effective way to guide them.
- Punishment is intended to hurt, humiliate, or pay a child back for something he has done.
- Guidance is intended to teach appropriate behavior.
- American Sign Language can support positive guidance.
- The use of time-out as a penalty does not support positive child guidance.

PRACTICAL APPLICATION

The Big Boys and the Very Muddy Day

Mrs. Belk had taught first graders in a neighborhood public school for several years. She decided to upgrade her skills by taking a graduate course in psychology at a nearby university. Only a few weeks after class began

the professor lectured on operant conditioning. What a great idea, she thought: ignore the negative and reinforce the positive.

Mrs. Belk was eager to try some new disciplinary techniques on several of her more difficult children, especially Chad, a six-year-old who tended to be her group's ringleader for inappropriate behavior. He seemed to be in a constant state of motion.

For two years he had been taking daily doses of a prescription medication for hyperactivity. The past week had been particularly stressful for Mrs. Belk. Chad had been even more out of control than usual. It had rained for so much of the week that the children had not played outside a single time. She looked out the window. The sun had come out and the only problem with the playground was that there were still some very large mud puddles here and there. When the room was clean and the children were all sitting around on the floor in a big circle, Mrs. Belk said, "How would you like to go outside to the playground?"

To their gleeful shouts of, "Yes, yes, yes!" Mrs. Belk answered, "We can go outside on one condition. Everyone has to agree to play only on the dry areas. There are mud puddles, and you will have to remember to walk around them." The children eagerly agreed to stay on dry land. As Mrs. Belk walked out into the bright sunlight, she took a deep breath of fresh air and felt a great sense of relief to be outside the stuffy classroom. After only a few seconds, she saw Chad running backward to catch a ball, and splat, he stepped right into the mud. Mrs. Belk stood with her hands on her hips, glaring at Chad and thinking about whether to have him sit on the bench for 10 minutes for breaking a class rule.

She knew that it was a real effort to keep Chad sitting for 10 minutes. Mrs. Belk dreaded a confrontation and decided that she just did not have the energy to deal with Chad at the moment.

She started thinking about what her professor had said about it being helpful to ignore inappropriate behavior—and besides, she thought, maybe his stepping in the mud was really an accident—so she looked the other way and decided to ignore Chad. Within seconds, several children were pulling at her shirt sleeves saying, "Mrs. Belk, Mrs. Belk, look, Chad is in the mud!" Mrs. Belk told them, "Go play and don't pay any attention to Chad."

Within minutes, two of Chad's favorite playmates, Eddie and John, also six, were hollering as Chad stamped his foot in the mud, splattering mud on them.

They found it necessary, of course (after they nervously looked back to make sure Mrs. Belk's back was still turned), to stamp their feet in the mud, splattering Chad from head to toe. The chase was on, with half the class frantically telling Mrs. Belk, "Look, look at Chad!" and the other half squealing and laughing as the three boys chased and slid in the mud.

Mrs. Belk saw that her strategy was not working. With the look of daggers in her eyes she shouted, "Okay, everybody line up at the door to go inside." All of the children (except Chad, Eddie, and John) hurried to the door and made a straight line. In a loud voice, Mrs. Belk stared straight at the three boys and said, "I'm waiting. Not everyone is ready to go inside." She thought, "There is no way I am going to chase those three around in this mud. They are just doing this to get attention. They'll come as soon as they think we are really going inside."

Mrs. Belk opened the door and said, "Everyone walk quietly in the hall, please." While the group of children were being led inside, they nervously glanced back and forth at Mrs. Belk and the three boys running around outside. They knew the three boys were in a lot of trouble, and they knew Mrs. Belk was angry. The three boys chased and played in the mud, pretending not to notice that the others were going inside, and trying to look tough and macho. By this time, their shoes and clothes were caked with mud and they were beginning to feel very uncomfortable.

Within five minutes, a teacher, whose room overlooked the playground, ran down the hall and said, "Mrs. Belk, you've got to get those boys inside! They've taken off all their clothes and they are on top of the fort throwing mud balls at the building and at cars."

The playground was a mess. The building and cars were a mess, and the boys were a mess. The situation was no longer salvageable. The boys had to be forcibly brought inside. The principal called their horrified parents to come and get them. There was no easy way for the boys to make amends for their behavior or to save face in front of their peers, parents, and teachers. They had taken part in an open rebellion, a serious and scary step for a child and a damaging precedent for future behavior.

DISCUSSION QUESTIONS

1. What are some possible reasons for Mrs. Belk's ignoring the muddy boys? Evaluate those reasons.
2. List some ways that you think these problems could have been avoided.
3. What could Mrs. Belk have done that might have prevented or stopped the inappropriate behavior?
4. What do you think the muddy boys were thinking and feeling throughout this episode?
5. What do you think the rest of the children were thinking and feeling?
6. How would you have responded if you were the principal? The parents? Another teacher in the building?
7. If you were Mrs. Belk, what would you say or do when the boys came back to school the next day?

STUDENT ACTIVITY

1. Isabella is five. She has painted yellow tempera paint all over the window. What is the most appropriate and authentic logical consequence for this misbehavior? Why did you select your choice?
   a. She is not allowed to paint ever again.
   b. She is required to sit in a "thinking chair" to consider what she has done.
   c. She is invited to use a small sponge and a small bucket of soapy water to clean the paint off the window.
   d. Are there any other appropriate consequences can you name?
2. Amália is three. She has been spitting water at the water fountain. She fills her mouth with water from the fountain then spews it at the wall and at anyone who happens to be nearby. What is the most appropriate and authentic consequence for this misbehavior? Why did you select your choice?
   a. She is forbidden to drink out of the water fountain.
   b. She is banished to time out for three minutes.
   c. She is invited to get paper towels to wipe off the wall where she got it wet.
   d. She is invited to bring a plastic cup to the sink in the bathroom, to explore spitting into the sink as long as she likes. (This is actually redirection rather than logical consequence.)
   e. Are there any other appropriate consequences can you name?
3. Trevor is seven. He is kicking the child next to him and disrupting group time while the children are hearing a story. What is the most appropriate and authentic consequence for this misbehavior? Why did you select your choice?
   a. He is sent away from the group time and not allowed to hear the story.
   b. He is ignored while the other children are lavishly praised for their excellent behavior.
   c. He is asked to sit by himself on a chair just behind the other children who are sitting on the floor, and he is told he can come back when he is sure he can be quiet and still.
   d. He is invited to sit next to the teacher so she can help him remember to be very still. (This is changing the surroundings rather than logical consequence.)
   e. Are there any other appropriate consequences you can name?

RELATED READINGS

Helping Children Develop Self-Control

Caulfield, R. (1996, Fall). Social and emotional development in the first two years. *Early Childhood Education Journal, 24*(1), 55–58.

Coon, C. (2005). *Books to grow with: A guide to using the best children's fiction for preteens—everyday issues and tough challenges.* Portland, OR: Lutra Press.

Crockenberg, S. (1997). How children learn to resolve conflicts in families. In E. N. Junn & C. Boyatzis (Eds.), *Annual editions: Child growth and development 97/98* (4th ed.). New York: McGraw-Hill. (Original work published in *Zero to Three,* April 1992).

> *According to Susan Crockenberg, children learn how to settle conflicts from early experiences in the home. When faced with a child's behavior problem or conflict, parents can model appropriate behavior and provide their young children with practice in conflict negotiation skills by using strategies that include directives, explanations, and compromise. Acquiring these skills early should have many long-term benefits.*

Crosser, S. (1997, March–April). Helping children to develop character. *Early Childhood News, 9*(2), 20–24.

Davis, J. (2001). Caregivers' corner. The day Pork Chop died (almost). *Young Children, 56*(3), 85.

> *This article describes how the impending death of a pet helped a group of preschoolers learn coping and grieving skills.*

Dowrick, N. (1997, October). "You can't shout at them because they just cry": Student teachers with nursery children. *International Journal of Early Years Education, 5*(3), 255–261.

Eaton, M. (1997, September). Positive discipline: Fostering the self-esteem of young children. *Young Children, 52*(6), 43–46.

Gartrell, D. (1997, September). Beyond discipline to guidance. *Young Children, 52*(6), 34–42.

Grossman, S. (1996, September–October). Passing Vickie's test: Building self-esteem and trust by following through with rules. *Early Childhood News, 8*(5), 6–12.

Honig, A. S. (1996). *Behavior guidance for infants and toddlers.* Little Rock, AR: SECA.

Honig, A. S., & Wittmer, D. S. (1996). Helping children become more prosocial: Ideas for classrooms, families, schools, and communities. *Young Children, 51*(2), 62–70.

Hunter, T. (2000). Modeling possibilities. *Young Children, 55*(5), 40.

> *The author presents strategies for indirect teaching through modeling to encourage discovery learning and problem solving.*

Kilpatrick, W. (1997). The moral power of good stories. In E. N. Junn & C. Boyatzis (Eds.), *Annual editions: Child growth and development 97/98* (4th ed.). New York: McGraw-Hill. (Original work published in *American Educator,* summer 1993).

> *Stories help children make sense of their lives, offer children concrete examples of morals and values, and stimulate discussion in the classroom and at home.*

Krogh, S. L., & Lamme, L. L. (1985). "But what about sharing?" Children's literature and moral development. *Young Children, 40*(4), 48–51.

> *Krogh and Lamme explain how children's books can be used to help children discuss moral issues. They review past views of moral understanding and examine how changes in children's cognitive, social, and emotional abilities, as well as changes in their family relationships, influence their development of moral understanding.*

Ogden, P. W. (1996). *The silent garden: Raising your deaf child.* Washington, DC: Gallaudet University Press.

Ogden, P. W. (2002). *El jardin silencioso: Criando a su hijo sordo.* Hillsboro, OR: Butte Publications.

Vander Wilt, J. (1996, Winter). Beyond stickers and popcorn parties. *Dimensions of Early Childhood, 24*(1), 17–20.

Wallace, E. (1997, May–June). Do you recognize this parent? *Early Childhood News, 9*(3), 32–33.

Resources for Signing with Young Children

Acredolo, L., Goodwyn, S., & Abrams, D. (2002). *Baby signs: How to talk with your baby before your baby can talk.* New York: McGraw-Hill.

Briant, M. Z. (2004). *Baby sign language basics: Early communication for hearing babies and toddlers.* Carlsbad, CA: Hay House.

Daniels, M. (2001). *Dancing with words: Signing for hearing children's literacy.* Westport, CT: Bergin & Garvey.

Glazer, S. (2001, March 13). Is it a sign? Babies with normal hearing are being taught sign language by parents hoping to produce a learning boost or tantrum relief. *The Washington Post,* pp. 1, 12.

Goodwyn, S. W., Acredolo, L. P., & Brown, C. (2000). Impact of symbolic gesturing on early language development. *Journal of Nonverbal Behavior, 24,* 81–103. Retrieved February 24, 2006, from http://www.babysigns.com.

Jaworski, M. (2000, October 3). Signs of intelligent life. *Family Circle,* 14.

Moore, B., Acredolo, L., & Goodwyn, S. (2001, April). *Symbolic gesturing and joint attention: Partners in facilitating verbal development.* California State University, Stanislaus University of California, Davis, Society for Research in Child Development.

Nakazawa, L. (2005, March 22). Infants use their hands to "talk." *The Christian Science Monitor, 1,* 14. Retrieved February 24, 2006, from http://www.csmonitor.com.

Snoddon, K. (2000, May). Sign, baby, sign! *World Federation of Deaf News,* 16–17. Retrieved September 2, 2008, from http://cas.la.psu.edu/faculty/daniels_article.htm.

The Online Companion™ to accompany the sixth edition of *Positive Child Guidance* is your link to additional guidance resources on the Internet. This supplement contains audio and visual materials; PowerPoint presentations; web activities with critical-thinking questions and practical-application assignments; and links to web resources. This additional content can be found at http://www.earlychilded.delmar.com.

Chapter 9

Misguided Behaviors and Mistaken Goals

Wadsworth/Cengage Learning

OBJECTIVES

After reading this chapter, you should be able to do the following:

- Identify persistent patterns of dysfunctional behaviors.
- Recognize hidden reasons for children's misbehavior.
- Categorize misguided behaviors in terms of their mistaken goal.
- Identify appropriate resources for problem solving.
- List steps to resolve conflicts in a positive manner.
- Reflect on your own emotional response to dealing with challenging children.

Feelings of self-worth make it possible for a child to learn acceptable behavior.

Developing a Plan for Guidance

Dealing with a child who constantly misbehaves strains the patience of any adult. It would be impossible to deal with a chronically misbehaving child without feeling some level of frustration. Having knowledge about *why* the child is behaving the way she does and having a clear plan for responding to the behavior will help the adult stay calm and positive. The adult needs to be in control, authoritative, and a good role model for the child, actively demonstrating the right way to handle stress and solve a tough problem.

Children who behave in ways that infringe on the rights of others, imperil their own or others' safety, destroy the environment, or simply annoy everyone around them must be helped to change. Tempting as it might be, it would be the worst possible thing to simply ignore their behavior. They deserve a chance to learn appropriate behavior. Their unproductive behavior is a cry for help.

To develop a plan to help, we must remember that children behave the way they do for a reason, almost always unconscious but still very real. Far too often their motive escapes us because our frustration focuses our attention on the results of children's inappropriate behavior—the turmoil they have created and the damage they have done. We forget to step back and wonder why they were motivated to behave that way. By seeking to understand behavior rather assign than blame for it, adults have an opportunity to open new doors of communication with children. Our plan for guidance must address the underlying cause of an individual child's inappropriate behavior.

As children mature and develop self-awareness, open lines of communication will help them assume greater responsibility for their actions and choices. By the time children reach adolescence, it is especially important that we have helped them develop conscious awareness of their motives and goals. It is important that open, honest communication has become an accepted and routine part of the child's daily life.

Misbehaviors Based on Mistaken Goals

Adler (1931), a colleague of Freud, theorized that inappropriate behavior stemmed from inadequate early guidance. He believed that some children were kept from developing a sense of competence and self-worth by doting or dominating parents who saddled them with an inferiority complex, causing them to adopt inappropriate ways to exert control and feel competent.

Dreikurs (Dreikurs et al., 2004) refined Adler's theory, distilling for teachers and parents a practical approach based on four **mistaken goals** that he hypothesized were the root of long-standing, habitual patterns of inappropriate behavior. He theorized that children behave inappropriately because of their overwhelming urge for the following:

1. Get attention from others.
2. Gain a sense of control.
3. Get revenge for their own perceived hurts.
4. Remove themselves from frightening or painful situations.

Each of these four mistaken goals is directed toward getting an emotional need met: the need for recognition, the need for a sense of control over one's life, the need for fairness, and the need to avoid stressful and frightening situations. Unfortunately, each behavior may seem to make the child feel a little better temporarily, but it actually compounds her problem in the long run.

The child's inappropriate responses increase the negativity and hostility in her environment, which in turn increases her emotional neediness and the likelihood of her behaving more and more inappropriately in the future. This is the **snowball**

■■ Sometimes children need to learn new ways to get their emotional needs met.

effect. Her misguided behavior increases the momentum in a negative cycle that continues to stimulate inappropriate behavior and push the child away from others around her.

Typically, we respond in a way that is precisely opposite to the response needed by the child. For example, we are tempted to ignore the child who is acting out to get attention, but that will cause her to have even more need to act out. We are tempted to get into a stern power struggle with the controlling child, "to show her who's boss," but this makes her feel even more powerless and out of control. We are sorely tempted to inflict pain on the aggressive child who bites or hurts another child, but angry aggression on our part can make the child even more resolved to get revenge. Additionally, we are tempted to shrug our shoulders and give up altogether on the withdrawn child who hides under a table, twisting her hair or bumping her head on the wall, but our abandonment only allows her to sink deeper and deeper into isolation.

To bring about real change, we must cure (or at least relieve) the problems that cause the child's persistent patterns of unproductive behavior and retrain her in appropriate methods to get her emotional needs met. It is not effective to tackle inappropriate behaviors as if they existed in a vacuum. When behavior is persistently inappropriate, the child's misbehaviors can be thought of as symptoms and the child's emotional neediness as the underlying disease. Suppressing behavioral symptoms without paying attention to the emotional well-being of the child may result in the

---

Children's Mistaken Goals

Children who are deprived of opportunities to gain status through useful contributions often seek attention by acting helpless, silly, bratty, artificially charming, lazy, inept, or obnoxious.
Mistaken goal: Get attention from others.

Children who do not feel they are accepted members of their family or social groups may seek power by acting bossy, rebellious, stubborn, vengeful, or disobedient.
Mistaken goal: Gain a sense of control.

Children who feel so beaten down that they no longer care about struggling for power retaliate by seeking revenge by hurting others the way they feel they have been hurt. They may injure peers, destroy property, express contempt, distrust others, and defy authority.
Mistaken goal: Get revenge for their own perceived hurts.

Children who become trapped in passive, self-destructive behavior because they have been overly stressed, criticized, or abused may eventually become so discouraged that they give up all hope and expect only failure and defeat. They seek only to be left alone. They may be passive, withdrawn, and depressed, paralyzed by feelings of inadequacy and hopelessness.
Mistaken goal: Remove themselves from frightening or painful situations.

---

eruption of new or different symptoms, just as treating the fever of an infection without giving an antibiotic to kill the bacteria that caused it might mean a return of the fever.

Healing can take place only when the child feels she is an accepted and worthwhile group member, she has some control over her life, she is treated fairly and respectfully, and she is optimistic that she can succeed in whatever is expected of her. If these feelings blossom in the child, then we can say that she has self-esteem and the four key reasons for persistent misbehavior no longer exist. The child will no longer need to rely on misbehavior for emotional survival and can begin to break habit patterns and learn more effective ways to get along with others.

Dreikurs recommends that children 5 to 12 years old be confronted in a caring, noncritical way at a relaxed time rather than during a time of conflict. The child can be engaged in conversation exploring the motives for her typical behaviors, then tactfully asked any of the following questions that seem relevant:

- Could it be that you want attention?
- Could it be that you want your own way and hope to be boss?
- Could it be that you want to hurt others as much as you feel hurt by them?
- Could it be that you want to be left alone?

Although these questions are not appropriate to ask infants and very young children, adults may find it helpful to mentally run through the list of questions to gain insight into possible unconscious causes of misbehavior in children under five. For children of any age, identifying the underlying feelings that motivate behavior make it possible to respond to children's emotional well-being rather than only to chase and eliminate symptomatic misbehaviors.

Once the motive for behavior is identified, adults can better respond to the misbehavior. If attention is the goal of the misbehavior, it can be removed as a response for inappropriate behaviors and instead given abundantly for appropriate or constructive behaviors. If bullying is the goal, adults can remove themselves from power struggles and focus on allowing children to feel they are respected and responsible group members. If revenge is the goal, adults can assist children in making friends and experiencing successful accomplishments. If solitude is the goal, adults can offer encouragement, persist in including the child, and find ways to make the child feel worthwhile.

Mistaken Goal Number One: Attention-Seeking Behavior

Clinging, Feigning Ineptness

Human babies are born helpless and vulnerable. It makes sense that they become emotionally attached to caregivers, and that they are most comfortable and secure when they can feel, see, or hear the caregiver's closeness. In a more primitive society, an infant's very survival could depend on staying close to a caring adult. As soon as infants are able to identify and distinguish among family members, caregivers, and strangers, they generally show signs of stranger anxiety and separation anxiety. A baby who has always cooed, gurgled, and smiled for anyone will suddenly cry when a stranger leans close to admire her and tickle her chin. A one-year-old who usually toddles around the house getting into everything may become subdued and clingy while a visitor is in the house.

bonding
The process of becoming emotionally attached to another.

This **bonding** is a healthy and normal phase of development. Attachment to a dependable caregiver is an essential factor in the development of trust. We do no favor to babies and toddlers when we push them too early to break away from the adults who care for them. Babies who are allowed to develop secure, loving bonds with responsive caregivers become friendlier, more independent, and more successful preschoolers later (Fonagy, 2001; Bretherton & Waters, 1985). Close attachment in infancy does not, as parents often worry, cause children to become spoiled, clingy attention seekers.

Clingy children who pretend they cannot do anything without help suffer from poor self-esteem. They have not been "loved" too much, although they may well have been overindulged and overprotected in ways that stunted their long-term development of healthy confidence and independence. Overindulgence and overprotection are poor excuses for real love, which is respectful and matched to a child's needs rather than being intrusive or overwhelming. In many cases, clingy children may have been given too little attention and attachment. Their need to bond may have never been fully satisfied, so they cling to baby behaviors. Clingy children feel comfortable and loved only when they are being fussed over and cared for. They long for the adult to cuddle them and to rescue them from their responsibilities.

Artificial Charm, Competitiveness

Children who are insecure in their sense of belonging often adopt an artificial charm. Younger children learn how to play the role of the adorable and irresistible child, and older children gush with insincere compliments. This niceness may vanish instantly, however, whenever the child feels threatened by attention directed toward someone else. The child may swing from absolute charmer to cold competitor in seconds. We need to focus on developing the child's sense of security and self-esteem by giving sincere affection and encouragement at appropriate times. We also need to set firm limits and help the child know that he is loved for himself, not for his fake charm.

Clowning, Acting Out, Silliness

Children use clowning, acting out, and silliness to get attention from not only adults but also other children. Some children seem to feel sure that they are loved and appreciated only when they are at the center of attention with everyone looking at them and either laughing or chiding. Children may be especially likely to get silly when they feel embarrassed or pushed into a corner. For some children, being a clown is a way of saving face and protecting damaged self-esteem.

We need to allow clowning children to save their dignity. They should be corrected privately and respectfully when their acting out is unacceptable. It is also essential that they be given opportunities for responsibility and leadership in positive settings as well as chances to entertain others in appropriate ways. For example, a child might be encouraged to plan a skit for classmates, chosen to pass out napkins or refreshments during a celebration, or allowed to sing, dance, or act out a story at group time.

Laziness, Compulsiveness, Obnoxiousness

Lazy, compulsive, or obnoxious behaviors may be a child's unconscious way of forcing adults to pay attention. They also signal a lack of self-esteem in the child. The child labeled as lazy may receive negative attention when adults nag, take over the child's responsibilities, or insist that other children help or do the child's work for her. Children who overeat, bite their nails, tease, or purposely disgust other children and adults are also giving strong indications that they do not feel good about themselves.

Persistent, assertive, and loving guidance will build the child's respect for herself by helping her know that the adult cares deeply enough to become actively involved in redirecting her inappropriate behaviors. For example, a child who persists in running around the playground terrifying other children with bugs and worms could be firmly redirected from poking the creatures in others' faces to constructing a terrarium for the science center out of an old aquarium, some rocks and dirt, and a

manipulative
Using clever or devious ways to control or influence another person into doing something that he or she may not want to do. (Be aware that *manipulative*, when used by early educators as a noun, refers to small objects that are used for fine-motor development. The fingers manipulate the objects, or move them around.)

few little plants. There, the insects and earthworms could be displayed in a socially acceptable manner that does not frighten or disgust others.

Mistaken Goal Number Two: Controlling Behavior
Manipulativeness, Vengefulness

Being **manipulative** usually involves trying to trick someone into doing something that she really does not want to do. Adults often set an example for this behavior in their attempts to gain control over the child's behavior. We tell children things such as "Eat your bread crusts because they will make your hair curly" or "Bend over, this shot won't hurt a bit!" We should not be surprised to hear a kindergartner say, "Give me your candy bar and I'll be your best friend forever."

Sometimes, manipulativeness can become excessive and vengeful as children struggle to gain control of the children and adults around them. Adults need to define clear limits and help children become aware of the feelings and reactions of those around them. Adults can recognize and verbalize feelings. For example, "Sallie, I know you really want Alvie's doll, but the doll belongs to Alvie. Alvie doesn't like to play with you when you try to take her doll. You may choose a different toy, or you may play by yourself."

Pouting, Stubbornness

Children who want control but fail to get their way with others may react by pouting, stubbornly refusing to participate, or causing a scene. The toddler who wants (but does not get) ice cream for dinner, for example, may push his plate off the high-chair tray, kick his feet, scream, shake his head, and generally refuse to have anything to do with carrots and roast beef.

Parents and early educators do no favor either by giving in to the toddler (and thus encouraging his controlling behavior) or by forcing nutritious food on him against his will. They can, however, avoid a power struggle by simply removing the toddler from the high chair and allowing him to express his anger. The adults can express sincere empathy but allow the child to be stubborn without showing a great deal of attention or concern.

Wadsworth/Cengage Learning

If others consistently see a child as lovable, capable, and worthwhile, he will probably feel high self-esteem. Exposure to racism and bigotry devastates self-esteem and sows the seeds of hatred.

For example, the adult may say, "It's okay to cry. When you feel better, your dinner is right here waiting for you." When the child has finished screaming, he may or may not want dinner. Either way, he will not starve before the next meal. The child's need for a sense of control can be met by allowing him to choose when he is ready to eat, not by letting him succeed in demanding things that are not in his best interest. Between the lines, the adult is saying, "You may make your own choices—within reasonable limits—but you must also deal with the consequences of your choices."

Bullying, Rebelling

Some children, when failing to gain control by other means, resort to bullying or rebelling. They gain control over smaller children by overwhelming them physically with their size and strength. Grown-ups are not usually so easy for a small child to bully. A child, consequently, might be tempted to control adults by being so rebellious, so out of control, that adults feel totally helpless. It is important, however, that adults not allow themselves to lapse into feelings of inadequacy. The child needs strong, reliable adult support to be able to give up inappropriate behaviors and form new habits.

It is also essential for adults to avoid power struggles with the bullying or rebelling child. Head-to-head confrontation will trigger an increase in angry rebellion and will not solve the problem. Aggressive, bullying behavior on the part of adults further establishes the role model for this undesirable behavior. Instead, adults must find ways to build a positive relationship with the child and help the child feel a sense of belonging. Clear limits are essential, as well as logical consequences, but the most important step is for the child to discover that she is loved, respected, and appreciated. Then she will be able to relax and relinquish her ham-handed attempt to control those around her.

> There is nothing so strong as gentleness, nothing so gentle as real strength.
>
> *St. Francis De Sales (1972)*

Prevent Bullying

Create a positive, calm environment   A well-planned, orderly, developmentally appropriate environment sets the stage for calm behavior. Additionally, calm, supportive adults provide excellent role models for children. Strictly limit books, television, and movies to age-appropriate materials featuring positive behavior.

Provide positive role models   Most importantly, be a positive role model for caring, respectful behavior. Don't say things such as "Do what I said because I said so" or "Do what I say or you'll be sorry." Don't angrily grab the child, shove her, or yank her arm. Harsh, controlling adults set an example for bullying. Stay calm and think before acting. Count to 10 backward. Regularly take steps to reduce your own stress: exercise, meditate, listen to music, laugh with friends, or whatever works for you. Seek information or help to cultivate more effective anger management skills. Consciously practice positive conflict resolution every day. Force yourself to try it even if it feels awkward at first.

Provide nurturing peer relationships   Never allow children to be abusive or cruel to each other. Help children learn that teasing is "good" teasing only if everyone is laughing and having fun. Hurtful teasing is bullying and will not be tolerated ever. Celebrate diversity. Help children learn to value individual differences. Teach them to be caring and compassionate. All people have feelings and deserve respect, regardless of their gender, race, religion, size, or special needs.

Help children recognize and understand their own and others' emotions Identify and label feelings for children: angry, sad, happy, frustrated, excited, worried, and so on. Encourage them to identify emotions in picture books. Encourage children to describe how they think friends or story characters might be feeling. Use reflective listening to get children to talk about their own feelings.

Explore strategies to strengthen children's self-esteem Research suggests that low self-esteem may cause children to be at more risk for bullying behavior. Steps should be taken to bolster the child's confidence and sense of being a valued member of the community. He may be given special responsibilities and leadership roles.

Help children learn to accurately perceive social situations so they can respond appropriately Stimulate children's thinking by asking questions and encouraging discussions about social situations. For example, while reading stories, ask questions such as "What does the boy see?" "What do you think is happening?" "How do you think the boy feels about that?" "What do you think he will do next?" "What do you think he should do?" "Why?" After disagreements or problems have occurred, encourage the children to discuss the incident objectively. Help them analyze why the disagreement might have taken place, what emotions they think each was feeling, and other ways they might have responded that would have been more positive.

Help children learn to predict the consequences of their actions, particularly those involving aggression Start early with babies and toddlers, helping them learn to predict simple cause-and-effect sequences in everyday activities. Playfully pretend to put your adult foot into the toddler's shoe. If the toddler is able to comprehend that the shoe will not fit, she will be delighted and want to repeat the game. "What will happen if I eat the banana without taking the peel off?" Continue to talk about consequences as the child matures. "What do you think will happen if you throw the blocks?" "How will your friend feel if you scream at her and push her?" "How would you feel if someone called you a hurtful name?"

Help children learn how to use group processes to resolve social problems Preschoolers and school-agers can learn to talk about problems as a group. Have a class meeting or a family meeting to talk through a problem together, to brainstorm possible solutions, and to decide on a plan. Children can be selected to role-play problem behaviors to help the group explore what is happening, why it's happening, and what can be done to prevent it or resolve it. Help children practice appropriate things to say to a bully. Remind them how to get adult help.

> ### Be Alert—Stop Bullying!
>
> Immediately intervene to stop bullies because
>
> - **Experiencing** bullying behavior—whether it's through threatening words or gestures or being physically hurt, called ugly names, mimicked, harassed, or shunned (isolated)—is a terribly destructive force in the life of a child.
>
> - **Being** a bully allows a child to develop dysfunctional behavior patterns that will affect him or her socially and professionally throughout life.
>
> - **Witnessing** bullying creates an upsetting, distracting, and threatening environment in which children cannot learn at their best.

Mistaken Goal Number Three: Disruptive Behavior

Destructiveness, Aggressiveness

Children whose self-esteem is lacking may deteriorate into disruptive habit patterns of destructiveness and aggression. These behaviors tell us that the child feels a sense of hopelessness. She may believe that she has already been rejected by others so that it really does not matter what she does; nobody will like her no matter how she behaves. These feelings discourage her from developing self-control over her impulses.

The destructive or aggressive child must know that she will be stopped and that others' rights will be protected. In an extreme situation, a parent or early educator may have no choice but to restrain a child to prevent her from harming herself or others. A caregiver in a child care facility who feels helpless and intimidated by a child does great harm to that child by allowing her to bite, kick, shove, pinch, or scratch other children and destroy shared toys. The caregiver must believe that she has two responsibilities: (1) to befriend the child during noncrisis times and rebuild her feelings of self-esteem and (2) to take steps to interrupt outbursts of aggression and protect other children and the physical environment. The caregiver may need to ask for help from another staff member or administrator or from the parents. However tempting it may be for adults to make excuses (no one will help me, I'm a single parent, my director is too busy, there is nowhere else for the child to be, psychologists are too expensive), the adult must not stop until she finds the support that is needed. Although it will probably not be necessary to call in local law enforcement for help with a 50-pound child who is throwing rocks, the caregiver must have confidence that if one strategy for stopping the child from hurting others does not work, then other strategies will be tried until something does work. Although it is rarely appropriate in early childhood settings, the adult must be willing, in a crisis situation, to physically restrain the child as firmly as necessary but as gently as possible.

Giving children undivided attention in the form of quality time is one way parents assure that their children know they are loved and valued.

In dealing with a very difficult child, behavior modification may be an essential and effective tool for regaining a manageable relationship with the child. A reinforcer (token reward) must be selected that is meaningful and desirable to the child; the specific desired behavior goal must be identified in concrete terms; and a schedule of when, how, and under what circumstances the reinforcement will be given should be planned with the child. Reinforcement must always be immediate. As the child makes little steps of progress toward the desired behavior, she is instantly reinforced with a reward (such as a sticker, a plastic disk, or checks on a chart) that can be exchanged at a predetermined number for special privileges or treats.

Behavior modification will be most successful (especially with an older child) if she has enthusiastically agreed to participate in the plan. If the child likes and respects the adult and really wants to change some behaviors and habits she knows are unacceptable, she may be surprisingly willing to participate in a voluntary behavior modification plan, at least during the brief periods in which she is calm and logical. During the entire process of behavior modification, the child must be helped toward eventual weaning from external control and toward increasing internal control.

She can be told from the very beginning, "Changing habits is very, very hard for anyone! These little prizes are just to help you get started, to help you remember to use words instead of hitting. After a while you can't rely on little prizes anymore. You must use words because it is the right thing. It is wrong to hit. Your best prize of all will be learning how to have fun with your friends without having fights that spoil everything."

Contempt, Mistrust

Contempt and mistrust in children sadden and dismay us. The child filled with contempt has so much mistrust of others that she seems to despise everyone. We may find it necessary to backtrack and work on the basic development of trust. Just as a first grader who lacked visual discrimination and vocabulary would need remedial work before she could learn to read, the child who feels contempt must relearn the essential lesson of infancy—to trust others, to believe that adults are reliable, predictable, and accepting—before she can learn to behave appropriately.

A child who feels that she has received a great deal of hurt and unfair treatment in her life will not easily place her trust in adults. Adults will have to earn that trust through consistent fairness and sincere interest in the child's well-being. Adults can facilitate the development of trust in the child by modeling trust. They can find opportunities to place trust in the mistrustful child in situations in which the child is very likely to succeed and in which a failure to live up to the adult's trust can safely be overlooked.

Fits of Anger, Tantrums, Defiance

Children who regularly indulge in fits of anger, tantrums, and defiance need to know that the adults who care for them are not cowed by these behaviors, but they also need to know that adults will not explode into their own fits of anger. Angry, defiant behaviors may unconsciously be intended to strike back at adults who are perceived to be enemies. Adults, consequently, must take steps to build a cooperative relationship with the defiant child, to become the child's ally and friend while refusing to participate in inappropriate interactions with the child.

We can help children let go of explosive behaviors by responding matter-of-factly but steadfastly to the child's eruptions. An adult may be forced to remove or restrain the child in extreme circumstances, but the adult can be very sure the child recognizes that there is no anger or punitiveness in those actions, just firmness and resolve. Also, the adult can avoid overreacting to expressions of defiance such as vulgar language or spitting (Greene, 2001).

No adult wants to be spit at or see a child spit on others, but our own angry or violent outburst will make the child's problem worse, not better. Instead, a patient but very firm adult might say, "If you need to spit, you may spit in the sink. Spitting in the sink is fine. Spitting on people is not allowed, though. It makes them angry, and it could get germs on them. If you spit, you can't play. You'll need to sit here by me until you are sure you are through spitting."

The child needs to learn that defiant tantrums are really a waste of time because they have no effect on the adult. The tantrums will not bring about special favors, and they will not succeed in annoying the adult. Because persistently disruptive behavior is unconsciously intended to hurt others as the child feels she has been hurt, the child may delight in seeing adults frustrated, angry, and helpless.

Mistaken Goal Number Four: Withdrawn, Passive Behavior

Cyclical Self-Stimulation

When a child is overwhelmed by fear, stress, and anxiety, she may withdraw into her own little world. Although most children do things to make themselves feel better from time to time, the withdrawn child may sink into constant self-stimulation. This pattern is referred to as cyclical, because the child repeats the behavior cycle over and over. The cycle may consist of excessive thumb-sucking, nail-biting, hair-twisting, overeating, head-banging, masturbating, or any number of other self-stimulating actions.

Adults frequently find these behaviors very embarrassing and may focus on forcing the child to end the behavior without addressing the cause of the behavior at all.

These behaviors tell us the child is feeling too stressed and overwhelmed to participate in usual activities. By focusing on reducing stress in the child's life and drawing the child out into pleasurable, nonthreatening activities, the child may be eased into more active involvement with things and people around her (Nelson et al., 2005).

Rejection of Social Interchange

The severely withdrawn child may avoid eye contact, refuse to talk or play, and stay apart from others most of the time. Adults may mistakenly focus all of their guidance efforts on children whose inappropriate behaviors are active and annoying. Teachers, parents, and caregivers may view the child who is a loner as a good child who never bothers anyone. In reality, the child who is a loner may be more at risk emotionally than the difficult, loud, aggressive child. Self-esteem, trust, and a sense of belonging are all essential to building contact with the child who seems to have no interest in others.

Rejection of social interchange is a very frightening and serious state for a child to be in. The child needs intervention and help. Think of the number of times you have seen a horrific crime story on the news in which the perpetrator was described as someone who was a quiet loner who kept to himself.

Internalization of Stress

Inhibited children sometimes turn all their bad feelings inward. Fear, anger, and frustration are not expressed; they are just held inside, and they may chip away at the child's sense of competence and self-worth. These children need opportunities to learn that they do not have to be perfect, it is okay to disagree, and they have a right to be who they are. As they develop stronger self-esteem, they will feel more comfortable expressing their feelings and actively standing up for themselves.

Children need opportunities to learn socially acceptable ways to express negative feelings. They need assertive role models and the freedom to say what they feel honestly (but respectfully). Adults should avoid telling children that their feelings are not real or valid by saying such things as "That scratch doesn't hurt," "There's nothing to cry about," or "You have no reason to be mad!" Children must be allowed to feel what they feel, even though they must also learn to express negative feelings without hurting, harassing, or humiliating others. When children know an acceptable way to express themselves, they are likely to feel much freer about exposing their inner feelings.

Display of Ineptness and Hopelessness

Feelings of depression are not the exclusive territory of adolescents and adults. Even very young children can show signs of depression. Overwhelming disruption in the child's daily life may contribute to her listlessness and display of ineptness and hopelessness. These children do not involve themselves in spontaneous play or creative expression. They seem to have no energy. They may sleep too much or too little. They are clearly at risk and need special guidance to rebuild self-esteem and give them the spark of hope that fuels healthy curiosity, spontaneous play, and active involvement with others.

Reacting to Needs— Maslow's Hierarchy

Another way to look at children's emotional needs comes from Abraham Maslow (1943). Human beings—children and adults—behave in many complicated ways to get their emotional needs met. At the heart of almost any behavior lies the desire to acquire something, whether an object, an experience, or a feeling. Although some behaviors may be directed toward frivolous whims, many behaviors focus on basic human needs. Maslow developed a theory of human motivation. He proposed that basic needs are arranged in a hierarchy, a pyramid in which each overriding level of need has to be met before successive levels of need can be addressed. Following is Maslow's list of emotional needs that motivate behavior:

- Fulfillment
- Self-esteem, responsibility, achievement
- Sense of belonging, attachment to family and friends
- Feeling of safety, security, order
- Basic life needs are met (food, shelter, air, warmth)

A sense of belonging is essential to the development of positive self-esteem. Positive self-esteem prevents misbehavior caused by mistaken goals.

In other words, a child who is hungry will be distracted from playing and learning. Her primary concern will be food. A child who is frightened and insecure will show little interest in making friends or building castles with blocks. A child who feels unloved will not be able to function independently and confidently. In fact, very young children will tend to do anything that seems to work to get their needs met, no matter how annoying or uncivilized their behavior appears to the adults around them. They have not yet developed the ability to inhibit their impulses. They are driven to get their basic emotional needs met, and only after these needs have been met can we expect them to be calm, cooperative, and curious learners (Brewer, 1998; Bullock, 1997; Feeney et al., 1996; Gibbs, 1997; Kagan, 1997; McAlister, 1997; Adler & Brett, 1998; Franken, 2001; Heylighen, 1992; Mittleman, 1991).

What Is the Role of Self-Esteem in Repeated Misbehavior?

Unmet needs are a hidden cause of repeated patterns of dysfunctional behavior in children. To behave well, children must have a strong sense of self-esteem. Many behavior-disordered children seem to be walking around with a big, black hole

Abraham Maslow's Hierarchy of Needs

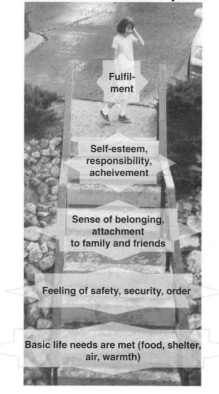

Fulfil-
ment

Self-esteem,
responsibility,
acheivement

Sense of belonging,
attachment
to family and friends

Feeling of safety, security, order

Basic life needs are met (food, shelter,
air, warmth)

Basic needs must be met before a child can strive for higher levels of achievement. (Abraham H. Maslow, *Motivation and Personality* (Robert D. Frager & James Fadiman, Eds., 3rd ed.). © 1987. Reproduced by permission of Pearson Education, Inc., Upper Saddle River, NJ.)

inside them where their self-esteem ought to be. Self-esteem has become more and more emphasized over the past few decades as a characteristic that seems closely tied to school success and social adjustment (Kokenes, 1974; Wittmer & Honig, 1997). Early childhood educators have especially focused on activities intended to foster self-esteem. Children, unfortunately, do not suddenly develop a sense of self-worth simply because they sing a cute song about being special or color in between the lines on a workbook sheet that says "I am special."

Authentic self-esteem activities involve valuing the child, giving the child positive recognition, treating the child with respect every day, listening to the child, protecting the child's rights, and nurturing the child by making frequent eye contact, using appropriate touch, and using the child's name while at eye level.

Every child has a right to achieve to the maximum of his own potential—however high or low that potential is. Our role is to support the child's achievement so he can reach for his dreams.

How Can I Support the Child's Development of Self-Esteem?

The perception of "value" that children place on themselves reflects the value that others who are important to them place on them (Coopersmith, 1967; Randy et al., 1997; Roberts, 1997; Ryan & Deci, 2000). If parents and caregivers consistently see a child as lovable, capable, and worthwhile, then the child will develop a positive self-esteem. Children begin to develop self-esteem from birth, but only if their needs are met by attentive caregivers, they feel safe and loved, and they are consistently treated with respect (even while they are being disciplined). Although it may be possible to rebuild damaged self-esteem, it is more effective to support the development of a positive self-concept from the very beginning.

If a child's early experiences have been damaging to her sense of self, it is essential to begin fostering self-esteem and to teach her appropriate ways to get her needs met. With a great deal of support and patience, children can unlearn old, inappropriate behaviors that may have been the only way they knew to get their needs met in a confusing or unsupportive environment. Repeated cycles of inappropriate behavior are difficult to handle, and adults easily fall into behaviors that are as inappropriate as that of the children they are trying to help. Verbal abuse, yelling, sarcasm, ridicule, and shoving are all inappropriate adult behaviors.

A key to success in dealing with children who have developed habit patterns of inappropriate behavior is for the adult to persistently pull the child up to a more acceptable level of behavior rather than allowing the child to pull the adult down to the child's level of immature and inappropriate interaction, advice that is easy to give but never easy to put into practice.

Meeting Adult Needs

Children definitely have needs, but adults have needs too. Caring for children is demanding, exhilarating, frustrating, and rewarding, but it is also exhausting. We can best care for children if our own social, emotional, physical, and intellectual needs have been met. We must set aside time for our own rest and recreation, and we must be able to admit to ourselves at times that we are not able to deal with children in a positive and productive manner. If children are dealt with in a caring and respectful manner most of the time, they will be likely to cope well and respect our own need when we say, "I'm too frustrated and angry to talk about this right now. I just want to be alone for a few minutes."

We can be patient and reasonable with ourselves, recognizing that we, too, are imperfect. It is easy to sit down and think carefully about an ideal response to a misbehaving child, but it is not so easy to respond perfectly when the response is instantaneous and in the heat of conflict with that child. It is important for adults to be supportive, calm, respectful, and consistent. Step back and give yourself a moment when you need to.

When we attempt to change our ways of dealing with children, we go through the same stages of learning that children go through when they learn new behaviors. For example, a toddler who has no concept of toileting will simply show no awareness when she makes a puddle on the floor. When she has developed recognition of the desired behavior but lacks practice carrying it out, she will make a puddle, look down, smile sweetly, and say, "Go potty!" Of course, it will be too late to go to the potty then. Finally, when she has fully developed both the awareness and the skill to carry out the new behavior, she will notice the sensation of a full bladder and do what needs to be done to successfully use the toilet.

We go through that same process. At first, we may be totally unaware of the negative, destructive, and hurtful things we say or do with youngsters in the name of disciplining them. As we discover more productive and effective ways to guide them, we begin, for the first time, to notice ourselves saying or doing negative things. We feel frustration because we seem to become aware of these actions only after we have done them. We become aware of our inappropriate actions, but only after it is too late. Gradually, however, with persistence and practice, we are able

> Ever tried?
> Ever failed?
> No matter.
> Try again.
> Fail again.
> Fail better.
>
> *Samuel Beckett (Knowlson, 1996)*

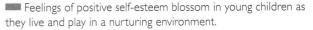 Feelings of positive self-esteem blossom in young children as they live and play in a nurturing environment.

to anticipate and respond more skillfully and appropriately—before we have done it wrong. Eventually, our new behaviors become so natural to us that we can behave the new way with almost no thought or effort.

Positive child guidance is a tool that can be used to help mature, caring adults teach young children the skills they need to lead productive, happy lives (Thompson et al., 2001).

Adult Coping Techniques

Caring for an unhappy child can be stressful and overwhelming. Early childhood educators need to have a plan to help them get through difficult times. Keep these tips in mind:

• Remember not to take the crying personally. Babies and young children are coping the best they know how at the moment.

• Take deep breaths. Try to relax as much as possible. A screaming child can be very frustrating. You will need to stay calm to figure out the best way to resolve the problem.

• Your first concern should be to make sure the child is safe and secure. An out-of-control child may harm herself or others. If necessary to protect the child or others, restrain the child as gently as possible but as firmly as necessary.

• Softly and calmly repeat reassuring statements such as "I know you're feeling angry now," "When you feel better, we'll talk," and "It's okay to cry. Sometimes I cry when I'm feeling angry." This will remind the child (and yourself) that you are not angry.

• Take turns with the child if another appropriate adult is available. Amazingly, having a calm, uninvolved adult take over in the middle of a tantrum may break the cycle and help the child gain control.

• Make it a point to talk later about stressful situations. Identify early childhood professionals who seem to have developed effective coping skills themselves. They may be able to give helpful suggestions.

• As negative influences build up in your life, consciously take time to create enough positive influences to bring about a balance.

• Exercise, pray, listen to music, meditate, read, visit friends—find ways that work for you to recharge your emotional reservoir.

• Our goal is not just to eliminate stress but also to develop skills to manage stress, to handle day-to-day challenges effectively without allowing stress to damage our bodies.

• Don't be afraid to accept or ask for help from experts. Seek out expertise in books, websites, college early childhood departments, college counselors, doctors, and therapists.

Do Behavioral Problems Indicate Child Abuse or Neglect?

A very serious potential cause of developmental and behavioral problems can be the presence of abuse or neglect in a child's life. Although virtually any normally developing child can experience a rare incident of inappropriate treatment, children who lead lives filled with abuse and neglect are profoundly affected by that experience, even if they are not maimed or killed. Every aspect of their development is affected: intellectual, physical, social, and emotional (Dean et al., 1986; Finkelhor & Dziuba-Leatherman, 1997; Heineman, 1998; Hoffman-Plotkin & Twentyman, 1984; Ingrassia & McCormick, 1997; Kempe & Kempe, 1978; Lamb et al., 1985; Brophy, 2007; Wallach, 1997; Wang & Daro, 1998; see Appendix B for additional resources).

KEEP YOUR LIFE IN BALANCE

Keep your life in balance.

Consequences of Maltreatment

The consequences of maltreatment are far-reaching and affect the whole child (Douglas & Finkelhor, 2005).

- Children who experience maltreatment are at increased risk for adverse health effects and behaviors as adults—including smoking, alcoholism, drug abuse, eating disorders, severe obesity, depression, suicide, sexual promiscuity, and certain chronic diseases (Felitti et al., 1998; Runyan et al., 2002).
- Maltreatment during infancy or early childhood can cause important regions of the brain to form improperly, leading to physical, mental, and emotional problems such as sleep disturbances, panic disorder, and attention deficit/hyperactivity disorder (U.S. Dept. of Health and Human Services, 2001).
- About 25 to 30 percent of infants with shaken baby syndrome (SBS) die from their injuries. Nonfatal consequences of SBS include varying degrees of visual impairment (for example, blindness), motor impairment (for example, cerebral palsy), and cognitive impairments (Jenny et al., 1999).
- Victims of childhood maltreatment who were physically assaulted by caregivers are twice as likely to be physically assaulted as adults (Tjaden & Thoennes, 2000).
- As many as one-third of parents who experienced maltreatment in childhood may victimize their own children (Fromm, 2001).

Treat people as if they are what they ought to be, and you help them to become what they are capable of being.

Johann Wolfgang Von Goethe, German Poet, 1749–1832 (Von Goethe, 1995)

- Children younger than four are at greatest risk of severe injury or death. In 2003, children younger than four accounted for 79 percent of child maltreatment fatalities, with infants younger than one year accounting for 44 percent of those deaths (U.S. Dept. of Health and Human Services, 2005).

How Can Child Abuse Fatalities Be Prevented?

Communities can help prevent child abuse deaths by fully supporting their child protective services agencies and ensuring the availability of treatment services for potential abusers. Additionally, alcohol and drug treatment services need to be expanded and made more accessible to pregnant and parenting women. Public agencies, however, cannot single-handedly prevent all fatalities. Other formal institutions such as schools, child care centers, and hospitals and members of the community must also play an active role in identifying and getting help for families at risk of abusive or neglectful behavior.

Child abuse is against the law. Every state has a designated agency that is mandated by federal law to receive and to investigate reports of suspected child abuse and neglect. Remember, reporting is a means of getting help for a child or family, not just a way to punish abusers. You do not have to prove that child abuse has occurred. That is up to the investigator to determine. To report a suspected case of child abuse, you should notify the designated agency in the state where the child lives. The agency is listed in the telephone directory, usually in the government pages under Rehabilitative Services or Children and Family Services. In some areas, it may also be listed in the yellow pages. If you have difficulty finding the agency in your community, call your local police department or call the ChildHelp USA/IOF Foresters National Child Abuse Hotline, 1-800-422-4453 (4-A-CHILD), which keeps national listings of child protective service agencies.

Abused and neglected children's behaviors tend toward extremes: there seems to be no happy middle ground for these children. They may be diagnosed as learning disabled, or they may be compulsive overachievers. They may be hyperactive or lethargic. They may be physically inept weaklings or street-smart, death-defying daredevils. They may cling relentlessly to others or shun all social interaction. They may appear dirty and unkempt or rigidly and spotlessly scrubbed, starched, and pressed. They may defy authority altogether or compulsively try to please everyone at all times in all ways. They may always play the role of victim or brutally victimize others. The one

Wadsworth/Cengage Learning

▪▪ Children who feel good about themselves feel comfortable behaving in a natural and spontaneous way, but they also are able to accept reasonable limits.

Child Abuse Fatalities

- Each day in the United States more than four children die of child abuse.

- About three-fourths of the children who die are younger than four.

- Of the children who die, more than 40 percent are babies younger than one year.

- The rate of infant homicide reached a 30-year high in 2000.

- Research studies indicate that the actual deaths of babies and children up to age four that are attributable to abuse or neglect are probably twice as high as the official rate reported on death records.

ChildHelp USA (2005).

Wadsworth/Cengage Learning

Adults can help children become aware of the feelings of others.

characteristic that is shared by all abused and neglected children is their lack of or stunted sense of self. They do not have that essential component of all fully functional human beings, which is the positive feeling of self-worth that comes with self-esteem (U.S. Department of Health and Human Services, Administration on Children, Youth, and Families, 2007).

Locating Community Resources

Adults caring for children who have persistent misbehavior problems need help. Once possible causes for behavior problems have been identified, a search for appropriate community resources should take place. Families, schools, and child care facilities all have the potential to serve as resources for each other, to share ideas and methods, and to give each other emotional support and encouragement. Parents can learn a great deal from teachers and caregivers, and teachers and caregivers can learn a great deal from parents. Additionally, almost any community setting offers a wealth of potential resources such as the following (see listings at the end of this chapter for organizations, websites, and telephone numbers):

- the medical community—physicians, psychologists, and other therapists
- governmental agencies—child protective services workers, child care licensing specialists, health departments, social workers, Head Start, and other publicly funded programs
- religious entities—churches, synagogues, priests, ministers, counselors, congregational support groups
- nonprofit organizations—self-help groups, associations
- treatment centers—special schools, testing clinics, or therapy facilities
- public school systems—educational programs for exceptional children, early intervention programs for children at risk, school psychologists, and counselors
- World Wide Web—in every chapter of this text you will find Internet starting points for early childhood development care and education

KEY TERMS

bonding   mistaken goals
manipulative   snowball effect

POINTS TO REMEMBER

- At the heart of almost any behavior lies the desire to acquire something that will meet a need.
- Dreikurs proposed that mistaken goals cause children to misbehave to get attention, gain control, get revenge, or remove themselves.

- Seeing children as lovable, capable, and worthwhile supports the growth of self-esteem.
- The destructive or aggressive child must know that she will be stopped and that others' rights will be protected.

- Intervene immediately to stop bullying.
- Children who regularly indulge in fits of anger, tantrums, and defiance need to know that the adults who care for them will not explode into their own fits of anger.

- Adults must recognize their own needs and imperfections to be effective in child guidance.
- Reporting child abuse and neglect can save children's lives.

PRACTICAL APPLICATION

"Please Wear This Dress!"

The day Minh Hoa Thi Nguyen started child care, both her mother and father took the morning off work to take her to school to make sure that she made a good transition into the early childhood program. The parents are extremely successful businesspeople. They had studied all their options and put Minh's name on the waiting list for Apple Valley Child Development Center when she was only a few months old.

Minh had always been cared for by her grandmother while her parents worked. Grandmother has moved away now and it is time for Minh to become part of a group of children. Minh is three and a half years old, but she arrives at Apple Valley carried in her father's arms and sucking on a pacifier. She is a beautiful little girl with wide dark eyes, porcelain skin, and shiny black hair. She is dressed in an expensive pink baby-doll-style dress that makes her look even younger than she is.

Over the first few weeks at Apple Valley, Minh seems to have a good time, although the teachers have to spend a lot of time reminding her to use words instead of just screeching when she needs something. Minh's parents, however, are at their wits' end.

In a meeting with the teachers, the parents report that mornings are a nightmare. Minh's mother says, "Every morning I get a nice dress out for Minh to wear and I say, 'Let's wear this one.' But Minh grabs it and runs down the hall and stuffs it into the laundry hamper. After we go through that for forty-five minutes, then I try to feed her some breakfast. It is awful! I give her eggs, and she throws them on the floor and says, 'No, I want oatmeal.' Then we go through that for a half hour! We don't believe in spanking and we don't know what to do. Please help us."

After some discussion, it is decided that Minh's favorite teacher, Miss Selena, should be invited to dinner at the Nguyen's house. At 6 p.m. on Thursday evening, Miss Selena arrives. Minh greets her at the door excitedly. The air is fragrant with the spicy Vietnamese stir-fry cooking in the kitchen. Minh says, "Miss Selena, come see my room!" Miss Selena is startled to discover that Minh's room is a perfectly appointed baby nursery, complete with beautifully decorated crib, a diaper-changing table that is no longer needed, and an adult rocking chair. The curtains and all the furniture are decorated in a frilly fabric that shows pictures of baby objects such as rattles, diapers, and baby bottles.

When the family and Miss Selena sit down to eat, Minh is placed in an infant high chair, even though her legs hang down far below the footrest. Every item of food Mr. and Mrs. Nguyen put on the highchair tray in front of Minh is refused. She refuses to drink any milk. As soon as the dishes are cleared away, Minh announces that she is hungry; Mr. Minh makes her a peanut butter sandwich. Before she even takes one bite, Minh throws the sandwich on the floor and demands an apple. She takes one bite of the apple and throws it on the floor. Her parents look embarrassed and helpless. They look at Miss Selena, "What are we supposed to do?" Wisely, Miss Selena says, "Let's all meet tomorrow at school to see if we can figure this out."

As the adults sit down the next day, it is obvious that the Nguyens love their daughter and want only the best for her. But it is also obvious that they are frustrated and overwhelmed by her behavior. Miss Selena begins the conversation by thanking the Nguyens for allowing her into their home and for the lovely dinner. Then she says, "Minh is three and a half. I was puzzled that she still needs a crib and a high chair." The Nguyens are surprised. "Well, we waited until we were a little older to have a child. We are both so involved in our careers that we haven't spent a lot of time around friends with babies or children. I guess it just didn't dawn on us that maybe she was outgrowing those things."

"I'm wondering," said Miss Selena, "if Minh is trying to gain control because she doesn't feel that she is completely accepted as a full-fledged, responsible member of the family. I'm wondering if there are some things that you could do at home, and that we could do at school, that would assure her that we all see her as a capable, responsible three-and-a-half-year-old who really belongs in the family and in the school."

Mr. Nguyen said, "Oh my god! I think my wife and I have been accustomed to being alone for so long, we just weren't prepared for a child. Yes, we'll go today

and find new furniture for her room. What should she have?" Miss Selena talked about giving Minh a voice in the family, giving her three options and letting her make her own choice. But she also talked to the Nguyens about allowing Minh to accept responsibility for her actions. Miss Selena explained how to apply logical consequences appropriately.

As the Nguyen's began to accept Minh as a responsible child instead of a helpless toddler, Minh's irresistible urge to control interactions with her parents began to fade. As her parents became more consistent in holding her responsible for her actions, she learned to think before she made impulsive choices. Miss Selena continued to provide the parents encouragement and information.

DISCUSSION QUESTIONS

1. What mistaken goal did Miss Selena refer to? Explain.
2. Describe some additional things her parents could do to assure that Minh really does feel accepted as a valued and responsible member of the family.
3. Give several examples of logical consequences that would have been appropriate for the Nguyens to use with Minh when she put her dresses in the laundry hamper or when she refused dinner and then demanded food immediately afterward.
4. List several other guidance techniques that you would share with the Nguyens.
5. What would you have done?

STUDENT ACTIVITY

1. Concetta is three. She has tantrums several times a week. Typically, another child will have something she wants and she will launch into a tantrum. What do you think is Concetta's misguided goal? How should you respond when Concetta has a tantrum?
2. Weimin is five. He is extraordinarily competitive. Anytime he is not first in line, first in a game, or first on the slide, he becomes upset. At times he becomes so upset that he cries and refuses to participate. He always rushes to the teacher for aid. What do you think is Weimin's misguided goal? How should you respond when Weimin cries and refuses to participate?
3. Armand is four. He is quarrelsome and begins a power struggle anytime he senses an adult is trying to get him to do something. What do you think is Armand's misguided goal? How should you respond when Armand is belligerent and refuses to cooperate?
4. Beth is eight. She is extremely silly. She follows the class leaders around making jokes and behaving outrageously. Beth is so annoying that most of her peers avoid her. What do you think is Beth's misguided goal? How should you respond when Beth is silly and out of control?

CHILDREN'S BOOKS RELATED TO MISTAKEN GOALS AND BULLYING

Bloch, D. (1993). *Positive self-talk for children: Teaching self-esteem through affirmations.* New York: Bantam Books.

Cooper, S. (2005). *Speak up and get along! Learn the mighty might, thought chop, and more tools to make friends, stop teasing, and feel good about yourself.* Minneapolis, MN: Free Spirit Publishing.

   For ages 8 to 12, this book offers a collection of 21 concrete strategies kids can use to express themselves, build relationships, end arguments and fights, halt bullying, and ease unhappy feelings. Each strategy is illustrated with examples and accompanied by dialogue children can practice and use. Stories and anecdotes show each tool in action.

Freedman, J. S., Ed. (1999a, July 10). Easing the teasing. *ERIC Digest.* Champaign, IL: ERIC Clearinghouse on Elementary and Early Childhood Education. Document # ED431555. Retrieved September 28, 2008, from http://www.uwsp.edu/education/block1/ED431555%201999-07-00%20Easing%20the%20Teasing%20How%20Parents%20Can%20Help%20Their%20Children_%20ERIC%20Digest.htm.

Freedman, J. S. (1999b). Preventing violence by elementary school children. *ERIC/CUE Digest, 149.* New York: ERIC Clearinghouse on Urban Education, Institute for Urban and Minority Education, Teachers College. Retrieved September 28, 2008, from http://www.ericdigests.org/2000-3/children.htm.

Ludwig, T. (2005). *My secret bully.* Minneapolis, MN: Free Spirit Publishing.

   When Monica is bullied by her friend Kate, it's not with fists or weapons. Instead, Kate uses name-calling, humiliation, and exclusion—emotional bullying, or relational aggression. Often dismissed as a normal rite of passage, it's as harmful as physical aggression, with devastating long-term effects. With the help of a supportive adult (her mother), Monica learns to reclaim her power. This book includes tips, discussion questions, and resources and is suitable for children ages 5 to 11 and parents and caregivers as well.

Moss, P. (2004). *Say something.* Minneapolis, MN: Free Spirit Publishing.

   Kids can help make school safe from bullying and teasing. But too many are silent bystanders, watching from the sidelines and not getting involved. In straightforward words and bright, realistic watercolor illustrations, this book for ages seven and older encourages children to "say something." It shows how a few words or an act of kindness can make a big difference. It is also suitable for educators, counselors, and youth workers.

Naylor, P. R. (2005). *King of the playground.* Minneapolis, MN: Free Spirit Publishing.

   Kevin's playtime is no fun anymore. Whenever he goes to the playground, Sammy starts bullying him with threats of horrible things he'll do. If Kevin goes on the slide, Sammy will tie him up! If he goes on the swing, Sammy will dig a hole and put Kevin in it! Fortunately, Kevin's dad believes that words are stronger than fists. When he suggests things Kevin might say or do in response to Sammy, Kevin starts to realize that Sammy isn't so scary after all. A story with subtlety, wit, and wonderful illustrations for ages four to eight.

Noddings, N. (1996). Learning to care and to be cared for. In A. M. Hoffman (Ed.), *Schools, violence, and society* (185–198). Westport, CT: Praeger.

Payne, L. M., & Rohling, C. (1997). *We can get along: A child's book of choices.* Minneapolis, MN: Free Spirit Publishing.

   We Can Get Along *teaches essential conflict resolution and peacemaking skills—think before you speak or act, treat others the way you want to be treated—in a way that young children ages three to nine can understand.*

Romain, T. (1997). *Bullies are a pain in the brain.* Minneapolis, MN: Free Spirit Publishing.

   This book blends humor with serious, practical suggestions for coping with bullies. Trevor Romain reassures kids ages 7 to 10 that they're not alone and it's not their fault if a bully decides to pick on them. He explains some people are bullies and describes realistic ways to become "bully-proof," stop bullies from hurting others, and get help in dangerous situations. And if bullies happen to read this book, they'll find ideas they can use to get along with others and feel good about themselves—without making other people miserable.

Romain, T., & Verdick, E. (2005). *Stress can really get on your nerves!* Minneapolis, MN: Free Spirit Publishing.

This is a book for ages 7 to 13.

Slaby, R. G., Roedell, W. C., Arezzo, D., & Kendrix, K. (1995). *Early violence prevention: Tools for teachers of young children.* Washington, DC: National Association for the Education of Young Children.

Sullivan, K. (2000). *The anti-bullying handbook.* Oxford, UK: Oxford University Press.

U.S. Department of Education, Office of Civil Rights. (1999). *Protecting students from harassment and hate crime: A guide for schools.* Washington, DC: U.S. Department of Education.

Verdick, E. (2003). *Teeth are not for biting board book.* Minneapolis, MN: Free Spirit Publishing.

This upbeat, colorful, virtually indestructible board book for infants and preschoolers helps prevent biting and teaches positive alternatives.

Verdick, E. (2004a). *Words are not for hurting.* Minneapolis, MN: Free Spirit Publishing.

The older children get, the more words they know and can use—including hurtful words. This book is suitable for ages four to seven.

Verdick, E. (2004b). *Feet are not for kicking.* Minneapolis, MN: Free Spirit Publishing.

This book helps infants and preschoolers learn to use their feet for fun, not in anger or frustration. It also includes tips.

Verdick, E., & Lisovskis, M. (2002). *How to take the grrrr out of anger.* Minneapolis, MN: Free Spirit Publishing.

Kids ages five to nine need help learning how to manage their anger. This book speaks directly to them and offers strategies they can start using immediately.

Wallach, L. B. (1994). Violence and young children's development. *ERIC Digest.* Champaign, IL: ERIC Clearinghouse on Elementary and Early Childhood Education. Document # ED369578. Retrieved September 28, 2008, from http://eric.ed.gov/ERICWebPortal/custom/portlets/recordDetails/detailmini.jsp?_nfpb=true&_&ERICExtSearch_SearchValue_0=ED369578&ERICExtSearch_SearchType_0=no&accno=ED369578.

RELATED READINGS

Bullying

Bauman, S. (2008) The role of elementary school counselors in reducing school bullying. *Elementary School Journal,* May, *108*(5), 362–375.

Clearinghouse on Elementary and Early Childhood Education. Exploring the nature and prevention of bullying. Retrieved June 9, 2008, from http://www.ed.gov/admins/lead/safety/training/bullying/index.html.

Child Abuse

Baker, L. L., & Cunningham, A. J. (2004). *Helping children thrive: Supporting woman abuse survivors as mothers: A resource to support parenting.* London, ON: Centre for Children and Families in the Justice System.

Banks, R. (1997). Bullying in schools. *ERIC Digest.* Champaign, IL: ERIC Clearinghouse on Elementary and Early Childhood Education. Document # ED 407 154. Retrieved September 28, 2008, from http://eric.ed.gov/ERICWebPortal/Home.portal?_nfpb=true&ERICExtSearch_SearchValue_0=%22Bullying+in+schools%22&searchtype=basic&ERICExtSearch_SearchType_0=ti&pageSize=10&eric_displayNtriever=false&eric_sortField=aau&eric_displayStartCount=1&_pageLabel=RecordDetails&objectId=0900019b800bf2ec&accno=ED407154&_nfls=false.

Barnett, O. W., Miller-Perrin, C. L., & Perrin, R. D. (2005). *Family violence across the lifespan: An introduction* (2nd ed.). Thousand Oaks, CA: Sage.

Berger, L. M. (2004). Income, family structure, and child maltreatment risk. *Children and Youth Services Review, 26*(8), 725–748.

Berger, L. M. (2005). Income, family characteristics, and physical violence toward children. *Child Abuse and Neglect, 29*(2), 107–133.

Berger, L. M., & Brooks-Gunn, J. (2005). Socioeconomic status, parenting knowledge and behaviors, and perceived maltreatment of young low-birth-weight children. *Social Service Review, 79*(2), 237–267.

Berger, L. M., & Waldfogel, J. (2000). Prenatal cocaine exposure: Long-run effects and policy implications. *Social Service Review, 74*(1), 28–54.

Carlson, M., & McLanahan, S. (2005). *Do good partners make good parents? Relationship quality and parenting in married and unmarried families.* Princeton, NJ: Wallace Hall, Princeton University, Center for Research on Child Well-being.

Djulus, J., Moretti, M., & Koren, G. (2005). Marijuana use and breastfeeding. *Canadian Family Physician, 51,* 349–350.

Douglas, E. M. (2005). Child maltreatment fatalities: What do we know, what have we done, and where do we go from here? In *Child victimization: Maltreatment, bullying and dating violence, prevention and intervention* (chap. 4, 1–17.) Kingston, NJ: Civic Research Institute.

Erikson, E. H. (1950). *Childhood and society.* New York: Norton.

Federal Interagency Forum on Child and Family Statistics (2005). *America's children in brief: Key national indicators of well-being.* Merrifield, VA: Health Resources and Services Administration Information Center.

Fontes, L. A. (2005). *Child abuse and culture: Working with diverse families.* New York: Guilford Publications.

Geffner, R., Ingleman, R. S., & Zellner, J. (2003). *The effects of intimate partner violence on children.* New York: Haworth Maltreatment & Trauma.

Goldstein, S., & Brooks, R. B. (2005). *Handbook of resilience in children.* New York: Kluwer Academic/Plenum Publishers.

Hanlong, T. E., Blatchley, R. J., Bennett-Sears, T., O'Grady, K. E., Rose, M., & Callaman, J. M. (2005). Vulnerability of children of incarcerated addict mothers: Implications for preventive intervention. *Children and Youth Services Review, 27,* 67–84. (Reprints available from Elsevier Customer Service Department, 6277 Sea Harbor Drive, Orlando, FL 32887.)

Hutchison, S. B. (2005). *Effects of and interventions for childhood trauma from infancy through adolescence: Pain unspeakable.* Binghamton, NY: Haworth Maltreatment and Trauma Press.

Kagan, R. (2004). *Rebuilding attachments with traumatized children: Healing from losses, violence, abuse and neglect.* New York: Haworth Maltreatment & Trauma.

McKenry, P. C., & Price, S. J., Eds. (2005). *Families and change: Coping with stressful events and transitions* (3rd ed.). Thousand Oaks, CA: Sage.

Miller, L. C. (2005). *The handbook of international adoption medicine: A guide for physicians, parents, and providers.* New York: Oxford University Press.

National Sexual Violence Resource Center (2005). *Preventing child sexual abuse: A national resource directory and handbook.* Enola, PA: National Sexual Violence Resource Center.

Regalado, M., Sareen, H., Inkelas, M., Wissow, L., & Halfon, N. (2004). Parents' discipline of young children: Results from the National Survey of Early Childhood Health. *Pediatrics, 113*(6), 1952–1958, June. (Reprints available from American Academy of Pediatrics.)

Stien, P. T., & Kendall, J. C. (2004). *Psychological trauma and the developing brain: Neurologically based interventions for troubled children.* New York: Haworth Maltreatment & Trauma.

Sullivan, K. (2000). *The anti-bullying handbook.* Oxford, UK: Oxford University Press.

Taylor, H. G., Fischer, K. W., Burdzovic, A. J., & Smith, K. W. (2004). Pathways to aggression in children and adolescents. *Harvard Educational Review, 74,* 404–430.

Zeanah, C. H., & Zeanah, P. D. (2001). Towards a definition of infant mental health. *Zero to Three, 22*(1), 13–20.

The Online Companion™ to accompany the sixth edition of *Positive Child Guidance* is your link to additional guidance resources on the Internet. This supplement contains audio and visual materials; PowerPoint presentations; web activities with critical-thinking questions and practical-application assignments; and links to web resources. This additional content can be found at http://www.earlychilded.delmar.com.

Chapter 10

Taking a New Look at Children

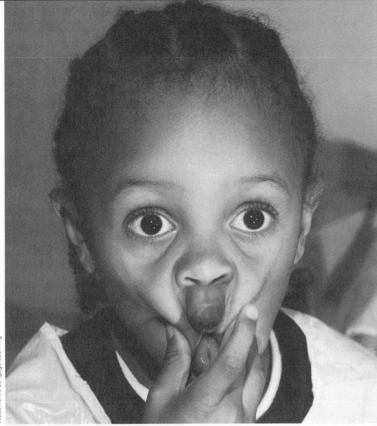

Wadsworth/Cengage Learning

OBJECTIVES

After reading this chapter, you should be able to do the following:

- Identify personal biases that affect guidance.
- Recognize the difference between objective and subjective observations.
- List effective observation strategies.
- Use observations for prescriptive guidance.
- Identify components of the observation sequence.
- Become more introspective about your level of cultural objectivity in observations.

Identifying Personal Biases

Gilda is a bright, gregarious ball of energy. When she was in kindergarten, she popped out of bed every morning before the sun was up because she loved going to school each day. Her teacher, Mr. Costa, seemed to really like her. He often invited her to help with classroom chores such as feeding the goldfish or passing out napkins for snack. Because she learned concepts very quickly, he encouraged her to help other children, a responsibility she took very seriously. Gilda liked pretending that she was a teacher, and the younger

(Continued)

To guide children effectively, we must become skillful observers.

children thrived on her persistent tutoring. Whenever anyone asked her what she wanted to be when she grew up, she always answered quickly, "A schoolteacher just like Mr. Costa!"

During Gilda's first day of first grade, she eagerly tried to get the attention of her new teacher, Mrs. Redwing, and jumped up to help pass out papers. Mrs. Redwing reprimanded Gilda for getting up out of her desk without asking and said, "Please stop asking me questions and just sit quietly and listen." Mrs. Redwing thought, "Oh, no, another hyperactive kid. That's all I need."

Over time, Gilda has become impatient and unhappy. She cries in the morning and tells her father that she does not want to go to school anymore. Mrs. Redwing is upset too. She is becoming more and more frustrated with Gilda's behavior, which eventually has become disruptive and, at times, even defiant. Mrs. Redwing has become especially exasperated with Gilda's attempts to help other children do their work whenever they have trouble, an action Mrs. Redwing considers a kind of cheating.

One day, Mr. Costa and Mrs. Redwing are sitting in the teacher's lounge drinking coffee. Mr. Costa says, "How is Gilda doing this year? I really miss her. What a terrific little girl she is." Mrs. Redwing chokes on her coffee and sputters, "Gilda? You've got to be kidding! She drives me absolutely up the wall."

How is it possible for two people to see the same child's behavior so differently? We see children differently because we are different. Everything that we perceive with our senses (eyes, ears, and so on) is filtered through layer upon layer of our personal views and biases.

Mr. Costa responds favorably to Gilda's energy and spontaneity because she reminds him of himself when he was younger. He values creativity so he is delighted by Gilda's bright mind. In contrast, because of her very strict upbringing, Mrs. Redwing learned early in life to suppress any fidgety impulses she had, so she finds particularly annoying Gilda's chattering and bounciness, behaviors her parents would never have tolerated. These behaviors strike Mrs. Redwing as rude and reckless, even though she can remember resenting her parents' rigidness toward her when she was a child.

Responding More Objectively to Individual Children

It is inevitable that some children will be more appealing than others to any given adult. Gender, culture, age, experiences, and temperament all affect our biases and shape our perceptions. Our own personality and style cannot be perfectly matched to the needs of every child; however, we can at least be honest about our bias and respectful in our treatment of children, regardless of their differences. Within families, parents sometimes admit that one of their own children seems easier to understand and manage whereas another child's behavior seems totally incomprehensible. In group settings, an adult may have difficulty admitting that he or she feels more comfortable with children who are small (or large), male (or female), black (or white), or rich (or poor).

To respond more effectively to children's behaviors, we must discover our own areas of bias. What preconceived notions do I have about children? Do I expect certain behaviors from children because of their ethnic, gender, or appearance differences? How can I learn who an individual child really is rather than focus on stereotypes associated with groups or categories of people? Do I tend to have favorite and least favorite children? How do I respond differently to them? How can I become more objective?

One way to increase objectivity is to consciously separate facts from opinions. What do I actually perceive, and what do I interpret intuitively based on my knowledge, experience, and bias? By sorting through our own thinking processes to separate facts from opinions, we can more accurately focus on actual child behaviors and scrutinize our interpretations of the meaning of those actions.

If Mrs. Redwing had separated the facts from her opinions, she might have seen Gilda differently.

> Objective observations (Mr. Costa and Mrs. Redwing both agree that these are accurate facts): Gilda talks frequently, begins tasks quickly, completes work before others in class, is active and quick in physical movements, and expresses interest in the progress of classmates.
>
> Mr. Costa's subjective interpretations: Gilda is very capable in oral communications; she is a competent, bright student; she is enthusiastic about her schoolwork; she has leadership potential; she cares intensely about others.
>
> Mrs. Redwing's subjective interpretations: Gilda ignores the teacher and class rules about talking, she rushes through her work because she does not take it seriously enough, she is overactive, and she worries about the affairs of other children that are none of her business.

When one's opinions are stated separately from observable facts and those opinions are clearly labeled "subjective," or interpretation, then it is much easier to recognize and deal with personal bias. If we trick ourselves into believing that our opinions are objective facts, then we lose an opportunity to see children as they really are. We can consciously learn to be more objective in our thinking.

For example, the following observation is filled with opinions: "Erik angrily stomped into the kitchen trying to pick a fight with someone. He taunted his sister and hurt her feelings just to see her cry. He hoped she would hit him so he would have an excuse to get her in trouble." These statements are pure fantasy. We cannot see into Erik's head to look at his intentions or hear his thoughts.

What we can actually see and hear is that Erik "stomped into the kitchen. He looked around with a frown on his face. He pointed to his sister's sandwich and said, 'Yuk, are you going to eat that gooey mess?' His sister began to cry and threatened to hit Erik. Erik said, 'If you hit me, I'll tell mom.'" What we may interpret is that Erik seemed irritable, unhappy, and in a mood to agitate his sister.

The first opinionated description tempts us to punish Erik for his obnoxious behavior because we assume we know why he behaved the way he did. The second,

Wadsworth/Cengage Learning

▬▬▬To be objective, we must focus on the things we actually see and hear.

more objective way of reporting Erik's behavior reminds us that we do not know everything that is going on in Erik's mind and heart. Objective observation encourages us to look further for reasons for actions and to better understand troublesome behavior.

The Observation Sequence

To be effective in working with children, we must become skilled observers so that we can constantly improve the quality of the care and education we provide. Our ongoing observations should result in concrete plans and changes in the curriculum and environment. Child guidance is much more an art than a science.

There is no recipe for treating children that works for all children in all circumstances, but with careful observation, the adult can gather the information needed to make intelligent decisions and to select appropriate methods to prevent or respond to various problems. Later, the adult can observe to evaluate how effective the chosen guidance technique has been in solving the problem.

How Observation Supports Positive Guidance

For any effort at resolving a behavior problem to be effective, it must be well matched to the child's ability and frame of mind as well as to the circumstances surrounding the behavior. Does the child appear to be feeling angry and destructive or just bored and silly? Is the behavior habitual or a rare event? Is the child capable of benefiting from verbal reminders or is direct physical redirection required? What actually is the problem? When, where, and why does it occur? These are all questions that should be answered through careful observation.

What Do I Need to Get Started?

There are many excellent checklists, kits, and observational instruments (assessments) available commercially to assist early childhood professionals in observing children. For most parents, caregivers, and preschool teachers, however, the most useful record-keeping tool (and definitely the least expensive) is a simple pocket-size spiral notepad and a pencil. If paper and pencil are available whenever something interesting occurs, it will be a great deal easier to get something written down. No record-keeping instrument of any kind is of value if it stays in a desk drawer or a file cabinet.

With a little pocket notepad, an anecdote can be described before the details are forgotten, tidbits can be added regularly to a running account, or some type of sampling checklist can be maintained. It is easy for us to think, "I don't need to write this down. I'm sure I'll remember it." But then, of course, we forget whatever it was that we were so sure we would remember.

What observations can you make from this picture? (Hint: this baby's arm is outstretched and stiffened, and she is peering at the adult out of the corner of her eye.)

How Will I Use My Observations?

Observations can be just for fun. Parents love observing their children, telling grandparents hilarious stories about the things the toddler has done or clever things the pre-schoooler has said. Many families treasure photographs showing their children's changes in size and appearance over the years. Educators can enrich families' lives by providing information, photographs, anecdotes, and child-made keepsakes showing children's friendships, accomplishments, field trips, and interests. Many early educators (especially those caring for infants and toddlers) collect anecdotes, pictures, and other items throughout the year, then present each child's family with a scrapbook that will help the child and family remember the events and activities of that year. Scrapbooks are a terrific way for adults to support the development of children's self-esteem. Photographs and mementos remind the child how much he is valued by parents and the educators who care for him.

Observations should routinely be used by parents and educators to determine developmentally appropriate activities for children. Is the child eagerly engaged in the toy, book, or activity? Or is he looking bored? The activity may not offer a challenge anymore. Does he seem frustrated? The game may be too complicated for his developmental level. Is the group of preschoolers fidgeting and misbehaving during story time? The story may be too long or not lively enough to hold their interest at that age.

Most important for the purposes of this book, observations must be used to lead early educators and parents through the daily process of positive child guidance. Positive child guidance is a problem-solving method. Adults observe how children are behaving at a given moment, figure out why they are behaving that way, and determine supportive methods to help the child become more responsible and self-disciplined. Positive child guidance cannot succeed without effective and ongoing child observations. It takes concentrated effort and practice to develop keen observation skills.

inferring meaning
Drawing conclusions from evidence perceived by one's senses or through communication.

Interpreting observations is the process of **inferring meaning** from what has been sensed (seen, heard, touched, tasted, or smelled). To interpret what has been observed, a knowledge of child development in general as well as of the unique development of an individual child is necessary. An additional help is firsthand experience with other children as well as with the individual child in question. All of this means we should take what we sense at the present time and mull it over using all of our past knowledge and experience to create new ideas about why the child may need to behave as he does.

Looking back over observation notes can be surprisingly enlightening. Children grow and change so quickly that we may be startled to look back at our notes about little Bronwyn and see that only three months ago she cried and clung to us when other children were around. Now, she confidently approaches others to initiate play. By seeing a child's progress over time, we can make better sense of the child's immediate behavior and know what help and guidance the child needs to behave more appropriately.

Personal bias must be kept in check while interpreting one's observations. Observation records, particularly objective checklists, may provide convincing evidence that our intuitive assumptions about a particular child have been wrong. Interpreting observations also gives us an opportunity to see things from the child's point of view. We may be annoyed with a child for interrupting our conversations but, after observing him carefully, realize that he really deserves to be included more in adult interactions and just needs to be taught how to join a conversation politely.

How Does My Observation Become a Plan?

In a doctor's office, a patient is seen and observations are recorded in a chart. The observations of the physician are then carefully interpreted (to make a diagnosis): what is the meaning of the rash? . . . of the fever? . . . of the pain in the left foot? Then, most importantly, a plan is formulated (a prescription) to remedy the problem. The doctor prescribes bed rest or an antibiotic. We prescribe five minutes away from an activity for the child; an understanding, heart-to-heart talk with the child about hurting people's feelings; or a change in our behavior toward the child by giving more positive attention or more developmentally appropriate activities.

What if My Plan Does Not Work?

After a plan is formulated, the next step is action. Some adults take a fatalistic attitude toward children's misbehavior. They think children will not change and consequently do not bother doing anything other than complain about their inappropriate or immature behaviors. Young children are avid learners. They learn new habits much more easily than do older children or adults. They just need time, effort, encouragement, and a great deal of practice to control impulses and master the social skills they need to be responsible, cooperative group members.

Sometimes, even if the plan we attempt does not really work, merely focusing on the child's problem (and caring enough to try to resolve it) may stimulate the child's own awareness of the problem and commitment to correct it. It will be very therapeutic for the child to see evidence from our actions that "I care about you. I am willing to make a real effort to help you learn to use words rather than fists to express your feelings. I won't give up on you."

As long as the action is positive and respectful of the child, it is far more important for us to formulate a plan and do something than it is to worry about being right every time. Perfectionists are often so paralyzed by their fear of making mistakes that they never get around to doing anything. Children can learn valuable lessons from our handling of our own mistakes. They can learn that everyone makes mistakes from time to time and that admitting mistakes is nothing to be ashamed of. We could set a good example by saying, "Joshua, I asked you to hold my hand on our walk to help you remember to stay on the sidewalk where it's safe. I made a mistake. I didn't think about how that might make you feel like a baby. Let's think of a different way to help you be safe."

> Think left
> and think right
> and think low
> and think high.
> Oh, the thinks
> you can think up
> if only you try!
>
> *Oh, the Thinks You
> Can Think!*
> *Dr. Seuss/Theodor Seuss
> Geisel. Copyright © 1975.
> New York: Random House
> Books for Young Readers.*

How Can I Be Sure My Plan Is Working?

Is what we are doing effective? In the evaluation phase, we make a complete circle and come back to observing. The only way we can be sure we were on target in our first observation, interpretation, plan, and resulting action is to observe again and look for indications that our plan is or is not working. If it is working, we can relax and go on to the next problem. If it is not, we return to square one, collect more information through observation, and develop a new and improved plan of action. This cycle repeats until we find a plan that works.

Observation Strategies

Researchers use carefully orchestrated strategies to collect objective data. Adults who care for young children rarely need such formal methodology; they need only a workable plan for finding out the what, when, where, and why of children's problem behaviors so that they can respond effectively and appropriately. The following sections describe some useful methods for keeping track and making sense of puzzling or upsetting behaviors (Barko, 1997; Bentzen, 2005; Billman & Sherman, 1997; Bredekamp & Copple, 1997; Green & Stafford, 1997; Harms & Clifford, 1998; McLean et al., 1997; Mindes et al., 1996).

What Is an Anecdotal Record?

anecdotal record
A short descriptive story about a child's specific behavior event that is of particular interest or concern. This may be firsthand information as observed by child care providers or recorded from secondhand information as provided by parents. It is qualitative, not quantitative data.

An **anecdotal record** is a detailed account of a specific episode that is of particular interest or concern. A specific event takes place that catches the attention of the adult. As soon as possible, the adult writes a narrative account; he tells the story of the event. He describes all of the pertinent details that he can recall such as what he saw, heard, or otherwise perceived with his senses. He will include verbatim quotes whenever possible to further clarify the account. Any personal opinions or interpretations will be set apart and clearly identified as observer's comments by such phrases as "It appeared to me that . . ." or "Therefore, it was my impression that. . . ."

Following is an example of an anecdotal record of a toddler biting incident:

Observations: Ricky wandered slowly around the room, whining and shaking his head. After about five minutes, he abruptly dropped to the floor and began to cry. Periodically, he stopped crying to sit up, suck his thumb, and twist a tuft of his hair while he looked around, and then he would close his eyes, drop back on the floor, and begin sobbing again.

I picked up a handful of picture books and sat down on the floor beside him. I said, "Ricky, would you like to read a book? Look, it's a book about kitty cats." At first he ignored me, but finally he crawled into my lap and laid his head on my chest as he continued to suck his thumb and make the jerky little sniffing sounds that follow a bout of hard crying. I began to read the story about kittens.

After only a few minutes, Katherine toddled over and plopped into my lap practically on top of Ricky. Before I had even a second to respond, Ricky had grabbed Katherine's face and hair and sunk his teeth into her cheek.

Comments/Interpretations: Ricky was probably frightened and anxious because he has not been away from his mother very often. He seems to be showing evidence of a great deal of separation anxiety. He may have felt threatened by Katherine's presence because he has no sisters or brothers and may not be accustomed to sharing adult attention with others. I will have to watch Ricky very carefully so that I can help him find ways to cope with his feelings and I can anticipate and intervene better in situations where he might hurt another child.

What Is a Running Account?

running account
A detailed commentary describing an event as it unfolds each time it occurs.

In a **running account,** a specific type of behavior is noted each time it occurs. A mother who worries that her child is not eating properly may keep a running account for a time, keeping track of when, where, and what her child eats during and between meals each day. After a few days or weeks, she could begin to see if specific eating patterns emerge. Does the child pick at meals but consume high-calorie junk food during frequent snacks? Does the child eat a well-balanced lunch and afternoon snack but often refuse supper? Does the child eat whatever is offered at home but get into power struggles over food with a caregiver in the child care center?

Following is an example of a running account of a four-year-old girl's incidences of nail-biting:

Home Observations

Monday, 8:00 a.m.—Celia bit her nails while watching cartoons on television; she had a very tense facial expression.

Monday, 3:30 p.m.—Celia and her best friend Joel had an argument; after he told her he wouldn't play with her anymore, she sat by herself on the steps for a long time, biting her nails; again, she appeared very tense.

Tuesday, 11:30 a.m.—Celia bit her nails while she waited for lunch; she appeared more bored than tense.

Tuesday, 4:30 p.m.—Celia bit her nails the whole time she watched a television cartoon; her whole body appeared to be tense as she sat on the edge of her chair and strained toward the television.

Comments/Interpretations: Tension (and possibly boredom) seems to be triggering Celia's nail-biting. She was not seen biting her nails when she was coloring, playing dolls, or putting together puzzles. It may be helpful to redirect Celia to more active play and to discourage her watching television cartoons.

What observations can you make from this picture? (Hint: look at the children's facial expressions and body postures.)

What Is Time Sampling?

The purpose of **time sampling** is to give a periodic snapshot of a certain behavior. In time sampling, a time interval is selected: 5 minutes, 30 minutes, an hour, or other interval. Then, at the designated time intervals, a checklist is marked to show whether the chosen behavior is or is not occurring at that moment. For example, an individual child could be watched at intervals to determine whether he is spending more time actively engaged in play or passively watching others. An entire class could be watched to see how often the reading center is used compared with the block center. This procedure can give factual evidence to support or refute an adult's intuitive impressions about the occurrence of various patterns of behavior.

Following is a time-sampling checklist used by a preschool teacher to help her study her students' patterns of being **on task** rather than misbehaving, wandering aimlessly, or just watching:

time sampling
A recording made at predefined intervals to determine the pattern of occurrence and the general frequency of a certain behavior either in an individual or in the entire group. Setting and sticking with specific time intervals for recording the behavior reduces the influence of observer bias.

on task
Focused on the activities at hand; fully involved in and attentive to productive skill development or learning activity.

Classroom Observations			
Time	**Misbehaving**	**Wandering**	**Watching**
8:15 a.m.	James, Jill	Suzette, Amy, Tyler	Ben, Ann
8:30 a.m.	James	Amy	Suzette
8:45 a.m.	Amy, Suzette	—	—
9:00 a.m.	Tyler	—	—
9:15 a.m.	—	—	—
9:30 a.m.	—	Suzette	—
9:45 a.m.	Amy, Ben	Jill, Tyler	Suzette
10:00 a.m.	Suzette, Ann	Tyler	Jill, Amy
10:15 a.m.	Suzette	Ann, Tyler, Ben	Amy

Comments/Interpretations: These children have more difficulty staying on task at the beginning and the end of the morning. Their most productive time is between 8:45 and 9:30. Suzette, Amy, and Tyler may need special attention to help them focus on productive activity. James seemed able to avoid misbehavior after he settled into productive activity.

What Is Event Sampling?

event sampling
A recording to determine the precise number of times a specific behavior occurs within a set period, as well as the pattern of occurrence.

The purpose of **event sampling** is to determine the exact number of times a specific behavior occurs. Individual children can be observed for occurrences of a specific behavior, or an entire group can be watched, and a total number of occurrences of a behavior (such as aggression) can be recorded and tallied. In event sampling, a specific action (or actions) is designated for observation. When the behavior occurs, a checklist is marked so that after a given period, the adult can tally the exact number of times the behavior took place.

Following is an event sampling checklist used by a child care worker to determine the individual daily progress of several toddlers in their toilet training (each accident has been recorded as an x):

Toileting Accidents					
Names	**Monday**	**Tuesday**	**Wednesday**	**Thursday**	**Friday**
Reily	xxx	xxx	xxx	x	
Joseph	xx				
Mariette	xxx	xx	x	x	
Ella	xxxx	xxxxx	xxxx	xxxx	xxxx
Prichart			x	xx	
Bethany	xx		x		

Comments/Interpretations: Ella may not be ready for toilet training yet. It may be helpful to observe Mariette more closely to determine if she is having difficulty at a specific time of day or under specific circumstances.

Reily had difficulty early in the week but managed to stay dry most of the day Thursday and all day Friday. He should probably be watched further to see what happens the following week.

What factual observations can you make from this picture? What can you infer about what is going on? What can you observe about their moods? Describe your inferences.

Which Method of Recording Observations Works Best?

Checklists and narrative accounts can be used as tools for gathering information in many different situations. The particular advantage of narrative accounts is that they create word pictures that may provide insight into a child's behavior far beyond that originally anticipated when the event was recorded.

The adult can look back over several anecdotal records and discover new, previously overlooked relationships or details each time. The biggest drawback to narratives is, of course, that they are very time-consuming and so can be relied on only for recording occasional rather than routine occurrences. Narratives collect **qualitative information** whereas checklists collect **quantitative information.**

Checklists leave out all of the details surrounding behaviors and focus only on the frequencies and distributions of occurrences. They are especially useful for making comparisons, not only of one child's behaviors to that of other children but also to the child's own behaviors at other times of day, in other settings, or at an earlier age. The major advantage of checklists is the ease with which they can be used. The major drawback is that a great deal of important information about the extenuating background circumstances of a behavior are not recorded. The checklist examples provided earlier gave a great deal more factual information about many more children than the anecdotal record and the running account; however, you probably feel that you know much more about what Ricky and Celia (described in the narrative accounts) are really like than any of the children listed on the checklists.

qualitative information
Unmeasurable descriptive qualities and characteristics of behaviors.

quantitative information
Measurable numerical data and statistical calculations that tell how often or to what degree behaviors occur.

KEY TERMS

anecdotal record
event sampling
inferring meaning
on task

qualitative information
quantitative information
running account
time sampling

POINTS TO REMEMBER

- Everything that we perceive with our senses (eyes, ears, and so on) is filtered through layer upon layer of our personal point of view (our bias).
- One way to increase objectivity is to make a conscious effort to separate facts from opinions.

- Observations help us evaluate how effective a chosen guidance technique has been in solving a problem.

PRACTICAL APPLICATION

The Mysterious Case of the Spinning Peg

Felicia, an afternoon assistant in an infant and toddler child care center, is sitting on the floor and pulling the string of a "See and Say" toy. Lisa is laughing. Felicia asks, "Where are the fish? Can you see the fish? There they are, seven of them." She laughs and tickles Lisa's tummy. Other toddlers push close to Felicia as they laugh and interact with her. They watch every move that Felicia makes.

Lisa, who is 18 months old, wanders away from them toward me as I sit on the vinyl padded tunnel. Lisa accidentally drops a large plastic peg she is carrying. When it hits the nearby wooden stair, it spins for several seconds. She stares at it with a look of wonder. She carefully picks it up and with great concentration, drops it on the step again, but this time it does not spin. She stares at it, squats beside the stairs, and then proceeds to drop it again and again on the carpet.

It does not spin. She stands up and throws it down on the carpet. It does not spin! She bites it hard and throws it two more times, but still it does not spin. She leaves the peg lying on the floor and walks away. Felicia picks it up and puts it away.

Lisa comes over to me, looks at my writing and at my face. She pats my tablet and then pulls at the pages. She looks very seriously at my eyes. She then walks away. I hear her whine as she walks over to the play sink. She stops abruptly, looks at a plastic fruit, then with great interest she watches it as she drops it to the floor. It does not spin.

She sucks her finger and starts to cry. Felicia picks her up, comforts her, then walks away saying, "You're getting a little fussy. I wonder if you're hungry. Let me see if you get an afternoon bottle."

DISCUSSION QUESTIONS

1. What are the objective observations you would have actually seen, heard, and so on, if you had been observing this interaction?
2. What are your own interpretations of the interaction?
3. Why do you think Lisa started to cry?
4. What can you tell about the relationship between Lisa and her caregiver, Felicia?

STUDENT ACTIVITY

1. Carry out an observation by creating an *anecdotal record* of the things you see and hear.
   a. Study your observations.
   b. What can you infer from your record?
   c. List three things you might do differently with the child or children on the basis of your observations.

2. Carry out an observation by creating a *running account* of the things you see and hear.
   a. Study your observations.
   b. What can you infer from your record?
   c. List three things you might do differently with the child or children on the basis of your observations.
3. Carry out an observation using *time sampling* to track a specific behavior you have selected.
   a. Study your observations.
   b. What can you infer from your record?
   c. List three things you might do differently with the child or children on the basis of your observations.
4. Carry out an observation using *event sampling* to track a specific behavior you have selected.
   a. Study your observations.
   b. What can you infer from your record?
   c. List three things you might do differently with the child or children on the basis of your observations.
5. Discuss your observations and decide what you might have done more effectively. What worked best? Why?

RELATED READINGS

Developmentally Appropriate Assessment

Barko, N. (1997). Labeled for life? In K. M. Paciorek & J. H. Munro (Eds.), *Annual editions: Early childhood education 97/98* (18th ed.). New York: McGraw-Hill. (Original work published in *Parents,* September 1996).

    The author addresses pragmatic reasons for children being labeled as "exceptional" but also looks at how this labeling may cause difficulties for a child if the diagnosis is wrong or if the child's ability level changes significantly over time.

Benjamin, A. C. (1994). Observations in early childhood classrooms: Advice from the field. *Young Children, 49*(6), 14–20.

Bentzen, W. R. (2005). *Seeing young children: A guide to observing and recording behavior* (5th ed.). Clifton Park, NY: Delmar Learning.

    Seeing Young Children is designed to provide essential background information on many aspects of child development and recording techniques. These two bodies of information then form the basis for observing and recording young children's behavior in child care centers, early childhood classrooms, homes, public schools, and other settings.

Billman, J., & Sherman, J. A. (1997). *Observation and participation in early childhood settings: A practicum guide, birth through age five.* Needham Heights, MA: Allyn & Bacon.

Bondurant-Utz, J. (2002). *A practical guide to assessing infants and preschoolers with special needs.* Columbus, OH: Merrill.

Curtis, D., & Carter, M. (2000). *The art of awareness: How observation can transform your teaching.* New York: RedLeaf Press.

Dodge, D., Colker, L. J., & Heroman, C. (2002). *The creative curriculum developmental continuum assessment system.* Washington, DC: Teaching Strategies.

Earl, L. M. (2003). *Assessment as learning: Using classroom assessment to maximize student learning.* Thousand Oaks, CA: Corwin.

Engel, B., & Gronlund G. (2001). *Focused portfolios: A complete assessment for the young child.* New York: RedLeaf Press.

Espinosa, L. M. (2002). High-quality preschool: Why we need it and what it looks like. NIEER policy brief. *Preschool Policy Matters, 1,* 1–11. Retrieved October 3, 2008, from http://nieer.org/docs/?DocID=58.

Feinburg, S. G., & Mindess, M. (1994). *Eliciting Children's Full Potential: Designing and evaluating developmentally based programs for young children.* Needham Heights, MA: Brooks/Cole.

    This book describes what makes a quality early childhood program and explains the procedures through which quality programs can be developed, nurtured, and maintained. The authors discuss the process of designing and maintaining excellent programs that develop children's full potential throughout the curriculum and offer a guide for an ongoing process of evaluation.

Frank Porter Graham Child Development Institute. (2002). Rating early childhood environments. Special issue, *Early Developments, 7*(2).

Freeman, N., & Brown, M. 2000. Evaluating the child care director: The collaborative professional assessment process. *Young Children, 55*(5), 20–28.

Gaustad, J. (1996). Assessment and evaluation in the multiage classroom. Special issue, *OSSC Bulletin, 39*(3–4).

Gronlund, G., & James, M. (2006). *Focused observations: How to observe children for assessment and curriculum planning.* New York: RedLeaf Press.

Hannon, J. (2000). Learning to like Matthew. *Young Children, 55*(6), 24–28.

   This article addresses strategies for authentic, holistic assessment practices in observation and note taking to better understand children, to effectively share information about the child's growth and learning with his family, and to continually improve teaching methods.

Hemmeter, M. L., Maxwell, K. L., Ault, M. J., & Schuster, J. W. (2001). *Assessment of practices in early elementary classrooms (APEEC).* New York: Teachers College Press. Available from NAEYC.

Hills, T. W. (1992). Reaching potentials through appropriate assessment. In S. Bredekamp & T. Rosegrant (Eds.), *Reaching potentials: Appropriate curriculum and assessment for young children.* Washington, DC: National Association for the Education of Young Children.

Hills, T. W. (1993). Assessment in context—Teachers and children at work. *Young Children, 48*(5), 20–28.

   To be developmentally appropriate and to best serve children's needs, assessment should be included as an integrated part of an overall program. It is most effective when it contributes positively to children's self-esteem and developmental process, recognizes children's individuality, and respects their family and community backgrounds.

Jones, J. (2003). *Early literacy assessment systems: Essential elements.* Princeton, NJ: Policy Information Center, Educational Testing Service.

Katz, L. G. (1995). *Talks with teachers of young children: A collection.* Norwood, NJ: Ablex.

Katz, L. G., & Chard, S. C. (1996). The contribution of documentation to the quality of early childhood education. *ERIC Digest.* Urbana, IL: ERIC Clearinghouse on Elementary and Early Childhood Education.

Kohn, A. (2001). Fighting the tests: Turning the frustration into action. *Young Children, 56*(2), 19–24.

Losardo, A., & Notari-Syverson, A. (2001). *Alternative approaches to assessing young children.* Baltimore, MD: Brookes.

Marsden, D. B., Dombro, A. L., & Dichtelmiller, M. L. (2003). *The ounce scale user's guide.* New York: Pearson Early Learning.

Marshall, H. (2003). Research in review. Opportunity deferred or opportunity taken? An updated look at delaying kindergarten entry. *Young Children, 58*(5), 84–93.

McAfee, O., & Leong, D. (2001). *Assessing and guiding young children's learning.* New York: Pearson/Allyn & Bacon.

McLean, M. E., Bailey, D. B., Jr., & Wolery, M. (1997). *Assessing infants and preschoolers with special needs* (2nd ed.). Upper Saddle River, NJ: Merrill Education/Prentice Hall.

   This text, written for early childhood special educators and other professionals who work with infants and preschoolers, focuses on assessment for planning effective intervention programs.

Meisels, S. (2000). On the side of the child-personal reflections on testing, teaching, and early childhood education. *Young Children, 55*(6), 16–19.

NAEYC & National Association of Early Childhood Specialists in State Departments of Education. (2003a). Executive Summary. Early learning standards: Creating the conditions for success. *Young Children, 58*(1), 69–70.

NAEYC & National Association of Early Childhood Specialists in State Departments of Education. (2003b). Joint Position Statement. *Early childhood curriculum, assessment, and program evaluation: Build-*

ing an effective, accountable system in programs for children birth through age 8. Retrieved October 3, 2008, from http://www.naeyc.org/about/positions/pdf/pscape.pdf.

National Association for the Education of Young Children. (1991). Guidelines for appropriate curriculum content and assessment in programs serving children ages 3 through 8. *Young Children, 46*(3), 21–38.

Owocki, G., & Goodman, Y. M. (2002). *Kidwatching: Documenting children's literacy development.* Portsmouth, NH: Heinemann.

Popham, W. J. (2000). *Testing! Testing! What every parent should know about school tests.* Boston, MA: Allyn & Bacon.

Popham, W. J. (2002). *Classroom assessment: What teachers need to know.* Boston, MA: Allyn & Bacon.

Project Zero. (2003). *Making teaching visible: Documenting individual and group learning as professional development.* Cambridge, MA: Project Zero. Available from NAEYC.

Project Zero & Reggio Children. (2001). *Making learning visible: Children as individual and group learners.* Reggio Emilia, Italy: Reggio Children. Available from NAEYC.

Puckett, M. B., & Black, J. (2000). *Authentic assessment of the young child.* Columbus, OH: Merrill.

Ridley, S., & McWilliam, R. A. (2001). Putting the child back into child care quality assessment. *Young Children, 56*(4), 92–93.

Saluja, G., Scott-Little, C., & Clifford, R. M. (2000). Readiness for school: A survey of state policies and definitions. *Early Childhood Research and Practice 2*(2). Retrieved February 26, 2006, from http://ecrp.uiuc.edu/.

Shepard, L. A. (1994). The challenges of assessing young children appropriately. *Phi Delta Kappan, 76*(3), 206–212.

Southern Association on Children Under Six. (1990). *Developmentally appropriate assessment.* Little Rock, AR: Author.

Wesson, K. A. (2001). The "Volvo effect"—Questioning standardized tests. *Young Children, 56*(3), 16–18.

Wheatley, K. (2003). Viewpoint. Promoting the use of content standards: Recommendations for teacher educators. *Young Children, 58*(2), 96–102.

Wortham, S. C. (2000). *Assessment in early childhood education* (3rd ed.). Upper Saddle River, NJ: Pearson Education.

The Online Companion™ to accompany the sixth edition of *Positive Child Guidance* is your link to additional guidance resources on the Internet. This supplement contains audio and visual materials; PowerPoint presentations; web activities with critical-thinking questions and practical-application assignments; and links to web resources. This additional content can be found at http://www.earlychilded.delmar.com.

Chapter 11

Historical Perspectives and Guidance Theories

OBJECTIVES

After reading this chapter, you should be able to do the following:

- Recognize historical events related to beliefs about children.
- Outline the child's role in society.
- Identify the role of child guidance in a democracy.
- List changes in disciplinary strategies over time.
- Outline tenets of various folk ideologies of child guidance.
- Identify behaviorist approaches to guidance.
- Identify maturationist approaches to guidance.
- Identify developmental interactionist approaches to guidance.
- Reflect on your own philosophy of child guidance.

Wadsworth/Cengage Learning

Our perspectives on babies and young children are constantly changing.

Historical Perspectives

Child care and guidance practices have changed drastically through the years. Many child care traditions from the past would seem strange, even cruel, to modern parents. For example, swaddling, the snug wrapping of infants in strips of cloth or blankets, is an ancient custom that has persisted for centuries in many parts of the world. Snugly wrapping newborns in blankets is considered to be a very appropriate tradition in most modern cultures, but the old practice of swaddling was intended to control the baby's movement and routinely continued until the child was old enough to walk. John Locke in 1699 described the customary child care of his day and how a baby was rolled and swathed, ten or a dozen times round; then blanket upon blanket, mantle upon that; its little neck pinned down to one posture; its head more than it frequently needs, triple crowned like a young page, with covering upon covering; its legs and arms as if to prevent that kindly stretching which we rather ought to promote . . . the former bundled up, the latter pinned down; and how the poor thing lies on the nurse's lap, a miserable little pinioned captive. (cited in Cunnington & Buck, 1965, p. 103)

In western Europe during the first half of the 18th century, infants were seen as not only somehow less human than older people but also somewhat expendable. A wealthy mother usually sent her newborn infant to the care of a hired wet nurse who was expected to breastfeed and care for the child, often at the expense of the life of the wet nurse's own infant. Infant mortality rates reportedly reached as high as 80 percent in some areas as wet-nurse mothers, to ensure their livelihood, gave birth to stimulate the production of breast milk, then sent their own infants to poorly maintained foundling homes (Weiser, 1982).

The writings of Rousseau toward the end of the 18th century both influenced and reflected a change in the cultural perception of childhood. He insisted that "everything is good as it comes from the hands of the Author of Nature" (Rousseau, l893, p. 1). He argued that, rather than being an evil creature who must have sin beaten out of him, the young child is born good and innocent. He believed that the harsh discipline techniques of that day, which were intended to provide the child salvation from original sin, tainted the child rather than provided healthy, normal growth. Rousseau's prescription for child care included breastfeeding by the natural mother, fresh air, loose clothing, and a minimum of interference from adults.

Certain tribes of Native Americans in the 1900s particularly valued physical toughness in their children. To build up the child's resistance, newborns were plunged into cold water several times at birth, regardless of the weather. Their version of swaddling was to fasten the baby securely onto a cradleboard that could be conveniently hung inside the lodge, from a tree branch, from a saddlebow, or wherever family members were clustered. Babies were not released from the confines of cradleboards until they were able to walk (Weiser, 1982).

American mothers of European descent sent their infants and young children to the neighborhood widow or spinster for care and teaching. In these "dame schools," a baby might nap on a quilt in a corner of the kitchen while older children practiced reading from the New Testament (Weiser, 1982). Farm and slave children were valued as a source of free labor. Toddlers barely able to walk were assigned chores and held accountable for them. By the early 1900s, momentum had begun to build for promoting the scientific study of the development of children and the dissemination of pertinent information to parents. Some of the writings of that day foretold trends in thinking about young children. For example, a book produced by the Institute of Child Welfare at the University of Minnesota in 1930 warned parents that children's personal characteristics were not necessarily inborn.

As a matter of fact, the modern study of young children is indicating that such traits are in large part due to the manner in which the child is treated by adults and other children, rather than to inheritance. The parent who has the ideal of complete and unquestioning obedience, and who is forceful and consistent enough to obtain it, is likely to have a child who, when he goes to school, distresses a good teacher and delights a poor one by always doing what he is told and furthermore by always waiting to be told what to do. His whole attitude is that of finding out what authority requires and then complying, an attitude which, if maintained, is apt to result in incompetence, inefficiency, and unhappiness in adulthood. (Faegre & Anderson, 1930, p. 45)

How the Modern World Has Influenced Thinking about Child Guidance

During the 20th century, ideas about children were influenced by two world wars, alternating periods of economic depression and prosperity, and by growing scientific interest in child development research. At the end of World War II, Maria Montessori wrote such books as *Peace and Education* (1971) and *Reconstruction in Education* (1968) to express her view that the hope for world peace lay in a new education for young children. Montessori (1971) wrote,

> Certainly we cannot achieve [peace] by attempting to unite all these people who are so different, but it can be achieved if we begin with the child. When the child

■ The early 1900s brought changes in people's beliefs about childhood and their expectations for children.

is born he has no special language, he has no special religion, he has not any national or racial prejudice. It is men [*sic*] who have acquired all these things. (p. 6)

In the late 1940s and into the 1950s, researchers began to unlock some of the mysteries of early learning. The common belief that experiences of the first years of life were inconsequential to later development was pushed aside by more complex theories explaining the development of intelligence and personality. These new theories placed greater emphasis on early social interaction and exploration of the physical environment (Erikson, 1963; Harlow & Zimmerman, 1959; Piaget, 1952, 1962, 1963, 1968, 1970; Skinner, 1953; Wolff, 1963). In the 1960s, research into the learning processes of children from birth to school age flourished, and an estimated 23 million books on child rearing were sold during the mid-1970s (Clarke-Stewart, 1978). Since the 1970s, there has been a mushrooming of parental as well as scientific interest in the processes of child growth and development (Elkind, 1997; Petersen, 1996).

Alfred Adler

Alfred Adler (1870–1937) developed a social constructivist view of human behavior based on value-oriented psychology. He believed human beings were capable of working cooperatively, living together peacefully, striving for self-improvement and self-fulfillment, and contributing to the common welfare of the community. He believed that people were not passive victims of heredity or environment but actively constructed their beings through their social interactions, experiences, and developing perceptions of the world. He saw human beings as constantly striving to compensate for their feelings of inferiority.

Adler's ideas are similar to those of Abraham Maslow, who envisioned individuals as striving toward self-actualization, toward the full realization of their potential (Maslow, 1970). Adler, like Sigmund Freud, believed that a person's personality was largely developed in the first five years of life. Adler's concepts for the guidance of young children include the following:

- Mutual respect is based on a belief that equality is the inalienable right of all human beings.
- Reward and punishment are outdated and less effective than logical consequences.
- Acting instead of talking in heated conflict situations avoids arguments and resolves problems quicker.
- It is appropriate to withdraw from provocation but not appropriate to withdraw emotionally from the child.
- Teaching and training take time and patience.
- Adults should never do for a child what she can do for herself.
- It is critical to recognize and understand a misbehaving child's goal.

Carl Rogers

Carl Rogers's (1902–1987) theory of personality evolved out of his work as a clinical psychologist and his deep respect for the dignity of all human beings. The clinical methods he developed focused specifically on the humane and ethical treatment of

We mark our progress as a civilization by what we see as advances in hardware, and that criterion, assumed so readily by the population at large, blinds us to other possible values such as community, reverence, wisdom, the care and education of children, and the condition of the natural world.

I would wish to be a member of a community that judged itself on the happiness of its children rather than on the unhindered flow of its mechanical inventions.

Thomas Moore (1994)

Over the years, educators, philosophers, and scientists have profoundly altered their views on child guidance.

persons. He believed that human beings have an underlying "actualizing tendency" that motivates them to achieve their potential.

The idea of self is central to his theory. He believed that the self is constructed through interactions with others. A child's self-concept is strongly influenced by the perceptions of those around her. Thus, valuing a child and treating her with dignity and respect would help her construct a strong, positive self-concept. Disrespectful, humiliating, and dehumanizing treatment would damage the child's development of self-esteem. Rogers argued that, to reach their full potential, human beings must have positive regard from others that eventually leads to the development of positive self-regard.

Rogers's focus on psychological therapy differentiates him from Maslow, although their ideas are similar. Although his person-centered approach was developed for use in therapy, it has been adopted by educators to manage conflict resolution.

Robert R. Carkhuff

Robert Carkhuff took the abstract theories of Carl Rogers and developed a systematic set of guidelines for effective interpersonal skills. The impact of his work has been dramatic. Numerous existing programs teaching appropriate interpersonal skills have been derived from this original source.

George Michael Gazda

George Gazda (1931–) took the work of Carkhuff and modified it further to create an effective system for solving classroom management problems and motivating children to change their inappropriate behaviors. His work focuses on effective strategies for perceiving and responding, ineffective communication styles, nonverbal behaviors, confrontation, and anger. Gazda defined strategies for teachers that correct behavior problems while strengthening children's self-concept and self-esteem.

Urie Bronfenbrenner

Urie Bronfenbrenner (1917–) worried that the unpredictability and instability of modern family life was undermining the well-being of our children. He theorized that modern society had allowed its economy to create forces that were especially destructive to children's development. Bronfenbrenner developed a bioecological model to explain expanding worries about school failure and behavioral, social, and emotional problems in children.

According to Bronfenbrenner's bioecological theory, when relationships in the immediate family break down, children fail to develop the tools they need to thrive as they grow up and move out into other parts of the community—school, religious groups, social organizations, and eventually work. Bronfenbrenner argued that technology has changed our society, but we have not responded to compensate for the negative effect of the work world on our families (Henderson, 1995).

Bronfenbrenner pointed out that, to develop well, young children need constant, stable, reciprocal interaction with attentive and caring adults. Children who don't get this kind of high-quality care eventually look for attention in inappropriate places. Children's deficiencies show up in adolescence as antisocial behavior, lack of self-discipline, rebelliousness, and lack of initiative.

To help solve some of the problems he identified, Bronfenbrenner cofounded Head Start. At the beginning, Bronfenbrenner convinced the other cofounders that Head Start would be most effective if it involved not just the child but the family and community. Parent and community involvement were unheard of at the time, but that became a cornerstone of Head Start and proved to be critical to its success. We know now that developmentally appropriate practice must include parent involvement (Addison, 1992; Bronfenbrenner, 1990).

Jean Piaget

Jean Piaget (1896–1980) studied the development of intelligence in children and proposed a theory based on four predetermined stages of mental growth. His studies have had a major impact on the fields of psychology and education. Piaget spent much of his professional life listening to children, watching children, and studying research reports from other cognitive psychologists. He concluded that children's learning was progressively constructed by the children themselves through their interaction with their environment. He believed that children's logic for thinking and problem solving was initially very different from the logic they would use later as they grew stage by stage toward adulthood. Children simply don't think like adults.

Piaget believed that children are little scientists who constantly create and test their own theories of the world. Children are not empty vessels to be filled with knowledge (as had been believed) but active builders of their own knowledge. Like John Dewey and Maria Montessori, Piaget took child learning very seriously. Montessori and Dewey set out to reform education, but Piaget tried only to understand and explain how children think and learn. Piaget, nonetheless, has had a profound effect on education throughout the world.

Lev Vygotsky

Lev Vygotsky (1896–1934) is remembered primarily for identifying what he called the "zone of proximal educational development" (sometimes referred to as the ZPD, ZoPED, or simply "the Zone"). He believed that children develop by exposure to skills, words, concepts, and tasks that are a little beyond their ability but within a "zone" of possible achievement. He believed that adults played an important coaching role in helping the child grasp this new knowledge or ability during these teachable moments.

Vygotsky believed that children developed primarily from their interactions with adults but also from those with other children. This is a collectivist view of psychological growth, as opposed to the individualism of behaviorism and predetermined growth stages of Piaget. Vygotsky believed that child learning was inseparable from human history and culture. He believed that psychological development was the process of children learning how to use the ideas and tools developed by people throughout history such as language, number concepts, music, art, and so forth. He emphasized that language was the most important of the cognitive tools passed down through the centuries. Without language, children cannot fully develop self-awareness. Without self-awareness, children cannot think about, evaluate, anticipate, and control their behavior. Words become the framework through which we think, perceive, experience, and act (Berk & Winsler, 1995).

Vygotsky believed the overarching goal of education was to generate and lead development. He believed that development occurred through the processes of social learning, social interactions, and the internalization of culture. Vygotsky emphasized the critical importance of prior knowledge for making sense of new experiences and situations. Everything has to be taught in context of what the child already knows. The child's culture, family background, and current skill level determine her curriculum (Feden & Vogel, 1993).

Vygotsky believed that language skills were critical for children to create meaning and link new information to past experiences and prior knowledge. He believed that a child's internalized learning became a psychological tool the child could use to gain control of her behavior and thinking. One of the most important tools the child could gain was the development of speech. Speech connected the child socially and culturally to others and dramatically increased her ability to share ideas and absorb culture (Hamilton & Ghatala, 1994).

Friedrich Froebel

Friedrich Froebel (1782–1852) transformed our thinking about early childhood education. Froebel realized that play was the engine that naturally drove learning in young children. He set about finding ways to guide children's natural desire to play and to help them find additional meaning in their play. He created learning materials for children he called "gifts"—small balls, rods and rings, wooden building blocks, rectangular tiles, and such. He invented games for children to play using these objects that would help them discover new concepts (Froebel, 1907).

Stimulating children's learning through interaction with these play objects was the focal point of Froebel's innovative demonstration kindergarten. His intention was for the materials to engage the child's intellect, creativity, and natural spirit of playfulness. Soon educators around the world took note of Froebel's gifts, or *Gaben*, as he called them. His idea was a huge success (Corbett, 1988).

Today we would expect any developmentally appropriate early childhood program to have wooden building blocks as essential classroom learning materials. Certainly there are other early childhood learning materials we use today that have evolved directly or indirectly from Froebel's original gifts.

John Dewey

John Dewey's (1859–1952) approach to education relied on learning by doing rather than learning through rigid lecture-based lessons, tedious memorization, and recitation of memorized material, which were all standard practices of that period.

Dewey's significance for educators lies in several key areas. His innovative exploration of thinking and reflection inspired continuing development and research by others such as Carl Rogers. Dewey's belief that education must engage with and expand experience to be meaningful has had a powerful effect on today's views of education.

Additionally, he raised awareness and concern for the development of learning environments in which students were able to actively interact with learning materials and find a concrete framework for continued practice of learning concepts. And most importantly, his passionate belief in democracy propelled him to advocate for schools that developed good citizens so that democracy could thrive (Caspary, 2000).

The Child in Society

Children occupy a very special niche in our society (Cowan & Cowan, 1992; Gutek, 1997; Hoffman & Manis, 1979). They are dressed in fancy clothing, photographed, given many colorful objects made especially for children (toys), fed special foods from tiny glass jars, and equipped with elaborate contraptions designed for sitting, swinging, strolling, eating, and crawling. Compared with previous cultures, children today are pampered and indulged. A bright-eyed baby decked out in several yards of lace, scented leak-proof disposable diapers, and a huge bonnet will bring oohs and ahhs from shoppers in a supermarket and comments such as, "Oh, isn't it adorable! Look at its little shoes and its tiny earrings!"

The practice of referring to infants (and sometimes toddlers) with impersonal pronouns such as *it* tells us a lot about our perception of babies. The use of such descriptors as "it" and "thing" in reference to children gives a subtle indication that babies are not perceived as real persons. Several centuries ago, impersonal references to children were even more pervasive than they are today. Children were commonly referred to as "it" well into early childhood: "In this age [birth to seven years] it cannot talk well or form its words perfectly, for its teeth are not yet well arranged or firmly implanted" (*Le Grand Proprietaire,* cited in Aries, 1962, p. 21). At the present time, despite remnants of belief

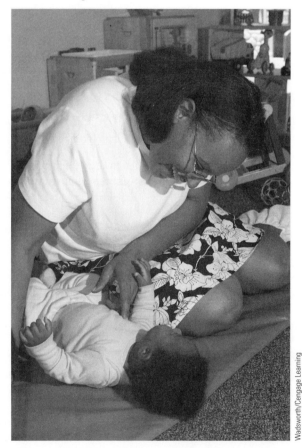

Wadsworth/Cengage Learning

▬ A contemporary newborn is almost always considered to be a "he" or "she" rather than an "it." Parents often have known the baby's gender and have decided on a name well before birth. Unfortunately, people sometimes forget to treat the infant as a real human being, with a full range of human rights and needs.

that infants are somewhat less than fully human, we place a great deal more emphasis on the value and importance of individual children's lives than we did in the past.

Parents may refer to a fetus as an "it" before the child's birth, but parents almost never refer to their baby as "it" afterward, especially after they have come to know and love the child. Strangers are always more likely to refer impersonally to a baby or child. For example, a newspaper account of an alleged brutal child abuse murder quoted a district attorney explaining to shocked citizens why the murder victim, a two-year-old boy, had been given back to his natural mother after having been removed since early infancy for neglect: "Most reasonable people . . . might say the decision to put it [the child] back was probably a bad call. . . ." (Krupinski & Weikel, 1986). When asked about the use of impersonal references for babies, people often explain that "it" is used because the baby's sex may not be known. Interestingly, in discussing older children and adults, even if that person's gender is not known, it would be considered highly inappropriate to refer to that person (a salesperson, a mail carrier, or an acquaintance's teenager) as an "it." Only after a person dies is that person's body referred to as an "it."

How Life Is Different for Contemporary Children in Today's Changing World

Children today are not only valued but also usually thought to have a fairly carefree existence, in contrast to earlier generations' use of child labor. In past years, young children have generally been allowed to spend a good portion of their days playing, fooling around, romping in the sunshine, and generally finding their own occupations (sometimes in front of a television set). Child care has brought new levels of structure to many children's lives. In many early childhood programs, this structure has enriched children's lives and assisted in their development of healthy and productive habits. In other child care settings, children spend a considerable amount of time sitting, waiting, being berated, standing in line, and taking part in activities that are initiated and controlled by adults and are carried out by groups of children in lockstep (Werner, 1987).

Because many affluent parents are having fewer children and waiting until their professional careers are well established before having them, there is new pressure on some children to live up to the "fast lane" expectations of their parents. In the push for superbabies and superior children, many youngsters may be given gymnastics, music lessons, dance lessons, tutoring, and yoga before they ever start kindergarten. Their lives may become so full of enrichment activities that they run out of time to lie in the clover and experience wonder as they watch clouds go by. In an era when parents feel pressured to create a superchild, they may inadvertently destroy some of the wonder and magic of early childhood.

The young child's role in contemporary society sometimes approaches that of a pet or a possession rather than a person deserving respect and dignity. From time to time, that role may mean that the child is indulged, pampered, forgotten, rushed, herded, and pushed (Kantrowitz & Wingert, 1997; Ladd, 1996; Silvers, 1997; Stengel, 1997). She may be expected to be perfect at all times, or be coerced to perform cute

If the only tool you have is a hammer, you tend to treat everything as if it were a nail.

Abraham Maslow (1993)

tricks on cue to entertain or impress adults. Our growing knowledge of and emphasis on early childhood has put youngsters on a pedestal. But, of course, being on a pedestal has distinct disadvantages as well as advantages. Being on a pedestal means that every move one makes is watched, judged, and managed. Early childhood experts have growing concerns that children are not being allowed the freedom to "just be children."

Preparation for Participation in a Democracy

Settings where young children live, work, and play (whether in a home or a child care facility) function as their small version of the world. As has been previously discussed, interaction in familial, educational, and caregiving communities helps children learn how to participate later in adult community life. Child guidance is the process by which adults help children learn appropriate ways to function as part of a group. In an **autocracy,** people would need to learn only blind obedience to function appropriately. A dictator who demands submission dominates people. In an **anarchy,** everyone follows his or her own desires and interests. Chaos prevails because no one governs. In a **democracy,** however, educated, responsible citizens are needed to provide effective self-governance through active participation.

The guidance practices carried out by adults can help children learn how to participate in a democracy by developing the necessary skills.

By playing and learning in a culturally diverse, developmentally appropriate learning environment, children develop citizenship skills, self-reliance, responsible work habits, and ability to cooperate in teamwork.

Wadsworth/Cengage Learning

autocracy
Control by a single person having unlimited power.

anarchy
Absence of any form of control; chaos and disorder.

democracy
The principles of social equality and respect for the individual within a cohesive community.

Critical Skills for Good Citizenship

- **Concept of citizenship**—being cooperative, having a sense of fair play, and respecting the rights of others
- **Initiative and self-reliance**—being a self-starter, a lifelong learner, and a creative problem solver
- **Appropriate work habits**—having established patterns of accomplishing tasks, taking pride in the accomplishments, and accepting responsibility for the results
- **Ability to cooperate in teamwork**—willingness to put aside one's immediate interests for the good of the team

How Early Influences Affect Children and Their Learning Appropriate Behavior

Researchers only recently, during the 1970s and 1980s, began studying how various approaches in early childhood programs affect children's development of characteristics, attitudes, and values. However, some educators have been focusing on personal development and citizenship as a part of early learning and guidance for more than 100 years. John Dewey wrote dozens of books describing his theories of learning as a part of daily living. His world-famous school, which included preschool and kindergarten and opened in 1894, was specifically designed to foster the characteristics that are essential for living in a democracy (Dewey, 1966).

It is essential for those parents, caregivers, and teachers who supervise young children to recognize that guidance is not just a process for getting children to behave appropriately today, but rather a process for helping children learn to live happy, productive lives. Guidance strategies cannot be judged only on the merits of how expedient they are at the moment; judgment must also consider how effective they are in instilling functional living skills that relate to the real world.

Disciplinary tactics are aimed at controlling children's behaviors, often by the use of punishment. Guidance procedures are focused on the development of children's self-control and self-discipline. They rely on authentic experiences, logical consequences, and intrinsic rewards. Positive guidance is not a bag of tricks for coaxing or coercing children to do what we want them to do.

In a democracy, people have rights. If I break a law by driving faster than the speed limit, I still have rights. A police officer is authorized to use only as much force as is appropriate and necessary to stop me. She is forbidden to hurt me, harass me, or humiliate me as a punishment or to get back at me for what I did. In fact, many police officers patiently persist with recalcitrant lawbreakers by politely but firmly insisting, "I know you don't like being pulled over, sir, but you were exceeding the speed limit. May I see your license?"

If officers of the law behaved the way some adults do in handling misbehaving children, we would be shocked. Imagine an officer yanking a driver out of the car, angrily shaking the driver while yelling at her, and snapping, "If you ever do this again, I'll use a paddle on you and you won't be able to sit down for a week!" We would probably feel very angry and misused. Children feel that same way too. It takes time and practice for children to grasp rules, but they can learn to be good citizens by the same technique that our judicial system is supposed to use: persistent and consistent guidance that is as firm as necessary but as respectful as possible.

The Strain of Changing Disciplinary Traditions

Changing one's methods of dealing with misbehaving children is not easy. During our own childhoods, we absorbed a great deal of unconscious information about how adults and children are expected to interact. It is as if we had mental videotapes of disciplinary interactions stored unconsciously but ready for instant replay at any time. Without thinking, we sometimes hear the voices of our parents and teachers as we scold the young children in our care. However, the disciplinary methods that were appropriate and functional generations ago may be inappropriate and nonfunctional in preparing today's children for life in the next century (deMelendez & Ostertag, 1997; Hildebrand et al., 1996; Thorne, 1997).

The world is changing at an astonishing rate. As it changes, children need different kinds of experiences to prepare them for the future. A hundred years ago,

Beliefs are altered primarily by experience, learning over a long period of time, and confidence in the authority of someone considered more knowledgeable.

Costley and Todd (1987)

children were not expected to prepare for a techno-logical world where adaptability and flexibility were more valued than adherence to set routines. Minorities and women were not expected to prepare for the likelihood that they would be competing ambitiously in the business world. And women were not expected to prepare for the distinct possibility that they would, at some time or other, function as head of household and sole breadwinner.

Once we recognize the necessity for updating strategies for guiding and teaching children, it can be difficult to change our old habits. Unfortunately, we adults experience confusion and stress when the methods for dealing with children that intellectually begin to seem logical and right do not match the methods we experienced and lived in our own childhoods. Beliefs cannot be turned on and off like a light switch. Instead, they must be studied and practiced for years.

Human beings, adults and children alike, are influenced by life experiences. But as human beings, we also have the ability to make choices, to take control of our lives, and even to make unexpected changes in our life journey. We are not merely leaves floating in the stream of life. Instead, we are fish, strongly influenced by currents and tides but free to swim upstream if we have the strength and motivation. We can choose to break old habits and establish new ones, but it is not easy. It requires stamina, determination, and a great deal of persistent practice over time.

One hundred years ago, a strong back and a willing attitude were generally considered to be all one needed to make a living. Today, success requires a very complicated set of skills and attitudes.

Philosophies of Guidance

Culture plays an important role in shaping parents', teachers', and caregivers' philosophies about children and child rearing. A person's philosophy affects her perception of children, how they learn, what their intentions are, and why they behave as they do. Ideas about child guidance that immediately seem logical and appropriate or sound ridiculous have been filtered by the set of beliefs and assumptions that make up one's philosophy.

Although parents, teachers, or caregivers may think that they have no particular philosophy, it is likely that they simply have never really analyzed how their beliefs compare with those held by others. Some people may mistakenly assume that everyone in the world naturally shares their underlying beliefs about how things should be and why they are as they are. The process of acquiring appropriate behavior is a learning process just as surely as the process of learning to read and write is. It is, therefore, essential for us to explore various philosophies related to how and why learning takes place.

Training and experience are not the only factors that shape our views on child guidance. Our cultural values profoundly influence our perceptions about what guidance practices are most appropriate for children.

Is a Child's Personality Mostly the Result of Nature or Nurture?

One of the oldest debates related to children is the old nature versus nurture controversy. People who believe that *nature* has the stronger effect believe that children become whatever they become owing to heredity, inborn traits, and inner motivation. People who believe that *nurture* has more effect believe that children become whatever they become owing to parental guidance, teaching effectiveness, television, and other external influences (Cohen, 1999; French, 2003; Kagan, 2004).

Whenever adults compare children, they can hardly resist venturing opinions about how children grow to be so different. Some will say, "Jennifer was born to be a little terror! She's just like her dad, never still for a minute," or "Rahul will undoubtedly be a talented musician. He has inherited musical ability from both sides of his family." These people emphasize the importance of children's internal nature in their development. They believe that children are predestined at birth to certain talents and personality traits because of genetic inheritance or inborn characteristics.

Others disagree. They say things such as "Of course Ming Li has become potty trained so early. Her child care teachers have trained hundreds of toddlers. They know how to do it." Or they say, "If that was my child, he wouldn't be whining and sucking his thumb. His parents must be overindulgent or he wouldn't behave that way." These people emphasize the importance of external nurturing in the development of children. They believe that children are all born pretty much the same, and their differences evolve because of differences in their treatment and teaching.

In past decades, cultural perceptions dictated that personality and potential were inborn. Some people even worried that an adopted child could carry a "bad seed." Human nature is such that we as parents or caregivers are often tempted to take credit for a child's accomplishments and exemplary behavior but blame failures and unacceptable behaviors on inborn traits of the child or on a conscious choice to be bad.

As research into human learning has mushroomed over recent years, a dawning awareness has blossomed in parents and caregivers of the role of environment (everything and everyone the child encounters) in child development. The pendulum has swung to the extreme opposite direction from blaming fate for child behaviors to attempting to manipulate them artificially, speeding the process of development and even attempting to create "better" babies.

In the early 1980s, a culturally popular trend began that has been referred to as the "superbaby" phenomenon. Many parents had only one or two children well after both parents' careers were established, and they began to place more and more emphasis on the optimal development of the child or children they had. People bought or made flashcards with abstract number concepts, names of famous composers, and anatomy terms to use in stimulating their infants. Some parents began to fear that their toddler would be left behind if she had not been enrolled in baby gymnastics, French tutoring, and violin lessons by the age of two. Guilt became a national pastime for trend-setting parents. Perhaps the pendulum will settle to a middle ground where popular culture encourages adults to recognize and appreciate the uniqueness of every individual child and her natural rate of development, and to take seriously the critically important role of play experiences and social interactions for the child's development to her fullest potential. As a society, we have not yet found that middle ground.

For example, cognitive stimulation is to psychic development much like food is to physical development. If enough food is not available, development will be stunted. However, forcing as much food as possible on a child is probably equally destructive. Making appropriate quantities of developmentally appropriate foods (or learning experiences) available while respecting the child's hunger (or readiness for learning) makes a great deal of sense (Elkind, 1997).

What Do Researchers Say about the Origin of Intelligence and Personality?

Lately, educators have been placing more emphasis on the range of philosophies that underlie various theoretical explanations of the origin of human intelligence and personality. These experts trace the ancient nature versus nurture controversy and add a new interactionist point of view that assumes a reciprocal relationship between nature and nurture.

The Nature versus Nurture Controversy

If human thinking could be neatly separated into simple categories, we would find three primary positions.

1. The **behaviorists** believe that behavior and learning result from external forces such as reinforcement; they focus on external strategies for managing (sometimes controlling) children's behavior.
2. The **maturationists** believe that behavior and learning hinge on internal processes such as maturation and motivation; they focus on nonintrusive ways to support children's naturally developing self-control.
3. The **developmental interactionists** (also called constructivists) believe that behavior and learning result from the interactions between internal development and external environment; they study child development, observe the child, and prepare a developmentally appropriate environment. They positively and proactively guide the child's inner development of self-control and respect for others.

behaviorists
Those holding the view that the environment is the primary determinant of human behavior and that objectively observable behavior constitutes the essential psychological makeup of a human being.

maturationists
Those holding the view that internal predisposition, physiological characteristics, or inherited traits account for the essential psychological makeup of a human being.

developmental interactionists
Those holding the Piagetian view that, rather than only passively absorbing information or emerging into a predestined form, a human being's essential psychological makeup derives from a dynamic interactive process that includes both innate cognitive structures and external experiences.

According to the developmental interactionist (or constructivist) point of view, nature lays the groundwork for a child's potential, but nurturing makes it possible for the child to achieve that potential.

tokens
Objects (for example, stars, points, stickers) given to children for performing specified behaviors that are then exchanged at prearranged times for their choice of activities or items from a menu of rewards (for example, toys, special food treats, field trips).

modify
The process of bringing about a change. In behavior modification, modifying is the process of changing a specific behavior through external reinforcement of some kind.

The Behaviorist Approach

The behaviorists incorporate the 17th-century tradition of John Locke, who viewed the newborn's mind as a tabula rasa, or empty slate. These theorists—the behaviorists, positivists, and empiricists—believe that human learning comes from outside the learner. They believe that environment accounts for nearly all that a person becomes.

Watson (1930), Skinner (1953, 1974), and others have theorized that human beings are really products of their environments. People become scholars or cat burglars, not because of their genetic makeup or by choice, but because their environment has conditioned them to behave as they do. Subscription to this view has powerful implications for parents and educators. It implies that human beings can be molded or shaped by controlling environmental experiences. This view also shifts emphasis away from focus on human will and predisposition.

Behaviorists view the development of appropriate behavior as the responsibility of the adult. The adult is responsible for identifying and selecting specific behavior goals for the child. Then the adult observes the child and monitors spontaneous behaviors that are slightly closer to the desired goal behavior, reinforcing each subsequent step closer to the desired goal by giving praise, treats, or **tokens.** The adult maneuvers the child's surroundings to **modify** (or change) specific behaviors in the child.

Behaviorists leave nothing to chance. They choose goal behaviors, select reinforcers, and even plan a reinforcement schedule of when, how often, and under exactly what circumstances reinforcers will be given. Behaviorist views are all focused on the idea that learning is an external process and that learning takes place in a child as a result of influences from the child's environment. Child guidance is seen as an adult-directed process.

The Maturationist Approach

From a point of view opposite to that of the behaviorists, the maturationists borrow from the tradition of Plato. These maturationists, innatists, and nativists believe that learning emerges from within. These educators and philosophers have theorized that human beings are born to be whatever they become; the human infant in this conception is like the rosebud, naturally unfolding into a preordained blossom as long as it is kept healthy. Well into the 1920s and 1930s, Arnold Gesell, a researcher at Yale, maintained that children's external environment did not control developmental outcomes. He claimed that children's own genetic and biological characteristics determined their intelligence and personality (Gesell et al., 1940).

The maturationists view the development of appropriate behavior as a natural process. They believe that as long as basic needs are met, the child will automatically develop the social skills, intelligence, and physical control necessary to behave properly. They see the role of the adult as that of a facilitator. The adult studies children, carefully observing and monitoring their behaviors and abilities. When there is a problem, the adult steps in to help the child understand what has happened in a specific situation and help the child resolve the problem as independently as possible.

Maturationists perceive that learning comes from inside the child. They believe that the processes of learning cannot be rushed. Adults view themselves as role models, guides, and consultants. They believe children are ultimately responsible for their behavior. Personality and growth traits inherited genetically and the child's own willpower play an important role in the maturationists' views on how children learn to behave appropriately. Maturationists see the development of proper behavior as a child-directed process.

Obviously, this type of perception has broad implications for parents and educators concerned with guiding children. If early experiences are relatively inconsequential to later development, then adults need be concerned only with providing the basic necessities for safety and health—custodial care—in the earliest years. This view implies that growth and learning proceed according to internal rules of physiological growth and as a result of personal decision making, not specific environmental circumstances.

The Developmental Interactionist or Constructivist Approach

Debate over the previous two contrasting views of human learning (the nature versus nurture controversy) has been complicated by a growing body of research compiled toward the end of the 20th century by the developmental interactionists, who believe that human learning results from the interaction between the learner and her environment.

Much research has made it clear that environmental factors influence human development (Berk, 1997; Gutek, 1997; Leong & Bodrova, 1996; Seefeldt & Barbour, 1998; Spafford et al., 1998; Piaget 1952, 1962, 1963, 1970, 1983; Chomsky, 1965; Kohlberg & DeVries, 1987; Hunt, 1976; Bloom, 1964; Kagan & Moss, 1962; Kagan, 1971; Kagan et al., 1978; White, 1975, 1995; White & Watts, 1973; White et al., 1979; Vardin, 2003; Csikszentmihalyi, 1996). But the research also supports the importance of individual readiness, personal learning styles, and reciprocal interaction as a part of the process. These factors have gained scientific credibility and are now recognized as part of neither a maturational nor a behaviorist view of learning. Piaget (1952), for example, termed himself a constructionist or cognitive interactionist (developmental interactionist). He asserted that infants are born with predispositions to certain kinds of thought and behavior but that they must create their own knowledge through stages of interaction with the environment. *Play* is the concept we use to refer to this early exploratory interaction with the environment.

Vygotsky's sociocultural theory of development states that children learn through social interactions by means of their culture. This approach is much different from Piaget's theory that children act on their environment to learn. Vygotsky

According to the developmental interactionists (or constructivist) point of view, children create their own learning; we are only their guides.

ethologists
Scientists who study the behavior of animals living under normal conditions. Ethology is the scientific study of animal behavior. (Ethnology is the study of the characteristics of cultures.)

asserted that children socially interact through what he called "dialogues," and through these dialogues they learn the cultural values of their society. Vygotsky also believed that all human activities occur in cultural settings and cannot be understood apart from the culture (Woolfolk, 2004).

White (1975) said that newborn children come into the world with an internal structure that sets an upper limit to their potential, but that the internal structure is not a guarantee of any level of development or learning. The child is programmed to learn, but without stimulation and reinforcement from the environment, no learning can take place (Petersen, 1996). This way of thinking about young children creates pressure on parents and child care providers to produce high-quality early experiences so that optimal experiences can be made available. Chugani (1993) has further emphasized the importance of early environments by showing that a baby's brain uses information from sensory experiences to design its own architecture. A kind of mapping takes place inside the brain with astounding rapidity as the number of synapses (or connections) among brain cells multiplies by the trillions in a very few months.

Lorenz (1966), Hess (1972), von Frisch (1974), and Lamb (1978, 1981) are **ethologists** (researchers who study behaviors in terms of natural processes and in natural settings). They have refined the idea of sensitive periods for learning in which environmental stimuli can have a maximum impact on a child's learning. Hunt (1976) described what he called the "match." He said that a match must be created between a child's level of readiness and the exact level of difficulty or discrepancy in a specific learning situation before optimal learning can take place.

If interactions in the environment are too difficult, children become frustrated and discouraged. If they are too easy, children become bored. Children actively seek out materials and activities that match their level. They enjoy and learn well from an environment that offers a fairly wide range of difficulty and in which they are allowed the freedom to choose toys, games, and interactions matched to their ability level, as well as the freedom to reject materials or activities that seem too easy or too difficult.

In terms of child guidance, the interactionists (constructionists) believe that children can learn to behave appropriately only when they have inner maturity as well as suitable external influences. Adults must study children and plan carefully, but they must also focus on the child's own interests and abilities. A few areas of child guidance seem more responsive to external behaviorist control or internal maturationist development. Mindless habits a child really wants to change can probably be treated quickly and effectively through behaviorist strategies. Long-standing problems that seem to have deeply rooted emotional causes are sometimes best treated with maturationist support of the natural processes of development.

Vygotsky stressed the importance of looking at each child as an individual who learns in a unique way and at a unique pace. To follow his teachings, we analyze what we know about child development in the context of day-to-day observations of the children in our care and strive to match the right activities and materials to the emerging abilities that we identify in each child.

The interactionist approach integrates the processes for inner and outer development. Interactionists see child guidance as not an adult-directed or a child-directed process but rather an interaction in which either can lead or follow. It is like a waltz with give and take, leading and following. The adult respects the child's interests and abilities but is also not afraid to take control when necessary. The child feels free to express herself but also knows and respects clearly defined limits. The interactionist approach provides the most broadly useful teaching and learning approach for use in developmentally appropriate programs.

How Do I Know Which Philosophy Is Right?

Within any group of people who care for and teach young children, there will be many successful and effective adults who tend to lean a bit toward either a more maturationist or a more behaviorist view of early growth and development. Generally, however, a predominant view in the field of early childhood education revolves around the belief that early development results from the interaction between children's inner capacity and motivation and their external environment.

Two basic assumptions fundamental to the procedures throughout this book are the following:

1. Babies and children develop skills and concepts by interacting (playing and living) in a stimulating and supportive environment.
2. The way children interact in their environment is triggered by their particular stage of development as well as their own interests and motives.

In other words, one might say that healthy, well-developed children come into the world preprogrammed to learn (Chomsky, 1965). They will automatically be motivated to explore the physical properties of the environment around them by using their senses, they will seek human social contact, and they will quickly absorb any language they hear. If these components of the environment are

Wadsworth/Cengage Learning

■ Babies thrive in a warm and nurturing environment. Babies require a great deal of time and attention to learn and grow to the best of their ability.

Wadsworth/Cengage Learning

Wouldn't it be a better world if children grew up remembering to be kind, neat, health and safety conscious, respectful of the rights of others, and thoughtful in preserving the environment?

marasmus
A disease associated with inadequate or inadequately assimilated nutrition that affects infants and causes a wasting away of the child's body. Also referred to as *failure to thrive syndrome*, this condition can result from prolonged absence of emotional nurturance as well as from malnutrition, and affected infants typically evidence delays in motor and intellectual development.

abundantly available, the interactions that ensue will foster development in a healthy and natural way. Children who come into the world without all five senses intact, with developmental delays, or with impaired motor capabilities need special equipment, extra stimulation, and skilled teaching to reach their full potential for development. Children with disabilities do not usually learn as easily and naturally as their peers.

Tragically, however, even an infant who is perfectly healthy at birth may eventually suffer from a hostile or non-nurturing environment and its effects:

- **marasmus** (failure to thrive syndrome)
- developmental delay
- permanent mental retardation
- death

Any of these effects can afflict potentially normal, healthy children if they are deprived of the essential elements of an appropriate environment with nurturing human contact, a sense of being wanted and accepted, the opportunity to share thoughts and feelings with others, and exposure to interesting things they can explore by seeing, touching, tasting, feeling, smelling, and moving around.

The development of an intelligent, responsible human being is not an automatic internal process that takes place whatever the environmental factors, and it is not an external process of molding a pliable child into a predetermined shape chosen by parents and teachers. It is a lively process of give-and-take in which children explore their boundaries and limits. Sometimes they accommodate adult expectations, and sometimes, quite naturally, they resist.

Children come equipped with individual personalities, likes, dislikes, interests, and motives. The role of the adult is to guide, assertively and respectfully, never forgetting that even the youngest child is truly a person with all the rights belonging to any other human being (even the right to be negative and recalcitrant on occasion). In the developmental interactionist perspective, child guidance is intended to give children feedback about the realities of their world, to allow them choices within reasonable limits, and to help them confront the logical consequences of their own actions.

KEY TERMS

anarchy
autocracy
behaviorists
democracy
developmental interactionists

ethologists
marasmus
maturationists
modify
tokens

POINTS TO REMEMBER

- Parents who depend on help from others in rearing their children want to be assured that their children will receive proper guidance.
- Adults may have difficulty changing old habit patterns in dealing with children, but change is possible with motivation and practice.

- People from different cultural and economic backgrounds often hold starkly contrasting views about the parameters of proper child care.
- Honoring cultural differences involves recognition and respect for the appearances, customs, and beliefs of others.

PRACTICAL APPLICATION

Bringing Home a Baby Bumblebee

In a medium-size neighborhood child care center, a group of preschool-age children cluster around their teacher and sing with her. They snatch invisible bumblebees out of the air and pretend to trap them in their clasped hands as they sing:

"I'm bringing home a baby bumblebee. Won't my mommy be so proud of me? I'm bringing home a baby bumblebee—bzzz bzzz bzzz bzzz. Ouch! [slap] He stung me!"

In another part of town, in a child care center located in a tiny building that is part of a low-income housing project, a group of children sit on chairs around long tables as they enthusiastically sing:

"I'm bringing home a baby bumblebee. Won't my mama be surprised of me? I'm bringing home a baby bumblebee—bzzz bzzz bzzz bzzz. Ouch! [slap] He stung me! I'm squashing up the baby bumblebee. Now there's bumblebee blood all over me. I'm wiping off the blood of the bumblebee. Now there's no more blood all over me."

In still another part of town, in a tastefully decorated private preschool, a third group of children sit cross-legged on the floor in a circle singing happily with their teacher:

"I'm bringing home a baby bumblebee. Won't my daddy be so proud of me? I'm opening up the window carefully, so my bee can fly away free—bzzz bzzz bzzz bzzz. Bye bye, baby bumblebee."

(See Miller, 1989, for more information on differences in linguistic code in toddlers.)

DISCUSSION QUESTIONS

1. How do the words to each of these songs reflect the differences in perspectives and expectations of childhood in these different communities?
2. Do you think that songs and games parents and child care workers use to entertain children pass cultural perceptions from one generation to the next?
3. What are your own cultural perceptions of children? Do you see children as innocent and pure, to be protected from anything violent, scary, or disgusting? Do you see children as regular people who enjoy raucous humor and vicarious aggression? Do you see children as "born sinners" who sometimes can have evil or cruel impulses?
4. Compare versions of songs and stories you have heard. Do the different versions reflect cultural experiences of children?
5. Why do you think the third teacher in the example replaced the word *mommy* or *mama* with the word *daddy?*
6. Do you think that children growing up in inner-city slums might like different songs and games than other, more sheltered children who have not experienced the discomfort and fear associated with poverty?

7. How are songs and stories purposely used by adults to instill in children an awareness of cultural values?

8. Identify a song or story you would feel uncomfortable using with children. What would you do to change it? Why?

STUDENT ACTIVITY

1. Because the behaviorists believe that behavior and learning result from external forces such as reinforcement, they focus on external strategies for managing children's behavior.
  a. Give an example of an external strategy for managing a child's behavior.
  b. When are external strategies for guidance appropriate?
  c. When are external strategies for guidance inappropriate?
  d. Give examples.

2. Because the maturationists believe that behavior and learning hinge on internal processes such as maturation and motivation, they focus on nonintrusive ways to support children's naturally developing self-control.
  a. Give examples of nonintrusive ways to support guidance.
  b. When is nonintrusive support appropriate for guidance?
  c. When is nonintrusive support inappropriate for guidance?
  d. Give examples.

3. Because the developmental interactionists (constructivists) believe that behavior and learning result from the interactions between internal development and external environment, they study child development, observe the child, and prepare a developmentally appropriate environment. They positively and proactively guide the child's inner development of self-control and respect for others.
  a. Give an example of developmentally appropriate ways to support guidance.
  b. How are developmentally appropriate practice, the developmental interactionist approach, and the authoritative guidance style similar?
  c. How is the application of logical consequences consistent with the philosophy of the developmental interactionists?

RELATED READINGS

Adler, A. (1963). *The problem child: The life style of the difficult child as analyzed in specific cases.* Oakville, Ontario: Capricorn Books.

Adler, A. (1998). *Understanding human nature* (reprint ed.). Center City, MN: Hazelden Information Education.

Ansbacher, H. L., & Ansbacher, R. R., Eds. (1989). *Individual psychology of Alfred Adler: A systematic presentation in selections from his writings.* New York: Harper Collins.

Bruner, J. (1996). *The culture of education.* Cambridge, MA: Harvard University Press.

DeVries, R., & Kohlberg, L. (1987). *Constructivist early education: Overview and comparison with other programs.* Washington, DC: National Association for the Education of Young Children.

DeVries, R., & Zan, B. (1994). *Moral classrooms, moral children: Creating a constructivist atmosphere in early education.* New York: Teachers College Press.

Duckworth, E., Easly, J., Hawkings, D., & Henriques, A. (1990). *Science education: A minds-on approach for the early elementary years.* Hillsdale, NJ: Erlbaum.

Furth, H. G. (1970). *Piaget for teachers.* Engelwood Cliffs, NJ: Prentice Hall.

Gazda, G. M., Asbury, F. R., Balzer, F. J., Childers, W. C., Phelps, R. E., & Walters, R. P., Eds. (1998). *Human relations development: A manual for educators* (6th ed.). Boston, MA: Allyn & Bacon.

Gruber, H. E., & Vonèche, J. (1995). *The essential Piaget.* Northvale, NJ: Aronson.

Krebs, D., & Blackman, R. (1988). *Psychology: A first encounter.* Toronto: Harcourt Brace Jovanovich.

Lourenco, O., & Machado, A. (1996). In defense of Piaget's theory: A reply to 10 common criticisms. *Psychological Review, 103*(1), 143–164.

Mooney, C. G. (2000). *Theories of childhood: An introduction to Dewey, Montessori, Erickson, Piaget and Vygotsky.* Saint Paul, MN: Redleaf Press.

Mosak, H. H., & Maniacci, M. (1999). *A primer of Adlerian psychology: The analytic-behavioral-cognitive psychology of Alfred Adler.* New York: Brunner-Routledge.

Piaget, J. (1985). *Equilibration of cognitive structures.* Chicago: University of Chicago Press.

Piaget, J., & Inhelder, B. (1969). *The psychology of the child.* New York: Basic Books.

Rogers, C. R. (1961). *On becoming a person.* Boston: Houghton Mifflin.

Van der Veer, R., & Valsiner, J. (1991). *Understanding Vygotsky: A quest for synthesis.* Cambridge, MA: Blackwell.

Wertsch, J. V. (1985). *Vygotsky and the social formation of mind.* Cambridge, MA: Harvard University Press.

Wertsch, J. V. (1988). *Vygotsky and the social formation of mind.* Boston, MA: Harvard University Press.

The Online Companion™ to accompany the sixth edition of *Positive Child Guidance* is your link to additional guidance resources on the Internet. This supplement contains audio and visual materials; PowerPoint presentations; web activities with critical-thinking questions and practical-application assignments; and links to web resources. This additional content can be found at http://www.earlychilded.delmar.com.

Chapter 12

Understanding Children with Disabilities

OBJECTIVES

After reading this chapter, you should be able to do the following:

- List characteristic features of a wide range of disabling conditions.
- Recognize behaviors associated with a wide range of disabling conditions.
- Identify strategies for effective guidance of children with disabilities.
- Discuss techniques for effective communication with families of disabled children.
- Describe the laws related to providing care and education for children with disabilities.
- Reflect on your own feelings about and attitudes toward people with disabling conditions.

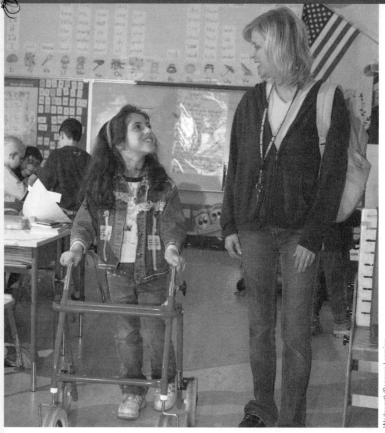

Wadsworth/Cengage Learning

Children with disabilities need, as all children do, care and education that follow developmentally appropriate practice (DAP)—and that, of course, includes positive, assertive guidance.

Why Do We Need to Know about Disabilities?

This chapter considers children with disabilities. To guide these children and their peers effectively, we must understand disabilities for several important reasons:

- to notice a child who may need to be screened by appropriate professionals
- to help the nondisabled children in our care become more sensitive, tolerant, and aware of children with disabilities

- to communicate knowledgeably with the parents of a child with a disability
- to avoid making offensive and embarrassing cultural mistakes related to disabilities
- to be enriched and ready for the opportunity to interact successfully with a wonderful little child who has faced challenges we can only imagine

Adults often find that their ability to cope with a child's behavior improves dramatically when they understand that the child's problems are based on a physical, mental, or emotional problem and are not the child's fault. The child is not simply being out of control, defiant, or stubborn. We should remember, however, that a child might have an undiagnosed disability. Children may have experienced abuse that affected their behavior or something else that we don't know about. We should always give children the benefit of the doubt. There *may be* some reason that they are behaving the way they are.

Do Children with Disabilities Need DAP?

Children with disabilities absolutely need DAP. They need it as much or more than any other children. Here is a summary of some DAP concepts that are especially important:

- a calm, peaceful, and orderly environment with a minimum of distractions
- skill development with age-appropriate, authentic, multisensory activities using real objects
- regular careful planning to meet *individual* children's needs
- individualized interactions that let children learn at their own pace
- sincere cultural respect, with every child intrinsically valued for who she is
- clear, simple instructions
- reasonable expectations
- positive, assertive communication
- support for a healthy lifestyle—stress reduction, good nutrition, and sufficient sleep and exercise
- careful observation and record keeping   *small moments of time*
- consistent follow-up

Does a Different Appearance Affect a Child's Life?

Some disabilities are hidden and can be identified only by a professional medical expert. Many other disabilities are so visible and so obvious that even a baby or toddler immediately recognizes that something is different. Children who live with a different physical appearance face very special obstacles.

Some time ago, I visited my three-year-old granddaughter at her preschool. At the time, my arm was in a cast. As I greeted and hugged my granddaughter, I asked her if she would like to introduce me to her friends. Her bright expression clouded and she said, "Okay, but first I have to go tell them that you are good." Surprised, I said, "Honey, why would your friends think I was bad?" She hung her head and said,

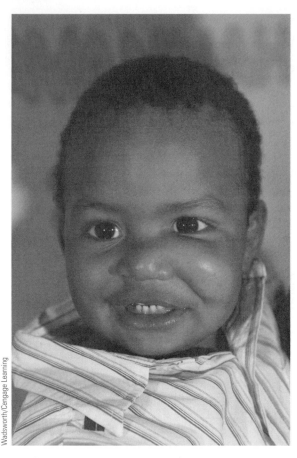

Wadsworth/Cengage Learning

■■■ Children can learn that beauty is in a person's heart. It's okay to look the way you look. Different is just different. Different is not bad.

"You know, 'cause of that." She tapped my cast. I learned something new about child development that day.

After researching the topic, I found that aversion to people who don't fit the familiar or typical image is an inborn survival mechanism. From infancy, our brains are constantly sensing, perceiving, and storing information from the outside world. Simultaneously, these sensations and perceptions are compared with patterns of sensations and perceptions that we have previously stored (Perry et al., 1998). If the new person a child sees doesn't fit the "normal" category she has established, she may react with curiosity, aversion, or disgust, depending on her temperament and life experiences.

Often, as I push my mother in her wheelchair in public places, I make it a point to observe babies, toddlers, and preschoolers stopping to stare at my mom in her chair with wheels. It is especially interesting to see a child in a stroller staring at her, trying to comprehend the connection between her chair with wheels and his chair with wheels. Fortunately, the more often very young children see people in wheelchairs, the more likely they are to include this image into their mental category of normal, acceptable things.

The value of inclusive early childhood programs is not only to challenge children with disabilities by allowing them to live in "real world" environments but also to allow children to grow up knowing that children with disabilities are real people with real feelings who have a lot to offer and who deserve to be treated well.

The role of physical attractiveness in society has been well documented. Studies have shown that attractive individuals have an advantage in employment settings and are more likely to be acquitted of a crime (Efran, 1974). This bias for beauty is also evident for children. Research suggests that unattractive children are generally treated more harshly by adults who do not know them (Berkowitz & Frodi, 1979) and are viewed as less developmentally competent (Ritter et al., 1991). Unattractive children are commonly not preferred as playmates by other children (Langlois & Downs, 1979) and are assumed by their peers and teachers to be more antisocial (Schneiderman & Harding, 1984; Lerner & Lerner, 1977). In addition, teachers expect attractive children to be more intelligent and well behaved than their unattractive peers.

We find that even parents are not immune to prejudice against unattractive babies and children:

Yet the influence of attractiveness is widely believed to not influence parents of children. It is assumed all children are viewed as beautiful by a parent's eye. And the phrase "a face only a mother could love" suggests this is true even for very unattractive children; however, recent studies have demonstrated that even parents are influenced by the attractiveness of their children. (Perry et al., 1998, p. 590)

Every adult who is experienced with young children knows that children are quite transparent in their insensitivity toward out-of-the-ordinary physical appearances such as that of burn victims.

In the less inhibited society of childhood, disapproval of deviant physical features is openly voiced, and in interviews held at outpatient clinics for children with deformities such as cleft lip and facial burns, most of the children were reported to be victims of frequent teasing and harassment (Shaw, 1980, p. 192).

Every day children are bombarded with messages from television, radio, magazines, movies, and elsewhere indicating that it's not okay to be different. To fit in and be popular you have to have white teeth, fresh breath, and glossy hair. Between the lines, the messages say that the heroes are all gorgeous and the villains are ugly, with irregular features and rough, scarred complexions.

The ax murderers in Halloween movies in our society usually have a face scarred by fire. We have to counter this pervasive and damaging cultural message in our society, letting children know that handsome people can harm them and people with damaged faces can be really good friends. The only way to know whether a person is good or bad (in my granddaughter's simple terms) is to find out what is inside them, not what they look like.

How Can I Help the Children in My Class Learn to Treat People with Disabilities with Respect?

Children—human beings—fear what they don't understand. Several years ago I had the good fortune to observe parents taking their young children through an exhibition of lifelike dinosaurs at Houston's Museum of Natural Science. The exhibit was set up to make you feel as if you had stepped into a foggy primeval lagoon at dawn, just as a bunch of massive dinosaurs had gathered to find food and water. You stood about ankle high to these dagger-toothed monsters—the effect was quite dramatic!

As parents brought their young children in, I watched their reactions carefully. The youngest children who didn't understand that the dinosaurs weren't real interested me most. Some cried; some "turned into Velcro" and couldn't be peeled off their parents. But some children immediately became aggressive. The aggressive ones (often little boys, but some girls) marched up to the border around the dinosaurs and planted one foot on the low rail. The child usually menacingly stuck out his fists toward the dinosaurs, making his most daunting growls and snarls. Some spit. Some, who had something in hand, threw what they had at the dinosaur, much to their parents' dismay. They weren't being bad; they were just reacting to their fear by attacking the source of their anxiety.

These are essentially the same reasons that children pick on a child who is different for some reason, such as a disability. Their immature brain tells them this person is not right, is not the way they expect that people are supposed to be. Their natural **fight or flight response** causes them to be prepared to run away or to try to hurt the person in some way.

> The highest result of education is tolerance.
>
> *Helen Keller,* Optimism: An essay, *1903*

fight or flight response The body's reaction to a perceived threat or danger. Our bodies react to threats by releasing hormones such as adrenalin and cortisol into our blood stream, giving us a burst of energy and strength to fight or flee. When the perceived threat is gone, our systems are designed to go back to normal levels by means of a relaxation response. But if a child is subjected to constant stress, relaxation is impaired and damage to physical health as well as sleeping, eating, and social and emotional problems may occur.

We can help children lose their fear of people who are different by replacing it with knowledge and tolerance. We are teachers; we know how to teach. We can take field trips to expose children to people who have differences; we can provide hands-on exploration of disability equipment and we can read disability related books. The Online Companion™ provides titles of hundreds of thought-provoking, sensitive, and reassuring children's books, sorted by disability, age level, and interest level. Never underestimate the power of bibliotherapy.

According to Easter Seals Wisconsin (2008),

Books should . . .

- Promote respect and empathy for individuals with disabilities
- Use a person's first language
- Promote understanding and acceptance
- Depict individuals with disabilities as complete human beings with the same types of strengths and weaknesses as their peers
- Provide accurate information about disabilities
- Focus on similarities between people with disabilities and people without disabilities
- Show people with disabilities taking on diverse and active roles within the community
- Depict inclusive schools, work places and communities
- Depict people with disabilities from different ethnic and racial backgrounds and from a variety of age groups

Avoid books that . . .

- Dwell on what people with disabilities can't do, rather than on what they can
- Depict people with disabilities as victims or only as objects of curiosity or seek to evoke pity
- Depict ordinary actions and achievements as heroic when performed by a person with a disability
- Depict people with disabilities as helpless or always dependent on others to function in the world
- Use unacceptable disability related language
- Depict people with disabilities as passive observers who take no active role in schools or in their communities
- Fail to show people with disabilities participating in activities accurate for their age group

What if the Child Is Not Anxious about the Disability, He Just Likes to Tease and Bully?

In Chapter 9 we discussed mistaken goals that are the root of inappropriate behavior. We learned that one reason children misbehave is to get revenge for perceived hurts. Children who feel they have been picked on, bullied, discriminated against, stigmatized, or looked down on by others probably have had their self-esteem damaged.

Their self-esteem may be at such a low level they feel compelled to pick on, bully, discriminate against, stigmatize, or generally look down on anyone they perceive to be inferior in some way. Dealing with their inappropriate behavior will never succeed until we address the self-esteem shortfall that is triggering the poor behavior. It is sort of like constantly bailing water out of a sinking boat. We need to fix the hole at the bottom of the boat to solve the problem. We need to address the child's self-esteem problem so that he is able to respect himself and learn to respect others.

If the child's self-esteem seems strong, look at other mistaken goals. Does the child have an inordinate need for attention? Is the child rebelling against authority? Go back to Chapter 9 for suggestions on responding to these mistaken goals.

> Never look down on anybody unless you're helping him up.
>
> *Jesse Jackson, "Dream of Things as They Ought to Be," speech delivered to Never Surrender, Young America, 1988*

What Do Children with Disabilities Need?

Children with disabilities have as many unique needs as there are children. Some of those specific needs will be addressed later in this chapter. Following is a summary of essential things we can do to make sure we meet the needs of individual children in our care:

- Provide unconditional acceptance.
- Focus positively on what the child can do.
- Set realistic goals cooperatively with the child, letting her take as much control as possible.
- Support the child and family in dealing with hygiene, assistive devices, and other medical concerns.
- Help the child deal with the emotional ups and downs of her disability.
- Recognize that even children with disabilities sometimes behave inappropriately and need to face consequences.
- Learn to deal honestly and caringly with the child's anger and fear, but set reasonable limits on behavior.
- Pay attention to nonoral as well as oral cues and let the child know you understand and care.
- Remember that children must be treated as much as possible as nondisabled children are, and this, of course, includes guidance.
- Stay in close contact with parents for suggestions on solving tactical how-to problems and for celebrating triumphs.
- Keep a written record of observations and progress.

Children with disabilities sometimes need special **accommodations** to help them interact, learn, and play as normally as possible with their nondisabled peers. But what they need most of all is exemplary DAP and positive guidance.

What Type of Disabilities Am I Most Likely to Encounter?

Behavior disorders are by far the most common reason children are referred to specialists for assessment and expert support. The category of behavior disorders may include the largest number of children who fall under the definition of disabled. Some

accommodations
Special aids for persons with disabilities that give them access to mainstream activities and environments. Accommodations can include such things as a ramp for a wheelchair, a lowered sink, special door handles, signs written in Braille, a sign language translator, or other changes to help the person with disabilities function equitably with nondisabled peers.

researchers suggest that as many as 10 percent of children have behavioral problems significant enough to cause serious problems at school and at home (Briggs-Gowan et al., 2001; Stallard, 1993; Zeanah, 2000; Zeanah et al., 1997).

Parents and teachers agonize especially over the following five categories of disorders, which can play havoc with children's educational success (Doll, 1996):

1. Attention problems
2. Conduct and behavior problems
3. Anxiety problems
4. Affect and mood problems
5. Social and interpersonal problems

How Can I Support Parents of Children with Disabilities?

Families learning that their young child has a disability go through a great deal of shock and pain. All parents need communication and support, but parents of children with disabilities have special needs and special vulnerabilities. Patience, understanding, and encouragement are especially required for these parents.

When parents learn that their child has a serious disability they often experience for months, even years, a rollercoaster ride of overwhelming emotions that may take them through many or most of the feelings described in the list below.

- **Shock or denial.** The parents may deny that there is any disability, or they may become preoccupied with thoughts such as "How can this be happening to me?" "Why is this happening to me?" What did I do to deserve this?"
- **Anger.** The parents may feel anger at themselves for "causing" the disability, or they direct their rage at others (medical personnel, the spouse, the teacher, the school, or God, and some parents may even feel unconscious anger toward the child).
- **Guilt.** Parents almost always go through a period of feeling that there was something they could and should have done to prevent the disability.
- **Rejection.** Some parents describe going through a period of hating the idea of the disability so much that they couldn't stop themselves from withdrawing from the child emotionally for a while, a few even silently wished the child had never been born.

Wadsworth/Cengage Learning

Discovering that one's dearly loved baby or young child has a disability can turn a family's world upside down.

- **Confusion.** Parents almost always feel confusion after diagnosis of a child's disability—opinions come from every direction, experts sometimes seem to give contradictory advice, and quack cures may seem unbearably tempting.
- **Fear.** Parents fear the worst for their disabled children; they wonder what will happen to their children when they die or become too old to care for them.
- **Isolation.** Dealing with a child with a profound disability can cause parents to feel very isolated. Eating out, visiting with friends, having a relaxing vacation, or creating romantic time alone with a spouse becomes so challenging it hardly seems worth it.
- **Envy.** Parents with a severely disabled child may listen to other parents talking about their children's accomplishments and feel envy, resentment, annoyance, and bitterness that is hard to control.
- **Relief.** Parents, especially those who have been struggling for a significant length of time with an undiagnosed disability, often report they are glad to have a name for their child's disorder. They are relieved to know that their child's problems are not imaginary or caused by bad parenting (Owens & Bassity, 2007, p. 26).

Parents may hold an idealized image of their child and resist the notion that their child is imperfect, having both strengths and weaknesses. They may need time to learn that there is no shame in having a special need or an imperfection. There is shame only in not dealing with reality and failing to take appropriate steps to help the child function as well as possible.

Many potentially disabling conditions can be prevented or alleviated if they are identified and treated during infancy or earliest childhood, so early screening for developmental problems has special importance. Resource lists in the appendixes offer many sources of free or inexpensive help for parents, teachers, and caregivers.

How Can I Help the Child with a Disability?

Welcome children with disabilities into your heart. Whether you realize it or not, you have a lot to offer a young child with a disability. Follow the key points below:

- Learn as much as possible about the child's disability.
- Show respect for the child and the family as they struggle to deal with the disability in their own way.
- Avoid being overprotective. Never do anything for the child that he can reasonably do for himself.
- Don't walk on eggshells when guiding the child's behavior. The disabled child needs calm, assertive, caring, positive child guidance as much as any nondisabled child.
- It's good to be optimistic, but have *realistic* expectations in guidance. Recognize limitations.

Individuals with Disabilities Education Act (IDEA)
A law ensuring that eligible infants, toddlers, and children with disabilities receive early intervention and special education and related services. It requires that students be provided a free appropriate public education (FAPE) preparing them for further education, employment, and independent living. Special education must provide the least restrictive environment (LRE), which is the environment most like that of typical children in which the child with a disability can succeed.

free appropriate public education (FAPE)
A directive requiring that school districts provide children with disabilities access to general education as well as specialized educational services to accommodate special needs. It also requires that children with disabilities receive support free of charge, the same as is provided to nondisabled students.

least restrictive environment (LRE)
The requirement in IDEA law that children with disabilities receive their education, to the maximum extent appropriate, with nondisabled peers and that special education pupils not be removed from regular classes unless, even with supplemental aids and services, education in regular classes cannot be achieved satisfactorily.

- Appreciate the uniqueness of each individual child. Never compare children.
- Focus on each child's strengths. Every child has positive characteristics and assets.
- Show unconditional affection to every child. Remember to communicate at eye level, use the child's name, and use appropriate touch to convey to every child how much she is valued.
- Teach all of the children how to celebrate differences, show compassion, and express caring for peers. Prevent bullying and stigmatizing.
- Have a sense of humor. Make sure that the environment is filled with joy.

What Are the Legal Rights of Children with Disabilities?

Parents and educators need to know as much as possible about the legal rights of children with disabilities and the legal responsibilities of educational professionals who work with them. Special education law—the **Individuals with Disabilities Education Act, or IDEA**—requires that students be provided a **free appropriate public education (FAPE)** preparing them for further education, employment, and independent living. Special education must provide the **least restrictive environment (LRE),**

Wadsworth/Cengage Learning

▬ Children with disabilities are to be included in the *least restrictive environment* possible. That means they must be included equally in all of the day-to-day activities with their peers unless their disability makes all or part of that impossible. Early childhood professionals should be very creative in finding ways to make inclusion in all activities possible.

which is the environment most like that of typical children in which the child with a disability can succeed.

Using a program called **Child Find,** state agencies are required to locate, evaluate, and identify children between the ages of 3 and 21 with disabilities. They must find children regardless of the severity of the disability, including children attending private schools and child care centers, highly mobile children such as migrant and homeless children, and children who are suspected of having a disability even though they may be progressing from grade to grade. Disabilities include autism, emotional disorders, hearing impairment and deafness, visual impairment and blindness, intellectual disability, orthopedic impairment, health impairments, specific learning disabilities, speech or language impairment, traumatic brain injury, developmental delay, attention deficit/hyperactivity disorder (ADHD), and oppositional defiance disorder.

Any public school child receiving special education is required to have what is called an **Individualized Education Program (IEP).** Each IEP must be designed individually to meet the specific needs of the student. An IEP requires parents, teachers, other school staff—and often the student—to come together, communicate, share their commitment and expertise, and gather further information about the student's unique needs. Then they collaborate to design a support plan that will help the student be successful in the mainstream curriculum. An effective IEP requires teamwork.

Child Find
A component of IDEA law that requires state agencies to locate, evaluate, and identify children between the ages of 3 and 21, who are in need of early intervention or special education services.

Individualized Education Program (IEP)
A written plan that describes exactly how teachers, parents, school administrators, related services personnel, and the student with a disability will work together to improve the student's educational results.

What Is the IEP Process?

IDEA specifies rules concerning IEPs in public schools, charter schools, and some private schools or child care programs that accept public funding. Although details of the IEP process can vary from one school to another, and from one state to another, and each school may have its own forms, the general process does not change. See Appendix D for a sample form and The Online Companion™ for an explanation of the IEP steps.

What if My Program Isn't Required to Provide an IEP?

Even if a formal IEP is not required, common sense dictates that a plan be put in place. Every special needs child deserves an individualized plan for

■ Planning for success

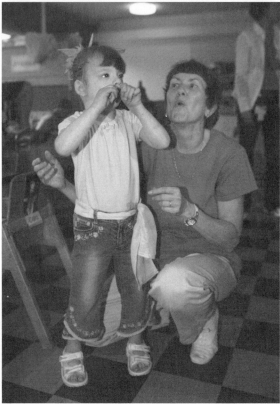

Wadsworth/Cengage Learning

Every early childhood program is ethically and legally responsible to ensure that doors are open to children with disabilities.

success, whether it is legally required or not. In any developmentally appropriate program, there will be a plan in place to bring parents together with teachers or caregivers and any other relevant resources to identify the child's needs, set goals, plan strategies for success, and track progress over time.

These meetings can be very informal in small, intimate programs, or they can be quite formalized and follow virtually every step of the IEP format in a more structured setting. The important thing is the quality and depth of the communication that takes among the parents, the teachers, the child (when appropriate), and resource personnel (a community volunteer, a social worker, the center director, and so on). This communication has the potential to generate creative approaches to troublesome problems, release pent-up emotions, provide warmth and support for all the parties involved, and keep the child's needs foremost in everyone's minds.

What if My Program Doesn't Want to Accept Children with Disabilities?

Some private child care programs and private schools may feel that it is outside their scope to care for children with disabilities. They may be surprised to learn that they can be held legally responsible if they turn away a child because of his or her disability. We are each responsible to ensure that doors are always open for children with disabilities.

For more information about IDEA regulations, contact the Department of Education at 202-205-5465 or 202-205-5507 or visit the department's website at http://www.ed.gov/offices/OSERS/IDEA. You will also find answers to commonly asked questions about the Americans with Disabilities Act and practical information on child care professionals' legal responsibilities at http://www.usdoj.gov/crt/ada/childq&a.htm.

Physical Conditions That Affect Behavior

Because irritability and discomfort are likely causes of misbehavior, any number of physical illnesses or conditions could result in behavior changes. Muscular disabilities could hamper a child's ability to carry out tasks, or developmental delays could make it impossible for a child to perform as expected. Parents, teachers, and caregivers can assist medical personnel in evaluating a child who has difficulty by observing and keeping daily records of behaviors that might indicate problems.

All children behave inappropriately from time to time, no matter how well they seem to be developing and how cooperative, competent, and confident they are generally. Some children, however, behave inappropriately often enough to cause us serious concern. It is essential that we consider the possibility of physical causes for severe, persistent misbehavior. Various cues or signals could be red flags, or warning indicators, that something is awry. Parents, teachers, and caregivers should never attempt to diagnose physical ailments or developmental delays. They should, however, watch carefully for indications that a child needs further evaluation by a physician or other expert to rule out or confirm physiological or psychological problems. (See Appendix B for additional resources.)

In addition to emotional neediness, numerous other illnesses and physiological conditions can cause children to behave unproductively. It is impossible to list every possibility, but some key conditions that affect behavior follow.

See the online resources for more information on the disorders listed here as well as information on a number of other disabling conditions. We are beginning to learn that these problems affect a surprisingly large number of children.

Fetal Alcohol Spectrum Disorders

The umbrella term **fetal alcohol spectrum disorders (FASDs)** covers a cluster of individual **syndromes,** each caused by prenatal alcohol exposure. The FASD group includes fetal alcohol syndrome (FAS), partial fetal alcohol syndrome (PFAS), alcohol-related neurodevelopmental disorder (ARND), alcohol-related birth defects (ARBDs), and fetal alcohol effect (FAE). Children with FAS are the most severely affected among this group of syndromes; those with FAE are the least affected, but they usually have significant behavioral and learning issues (National Task Force on Fetal Alcohol Syndrome and Fetal Alcohol Effect, 2004; Streissguth, 1997; Tanner-Halverson, 1996).

Alcohol use during pregnancy is a leading preventable cause of physical, cognitive, and behavioral problems. According to the National FASD Center for Excellence, 1 in 10 U.S. women drinks alcohol while pregnant and at least 40,000 babies are born each year affected by maternal drinking (Sood et al., 2001; Gmel & Rehm, 2003).

There is no known safe amount of alcohol for a woman who is pregnant (Sood et al., 2001). Sadly, even drinking low (that is, one drink per week) to average quantities of alcohol, particularly during the first three months of pregnancy, increases the risk of

fetal alcohol spectrum disorders (FASDs)
A group of permanent birth defects caused by a mother drinking alcohol during pregnancy.

syndrome
A disease or disorder that has more than one feature or symptom.

Wadsworth/Cengage Learning

 To help your future children reach their maximum potential, never drink if you are pregnant, are trying to get pregnant, or think you might be pregnant.

low birth weight, prematurity, delayed or irregular development, behavior problems, and learning disabilities in a child. Children of heavy drinkers can suffer a wide range of serious and permanent mental, physical, and behavioral disorders (Gunzerath et al., 2004; Jacobson & Jacobson, 1994, 2002; Lasser, 1999; Abel & Sokol, 1987).

Visual Impairment and Blindness

visual impairment and blindness
Inability to see details at near and far distances; defects in the field of vision or visual distortions. No vision and low vision can be caused by several different diseases, conditions, or accidents.

congenital
A condition that is inborn or existing at birth.

acquired
Developed after birth, at some time during life in response to environmental interactions, injuries, or illness.

Childhood **visual impairment and blindness** most commonly occurs before birth but can happen later due to injury or illness. Blind and visually impaired children need intervention as early as possible so they and their families can receive the specialized support necessary to help the child develop independence and confidence in a mainstream environment. Some eye conditions are **congenital** (or present at or near birth), and others are **acquired** later due to a disease, infection, or accident.

In the first few years of life, vision is usually the most effective way for babies and toddlers to take in a wide range of information to support their earliest learning. Babies spend long periods watching and staring. No other sense arouses curiosity and integrates information as efficiently as vision. Thus, infant vision loss has serious consequences. Early vision loss can affect virtually every area of development, including cognitive, social, emotional, communication, self-help, and fine- and gross-motor skills.

A baby who is born blind or severely visually impaired experiences the world differently from typically developing children. The child who is blind or visually impaired is at great risk for developmental delays. Effective, intensive intervention is essential in the early years (American Foundation for the Blind, 1993).

Hearing Impairment and Deafness

Hearing loss is the most common type of sensory disability. About 1 in 1,000 children is born permanently hearing impaired or will develop severe to profound **hearing impairment** before developing verbal communication. About 3 to 5 in 1,000 are born with less severe degrees of hearing impairment (Kumar & Dhanda, 1997).

Research has shown that children whose hearing loss is identified while they are still babies learn language more easily and more completely than those whose hearing loss is identified later. Additionally, congenitally deaf or hard of hearing children are able to develop and learn more effectively if they are identified early in infancy so they can receive appropriate early intervention. Because early detection is key to effective treatment, some states now require hearing tests for infants soon after birth. This may give parents

Wadsworth/Cengage Learning

▬▬ Early childhood professionals must watch children carefully for indications of a vision problem. Sending a child for screening and correcting a vision problem may correct what had been thought to be a behavior problem. The child may not have been interested in puzzles, books, and other manipulatives simply because he couldn't see them very well.

a great advantage in seeking and providing the kind of support that enables children to learn to communicate naturally and avoid severe developmental delay. Even with prompt intervention, however, the effects of deafness on language acquisition and learning can be almost overwhelming to overcome (Snashall, 1985).

Parents need to decide how to communicate with the infant. Communication is pivotal in a child's development, but oral language development hinges on hearing. Learning to communicate effectively in sign language may open a whole world of possibilities for a young child. Early access to specialized therapies and educational resources supports the child's long-term success (Harris, 1998; Harris et al., 1989).

Proprioceptive Dysfunction and Sensory Integration Dysfunction

Working closely with the **tactile sense** and **vestibular function, proprioceptive sensation** tells the brain where one's body is in space. When signals of body position brought in through the muscles, connecting tissue, skin, and joints are not properly conveyed to the brain, a child with **proprioceptive dysfunction** may appear clumsy, have difficulty sitting up without support, and have problems with motor activities (Smyth & Mason, 1998; Shumway-Cook & Woollacott, 1995; Sigmundsson et al., 1999).

Children with proprioceptive dysfunction typically have the following characteristics:

- aversion to or an excessive need for vestibular and sensory stimuli
- difficulty coordinating their body to move a certain way or complete a task
- difficulty sensing how much pressure is needed to complete a task
- difficulty with postural muscles and responses

Sensory integration dysfunction (SID), also called sensory processing disorder, is a disorder characterized by the inability of the brain to correctly process information brought in by the senses. SID is associated with autism, cerebral palsy, ADHD, and other neurological conditions, or it can be present by itself.

Muscular Dystrophy

Muscular dystrophy is a genetic condition that causes increasing weakness in muscle tissue. There are a number of different dystrophies with different names and slightly different causes. The environment will need to be modified to meet the needs of the individual child. A preschooler may enjoy putting a walker or wheelchair aside so he can get down on the floor to crawl (or belly-drag) from shelf to shelf, get work, and drag it to a spot to work with friends on the floor. Ideally, the early childhood staff should meet with the child's therapist or medical expert in the learning environment to find out how best to support him. In the real world, however, that isn't always possible.

---

hearing impairment and deafness
Inability to respond to a normal range of sound frequencies because of an injured eardrum, malformed or damaged inner ear, clogged outer ear, or brain problem. Genetic defects are the most common cause of hearing deficits in newborns, but ear infections are the most common cause of hearing deficits in older children.

tactile sense
Perception through touch that provides input from textures, temperature, and pressure.

vestibular function
The body's balance system, which provides perception of movement and orientation in space. The vestibular function is essential for a person to maintain muscle tone, coordinate both sides of the body, and know the difference between up and down.

proprioceptive sensation
Sensory information taken in through the muscles, connecting tissue, skin, and joints that informs the brain where one's body is in space. Proprioception makes it possible for a person to move body parts without having to observe the movement to make sure it is happening.

proprioceptive dysfunction
Malfunction of input and feedback on body position. This disorder causes the child to appear clumsy, have difficulty sitting up without support, and have problems with motor activities.

sensory integration dysfunction (SID)
A disorder characterized by the inability of the brain to correctly process information brought in by the senses.

muscular dystrophy
A genetic disorder that causes progressive weakness in muscle tissue.

Children with muscular dystrophy typically exhibit the following characteristics:

- lack of muscle tone, abnormal muscle weakness, or difficulty breathing
- severe delay in reaching motor milestones (such as walking and running)
- abnormally enlarged calf muscles
- cataracts, heart problems, eye disorders, and learning problems (in some dystrophies)
- cognitive problems; although most dystrophies do not cause cognitive problems, affected children's distorted facial muscles may mislead people into thinking the children have cognitive problems. Be proactive in pointing out these children's strengths
- back curvature, which may cause pain and breathing and mobility problems
- constipation and slower swallowing
- excessive weight gain as children become full-time wheelchair users
- nutritional defects, caused by inability to take in optimal nutrition

Rehabilitation professionals are important in helping the child with muscular dystrophy develop the best possible quality of life. These professionals include physical therapists, occupational therapists, speech therapists, respiratory therapists, orthotists (brace-makers), social workers, and rehabilitative medical staff. The child's doctor can assist with ordering special equipment, including such things as wheelchairs, seating support systems, braces, and other aids to help the child move freely.

A child with muscular disabilities may need accommodations such as a specially designed chair to assist her in sitting up to access learning materials.

The occupational therapist can make recommendations with regard to school issues and can recommend adaptive equipment to help the child eat, draw, and play. The occupational therapist can make sure the child's health care plan is properly coordinated with specialists from pulmonology, cardiology, orthopedic surgery, ophthalmology, or neurology if needed.

Early childhood professions must rely heavily on input from families, medical professionals, and therapists to care properly for the child with muscular dystrophy.

Cerebral Palsy

Cerebral palsy is a group of disorders that affect a person's ability to move and to maintain balance and posture. The disorders are usually diagnosed very early in the child's life and do not get worse over time. Children with cerebral palsy may have stiff limbs and poor muscle control, causing difficulty with such activities as crawling, walking, rolling over, sitting, writing, and using scissors. Some have medical problems such as **seizure** disorders or intellectual disability. Others have normal or above normal intelligence. Cerebral palsy may be congenital or acquired. There is no cure for cerebral palsy, but treatment usually includes medicines and braces as well as physical, occupational, and speech therapy (Liptak, 2001; Kutscher, 2006; Martin, 2006).

As with muscular dystrophy, therapists and medical professionals will help you determine the accommodations needed to assist the child with cerebral palsy in day-to-day activities in early childhood programs. A seizure response plan should be in place.

Infants with cerebral palsy typically exhibit the following characteristics:

- sluggishness, lack of alertness, irritability, fussiness
- uncharacteristic, high-pitched cry
- trembling of the arms and legs
- difficulty sucking and swallowing
- poor muscle tone
- unusual posture, such as favoring one side of the body
- seizures, staring spells, eye fluttering, body twitching

Children with cerebral palsy may exhibit a few or many of the following characteristics:

- spasms, sudden shudders, or muscle contractions
- problems with muscle tone
- unintentional movement
- problems crawling and walking; awkward, jerky gait
- seizures
- abnormal sensations and perceptions
- visual impairment
- hearing impairment
- speech problems
- intellectual disability

cerebral palsy
A group of disorders that affect a person's ability to move and to maintain balance and posture.

seizure
A sudden disruption of the brain's normal electrical activity accompanied by a change in consciousness or neurological and behavioral symptoms such as breathing problems, a bizarre feeling of déjà vu, changes in muscle tone, and convulsions.

Wadsworth/Cengage Learning

Every child is a valuable human being with something to offer to the world. We must remember to focus on a child's strengths instead of being preoccupied with her areas of weakness.

Teachers who care for children with cerebral palsy should heed the following tips:

- Learn more about cerebral palsy. Parents, community organizations, and the Internet and research resources at the end of this section will help you.
- Be patient and optimistic about improvement. This child, like every other child, has a whole lifetime to learn and grow.
- As with children with muscular dystrophy, a child who lacks facial muscular control may give the impression of cognitive impairment. Assuming this is prejudiced and unfair. Focus on the individual child and learn firsthand what capabilities she has. Emphasize her capabilities to other children and adults.
- Be creative. Ask yourself, "How can I teach a certain concept to this child while maximizing active, hands-on learning with three-dimensional, sensory-rich materials?"
- Find out about different learning styles. Use the approach best suited for each child and based on that child's learning strengths as well as physical abilities (remembering that all young children learn best in hands-on interaction with three-dimensional, sensory materials).
- Learn to use assistive technology. Find experts within and outside your school to help you. Assistive technology can mean the difference between independence for a child or not.
- Always remember that parents are experts when it comes to their child. Listen to them and show them respect. They can tell you a great deal about their child's special needs and abilities.
- Create a cooperative team made up of the teacher, the parents, and the medical and therapeutic professionals with diverse backgrounds and expertise. The team must combine the knowledge of its members to plan, implement, and coordinate the child's services.

Asthma

asthma
Chronic illness of the respiratory system in which the airway occasionally constricts, becomes inflamed, and is lined with excessive amounts of mucus.

Asthma is a chronic illness involving the respiratory system in which the airway occasionally constricts, becomes inflamed, and is lined with excessive amounts of mucus. In children, the most common triggers are viral illnesses such as the common cold. Environmental irritants or allergens; overly cold, warm, or humid air; exertion; or emotional stress may also trigger an asthma episode. Airway narrowing causes wheezing, shortness of breath, chest tightness, and coughing. Between episodes, the child may have no or mild symptoms. The symptoms of asthma, which can range from mild to life threatening, can usually be controlled with a combination of medication and environmental changes (Akinbami, 2006; Faniran et al., 1998; von Mutius, 2000).

Epilepsy

Epilepsy is a condition characterized by persistent seizures that may include brutal muscle jerking episodes called **convulsions.** Epilepsy can cause seizures several times a day or only once every few months. Normally, millions of very small electrical charges pass between our nerve cells, our brain, and throughout our body to control our body's many functions. Epileptic seizures are caused by strong surges of misplaced electrical energy in the brain. This tiny electrical storm in the brain may affect a person's consciousness, bodily movements, or sensations for a short time. Normal brain function cannot return until the electrical bursts subside. Fortunately, many children respond well to epilepsy treatment. Children are usually treated with medications, but surgery is also an option in some extremely severe cases (Appleton et al., 1997; Lynch, 2000; Scherer, 1988). If you care for a child who might have seizures, you must put a seizure response plan in place and make sure that everyone knows how to respond appropriately. Let the other children know, based on their age, an appropriate amount of information so they will be understanding, kind, and caring rather than frightened.

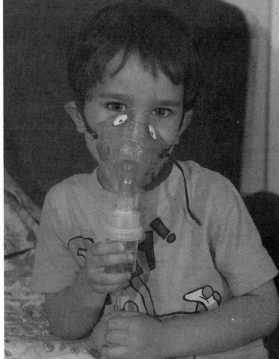

Wadsworth/Cengage Learning

▬ Early childhood staff must have a response plan ready for asthma attacks. But a plan is meaningless unless every staff member who might be alone with the child is properly trained in how to recognize an attack and what to do about it.

Diabetes Mellitus

In **diabetes mellitus,** blood sugar (glucose) levels can become dangerously high because the body does not produce enough insulin. The symptoms, diagnosis, and treatment of diabetes in children are similar to those for adults, but the management of diabetes in children can be more challenging. Treatment must be adapted to the child's maturity and ability to be responsible and to continuous changes in her food intake, physical activity, and stress (American Diabetes Association, 2006).

Cystic Fibrosis

Cystic fibrosis affects the lungs and digestive system. An inherited defective gene and its protein product cause the body to produce unusually thick, sticky mucus that clogs the lungs, which can lead to life-threatening lung infections, and obstructs the pancreas, which hinders food digestion.

epilepsy
A condition characterized by persistent seizures that may include brutal muscle jerking episodes called convulsions.

convulsions
A violent shaking of body or limbs caused by involuntary muscle contractions.

diabetes mellitus
A condition in which blood sugar level can become dangerously high because the body does not produce enough insulin to regulate it.

Wadsworth/Cengage Learning

Today, as many as 40 percent of children diagnosed with diabetes may have the kind of diabetes that is associated with obesity—a kind of diabetes that in the past was thought only adults could have. We may be able to help children avoid this deadly disease by ensuring they have nutritious food, daily vigorous exercise, and strict limits on television time.

cystic fibrosis
An inherited chronic disease that affects breathing and digestion. A defective gene causes the body to produce unusually thick, sticky mucus that clogs the lungs and obstructs the pancreas.

In the early 1950s, few children with cystic fibrosis lived long enough to start school. Today, advances in research and medical treatment are extending life expectancies for children and adults with cystic fibrosis at a remarkable rate. Now school children with cystic fibrosis have a good chance of living to be middle aged or older (Kepron, 2004; Hopkin, 1998; Pitts, 2007).

Heart Defect/Heart Disease

heart defect/heart disease
A congenital cardiovascular defect that occurs when the heart or blood vessels near the heart fail to develop normally before birth.

When a baby's heart or blood vessels near the heart fail to develop normally before birth it can be due to a congenital defect or have another causes. A woman who contracts German measles (or rubella) or another viral infection while pregnant could have a baby with a malformed heart. Although it rarely occurs, more than one child in a family may have a congenital cardiovascular defect (Clark et al., 2001).

Other conditions, such as Down syndrome, affect multiple organs and can also involve the heart. Some prescription drugs, over-the-counter medicines, alcohol, and illegal drugs increase the risk of a child being born with a heart defect. Researchers are studying other factors, but in many cases we don't know why congenital heart defects occur. Most children with heart defects can benefit from surgery and many medical treatments are available to control symptoms.

Although congenital heart defects are the most common cause of heart problems for children younger than 12, overweight children are increasingly at risk for heart disease, stroke, and other cardiovascular diseases (Elder & King, 1994).

A few years ago at the Seattle Special Olympics, nine children gathered at the starting line for the 100-yard dash. All nine were either physically or mentally disabled. When the gun went off, they all went out with the burning desire to run the race to the end and win. One little boy tripped and fell to the asphalt. He sat there and began to cry. As the other children heard him crying, they began to slow down. All eight of them stopped, turned around, and walked back to the starting line. One little girl with Down syndrome bent over and kissed the crying boy on the cheek, saying, "This will make it better." Then all nine children linked arms and walked together across the finish line. Everyone in the stadium stood up and cheered for several minutes. *Families Across Michigan reported this oft-repeated anecdote, October/November, 2001, http://www .mare.org.*

Down Syndrome

Down syndrome causes children some degree of cognitive and developmental delay (there is a wide range). Children with Down syndrome tend to be endearing and affectionate, but they desperately need consistent, loving, solid guidance or they too can be out of control and disrespectful.

- Set limits that are within the child's capability and then firmly but gently see that they are kept. Although children with Down syndrome are often perceived as gentle and mild tempered, they too are at risk for developing significant behavior problems.
- Support the development of self-competence, self-esteem, and self-determination that can bring about social and emotional well-being.
- Support healthy dietary and active physical exercise patterns that will help prevent obesity.
- Be alert to the possibility of hearing problems.
- Provide closeness, attachment, and personal interaction with at least one *special* adult in care situations.
- Assist the child in developing friendships with peers.

The presence of an extra chromosome causes Down syndrome. Children with Down syndrome usually have a small head, a face that is flat and broad, slanting eyes, and a short nose. The tongue tends to protrude and the ears are set low on the head and may be small. The hands are short and broad, with a single distinct crease through each palm (Hanson, 1996).

Infants with Down syndrome tend to be quiet, passive, and have somewhat limp muscles. The **intelligence quotient (IQ)** among children with Down syndrome varies but averages about 50, compared with normal children, whose average IQ is 100.

down syndrome
A disorder that causes mild to severe learning disabilities and distinctive physical characteristics due to the child having an extra chromosome.

intelligence quotient (IQ)
A numerical score resulting from one of several different standardized tests that make an attempt to measure intelligence. The score is used as a predictor of educational achievement and is intended to reflect a person's general capacity for performing intellectual tasks.

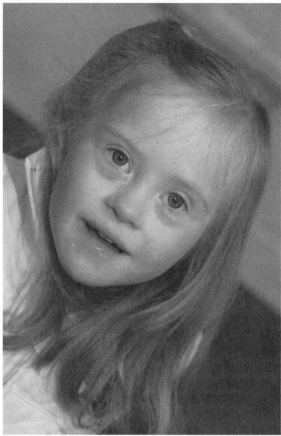

Wadsworth/Cengage Learning

■■■ Children with Down syndrome may have slight intellectual disabilities or they may have profound learning problems. Making prejudicial assumptions about children because they have Down syndrome would be unfair and unethical. Each child must be approached as an individual and helped to make the most of her potential.

Children with Down syndrome have better visual-motor skills (such as drawing) than skills that require hearing. Consequently, their language skills usually develop very slowly. Early intervention with educational and other support services significantly increases the functioning of young children with Down syndrome (Pueschel, 2000).

Any family from any racial or ethnic background may give birth to a child with Down syndrome, although it's more likely in mothers older than 35. Children with Down syndrome are especially vulnerable to colds, ear infections, and pneumonia. They usually have heart defects and a range of other underlying health problems that cause them to have a shorter than usual life expectancy (Stray-Gundersen, 1995).

In the past, this condition was sometimes called "mongolism" because the features of people with Down syndrome were thought to resemble those of Mongolian Asians. This term is now considered offensive and inappropriate and should never be used.

Spina Bifida

Spina bifida (Latin for "split spine") is the incomplete development of the spinal cord, the protective covering around the spinal cord, and possibly the brain that leaves them "split open" and exposed. The human nervous system develops from a special strip of cells along the embryo's back. Early in development, the edges of this strip begin to curl back up toward each other. By the 28th day of pregnancy, this strip should be a closed cylinder, called the **neural tube,** that protects the developing brain and spinal cord of the embryo. But neural tube defects can occur, one of them being spina bifida (ICON Health Publications, 2004e).

spina bifida
Incomplete development of the protective covering around the spinal cord that leaves the covering "split open" and the spinal cord exposed to injury and infection. This can happen anywhere from the tailbone to the brain, with mild to devastating results.

Three types of spina bifida can occur:

- An opening in one or more of the vertebrae (bones) of the spinal column with no damage to the spinal cord. This form usually causes no symptoms.
- An opening in the protective covering around the spinal cord without damage to the spinal cord. This birth defect can be surgically repaired with little or no damage to the nerve pathways. This form usually causes few or no symptoms after surgical repair.
- Opening in the bone and protective covering around the spinal cord with the spinal cord bulging out. The spinal cord may have a covering or the tissue and nerves may be raw and exposed. This is the most severe form of spina bifida and often has terribly damaging consequences.

The most severe form of spina bifida can cause paralysis with urinary and bowel dysfunction. In addition, fluid may accumulate in the brain, a condition known as **hydrocephalus.** Hydrocephalus is often treated by shunting, a surgical procedure that drains fluid buildup in the brain. Without shunting, the pressure buildup in the brain can crush brain tissue, damaging the brain and causing intellectual disability, seizures, or blindness (ICON Health Publications, 2004e).

Some children with spina bifida need braces, crutches, or wheelchairs to move around. Treatment for paralysis and bladder and bowel problems usually begins in infancy. A child with spina bifida may use an electric wheelchair to move around. She may have very small arms, legs, hands, and feet, so crawling or dragging herself around on the floor to access toys without the chair may be impossible. Additionally, she may be wearing equipment to handle her body wastes (she may be unable to use the toilet). Physical therapy for a young spina bifida patient may include special exercises to help her prepare for walking with braces or crutches when she is older (Lutkenhoff, 1999).

If spina bifida causes a child in your care to be in a wheelchair, borrow a wheelchair from a nonprofit organization, church, synagogue, or university or rent one for a weekend. See for yourself what it feels like to move through every area of your parking lot, your building, and your learning environment in a wheelchair. You can use this test to determine the changes needed to make the environment truly accessible for a child, a staff member, or a parent in a wheelchair.

neural tube
A hollow tube developing along the back of the embryo that becomes the brain and spinal cord.

hydrocephalus
Fluid accumulation in the brain. Shunting is a process used to drain excess brain fluid to prevent brain damage and blindness.

Traumatic Brain Injury

Traumatic brain injury is damage to the brain causing cognitive, social, or psychomotor disability. Children with this condition may be at risk for behavior problems related to anger management and inhibition control, so we must keep a watchful eye over them as we nurture and guide them (Blosser & DePompei, 1994).

Moderate to severe pediatric traumatic brain injury has varied effects:

- intellectual disability
- long- or short-term memory problems
- behavior problems, disruptiveness, aggressiveness
- difficulty learning negotiation skills
- social and emotional difficulties; difficulties establishing and maintaining friendships

traumatic brain injury
Caused when the head is struck or shaken violently and resulting in cognitive, social, or psychomotor disability.

Cleft Lip and Cleft Palate

Cleft lips and palates are the most common birth defect in the United States. A **cleft palate** is an incompletely fused roof of the mouth (palate), leaving a gap, that is present at birth. When the gap proceeds through the teeth and gums, cutting through the lip toward the nose, **cleft lip** is also present. Clefts happen when the lip or palate doesn't completely develop while the baby is forming before birth. Babies' lips and palates develop separately during the first three months of pregnancy. In most

cleft palate
An opening in the center of the roof of the mouth.

cleft lip
An opening in the center of the top lip.

intellectual disability (ID)
Mismatch between an individual's capabilities and the demands of daily life to communicate, handle self-care and hygiene needs, participate in community life, make appropriate decisions, solve problems, carry out tasks, and follow safety rules.

cases, the left and right sides of the lip come together, or fuse, creating the two little lines on our upper lip, under our nose. The palate develops this same way. The front-to-back line that can be felt along the roof our mouth indicates where the fusion occurred.

Often, doctors repair cleft lips in the first few months of life. Cleft palates are often repaired several months later, although timing of these surgeries depends on many considerations. Some babies with clefts have very few or no problems feeding, but others have great difficulty. Use of special bottles and careful positioning of the baby may be needed. The child's family may need help in the coordination of services by professionals such as a surgeon, social worker, dentist, orthodontist, speech therapist, and so on.

Babies and young children with birth defects and their families need a great deal of support in fostering the child's self-esteem. Young children tend to stare at anything that looks different—they are naturally curious. Children and adults may be perplexed, uncomfortable, and awkward around a child with a significant facial malformation. Babies and young children are extremely sensitive to the body language and facial expressions of those around them. Routinely seeing adults cringing or averting their faces when they look at you can shatter your self-esteem.

The family, the school, and the community have a responsibility to work together to let the child know from infancy, not only through actions and words but also through body language and facial expressions, that they truly value the child as a worthwhile human being.

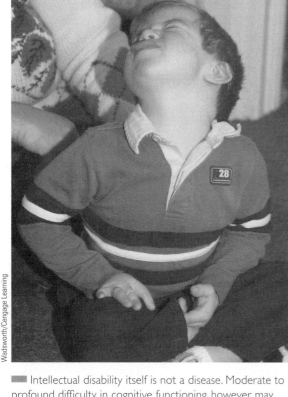

Wadsworth/Cengage Learning

▬ Intellectual disability itself is not a disease. Moderate to profound difficulty in cognitive functioning, however, may be caused by any number of things—brain injury, inherited disorder, certain types of diseases, child abuse, child neglect, and the list goes on and on.

Intellectual Disability

The traditional term "mental retardation" has taken on an objectionable social stigma. Because of this negative connotation, doctors, health care practitioners, and educators have begun replacing the term with "intellectual disability." Because this change is so recent, "mental retardation/intellectual disability" (MR/ID) is used to indicate the transition in terminology (Byrne, 2000).

Intellectual disability (ID) is not a specific medical disorder or illness like chicken pox or diabetes, and it is not a mental health condition like depression or obsessive-compulsive disorder. MR/ID can be caused by a specific medical disorder or illness, but MR/ID itself is simply a mismatch between the capabilities of an individual and the demands daily life in the mainstream community makes on community members.

A person is intellectually disabled if her ability to manage the basic activities of daily living is significantly limited. Essential daily activities include communicating, self-care and hygiene, participating in community life, making decisions, solving problems, carrying out tasks, and following safety rules. Children with this disorder need a great deal of specialized support and guidance throughout their schooling to prepare them for maximum independence (Bouras, 1995; Bogdan et al., 1982; Bouras, 1999; Byrne, 2000; Koskentausta, 2006).

Dyslexia and Learning Disabilities

A **learning disability** is a neurological disorder that causes a difference in the way a person's brain takes in information and processes learning. "Learning disability" is a general term that identifies very specific problems in ability to learn and perform intellectual tasks. The skills most often affected are reading, writing, listening, speaking, reasoning, and mathematics (Seabrook, 1988; Wong, 2004).

Children with learning disabilities have normal to high intelligence, but they may have severe difficulty organizing information for themselves in one or more critical areas of learning. Without special help, these children risk falling far behind their peers in school learning. A learning disability can't be cured or corrected—it is considered permanent. With the right support and intervention, however, children with learning disabilities can thrive in school and go on to successful adulthood (Cicci, 1995).

Adults can help children with learning disabilities succeed by recognizing and appreciating their areas of strength, identifying their specific areas of weakness and teaching them simple methods to reduce the effect of their individual limitations. Children with learning disabilities need to be taught organization skills, memory aids, strategies to break down complex tasks into individual steps, and relaxation techniques to let go of stress and frustration (Ariel, 1992; Lerner & Kline 2005).

Dyslexia is a difference in cognitive function related to difficulty in reading. Children with dyslexia have great difficulty in learning to read because of a perceptual disorder in their brain's information processing system. Children with dyslexia often have difficulty remembering and recognizing letters. They may reverse letters, numbers, and words. They may even read or write backward on occasion. Most have poor handwriting. Recent research guides specific methods of instruction that can help children learn to read well in spite of their learning disability (Spilsbury, 2002; Clark & Uhry, 1995; Reid, 2003).

Pica

The term **pica** comes from the Latin word for magpie, a bird known for its peculiar eating habits. Pica describes the compulsive eating of non-nutritive substances at an age for which this behavior is no longer developmentally inappropriate (past 24 months) and that are not culturally sanctioned. A child with pica persists in eating substances such as a building's wallboard, paper, Play-Doh, dirt, or small objects

---

Disability is a matter of perception. If you can do just one thing well, you're needed by someone.

Martina Navratilova, Retrieved September 30, 2007, from http://www.legendspeak.com/MartinaNavratilova.htm

learning disability
Disorder that affects the brain's ability to receive, process, analyze, or store information.

dyslexia
Cognitive problems in which a person's reading or writing ability is significantly lower than expected given his exposure to appropriate instruction, his intellectual ability, and his lack of other disabilities that might explain his poor progress. Because reading is a complex mental process, dyslexia has many potential causes.

pica
An eating disorder in which one eats nonfood substances such as dirt, chalk, paper, or other items.

found in the indoor and outdoor environment. Children with an existing disability such as pervasive developmental disorder, epilepsy, head injury, or MR/ID are at the greatest risk for pica (Bicknell, 1975).

Children with pica must be supervised very closely (just as we look after toddlers) because eating non-nutritive objects is dangerous. Children eating paint chips containing lead may suffer brain damage from lead poisoning. The same risk exists from eating dirt on playgrounds near one of the many roads that existed when lead was used in gasoline. In addition to poisoning, pica can cause obstruction or tearing in the stomach. Children eating sand and dirt may swallow animal feces, exposing themselves to parasites and illness (Cooper, 1957; Kalisz et al., 1978; Oliver & O'Gorman, 1966).

Pervasive Developmental Disorders

pervasive developmental disorders (PDDs)
A group of neurodevelopmental disorders characterized by severe delays in the development of socialization and communication skills.

neurodevelopment
The development of the brain pathways that make the integration of sensory information possible; these pathways increase in capacity and complexity as children play, learn, and grow.

autism
A developmental brain disorder characterized by impaired social interaction and communication skills, avoidance of eye-to-eye gaze, and a limited range of activities and interests.

mind blindness
A brain disorder that impairs one's ability to "read minds" by noticing gestures, facial expressions, and changes in tone of voice. An inability to fathom what is in the mind of another person.

Pervasive developmental disorders (PDDs) are a group of disorders affecting **neurodevelopment** that are characterized by severe delays in the development of socialization and communication skills. Autism is the most characteristic and best-studied PDD. Other types of PDD include Asperger's syndrome, fragile X syndrome, and Rett's syndrome. It also includes childhood disintegrative disorder, which is very rare, and pervasive developmental disorder not otherwise specified (PDDNOS), which is an umbrella term for PDDs used in cases where doctors may not be ready or able to specify the appropriate categorization. Sometimes persons with these types of disorders are said to be "on the autistic spectrum" (Bruey, 2004; Cohen & Volkmar, 1997).

Parents sometimes identify PDD symptoms as early as infancy, but the usual age for diagnosis of these disorders is around three. Children with PDDs have in common conditions such as mild to severe problems with using and understanding language, difficulty relating socially to people, unusual play with toys and other objects, difficulty with changes in routine or familiar surroundings, and repetitive body movements or behavior patterns (Gupta, 2004; Coleman, 1976).

Autism

Autism, sometimes called **mind blindness,** is a brain disorder that affects a person's sense of self. Infants, toddlers, and children not affected with this disorder easily infer others' state of mind by noticing gestures, facial expressions, and changes in tone of voice. Children with the disorder are unable to detect or guess other people's moods. They fail to distinguish themselves as separate and have trouble picking up language. They often avoid eye contact and sometimes even avoid physical contact.

It is easy to see why these children are emotionally fragile. They begin with a special risk for developing inappropriate behaviors to help sooth themselves, such as flapping their arms, bumping their heads, or running around in circles. They especially need structured observation to learn the child's requirements; nurturance at their own pace; a modified environment to tone down stimuli; and consistency, consistency, consistency.

It is important for the child to make a personal connection with a consistent person. Spending a few minutes of quiet time with that person should help alleviate whatever stresses the child has encountered. Once the level of stress is reduced and the child is more relaxed, she may then become more responsive to guidance suggestions and be able to cope with the problem at hand.

In some cases a child's behavior can get back on track when her daily routines are simplified. A preschooler with autism or Asperger's would have a hard time coping with frequent, unexpected changes in the environment. Disruptions cause the child to be unresponsive and uncooperative, and the child might be unable to exercise self-control or to be self-sufficient.

Children with autism often avoid eye contact and may avoid physical contact. They are likely to become agitated if you use the recommended "eye contact at eye level with appropriate touch." The human closeness typically developing children long for is repulsive to the child with autism. The world is frightening, overwhelming, and overstimulating.

For children with autism, the caregiver must reduce the number and rate of changes to the absolute minimum.

- Set a clear schedule and daily routine. Make sure the child knows the daily routine at the start of each day and can make frequent reference to it throughout the day—for example, lay out the day's scheduled activities on a felt board.
- Give five-minute warnings of each impending switch of activity or change in the day's routine.
- Use literal, unambiguous language. Avoid ironic humor with this child (she won't understand phrases such as "I'm so hungry I could eat a horse," which will just cause confusion and bewilderment).
- Call the child by her name (the child may not realize that an instruction given to the whole class also includes her).
- Use short sentences to ensure clarity of communication.
- Incorporate multiple learning styles—involve sensory learning.
- Teach, practice, and model social rules and skills, such as taking turns and maintaining social distance when the child is willing.
- Protect the child from teasing.

Many children with autism have **hypersensitivity;** that is, they are overly sensitive to stimuli. For example, an autistic child may be overly sensitive to changes in his familiar environment. A simple change, such as switching to daylight saving time, alters the environment at preschool when the autistic child arrives (less light) and may cause him to feel extreme distress. His distress may be expressed in tantrums or other inappropriate behavior. He may also overreact to smells, food textures, sounds, or other different sensory stimuli or abrupt changes in them (Bonnice, 2004; Bogdashina, 2003).

Autistic children also experience a phenomenon referred to as **auditory figure-ground dysfunction.** The child may hear a distant siren on the freeway, the class singing in the next room, and the hamster scratching in the cage all at the same volume as the teacher speaking directly to him. Most of us would tune these background noises out and notice only the voice of the speaker. The autistic child is incapable of tuning out the unneeded sounds (Bogdashina, 2003).

hypersensitivity
Overreaction to sensory input from one of the senses (for example, sight, sound, taste, smell, touch).

auditory figure-ground dysfunction
An inability to distinguish between levels of sounds in the environment, to focus on significant sounds, and tune out irrelevant sounds. This is a common characteristic in PDDs and some learning disorders.

echolalia
A speech disorder that causes compulsive repetition of words spoken by others. In most cases, echolalic speech is a habitual form of cyclical self-stimulation that is not intended as communication, but in some cases echolalia may be used as the child's only available tool in an improvised attempt at communication.

Echolalia, a speech disorder, is the compulsive repetition of words spoken by someone else or heard on television or radio. In most cases, echolalic speech is cyclical self-stimulation (like hand flapping or rocking) that is not really intended as communication to anyone. The child with echolalia is able to repeat language she has heard and memorized even though she cannot generate her own speech to express her thoughts. Occasionally echolalia is intended as communication. For example, a well-functioning first grader with autism might say, "Let me tie your shoes," when she is actually asking for her own shoes to be tied. She can't create the words she needs to say, but she knows that "Let me tie your shoes" is what she hears when her shoes get tied. No matter how often her mistake is explained to her, she is unlikely to comprehend the language rules (Frith, 2003).

Even very young children can be diagnosed and treated for autism; in fact, the sooner the disorder is identified in a child, the better the outcome (American Psychiatric Association, 2004).

Children with autism often have differences in communication compared with their peers:

- have difficulty in expressing needs, often using negative behavior instead of words
- show delayed speech or no speech; stereotyped and repetitive language
- use echolalic speech
- are unresponsive to voices and sounds, as if deaf although tests prove hearing is normal
- are not able to share joint attention, showing or sharing something with another person by using gestures, particularly pointing

Children with autism often have differences in socialization compared with their peers:

- avoid eye-to-eye gaze
- may not want physical contact; avoids cuddling, touching, hugging
- do not develop peer relationships
- may prefer to be alone, appears aloof
- have difficulty interacting with other children
- can't carry on social and emotional give-and-take
- lack ability for spontaneous make-believe play or social imitative play
- act or speak in a socially inappropriate manner
- have difficulty interpreting facial expressions and body language
- have difficulty understanding and interpreting emotions in self and others

Wadsworth/Cengage Learning

■■■ Typically developing children may tend to ignore and stay away from a child with autism. Efforts should be made to help the other children understand the needs of the child with autism so they will be kind, supportive, and helpful to him.

Children with autism often have differences in behavior compared with their peers:

- are preoccupied with one or more stereotyped and restricted patterns of interest
- adhere inflexibly to specific, nonfunctional routines or rituals
- have persistent preoccupation with parts of objects
- are inappropriately attached to objects
- spin or line up objects
- display stereotypical or self-stimulatory behaviors such as hand flapping, rocking, flicking fingers in front of face
- have difficulty transitioning from one activity or setting to another
- resist changes in the environment
- have frequent tantrums or meltdowns
- are subject to self-injurious behaviors
- walk on tiptoe often

Asperger's Syndrome

Asperger's syndrome is a neurological condition very similar to autism. All of the guidance suggestions for children with autism should be considered as possible strategies to support children with Asperger's. A critical difference, however, is that children with autism will have developmental delays in one or more significant learning areas, whereas children with Asperger's will have average or perhaps even gifted intellectual capacity in one or more intellectual areas. For the sake of the child's self-esteem, it is crucial to find and nurture development of the child's special areas of talent or giftedness.

A child with Asperger's has a marked impairment in social development and may not use language in a socially appropriate way or with cognitive understanding of the social significance of the language he is using. He may be brilliant in math but not be able to decipher the meaning of another person's facial expression. He finds it challenging, even impossible, to connect with others; he can't hold eye contact and can't read other people's body language.

Typical symptoms of Asperger's syndrome include the following:

- possible language delay
- average or above-average intellectual capacity in one or more areas
- lack of social communication through body language, gestures, and facial expressions
- poor eye contact
- lack of spontaneity
- inability (or difficulty) comprehending social interactions
- repetitious or stereotypical behaviors

Having a classmate who is the smartest one in the class but who makes strange sounds, flaps his arms, and looks only at the floor can be very confusing to nondisabled children in the class. The teacher can help *all* the children through bibliotherapy.

asperger's syndrome
A neurological condition that is part of the autistic spectrum but includes only persons of average or above intelligence who are verbal.

Read books to the children about autism and Asperger's syndrome. Ask the child with Asperger's if he would like to talk about Asperger's and how others could be helpful.

Celiac Disease

celiac disease
A digestive disease that damages the small intestine and interferes with absorption of nutrients from food. People who have celiac disease cannot tolerate a protein called gluten, found in wheat, rye, and barley.

People who have **celiac disease** cannot tolerate a protein called gluten, found in wheat, rye, and barley. Gluten is found mainly in foods but may also be ingested from other products—such as when licking a stamp or taking a pill. The toddler with celiac disease can become ill by eating a crumb he has found on the floor.

Early childhood professionals play an important role in protecting the health of children with celiac disease, just as they do when caring for children who have life-threatening allergies to peanuts, bees, or other substances.

Most of the gastrointestinal symptoms of celiac disease are due to inadequate absorption of fat. This causes diarrhea, foul-smelling gas, abdominal bloating, and fat in the stool. When people with celiac disease eat foods or use products containing gluten, their immune system responds by further damaging the tiny, fingerlike protrusions lining the small intestine. These protrusions, called **intestinal villi,** normally allow nutrients from food to be absorbed into the bloodstream. Without healthy villi, a person becomes malnourished, regardless of the quantity of food eaten (ICON Health Publications, 2004b; Bower et al., 2006).

intestinal villi
Tiny, fingerlike protrusions lining the small intestine that absorb nutrients and make them available to the bloodstream. *Villi* is Latin for "shaggy hair."

Birthday parties are an important part of many early childhood programs. If you have a child with celiac disease in your program, don't let him feel left out if the other children eat special foods to celebrate birthdays and holidays. Collaborate with the parents to have something special on hand for the child with gluten intolerance. For example, you could store a box of rice cakes, a can of frosting, and some candy sprinkles. Whenever there is a birthday party or other event with special celebration food containing food the child with celiac disease can't have, create a pretty little frosted rice cake with sprinkles for the child. He will appreciate being included.

Human Immunodeficiency Virus and Acquired Immune Deficiency Syndrome

human immunodeficiency virus and acquired immune deficiency syndrome
Human immunodeficiency virus (HIV) is the virus that causes acquired immune deficiency syndrome (AIDS). AIDS attacks a person's immune system, leaving the person vulnerable to infection.

Human immunodeficiency virus (HIV) is the virus that causes **acquired immune deficiency syndrome (AIDS).** AIDS attacks a person's immune system, leaving the person vulnerable to infection. Although some children with HIV infection remain quite healthy through adolescence, others unfortunately, do not gain weight or grow normally as their HIV progresses to full-blown AIDS. These children are usually slow to reach important milestones in motor skills and mental development such as crawling, walking, and talking. If the disease progresses to AIDS, these children are at great risk of neurological problems, which show up in poor school performance, seizures, and other signs of brain involvement (Grodeck & Berger, 2007).

Children with HIV/AIDS experience the usual childhood infections along with their peers, but they are sick more frequently and more severely. Just as for adults with

HIV/AIDS, these opportunistic infections can become life threatening for children. The infections can cause high fever, seizures, pneumonia, diarrhea, dehydration, and other conditions that can result in frequent or long hospital stays and severe problems with malnutrition. Difficult, complex regimens of powerful drug combinations extend lives dramatically but can be exhausting for children. Their families also suffer—emotionally and financially as well as physically (ICON Health Publications, 2003).

Can I Catch HIV from a Child?

The primary ways that people get HIV/AIDS is by sexual contact with an infected person, by sharing syringes for drug injection with an infected person, or less commonly (and now very rarely where blood supplies are well regulated), from transfusions of infected blood or blood-clotting factors. Babies born to HIV-infected women may become infected before or during birth or through breast-feeding after birth. A few health care workers have become infected with HIV.

But casual, day-to-day contact has never been shown to be a risk factor for HIV/AIDS transmission.

Workers who are fearful about being around a child who is known or suspected to have HIV or AIDS are not behaving as ethical early childhood professionals. They are also not rational. People are not required to tell schools if their child has HIV/AIDS, so any child or coworker could be infected and we wouldn't know it.

Today, proper hygiene requires us, as a general rule, not to touch bodily fluids (blood, urine, breast milk) from *any* person without wearing rubber gloves, especially if we have an open cut or sore. We need to be careful if a child's (especially a toddler's) vomit or diarrhea ends up on the floor. Other babies or toddlers can be quick to get into the fluid, and we must block it off from them immediately.

Tourette's Syndrome

Children with **Tourette's syndrome** have multiple **motor tics** and **vocal tics.** These tics occur many times throughout the day and may be aggravated by stress. Tourette's syndrome is often accompanied by ADHD or obsessive-compulsive disorder. A child with Tourette's often suffers self-esteem difficulties and may be severely embarrassed by her tics. Children must be closely supervised in early childhood programs, classrooms, or any other group situations when the group includes a child with Tourette's. Allowing children to tease, bully, and stigmatize the child with tics is not only cruel but also damaging to the child's social and emotional development and can leave lifelong scars (Waltz, 2001).

Coprolalia and **copropraxia** are rare, but characteristic, offensive outbursts from individuals with Tourette's syndrome (Bruun & Bruun, 1994). The words or actions are not done out of anger. They burst out uncontrollably, almost always to the person's embarrassment and dismay. It is almost as if the very mechanism in the brain that suppresses disturbing or inappropriate thoughts instead forces them to be yelled or acted out. Although these outbursts are closely linked with Tourette's syndrome in the public consciousness, the vast majority of persons with Tourette's

tourette's syndrome
A disorder characterized by multiple motor and vocal tics.

motor tic
A sudden involuntary muscular contraction, often of the facial, shoulder, or neck muscles. Complex motor tics include distinct, obsessively repeated, intricate actions or behaviors such as twirling, hopping, or obsessively lining things up in straight rows. Tics tend to become more pronounced when one is under stress.

vocal tic
A sudden involuntary vocalization such as a yip, whistle, grunt, or cough. A complex vocal tic is a distinct, obsessively repeated phrase or the intricate obsessive use of words, such as repeating everything other people say.

coprolalia
Copro is the Greek term for "feces" and *lalia* is Greek for "babbling, meaningless talk." Literally, it means "manure talking." People with coprolalia make sudden, unexpected outbursts of inappropriate words or phrases.

copropraxia
Praxia is the Greek word for "act or action." Combined with *copro*, it means "manure behavior." People with copropraxia act out involuntarily, producing obscene, offensive, or shocking gestures and actions.

will never experience either type of outburst (Education and Advocacy Committee, Tourette Syndrome Foundation of Canada, 2001).

Typical symptoms of Tourette's syndrome include the following:

- vocal tics—uncontrollable repetitive sounds
  - coughing, throat clearing
  - whistling
  - grunting
  - hissing
  - barking
- complex vocal tics—uncontrollable, compulsive, repeated intricate verbalizations
  - repetitions of clichés such as "Wow," "Yup, that's it," "but, but . . ."
- motor tics—uncontrollable repetitive actions
  - neck twisting
  - excessive blinking
  - clapping
  - hopping
  - arm flailing
  - lip biting
  - head banging (this and some other tics are harmful to the child)
- complex motor tics—uncontrollable, compulsive, repeated intricate actions
  - sorting and lining up items up obsessively
  - drawing over letters again and again until the paper tears

Post-Traumatic Stress Disorder (PTSD)

post-traumatic stress disorder (PTSD)
A condition that follows a psychologically distressing event that can occur at any age and from any number of reasons.

Post-traumatic stress disorder (PTSD) is a condition that develops after a psychologically distressing event and can occur at any age. Common triggers of PTSD are child abuse, a natural disaster like a hurricane, a fire, a car wreck, seeing a horrible event such as a murder, being exposed to a war, or any other distressing event. A child with PTSD might relive the event over and over again—like a mental movie that won't stop playing. Or she may avoid all thoughts and feelings about the event. She may feel disconnected from reality and from other people and have a hard time concentrating. PTSD can even be expressed through physical symptoms such as nausea, body aches, headaches, and other problems (Dwivedi, 2000; Schiraldi, 2000; Stien & Kendall, 2003).

Childhood abuse may be the most common cause of PTSD. Ten percent of women and 5 percent of men in the United States suffer from PTSD caused by abuse they suffered as children (McCauley et al., 1997; Kessler et al., 1995). Children develop PTSD because of being exposed to violence at school, in the community, or in the home.

Typical indications of PTSD include the following:

- excessive startle response
- memory loss

- irritability
- angry outbursts
- nightmares
- flashbacks
- emotional detachment
- depression
- loss of appetite
- numbed feelings

How much an individual child may be at risk for PTSD depends on several factors:

- the child's temperament, coping skills and resiliency
- quality and availability of emotional and social support
- the severity of the trauma
- the type of ordeal the child has faced
- length or frequency of the traumatic events
- whether the trauma recurs

Depression

People use the term *depression* to describe gloomy moods that range from feeling blue to feeling suicidal. But in clinical depression a person can't just snap out of a gloomy mood. **Depression** is a psychological state of dejected mood characterized by feelings of discouragement, dejection, sadness, despair, and hopelessness. A child who is clinically depressed can't pull herself up by her bootstraps and wish depression away. A depressive disorder is an illness that depresses her bodily functions, her mood, her feelings, and her thoughts. Without treatment, depressive symptoms can last for weeks, months, or years. Appropriate treatment, however, can be very effective (Lyness, 2005).

Anhedonia is recognized as one of the key symptoms of depression. When anhedonic it is difficult or impossible to gain pleasure from activities or events that had been enjoyable. Everyday activities such as eating favorite foods, interacting with friends, playing, or participating in family activities have become dull and unappealing. A child with anhedonia may feel secure wearing a heavy hooded jacket. She may resist removing it regardless of the weather and not even realize that the jacket should feel very uncomfortable in hot weather (Miller, 1999).

Children who are depressed tend to have negative and self-critical thoughts. Sometimes, even if there is a strong caring support system around them, they can feel worthless and unlovable. Depression can cloud thinking, making even small problems seem overwhelming. A depressed child may cry at small things or cry for no reason at all (Barnard, 2003).

Typical symptoms of depression include the following:

- anhedonia
- dejected mood

depression
A psychological state of dejected mood characterized by feelings of discouragement, dejection, sadness, despair, and hopelessness.

anhedonia
Inability to gain pleasure from normally pleasurable activities. A person seems almost anesthetized against normally stimulating sensations and events in the environment. This phenomenon is a key symptom of depression.

- anxiety
- feelings of helplessness, hopelessness
- sleep problems, not being able to fall asleep, not being able to get up in the morning
- appetite changes
- feelings of exhaustion, fatigue
- trouble concentrating
- restlessness, irritability
- feelings of worthlessness
- bodily complaints
- dread, fear, anticipation of danger
- sweating, palpitations, or butterflies in the stomach

bipolar disorder
A disorder in which episodes of depression alternate with mania.

mania
A severe medical condition characterized by abnormally elevated mood, high energy, and bizarre thought patterns.

Bipolar Disorder

Bipolar disorder (also known as manic depression) causes episodes of mania followed by depression. Research indicates that bipolar disorder that begins in childhood may be more severe than older-adolescent- and adult-onset bipolar disorder (Carlson et al., 1998; Geller & Luby, 1997). A child who appears to be depressed for a significant period but also has extreme temper outbursts, has persistent moodiness, and is extremely fidgety and distracted should be referred for medical evaluation.

Bipolar disorder is different in children than it is in adults. Children usually have a continuing, ongoing mood disturbance that is a mix of **mania** and depression. This quick but severe rotation between manic and depressive moods produces chronic irritability and few noticeable periods of wellness between episodes. Mania causes a worrisome combination of fearlessness, an overblown belief in one's abilities, racing thoughts, poor judgment, irritability, and anger. Children with this difficult disorder are often treated with medication (frequently several drugs in combination) and counseling, for the child as well as the parents (Maj et al., 1994; Geller, Fox, & Clark, 1994; McClellan & Werry, 1997).

Early identification, diagnosis, and treatment of bipolar disorder will help children reach their full potential. However, children who have bipolar disorder are at a greater risk of having anxiety disorders or ADHD, and having these disorders often contributes to a misdiagnosis or lack of diagnosis of bipolar disorder in young children.

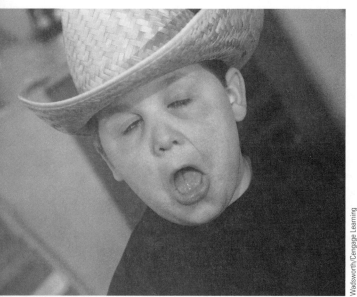

Wadsworth/Cengage Learning

Parents of children with bipolar disorder often describe them as unpredictable—quickly alternating between acting belligerent, silly, and withdrawn.

Manic symptoms include the following:

- stark changes in mood—irritability, rage, extreme silliness, or intense euphoria
- overblown, grandiose sense of self
- difficulty falling asleep, waking after only a short sleep
- increased talking; won't let anyone else speak
- extremely short attention span
- burst of energy, increased physical activity
- agitation; disregard for risk
- depressive symptoms (see earlier description of depression)

Attention Deficit/Hyperactivity Disorder

Attention deficit/hyperactivity disorder (ADHD) is one of the most common behavioral disorders that develop in children. It has forms that are characterized by inattention, impulsiveness, or extremely high levels of physical activity. ADHD has had different names in past years. Children with this disorder have been called hyperactive, hyperkinetic, and even brain damaged. Those terms are no longer considered appropriate or accurate (Bramer, 2006).

ADHD is often marked by excessive physical activity at inappropriate times. Obviously, these children need special support to achieve their maximum potential. They need to learn strategies to focus and how to set priorities.

- Remember that children with ADHD require more immediate and more frequent feedback for their behavior and activities than do more typically developing children.
- Regularly provide these children with natural and logical consequences.
- Routinely draw the child's attention to the consequences of her actions.
- Help her learn to identify and state the potential consequences of actions.
- Before beginning a potential problem situation, pause to talk about what is going to happen and what is needed from the child.
- Review rules that the child may have trouble following: "What are our special rules for staying safe when we go outside?" "That's right, no climbing on the fence."
- Review the logical consequences when someone forgets the rule and climbs on the fence. "They don't get to play near the fence. They have to play in the sand box away from the fence for the rest of play time so they will be safe."
- Remember that the child isn't constantly wriggling or not paying attention to annoy you. That is just the way his brain operates. Keep a caring perspective.

Parents or teachers may question a diagnosis of ADHD. How can a very bright child be unable to pay attention to a lesson but be able to focus on something that strongly interests him? This is not a matter of willpower. Bramer (2006) explains that the **executive system** of the brain controls the child's attention and ADHD may

**attention deficit/
hyperactivity disorder
(ADHD)**
A common developmental disorder that appears during childhood and is characterized by a persistent pattern of inattention as well as forgetfulness, poor impulse control, and distractibility.

executive system
A theorized system of the brain that controls and organizes other mental processes. It manages processes such as planning, abstract thinking, rule learning, screening out irrelevant sensory information, and inhibiting inappropriate actions; also referred to as executive function or the central executive.

interfere with this crucial aspect of self-regulation. ADHD causes malfunctions of the brain's executive system that can prevent the child from being able to deal with tasks that challenge him, even though he can succeed at easier tasks. Consequently, ADHD can significantly disrupt cognitive, behavioral, social, and educational parts of the child's daily life.

Effective treatments for ADHD are available and include behavioral therapy and medications. Most doctors believe that the potential side effects of using medications should be carefully weighed against the benefits before prescribing the drugs. While on these medications, some children may lose weight, have less appetite, and grow more slowly. Others may have problems falling asleep. Some doctors believe that stimulants may also make the Tourette's-like symptoms worse, although recent research suggests this may not be true. Other doctors say that if they carefully watch the child's height, weight, and overall development, the benefits of medication far outweigh the potential side effects. Physical problems or unexplained changes in behavior should be reported immediately to parents. Side effects that do occur can usually be handled by the doctor's changing the dosage or the medicine.

Stimulant medications increase activity in parts of the brain that aren't working properly. They aren't tranquilizers or sedatives, and they aren't addictive. A doctor might choose, based on an individual child's symptoms and needs, to use another medication that affects the brain differently from stimulants. All of these approaches, medication, and therapy help many children with serious ADHD to be happier and more at peace with their environment and the expectations of others (Manassis, 2007; MTA Cooperative Group, 2004; Adesman & Morgan, 1999; Bauermeister, 2003; Jensen, 1999).

Myths about ADHD abound. ADHD is a complex biologic disorder; too much television, bad parenting, inadequate teachers, food allergies, or excess sugar do not cause ADHD. A massive amount of international research demonstrates ADHD in some children regardless of their culture and parenting. Still, how parents and teachers respond to the child's ADHD may go a long way in bringing about a positive ultimate outcome. The child will need treatment through childhood, adolescence, and possibly adulthood to function optimally (Sherman et al., 2006; Swanson et al., 1999; Copeland & Love, 1995).

Life is challenging for children with ADHD. They get in trouble with adults, get into quarrels with their friends, and bump into one frustration after another. School-age children spend agonizing hours struggling to keep their mind on their homework project and then forget to bring it to school the next morning.

A child with ADHD is in trouble with adults so often that he develops poor self-esteem. The adult should find a way to make the majority of interactions with the child positive. Early childhood professionals must break the cycle of negative interactions with the child, and establish a new pattern of mutual respect and caring. Respect and caring create a foundation for self-esteem.

Some children with ADHD unleash their pent-up annoyance and frustration by having tantrums, being aggressive, or destroying property. Others hold the frustration inside and begin to have stomachaches, headaches, or other physical symptoms (Bramer, 2006; Sherman et al., 2006).

Siblings and classmates of a child who has ADHD are challenged too. They may feel neglected as their parents or teachers try to cope with the hyperactive child. They may resent their brother, sister, or classmate who is distressingly active, leaves messes, throws tantrums, and doesn't listen. They may especially resent that the child with ADHD doesn't seem to behave properly but still seems to have a disproportionate amount of the adult's time and attention (Johnson, 1992).

It's also hard for the adult. She may feel helpless and frustrated. Guidance techniques don't seem to work. The adult may be tempted to resort to negative discipline techniques, but these are even more troublesome and ineffective for the child with a disability than for other children. The child needs more calm and less stress—and most importantly, caring, consistent, assertive positive guidance.

Symptoms of the hyperactive form of ADHD include the following:

- extraordinary difficulty concentrating or paying attention
- distraction, forgetfulness
- extremely short interest span, bounces from one activity to another
- fidgeting and squirming
- impulsiveness, lack of self-control
- excessive talking
- difficulty waiting for a turn
- problems getting along with peers
- problems with erratic eating or sleeping

Some warning signs can be mistaken for indicators of ADHD:

- school problems due to a learning disability
- undiagnosed hearing problems (may be caused by chronic ear infections)
- distracted or disruptive behavior caused by depression or bipolar disorder
- attention lapses caused by hidden seizures

Oppositional Defiant Disorder and Intermittent Explosive Disorder

Oppositional defiant disorder (ODD) can seriously interfere with a child's day-to-day functioning. At a glance, it may seem difficult to tell the difference between a particularly strong-willed child and a child who has ODD. There is a big difference, however. Children afflicted with ODD are disobedient, hostile, and defiant to a degree not seen in typically developing children.

Most children have tantrums as toddlers. But by the preschool years, most children develop the social skills and **self-regulation** necessary to handle frustrating situations without resorting to tantrums—at least not very often. For reasons not yet well understood, the child with ODD is not able to develop essential self-regulation. These children regularly lose control of their emotions and feel compelled to defy authority. Children with ODD are clearly disruptive to home, community, and school environments. ODD is frequently identified in combination with other behavioral or mental health problems such as ADHD, anxiety, and depression. These children

oppositional defiant disorder (ODD)
A condition in which an ongoing pattern of disobedient, hostile, and defiant behavior toward authority figures goes well beyond the bounds of normal childhood behavior.

self-regulation
A critical developmental process by which one learns to function without external control; being able to deal with problems appropriately and independently.

need educational, medical, or therapeutic intervention to support them in managing this very challenging disorder (Keenan & Wakschlag, 2000).

intermittent explosive disorder (IED)
A mental disorder typified by outbreaks of violent and aggressive behavior that may harm others or destroy property.

Intermittent explosive disorder (IED) is a behavior disorder characterized by sudden extreme expressions of anger, often to the point of uncontrollable rage. These outbursts are totally out of proportion to the provocation and are sometimes accompanied by outbursts of physical aggression (Franz, 2004).

Because the child with ODD or IED may be argumentative, defiant, negative, and annoying to others, she may begin to feel rejected and unloved. Much of her time is spent in conflict with others at home, at school, and in child care. The child may know intellectually that she is loved but not really feel loved. Adults must be able to show unconditional caring so they can soothe and nurture this troubled child. This is not always easy to accomplish, especially when the child's previous negative behavior patterns have become ingrained habits (Speltz, 1999; Lavigne et al., 2001; Loeber et al., 2000; Ross et al., 1998).

Research is beginning to emerge that may connect maternal smoking during pregnancy to behavior problems. Children whose mothers smoked while they were pregnant have been identified as more likely to be socially defiant and impulsively aggressive (Williams et al., 1998). We don't know with certainty yet whether prenatal smoking directly causes or is only a risk indicator for the development of behavior problems in nicotine-exposed babies. But indications are that exposure to cigarette smoke (or other sources of nicotine) in the womb puts children on a path toward behavior problems (Wakschlag et al., 2006; Huizink & Mulder, 2006; Weitzman et al., 2002; Wakschlag et al., 2002; Kahn et al., 2003).

Because ODD and IED create tremendous challenges for children as they grow up, it is critical for adults to create a calm, supportive environment with clear boundaries, consistent limits and appropriate consequences (Greene et al., 2002).

The child with ODD routinely acts out with aggression and defiance and seems to feel a constant need to irritate others. Adults often have extreme difficulty staying calm, peaceful, and focused on assertive positive guidance. What the child needs most is a calm adult to rely on for stable, consistent guidance.

The child with ODD may or may not show signs of remorse for the harm he does. If he shows any small indication that he regrets what he has done, encourage this budding sense of conscience. Help him figure out how to make amends for the damage he caused. Encourage him to describe his feelings in words or to paint a picture showing how he feels when he has hurt someone.

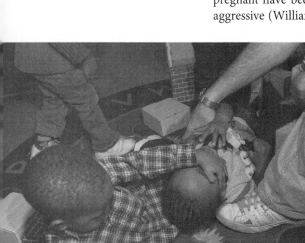

Wadsworth/Cengage Learning

■■■ Early detection of ODD and IED is meant for intervention and *not* for labeling the child a problem child. Identifying the problem makes sense only if we do something to solve it. Conflict resolution skills and anger management training should be provided at the appropriate levels for both the child and the family. Relevant early intervention may interrupt the pattern of oppositional and defiant behavior in the child. The goal of early intervention is to improve the child's natural growth and development and improve the quality of life experienced by the child, the child's family, the school, and the community.

Children with ODD may exhibit the following characteristics:

- losing their temper frequently and showing low tolerance for frustration
- arguing, being angry and resentful
- being spiteful or vindictive
- refusing to follow adult direction or rules
- deliberately bothering other people
- blaming others for their own mistakes

Follow these tips to guide children with ODD:

- Develop consistent behavior expectations.
- Communicate with parents so that guidance is consistent at home and school.
- Provide a positive and encouraging classroom environment.
- Use logical and natural consequences immediately, consistently, and fairly.
- Recognize appropriate behavior.

Children with ODD are often guided using behavior modification. Set up a behavior modification chart of desired positive actions—for example, safety, kindness, and neatness (responsibility). Discuss with the child what is expected:

- Select times to apply behavior modification when the child is most likely to succeed.
- Ensure that the periods of time and actions expected are small enough to be achievable.
- Set a timer occasionally during the first day for five minutes, and give the child a sticker each time the timer rings and she hasn't broken the rules (be safe, be kind, and be neat and responsible). If she has broken rules, give her encouragement and decrease the time interval while trying again.
- Recognition rather than praise is appropriate.
- Increase the time on the timer each day as the child's ability increases.
- When her chart is full (make sure it is not too hard to get the chart full) allow the child to take the chart home to parents with a note explaining what a significant accomplishment it is.
- Develop classroom strategies to relieve stress and anxiety.
- Avoid power struggles.

Conduct Disorder

Conduct disorder is a severe form of ODD that may, if not resolved, lead to adult antisocial personality disorder. Conduct disorder is a complex cluster of severe behavioral and emotional problems in children and adolescents. Children with this disorder have never learned to behave in a socially acceptable way. Children with conduct disorder typically exhibit aggression to people and animals, destroy property, are deceitful, lie, steal, and defy authority. Some children with conduct disorder may be drawn to violent gang involvement as young as 11 or 12 (Allen et al., 2005; Frick & Dickens, 2006).

conduct disorder
A mental condition typified by a repetitive and persistent pattern of socially unacceptable behavior that violates the rights of others. Typical symptoms include strongly aggressive behavior, bullying, cruelty, and destructiveness.

Adults, teachers, and peers might perceive children with conduct disorder to be juvenile delinquents rather than children who are disabled, emotionally disturbed, mentally ill, and deserving of compassion. Many factors can contribute to a child developing conduct disorder. This disorder may have initially been triggered by any of the following:

- brain injury
- fetal alcohol spectrum disorder
- exposure to lead before birth or in early childhood (Marlowe, 1986)
- exposure to maternal smoking before birth (Williams et al., 1998)
- genetic susceptibility, family history of behavioral disorders or mental illness
- child abuse or neglect
- traumatic, violent life experiences
- learning disability causing school failure
- social rejection, being stigmatized (because of race, cultural differences, appearance)
- failure to receive adequate treatment for one or more other underlying mental disorders

Many children with conduct disorder have earlier experienced ODD or ADHD. In some cases, we may never know why this condition evolved in a particular child (Dupéré et al., 2007; Boxer et al., 2005; Caspi et al., 1998; Coie & Dodge, 1998). We do know that the younger the child's age when we intervene with assertive positive guidance, appropriate resources, therapies, counseling, medication, or whatever is needed to help the child, the better the chances this child can grow up to enjoy a productive adulthood (Lier et al., 2007; Welsh & Farrington, 2007). Physically punishing or socially rejecting the child with a conduct disorder pushes him further into his disorder. Finding some way to accept and include the child may open communication with the child (Coie & Koeppl, 1990; Green, 1998; Hutchings & Lane, 2005).

The future for most children with conduct disorder is often very grim if they don't get early intervention and a great deal of support. A consistent, nurturing, and structured home environment is believed to be the best protection for children with conduct disorder. Child abuse and neglect are great risk factors for conduct disorder. Children with ADHD, behavior disorders, learning disabilities, or general difficulties in school need special help to avoid having these problems escalate. Addressing problems when they first appear helps prevent the frustration and low self-esteem that may lead to conduct disorder later on.

A child with conduct disorder typically exhibits some of the following behaviors while maturing into a school-ager:

- is persistently and severely aggressive
  - bullies, threatens, and intimidates
  - initiates fights
  - uses an object other than hands to hurt a person or animal
  - is cruel to animals

- destroys property
  - sets fires
  - vandalizes
- is deceitful
  - steals items
  - lies to obtain desire or avoid responsibility
  - breaks into locked property
- defies authority
  - defies parents, stays out at night
  - is truant from school
  - runs away from home

Follow these tips to deal with this disorder:

- Make use of all available professional and community resources.
- Remain assertive and persistent.
- Set realistic, achievable goals.
- Never give up!

Teachers and families dealing with a profound behavioral disability should develop strategies to cope with frustration:

- Stay calm, cool, and collected—maintaining your self-control models the behavior you want from the child.
- Forgive and forget—forget yesterday; start every day with a fresh outlook and a clean slate.
- You deserve a break today—arrange for regular periods of time away from the child; develop outside interests; get exercise; get therapy.

See Appendix C for information about less-common disabling conditions.

KEY TERMS

accommodations
acquired
anhedonia
Asperger's syndrome
asthma
attention deficit/hyperactivity disorder (ADHD)
auditory figure-ground dysfunction
autism
bipolar disorder (manic depression)
celiac disease
cerebral palsy
Child Find
cleft lip

cleft palate
conduct disorder
congenital
convulsions
coprolalia
copropraxia
cystic fibrosis
depression
diabetes mellitus
Down syndrome
dyslexia
echolalia
epilepsy

executive system
fetal alcohol spectrum disorders (FASDs)
fight or flight response
free appropriate public education (FAPE)
hearing impairment and deafness
heart defect/heart disease
human immunodeficiency virus and acquired
    immune deficiency syndrome
hydrocephalus
hypersensitivity
Individualized Education Program (IEP)
Individuals with Disabilities Education Act (IDEA)
intellectual disability (ID)
intelligence quotient (IQ)
intermittent explosive disorder (IED)
intestinal villi
learning disability
least restrictive environment (LRE)
mania
mind blindness
motor tic

muscular dystrophy
neural tube
neurodevelopment
oppositional defiant disorder (ODD)
pervasive developmental disorders (PDDs)
pica
post-traumatic stress disorder (PTSD)
proprioceptive dysfunction
proprioceptive sensation
seizure
self-regulation
sensory integration dysfunction (SID)
spina bifida
syndrome
tactile sense
Tourette's syndrome
traumatic brain injury
vestibular function
visual impairment and blindness
vocal tic

POINTS TO REMEMBER

- Children with disabilities sometimes need special accommodations.
- Children with disabilities need exemplary DAP and positive guidance.
- Behavior disorders are the most common reason children are referred to specialists.
- Families learning that their young child has a disability go through phases of shock and pain.
- Learn as much as possible about a child's disability.
- Show respect for the child and the family as they struggle to deal with the disability in their own way.
- Avoid being overprotective. Never do anything for the child that he can reasonably do for himself.
- The disabled child needs calm, assertive, positive child guidance as much as any nondisabled child.
- It's good to be optimistic, but have realistic expectations in guidance. Recognize limitations.

- Appreciate the uniqueness of each child. Never compare children.
- Focus on each child's strengths. Every child has positive characteristics and assets.
- Show unconditional affection to every child.
- Teach all of the children how to celebrate differences, show compassion, and express caring.
- Prevent bullying and stigmatizing.
- Have a sense of humor. Make sure that the environment is filled with joy.
- Any public school child receiving special education is required to have an IEP.
- In any developmentally appropriate program, there will be a plan in place to bring parents together with teachers to set goals, plan strategies for success, and track progress over time.
- We are each responsible to ensure that doors are always open for children with disabilities.

PRACTICAL APPLICATION

"Thank Heaven for Sarah"

Sarah taught and cared for a small group of children in her home. She felt strong commitment to her work and believed that she made a difference in children's lives. She took great pride in operating her home-based child care program in a professional and responsible manner. She bristled at the term *babysitter* and referred to herself as a teacher, because that is what she believed she was for the babies, toddlers, and preschoolers in her care.

Robert was three. Sarah had been caring for him for several months and had become very concerned about his behavior. He always seemed to be in conflict with the other children, and he never seemed to listen or follow even the simplest of Sarah's directions. Sarah began to wonder if Robert had some problem that was causing him to misbehave. She watched him carefully and wrote down her observations about when, where, and why he seemed to get into trouble.

Sarah began to suspect that Robert could not hear as well as he should. She noticed that whereas all the other children ran to the window each morning when they heard the garbage truck, Robert either did not respond at all or was the last to look up and run to the window. One day, Sarah stood quietly behind Robert and said very softly, "Robert, it's time for lunch." Although other children quickly responded, Robert never even looked up from his puzzle.

Sarah approached Robert's parents about the problem on several occasions. She said, "I'm not an expert in hearing problems, but I'm wondering if Robert could have a hearing problem. Has his pediatrician ever tested his hearing?" Robert's father said, "That's ridiculous. He hears whatever he wants to hear. He just chooses to ignore grown-ups most of the time." Robert's mother said, "His doctor hasn't ever mentioned a problem, and I don't see any reason to think anything is wrong."

Sarah continued caring for and working with Robert, but she still had a nagging feeling that his behavior was just not up to par for a child who seemed very bright in other ways. She noticed that his relationship with his parents had deteriorated and that he was almost constantly in trouble with adults or other children. Finally, she set an appointment to sit down privately to talk with Robert's parents.

Sarah, with kindness and respect in her voice, said, "I know that you have to do whatever you think is right for Robert, but I have to do what is right for me and for the other children in my care. I have become very attached to Robert. He is so full of creative energy. However, much of the time, his behavior is out of control and I don't know if I am doing the right thing for him. I worry that he may not be able to hear, and I wonder if that is part of the problem. I just don't feel comfortable caring for him without some kind of screening to at least rule out the possibility of a hearing problem."

Robert's father blurted out, "Fine! We'll just find someone else to care for him. We are not about to set out on some wild goose chase, looking for problems that don't exist." Sarah responded, "I understand. You have every right to do only what you believe is the best thing for your child. I'm sure that I would do the same myself. I need you to understand, though, that I am having real difficulty with Robert's behavior, and I just don't feel comfortable caring for him if I'm not sure I'm doing the right thing for him and for the other children. I am willing to accept your decision, and I'll do anything I can to help with the transition to a different child care situation. The important thing is for each of us to feel comfortable with what we do."

Robert's mother was not eager to find new child care for Robert. She really liked the way Sarah cared for the children. Robert's mother had several long discussions with her child's doctor and with her husband and finally convinced her husband that Robert should have his hearing tested in a medical clinic that could do specialized testing.

A few weeks later, Robert's father stopped by to talk to Sarah. He said, "You know, I was so sure that nothing was wrong with Robert's hearing that I really resented you insisting on a hearing test. I can't believe it, but the doctor says he has a 75 percent hearing loss in one ear and a slight loss in the other. I just didn't know."

Sarah responded, "I could have been right, or I could have been wrong. I'm no expert on hearing, but I do appreciate knowing more about why he may have been having such a hard time behaving. Thank you for being so tolerant of my questions and concerns. I think we can all work together now much more effectively to help Robert get his act together."

As Robert's father turned to leave, he patted Robert's head and said softly, "Thank heaven for Sarah."

DISCUSSION QUESTIONS

1. Do you think Sarah's actions were within her role as a caregiver?
2. Do you think Sarah went too far in insisting that Robert's hearing be checked?
3. How do you think this story would have ended if nothing had been wrong with Robert's hearing?
4. Specifically, what things did Sarah say or do that made her assertiveness more tolerable to Robert's parents?
5. What would you have done?

STUDENT ACTIVITY

1. Offer your services as a volunteer for an organization in your community that serves children with disabilities (Special Olympics, Down Syndrome Buddy Walk, a local hospital program, and so on).
2. Interview the parent of a child with a disability.
   a. How did the parent first discover the child had a disability?
   b. What has been most difficult for the parent in caring for the child and meeting the child's needs?
   c. What has the parent found most rewarding?
   d. What does the parent think is the child's greatest strength?
   e. What does the parent think is the child's greatest weakness?
   f. Are there any community resources that the parent takes advantage of? Have they been helpful?

The Online Companion™ to accompany the sixth edition of *Positive Child Guidance* is your link to additional guidance resources on the Internet. This supplement contains audio and visual materials; PowerPoint presentations; web activities with critical-thinking questions and practical-application assignments; and links to web resources. This additional content can be found at http://www.earlychilded.delmar.com.

Children's Books Addressing Values and Feelings

The Bully-Free Classroom: Over 100 Tips and Strategies for Teachers K–8

by Alan L. Beane. Minneapolis, MN: Free Spirit Publishing, 1999.

Alan Beane spells out more than 100 prevention and intervention strategies for use in the classroom. Some are classroom-centered—designed to change everyone's attitudes, thinking, and behaviors. Some are victim-centered—focusing on students who are current or potential victims of bullying. Some are bully-centered—because bullies need help as much as victims.

Get Organized Without Losing It

by J. S. Fox. Minneapolis, MN: Free Spirit Publishing, 2005.

For ages 7 through 13, this 112-page book offers tips, techniques, strategies, and examples that will empower older school-age children to conquer clutter, prioritize tasks, handle homework, prepare for tests, plan projects, stop procrastinating, and start enjoying the benefits of being organized. Children can learn how to be less stressed and more successful. Lists and steps make this little book effective while humor and cartoons make it fun to read.

Hands Are Not for Hitting

by Martine Agassi, Marieka Heinlen (Illus.). Minneapolis, MN: Free Spirit Publishing, board ed., April 2002.

For ages 2 through 5, this book stimulates children to think and talk about alternatives to hitting and other forms of hurtful behavior. The repeated phrase "hands are not for hitting" is accompanied by suggestions for positive uses for hands, such as waving, helping, drawing, and making music.

Don't Despair on Thursdays! The Children's Grief-Management Book

by Adolph J. Moser, David Melton (Illus.), Nancy R. Thatch (Ed.). Kansas City, MO: Landmark Editions (Emotional Impact Series), 1998.

This book is a useful resource for children ages 5 through 9 experiencing grief.

Don't Feed the Monster on Tuesdays! The Children's Self-Esteem Book

by Adolph J. Moser, David Melton (Illus.), Nancy R. Thatch (Ed.). Kansas City, MO: Landmark Editions (The Emotional Impact Series), 1991.

Showing numerous ways children ages 5 through 9 are critical of themselves, before the list is over, this book has kids laughing and realizing the importance of self-esteem.

Don't Tell a Whopper on Fridays! The Children's Truth-Control Book

by Adolph J. Moser, David Melton (Illus.). Kansas City, MO: Landmark Editions (Emotional Impact Series), 1999.

Adolph Moser discusses the problems of lying and the importance of telling the truth for children ages 5 through 9.

When Dinosaurs Die: A Guide to Understanding Death

by Marc Tolon Brown (Illus.), Laurie Krasny Brown. Boston, MA: Little, Brown (reprint ed.), 1998.

This book answers very basic questions about death, such as what it is and what it means and explores emotions related to grief, for ages 5 through 8. It is more appropriate for home than school settings as questions of a religious nature will probably arise.

Don't Fall Apart on Saturdays! The Children's Divorce-Survival Book

by Adolph J. Moser, David Melton (Illus.). Kansas City, MO: Landmark Editions (The Emotional Impact Series), 2000.

This book helps children ages 5 through 9 understand what divorce is and why their parents are getting a divorce.

It's Not Your Fault, Koko Bear: A Read-Together Book for Parents and Young Children During Divorce

by Vicki Lansky, Jane Prince (Illus.). Minnetonka, MN: Book Peddlers, 1998.

This book, for ages 3 through 7 and parents, provides a reassuring message to children that their feelings are natural, that their parents still love and will care for them, and that the divorce is not their fault. Each page includes endnotes for parents with information and advice about what children are experiencing and tips for handling each issue as it arises.

Dear Mr. Henshaw

by Beverly Cleary, Paul O. Zelinsky (Illus.). Glenview, IL: Scott Foresman (reprint ed.), 2000.

This award-winning book by Beverly Cleary will be appreciated by any youngster (ages 8 through 12) who feels lonely and troubled during the difficult transition into adolescence.

How Tia Lola Came to Stay

by Julia Alvarez, Andrea Cascardi (Ed.). New York: Knopf, 2001.

This is a story about Miguel's move to Vermont after his parents separate. It is a difficult time for him, and Tía Lola, his amazing aunt from the Dominican Republic, makes his life even more confusing when she arrives to help out his mami. This delightful story has a wonderful lesson to teach in a way that is simple and beautiful as it helps us experience the world of a child living in two cultures.

Vicki Lansky's Divorce Book for Parents: Helping Your Children Cope with Divorce and Its Aftermath

by Vicki Lansky. Minnetonka, MN: Book Peddlers, 2000.

This story of a young girl whose parents have just told her they are getting a divorce goes through the range of the child's possible emotions. The adults suggest how she might be feeling, and she imagines herself to be an animal that would adequately express her emotions. It is suitable for ages 5 through 8.

What Children Need to Know When Parents Get Divorced

by William L. Coleman. Minneapolis, MN: Bethany House (revised & updated ed.), 1998.

This practical guide from a licensed family counselor is designed to be read with elementary age children (ages 6 through 12) facing the agonizing trauma of divorce. When read with a caring adult, this book can be the first step in bringing children of divorce toward much-needed emotional healing.

Help! A Girl's Guide to Divorce and Stepfamilies

by Nancy Holyoke, Scott Nash (Illus.). Middleton, WI: Pleasant, 1999.

An appropriate resource of stories, for girls ages 7 through 12, shared by other girls to open the doors of communication about divorce and provide comfort.

Sad Isn't Bad: A Good-Grief Guidebook for Kids Dealing with Loss

by Michaelene Mundy, R. W. Alley (Illus.). St. Meinrad, IN: Abbey Press, 1998.

Written by a school counselor, this book helps comfort children ages 5 through 8 facing loss.

Grandmother's Song

by Barbara Soros, Jackie Morris (Illus.). Cambridge, MA: Barefoot Books, 2000.

A girl learns to pass on the wonderful lessons she learned from her late grandmother. This book is suitable for ages 7 through 10.

Play Lady: La Senora Juguetona

by Eric Hoffman, Suzanne Tornquist (Illus.), Carmen Sosa Masso (Trans.). St. Paul, MN: Redleaf Press, 1999.

When her mobile home is vandalized, neighbors come to the aid of their friend, Senora Juguetona. The children who visit to play with her are of many cultures and colors, and one, Kayla, is in a wheelchair. The children enlist their parents' help in repairing the Play Lady's house and yard. The illus-

trations express the feelings of the characters, enhancing the book's message of accepting diversity. This book is suitable for ages 3 through 7.

Bright Eyes, Brown Skin

by Cheryl Willis Hudson, Bernette G. Ford (Contributor), George Cephas Ford (Illus.). East Orange, NJ: Just Us Books, 2006.

Four African American children interact with one another in a preschool environment and, in so doing, explore their facial features, skin tones, activities, personalities, and how they learn from and appreciate each other. This book is suitable for ages 3 through 5.

Uncle Jed's Barbershop

by Margaree King Mitchell, James Ransome (Illus.). New York: Aladdin Paperbacks (reprint ed.), 1998.

Sarah Jean's favorite relative is her great-uncle Jed, who is the only black barber in the county. Great-uncle Jed travels from house to house cutting hair. His dream is to have his own barber shop. Unfortunately, segregation and the Depression present huge obstacles, and he puts aside his dream to pay Sarah Jean's hospital bill. When he finally opens his own shop on his 79th birthday, a grown-up Sarah Jean and the whole community share the joy of his dream come true. This book is suitable for ages 4 through 8.

Nappy Hair

by Carolivia Herron, Joe Cepeda (Illus.) New York: Random House (reprint ed.), 1998.

At the family picnic, Uncle Mordecai calls out the story of Brenda's hair—the nappiest hair in the world—while everyone else chimes in with "Yep," "You said it," and "Ain't it the truth." The traditional African American call and response style, and Cepeda's vibrant, folk-art paintings capture children's imagination and hold their attention. This book is suitable for ages 3 through 9.

In Daddy's Arms I Am Tall: African Americans Celebrating Fathers

by Javaka Steptoe (Illus.). New York: Lee & Low Books, 2001.

This award-winning book for ages 9 through 12 creates a beautiful series of images in mixed media—torn and cut paper, found objects, and color—to illustrate short poems about fathers.

My Dream of Martin Luther King

by Faith Ringgold (Illus.). New York: Dragonfly Books, 1998.

The author looks at the life of Martin Luther King Jr. to narrate a dream story in which King is a child who must go to a segregated school and hear his daddy called "boy." He watches police on horseback beat up protesters and is taken to prison where his grandmother holds him and tries to explain segregation. The book, for children ages 6 through 9, teaches about King's life through an impressionistic dream sequence.

Virgie Goes to School with Us Boys

by Elizabeth Fitzgerald Howard, Earl B. Lewis (Illus.). New York: Simon & Schuster Juvenile Books, 2000.

This family story for ages 5 through 10 is about five brothers and one little sister growing up in Tennessee just after the Civil War. Virgie, the daughter, wants to learn to read and write like her older brothers. But the boys have to walk seven miles to Jonesborough each Monday morning, carrying their clothes and enough food for the week in a tin pail. They sleep all week at the school and walk home on Friday evening. Although her parents are frightened about letting her go to school with her brothers, she begs until her father finally gives in. He says, "All free people need learning. Old folks, young folks . . . small girls, too."

My Man Blue

by Nikki Grimes, Jerome Lagarrigue (Illus.), Toby Sherry (Ed.). New York: Dial Books for Young Readers, 1999.

Through a series of poems, an African American boy living in a tough neighborhood tells about his friend Blue. Damon and his mother have just moved to a new apartment when an old friend of the mother's, named Blue, befriends Damon. Blue lost one boy to the streets and is determined to keep Damon on the right track. Blue shoots hoops with Damon, listens to him, and shares laughs and hot dogs. Blue always stands steadfast in Damon's corner and keeps him headed in the right direction. This book is suitable for ages 7 through 10.

Danitra Brown Leaves Town

by Nikki Grimes, Floyd Cooper (Illus.). New York: HarperCollins Juvenile Books, 2001.

When best friends Zuri Jackson and Danitra Brown are split up for summer vacation, Danitra goes off to the country to visit relatives and Zuri is stuck in the city. They write letters to each other all summer—in richly descriptive poetry—sharing their feelings and experiences. This book is suitable for ages 4 through 8. We met these two unforgettable best friends in the Coretta Scott King Honor Book, Meet Danitra Brown (1994).

Night Golf

by William Miller, Cedric Lucas (Illus.). New York: Lee & Low Books, 1999.

Before 1961 golf courses were closed to people who were not white. James finds a rusty old golf club and becomes interested in golf. Barred from the course except as a caddy, he is befriended by an older black caddy who invites him back into the golf course after the sun goes down so he can practice. This book is suitable for ages 7 through 12.

A Pig Is Moving In

by Claudia Fries (Illus.). New York: Orchard Books, 2000.

Doctor Fox, Henrietta Hen, and Nick Hare see a pig moving into their cozy apartment building and quickly jump to the conclusion that he will be "messy and dirty and sloppy." They assume that every mess they encounter was left by this pig but discover that they were wrong. The pig was cleaning up their messes. Their tidy pig neighbor turns out to be a clever and generous neighbor. This book is suitable for ages 4 through 7.

Jack and Jim

by Kitty Crowther. New York: Hyperion Press, 2000.

Jack, a blackbird, decides to venture out of his forest home to explore the nearby ocean. He makes friends with a dashingly handsome seagull named Jim. Unfortunately, the other white gulls aren't so hospitable. In spite of Jim's efforts to defend his friend, the village gulls can't seem to get beyond Jack's different appearance until they discover he has a talent none of them have. Jack reads funny stories to them from an old box of books that washed up on the shore. Finally, he wins the admiration and friendship of the narrow-minded gulls. This book is suitable for ages 4 through 7.

Sister Anne's Hands

by Marybeth Lorbiecki, K. Wendy Popp (Illus.), Joy Peskin (Ed.). New York: Dial Books for Young Readers, 2000.

This touching story, suitable for ages 8 through 12, is about a black nun in the early 1960s and the lessons she imparts and is based on the author's own childhood experiences. From the first day of second grade, Sister Anne lights up Anna's classroom. But it's the early 1960s and not everyone in Anna's small town is ready to accept Sister. How she deals with prejudice and the profound impact she has on her students is at the heart of this beautiful, timeless story about tolerance, and how a devoted teacher can change a child's life.

Companeros de Equipo/Teammates

by Peter Golenbock, F. Isabel Campoy, Alma Flor Ada (Trans.). San Diego, CA: Libros Viajeros (Spanish translation, original language English), 2002.

In a time of racial inequality, two teammates overcome boundaries and learn they are brothers despite the color of their skin. The story, suitable for ages 8 through 12, focuses on standing up for one's beliefs, fighting injustice, and respecting the rights of others.

Pelitos/Hairs

by Sandra Cisneros, Terry Ybanez (Illus.). New York: Random House, 1997.

This bilingual story for ages 3 through 7 describes differences between family members' hair. It helps children celebrate the experience of differences even within their own family. Classroom discussion can be extended from children's own family traditions and similarities and differences. The story encourages them to write their own stories.

My Very Own Room/Mi Propio Cuartito

by Amada Irma Pérez, Maya Christina Gonzalez (Illus.). San Francisco, CA: Children's Book Press (bilingual ed.), 2000.

The eight-year-old telling this touching family story (for ages 5 through 9) shares a noisy, crowded little room with her five brothers. She wishes she had her own room where she could write in her diary, read, and dream undisturbed. She claims a tiny storage closet behind a flour-sack curtain and imagines that she has a bedroom with her own bed, table, and lamp. The whole family pitches in to help her empty the closet and piece together her very own little room.

Carlos and the Cornfield/Carlos y la Milpa de Maiz

by Jan Romero Stevens, Jeanne Arnold (Illus.), Patricia Davison (Trans.). New York: Rising Moon, 1995.

Before Carlos plants seed corn, his papa warns him, "Remember, 'Cosechas lo que siembras': You reap what you sow." Carlos is so excited about earning money to buy a new red pocketknife that he plants all of the seeds in the first few rows, leaving no seed to plant in the last rows. He gives up his beloved knife to buy more seed corn for the empty rows. When the corn is harvested, the error of his ways is discovered: the last rows turn out to be blue rather than yellow corn, so mama serves blue corn cakes for breakfast. Bilingual and complete with a recipe for blue corn pancakes, this beautifully written sequel to Carlos y la Planta de Calabaza/ Carlos and the Squash Plant (1993) presents a valuable lesson on being responsible for one's own actions. The book is suitable for ages 5 through 8.

Chato's Kitchen

by Gary Soto, Susan Guevara (Illus.). New York: Paper Star (reprint ed.), 1997.

This award-winning book for ages 4 through 8 tells the story of Chato, a sly, mustachioed "cool cat" from an East Los Angeles barrio. Five mice, the color of gray river rock, move next door. Chato promptly invites the mice over for dinner— unfortunately, as the main course. Instead of the gruesome outcome you might expect, the author creates a delightfully surprising ending.

Too Many Tamales

by Gary Soto, Ed Martinez (Illus.). New York: Putnam, 1993.

In preparation for a family Christmas fiesta, Maria and her parents are busy making tamales. Maria can't resist trying on her mother's diamond ring, but she forgets all about the ring until she realizes it has disappeared. Maria is sure the ring must be inside a tamale, so she talks her cousins into eating all 24 to help her find it. The overstuffed cousins are greatly relieved to discover that the ring really isn't lost after all. Children ages 4 and older will empathize with mischievous Maria and appreciate this playful reminder about the importance of forgiveness.

Goin' Someplace Special

by Patricia C. McKissack, Jerry Pinkney (Illus.). New York: Atheneum Press, 2001.

This 2002 Coretta Scott King Illustrator Award Winner is about Tricia Ann's first solo trip out of her neighborhood. Tricia Ann is confronted by the segregation of Nashville in the 1950s, but her confidence, intelligence, pride in her heritage, and sense of self-worth make this a victorious journey for her

as she searches for truth. The story, suitable for ages 7 through 10, is based on the author's own experiences and the many indignities she encountered during that troubled period.

Markita

by Alissa Nash, Doby London (Illus.). Chicago, IL: African American Images, 1997.

Nice stories about beautiful flowers in a colorful human bouquet offer little comfort to a young girl who never feels as special as her lighter complexioned cousins. This book for ages 6 through 9 offers a compassionate look at diversity and self-esteem.

Oliver's High Five

by Beverly Swerdlow Brown, Margot J. Ott (Illus.). Santa Fe, NM: Health Press, 1998.

Oliver Octopus has only five arms, but he doesn't mind. Young children ages 3 through 9 with any kind of disability or difference will enjoy reading about Oliver's adventures above the sea. Through determination and a positive attitude, he changes the way others think about his uniqueness.

Harry and Willy and Carrothead

by Judith Caseley. New York: Greenwillow, 1991.

Harry, born without a left hand, is a lively, confident, and lovable child. His physical difference doesn't keep him from becoming a good baseball player. His red-headed friend Oscar is not so self-assured and is hurt by taunts of "carrot head." Harry stands up to Oscar's tormentor, Willy, and soon the three are best friends. This book is suitable for ages 3 through 9.

If the Shoe Fits

by Gary Soto, Terry Widener (Illus.). New York: Putnam Juvenile Press, 2002.

As the youngest son in a large Mexican American family, Rigo often gets stuck wearing worn-out hand-me-downs. He's thrilled to receive a pair of brand new penny loafers for his ninth birthday, but when a neighborhood bully makes fun of his fancy shoes, Rigo hides the shoes in his closet. A few months later, he tries to wear the shoes to a party, but they no longer fit. Rigo's disappointment helps him see hand-me-downs in a new light. He thoughtfully gives the almost new shoes to Uncle Celso, who needs good shoes for his new job as a waiter. This book is suitable for ages 5 and up.

Dancing in the Wings

by Debbie Allen, Kadir Nelson (Illus.). New York: Dial Books for Young Readers, 2000.

Though tall and lanky for a ballerina, African American Sassy loves to dance and dreams of performing on stage. She is hurt by teasing from classmates about her long legs but encouraged by her uncle's belief that she is beautiful. A Russian ballet master believes in her and she finally finds herself on stage, in the spotlight, partnered with an even taller young man. The book is suitable for ages 5 through 8.

Simon's Hook: A Story about Teases and Put-downs

by Karen Gedig Burnett, Laurie Barrows (Illus.). New York: GR Lockwood, 1999.

This book for ages 6 and up helps children learn appropriate ways to respond to teasing. Through his use of a fishing analogy, Burnett shows children how to "swim free" from feeling helpless, trapped, stuck, or powerless. The book teaches alternatives to hitting back.

The First Strawberries: A Cherokee Story

by Joseph Bruchac, Anna Vojtech (Illus.). New York: Puffin (reprint ed.), 1998.

This native Cherokee folktale, written for ages 5 through 10, reminds people to be kind to each other. In this creation story, the first man and woman have an angry quarrel that is forgotten when they share delicious strawberries she has discovered.

Coyote: A Trickster Tale from the American Southwest

by Gerald McDermott. New York: Voyager Books (reprint ed.), 1999.

Coyote, the trickster in this native legend, is rude, boastful, vain, and always in trouble. Young children (ages 2 through 5) will identify with this foolish but very human character who has a nose for trouble and always manages to find it.

Kids Like Me in China

by Ying Ying Fry and Amy Klatzkin, Brian Boyd, Terry Fry (Photographers). St. Paul, MN: Yeong & Yeong, 2001.

This touching, enlightening, and entertaining book provides children ages 7 through 12 with an opportunity to see China through a child's eyes. Ying Ying tells her own story as readers learn about ordinary life in China (schools, homes, and families).

Lucy and the Liberty Quilt

by Victoria London, Angela Liang (Illus.). Irving, TX: A Gifted Girls Series, Book 1; Sparklesoup Studios, 2001.

This book combines lessons in life, history, and culture to provide positive themes for girls ages 5 through 10 growing up today.

Come and Abide (We Are All the Same Inside)

by Timothy D. Bellavia, Randi Cannata's 4th Grade T.A.G. @ P.S. 175 Q. District 28 N.Y.C. (Collaborator). New York: T.I.M.M.E. (Tolerance in Multi Media Education), 2002.

Come and Abide, *a result of the author's collaboration with 26 fourth graders, helps children better understand tolerance and diversity.*

Somewhere Today: A Book of Peace

by Shelly Moore Thomas, Eric Futran (Photographer), Shelley Moore Thomas and Abby Levine (Eds.). Grove, IL: Albert Whitman, 1998.

This simple, readable picture book reminds children ages 4 through 8 how to behave positively rather than aggressively.

Something Beautiful

by Sharon Dennis Wyeth, Chris K. Soentpiet (Illus.). New York: Dragonfly Books (reprint ed.), 2002.

A small African American girl living in a very scary neighborhood searches for something beautiful. She sees garbage, broken glass, angry graffiti, and a homeless woman sleeping under plastic covers. The little girl manages, however, to find beauty and warmth in unlikely places. This book is suitable for all ages.

Five Minutes' Peace

by Jill Murphy. New York: Paper Star, 1999.

A humorous book for ages 4 through 7 about a mother searching for five minutes' peace. Unfortunately, chaos follows her around the house.

Harvesting Hope: The Story of Cesar Chavez

by K. Krull. Orlando, FL: Harcourt, 2003.

Cesar Chavez wanted justice for farmworkers, so he organized them. He became to Mexicans what Martin Luther King Jr. is for blacks. Although the book is recommended for children ages 6 through 9, middle school students, ages 9 through 12, especially those with limited English proficiency, can benefit from this story. This book can help instill pride and understanding as to how determination, perseverance, and hard work can overcome even the greatest odds.

I'm Like You, You're Like Me: A Child's Book about Understanding and Celebrating Each Other

by C. Gainer. Minneapolis, MN: Free Spirit Publishing, 1998.

This book for ages 3 through 8 presents diversity on children's level: hair that's straight or curly, families with many people or few, bodies that are big or small—each one unique but just right for that person. Boys and girls discover that even though people are different, they can enjoy being together and learning about each other.

Iceberg/Fetal Alcohol Syndrome Information Service (FASIS)

Iceberg is a quarterly international educational newsletter on FASD (fetal alcohol spectrum disorders). It is called *Iceberg* because the childhood problems that are easily seen are only the "tip of the iceberg." The organization producing *Iceberg*, Fetal Alcohol Syndrome Information Service (FASIS), has provided information about prenatal exposure to alcohol, fetal alcohol spectrum disorder (FASD), fetal alcohol syndrome (FAS), fetal alcohol effects (FAE), alcohol-related birth defects (ARBD), and alcohol-related neurodevelopmental disorders (ARNDs), since 1991.

FASIS
P.O. Box 95597
Seattle, WA 98145-2597
E-mail: iceberg_fas@yahoo.com
http://www.fasiceberg.org

FAS Community Resource Center

The focus of the FAS Center is prevention: Primary prevention raises awareness in the general population to reduce the incidence of FASD. Secondary prevention focuses on women at high risk—those who have already had a child with FASD. Tertiary prevention focuses on reducing the incidence of secondary conditions associated with FASD. The FAS Community Resource Center comprises two communities: a local community in Tucson, Arizona, and a virtual Internet community that reaches around the world.

Teresa Kellerman
FAS-CRC
7725 East 33rd Street
Tucson, Arizona 85710-6059
Telephone: (520) 296-9172
http://www.come-over.to/FASCRC/

The National Organization on Fetal Alcohol Syndrome (NOFAS)

This international FASD nonprofit organization is committed to prevention, advocacy, and support. NOFAS increases public awareness and mobilizes grassroots action in diverse communities and represents the interests of those with FASD and their caregivers as the liaison to researchers and policymakers. By ensuring that FASD is broadly recognized as a developmental disability, NOFAS strives to reduce the stigma and improve the quality of life for affected individuals and families.

NOFAS
900 17th Street, NW, Suite 910
Washington, DC 20006
Telephone: (202) 785-4585 or (800) 66NOFAS
Fax: (202) 466-6456
http://www.nofas.org/

Allergy and Asthma Network, Mothers of Asthmatics, Inc. (AAN-MA)

AAN-MA is an international, nonprofit organization dedicated to educating families dealing with asthma and allergies. Members of AAN-MA receive a monthly newsletter that includes information on medical research, current treatments and therapies, new products, and coping techniques.

Allergy and Asthma Network Mothers
    of Asthmatics, Inc.
2751 Prosperity Ave., Suite 150
Fairfax, VA 22031
Telephone: (800) 878-4403
Fax: (703) 573-7794
E-mail: aanma@aol.com
http://www.aanma.org/

American Academy of Child and Adolescent Psychiatry

This is a professional organization for child and adolescent psychiatrists conducting research and diagnosing and treating psychiatric disorders of children, adolescents, and their families. It publishes "Facts for Families," a series that includes more than 50 informational sheets on topics such as the depressed child, suicide, discipline, and child sexual abuse.

American Academy of Child and Adolescent
   Psychiatry
3615 Wisconsin Avenue, NW
Washington, DC 20016
Telephone: (202) 966-7300
Fax: (202) 966-2891
E-mail: membership@aacap.org
http://www.aacap.org/

The Arc

The Arc is the country's largest voluntary organization committed to the welfare of all children and adults with mental retardation and their families.

The Arc
1010 Wayne Avenue, Suite 650
Silver Spring, MD 20910
Telephone: (301) 565-3842 or (800) 433-5255
Fax: (301) 565-3843 or (301) 565-5342
E-mail: info@thearc.org
http://www.TheArc.org/

Birth Defect Research for Children, Inc. (BDRC)

A charitable organization that provides free information by telephone to parents and professionals about birth defects, BDRC also sponsors the National Birth Defect Registry, a birth defect prevention project that provides information on possible links between specific birth defects and their causes (for example, exposures to chemicals during the Gulf War). Members of BDRC receive fact sheets, special reports, and a newsletter.

BDRC
800 Celebration Ave, Suite 225
Celebration, FL 34747

Telephone: (407) 566-8304
http://www.birthdefects.org/

Association for Special Kids, Inc. (A.S.K.)

A.S.K. is a financial planning organization dedicated to helping parents of children with disabilities protect their children's future. Counselors work individually with parents and with a network of qualified attorneys and accountants to set parents' plans into action. There is a fee for these services. Most of the counselors are parents of children with disabilities.

A.S.K.
2241 Hollywood Blvd.
Hollywood, FL 33020
Telephone: (888) 342-4077 or (954) 342-4077
http://www.specialkidslawcenter.com/

ASPIRA Association, Inc.: An Investment in Latino Youth

This national, nonprofit organization serves Puerto Rican and other Hispanic youth and their families through leadership and education. (ASPIRA is taken from the Spanish word *aspirar,* which means "to aspire to something greater.") It provides bilingual publications at low cost related to Hispanic health, education, violence, and the like.

ASPIRA Association, Inc.
1444 I Street, NW, Suite 800
Washington, DC 20005
Telephone: (202) 835-3600
Fax: (202) 835-3613
E-mail: aspira1@aol.com
http://www.aspira.org/

Asthma and Allergy Foundation of America (AAFA)

This organization supports families by providing a bi-monthly newsletter with practical articles on asthma and allergies. AAFA also maintains a clearinghouse of current and affordable educational materials, funds medical research, and sponsors a nationwide network of affiliated AAFA chapters.

Asthma and Allergy Foundation of America
1233 20th Street, NW, Suite 402
Washington, DC 20036
Telephone: (800) 7-ASTHMA (800-727-8462)
E-mail: info@aafa.org
http://www.aafa.org/

Attention Deficit Disorders Association

This independent, nonprofit organization provides a re-source network for parents, educators, and health care professionals. ADDA keeps the public informed about ADD/ADHD through educational and support programs and services.

Attention Deficit Disorders Association
15000 Commerce Parkway, Suite C
Mount Laurel, NJ 08054
Telephone: (856) 439-9099
Fax: (856) 439-0525
E-mail: adda@add.org
http://www.add.org/

Child Attention Deficit Disorder/Attention Deficit Hyperactivity Disorder (CH.A.D.D.)

This is a support organization for families coping with ADD/ADHD.

CHADD National Office
8181 Professional Place, Suite 150
Landover, MD 20785
Telephone: (301) 306-7070
Fax: (301) 306-7090
http://chadd.org/

Children's Hospice International

This nonprofit organization provides medical, psychological, emotional, and spiritual support to seriously ill children and their families, as well as to families recovering from the loss of child.

Children's Hospice International
1101 King Street, Suite 360
Alexandria, VA 22314
Telephone: (703) 684-0330 or (800) 24-CHILD
Fax: (703) 684-0226
http://www.chionline.org/

The Council for Exceptional Children (CEC): The Voice and Vision of Special Education

CEC provides information through its library and database of professional literature to those concerned with the education of children who are gifted and have special needs. CEC also convenes conferences, assists lawmakers, and coordinates the North American Political Action Network.

The Council for Exceptional Children
1110 North Glebe Road, Suite 300
Arlington, VA 22201
Telephone: (800) 224-6830 or (888) 232-7733
    (membership services)
http://www.cec.sped.org

Education for Parents of Indian Children with Special Needs (EPICS)

This is a national project providing parent training and information for Native American families with special needs children.

Indian Children with Special Needs
P.O. Box 788
Bernalillo, NM 87004
Telephone: (505) 867-3396
Fax: (505) 867-3398
E-mail: JeanetteT@EpicsProject.org
http://www.abrazosnm.org/

Educators for Social Responsibility

ESR develops curricula and trains teachers with a particular focus on conflict resolution.

ESR
23 Garden Street
Cambridge, MA 02138
Telephone: (617) 492-1764 or (800) 370-2515
E-mail: educators@esrnational.org
http://www.esrnational.org/

Families Anonymous

A national group that provides support for individuals who are concerned about drugs and drug-related behavioral problems of friends and relatives.

Families Anonymous
P.O. Box 3475

Culver City, CA 90231-3475
Telephone: (800) 736-9805 or (310) 313-5800
Fax: (310) 815-9682
E-mail: famanon@FamiliesAnonymous.org
http://www.familiesanonymous.org/

The Institute on Violence, Abuse and Trauma (IVAT)

IVAT strives to be a comprehensive resource, training, and research center dealing with all aspects of violence, abuse, and trauma.

IVAT
10065 Old Grove Road
San Diego, CA 92131
Telephone: (858) 527-1860 x 4160
Fax: (858) 527-1743
http://www.ivatcenters.org/

Federation for Children with Special Needs

This center is for parents and parent organizations to work together on behalf of children with special needs and their families.

Federation for Children with Special Needs
1135 Tremont Street, Suite 420
Boston, MA 02120
Telephone: (617) 236-7210 or (800) 331-0688
    (in Massachusetts)
Fax: (617) 572-2094
E-mail: fcsninfo@fcsn.org
http://www.fcsn.org/

Federation of Families for Children's Mental Health

This national organization focuses on the needs of children and youth with emotional, behavioral, or mental disorders and their families.

Federation of Families for Children's Mental
    Health
FFCMH
9605 Medical Center Drive, Suite 280
Rockville, MD 20850
Telephone: (240) 403-1901
Fax: (240) 403-1909

E-mail: ffcmh@ffcmh.org
http://www.ffcmh.org/

National Association for Visually Handicapped

This private, nonprofit organization serves visually impaired—not totally blind—children, their parents, and professionals who work with them, as well as adults with vision loss. The organization provides large-print visual aids, a newsletter, and brochures with information about commercially manufactured optical aids.

National Association for Visually Handicapped
22 West 21st Street
New York, NY 10010
Telephone: (212) 889-3141
Fax: (212) 727-2931
E-mail: navh@navh.org
http://www.navh.org/

National Black Child Development Institute (NBCDI)

This organization provides community and direct services to African American children, families, and advocates.

National Black Child Development Institute
1313 L Street, NW, Suite 110
Washington, DC 20005-4110
Telephone: (202) 833-2220
Fax: (202) 833-8222
E-mail: moreinfo@nbcdi.org
http://www.nbcdi.org

United States Burn Support Organization (USBURN)

The mission of USBURN is to help those who have suffered minor to severe burns and their families rebuild their lives, which have been forever changed as a result of the burn injuries.

USBURN
P.O. Box 26001
Philadelphia, PA 19128
Telephone: (215) 473-2955 or (215) 577-0631
    (burn pager)
E-mail: usburnsupport@usburn.org
http://www.usburn.org/

National Clearinghouse for Alcohol and Drug Information (NCADI)

Serving as the world's largest resource for current information and materials concerning substance abuse prevention, NCADI has an information services staff equipped to respond to the public's alcohol, tobacco, and illicit drug inquiries. The program is a service of the Center for Substance Abuse Prevention, Substance Abuse and Mental Health Services Administration, U.S. Public Health Service, U.S. Department of Health and Human Services.

National Clearinghouse for Alcohol and Drug
   Information
P.O. Box 2345
Rockville, MD 20847-2345
Telephone: (240) 221-4017 or (800) 729-6686; (877)
   767-8432 (Spanish)
TDD: (800) 487-4889
Fax: (240) 221-4292
E-mail: info@health.org or ncadi.samhsa.gov
http://ncadi.samhsa.gov/

National Latino Children's Institute (NLCI)

NLCI promotes and implements the National Latino Children's Agenda, which is a statement of principles essential for the healthy and complete development of Latino children. NLCI identifies and recognizes best practices in the areas of children's health, environment, economic, and educational conditions that are respectful of Latino cultural values and language.

National Latino Children's Institute
1115 South St. Mary's Street
San Antonio, TX 78210
Telephone: (210) 228-9997
Fax: (210) 228-9972
E-mail: nlci@nlci.org
http://www.nlci.org

National Organization of Parents of Blind Children (NOPBC)

Facilitating the sharing of experience and concerns among parents of blind children and visually impaired children, providing information and support, and developing resources for them, NOPBC conducts seminars and workshops, and publishes free or low-cost brochures.

Mrs. Barbara Cheadle, President
National Organization of Parents of Blind Children
1800 Johnson Street
Baltimore, MD 21230
Telephone: (410) 659-9314
Fax: (410) 685-5653
http://www.nfb.org/

The Stuttering Foundation of America (SFA)

SFA maintains a toll-free hotline on stuttering. Call for free information, brochures, and a nationwide referral list of speech-language pathologists who specialize in stuttering. SFA has also produced *Stuttering and Your Child: A Videotape for Parents,* which is offered free of charge to public libraries. Provide your local library with the toll-free telephone number below and ask that they obtain a copy of the video for their collection. The video is geared toward parents, teachers, child care professionals, and others interested in helping a child who stutters.

Stuttering Foundation of America
3100 Walnut Grove, Suite 603
P.O. Box 11749
Memphis, TN 38111-0749
Telephone: (800) 992-9392 or (901) 452-7343
Fax: (901) 452-3931
E-mail: info@stutteringhelp.org
http://www.stutteringhelp.org/

Uncommon Disabling Conditions

Sickle Cell Disease

Sickle cell disease is an inherited disorder of the blood resulting in abnormal red blood cells that are not able to carry enough oxygen around the body. The abnormal red blood cells are distorted into a crescent shape, which is why the disease is called "sickle cell" disease. These misshapen red blood cells are fragile and rupture easily. When the number of red blood cells drops dangerously low because too many fragile blood cells have disintegrated, **anemia** results. This is called sickle cell anemia (Sacerdote, 2003).

Additionally, because of their curved shape, sickled cells tend to block blood vessels, causing tissue and organ damage and pain. Episodes of pain may last hours or days. The bones of the back, the long bones in the legs and arms and the chest are all areas that are particularly vulnerable to pain. Over time, the severe anemia from sickle cell disease can damage the kidneys, lungs, bone, liver, and central nervous system. Blocked blood vessels in the brain can cause a stroke. This can cause brain cells to die. Strokes affect about 1 in every 10 children with sickle cell disease.

Sickle cell disease primarily affects Africans and African Americans, but people with other ethnic backgrounds may also be affected. Sickle cell disease has been known in Africa for hundreds of years. In west Africa ethnic groups gave the disorder names in their local dialect: *chwechweechwe, nwiiwii, nuidudui,* and *ahotutuo* (Wailoo, 2001). In the United States, it is estimated that about 50,000 African Americans are afflicted with the most severe form of sickle cell anemia (Parker & Parker, 2005; Sickle Cell Advisory Committee, 1999).

For more information, see http://www.sicklecelldisease .org; www.sicklecellct.org; http://www.cqscc.org; www .cscsginc.org; www.scinfo.org; http://www.sickle.bwh .harvard.edu.

American Academy of Pediatrics. (2002). Health supervision for children with sickle cell disease. *Pediatrics, 109,* 526–535.

Ballas, S. K. (1998). *Sickle cell pain: Progress in pain research and management* (Vol. 11). Seattle, WA: IASP Press.

Mehta, S. R., Afenyi-Annan, A., Byrns, P. J., & Lottenberg, R. (2006). Opportunities to improve outcomes in sickle cell disease. *American Family Physician,* July, *74*(2), whole issue.

Parker, J. N., & Parker, P. M., Eds. (2005). *The official patient's sourcebook on sickle cell anemia.* San Diego, CA: ICON Health Publications.

Platt, O. S., Brambilla, D. J., Rosse, W. F., Milner, P. F., Castro, O., Steinberg, M. H., & Klug, P. P. (1994). Mortality in sickle cell disease: Life expectancy and risk factors for early death. *New England Journal of Medicine, 330,* 1639–1644.

Powars, D., Wilson, B., Imbus, C., Pegelow, C., Allen, J. (1978). The natural history of stroke in sickle cell disease. *American Journal of Medicine, 65,* 461–471.

Sacerdote, A. (2003). *Hope and destiny: A patient's and parent's guide to sickle cell anemia.* Munster, IN: Hilton.

Schechter, A. N., & Bunn, H. F. (1982). What determines severity in sickle cell disease? (Editorial) *New England Journal of Medicine, 306,* 295.

Sickle Cell Advisory Committee. (1999). *Sickle cell disease: Information for school personnel.* Trenton: New Jersey Department of Health and Senior Services.

Wailoo, K. (2001). *Dying in the city of the blues: Sickle cell anemia and the politics of race and health.* Chapel Hill: University of North Carolina Press.

Walters, M. C., Patience, M., Leisenring, W., Eckman, J. R., Scott, J. P., Mentzer, W. C., Davies, S. C., Ohene-Frempong, K., Bernaudin, F., Matthews, D. C., Storb, R., & Sullivan, K. M. (1996). Bone marrow transplantation for sickle cell disease. *New England Journal of Medicine, 335,* 369–376.

CHARGE Syndrome

Individuals with **CHARGE syndrome** are born with an extremely complex set of birth defects. This syndrome involves extensive medical and physical disorders that can differ from child to child. Most have hearing loss, vision loss, and balance problems, which seriously delay their development and communication. All are likely to require medical and educational intervention for many years (Pagon et al., 1981; Davenport et al., 1986).

The term CHARGE came from taking the first letter of each of the primary features seen in this condition (Davenport et al., 1986):

- **c**oloboma (eye defects, blindness)
- **h**eart defects
- **a**tresia of the choanae (nasal blockage)
- **r**etardation (of growth and developmental delay)
- **g**enitalia (undescended testicles, urinary abnormalities)
- **e**ar (anomalies, deafness)

For more information, see http://www.chargesyndrome .org/.

Davenport, S. L. H., Hefner, M. A., & Mitchell, J. A. (1986). The spectrum of clinical features in CHARGE syndrome. *Clinical Genetics, 29,* 298–310.

Hartshorne, T. S., & Cypher, A. D. (2004). Challenging behavior in CHARGE syndrome. *Mental Health Aspects of Developmental Disabilities, 7*(2), 41–52.

Hartshorne, T. S., Grialou, T. L., & Parker, K. R. (2005). Autistic-Like Behavior in CHARGE Syndrome. *American Journal of Medical Genetics, 133A,* 257–261.

Hartshorne, T. S., Hefner, M. A., & Davenport, S. L. H. (2005). Behavior in CHARGE Syndrome: Introduction to the series. *American Journal of Medical Genetics, 133A,* 228–231.

Pagon, R. A., Graham, J. M., Zonana, J., & Yong, S. L. (1981). Coloboma, congenital heart disease, and choanal atresia with multiple anomalies: CHARGE association. *Journal of Pediatrics, 99,* 223–227.

Thelin, J. W., & Fussner, J. C. (2005). Factors related to the development of communication in CHARGE syndrome. *American Journal of Medical Genetics, 133A,* 228–231.

Williams, G. L., & Hartshorne, T. S. (2005). Understanding balance problems in children with CHARGE syndrome. *Deaf-Blind Perspectives, 12*(2), 5–7.

Turner's Syndrome

Turner's syndrome is a genetic disorder that can affect a girl's development. The cause is a missing or incomplete Y chromosome. Girls who have it tend to be very short and their ovaries and genitalia don't usually become sexually mature at puberty. Girls with Turner's syndrome are at risk for health difficulties such as high blood pressure, kidney disorders, eye defects, diabetes, thyroid disorders, and spatial perceptual problems (Saenger, 1996; Frias & Davenport, 2003).

Physical features typical of Turner's syndrome are the following:

- short stature
- short "webbed" neck
- low hairline in the back
- low-set ears
- swelling on tops of hands and feet

For more information, see http://www.turner-syndrome-us.org/.

Frias, J. L., & Davenport, M. L. (2003). Health supervision for children with Turner syndrome. *Pediatrics,* March, *111*(3), 692–702.

ICON Health Publications (2004). *Turner syndrome: A medical dictionary, bibliography, and annotated research guide to internet references.* San Diego, CA: Author.

Saenger, P. (1996). Turner's syndrome. *New England Journal of Medicine,* December, *335*(23), 1749–1754.

Stratakis, C. A., & Rennert, O. M. (2005). Turner syndrome: An update. *The Endocrinologist, 15,* 27–36.

Tay-Sachs Disease

Tay-Sachs disease is a genetic disorder that occurs in the Jewish population. Tay-Sachs is characterized by severe mental and developmental delay that begins during the first four to eight months of life. The involvement of the central nervous system progresses quickly so that children with Tay-Sachs become profoundly disabled by preschool age. Typically, these children also develop uncontrollable seizures and are vulnerable to infection. Sadly, most die before kindergarten (Desnick & Kaback, 2001; ICON Health Publications, 2004f).

For more information, see http://www.ntsad.org; http://www.ntsad-ny.org.

Bach, G., Tomczak, J., Risch, N., & Ekstein, J. (2001). Tay-Sachs screening in the Jewish Ashkenazi population: DNA testing is the preferred procedure. *American Journal of Medical Genetics,* February, *99*(1), 70–75.

Desnick, R. J., & Kaback, M. M., Eds. (2001). *Tay-Sachs disease.* San Diego, CA: Academic Press.

ICON Health Publications. (2004f). *Tay-Sachs disease: A medical dictionary, bibliography, and annotated research guide to internet references.* San Diego, CA: Author.

Kaback, M. M. (2000). Population based genetic screening for reproductive counseling: The Tay-Sachs disease model. *European Journal of Pediatrics,* December, *159*(3), 192–195.

Kaback, M. M., & Desnick, R. J. (2001). Tay-Sachs disease: From clinical description to molecular defect. *Advances in Genetics, 44,* 1–9.

Kaback, M., Steele, J., Dabholkar, D., Brown, D., Levy, N., & Zeiger, K. (1993). Tay-Sachs disease-carrier screening, prenatal diagnosis, and the molecular era. *Journal of the American Medical Association, 270,* 2307–2315.

Kaplan, F. (1998). Tay-Sachs disease carrier screening: A model for prevention of genetic disease. *Genetic Testing, 2*(4), 271–292.

Myerowitz, R. (2001). The search for the genetic lesion in Ashkenazi Jews with Classic Tay-Sachs disease. *Advances in Genetics, 44,* 137–143.

Risch, N. (2001). Molecular epidemiology of Tay-Sachs disease. *Advances in Genetics, 44,* 233–252.

Walker, J. (2006). *Tay-Sachs disease.* New York: Rosen.

Rett Syndrome

Rett syndrome is a devastating brain and developmental disorder that is the second-most-common cause of severe intellectual disability in females, after Down syndrome. Its many characteristics include epilepsy and scoliosis as well as problems with nutrition, learning, development, mood, and behavior. Rett syndrome affects only girls. This pervasive disorder is caused by a defect in the X chromosome. Although Rett disorder is genetic—resulting from a faulty gene—it is not inherited from parents (Ingegerd & Engerstrom, 2005; ICON Health Publications, 2002).

Rett syndrome is characterized by normal early development followed by loss of purposeful use of the hands, walking abnormalities, slowing of head growth, seizures, and intellectual disability. The course and severity of Rett syndrome varies greatly. Some girls have symptoms from birth proceeding to devastating symptoms in early childhood, whereas others have later onset, milder deterioration, and fewer symptoms through life (Ingegerd & Engerstrom, 2005).

Symptoms of Rett syndrome at different stages include the following:

- normal development during the first few months of life, followed by a rapid worsening in development
- loss of motor skills and coordination
- poor language and cognitive skills, intellectual disability
- constant hand movements when awake such as wringing, tapping, and clasping
- slowed brain and head growth

For more information, see http://www.rettsyndrome.org/; http://www.rettillinois.org; www.rett.ca; http://www.rsrf.org; http://www.disabilityresources.org/RETT.html.

ICON Health Publications (2002). *The official parent's sourcebook on Rett syndrome: A revised and updated directory for the internet age.* San Diego, CA: Author.

Ingegerd, A. K., & Engerstrom, W., Eds. (2005). *Rett disorder and the developing brain.* New York: Oxford University Press.

Lewis, J., & Wilson, D. (1998). *Pathways to learning in Rett syndrome.* London: David Fulton.

Zimmerman, S. (1996). *Grief dancers: A journey into the depths of the soul.* Golden, CO: Nemo Press.

Noonan Syndrome

Noonan syndrome is a rare genetic disorder that causes abnormal development of many parts of the body. It initially was called Turner-like syndrome because certain symptoms (webbing of neck and short stature) were so similar to Turner's syndrome (ICON Health Publications, 2004d).

The typical characteristics of Noonan syndrome include the following:

- short stature
- delayed puberty
- slanting, wide-set eyes
- webbed and shortened neck
- drooping eyelids
- low-set or abnormally shaped ears
- unusual chest shape (usually a sunken chest)
- hearing disability

- small penis, undescended testicles
- speech and behavior problems
- mild developmental delay in a minority of children

For more information, see http://www.noonansyndrome.org/; http://www.rarediseases.org.

Allanson, J. E. (1987). Noonan syndrome. *Journal of Medical Genetics,* January, *24*(1), 9–13.

ICON Health Publications (2004d). *Noonan syndrome: A medical dictionary, bibliography, and annotated research guide to internet references.* San Diego, CA: Author.

Noonan, J. A. (1994). Noonan syndrome. An update and review for the primary pediatrician. *Clinical Pediatrician,* September, *33*(9), 548–555.

Sharland, M., Burch, M., McKenna, W. M., & Paton, M. A. (1992). A clinical study of Noonan syndrome. *Archives of Disease in Childhood,* February, *67*(2), 178–183.

Williams Syndrome

Williams syndrome is a rare genetic condition that causes serious medical and developmental problems. It is characterized by learning difficulties and intellectual disability. Children with this syndrome have a distinctive facial appearance and a unique personality that combines excessive friendliness and high levels of empathy with anxiety (ICON Health Publications, 2004g; Semel & Rosner, 2003).

Children with Williams syndrome typically love music and will spend long periods listening to music or creating musical sounds. Despite serious developmental delays, many children with Williams syndrome seem to have a great memory for songs, a remarkable sense of rhythm, and outstanding auditory skill. They spend much more time in focused concentration when music is included as part of a learning activity (Don et al., 1999).

Characteristics include the following:

- feeding problems and low weight gain in infancy
- irritability and colic during infancy
- distinctive facial appearance
- extremely social personality
- developmental delay
- learning disabilities
- ADD/ADHD
- musculoskeletal problems
- heart and blood vessel problems
- dental abnormalities
- kidney abnormalities

For more information, see http://www.williams-syndrome.org/; http://www.rarediseases.org; http://www.wsf.org.

Bellugi, U., & St. George, M. I. (2001). *Journey from cognition to brain to gene: Perspectives from Williams Syndrome.* Cambridge, MA: MIT Press.

Don, A., Schellenberg, G., & Rourke, B. (1999). Music and language skills of children with Williams syndrome. *Child Neuropsychology, 5,* 154–170.

Dykens, E. M., Rosner, B. A., Ly, T., & Sagun, J. (2005). Music and anxiety in Williams syndrome: A harmonious or discordant relationship? *American Journal of Mental Retardation, 110*(5), 346–358.

Hickock, G., Bellugi, U., & Jones, W. (1995). Asymmetrical ability. *Science, 270*(5234), 219–220.

ICON Health Publications (2004g). *Williams syndrome: A medical dictionary, bibliography, and annotated research guide to internet references.* San Diego, CA: Author.

Lenhoff, H., Wang, P., Greenberg, F., & Bellugi, U. (1997). Williams syndrome and the brain. *Scientific American, 277*(6), 68–73.

Levitin, D. (2005). Musical behavior in a neurogenetic developmental disorder: Evidence from Williams Syndrome. *Annals of the New York Academy of Sciences, 1060,* 325–334.

Semel, E., & Rosner, S. R. (2003). *Understanding Williams syndrome: A guide to behavioral patterns and interventions.* Mahwah, NJ: Erlbaum.

Prader-Willi Syndrome

Prader-Willi syndrome is an incurable genetic disability that is sometimes mistaken for bulimia. This syndrome is the result of a dysfunction in part of the brain that signals satisfaction when enough food has been ingested. People with Prader-Willi syndrome never feel satisfied or full, no matter how much they eat (Hodapp et al., 1997; Lupi, 1988).

Typical characteristics include the following:

- constant, ravenous food cravings that do not stop even after life-threatening binges
- feeding problems and poor weight gain in infancy
- obesity due to overeating
- medical problems associated with obesity, such as diabetes, heart disease, gall bladder disease, sleep apnea, blood vessel disease, and so on

- severe behavior problems such as temper tantrums, violent outbursts, obsessive-compulsive behavior, argumentativeness, defiance, manipulativeness, possessiveness, stubbornness, stealing, and lying—almost always to get food
- distinctive facial features, narrow face, almond-shaped eyes, small-appearing mouth with thin upper lip and down-turned corners of mouth
- mild to moderate intellectual disability (mental retardation)
- skin that is easily irritated, tendency to scratch skin causing bloody abrasions
- speech problems, thick saliva crusting at corners of mouth
- muscle weakness, slack muscle tone

For more information, see http://www.pwsausa.org/; http://www.lpch.org/DiseaseHealthInfo/HealthLibrary/genetics/uniparen.html.

Hodapp, R. M., Dykens, E. M., & Masino, L. (1997). Stress and support in families of persons with Prader-Willi syndrome. *Journal of Autism and Developmental Disorders, 27,* 11–24.

Lupi, M. H. (1988). Education of the child with Prader-Willi syndrome. In Greenswag, L. R., & Alexander, R. C. (Eds.), *Management of Prader-Willi syndrome* (113–123). New York: Springer-Verlag.

Waters, J. (1999). *Prader-Willi syndrome: A practical guide.* London: David Fulton.

Whittington, J., & Holland, T. (2004). *Prader-Willi syndrome: Development and manifestations.* New York: Cambridge University Press.

Kawasaki Disease

Kawasaki disease is a rare condition in children that involves inflammation of the blood vessels. Kawasaki disease can cause inflammation of blood vessels in the coronary arteries, which can lead to aneurysms. Although it is rare, an aneurysm can lead to a heart attack, even in a young child. In as many as 15 to 25 percent of children with Kawasaki disease, the heart is permanently affected. The coronary arteries or the heart muscle itself can be damaged (Shulman, 1987).

Kawasaki disease occurs most frequently in Japan, where the disease was first discovered. In the United States, Kawasaki disease is the leading cause of acquired heart disease in children. Eighty percent of U.S. citizens infected each year are younger than five. Older children and adults are rarely affected. The disorder affects the mucus membranes, lymph nodes, walls of the blood vessels, and the heart (ICON Health Publications, 2004). Its cause is unknown.

Symptoms of Kawasaki disease include the following:

- fever between 102°F and 104°F lasting five days or longer
- extremely bloodshot or red eyes
- swollen lymph nodes (frequently only one neck lymph node is swollen)
- bright red, chapped, or cracked lips
- red bumpy tongue, white coating on the tongue
- red palms of the hands and the soles of the feet
- swollen hands and feet
- joint pain and swelling
- skin rashes on the middle of the body, no blisters
- peeling skin in the genital area, hands, and feet

For more information, see http://www.vasculitisfoundation.org/kawasakidisease.

ICON Health Publications (2004c). *Kawasaki disease: A medical dictionary, bibliography, and annotated research guide to Internet references.* San Diego, CA: Author.

Shulman, S. T. (1987). *Kawasaki disease.* New York: Wiley.

Childhood-Onset Schizophrenia

Schizophrenia is a psychotic disorder that is most distinctly characterized by disintegration of personality. Childhood-onset schizophrenia (COS) begins in a child younger than 13.

Fortunately, schizophrenia is rare in children. It affects only 1 in 40,000 children, compared with 1 in 100 adults. Although schizophrenia normally is diagnosed in young adulthood, the average onset of COS occurs around age nine. Because COS is so rare and because schizophrenia is a broad term including a variety of symptoms, it is sometimes difficult to identify in children (Torrey, 2001).

Symptoms typically include the following:

- hearing voices
- hearing one's own thoughts
- fearing that people are watching and plotting
- believing something or someone is controlling one's thoughts, delusional beliefs
- believing one's actions are controlled from something on the outside

- irregular speech, inability to carry on a focused, coherent conversation
- bizarre behavior, developmentally inappropriate mannerisms

For more information, see http://www.nami.org; http://www.nascos.org; http://www.childhood-schizophrenia.org.

Rapoport, J. L., Giedd, J., Kumra, S., Jacobsen, L., Smith, A., Lee, P., Nelson, J., & Hamburger, S. (1997). Childhood-onset schizophrenia. Progressive ventricular change during adolescence. *Archives of General Psychiatry, 54,* 897–903.

Sowell, E. R., Toga, A. W., & Asarnow, R. (2000). Brain abnormalities observed in childhood-onset schizophrenia: A review of the structural magnetic resonance imaging literature. *Mental Retardation and Developmental Disabilities Research Review, 6,* 180–185.

Torrey, E. F. (2001). *Surviving schizophrenia: A manual for families, consumers, and providers* (4th ed.). Burlington, MA: Quill Pen Press.

Velocardiofacial Syndrome

Velocardiofacial syndrome is a rare genetic condition that causes cleft palate, heart malformations, severe speech problems, and learning disabilities. It has been linked with more than 30 different features or abnormalities. The name *velocardiofacial syndrome* comes from Latin *velum,* meaning palate; *cardia,* meaning heart; and *facies,* having to do with the face. Feeding problems with regurgitation of milk through the nose are a frequent problem for babies with this disorder (Parker & Parker, 2002).

Typical characteristics include the following:

- short stature
- long face and prominent upper jaw
- small ears
- middle-ear infections
- prominent nose and narrow nasal passages
- flattening of the cheeks
- bluish color below the eyes
- eye problems
- underdeveloped lower jaw
- cleft palate
- heart problems
- thyroid problems

- immune system problems
- curvature of the spine
- learning difficulties and speech problems
- extremes of behavior

For more information, see http://www.vcfsef.org/; http://www.rarediseases.org; http://www.faces-cranio.org/.

Antshel, K. M., Stallone, K., AbdulSabur, N., Shprintzen, R., Roizen, N., Higgins, A. M., & Kates, W. R. (2007). Temperament in velocardiofacial syndrome. *Journal of Intellectual Disability Research,* March, *51*(3), 218–227.

Golding-Kushner, K. J., & Shprintzen, R. J. (2007). *Velo-cardio-facial syndrome: Treatment of communication disorders.* San Diego, CA: Plural Publishing.

Murphy, K. C., & Scambler, P. J., Eds. (2005). Velo-cardio-facial syndrome: A model for understanding microdeletion disorders. New York: Cambridge University Press.

Parker, J. N., & Parker, P. M., Eds. (2002). *The official parent's sourcebook on velocardiofacial syndrome.* San Diego, CA: ICON Health Publications.

Shprintzen, R. J., & Bardach, J. (1995). *Cleft palate speech management: A multidisciplinary approach.* Oxford, UK: Elsevier Science.

Shprintzen, R. J., & Kushner, K. G. (2007). *Velo-cardio-facial syndrome: The path to normal speech.* San Diego, CA: Plural Publishing.

Angelman Syndrome

Angelman syndrome is a genetic disorder caused by a chromosome abnormality. It is characterized by a stiff, jerky way of walking, severely delayed speech, excessive laughter, and seizures. This syndrome is usually not recognized until at least the preschool years, when the distinctive behaviors and features become most evident.

Typical characteristics of Angelman syndrome include the following:

- normal prenatal development and birth, no visible birth defects
- severe developmental delay becomes evident by 6 to 12 months of age
- severe speech impairment
- movement or balance disorder, uncoordinated and trembling movement of limbs

- behavioral differences, frequent laughter or smiling, happy demeanor, excitable personality (often with hand flapping)
- ADD/ADHD, short attention span
- delayed, disproportionately small head circumference
- seizures, usually beginning by three years of age

Angelman, H. (1965). "Puppet" children: A report on three cases. *The Journal of Developmental Medicine and Child Neurology, 7,* 681–688.

ICON Health Publications (2004a). *Angelman Syndrome: A medical dictionary, bibliography, and annotated research guide to internet references.* San Diego, CA: Author.

Ohtsuka, Y., Kobayashi, K., Yoshinaga, H., Ogino, T., Ohmori, I., Ogawa, K., & Oka, E. (2005). Relationship between severity of epilepsy and developmental outcome in Angelman syndrome. *Brain Development,* March, *27*(2), 95–100.

Parker, J. N., & Parker, P. M., Eds. (2005). *The official parent's sourcebook on Angelman syndrome: A revised and updated directory for the internet age.* San Diego, CA: ICON Health Publications.

Peters, S. U., Beaudet, A. L., Madduri, N., & Bacino, C. A. (2004, December). Autism in Angelman Syndrome: Implications for autism research. *Clinical Genetics, 66,* 530–536.

Williams, C. A., Beaudet, A. L., Clayton-Smith, J., Knoll, J. H., Kyllerman, M., Laan, L. A., Magenis, R. E., Moncla, A., Schinzel, A. A., Summers, J. A., & Wagstaff, J. (2006). Angelman syndrome 2005: Updated consensus for diagnostic criteria. *American Journal of Medical Genetics,* March, *140*(5), 413–418.

School:

Individualized Education Program (IEP)

IEP Dates: from _____ to _____

Child: Name: _____ **DOB:** _____ **Level or Grade:** _____

Parents' Names: **Phone:**

IEP Team Leader: **Phone:**

Other IEP Team Members

Name:	Role:	**Phone:**
Name:	Role:	**Phone:**
Name:	Role:	**Phone:**
Name:	Role:	**Phone:**

Parent or Child Concerns
What concerns do the parent or child want to see addressed in this plan to enhance the child's learning?

Child Strengths and Evaluation Results Summary
What are the child's educational strengths, interest areas, personal attributes and abilities?
What has been determined to be the child's disability?

Current Skill Level

Check all that apply.   **How is this area of learning affected by the disabilities?**

☐ Self-Care Skills/Independence

☐ Self-Control/Concentration

☐ Social and Emotional Development

☐ Fine and Gross Motor Development

☐ Language Development

☐ Problem Solving/Analytical Thinking

☐ Science and Environment Learning

☐ Number Concepts

☐ Other Development Areas   Specify:

Check all that apply.   **How is this area of learning affected by the disabilities?**

☐	English Language Arts	
☐	History and Social Sciences	
☐	Mathematics	
☐	Science and Technology	
☐	Reading	

☐ Other Curriculum Areas   Specify:

How do the child's disabilities affect learning?

Would accommodations make learning easier for the child? What types? How?

How will specially modified care, instruction, and environment will help the child make effective progress in all areas of learning?

Describe the necessary instructional modifications and describe how such modifications will be made.

☐ Teaching Methods:

☐ Guidance Methods:

☐ Environmental Changes:

☐ Special Equipment:

General Considerations

Check all that apply.

☐ Physical Movement Issues	☐ Braille Needs (blind/visually impaired)	☐ Behavior Intervention
☐ Assistive Devices/Services	☐ ASL Needs (deaf/hard of hearing)	☐ Self-Control Issues
☐ Emotional Needs	☐ Limited English Proficiency (LEP)	☐ Personal Hygiene Needs
☐ Social Development	☐ Communication (speech issues)	☐ Medical Support

☐ Other _____

How will these considerations be addressed?

Developmentally Appropriate Practice Considerations

☐ **For children ages birth to 5:**

How will the child participate in developmentally appropriate play and exploration activities with nondisabled peers?

☐ **For children ages 6 to 12:**

How will the child participation in developmentally appropriate academic curriculum and extracurricular activities with nondisabled peers?

Current Performance Levels and Measurable Annual Goals
There must be a direct correlation between the annual goals and the present level of educational performance

Goal 1	Specific Goal Focus:

Current Performance Level: What can the child currently do?

Measurable Annual Goal:

What challenging, yet attainable, goal can we expect the child to meet by the end of this IEP period?
How will we know that the child has reached this goal?

Benchmark/Objectives:

What will the child need to do to complete this goal?

Current Performance Levels and Measurable Annual Goals

There must be a direct correlation between the annual goals and the present level of educational performance

Goal 2	Specific Goal Focus:

Current Performance Level: What can the child currently do?

Measurable Annual Goal:

What challenging, yet attainable, goal can we expect the child to meet by the end of this IEP period?
How will we know that the child has reached this goal?

Benchmark/Objectives:

What will the child need to do to complete this goal?

Current Performance Levels and Measurable Annual Goals

There must be a direct correlation between the annual goals and the present level of educational performance

Goal 3	Specific Goal Focus:

Current Performance Level: What can the child currently do?

Measurable Annual Goal:

What challenging, yet attainable, goal can we expect the child to meet by the end of this IEP period?
How will we know that the child has reached this goal?

Benchmark/Objectives:

What will the child need to do to complete this goal?

Current Performance Levels and Measurable Annual Goals

There must be a direct correlation between the annual goals and the present level of educational performance

Goal 4	Specific Goal Focus:

Current Performance Level: What can the child currently do?

Measurable Annual Goal:

What challenging, yet attainable, goal can we expect the child to meet by the end of this IEP period?
How will we know that the child has reached this goal?

Benchmark/Objectives:

What will the child need to do to complete this goal?

Current Performance Levels and Measurable Annual Goals

There must be a direct correlation between the annual goals and the present level of educational performance

Goal 5	Specific Goal Focus:

Current Performance Level: What can the child currently do?

Measurable Annual Goal:

What challenging, yet attainable, goal can we expect the child to meet by the end of this IEP period?
How will we know that the child has reached this goal?

Benchmark/Objectives:

What will the child need to do to complete this goal?

Current Performance Levels and Measurable Annual Goals

There must be a direct correlation between the annual goals and the present level of educational performance

Goal 6	Specific Goal Focus:

Current Performance Level: What can the child currently do?

Measurable Annual Goal:

What challenging, yet attainable, goal can we expect the child to meet by the end of this IEP period?
How will we know that the child has reached this goal?

Benchmark/Objectives:

What will the child need to do to complete this goal?

Current Performance Levels and Measurable Annual Goals

There must be a direct correlation between the annual goals and the present level of educational performance

Goal 7	Specific Goal Focus:

Current Performance Level: What can the child currently do?

Measurable Annual Goal:

What challenging, yet attainable, goal can we expect the child to meet by the end of this IEP period?
How will we know that the child has reached this goal?

Benchmark/Objectives:

What will the child need to do to complete this goal?

Services Needed

What are the total special needs of this child?

Include services, related services, program modifications, and supports (including positive behavioral supports, school personnel, and parent training/supports). Services should assist the child in reaching IEP goals, being involved in and progressing in the general curriculum, participating in extracurricular/nonacademic activities, and participating with nondisabled students while working toward IEP goals.

A. Special Services, Activities Provided by School					
Goal #	Type of Service	Person Responsible	Desired Outcome	Start Date	End Date
Frequency of service: ☐ Daily ☐ Weekly ☐ Monthly ☐ other:					
Frequency of service: ☐ Daily ☐ Weekly ☐ Monthly ☐ other:					
Frequency of service: ☐ Daily ☐ Weekly ☐ Monthly ☐ other:					
Frequency of service: ☐ Daily ☐ Weekly ☐ Monthly ☐ other:					

Schedule Accommodations

Less Time: Does this child require a shorter school day or shorter school year?

☐ No   ☐ Yes — shorter day   ☐ Yes — shorter year   Why?

More Time: Does this child require a longer school day or a longer school year to prevent significant loss of skills or difficulty in relearning?

☐ No   ☐ Yes — longer day   ☐ Yes — longer year   Why?

Will the child's schedule be changed? Why is this schedule change being recommended?
How will services be coordinated?

Transportation Services

Does the child require transportation assistance as a result of the disabilities?

☐ No   Transportation will be provided by the parent.

☐ No   Transportation will be provided by the school in the same manner as provided for children without disabilities.

☐ Yes   Special transportation will be provided in the following manner:

   ☐ Using a school transportation vehicle with the following changes or specialized equipment and precautions:

Specify:

   ☐ Using a community transportation vehicle with the following changes or specialized equipment and precautions:

Specify:

B. Special Classroom Activities					
B. Special Classroom Activities					
Focus on Goal #	Type of Activity	Person Responsible	Frequency and Duration	Start Date	End Date

C. Special Services/Therapies Provided Outside the School					
Focus on Goal #	Type of Service/Therapy	Person Responsible	Frequency and Duration	Start Date	End Date

Routine Evaluation/Assessment

EARLY CHILDHOOD DEVELOPMENT AREAS

Check all that apply.

Will the child need special accommodations/considerations in regard to this assessment? How will that be accomplished?

☐ Self-Care Skills/Independence

☐ Self-Control/Concentration

☐ Social and Emotional Development

☐ Fine and Gross Motor Development

☐ Language Development

☐ Problem Solving/Analytical Thinking

☐ Science and Environment Learning

☐ Number Concepts

☐ Other Development Areas   Specify:

ELEMENTARY LEVEL CURRICULUM AREAS

Check all that apply.

Will the child need special accommodations/considerations in regard to this assessment? How will that be accomplished?

☐	English Language Arts	
☐	History and Social Sciences	
☐	Mathematics	
☐	Science and Technology	
☐	Reading	

☐ Other Curriculum Areas   Specify:

Special Observations/Assessments
Related to Disabilities

Identify and describe observations/assessments planned during the IEP period to confirm goal achievement:

Goal 1:

Goal 2:

Goal 3:

Goal 4:

Goal 5:

Goal 6:

Goal 7:

Schedule for Meeting and Communicating With Parents

Identify and describe strategies planned for meeting and communicating with parents during the IEP period:

Timetable for Reporting Progress to Parents

Identify and describe timetable for reporting progress to parents during the IEP period:

Supplementary Information

☐ The anticipated completion date of grade or level:

☐ Coordination of transition to next level:

☐ Interagency collaboration:

☐ Evidence of efforts to obtain parental IEP participation if parent did not attend meeting or provide input:

☐ Evidence of efforts to obtain child's IEP participation or reasons for nonparticipation if child did not provide input:

☐ Other relevant information not previously stated:

Response Section

School Assurance

I certify that the goals in this IEP are those recommended by the planning team and that the indicated plan will be carried out.

Signature and Role of Planning Team Leader: **Date:**

Parent Response

It is important for the IEP team to know your response as soon as possible. Please indicate by checking at least one of the boxes below and returning a signed copy to the school. Thank you.

☐ I accept the IEP as developed.   ☐ I reject the IEP as developed.

☐ I reject the following sections of the IEP with the understanding that any portions that I do not reject will be considered accepted and will be implemented.

☐ I request a meeting to discuss the rejected IEP or rejected portions.

Signature of Parent or Guardian: **Date:**

Parent Comment: I would like to make the following comments. I realize any comments made that suggest changes to the IEP will not be implemented unless the IEP is changed.

Glossary

A

accommodations Special aids for persons with disabilities that give them access to mainstream activities and environments. Accommodations can include such things as a ramp for a wheelchair, a lowered sink, special door handles, signs written in Braille, a sign language translator, or other changes to help the person with disabilities function equitably with nondisabled peers.

acquired Developed after birth, at some time during life in response to environmental interactions, injuries, or illness.

active listening A form of attentive listening in which one concentrates on what is being said, then reflects the ideas back to the speaker to show an understanding of what the speaker is feeling and saying.

adult One who seeks not to gain control over children but rather to guide them effectively, while setting for them an immediate and tangible example of appropriate coping and assertive negotiation.

age-typical behavior Behavior that is characteristic to specific developmental stages, thus it is typically seen in children of a certain age.

anarchy Absence of any form of control; chaos and disorder.

anecdotal record A short descriptive story about a child's specific behavior event that is of particular interest or concern. This may be firsthand information as observed by child care providers or recorded from secondhand information as provided by parents. It is qualitative, not quantitative data.

anemia A blood condition in which there are not enough red blood cells to carry essential oxygen around the body. Because all cells in the body rely on oxygen to live, anemia has a damaging effect on a person's health and may cause a variety of symptoms.

Angelman syndrome A genetic disorder caused by a chromosome abnormality. It is characterized by a stiff, jerky way of walking, severely delayed speech, excessive laughter, and seizures.

anhedonia Inability to gain pleasure from normally pleasurable activities. A person almost seems anesthetized against normally stimulating sensations and events in the environment. This phenomenon is a key symptom of depression.

antisocial Behavior that detracts from the welfare of others or has a generally negative effect on persons with whom one comes in contact. Antisocial personality behaviors are typically marked by lack of ethical restraint, lack of moral control, impulsiveness, and an inability to experience feelings of guilt.

apnea A breathing abnormality marked by momentary delays in breathing.

appropriate touch Suitable for the occasion and the person affected, nonexploitative, and having no concealed intention; physical contact that is casual, affectionate, reciprocal, and welcome, but never sexual or controlling.

Asperger's syndrome A neurological condition that is part of the autistic spectrum but includes only persons of average or above intelligence who are verbal.

asthma Chronic illness of the respiratory system in which the airway occasionally constricts, becomes inflamed, and is lined with excessive amounts of mucus.

attention deficit/hyperactivity disorder A common developmental disorder that appears during childhood and is characterized by a persistent pattern of inattention as well as forgetfulness, poor impulse control, and distractibility.

auditory figure-ground dysfunction An inability to distinguish between levels of sounds in the environment, to focus on significant sounds, and tune out irrelevant sounds. This is a common characteristic in PDDs and some learning disorders.

auditory physiology The physical makeup of the ear that enables hearing. Sounds are channeled through the external auditory canal to the tympanic membrane (eardrum) and the middle ear (ossicles), and then through the auditory nerve to the brain for interpretation of what has been heard. Auditory perception encompasses the ability to understand what has been heard.

authentic learning A family of research efforts that explain cognition in terms of the relationship between learners and the properties of specific environments. The emphasis of research on authentic learning (or situated cognition as it is often called) is to study complex learning, problem solving, and thinking in a realistic environment.

authoritarian style Interactive (or control) style relying on one-way communication, rigid rules, and punishment—"the sledgehammer."

authoritative style Interactive (or control) style relying on two-way communication, collaboratively developed rules, and positive guidance—"the guide."

autism A developmental brain disorder characterized by impaired social interaction and communication skills, avoidance of eye-to-eye gaze, and a limited range of activities and interests.

autocracy Control by a single person having unlimited power.

autonomy A person's self-reliance, independence, and self-sufficiency. One's capacity to make decisions and act on them.

B

behavior modification A specific method for changing a child's behavior by following a highly structured process.

behaviorists Those holding the view that the environment is the primary determinant of human behavior and that objectively observable behavior constitutes the essential psychological makeup of a human being.

bias One's own set of beliefs, values, and assumptions that develop from one's upbringing, past experience, and personal philosophy of life; bias can include an unfair preference for or dislike of something or someone.

bibliotherapy The use of literature by children or adults to aid them in processing specific problems (for example, depression, anxiety, stress, and frustration). Many libraries have listings of bibliotherapy selections categorized by concerns (divorce, death and dying, new baby, stepparenting, and so on).

bipolar disorder A disorder in which episodes of depression alternate with mania.

body language The gestures, facial expressions, and body postures that people use to communicate along with or instead of speech.

bonding The process of becoming emotionally attached to another.

C

celiac disease A digestive disease that damages the small intestine and interferes with absorption of nutrients from food. People who have celiac disease cannot tolerate a protein called gluten, found in wheat, rye, and barley.

cephalocaudal Development in a pattern from the head downward, toward the feet (head to toe).

cerebral palsy A group of disorders that affect a person's ability to move and to maintain balance and posture.

CHARGE syndrome An extremely complex set of birth defects that can differ from child to child. Most have hearing loss, vision loss, and balance problems, which seriously delay their development and communication.

Child Find A component of IDEA law that requires state agencies to locate, evaluate, and identify children between the ages of 3 and 21, who are in need of early intervention or special education services.

child guidance Contrived methods for external control, as well as interaction with and extension of the development of naturally unfolding internal mechanisms and motivations for self-control and self-discipline.

child-directed Learning activity instigated by the child's natural curiosity and desire to learn rather than by the adult's direction, manipulation, or coercion.

classical conditioning Teaching a new response triggered by a new stimulus by pairing it repeatedly with a stimulus for which there is a physiological reflex (sometimes called Pavlovian conditioning). This term derives from an experiment originally performed by Ivan Pavlov in which a bell was rung just as food was offered to a hungry dog. Soon the dog would salivate at the sound of the bell whether or not food was offered, demonstrating that the this association had become learned.

cohesive interaction Reciprocal teamwork; sticking together to carry out tight-knit group activity.

cleft lip An opening in the center of the top lip.

cleft palate A gap in the center of the roof of the mouth.

collaborative Cooperative interaction of two or more people who are trying achieve a common goal.

community of learners A group of individuals who share similar educational principles, who work toward common goals, whose activities are linked, and whose collaborative efforts create a synchronized energy in which the power of the group is more profound than that of any one individual. For children, a group that nurtures a sense of belonging among the children and adults in a program where children learn that all contribute to each other's learning.

concept An idea, understanding, or belief formed by organizing images or mental pictures from specific occurrences and experiences.

concrete operational In Jean Piaget's theory the third stage of cognitive development, which begins with the ability to analyze thoughts concerning a concrete idea (as opposed to an abstract idea).

conduct disorder A mental condition typified by a repetitive and persistent pattern of socially unacceptable behavior that violates the rights of others. Typical symptoms include strongly aggressive behavior, bullying, cruelty, and destructiveness.

conflict resolution A problem-solving strategy to help two disagreeing parties dissipate their frustration and bring their opposing views to a common solution. The method requires active listening and respectful, non-judgmental communication.

congenital A condition that is inborn or existing at birth.

control of error A teaching strategy originally developed by Maria Montessori and also known as self-correction. Materials are designed to provide instant feedback to the child if he has made a mistake, or they are designed to make it impossible to make a mistake. This puts control in the hands of the learner and protects the child's self-esteem and self-motivation.

convulsions A violent shaking of body or limbs caused by involuntary muscle contractions.

coprolalia *Copro* is the Greek term for "feces" and *lalia* is the Greek for "babbling, meaningless talk." Literally, it means manure talking. People with coprolalia make sudden, unexpected outbursts of inappropriate words or phrases.

copropraxia *Praxia* is the Greek word for "act or action." Combined with *copro*, it means "manure behavior." People with copropraxia act out involuntarily, producing obscene, offensive, or shocking gestures and actions.

cues Indications of interest or need.

cultural adaptation The process of human societies making cultural changes to better accommodate diverse environments across the globe. Slowly evolving adaptations may have neutral or even maladaptive effects in a rapidly changing cultural environment.

cultural bias Unfair preference for or dislike of something or someone based on culture.

cultural context The situation or circumstance in which a particular cultural event, action, behavior, or imagery occurs. Actions, events, and behaviors can have different meanings, depending on their cultural context.

cultural pluralism The peaceful coexistence of numerous distinct ethnic, religious, or cultural groups within one community or society.

culture The traditional beliefs and patterns of behavior that are passed down from parents to children by a society; beliefs, customs, practices, and social behavior of any particular cluster of people whose shared beliefs and practices identify the particular nation, religion, ability, gender, race, or group to which they belong.

culture shock A feeling of confusion, alienation, and depression that can result from the psychological stress that typically occurs during a person's initial immersion in a new culture.

cystic fibrosis An inherited chronic disease that affects breathing and digestion. A defective gene causes the body to produce unusually thick, sticky mucus that clogs the lungs and obstructs the pancreas.

D

delay gratification The process of putting off something desired until a later time. This skill can be learned gradually during early childhood by children who develop a strong sense of trust that their essential needs will be met.

demandingness Requiring certain behaviors from children. Having high expectations for children that are reasonable and supported with encouragement and optimism.

democracy The principles of social equality and respect for the individual within a cohesive community.

depression A psychological state of dejected mood characterized by feelings of discouragement, dejection, sadness, despair, and hopelessness.

developmental interactionists Those holding the Piagetian view that, rather than only passively absorbing information or emerging into a predestined form, a human being's essential psychological makeup derives from a dynamic interactive process that includes both innate cognitive structures and external experiences.

developmentally appropriate practice Early education and care that is carefully planned to match the diverse interests, abilities, and cultural needs of children at various ages and that is carried out with respect for and in cooperation with their families.

diabetes mellitus A condition in which blood sugar level can become dangerously high because the body does not produce enough insulin to regulate it.

differentiated Made apparent or categorized differences between two or more things.

discrimination Participation in harmful actions toward others because of their membership in a particular group. The behavioral manifestation of negative prejudice.

doubt A feeling of questioning, uncertainty, and hesitation.

Down syndrome A disorder that causes mild to severe learning disabilities and distinctive physical characteristics due to the child having an extra chromosome.

dual-earner couples Couples in which both partners are gainfully employed.

dysfunctional Inappropriate or self-destructive behavior not serving any positive or productive function in a child's life.

dyslexia Cognitive problems in which a person's reading or writing ability is significantly lower than expected given his exposure to appropriate instruction, his intellectual ability, and his lack of sensory problems such as poor eyesight. Because reading is a complex mental process, dyslexia has many potential causes.

E

echolalia A speech disorder that causes compulsive repetition of words spoken by others. In most cases, echolalic speech is a habitual form of cyclical self-stimulation that is not intended as communication, but in some cases echolalia may be used as the child's only available tool in an improvised attempt at communication.

egocentric Seeing oneself as the center of the universe, self-centered, selfish. This point of view is a perfectly normal development characteristic of babies and very young children.

egocentrism The inability to view reality from the standpoint of another person, which is an intellectual limitation of very young children.

emotional growth Developing and learning to manage the feelings that affect behavior and self-esteem.

emotional intelligence The level of one's self-awareness, mood management, self-motivation, empathy, and understanding of one's inner feelings.

empathetic Taking the time to learn about a person to better understand situations and issues from his or her perspective.

empathy The ability to understand or have concern for someone other than oneself, marked by identification with and understanding of another's situation, feelings, and motives.

enculturation The process whereby an established culture teaches an individual its accepted norms and values, so that the individual can become an accepted member of that society. It is the process of passing the culture down to the child through teaching, learning, and guiding at a given time in a given place.

epilepsy A condition characterized by persistent seizures that may include brutal muscle jerking episodes called convulsions.

ethics The ideals and the shared conceptions of professional responsibility that reflect the aspirations of a group of practitioners and affirm their commitment to the core values of their field. The basic principles that are intended to guide their conduct and assist them in resolving ethical dilemmas encountered in their field.

ethnocentrism The deeply felt belief (possibly unconsciously held) that one's own culture is superior to all others. Being unyielding in attachment to one's own way of life and condescending and intolerant toward other cultures. Alien cultural practices are often viewed as being not just different but silly, weird, evil, or unnatural.

ethologists Scientists who study the behavior of animals living under normal conditions. Ethology is the scientific study of animal behavior. (Ethnology is the study of the characteristics of cultures.)

event sampling A recording to determine the precise number of times a specific behavior occurs within a set period, as well as the pattern of occurrence.

executive system A theorized system of the brain that controls and organizes other mental processes. It manages processes such as planning, abstract thinking, rule learning, screening out irrelevant sensory information, and inhibiting inappropriate actions; also referred to as executive function or the central executive.

expressive language Communication with others by oral or written language.

external environment The physical surroundings or conditions around a child that influence his or her growth, development, and learning. A young child's environment can be described as everything the child sees, hears, touches, or experiences.

F

family structures Various arrangements of people living together with children and possibly other generations of relatives.

fetal alcohol spectrum disorders A group of permanent birth defects caused by a mother drinking alcohol during pregnancy.

fight or flight response This body's reaction to a perceived threat or danger. Our bodies react to threats by releasing hormones such as adrenalin and cortisol into the blood stream, giving us a burst of energy and strength to fight or flee. When the perceived threat is gone, our systems are designed to go back to normal levels by means of a relaxation response. But if a child is subjected to constant stress, relaxation is impaired and damage to physical health as well as sleeping, eating, social, and emotional problems may occur.

free appropriate public education (FAPE) A directive requiring that school districts provide children with disabilities access to general education as well as spe-

cialized educational services to accommodate special needs. It also requires that children with disabilities receive support free of charge, the same as is provided to nondisabled students.

fulfillment Completely developing one's abilities and interests; a feeling of pleasure because you are getting what you want from life.

functional Appropriate actions or behaviors that serve some productive or positive function in a child's life and patterns of interactions.

G

goal Overarching purpose or aspiration.

group contagion Typical toddler group behavior in which one child's gleeful action, for example, foot stamping, head shaking, or squealing, is quickly imitated by the whole group of toddlers.

group identity A young child constructs group identity primarily by internalizing whatever that child's family considers important in defining who is "like us." Creating a strong and positive group identity is essential for young children who happen to be part of a cultural grouping that has been devalued or stigmatized by the larger society.

H

habituated The process of becoming accustomed to frequent repetition or pattern of behavior.

hearing impairment and deafness Inability to respond to a normal range of sound frequencies because of an injured eardrum, malformed or damaged inner ear, clogged outer ear, or brain problem. Genetic defects are the most common cause of hearing deficits in newborns, but ear infections are the most common cause of hearing deficits in older children.

heart defect/heart disease A congenital cardiovascular defect that occurs when the heart or blood vessels near the heart fail to develop normally before birth.

human ecology The theory that people don't develop in isolation, but in relation to their family, home, school, community, and society. Each of these constantly changing multilevel environments, as well as the interactions among these environments, is key to a human being's development.

human immunodeficiency virus and acquired immune deficiency syndrome Human immunodeficiency virus (HIV) is the virus that causes acquired immune deficiency syndrome (AIDS). AIDS attacks the person's immune system leaving them vulnerable to infection.

hydrocephalus Fluid accumulation in the brain. Shunting is a process used to drain excess brain fluid to prevent brain damage and blindness.

hypersensitivity Overreaction to sensory input from one of the senses (for example, sight, sound, taste, smell, touch).

I

imprinting A kind of early bonding in an animal's development that normally results in significant recognition ability and social attraction to members of its own species, especially to its mother.

inappropriate behavior Behavior that is out of place, immature, unproductive, or socially inept.

individual development A particular person, distinct from others in a group, changes, advances, or progresses to a more advanced state.

Individualized Education Program (IEP) A written plan that describes exactly how teachers, parents, school administrators, related services personnel, and the student with a disability will work together to improve the student's educational results.

Individuals with Disabilities Education Act (IDEA) A law ensuring that eligible infants, toddlers, and children with disabilities receive early intervention and special education and related services. It requires that students be provided a free appropriate public education (FAPE) preparing them for further education, employment, and independent living. Special education must provide the least restrictive environment (LRE), which is the environment most like that of typical children in which the child with a disability can succeed.

induction The process of inducing a state, feeling, or idea. Here we are inviting the child to think through the cause–effect sequence to understand better why certain behaviors hurt others, are unsafe, or damage the environment.

industry One's motivation to work constructively, to be diligent and productive.

inferiority The feeling of being incapable, having a pervasive sense of inadequacy and experiencing a tendency toward self-diminishment.

inferring meaning Drawing conclusions from evidence perceived by one's senses or through communication.

intellectual disability Mismatch between an individual's capabilities and the demands of daily life to communicate, handle self-care and hygiene needs, participate in community life, make appropriate decisions, solve problems, carry out tasks, and follow safety rules.

intelligence The aggregate or global capacity of a person to act purposefully, think rationally, and deal effectively with his or her environment.

intelligence quotient (IQ) A numerical score resulting from one of several different standardized tests that make an attempt to measure intelligence. The score is used as a predictor of educational achievement and is intended to reflect a person's general capacity for performing intellectual tasks.

intermittent explosive disorder A mental disorder typified by outbreaks of violent and aggressive behavior that may harm others or destroy property.

intermittent reinforcers The presence of a reinforcer after some, but not all, occurrences of a particular behavior. This process tends to result in an increase in the specific behavior that is reinforced, even if the reinforcement is only sporadic.

internal sensations The physical feelings that are caused by one or more of the sense organs being stimulated. The feelings sensed by one's own body such as hunger or fear.

internalize The process of taking in experiences and absorbing learning, then making them part of one's own behavior or belief.

intestinal villi Tiny fingerlike protrusions lining the small intestine that absorb nutrients and make them available to the bloodstream. *Villi* is Latin for "shaggy hair."

J

judging The process of using perceptions to create conclusions.

justice orientation Perspective in which integrity tends to be the dominant moral compass for making autonomous, independent, and *self-oriented* ethical and principled decisions.

L

learned behavior An action repeated because it produced a favorable response in the past. A behavior that is taught by the reinforcing response of another person. This develops in children in the preoperational stage of cognitive growth in Piaget's theory.

learned helplessness A person's inability to take action to make his or her life better, arising out of a sense of not being in control.

learning disability Disorder that affects the brain's ability to receive, process, analyze, or store information.

least restrictive environment (LRE) The requirement in IDEA law that children with disabilities receive their education, to the maximum extent appropriate, with nondisabled peers and that special education pupils not be removed from regular classes unless, even with supplemental aids and services, education in regular classes cannot be achieved satisfactorily.

logical consequence An outcome that results from a situation where adults determine and control the conclusion.

M

mania A severe medical condition characterized by abnormally elevated mood, high energy, and bizarre thought patterns.

manipulative Using clever or devious ways to control or influence another person into doing something that he or she really does not want to do. (Be aware that *manipulative,* when used by early educators as a noun, refers to small objects that are used for fine-motor development. The fingers manipulate the objects, or move them around.)

marasmus A disease associated with inadequate or inadequately assimilated nutrition that affects infants and causes a wasting away of the child's body. Also referred to as *failure to thrive syndrome,* this condition can result from prolonged absence of emotional nurturance as well as from malnutrition, and affected infants typically evidence delays in motor and intellectual development.

maturationists Those holding the view that internal predisposition, physiological characteristics, or inherited traits account for the essential psychological makeup of a human being.

media Materials that convey information and cultural expression. Media can bring data by paper (books), film (videos), plastic (CDs), electronic wires, and so on.

metacognition The ability to reflect or evaluate one's behavior or actions.

mind blindness A brain disorder that impairs one's ability to "read minds" by noticing gestures, facial expressions, and changes in tone of voice. An inability to fathom what is in the mind of another person.

mirror Reflect the feelings expressed by someone else—repeating what you understood someone to say (*see* active listening).

misbehavior Inappropriate, troublesome, and sometimes unsafe behavior.

mistaken goals The motivation that Dreikurs theorized caused children to behave inappropriately. The mistaken logic causing children to misbehave to get attention from others, gain a sense of control, get revenge for their own perceived hurts, and remove themselves from frightening or painful situations.

modeling Providing an example, being a role model. In positive child guidance, the adult is the primary role model.

modify The process of bringing about a change. In behavior modification, modifying is the process of changing a specific behavior through external reinforcement of some kind.

moral affect The ability to feel guilt or shame—feelings associated with a guilty or clear conscience indicate whether behavior was appropriate and guide one to choose appropriate or desired behaviors.

moral reasoning The thinking processes that guide people in deciding what is or is not moral behavior.

motor tic A sudden involuntary muscular contraction, often of the facial, shoulder, or neck muscles. Complex motor tics include distinct, obsessively repeated, intricate actions or behaviors such as twirling, hopping, or obsessively lining things up in straight rows. Tics tend to become more pronounced when one is under stress.

muscular dystrophy A genetic disorder that causes progressive weakness in muscle tissue.

N

National Association for the Education of Young Children (NAEYC) This professional organization for early childhood educators is dedicated to improving the well-being of all young children, with particular focus on the quality of educational and developmental services for all children from birth through age eight.

natural consequence An outcome that results from a situation without any external intervention to change or control the conclusion.

negative stereotyping To categorize individuals in a group according to an oversimplified, standardized (usually racist or sexist) image or idea that ignores the unique characteristics of the individual.

negotiate The process of settling disputes through interactive verbal exchanges rather than by physical force.

nested structures An individual's interactive experience; that is, how the parents, their workplace, the community, the society, the school, and even the economy all interact and affect the children.

neural tube A hollow tube developing along the back of the embryo that becomes the brain and spinal cord.

neurodevelopment The development of the brain pathways that make the integration of sensory information possible; these pathways increase in capacity and complexity as children play, learn, and grow.

nonverbal communication Communicating ideas without the use of speech through such cues as gesture, tone of voice, facial expression, or body posture.

O

object permanence The knowledge that something hidden from view is not gone forever but rather is in another location at that time and likely to reappear.

objective Immediate aim or purpose.

on task Focused on the activities at hand; fully involved in and attentive to productive skill development or learning activity.

operant conditioning A kind of learning that occurs when a spontaneous behavior is either reinforced by a reward or discouraged by punishment. For example, mice who go through a maze the wrong way get a shock. If they go the right way, they get some cheese. So they eventually learn to go the right way every time.

oppositional defiant disorder A condition in which an ongoing pattern of disobedient, hostile, and defiant behavior toward authority figures goes well beyond the bounds of normal childhood behavior.

osmosis A gradual, often unconscious mental process of assimilating ideas or absorbing information that resembles the tendency of fluids to gradually flow through an absorbent material.

P

parent–teacher resource team Teachers and parents working together as a cooperative, respectful, and cohesive team.

perceiving Becoming aware of, by direct use of senses; noticing; or understanding in one's own mind.

permissive style Interactive (or control) style relying on neglect, abdication of responsibility, or overindulgence—"the doormat."

personal interaction Reciprocal social activity that should express genuine interest and respect for the other individual.

pervasive developmental disorders A group of neurodevelopmental disorders characterized by severe delays in the development of socialization and communication skills.

pica An eating disorder in which one eats nonfood substances such as dirt, chalk, paper, or other items.

pluralistic culture (*See* cultural pluralism.)

positive child guidance Relying on the "developmental interactionist" perspective to create guidance that is primarily based on an interweaving between external forces and internal processes.

positive, assertive guidance Guidance that bolsters self-esteem, nurtures cooperativeness, and models socially acceptable coping skills.

post-traumatic stress disorder A condition that follows a psychologically distressing event that can occur at any age and from any number of reasons.

prejudice As the name implies, prejudice is the process of *prejudging* someone. Racial prejudice comprises negative attitudes, beliefs, and rigid stereotypes against an ethnic group that are resistant to change despite contradictory evidence.

preoperational The second stage of cognitive development in Jean Piaget's theory that begins with the achievement of object permanence. This stage is typified by imaginative play, egocentricity, the inability to take another person's point of view, and the belief that the number or amount is changed when objects are rearranged.

prevention techniques A specific procedure or special type of action taken to make it difficult or impossible for someone to do a certain thing or for a certain type of thing to happen.

problem behavior Difficult and troubling behavior that requires planning and problem solving to resolve.

proprioceptive dysfunction Malfunction of input and feedback on body position. This disorder causes the child to appear clumsy, have difficulty sitting up without support, and have problems with motor activities.

proprioceptive sensation Sensory information taken in through the muscles, connecting tissue, skin, and joints that informs the brain where one's body is in space. Proprioception makes it possible for a person to move body parts without having to observe the movement to make sure it is happening.

prosocial Behavior that improves the welfare of others or has a generally positive effect on persons with whom one comes in contact.

proximodistal Development in a direction from closest to the body's trunk to the farthest, such as controlling the muscles of the trunk, then the muscles down the arms, and finally the hands (close to far).

pseudoconditioning The pairing of an unconditioned stimuli with a naturally occurring stimulus–response connection.

Q

qualitative information Unmeasurable descriptive qualities or characteristics of behaviors.

quantitative information Measurable numerical data and statistical calculations that tell how often or to what degree behaviors occur.

quick response techniques A specific procedure or special type of action done swiftly in reaction to a situation.

R

racism Founded on a belief that race is a major determinant of human characteristics and causes the superiority of some races over others. Racism is a combination of racial prejudice and discrimination. Racism uses the inflexible assumption that group differences are biologically determined and therefore inherently unchangeable. Racism does not exist in a vacuum but rather is enacted and reinforced through social, cultural, and institutional practices that endorse the hierarchical power of one racial group over another.

receptive language Comprehension of written or spoken communication expressed by others.

redirection The process of offering a substitute focus to distract the child from a current undesirable one. For example, a child may be offered a developmentally appropriate water play activity to refocus his or her inappropriate interest in pouring milk from a cup onto the floor.

replaces Substitutes one action for another when both cannot be done at the same time, so that an undesired behavior must be given up or suspended for the new action to take place.

rescued A situation in which one has been removed from experiencing the logical consequence of an inappropriate behavior. Typically, a child acted improperly without any negative results because an adult intervened to extricate the child from a precarious situation the child has created.

respect The process of showing regard for the rights and needs of another. To display polite expressions of consideration for another.

responsibility Individual accountability and answerability.

responsibility orientation Perspective in which sensitivity to others, loyalty, responsibility, self-sacrifice, and peacemaking reflect *interpersonal* involvement and caring guides and ethical and moral decision making.

running account A detailed commentary describing an event as it unfolds each time it occurs.

S

scapegoating Putting blame on another by someone who wants to cause harm or is unwilling to take responsibility for his or her own actions.

secure attachment Healthy emotional ties to caregiver. Typical signs include brightening at the sight of caregiver, visually following caregiver's movements, smiling or vocalizing to get attention, holding out arms to be picked up, or clinging to the caregiver.

seizure A sudden disruption of the brain's normal electrical activity accompanied by a change in consciousness or neurological and behavioral symptoms such as breathing problems, a bizarre feeling of déjà vu, changes in muscle tone, and convulsions.

self-concept Perception of oneself in terms of personal worth, life and school successes, and perceived social status.

self-esteem Seeing oneself as a worthwhile individual.

self-identity The set of characteristics that a person recognizes as belonging uniquely to himself or herself and constituting his or her own individuality.

self-regulation A critical development process by which one learns to function without external control; being able to deal with problems appropriately and independently.

sensory integration dysfunction is a disorder characterized by the inability of the brain to correctly process information brought in by the senses.

sexism Historically, sexism has been male-driven and accompanied by a belief in male superiority.

sexual harassment Harassment, or unwelcome attention, of a sexual nature. It includes a range of behavior from mild annoyances to serious abuses and even forced sexual activity for sexual gratification; for personal sexual stimulation; or to antagonize, bully, and dehumanize another person by using sexually related activity.

shaken baby syndrome (SBS) A particularly devastating type of child abuse that is caused by forcefully shaking a baby or young child. It can cause brain damage, blindness, learning impairment, and death.

shame A negative feeling or emotion of embarrassment, unworthiness, or disgrace.

sickle cell disease An inherited disorder of the blood resulting in abnormal red blood cells that are not able to carry enough oxygen around the body.

single parents Mothers, fathers, grandparents, or guardians rearing children alone.

social growth Learning to understand and function appropriately in one's social environment; learning how to effectively interact with others.

social intelligence An individual's fund of knowledge about the social world and ability to act wisely in human relations, to get along with others, and to interact with skill and ease in social matters.

socialization The process by which children learn acceptable behavior.

snowball effect The cycle in which an emotionally needy child's inappropriate behavior causes others to treat her negatively, causing her to feel more emotionally needy, which causes her to increase her misbehavior to achieve goals she mistakenly believes will meet her emotional needs. This in turn speeds up the tailspin cycle of more and more negative behavior patterns and habits, pushing others further and further away.

spina bifida Incomplete development of the protective covering around the brain and spinal cord that leaves the covering split open and the spinal cord exposed.

stigmatized Labeled as socially undesirable on the basis of some specific characteristic, damaging the stigmatized person's self-esteem and excluding him or her socially.

stimuli Something taken in through the senses that might incite activity or thought, something seen, smelled, heard, felt, or tasted; an incentive for action.

stress The process of recognizing and responding to threat or danger.

syndrome A disease or disorder that has more than one feature or symptom.

T

tactile sense Perception through touch that provides input from textures, temperature, and pressure.

temperament Clusters of personality traits with individual and distinctive behavioral patterns.

time sampling A recording made at predefined intervals to determine the pattern of occurrence and the general frequency of a certain behavior either in an individual or in the entire group.

time-away Removing a child from an overwhelming situation to provide a supportive cooling off time with an adult present.

tokens Objects (for example, stars, points, stickers) given to children for performing specified behaviors that are then exchanged at prearranged times for their choice of activities or items from a menu of rewards (for example, toys, special food treats, field trips).

Tourette's syndrome A disorder characterized by multiple motor and vocal tics.

traffic patterns The most obvious routes children will take as they move around the classroom.

transitions Phase in daily activities in which a child must give up or leave one activity and begin another activity. These difficult phases between activities may cause children to balk at moving from one thing to the next. Additionally, the confusion and stress of the changeover may trigger misbehavior.

traumatic brain injury Caused when the head is struck or shaken violently and resulting in cognitive, social, or psychomotor disability.

trust Sense of security; belief that one's needs will be met.

Turner's syndrome A genetic disorder that can affect a girl's development. The cause is a missing or incomplete Y chromosome. Girls who have it tend to be very short and their ovaries and genitalia don't usually become sexually mature at puberty.

U

unconditional acceptance The process of accepting someone as a worthwhile human being; recognition and appreciation without any strings attached.

unconscious conditioning A response developed through the use of all the senses; an association of things seen, felt, heard, tasted, and smelled with other meaningful sensations or events.

unconscious reactions Actions that are unplanned, devoid of forethought.

V

vestibular function The body's balance system, which provides perception of movement and orientation in space. The vestibular function is essential for a person to maintain muscle tone, coordinate both sides of the body, and know the difference between up and down.

visceral Proceeding more from instinct rather than from logical thinking; characterized by or showing emotion.

visual impairment and blindness Inability to see details at near and far distances; defects in the field of vision or visual distortions. No vision and low vision can be caused by several different diseases, conditions, or accidents.

vocal tic A sudden involuntary vocalization such as a yip, whistle, grunt, or cough. A complex vocal tic is a distinct, obsessively repeated phrase or the intricate obsessive use of words, such as repeating everything other people say.

References

Abel, E. L., & Sokol, R. J. (1987). Incidence of fetal alcohol syndrome and economic impact of FAS-related anomalies. *Drug and Alcohol Dependence, 19,* 51–70.

Ackerman, D. J. (2006). The costs of being a child care teacher: Revisiting the problem of low wages. *Educational Policy, 20*(1), 85.

Acredolo, L., Goodwyn, S., & Abrams, D. (2002). *Baby signs: How to talk with your baby before your baby can talk.* New York: McGraw-Hill.

Adams, G., & Rohacek, M. (2002, February). *Child care and welfare reform.* WR&B Policy Brief #14. Washington, DC: Brookings Institution.

Addison, J. T. (1992). Urie Bronfenbrenner. *Human Ecology, 20*(2), 16–20.

Adesman, A. R., & Morgan, A. M. (1999). Management of stimulant medications in children with attention-deficit/hyperactivity disorder. *Pediatric Clinics of North America, 46*(5), 945–963.

Adlam, D. (1977). *Code in context.* London: Routledge & Kegan Paul.

Adler, A. (1931). *The pattern of life.* London: Kegan, Paul, Trench, Tutner.

Adler, A. (1963). *The problem child: The life style of the difficult child as analyzed in specific cases.* Oakville, Ontario: Capricorn Books.

Adler, A., & Brett, C. (Translator). (1998). *Understanding human nature.* Center City, MN: Hazelden.

Administration on Children and Families, Child Care Bureau. (2005). FY 2004 CCDF data tables (preliminary estimates). Washington, DC: U.S. Department of Health and Human Services.

AFL-CIO. (2004). *Ask a working woman survey report.* Washington, DC: AFL-CIO.

AFL-CIO Working Women's Department. (2000, November). Working together for kids. *Labor Project for Working Families and the AFL-CIO Working Women's Department.* Online document no longer available, but similar updated articles are available, http://www.aflcio.org/issues/workfamily/.

Aidman, A. (1997). *Television violence: Content, context, and consequences.* Champaign, IL: ERIC Digest, document no. ED414078. Retrieved from http://www.eric.ed.gov/.

Ainsworth, M. D. S. (1973). The development of the infant-mother attachment. In B. M. Caldwell & H. N. Ricciuti (Eds.), *Review of child development research* (vol. 3, 1–94). Chicago: University of Chicago Press.

Aitken, J., & Shedletsky, L., Eds. (1995). *Intrapersonal communication processes.* Annandale, VA: National Communication Association.

Akinbami, L. (2006). The state of childhood asthma. *United States, Centers for Disease Control and Prevention National Center for Health Statistics, 1980–2005 Advance Data,* December, *12*(381), 1–24.

Allanson, J. E. (1987). Noonan syndrome. *Journal of Medical Genetics,* January, *24*(1), 9–13.

Allen, J. P., Porter, M. R., McFarland, F. C., Marsh, P., & McElhaney, K. (2005). The two faces of adolescents' success with peers: Adolescent popularity, social adaptation, and deviant behavior. *Child Development, 76,* 747–760.

Alley, T. R. (1981). Head shape and the perception of cuteness. *Developmental Psychology, 17,* 650–654.

Allinsmith, W., & Greening, T. C. (1955). Guilt over anger as predicted from parental discipline: A study of superego development. *American Psychologist, 10,* 320.

Allport, G. W. (1954). *The nature of prejudice.* Cambridge, MA: Addison-Wesley.

Altenor, A., Kay, E., & Richter, M. (1977). The generality of learned helplessness in the rat. *Learning & Motivation, 8,* 54–61.

Amato, P. R. (1997). Life-span adjustment of children to their parents' divorce. In E. N. Junn & C. Boyatzis (Eds.),

Annual editions: Child growth and development 97/98 (4th ed.). New York: McGraw-Hill. (Original work published in *The Future of Children,* Spring 1994).

American Diabetes Association. (2006). *American Diabetes Association complete guide to diabetes* (4th ed.). New York: Bantam.

American Foundation for the Blind. (1993). *First steps.* Los Angeles, CA: Blind Childrens' Center.

American Psychiatric Association. (2004). *Diagnostic and statistical manual of mental disorders* (DSMIV-TR, 4th ed.). Washington, DC: Author.

Anyon, J. (1983). Intersections of gender and class: Accommodation and resistance by contradictory sex-role ideologies. In S. Walker & L. Barton (Eds.), *Gender, class and education* (21–37). London: Falmer.

Appleton, R., Chappell, B., Beirne, M., & Hastings, L. (1997). *Your child's epilepsy.* London: Class Publishing.

Ariel, A. (1992). *Education of children and adolescents with learning disabilities.* New York: Macmillan.

Aries, P. (1962). *Centuries of childhood.* New York: Random House.

Ashcraft, R., Ed. (1991). John Locke: Critical assessments. New York: Routledge.

Ashworth, M. (1992). *The first step on the longer path: Becoming an ESL teacher.* Markham, ON: Pippin.

Atherton, J. S. (2005). *Learning and teaching: Piaget's developmental theory.* UK: Available online at http://www.learningandteaching.info/.

Baillargeon, R. (1997). How do infants learn about the physical world? In E. N. Junn & C. Boyatzis (Eds.), *Annual editions: Child growth and development 97/98* (4th ed.). New York: McGraw-Hill. (Original work published in *Current Directions in Psychological Science,* October 1994).

Ball, J., & Pence, A. R. (1999, March). Beyond developmentally appropriate practice: Developing community and culturally appropriate practice. *Young Children, 54*(2), 46–50.

Bandura, A. (1977). *Social learning theory.* Englewood Cliffs, NJ: Prentice Hall.

Banich, M. T. (1997). *Neurology: The neural bases of mental function.* Boston, MA: Houghton Mifflin.

Bardige, B. S., & Segal, M. M. (2005). *Building literacy with love: A guide for teachers and caregivers of children birth through age 5.* Washington, DC: Zero to Three.

Barko, N. (1997). Labeled for life? In K. M. Paciorek & J. H. Munro (Eds.), *Annual editions: Early childhood education 97/98* (18th ed.). New York: McGraw-Hill. (Original work published in *Parents,* September 1996).

Barnard, M. U. (2003). *Helping your depressed child: A step-by-step guide for parents.* Oakland, CA: New Harbinger.

Barnett, R. C., & Rivers, C. (1998). *She works, he works: How two income families are happy, healthy and thriving.* Cambridge, UK: Harvard University Press.

Barnett, W. S., & Ackerman, D. J. (2006). Costs, benefits, and the long-term effects of preschool programs. *Community Development: Journal of the Community Development Society, 37*(2).

Bar-On, R. (1997). *The Emotional Quotient Inventory (EQ-i): Technical manual.* Toronto, Canada: Multi-Health Systems.

Bar-On, R. (2000). Emotional and social intelligence: Insights from the Emotional Quotient Inventory (EQ-i). In R. Bar-On & J. D. A. Parker (Eds.), *Handbook of emotional intelligence.* San Francisco, CA: Jossey-Bass.

Bar-On, R. (2005). The Bar-On model of emotional-social intelligence. In P. Fernández-Berrocal & N. Extremera (Guest Eds.), Special issue on emotional intelligence. *Psicothema, 17.*

Bauermeister, J. J., Canino, G., Bravo, M., Ramirez, R., Jensen, P. S., Chavez, L., Martinez-Taboas, A., Ribera, J., Alegria, M., & Garcia, P. M. (2003). Stimulant and psychosocial treatment of ADHD in Latino/Hispanic children. *Journal of the American Academy of Child and Adolescent Psychiatry, 42,* 851–855.

Baumrind, D. (1967). Child care practices anteceding three patterns of preschool behavior. *Genetic Psychology Monographs, 75,* 43–88.

Baumrind, D. (1971). Current patterns of parental authority. *Developmental Psychology Monographs, 4*(1), 1–103.

Baumrind, D. (1978). Parental disciplinary patterns and social competence in children. *Youth and Society, 9*(3), 239–276.

Baumrind, D. (1980). New directions in socialization research. *Psychological Bulletin, 35,* 639–652.

Baumrind, D. (1993). The average respectable environment is not good enough: A response to Scarr. *Child Development, 64,* 1299–1317.

Baumrind, D. (1995). *Child maltreatment and optimal caregiving in social contexts.* New York: Garland.

Beaty, J. J. (1997). Building bridges with multicultural picture books: For children 3–5. Upper Saddle River, NJ: Merrill Education/Prentice Hall.

Beck, R. (1973). White House conferences on children: An historical perspective. *Harvard Educational Review, 43*, 4.

Begley, S. (1997a). Your child's brain. In K. M. Paciorek & J. H. Munro (Eds.), *Annual editions: Early childhood education 97/98* (18th ed.). New York: McGraw-Hill. (Original work published in *Newsweek*, February 19, 1996.)

Begley, S., & Springen, K. (1997). Life in a parallel world. In E. N. Junn & C. Boyatzis (Eds.), *Annual editions: Child growth and development 97/98* (4th ed.). New York: McGraw-Hill. (Original work published in *Newsweek*, May 13, 1996.)

Bentzen, W. R. (2005). *Seeing young children: A guide to observing and recording behavior* (5th ed.). Clifton Park, NY: Thomson Delmar Learning.

Berens, L. V. (2000). *Understanding yourself and others: An introduction to temperament—2.0.* Huntington Beach, CA: Telos Publications.

Berk, L. E. (1997). Vygotsky's theory: The importance of make-believe play. In E. N. Junn & C. Boyatzis (Eds.), *Annual editions: Child growth and development 97/98* (4th ed.). New York: McGraw-Hill. (Original work published in *Young Children*, November 1994.)

Berk, L. E. (2001). *Awakening children's minds: How parents and teachers can make a difference.* New York: Oxford University Press.

Berk, L. E., & Winsler, A. (1995). *Scaffolding children's learning: Vygotsky and early childhood education.* Washington, DC: National Association for the Education of Young Children.

Berkowitz, L., & Frodi, A. (1979). Reactions to a child's mistakes as affected by her/his looks and speech. *School Psychology Quarterly, 42*, 420–425.

Berkowitz, M. W. (1997). The complete moral person: Anatomy and formation. In J. M. Dubois (Ed.), *Moral issues in psychology: Personalist contributions to selected problems* (11–41). Lanham, MD: University Press of America.

Berkowitz, M. W., & Gibbs, J. C. (1983). Measuring the developmental features of moral discussion. *Merrill-Palmer Quarterly, 29*, 399–410.

Berkowitz, M. W., & Grych, J. H. (1998). Fostering goodness: Teaching parents to facilitate children's moral development. *Journal of Moral Education, 27*(3), 371–391.

Berndt, T. J. (1997). *Child development* (2nd ed.). New York: McGraw-Hill.

Betz, C. (1994). Beyond time-out: Tips from a teacher. *Young Children, 4*(3), 10–14.

Bicknell, J. (1975). *Pica, a childhood symptom.* Southampton, UK: Camelot Press.

Billman, J., & Sherman, J. A. (1997). *Observation and participation in early childhood settings: A practicum guide, birth through age five.* Needham Heights, MA: Allyn & Bacon.

Blau, F. (1998, March). Trends in the well-being of American women, 1990–1995. *Journal of Economic Literature, 36*, 112–165.

Bloom, B. S. (1964). *Stability and change in human characteristics.* New York: Wiley.

Blosser, J., & DePompei, R. (1994). *Pediatric traumatic brain injury: Proactive intervention.* San Diego, CA: Singular.

Bodrova, E., & Leong, D. J. (1996). *Tools of the mind: The Vygotskian approach to early childhood education.* Englewood Cliffs, NJ: Prentice Hall.

Bogdan, R., Bogdan, R., & Taylor, S. J. (1982). *Inside out: The social meaning of mental retardation.* Toronto, Canada: University of Toronto Press.

Bogdashina, O. (2003). *Sensory perceptual issues in autism: Different sensory experiences, different perceptual worlds.* Philadelphia, PA: Jessica Kingsley.

Bond, J. T., Galinsky, E., & Swanberg, J. E. (1998). *The 1997 national study of the changing workforce.* New York: Families & Work Institute.

Bonnice, S. (2004). *The hidden child: youth with autism. Part of the series youth with special needs.* Broomall, PA: Mason Crest.

Bouras, N., Ed. (1995). *Mental health in mental retardation: Recent advances and practices.* New York: Cambridge University Press.

Bouras, N., Ed. (1999). *Psychiatric and behavioural disorders in developmental disabilities and mental retardation.* New York: Cambridge University Press.

Bower, S. L., Sharrett, M. K., & Plogsted, S. (2006). *Celiac disease: A guide to living with gluten intolerance.* New York: Demos Medical.

Bowlby, J. (1958). The nature of the child's tie to his mother. *International Journal of Psychoanalysis, 39*, 350–373.

Boxer, P., Guerra, N. G., Huesmann, L. R., & Morales, J. (2005). Proximal peer-level effects of a small-group selected prevention on aggression in elementary school children: An investigation of the peer contagion hypothesis. *Journal of Abnormal Child Psychology, 33,* 325–338.

Boyatzis, C. (1997). *Annual editions: Child growth and development 97/98.* New York: McGraw-Hill.

Brady, K., Forton, M. B., Porter, D., & Wood, C. (2003). *Rules in school.* Greenfield, MA: Northeast Foundation for Children.

Bramer, J. S. (2006). *Attention deficit disorder: The unfocused mind in children and adults.* New Haven & London: Yale University Press.

Brazelton, T. B. (1985). *Working and caring.* Reading, MA: Addison-Wesley.

Brazelton, T. B., Koslowski, B., & Main, M. (1974). The origins of reciprocity. In M. Lewis & L. Rosenblum (Eds.), *The effect of the infant on its caregiver.* New York: Wiley-Interscience.

Bredekamp, S., & Copple, C., Eds. (1997). *Developmentally appropriate practice in early childhood programs* (rev. ed.). Washington, DC: National Association for the Education of Young Children.

Bremner, R. H., Ed. (1974). *Children and youth in America: A documentary history* (vols. 1–3). Cambridge, MA: Harvard University Press.

Bretherton, I., & Waters, E. (1985). Security in infancy, childhood and adulthood. *Monographs of the Society for Research in Child Development, 5,* 1–2.

Brewer, A. (1998). *Introduction to early childhood education: Preschool through primary grades* (3rd ed.). Needham Heights, MA: Allyn & Bacon.

Briant, M. Z. (2004). *Baby sign language basics: Early communication for hearing babies and toddlers.* Carlsbad, CA: Hay House.

Briggs-Gowan, M. J., Carter, A. S., Skuban, E. M., & Horwitz, S. M. (2001). Prevalence of social-emotional and behavioral problems in a community sample of 1- and 2-year-old children. *Journal of the American Academy of Child & Adolescent Psychiatry, 40*(7), 811.

Bronfenbrenner, U. (1979). *The ecology of human development: Experiments by nature and design.* Cambridge, MA: Harvard University Press.

Bronfenbrenner, U. (1988). Interacting systems in human development: Research paradigms: Present and future. In N. Bolger, A. Caspi, G. Downey, & M. Moorehouse (Eds.), *Persons in context: Developmental processes* (25–49). New York: Cambridge University Press.

Bronfenbrenner, U. (1990). Discovering what families do. In *Rebuilding the nest: A new commitment to the American family.* Family Service America. Retrieved October 5, 2008, from http://www.montana.edu/www4h/process.html.

Bronfenbrenner, U. (1993). The ecology of cognitive development: Research models and fugitive findings. In R. H. Wozniak & K. W. Fischer (Eds.), *Development in context: Acting and thinking in specific environments* (3–44). Hillsdale, NJ: Erlbaum.

Bronfenbrenner, U. (1994). Who cares for the children? In H. Nuba, M. Searson, & D. L. Sheiman (Eds.), *Resources for early childhood: A handbook.* New York: Garland.

Bronfenbrenner, U. (1995). The bioecological model from a life course perspective: Reflections of a participant-observer. In P. Moen, G. H. Elder, & K. Luscher (Eds.), *Examining lives in context: Perspectives on the ecology of human development.* Cambridge, MA: Harvard University Press.

Bronfenbrenner, U., & Morris, P. A. (1998). The ecology of developmental processes. In W. Damon (Series Ed.) & R. M. Lerner (Vol. Ed.), *Handbook of child psychology: Theoretical models of human development* (Vol. 1, 5th ed.; 993–1027). New York: Wiley.

Bronson, M. B. (2001). *Self-regulation in early childhood: Nature and nurture.* New York: Guilford.

Brophy, J. (2007). Child maltreatment in diverse households: Challenges to child care law, theory and practice. In S. Meuwese, S. Detrick, & S. Jansen (Eds.), *100 years of child protection.* The Netherlands: Wolf Legal.

Bruey, C. T. (2004). *Demystifying autism spectrum disorders: A guide to diagnosis for the parents and professionals.* Bethesda, MD: Woodbine House.

Bruner, J. (1978a, September). Learning the mother tongue. *Human Nature, 1,* 43–48.

Bruner, J. (1978b). Learning how to do things with words. In J. S. Bruner & A. Garton (Eds.), *Human growth and development: Wolfson College lectures.* Oxford, UK: Clarendon Press.

Bruns, D. A., & Corso, R. M. (2001). *Working with culturally and linguistically diverse families.* Champaign, IL: ERIC Clearinghouse on Elementary and Early Childhood Education, document no. ED455972. Retrieved from http://www.eric.ed.gov.

Bruun, R. D., & Bruun, B. (1994). *A mind of its own: Tourette's syndrome: A story and guide.* New York: Oxford University Press.

Bullock, B. M., & Dishion, T. J. (2003). Conduct disorder. In J. J. Ponzetti Jr., R. R. Hanom, Y. Kellar-Guenther, P. K. Kerig, T. L. Scales, & J. M. While (Eds.), *The international encyclopedia of marriage and family relationships* (2nd ed.). New York: Macmillan Reference USA.

Bullock, J. R. (1997). Children without friends. In E. N. Junn & C. Boyatzis (Eds.), *Annual editions: Child growth and development 97/98* (4th ed.). New York: McGraw-Hill. (Original work published in *Childhood Education,* Winter 1992).

Buysse, V., Castro, D. C., West, T., & Skinner, M. L. (2005). Addressing the needs of Latino children: A national survey of state administrators of early childhood programs. *Early Childhood Research Quarterly, 20*(2), 146–163.

Byrne, P. (2000). *Philosophical and ethical problems in mental handicap.* New York: Palgrave Macmillan.

Cairns, R. B. (1979). *Social development: The origins and plasticity of interchanges.* San Francisco, CA: Freeman.

Capizzano, J., & Main, R. (2005). *Many young children spend long hours in child care.* Urban Institute: Online research report, March 31, 2005. Retrieved March 3, 2006, from http://www. urban.org/.

Capps, R., Fix, M. E., Ost, J., Reardon-Anderson, J., & Passel, J. S. (2005). *The health and wellbeing of young children of immigrants.* Urban Institute: Online research report, February 8, 2005. Retrieved March 3, 2006, from http://www.urban.org/.

Cárdenas, J. A. (1995). *Multicultural education: A generation of advocacy.* Needham Heights, MA: Allyn & Bacon.

Carkhuff, R. (1994). *The art of helping* (7th ed.). Amherst, MA: Human Resource Development.

Carlson, G. A., Jensen, P. S., & Nottelmann, E. D., Eds. (1998). Special issue: current issues in childhood bipolarity. *Journal of Affective Disorders, 51,* entire issue.

Carlsson-Paige, N., & Levin, D. E. (1998). *Before push comes to shove: Building conflict resolution skills with children.* St Paul, MN: Redleaf.

Carnegie Corporation of New York. (1994). Starting points: Meeting the needs of our youngest children: The report of the Carnegie Task Force on Meeting the Needs of Young Children. Waldorf, MD: Author.

Carr, E. G., Dunlap, G., Horner, R. H., Koegel, R. L., Turnbull, A. P., Sailor, W., Anderson, J., Albin, R. W., Koegel, L. K., & Fox, L. (2002). Positive behavior support: Evolution of an applied science. *Journal of Positive Behavior Interventions 4,* 4–16.

Caspary, W. R. (2000). *Dewey on democracy.* Ithaca, NY: Cornell University Press.

Caspi, A., Moffitt, T. E., Newman, D. L., & Silva, P. A. (1998). Behavioral observations at age 3 years predict adult psychiatric disorders: Longitudinal evidence from a birth cohort. In M. E. Hertzig & E. A. Farber (Eds.), *Annual progress in child psychiatry and child development: 1997* (319–331). Bristol, PA: Brunner/Mazel.

Center for Policy Alternatives. (2002). *Kids count data book: State profiles of child wellbeing.* Washington, DC: Author.

Charlesworth, R. (2004). *Understanding child development* (6th ed.). Clifton Park, NY: Thomson Delmar Learning.

Charney, R. S. (1997). *Habits of goodness: Case studies in the social curriculum.* Greenfield, MA: Northeast Foundation for Children.

Charney, R. S. (2002). Teaching children to care: Classroom management for ethical and academic growth, K–8. Greenfield, MA: Northeast Foundation for Children.

Chen, D. (1999c). Interactions between infants and caregivers: The context for early intervention. In D. Chen (Ed.), *Essential elements in early intervention: Visual impairment and multiple disabilities* (22–48). New York: American Foundation for the Blind.

ChildHelp USA. (2005). *National child abuse statistics.* Scottsdale, AZ: Author, Treatment & Prevention of Child Abuse.

Child Welfare League of America. (2005). *National fact sheet 2005: America's children: A snapshot.* Washington, DC: Child Welfare League of America.

Chomsky, N. (1965). *Aspects of the theory of syntax.* Cambridge, MA: MIT Press.

Chugani, H. (1993, June). Positron emission tomography scanning: Applications in newborns. *Clinics in Perinatology, 20*(2), 398.

Ciaramicoli, A. P., & Ketcham, K. (2000). *The power of empathy: A practical guide to creating intimacy, self-understanding, and lasting love in your life.* New York: Dutton/Penguin.

Cicci, R. (1995). *What's wrong with me?* Baltimore, MD: York Press.

Clampet-Lundquist, S., Edin, K., London, A., Scott, E., & Hunter, V. (2003). Making a way out of no way: How mothers meet basic family needs while moving from welfare to work. In A. C. Crouter & A. Booth (Eds.), *Work-Family Challenges for Low-Income Parents and Their Children.* Mahwah, NJ: Erlbaum.

Clark, D. B., & Uhry, J. K. (1995). *Dyslexia: Theory and practice of remedial instruction*. Baltimore, MD: York Press.

Clark, E. B., Clark, C., & Neill, C. A. (2001). *The heart of a child: What families need to know about heart disorders in children* (2nd ed.). Baltimore, MD: Johns Hopkins University Press.

Clark, L., DeWolf, S., & Clark, C. (1992). Teaching teachers to avoid having culturally assaultive classrooms. *Young Children, 47*(5), 4–9.

Clarke, J. I. (1978). *Self-esteem: A family affair*. New York: Winston Press.

Clarke-Stewart, A. (1978). Popular primer for parents. *American Psychologist, 33,* 359.

Claxton, G., & Carr, M. (2004). A framework for teaching learning: The dynamics of disposition. *Early Years, 24*(1), 87–97.

Clewett, A. S. (1988). Guidance and discipline: Teaching young children appropriate behavior. *Young Children, 43*(4), 26–31.

Close, N. (2002). *Listening to children: Talking with children about difficult issues*. Boston, MA: Allyn & Bacon.

Cohen, D. B. (1999). *Stranger in the nest: Do parents really shape their child's personality, intelligence and character?* New York: Wiley.

Cohen, D. J., & Volkmar, F. R., Eds. (1997). *Handbook of autism and pervasive developmental disorders* (2nd ed.). New York: Wiley.

Coie, J. D., & Dodge, K. A. (1998). Aggression and antisocial behavior. In W. Damon & N. Eisenberg (Eds.), *Handbook of child psychology: Social, emotional, and personality development* (vol. 3, 779–862). New York: Wiley.

Coie, J. D., & Koeppl, G. (1990). Adapting intervention to the problems of aggressive and disruptive rejected children. In S. A. Asher & J. D. Coie (Eds.), *Peer rejection in childhood* (309–337). New York: Cambridge University Press.

Colby, A., & Damon, W. (1992). *Some do care: Contemporary lives of moral commitment*. New York: Free Press.

Cole, L. (1950). *A history of education*. New York: Rinehart.

Coleman, M., Ed. (1976). *The autistic syndromes*. New York: Elsevier.

Coleman, P. T. (2004, Winter). Conflict resolution at multiple levels across the lifespan: The work of the ICCCR. *Theory Into Practice, 43*(1), 31–38.

Collins, W. A., & Gunnar, M. R. (1990). Social and personality development. *Annual Review of Psychology, 41,* 387–416.

Condon, W. S., & Sander, L. (1974). Neonate movement is synchronized with adult speech: Interactional participation and language acquisition. *Science, 183,* 99–101.

Cook-Gumperz, J. (1973). *Social control and socialization*. London: Routledge & Kegan Paul.

Coontz, S. (1997). Where are the good old days? In K. M. Paciorek & J. H. Munro (Eds.), *Annual editions: Early childhood education 97/98* (18th ed.). New York: McGraw-Hill. (Original work published in *Modern Maturity,* May/June 1996).

Cooper, M. (1957). *Pica*. Springfield, IL: Charles C. Thomas.

Coopersmith, S. (1967). *The antecedents of self-esteem*. San Francisco, CA: W. H. Freeman.

Copeland, E., & Love, V. (1995). *Attention without tension: A teacher's handbook on attention disorders*. Plantation, FL: Specialty Press.

Copeland, M. L., & McCreedy, B. S. (1997, January–February). Creating family-friendly policies: Are child care center policies in line with current family realities? *Child Care Information Exchange, 113,* 7–10, 12.

Corbett, B. (1988). *A garden of children*. Mississauga, Ontario, Canada: The Froebel Foundation.

Corsaro, W. A. (1981). Friendship in the nursery school: Social organization in a peer environment. In S. R. Asher and J. M. Gottman (Eds.), *The development of children's friendships*. New York: Cambridge University Press.

Costley, D., & Todd, R. (1987). *Human relations in organization* (3rd ed.). New York: West.

Cotton, N. (1984). The development of self-esteem and self-esteem regulation. In J. E. Mack & S. L. Ablon (Eds.), *The development and sustaining of self-esteem in childhood*. New York: International Universities Press.

Council on Interracial Books for Children. (1998). *Bulletin of the council on interracial books for children*. Sacramento, CA: Bill Honig, Superintendent of Public Instruction, California State Department of Education.

Cowan, C. P., & Cowan, P. (1992). *When partners become parents*. New York: Basic Books.

Crockenberg, S. (1997). How children learn to resolve conflicts in families. In E. N. Junn & C. Boyatzis (Eds.),

Annual editions: Child growth and development 97/98 (4th ed.). New York: McGraw-Hill. (Original work published in *Zero to Three,* April 1992).

Cronen, V. E. (1995). Practical theory and the tasks ahead for social approaches to communication. In W. Leeds-Hurwitz (Ed.), *Social approaches to communication* (217–242). New York: Guilford.

Cronen, V. E. (2001). Practical theory, practical art, and the pragmatic-systemic account of inquiry. *Communication Theory, 11,* 14–35.

Crosser, S. (2002). *Time out: insights from football.* Published online by Excelligence Learning Corporation. Retrieved March 4, 2006, from http://www.earlychildhood.com.

Csikszentmihalyi, M. (1996). *Creativity: Flow and the psychology of discovery and invention.* New York: Harper Collins.

Cunnington, P., & Buck, A. (1965). *Children's costume in England.* New York: Barnes & Noble.

Curran, D. (1985). *Stress and the healthy family.* Minneapolis, MN: Winston Press.

Currie, J. (2005). Health disparities and gaps in school readiness. *The future of children—School readiness: Closing racial and ethnic gaps, 15*(1), 117–138.

Daly, K. (1996). *Families and time: Keeping pace in a hurried culture.* Thousand Oaks, CA: Sage.

Daly, K. (2000). *It keeps getting faster: Changing patterns of time in families.* Guelph, Ontario, Canada: Vanier Institute of the Family, University of Guelph. Retrieved from http://www.vifamily.ca/library/cft/faster.html.

Damon, W. (1988). *The moral child: Nurturing children's natural moral growth.* New York: Free Press.

Daniels, M. (2001). *Dancing with words: Signing for hearing children's literacy.* Westport, CT: Bergin & Garvey.

Davenport, S. L. H., Hefner, M. A., & Mitchell, J. A. (1986). The spectrum of clinical features in CHARGE syndrome. *Clinical Genetics, 29,* 298–310.

Davis, L. E., & Proctor, E. K. (1989). *Race, gender, and class.* Englewood Cliffs, NJ: Prentice Hall.

Day, R., Peterson, G., & McCracken, C. (1998). Predicting spanking of younger and older children by mothers and fathers. *Journal of Marriage and the Family, 60,* 79–94.

Dean, A. L., Malik, M. M., Richards, W., & Stringer, S. A. (1986). Effects of parental maltreatment on children's conceptions of interpersonal relationships. *Developmental Psychology, 22,* 617–626.

DeCasper, A. J., & Fifer, W. P. (1980). Of human bonding: Newborns prefer their mothers' voices. *Science, 208,* 1174–1176.

Denby, D. (1997). Buried alive. In E. N. Junn & C. Boyatzis (Eds.), *Annual editions: Child growth and development 97/98* (4th ed.). New York: McGraw-Hill. (Original work published in *The New Yorker,* July 15, 1996.)

Dennis, R. E., & Giangreco, M. F. (1996). Creating conversation: Reflections on cultural sensitivity in family interviewing. *Exceptional Children, 63*(1), 103–116.

Dennis, W. (1960). Causes of retardation among institutional children: Iran. *The Journal of Genetic Psychology, 96,* 47–59.

Dennis, W. (1973). *Children of the Creche.* New York: Appleton-Century-Crofts.

Derman-Sparks, L., & Ramsey, P. G. (2005). What if all the children in my class are white? Anti-bias/multicultural education with white children. *Young Children, 60*(6), 20–24, 26–27 SL.

Derman-Sparks, L., & ABC Task Force. (1989). *Anti-bias curriculum: Tools for empowering young children.* Washington, DC: National Association for the Education of Young Children.

de Sales, F. (1972). *Introduction to the devout life* (reissue ed.). Transl. & Ed. J. K. Ryan. New York: Image Books.

Desnick, R. J., & Kaback, M. M. (2001). *Tay-Sachs disease.* Burlington, MA: Academic Press.

DeVries, R., & Zan, B. (1994). *Moral classrooms, moral children: Creating a constructivist atmosphere in early education.* New York: Teachers College Press.

Dewey, J. (1959). *Dewey on education.* S. Dworkin (Ed.). New York: Bureau of Publications, Teachers College, Columbia University.

Dewey, J. (1966). *Experience and education.* New York: Collier.

Dinkmeyer, D. C., & McKay, G. D. (1982). *The parent's handbook: Systematic training for effective parenting.* Circle Pines, MN: American Guidance Service.

Dinnebeil, L. A., & Rule, S. (1994). Variables that influence collaboration between parents and service providers. *Journal of Early Intervention, 18*(4), 349–361.

Dinwiddie, S. (1994). The saga of Sally, Sammy, and the red pen: Facilitating children's social problem solving. *Young Children, 49,* 13–19.

Dinwiddie, S. (1997). *I want it my way!: Problem-solving techniques with children two to eight.* Palo Alto, CA: Better World Press.

Dishion, T. J., & Bullock, B. M. (2002). Parenting and adolescent problem behavior: An ecological analysis of the nurturance hypothesis. In J. G. Borkowski (Ed.) *Parenting and your child's world* (231–250). Hillsdale, NJ: Erlbaum.

Doll, B. (1996). Prevalence of psychiatric disorders in children and youth: An agenda for advocacy by school psychology. *School Psychology Quarterly, 11,* 20–47.

Don, A., Schellenberg, E., & Rourke, B. (1999). Music and language skills of children with Williams Syndrome. *Child Neuropsychology, 5,* 154–170.

Donohue-Carey, P. (2002). Solitary or shared sleep: What's safe? *Mothering: Natural Family Living, 114,* September/October.

Donohue-Colletta, N. (1995). *What parents should know about school readiness.* Washington, DC: National Association for the Education of Young Children.

Douglas, E. M., & Finkelhor, D. (2005). *Child maltreatment fatalities fact sheet.* Durham, NH: Crimes Against Children Research Center.

Dreikurs, R., & Grey, L. (1968). *A New Approach to Discipline: Logical Consequences.* New York: Hawthorn Books.

Dreikurs, R., Cassel, P., & Ferguson, E. D. (2004). *Discipline without tears: How to reduce conflict and establish cooperation in the classroom.* Canada: Wiley.

Dunn, L., & Kontos, S. (1997). Research in review. What have we learned about developmentally appropriate practice? *Young Children, 52*(5), 4–13.

Dupéré, V., Lacourse, É., Willms, J. D., Vitaro, F., & Tremblay, R. E. (2007). Affiliation to youth gangs during adolescence: The interaction between childhood psychopathic tendencies and neighborhood disadvantage. *Journal of Abnormal Child Psychology.* Published online, July. Retrieved September 19, 2007, from http://www.springerlink.com/content/e162227q7l214121/.

Dwivedi, K. (2000). *Post-traumatic stress disorder in children and adolescents.* London: Whurr.

Dykeman, C., Nelson, J. R., & Appleton, V. (1996). Building strong working alliances with American Indian families. In P. L. Ewalt, E. M. Freeman, S. A. Kirk, & D. L. Poole (Eds.), *Multicultural issues in social work.* Washington, DC: NASW Press.

Eddowes, E. A., & Ralph, K. S. (1998). *Interactions for development and learning: Birth through eight years.* Upper Saddle River, NJ: Merrill Education/Prentice Hall.

Education and Advocacy Committee, Tourette Syndrome Foundation of Canada. (2001). *Understanding Tourette syndrome: A handbook for educators.* Toronto, Canada: The TS Foundation of Canada.

Edwards, C. H. (1997). *Classroom discipline and management* (2nd ed.). Upper Saddle River, NJ: Merrill Education/Prentice Hall.

Efran, J. G. (1974). The effect of physical appearance on the judgment of guilt, interpersonal attraction, and severity of recommended punishment in a simulated jury task. *Journal of Research in Personality, 8,* 45–54.

Egan, G. (2002). Exercises in helping skills for Egan's the skilled helper: A problem-management and opportunity-development approach to helping. New York: Brooks/Cole.

Egan, G. (2006). *Essentials of skilled helping: Managing problems, developing opportunities.* New York: Brooks/Cole.

Eisenberg, R. B. (1976). *Auditory competence in early life.* Baltimore, MD: University Park Press.

Eisenberg-Berg, N. (1979). Development of children's prosocial moral judgment. *Developmental Psychology, 15,* 128–138.

Elder, V., & King, A. (1994). Cardiac kids: A book for families who have a child with heart disease. Lake Forest, IL: Tenderhearts.

Elkind, D. (1981). *The hurried child.* Reading, MA: Addison-Wesley.

Elkind, D. (1997). School and family in the post-modern world. In E. N. Junn & C. Boyatzis (Eds.), *Annual editions: Child growth and development 97/98* (4th ed.). New York: McGraw-Hill.

Elman, J., Bates, E. A., Johnson, M., Kaemiloff-Smith, A., Parisi, D., & Plunkett, K. (1997). *Rethinking innateness.* Cambridge, MA: MIT Press.

Emde, R. N., Wolf, D. P., & Oppenheim, D. (2003). *Revealing the inner worlds of young children.* New York: Oxford University Press.

Erikson, E. (1963). *Childhood and society* (2nd ed.). New York: W. W. Norton.

Erikson, E. (1982). *The life cycle completed: A review.* New York: W. W. Norton.

Erikson, E. H. (1959). Growth and crises of the healthy personality. *Psychological Issues, 1,* 50–100.

Faegre, M., & Anderson, J. (1930). *Child care and training* (3rd ed.). Minneapolis: University of Minnesota Press.

Faniran, A. O., Peat, J. K., & Woolcock, A. J. (1998). Persistent cough: Is it asthma? *Archives of Disease in Childhood,* November, *79,* 411–414.

Fantuzzo, J. W., Rohrbeck, C. A., Hightower, A. D., & Work, W. C. (1991). Teacher's use and children's preferences of rewards in elementary school. *Psychology in the Schools, 28*(2), 175–181.

Favez, N. (2006). From family play to family narratives. *Signal Newsletter* of *World Association of Infant Mental Health,* July–December.

Feden, P. D., & Vogel, R. M. (1993). *Methods of teaching: Applying cognitive science to promote student learning.* New York: McGraw-Hill.

Federal Interagency Forum on Child and Family Statistics. (2005). *America's children: Key national indicators of well-being.* Washington, DC: U.S. Government Printing Office.

Feeney, S. S., Christensen, D., & Moravcik, E. R. (1996). *Who am I in the lives of children? An introduction to teaching young children* (5th ed.). Upper Saddle River, NJ: Merrill Education/Prentice Hall.

Feldman, J., & Jones, R. (1995). *Transition time: Let's do something different!* Beltsville, MD: Gryphon House.

Felitti, V., Anda, R., Nordenberg, D., Williamson, D., Spitz, A., Edwards, V., Koss, M. P., & Marks, J. (1998). Relationship of childhood abuse and household dysfunction to many of the leading causes of death in adults. *American Journal of Preventive Medicine, 14*(4), 245–258.

Ferguson, T. J., & Rule, B. G. (1982). Influence of inferential set, outcome intent, and outcome severity on children's moral judgments. *Developmental Psychology, 18,* 843–851.

Field, T. M. (1982). Affective and physiological changes during manipulated interactions of high-risk infants. In T. Field & A. Fogel (Eds.), *Emotion and early interaction.* Hillsdale, NJ: Erlbaum.

Fields, M. V., & Boesser, C. (1998). *Constructive guidance and discipline: Preschool and primary education* (2nd ed.). Upper Saddle River, NJ: Merrill Education/Prentice Hall.

Finkelhor, D., & Dziuba-Leatherman, J. (1997). Victimization of children. In E. N. Junn & C. Boyatzis (Eds.), *Annual editions: Child growth and development 97/98* (4th ed.). New York: McGraw-Hill. (Original work published in *American Psychologist,* March 1994.)

Finkelstein, N. W., & Ramey, C. T. (1977). Learning to control the environment in infancy. *Child Development, 48,* 806–819.

Fishbein, H. D. (2002). *Peer prejudice and discrimination.* Mahwah, NJ: Erlbaum.

Flavell, J. H., Miller, P. H., & Miller, S. (2002). *Cognitive development* (4th ed.) Englewood Cliffs, NJ: Prentice Hall.

Fleming, R., Baum, A., & Singer, J. E. (1984). Toward an integrative approach to the study of stress. *Journal of Personality and Social Psychology, 46*(4), 939–949.

Flynn, C. (1996). Regional differences in spanking experiences and attitudes: A comparison of northeastern and southern college students. *Journal of Family Violence, 11*(1), 59–80.

Focus Council on Early Childhood Education. (2004). *The early childhood challenge: Preparing high-quality teachers for a changing society.* Washington, DC: American Association of Colleges for Teacher Education.

Fonagy, P. (2001). *Attachment theory and psychoanalysis.* New York: Other Press.

Fox, L., Dunlap, G., & Buschbacher, P. (2000). Understanding and intervening with young children's problem behavior: A comprehensive approach. In A. M. Wetherby & B. M. Prizan (Eds.). *Communication and language issues in autism and pervasive developmental disorder: A transactional developmental perspective.* Baltimore, MD: Paul H. Brookes.

Fox, L., Dunlap, G., & Cushing, L. (2002). Early intervention, positive behavior support, and transition to school. *Journal of Emotional and Behavioral Disorders, 10,* 149–157.

Francke, L. B. (1983). *Growing up divorced.* New York: Fawcett Crest.

Franken, R. (2001). *Human motivation* (5th ed.). Pacific Grove, CA: Brooks/Cole.

Franz, J. (2004). *Gale encyclopedia of psychology: Intermittent explosive disorder.* White Plains, NY: Thomson Gale.

Frederickson, G. M., & Knobel, D. T. (1980). A history of discrimination. In T. F. Pettigrew, G. M. Frederickson, D. T. Knobel, N. Glazer, & R. Ueda (Eds.), *Prejudice.* Cambridge, MA: Harvard University Press.

French, L. (1996). I told you all about it, so don't tell me you don't know. *Young Children, 5*(2), 17–20.

Frias, J. L., & Davenport, M. L. (2003). Health supervision for children with Turner syndrome. *Pediatrics,* March, *111*(3), 692–702.

Frick, P. J., & Dickens, C. (2006). Current perspectives on conduct disorder. *Current Psychiatry Reports, 8*(1), 59.

Frith, U. (2003). *Autism: Explaining the enigma* (2nd ed.). Oxford, UK: Blackwell.

Froebel, F. (1887). *The education of man: The art of educa-tion, instruction and training.* New York: Appleton.

Froebel, F. (1907). *The education of man* (W. N. Hailmann, Trans.). New York, NY: Appleton & Co. (Original work published 1826).

Fromm, S. (2001). Total estimated cost of child abuse and neglect in the United States—statistical evidence. Chi-cago: *Prevent Child Abuse America* (PCAA). Retrieved November 19, 2005, from http://www.preventchild abuse.org.

Gaetano, Y. D., Williams, L. R., & Volk, D. (1998). *Kaleido-scope: A multicultural approach for the primary school classroom.* Upper Saddle River, NJ: Merrill Education/ Prentice Hall.

Galinsky, E., & Bond, J. T. (2000). Helping families with young children navigate work and family life. In E. Applebaum (Ed.), *Balancing acts: Easing the burdens and improving the options for working families* (95–114), Washington, DC: Economic Policy Institute.

Gallagher, C. K. (2005, July). Brain research and early childhood development: A primer for developmen-tally appropriate practice. *Young Children, 60*(4), 12–20.

Gallo, N. (1997). Why spanking takes the spunk out of kids. In E. N. Junn & C. Boyatzis (Eds.), *Annual edi-tions: Child growth and development 97/98* (4th ed.). New York: McGraw-Hill. (Original work published in *Child,* March/April 1989).

Galston, W. (1993, Winter). Causes of declining well-being among U.S. children. *The Aspen Institute Quarterly, 5*(1), 52–77.

Garces, E., Thomas, D., & Currie, J. (2002). Longer-term ef-fects of head start. *American Economic Review, 92*(4), 999–1012.

Gardner, H. (1983). *Frames of mind.* New York: Basic Books.

Gartrell, D. (1997). Misbehavior or mistaken behavior? In K. M. Paciorek & J. H. Munro (Eds.), *Annual editions: Early childhood education 97/98* (18th ed.). New York: McGraw-Hill. (Original work published in *Young Children,* July 1995).

Gartrell, D. (2001). Replacing time-out: Part one—Using guidance to build an encouraging classroom. *Young Children, 56*(6), 8–16.

Gartrell, D. (2002). Replacing time-out: Part two—Using guidance to maintain an encouraging classroom. *Young Children, 57*(2), 36–43.

Gazda, G. M., Balzer, F. J., Childers, W. C., Nealy, A., Phelps, R. E., & Walters, R. P. (2006). *Human relations development: A manual for educators.* New York: Allyn & Bacon.

Geller, B., Fox, L. W., & Clark, K. A. (1994). Rate and pre-dictors of prepubertal bipolarity during follow-up of 6- to 12-year-old depressed children. *Journal of the American Academy of Child & Adolescent Psychiatry. 33*(4), 461–468.

Geller, B., & Luby, J. (1997). Child and adolescent bipolar disorder: A review of the past 10 years. *Journal of the American Academy of Child and Adolescent Psychiatry, 36*(9), 1168–1176.

Gerbner, G., & Gross, L. (1980). The violent face of tele-vision and its lessons. In E. L. Palmer and A. Dorr (Eds.), *Children and the faces of television: Teaching, violence, selling.* New York: Academic Press.

Gerhardt, S. (2004). *Why love matters: How affection shapes a baby's brain.* London: Routledge.

Gershoff, E. T. (2002). Corporal punishment by parents and associated child behaviors and experiences: A meta-analytic and theoretical review. *American Psy-chological Association, 128*(4), 539–579.

Gesell, A., Halverson, H. M., Thompson, H., Ilg, F. L., Cast-ner, B. M., Ames, L. B., & Amatruda, C. S. (1940). *The first five years of life: A guide to the study of the pre-school child.* New York: Harper & Row.

Gestwicki, C. (1999). *Developmentally appropriate practice.* Clifton Park, NY: Thomson Delmar Learning.

Gibbs, N. (1997). The EQ factor. In E. N. Junn & C. Boy-atzis (Eds.), *Annual editions: Child growth and de-velopment 97/98* (4th ed.). New York: McGraw-Hill. (Original work published in *Time,* October 2, 1995).

Gilliam, W. S. (2004). *Prekindergarteners left behind: Ex-pulsion rates in state prekindergarten systems.* Yale University Child Study Center. Retrieved November 19, 2005, from http://www.med.yale.edu/chldstdy/ faculty/pdf/Gilliam05.pdf.

Gilligan, C. (1982). *In a different voice: Psychological theory and women's development.* Cambridge, MA: Harvard University Press.

Gladwell, M. (2000). *The tipping point: How little things can make a big difference.* New York: Little, Brown.

Glazer, S. (2001). Is it a sign? Babies with normal hearing are being taught sign language by parents hoping to produce a learning boost or tantrum relief. *The Wash-ington Post,* March 13, p. 12, section 1.

Glubok, S., Ed. (1969). *Home and child life in colonial days.* New York: Macmillan.

Gmel, G., & Rehm, J. (2003). Harmful alcohol use. *Alcohol Research and Health, 2,* 52–62.

Goleman, D. (1995). *Emotional intelligence.* New York: Bantam Books.

Gonzalez-Alvarez, L. I. (1998). A short course in sensitivity training: Working with Hispanic families of children with disabilities. *Teaching Exceptional Children, 31*(2), 73–77.

Gonzalez-Mena, J. (1998a). *The child in the family and in the community* (2nd ed.). Upper Saddle River, NJ: Merrill Education/Prentice Hall.

Gonzalez-Mena, J. (1998b). *Foundations: Early childhood education in a diverse society.* Mountain View, CA: Mayfield.

Gonzalez-Mena, J. (2008). *Diversity in early care and education: Honoring differences.* Washington, DC: NAEYC.

Goodwyn, S. W., Acredolo, L. P., & Brown, C. (2000). Impact of symbolic gesturing on early language development. *Journal of Nonverbal Behavior, 24,* 81–103. Retrieved March 4, 2006, from http://www.babysigns.com.

Gordon, A., & Browne, K. W. (1996). *Guiding young children in a diverse society.* Needham Heights, MA: Allyn & Bacon.

Gordon, T. (1970). *Parent effectiveness training.* New York: Peter Wyden.

Gough, P. B. (1993). Dealing with diversity. *Phi Delta Kappan, 75*(1), 3.

Gowen, J. W., & J. B. Nebrig. (2002). *Enhancing early emotional development: Guiding parents of young children.* Baltimore, MD: Paul H. Brookes.

Graziano, A. M., Hamblen, J. L., & Plante, W. A. (1996). Subabusive violence in child rearing in middle-class American families. *Pediatrics,* October, *98,* 845–848.

Green, R. W. (1998). *The explosive child.* New York: Harper Collins.

Green, V., & Stafford, S. H. (1997). Preschool integration: Strategies for teachers. In K. M. Paciorek & J. H. Munro (Eds.), *Annual editions: Early childhood education 97/98* (18th ed.). New York: McGraw-Hill. (Original work published in *Childhood Education,* Summer 1996).

Greene, R. W. (2001). *The explosive child: A new approach for understanding and parenting easily frustrated, chronically inflexible children.* New York: HarperCollins.

Greene, R. W., Biederman, J., Zerwas, S., Monuteaux, M. C., Goring, J. C., & Faraone, S. V. (2002). Psychiatric comorbidity, family dysfunction, and social impairment in referred youth with oppositional defiant disorder. *The American Journal of Psychiatry, 159*(7), 1214–1224.

Greenenough, W. E., Black, J. E., & Wallace, C. S. (1993). Experience and brain development. In M. Johnson (Ed.), *Brain development and cognition: A reader.* Oxford, UK: Blackwell.

Griffin, E. (1997). *A first look at communication theory.* New York: McGraw-Hill.

Grodeck, B., & Berger, D. S. (2007). *The first year: HIV: An essential guide for the newly diagnosed.* Washington, DC: Marlowe.

Grolnick, W. S., & Ryan, R. M. (1989). Parents' styles associated with children's self-regulation and competence in school. *Journal of Educational Psychology, 81,* 143–154.

Gronlund, G. (1997). Families and schools: Bringing the DAP message to kindergarten and primary teachers. In K. M. Paciorek & J. H. Munro (Eds.), *Annual editions: Early childhood education 97/98* (18th ed.). New York: McGraw-Hill. (Original work published in *Young Children,* July 1995).

Grusec, J. E., Kuczynski, L., Rushton, J. P., & Simutis, Z. (1979). Learning resistance to temptation through observation. *Developmental Psychology, 15,* 233–240.

Grych, J. H., & Fincham, F. D. (1990). Marital conflict and children's adjustment: A cognitive-contextual framework. *Psychological Bulletin, 108,* 267–290.

Grych, J. H., & Fincham, F. D. (1993). Children's appraisals of marital conflict: Initial investigations of the cognitive-contextual framework. *Child Development, 64,* 215–230.

Gudykunst, W. B., Ting-Toomey, S., & Nishida, T. (1996). *Communication in personal relationships across cultures.* Thousand Oaks, CA: Sage.

Gunzerath, L., Faden, V., Zakhari, S., & Warren, K. (2004). National Institute on Alcohol Abuse and Alcoholism report on moderate drinking. *Alcoholism: Clinical and Experimental Research, 28,* 829–847.

Gupta, V. B., Ed. (2004). *Autistic spectrum disorders in children.* New York: Marcel Dekker.

Gutek, G. L. (1997). *Historical and philosophical foundations of education: A biographical introduction* (2nd ed.). Upper Saddle River, NJ: Merrill Education/Prentice Hall.

Hall, J. A. (1997). *Nonverbal communication in human interaction* (4th ed.). Fort Worth, TX: Harcourt Brace.

Hamburg, D. A. (1992). *Today's children.* New York: Times Books.

Hamilton, R., & Ghatala, E. (1994). *Learning and instruction.* New York: McGraw-Hill.

Hanson, M. J. (1996). *Teaching the infant with Down syndrome: A guide for parents and professionals* (2nd ed.). Austin, TX: Pro-Ed.

Harding, C. G., & Golinkoff, R. M. (1979). The origins of intentional vocalizations in prelinguistic infants. *Child Development, 50,* 33–40.

Harlow, H., & Zimmerman, R. (1959). Affectional responses in the infant monkey. *Science, 130,* 421–432.

Harms, T., & Clifford, R. (1998). *Early childhood environment rating scale* (rev. ed.). New York: Teachers College Press.

Harris, J. (1998). Hearing loss. *Audio-Digest Otolaryngology, 31,* 2.

Harris, M., Clibbens, J., Chasin, J., & Tibbitts, R. (1989). The social context of early sign language development. *First Language, 9,* 81–97.

Harrison, A. O., Wilson, M. N., Pine, C. J., Chan, S. Q., & Buriel, R. (1990). Family ecologies of ethnic minority children. *Child Development, 61,* 347–362.

Hartshorne, H., & May, M. A. (1928). *Studies in the nature of character* (Vol. 1). New York: Macmillan.

Hatch, J. A. (2005). *Teaching in the new kindergarten.* Clifton Park, NY: Thomson Delmar Learning.

Hauck F. R., Herman, S. M., Donovan, M., Iyasu, S., Merrick Moore, C., Donoghue, E., Kirschner, R. H., & Willinger, M. (2003). Sleep environment and the risk of Sudden Infant Death Syndrome in an urban population: The Chicago infant mortality study. *Pediatrics, 111,* 1207–1214.

Heineman, R. V. (1998). *The abused child psychodynamic: Understanding and treatment.* New York: Guilford.

Helm, J. H. (2004). Projects that power young minds. *Educational leadership, 62*(1), 58–62.

Henderson, Z. P. (1995). Renewing our social fabric. *Human Ecology, 23*(1), 16–19.

Hernandez, D. J. (1997). Changing demographics: Past and future demands for early childhood programs. In K. M. Paciorek & J. H. Munro (Eds.), *Annual editions: Early childhood education 97/98* (18th ed.). New York: McGraw-Hill. (Original work published in *The Future of Children,* Winter 1995).

Hess, E. (1972). Imprinting in a natural laboratory. *Scientific American, 227,* 24–31.

Hess, R., & Shipman, V. (1967). Parents as teachers: How lower and middle class mothers teach. In C. S. Lavatelli & F. Stendler (Eds.), *Readings in child behavior and development* (3rd ed.). New York: Harcourt Brace Jovanovich.

Heylighen, F. (1992). A cognitive systematic reconstruction of Maslow's theory of self-actualization. *Behavioral Science, 37,* 39–58.

Hildebrand, V. (1997). *Introduction to early childhood education* (6th ed.). Upper Saddle River, NJ: Merrill Education/Prentice Hall.

Hildebrand, V., Phenice, L. A., Gray, M. M., & Hines, R. P. (1996). *Knowing and serving diverse families.* Upper Saddle River, NJ: Merrill Education/Prentice Hall.

Hill, W. M. (2004). *Head start info: Time out letter 2.* Washington, DC: Head Start Bureau. Retrieved March 4, 2006, from http://www.headstartinfo.org/.

Hochschild, A. R. (1997). *The time bind: When work becomes home and home becomes work.* New York: Holt.

Hodapp, R. M., Dykens, E. M., & Masino, L. (1997). Stress and support in families of persons with Prader-Willi syndrome. *Journal of Autism and Developmental Disorders, 27,* 11–24.

Hoffman, L., & Manis, J. D. (1979). The value of children in the United States: A new approach to the study of fertility. *Journal of Marriage and the Family, 41,* 583–596.

Hoffman, M. L. (1979). Development of moral thought, feeling, and behavior. *American Psychologist, 34,* 958–967.

Hoffman, M. L., & Saltzstein, H. D. (1967). Parent discipline and the child's moral development. *Journal of Personality and Social Psychology, 5,* 45–57.

Hoffman-Plotkin, D., & Twentyman, C. T. (1984). A multimodal assessment of behavioral and cognitive deficits in abused and neglected preschoolers. *Child Development, 55,* 794–802.

Holmes-Lonergan, H. A. (2003, June). Preschool children's collaborative problem-solving interactions: The role of gender, pair type, and task—1. *Sex Roles: A Journal of Research, 48*(13), 505–517.

Honig, A. S. (2000). *Love and learn: Positive guidance for young children.* Brochure. Washington, DC: Author.

Honig, A. S., & Wittmer, D. S. (1997). Helping children become more prosocial: Ideas for classrooms. In

K. M. Paciorek & J. H. Munro (Eds.), *Annual editions: Early childhood education 97/98* (18th ed.). New York: McGraw-Hill. (Original work published in *Young Children*, January 1996).

Hopkin, K. (1998). *Understanding cystic fibrosis.* Oxford: University Press of Mississippi.

Howard, F., & Toossi, M. (2001, November). Labor force projections to 2010: Steady growth and changing composition. *Monthly Labor Review, 21–38.*

Howard, G. R. (1993). Whites in multicultural education: Rethinking our role. *Phi Delta Kappan, 75*(1), 36–41.

Huizink, A. C., & Mulder, E. J. (2006). Maternal smoking, drinking or cannabis use during pregnancy and neurobehavioral and cognitive functioning in human offspring. *Neuroscience and Biobehavioral Reviews, 30,* 24–41.

Hunt, J. (1976). The psychological development of orphanage-reared infants: Interventions with outcomes (Tehran). *Genetic Psychology Monographs, 94,* 177–226.

Hutchings, J., & Lane, E. (2005). Parenting and the development and prevention of child mental health problems. *Current Opinion in Psychiatry, 18*(4), 386–391.

Hyman, I. A. (1997). *The case against spanking: How to discipline your child without hitting.* San Francisco, CA: Jossey-Bass.

ICON Health Publications. (2002). *The official parent's sourcebook on Rett syndrome: A revised and updated directory for the internet age.* San Diego, CA: Author.

ICON Health Publications. (2003). *Human immunodeficiency virus: A bibliography, medical dictionary, and annotated research guide to internet references.* San Diego, CA: Author.

ICON Health Publications. (2004a). *Angelman Syndrome: A medical dictionary, bibliography, and annotated research guide to internet references.* San Diego, CA: Author.

ICON Health Publications. (2004b). *Celiac Sprue: A medical dictionary, bibliography, and annotated research guide to internet references.* San Diego, CA: Author.

ICON Health Publications. (2004c). *Kawasaki disease: A medical dictionary, bibliography, and annotated research guide to Internet references.* San Diego, CA: Author.

ICON Health Publications. (2004d). *Noonan syndrome: A medical dictionary, bibliography, and annotated research guide to internet references.* San Diego, CA: Author.

ICON Health Publications. (2004e). *Spina bifida: A medical dictionary, bibliography, and annotated research guide to internet references.* San Diego, CA: Author.

ICON Health Publications. (2004f). *Tay-Sachs disease: A medical dictionary, bibliography, and annotated research guide to internet references.* San Diego, CA: Author.

ICON Health Publications. (2004g). *Williams Syndrome: A medical dictionary, bibliography, and annotated research guide to internet references.* San Diego, CA: Author.

Improving School Readiness Project. (2001). *Early to rise: Improving the school readiness of Philadelphia's young children.* Philadelphia, PA: United Way of Southeastern Pennsylvania and School District of Philadelphia.

Ingegerd, A. K., & Engerstrom, W., Eds. (2005). *Rett disorder and the developing brain.* New York: Oxford University Press.

Ingrassia, M., & McCormick, J. (1997). Why leave children with bad parents? In E. N. Junn & C. Boyatzis (Eds.), *Annual editions: Child growth and development 97/98* (4th ed.). New York: McGraw-Hill. (Original work published in *Newsweek*, April 25, 1994).

Jackson, B. R. (1997, November). Creating a climate for healing in a violent society. *Young Children, 52*(7), 68–70.

Jacobson J. L., & Jacobson, S. W. (1994). Prenatal alcohol exposure and neurobehavioral development: where is the threshold? *Alcohol Health & Research World, 18,* 30–36.

Jacobson, J. L., & Jacobson, S. W. (2002). Effects of prenatal alcohol exposure on child development. *Alcohol Research & Health, 26*(4), 282–286.

Jaworski, M. (2000, October 3). Signs of intelligent life. *Family Circle, 14.*

Jenkins, J., Simpson, A., Dunn, J., Rasbash, J., & O'Connor, T. G. (2005). Mutual influence of marital conflict and children's behavior problems: Shared and nonshared family risks. *Child Development, 76,* 24–39.

Jenny, C., Hymel, K. P., Ritzen, A., Reinert, S. E., & Hay, T. C. (1999). Abusive head trauma: An analysis of missed cases. *Journal of the American Medical Association, 281,* 621–626.

Jensen, P. S. (1999). Are stimulants overprescribed? Treatment of ADHD in four U.S. communities. *Journal of the American Academy of Child and Adolescent Psychiatry, 38*(7), 797–804.

Joe, J. R., & Malach, R. S. (1998). Families with Native American roots. In E. W. Lynch & M. J. Hanson (Eds.), *Developing cross-cultural competence: A guide for working with young children and their families.* Baltimore, MD: Paul H. Brookes.

Johnson, D. (1992). I can't sit still: Educating and affirming inattentive and hyperactive children: Suggestions for parents, teachers, and other care providers of children to age 10. Santa Cruz, CA: ETR Associates.

Kagan, J. (1971). *Change and continuity in infancy.* New York: Wiley.

Kagan, J. (1984). *The nature of the child.* New York: Basic Books.

Kagan, J. (1998). Biology and the child. In W. Damon (Series Ed.) & N. Eisenberg (Vol. Ed.), *Handbook of child psychology: Vol. 3. Social, emotional, and personality development* (pp. 177–236). New York: Wiley.

Kagan, J. (2004). The uniquely human in human nature. *Daedalus, 133*(4), 77–89.

Kagan, J., Kearsley, R. B., & Zelazo, P. R. (1978). *Infancy: Its place in human development.* Cambridge, MA: Harvard University Press.

Kagan, J., & Moss, H. (1962). *Birth to maturity.* New York: Wiley.

Kagan, J., & Snidman, N. (2004). *The long shadow of temperament.* Cambridge, MA: Harvard University Press.

Kagan, J., Snidman, N., Arcus, D., & Reznick, J. S. (1998). *Galen's prophecy: Temperament in human nature.* Boulder, CO: Basic Books.

Kagan, J., Snidman, N., Zentner, M., & Peterson, E. (1999). Infant temperament and anxious symptoms in school age children. *Development and Psychopathology, 11,* 209–224.

Kagan, S. L. (1997, May). Support systems for children, youths, families, and schools in inner-city situations. *Education and Urban Society, 29*(3), 277–295.

Kahn, R. S., Khoury, J., Nichols, W. C., & Lanphear, B. P. (2003). Role of dopamine transporter genotype and maternal prenatal smoking in childhood hyperactive-impulsive, inattentive, and oppositional behaviors. *Journal of Pediatrics, 143,* 104–110.

Kalisz, K., Ekvall, S., & Palmer, S. (1978). Pica and lead intoxication. In S. Palmer & S. Ekvall (Eds.), *Pediatric nutrition in developmental disorders* (150–155). Springfield, IL: Charles C. Thomas.

Kalyanpur, M., & Harry, B. (1999). *Culture in Special Education: Building reciprocal family-professional relationships.* Baltimore, MD: Paul H. Brookes.

Kamerman, S. B., & Gatenio, S. (2003). Overview of the current policy context. In D. Cryer & R. M. Clifford (Eds.), *Early childhood education and care in the USA.* Baltimore, MD: Paul H. Brookes.

Kantrowitz, B., & Wingert, P. (1997). How kids learn. In E. N. Junn & C. Boyatzis (Eds.), *Annual editions: Child growth and development 97/98* (4th ed.). New York: McGraw-Hill. (Original work published in *Newsweek,* April 17, 1989).

Katz, I. (1981). *Stigma: A social psychological analysis.* Hillsdale, NJ: Erlbaum.

Katz, L. G., & McClellan, D. E. (1997). *Fostering children's social competence: The teacher's role.* Washington, DC: NAEYC.

Katz, P. A. (1982). Development of children's racial awareness and intergroup attitudes. In L. Katz (Ed.), *Current topics in early childhood education* (Vol. 4). Norwood, NJ: Ablex.

Kaye, K. (1982). *The mental and social life of babies.* Chicago: University of Chicago Press.

Keenan, K., & Wakschlag, L. S. (2000). More than the terrible twos: The nature and severity of disruptive behavior problems in clinic-referred preschool children. *The Journal of Abnormal Child Psychology, 28,* 33–46.

Keirsey, D. (1998). *Please understand me II: Temperament, character, intelligence* (5th ed.). Del Mar, CA: Prometheus Nemesis.

Keller, H. (1903). *Optimism: An essay.* New York: T. Y. Crowell.

Kempe, R. S., & Kempe, C. H. (1978). *Child abuse.* Cambridge, MA: Harvard University Press.

Kepron, W. (2004). *Cystic fibrosis: Everything you need to know.* Ontario, Canada: Firefly Books.

Kessler, R. C., Sonnega, A., Bromet, E., Hughes, M., & Nelson, C. B. (1995). Posttraumatic stress disorder in the national comorbidity survey. *Arch Gen Psychiatry, 52,* 1048–1060.

Kimmel, M. (2000). *Gendered lives.* New York: Oxford University Press.

Kimmel, M. A. (2004). *The gendered society* (2nd ed.). New York: Oxford University Press.

Kivel, P. 2002. *Uprooting racism: How White people can work for racial justice* (2nd ed.). Gabriola Island, BC, Canada: New Society.

Knapp, M., & Vangelisti, A. (1992). *Interpersonal communication and human relationships.* Boston, MA: Allyn & Bacon.

Knowlson, J. (1996). *Damned to fame: The life of Samuel Beckett.* New York: Simon & Schuster.

Kochanek, T. T., & Buka, S. L. (1998). Influential factors in the utilization of early intervention services. *Journal of Early Intervention, 21*(4), 323–338.

Kochanska, G. (1997). Mutually responsive orientation between mothers and their young children: Implications for early socializaton. *Child Development, 68,* 94–112.

Kochanska, G., & Aksan, N. (1995). Mother-child mutually positive affect, the quality of child compliance to requests and prohibitions, and maternal control as correlates of early internalization. *Child Development, 66,* 236–254.

Kohlberg, L. (1969). Stage and sequence: The cognitive-developmental approach to socialization. In D. Goslin (Ed.), *Handbook of socialization theory and research.* Skokie, IL: Rand-McNally.

Kohlberg, L. (1976). Moral stages and moralization: The cognitive-developmental approach. In T. Lickona (Ed.), *Moral development and behavior.* New York: Holt, Rinehart & Winston.

Kohlberg, L., & DeVries, R. (1987). *Constructivist early education: Overview and comparison with other programs.* Washington, DC: National Association for the Education of Young Children.

Kohn, A. (1990). *The brighter side of human nature: Altruism and empathy in everyday life.* New York: Basic Books.

Kohn, A. (1993). *Punished by rewards: The trouble with gold stars, incentive plans, A's, praise, and other bribes.* Boston, MA: Houghton Mifflin.

Kohn, A. (1994). *The risks of rewards.* ERIC Clearinghouse on Elementary and Early Childhood Education. Urbana, IL: Eric Clearinghouse, document no. ED376990. Retrieved April 22, 2006, from http://www.ed.gov/.

Kokenes, B. (1974). Grade level differences in factors of self-esteem. *Developmental Psychology, 10,* 954–958.

Koplow, L. (2002). *Creating schools that heal: Real-life solutions.* New York: Teachers College Press.

Koskentausta, T. (2006). *Psychiatric disturbances in children with intellectual disability: Prevalence, risk factors and assessment.* Helsinki, Finland: University of Helsinki.

Kottler, J. A. (2000). *Nuts and bolts of helping.* Boston, MA: Pearson Education.

Kras, E. (1995). *Management in two cultures—Bridging the gap between U.S. and Mexico.* Yarmouth, ME: Intercultural Press.

Kreidler, W. J. (1984). *Creative conflict resolution: More than 200 activities for keeping peace in the classroom.* Goodyear Education Series. Santa Monica, CA: Goodyear.

Krupinski, E., & Weikel, D. (1986). *Death from child abuse and no one heard.* Winter Park, FL: Currier-Davis.

Kuhl, P. K. (1981). Auditory category formation and developmental speech perception. In R. Stark (Ed.), *Language behavior in infancy and early childhood.* New York: Elsevier.

Kumar, A., & Dhanda, R. (1997). The identification and management of deaf children. *Indian Journal of Pediatrics,* November–December, *64*(6), 785–792.

Kurcinka, M. S. (1991). *Raising your spirited child: A guide for parents whose child is more intense, sensitive, perceptive, persistent, energetic.* New York: Harper Perennial.

Kutscher, M. L. (2006). *Children with seizures: A guide for parents, teachers, and other professionals.* Philadelphia, PA: Jessica Kingsley.

Ladd, R. E., Ed. (1996). *Children's rights revisioned: Philosophical readings.* Belmont, CA: Wadsworth.

Lamb, M. E. (1978). Infant social cognition and "second-order" effects. *Infant Behavior and Development, 1,* 1–10.

Lamb, M. E. (1981). *The role of the father in childhood development* (2nd ed.). New York: Wiley.

Lamb, M. E., Gaensbauer, T. J., Malkin, C. M., & Schultz, L. A. (1985). The effects of child maltreatment on security of infant-adult attachment. *Infant Behavior and Development, 8,* 35–45.

Lamborn, S. D., Mounts, N. S., Steinberg, L., & Dornbush, S. M. (1991). Patterns of competence and adjustment among adolescents from authoritative, authoritarian, indulgent, and neglectful families. *Child Development, 62,* 1049–1065.

Landreth, C., & Johnson, B. (1953). Young children's responses to a picture inset test designed to reveal reactions to persons of different skin color. *Child Development, 24,* 63–80.

Landy, S. (2002). *Pathways to competence: Encouraging healthy social and emotional development in young children.* Baltimore, MD: Paul H. Brookes.

Lane, R. D. (2000). Levels of emotional awareness: Neurological, psychological and social perspectives. In R. Bar-On and J. D. A. Parker (Eds.), *Handbook of emotional intelligence.* San Francisco, CA: Jossey-Bass.

Lane, R. D., & McRae, K. (2004). Neural substrates of conscious emotional experience: A cognitive-neuroscientific perspective. In B. M. Amsterdam & J. Benjamins

(Eds.), *Consciousness, emotional self-regulation and the brain.* San Francisco, CA: Jossey-Bass.

Langlois, J. H., & Downs, A. C. (1979). Peer relations as a function of physical attractiveness: The eye of the beholder or behavioral reality? *Child Development, 50,* 409–418.

Larzelere, R. E. (1986). Moderate spanking: Model or deterrent of children's aggression in the family? *Journal of Family Violence, 1*(1), 27–36.

Lasser, P. (1999). *Challenges and opportunities–A handbook for teachers of students with special needs with a focus on Fetal Alcohol Syndrome (FAS) and partial Fetal Alcohol Syndrome (pFAS).* Vancouver, BC: Vancouver School Board of Education.

Lavigne, J. V., Cicchetti C., Gibbons, R. D., Binns, H. J., Larsen, L., & Devito, C. (2001). Oppositional defiant disorder with onset in preschool years: Longitudinal stability and pathways to other disorders. *Journal of the American Academy for Child and Adolescent Psychiatry, 40*(12), 1393–1400.

Leach, P. (1996, July 9). *Spanking: A shortcut to nowhere.* Retrieved April 22, 2006, from http://www.nospank.net/leach.htm/.

Lefkowitz, M. M., & Tesiny, E. P. (1980). Dejection and depression: Prospective and contemporaneous analyses. *Developmental Psychology, 20, 776–786.*

Leland, J. (1997). Violence, reel to real. In E. N. Junn & C. Boyatzis (Eds.), *Annual editions: Child growth and development 97/98* (4th ed.). New York: McGraw-Hill. (Original work published in *Newsweek*, December 11, 1995).

Leong, D., & Bodrova, E. (1996). *Tools of the mind: A Vygotskian approach to early childhood education.* Upper Saddle River, NJ: Merrill Education/Prentice Hall.

Lerner, J. W., & Kline F. (2005). *Learning disabilities and related disorders: Characteristics and teaching strategies.* Boston, MA: Houghton Mifflin.

Lerner, R. M., & Lerner, J. V. (1977). Effects of age, sex, and physical attractiveness on child-peer relations, academic performance, and elementary school adjustment. *Developmental Psychology, 13,* 585–590.

Lickona, T. (1983). *Raising good children.* New York: Bantam Books.

Lickona, T. (1991). *Educating for character: How our schools can teach respect and responsibility.* New York: Bantam Books.

Lier, P., Vitaro, F., & Eisner, M. (2007). Preventing aggressive and violent behavior: Using prevention programs to study the role of peer dynamics in maladjustment problems. *European Journal on Criminal Policy and Research.* Published online, June. Retrieved September 19, 2007, from http://www.springerlink.com/content/tu7t754485u15041/.

Lindjord, D. (1997, November–December). Child care: The continuing crisis for working families and child care teachers. *Journal of Early Education and Family Review, 5*(2), 6–7.

Lindsay, R. L. (2002). Bedsharing/cosleeping: The data neither condemns nor endorses. *AAP Grand Rounds, 8,* 46–47.

Liptak, G. S. (2001). Cerebral palsy. In R. A. Hoekelman (Ed.), *Primary pediatric care,* 468–473. St. Louis, MO: Mosby.

Loeb, S., Fuller, B., Kagan, S. L., & Carrol, B. (2004). Child care in poor communities: Early learning effects of type, quality, and stability. *Child Development, 75,* 47–65.

Loeber, R., Burke, J. D., Lahey, B. B., Winters, A., & Zera, M. (2000). Oppositional defiant and conduct disorder: A review of the past 10 years, part I. *Journal of the American Academy for Child and Adolescent Psychiatry, 39*(12), 1468–1484.

Lorenz, K. (1966). *On aggression.* New York: Harcourt, Brace & World.

Lubeck, S. (1985). *Sandbox society: Early education in black and white America.* London: Falmer.

Lum, D. (1992). *Social work practice & people of color.* Brooks/Cole.

Lupi, M. H. (1988). Education of the child with Prader-Willi syndrome. In L. R. Greenswag & R. C. Alexander (Eds.), *Management of Prader-Willi syndrome* (113–123). New York: Springer-Verlag.

Lutkenhoff, M. (1999). *Children with spina bifida: A parent's guide.* Bethesda, MD: Woodbine House.

Lynch, B. J. (2000). *Guide to diagnosis, investigation and treatment of epilepsy.* Cambridge, MA: Novartis.

Lynch, E. W., & Hanson, M. J., Eds. (1998). *Developing cross-cultural competence: A guide for working with children and their families* (2nd ed.). Baltimore, MD: Paul H. Brookes.

Lyness, D. (2005). Depression. *Teens Health,* September. Retrieved September 14, 2007, from http://www.kidshealthorg/teen/your_mind/mental_health/depression.html.

Maj, M., Magliano, L., Pirozzi, R., Marasco, C., & Guarneri, M. (1994). Validity of rapid cycling as a course specifier for bipolar disorder. *American Journal of Psychiatry, 151,* 1015–1029.

Majors, R., & Billson, J. M. (1992). *Cool pose: The dilemmas of black manhood in America.* New York: Touchstone.

Manassis, K. (2007). When attention-deficit/hyperactivity disorder co-occurs with anxiety disorders: Effects on treatment. *Expert Review of Neurotherapeutics,* August, *7*(8), 981–988.

Mantagu, A. 1986. *Touching: The significance of the skin.* New York: Harper & Row.

Marlowe, M. (1986). Metal pollutant exposure and behavior disorders: Implications for school practices.

Marshall, M. J. (2002). *Why spanking doesn't work: Stopping this bad habit and getting the upper hand on effective discipline.* Springville, UT: Bonneville Books.

Martin, S. (2006). *Teaching motor skills to children with cerebral palsy and similar movement disorders: A guide for parents and professionals.* Bethesda, MD: Woodbine House.

Maslow, A. (1993). *The farther reaches of human nature* (Esalen Book reprint ed.). Manhattan Beach, CA: Arkana.

Maslow, A. H. (1943, July). A theory of human motivation. *Psychological Review, 50,* 370–396.

Maslow, A. H. (1970). *Motivation and personality* (2nd ed.). New York: Harper & Row.

Matthews, G., Roberts, R. D., & Zeidner, M. (2003). Development of emotional intelligence: A skeptical—but not dismissive—perspective. *Human Development, 46,* 109–114.

Matthews, G., Zeidner, M., & Roberts, R. D. (2002). *Emotional intelligence: Science and myth.* Cambridge, MA: MIT Press.

Mayes, L. C., & Cohen, D. (2001). *The Yale child study center guide to understanding your child.* New York: Little Brown.

McAlister, B. G. (1997, Spring). Growing up in a violent world: The impact of family and community violence on young children and their families. *Topics in Early Childhood Special Education, 17*(1), 74–102.

McCauley, J., Kern, D. E., Kolodner, K., Dill, L., Schroeder, A. F., DeChant, H. K., Ryden, J., Derogatis, L. R., & Bass, E. G. (1997). Clinical characteristics of women with a history of childhood abuse: Unhealed wounds. *JAMA, 277,* 1362–1368.

McClellan, J., & Werry, J. (1997). Practice parameters for the assessment and treatment of adolescents with bipolar disorder. *Journal of the American Academy of Child and Adolescent Psychiatry, 36*(10), 157S–176S.

McClelland, M. M., Morrison, F. J., & Holmes, D. L. (2000). Children at risk for early academic problems: The role of learning-related social skills. *Early Childhood Research Quarterly, 15*(3), 307–329.

McCloskey, C. M. (1997). Taking positive steps toward classroom management in preschool: Loosening up without letting it all fall apart. In K. M. Paciorek & J. H. Munro (Eds.), *Annual editions: Early childhood education 97/98* (18th ed.). New York: McGraw-Hill. (Original work published in *Young Children,* March 1996.)

McGraw, M. (1941). *The child in painting.* New York: Greystone Press.

McLean, M. E., Bailey, D. B., Jr., & Wolery, M. (1997). *Assessing infants and preschoolers with special needs* (2nd ed.). Upper Saddle River, NJ: Merrill Education/Prentice Hall.

McLoyd, V. C. (1990). The impact of economic hardship on black families and children: Psychological distress, parenting, and socioemotional development. *Child Development, 61,* 311–346.

McMillan, M. (1930). *The nursery school.* New York: E. P. Dutton.

Meece, J. (1997). *Child and adolescent development for educators.* New York: McGraw-Hill.

Meyers, M., & Jordan, L. (2006). Choice and accommodation in parental child care decisions. *Community Development: Journal of the Community Development Society, 37*(2).

Miller, D. (1986). *Infant/toddler day care in high, middle, and low socio-economic settings: An ethnography of dialectical enculturation and linguistic code.* Unpublished doctoral dissertation, University of Houston, TX.

Miller, D. F. (1989). *First steps toward cultural difference: Socialization in infant/toddler day care.* Washington, DC: Child Welfare League of America.

Miller, J. A. (1999). *The childhood depression sourcebook.* New York: McGraw-Hill.

Miller, N. B., Cowan, P. A., Cowan, C. P., Heatherington, E., & Clingempeel, W. G. (1993). Externalizing in preschoolers and early adolescents: A cross-study replication of a family model. *Developmental Psychology, 29,* 3–18.

Milner, D. (1983). *Children and race.* London: Sage.

Mindes, G., Ireton, H., & Mardell-Czudnowski, C. (1996). *Assessing young children.* Clifton Park, NY: Thomson Delmar Learning.

Mittelman, W. (1991). Maslow's study of self-actualization: A reinterpretation. *Journal of Humanistic Psychology, 31*(1), 114–135.

Moen, P., Elder, G. H., & Luscher, K., Eds. (1995). *Examining lives in context: Perspectives on the ecology of human development*. Washington, DC: American Psychological Association.

Montessori, M. (1968). *Reconstruction in education.* Adyar, Madras, India: Theosophical Publishing House.

Montessori, M. (1971). *Peace and education.* Adyar, Chennai, India: Theosophical Publishing House.

Montessori, M., & Hunt, J. M. (1989). *The Montessori method.* New York: Schocken Books.

Moore, T. (1994). *Care of the soul: A guide for cultivating depth and sacredness in everyday life* (reprint ed.). New York: Harper.

Morland, J. (1972). Racial acceptance and preference in nursery school children in a southern city. In A. R. Brown (Ed.), *Prejudice in children.* Springfield, IL: Charles C. Thomas.

MTA Cooperative Group. (2004). 24-month outcomes of treatment strategies for attention-deficit/hyperactivity disorder (ADHD): The NIMH MTA follow-up. *Pediatrics, 113,* 754–761.

Musher-Eizenman, D. R., Holub, S. C., Miller, A. B., Goldstein, S. E., & Edwards-Leaper, L. (2004). Body size stigmatization in pre-school children: The role of control attributions. *Journal of Pediatric Psychology, 29,* 613–620.

Mussen, P. H., & Eisenberg-Berg, N. (1977). *Roots of caring, sharing and helping.* San Francisco, CA: Freeman.

National Association for the Education of Young Children (NAEYC). (1993). Enriching classroom diversity with books for children, in-depth discussion of them, and story-extension activities. *Young Children, 48*(3), 10–12.

National Association for the Education of Young Children (NAEYC) Position Paper (1997). *Time out for "timeout.* Washington, DC: Author. Retrieved March 4, 2006, from http://www.naeyc.org/.

National Association for the Education of Young Children. (2005). *Code of ethical conduct and statement of commitment: A position statement of the National Association for the Education of Young Children.* Washington, DC: Author.

National Association of Child Care Resource and Referral Agencies. (2006). *Why care about child care?* Arlington, VA: NACCRRA.

National Association of Child Care Resource and Referral Agencies. (2004). *Child Care in America.* Washington, DC: Author.

National Center for Children in Poverty. (2004). *Low-Income Children in the United States.* New York: Author. Retrieved January 18, 2005.

National Task Force on Fetal Alcohol Syndrome and Fetal Alcohol Effect. (2004). *Fetal alcohol syndrome: Guidelines for referral and diagnosis.* Retrieved September 14, 2007, from http://www.cdc.gov/ncbddd/fas/documents/FAS_guidelines_accessible.pdf.

Nelson, L. J., Rubin, K., & Fox, N. (2005). Social withdrawal, observed peer acceptance, and the development of self-perceptions in children ages 4 to 7 years. *Early Childhood Research Quarterly, 20*(5), 185–200.

O'Brien, J., & Kollock, P. (1997). *The production of social reality: Essays and readings on social interaction.* Thousand Oaks, CA: Pine Forge Press.

O'Donnell, N. S. (2006). *Sparking connections phase II: A multi-site evaluation of community-based strategies to support family, friend and neighbor caregivers of children: Part I: Lessons learned and recommendations.* New York: Families and Work Institute.

Ohtake, Y., Santos, R. M., & Fowler, S. A. (2000). It's a three way conversation: Families, service providers, and interpreters working together. *Young Exceptional Children, 4*(1), 12–18.

Okami, P., Weisner, T., & Olmstead, R. (2002, August). Outcome correlates of parent-child bedsharing: An eighteen-year longitudinal study. *Journal of Developmental & Behavioral Pediatrics, 23*(4), 244–253.

Oliner, S. P., & Oliner, P. M. (1988). *The altruistic personality: Rescuers of Jews in Nazi Europe.* New York: Free Press.

Oliver, B. E., & O'Gorman, G. (1966). Pica and blood lead in psychotic children. *Developmental Medicine and Child Neurology, 8,* 704–706.

Osborn, D. (1980). *Early childhood education in historical perspective.* Athens, GA: Education Association.

Owens, D., & Bassity, K. (2007). *Ohio's parent guide to autism spectrum disorders.* Columbus: Ohio Center for Autism and Low Incidence (OCALI). Retrieved September 29, 2007, from http://www.ocali.org/pdf_family/Parent_Guide.pdf.

Pagon, R. A., Graham, J. M., Zonana, J., & Yong, S. L. (1981). Coloboma, congenital heart disease, and choanal atresia with multiple anomalies: CHARGE association. *Journal of Pediatrics, 99,* 223–227.

Paley, V. (1992). *You can't say you can't play.* Cambridge, MA: Harvard University Press.

Papousek, H. (1967). Conditioning during postnatal development. In Y. Brackbill & G. G. Thompson (Eds.), *Behavior in infancy and early childhood* (259–284). New York: Free Press.

Parke, R. D., & Slaby, R. G. (1983). The development of aggression. In E. M. Hetherington (Ed.), *Handbook of child psychology: Socialization, personality and social development* (4th ed.; Vol. 4, 537–643). New York: Wiley.

Parker, J. N., & Parker, P. M., Eds. (2002). *The official patient's sourcebook on velocardiofacial syndrome.* San Diego, CA: Icon Health Publications.

Parker, J. N., & Parker, P. M. (2005). *The official patient's sourcebook on sickle cell anemia.* San Diego, CA: Icon Health Publications.

Parrillo, V. N. (1985). *Strangers to these shores: Race and ethnic relations in the United States* (2nd ed.). Boston, MA: Houghton Mifflin.

Patterson, C. H., & Hidore, S. C. (1997). *A caring, loving relationship.* Northvale, NJ: Jason Aronson.

Patterson, G. R., Reid, J. B., & Dishion, T. (1992). *Antisocial boys: A social interactional approach* (Vol. 4). Eugene, OR: Castalia.

Pearce, K. A., & Pearce, W. B. (2001). The public dialogue consortium's school-wide dialogue process: A communicative approach to develop citizenship skills and enhance school climate. *Communication Theory, 11,* 105–123.

Pearce, W. B., & Pearce, K. A. (2000). Extending the theory of the coordinated management of meaning (CMM) through a community dialogue process. *Communication Theory, 10,* 405–424.

Pearson, J. C., & Nelson, P. (1994). *Understanding and sharing: An introduction to speech communication.* Madison, WI: Brown & Benchmark.

Perry, B. D., Czyzewski, D., Lopez, M., Spiller, L., & Treadwell-Deering, D. (1998). Neuropsychologic impact of facial deformities in children: Neurodevelopmental role of the face in communication and bonding. *Clinics in Plastic Surgery, 25,* 587–597. Retrieved from http://www.childtrauma.org/ctamaterials/craniocy.asp.

Petersen, E. A. (1996). *A practical guide to early childhood planning, methods and materials: The what, why and how of lesson plans.* Needham Heights, MA: Allyn & Bacon.

Peterson, L. (1983). Influence of age, task competence, and responsibility focus on children's altruism. *Developmental Psychology, 19,* 141–148.

Phillips, C. B. (1988). Nurturing diversity for today's children and tomorrow's leaders. *Young Children, 43*(2), 42–47.

Piaget, J. (1952). *The origins of intelligence in children.* New York: International University Press.

Piaget, J. (1962). *Play, dreams, and imitation in childhood.* New York: W. W. Norton.

Piaget, J. (1963). *The origins of intelligence in children.* New York: W. W. Norton.

Piaget, J. (1968). *On the development of memory and identity.* Barre, MA: Clark University Press.

Piaget, J. (1970). *Science of education and the psychology of the child.* New York: Orion Press.

Piaget, J. (1983). Piaget's theory. In P. H. Mussen (Ed.), *Handbook of child psychology* (4th ed.), and W. Kessen (Ed.), *History, theory, and methods* (Vol. 1). New York: Wiley.

Pitts, D. (2007). *Living on borrowed time: Life with cystic fibrosis.* Bloomington, IN: AuthorHouse.

Pitzer, R. L. (1997, November 9). *Corporal punishment in the discipline of children in the home.* Research update for practitioners presented at the National Council on Family Relations Annual Conference, Washington DC.

Poussaint, A. F., & Linn, S. (1997, Spring/Summer). Fragile: Handle with care. *Newsweek* [Your Child: From Birth to Three, Special Issue], *33.*

Power, F. C., Higgins, A., & Kohlberg, L. (1989). *Lawrence Kohlberg's approach to moral education.* New York: Columbia University Press.

Powers, S. I. (1982). *Family interaction and parental moral development as a context for adolescent moral development.* Unpublished doctoral dissertation, Harvard University.

Pransky, J. (1991). *Prevention: The critical need.* Springfield, MO: Burrell Foundation and Paradigm Press.

Prothrow-Stith, D., & Quaday, S. (1995). *Hidden casualties: The relationship between violence and learning.* Washington, DC: National Health & Education Consortium and National Consortium for African-American Children.

Provence, S., & Lipton, R. C. (1967). *Infants in institutions: A comparison of their development during the first year of life with family-reared infants.* Madison, CT: International Universities Press.

Pueschel, S. M. (2000). *A parent's guide to Down syndrome: Toward a brighter future* (2nd ed.). Baltimore, MD: Paul H. Brooks.

Raikes, H. (1996). A secure base for babies: Applying attachment concepts to the infant care settings. *Young Children, 51*(95), 59–67.

Ramsey, R. G., & Williams, L. R. (2003). *Multicultural education: A resource book.* New York: Routledge Farmer.

Randy, L., Hoover, R. L., & Kindsvatter, R. (1997). *Democratic discipline: Foundation and practice.* Upper Saddle River, NJ: Merrill Education/Prentice Hall.

Raver, C. C. (2002). Emotions matter: Making the case for the role of young children's emotional development for early school readiness. *Social Policy Report, 16*(3), 3–19.

Raver, C. C., & Zigler, E. F. (1997). Social competence: An untapped dimension in evaluating Head Start's success. *Early Childhood Research Quarterly, 12*(4), 363–385.

Reid, G. (2003). *Dyslexia: A practitioners handbook* (3rd ed.). Chichester, UK: Wiley.

Rimm-Kaufman, S. E., La Paro, K. M., Downer, J. T., & Pianta, R. C. (2005). The contribution of classroom setting and quality of instruction to children's behavior in kindergarten classrooms. *The Elementary School Journal, 105*(4), 377–394.

Ritter, J. M., Casey, R. J., & Langlois, J. H. (1991). Adults' responses to infants varying in appearance of age and attractiveness. *Child Development, 62,* 68–82.

Roberts, P. (1997). Fathers' time. In E. N. Junn & C. Boyatzis (Eds.), *Annual editions: Child growth and development 97/98* (4th ed.). New York: McGraw-Hill. (Original work published in *Psychology Today,* May/June 1996).

Robles de Melendez, W., & Ostertag, V. (1997). *Teaching young children in multicultural classrooms: Issues, concepts and strategies.* Clifton Park, NY: Thomson Delmar Learning.

Rose, S., & Meezan, W. (1996). Variations in perceptions of child neglect. *Child Welfare, 75*(2), 139–160.

Rosenblith, J. F., Sims-Knight, J. (1985). *In the beginning: Development in the first two years.* Monterey, CA: Brooks/Cole.

Rosenthal, R., & Jacobson, L. (1968). *Pygmalion in the classroom: Teacher expectations and pupils' intellectual development.* New York: Holt, Rinehart & Winston.

Ross, C., Blanc, H., McNeil, C., Eyberg, S., Hembree-Kigin, T. (1998). Parenting stress in mothers of young children with oppositional defiant disorder and other severe behavior problems. *Child Study Journal, 28,* 93–110.

Rothbart, M. K., & Derryberry, D. (1981). Development of individual differences in temperament. In M. E. Lamb & A. L. Brown (Eds.), *Advances in developmental psychology* (Vol. 1, 37–86). Hillsdale, NJ: Erlbaum.

Rothbart, M. K., Ahadi, S. A., & Evans, D. E. (2000). Temperament and personality: Origins and outcomes. *Journal of Personality and Social Psychology, 78,* 122–135.

Rouse, C., Brooks-Gunn, J., & McLanahan, S. (2005). Introducing the issue. *The Future of Children—School Readiness: Closing Racial and Ethnic Gaps, 15*(1), 12.

Rousseau, J. (1893). *Emile: Or treatise on education.* New York: Appleton.

Ruble, D., & Martin, M. (1998). Gender development. In N. Fisenberg (Vol. Ed.), *Social, emotional, and personality development* (Vol. 3, 933–1016). In W. Damon (Gen. Ed.), *Handbook of child psychology.* New York: Wiley.

Runyan, D., Wattam, C., Ikeda, R., Hassan, F., & Ramiro, L. (2002). Child abuse and neglect by parents and caregivers. In E. Krug, L. L. Dahlberg, J. A. Mercy, A. B. Zwi, & R. Lozano (Eds.). *World Report on Violence and Health.* Geneva, Switzerland: World Health Organization.

Rutter, M. (1976). Family, area, and school influences in the genesis of conduct disorders. In L. Hersov, M. Berber, & D. Shaffer (Eds.), *Aggression and antisocial behavior development.* Oxford, UK: Pergamon Press.

Ryan, R., & Deci, E. (2000). Self-determination theory and the facilitation of intrinsic motivation, social development, and wellbeing. *American Psychologist, 55*(1), 68–78.

Saarni, C. (1990). Emotional competence: How emotions and relationships become integrated. In R. A. Thompson (Ed.), *Socioemotional development. Nebraska symposium on motivation* (Vol. 36, 115–182). Lincoln: University of Nebraska Press.

Sacerdote, A. (2003). *Hope and destiny: A patient's and parent's guide to sickle cell anemia.* Munster, IN: Hilton Publishing.

Saenger, P. (1996). Turner's syndrome. *New England Journal of Medicine,* December, *335*(23), 1749–1754.

Salk, L. (1992). *Familyhood.* New York: Simon & Schuster.

Salovey, P., & Mayer, J. D. (1990). Emotional intelligence. *Imagination, Cognition, and Personality, 9,* 185–211.

Sameroff, J. J., & Cavanagh, P. J. (1979). Learning in infancy: A developmental perspective. In J. D. Osofsky (Ed.), *Handbook of infant development.* New York: Wiley.

Sanders, S. (2002). *Active for life: Developmentally appropriate movement programs for young children.* Washington, DC: NAEYC.

Santrock, J. W. (1997). *Children.* New York: McGraw-Hill.

Schaefer, C. E., & Digeronimo, T. F. (2000). *Ages and stages: A parent's guide to normal childhood development.* New York: Wiley.

Scherer, A. (1988). The epilepsy foundation of America. In H. Reisner (Ed.), *Children with epilepsy: A parent's guide.* Bethesda, MD: Woodbine House.

Schiraldi, G. R. (2000). *Post-traumatic stress disorder sourcebook.* New York: McGraw-Hill.

Schneiderman, C. R., & Harding, J. B. (1984). Social ratings of children with cleft lip by school peers. *Cleft Palate Journal, 21,* 219.

Schulman, K., & Blank, H. (2004). *Child care assistance policies 2001–2004: Families struggling to move forward, states going backward.* Washington, DC: National Women's Law Center.

Schulman, K., & Barnett, W. S. (2005). *The benefits of prekindergarten for middle-income children, NIEER policy report.* New Brunswick, NJ: NIEER.

Schwartz, W. (1995). *A guide to communicating with Asian-American families: For parents/about parents.* New York: ERIC Clearinghouse on Urban Education, document no. ED396014. Retrieved from http://www.eric.ed.gov.

Schweinhart, L. J. (2004). *The High/Scope Perry Preschool study through age 40: Summary, conclusions, and frequently asked questions.* Ypsilanti, MI: High/Scope Educational Research Foundation.

Scott, G., Gillespie, M., & Innes, S. (2003). *Breaking barriers: Poverty, childcare and mothers' transitions to work.* Glasgow, Scotland: Rosemount Lifelong Learning/Scottish Poverty Information Unit.

Seabrook, J. A. (1988). *Introducing children with specific learning disabilities.* Christchurch, New Zealand: McKenzie House.

Sears, R. R., Maccoby, E. E., & Lewin, H. (1957). *Patterns of child rearing.* Evanston, IL: Row & Peterson.

Sears, W. (2008). *Nighttime parenting: How to get your baby and child to sleep.* New York: Plume and La Leche League International Books.

Sears, W., & Sears, M. (2001). *How to get your baby to sleep: America's foremost baby and childcare experts answer the most frequently asked questions.* Charlottesville, VA: LB Collection Books.

Seefeldt, C., & Barbour, N. (1998). *Early childhood education: An introduction* (4th ed.). Upper Saddle River, NJ: Merrill Education/Prentice Hall.

Semel, E., & Rosner, S. R. (2003). *Understanding Williams Syndrome: A Guide to Behavioral Patterns and Interventions.* Mahwah, NJ: Erlbaum.

Shaw, W. C. (1980). Social aspects of dentofacial anomalies. In T. R. Alley, *Social and Applied Aspects of Perceiving Faces.* Hillsdale, NJ: Erlbaum.

Sheldon, A. (1990). Pickle fights: Gendered talk in preschool disputes. *Discourse Processes, 13,* 5–31.

Sherman, J., Rasmussen, C., & Baydala, L. (2006). Thinking positively: How some characteristics of AD/HD can be adaptive and accepted in the classroom. *Childhood Education,* Summer issue, *82,* 4.

Shonkoff, J. P., & Phillips, D. A. (2000). *From neurons to neighborhoods: The science of early childhood development.* Washington, DC: National Academy Press.

Shore, R. (1997). *Rethinking the brain: New insights into early development.* [Executive Summary]. New York: Families & Work Institute.

Shulman, S. T. (1987). *Kawasaki disease.* New York: Wiley.

Shumway-Cook, A., & Woollacott, M. (1995). The growth of stability: Postural control from a developmental perspective. *Journal of Motor Behaviour, 17,* 130–147.

Sickle Cell Advisory Committee. (1999). *Sickle cell disease: Information for school personnel.* Trenton: New Jersey Department of Health and Senior Services.

Sigmundsson, H., Whiting, H. T. A., & Ingvaldsen, R. P. (1999). Clumsy behaviour. *Behavioural Brain Research, 102,* 129–136.

Silvers, J. (1997). Child labor in Pakistan. In E. N. Junn & C. Boyatzis (Eds.), *Annual editions: Child growth and development 97/98* (4th ed.). New York: McGraw-Hill. (Original work published in *The Atlantic Monthly,* February 1996).

Simons, R., Johnson, C., & Conger, R. (1994). Harsh corporal punishment versus quality of parental involvement as an explanation of adolescent maladjustment. *Journal of Marriage and the Family, 56,* 591–607.

Skinner, B. (1953). *Science and human behavior.* New York: Macmillan.

Skinner, B. (1974). *About behaviorism.* New York: Knopf.

Skolnick, A. (1991). *Embattled paradise: The American family in an age of uncertainty.* New York: Basic Books.

Smyth, M. M., & Mason, U. C. (1998). Use of proprioception in normal and clumsy children. *Developmental Medicine and Child Neurology, 40,* 672–681.

Snashall, S. E. (1985). Deafness in children. *British Journal of Hospital Medicine,* April, *33*(4), 205–209.

Snoddon, K. (2000, May). Sign, baby, sign! *World Federation of Deaf News,* 16–17. Retrieved from http://www.hand speak.com/tour/kids/index.php?kids=signbabysign.

Socha, T., & Stamp, G. (1995). *Parents, children and communication: Frontiers of theory and research.* Mahwah, NJ: Erlbaum.

Solomon, D., Watson, M., Battistich, V., Schaps, E., & Delucchi, K. (1992). Creating a caring community: Educational practices that promote children's prosocial development. In F. K. Oser, A. Dick, & J. L. Patry (Eds.), *Effective and responsible teaching: The new synthesis.* San Francisco, CA: Jossey-Bass.

Sood, B., Delaney-Black, V., Covington, C., Nordstrom-Klee, B., Ager, J., & Templin, T. (2001). Prenatal alcohol exposure and childhood behaviour at age 6–7 years: Dose response effect. *Paediatrics, 108*(2), E34–E35.

Spafford, C. S., Pesce, A. I., & Grosser, G. (1998). *The cyclopedic education dictionary.* Clifton Park, NY: Thomson Delmar Learning.

Speltz, M. L., McClellan, J., DeKlyen, M., & Jones, K. (1999). Preschool boys with oppositional defiant disorder: Clinical presentation and diagnostic change. *Journal of the American Academy for Child and Adolescent Psychiatry, 38*(7), 838–845.

Spielberger, C., Ed. (2004). *Encyclopedia of applied psychology.* San Diego, CA: Academic Press.

Spilsbury, L. (2002). *What does it mean to have dyslexia?* Oxford, UK: Heinemann Library.

Sroufe, L. A. (1979). Socioemotional development. In J. Osofsky (Ed.), *Handbook of infant development.* New York: Wiley.

Sroufe, L. A. (1996). *Child development: Its nature and course.* New York: McGraw-Hill.

Stallard, P. (1993). The behaviour of 3-year-old children: Prevalence and parental perception of problem behaviour: A research note. *Journal of Child Psychology and Psychiatry,* March, *34*(3), 413–421.

Steinberg, L. (1995). *Childhood.* New York: McGraw-Hill.

Steinberg, L., Lamborn, S. D., Darling, N., Mounts, N. S., & Dornbush, S. M. (1994). Over-time changes in adjustment and competence among adolescents from authoritative, authoritarian, indulgent, and neglectful families. *Child Development, 65,* 754–770.

Stengel, R. (1997). Fly till I die. In K. M. Paciorek & J. H. Munro (Eds.), *Annual editions: Early childhood education 97/98* (18th ed.). New York: McGraw-Hill. (Original work published in *Time,* April 22, 1996).

Stern, D. N. (1974). Mother and infant at play: The dyadic interaction involving facial, vocal and gaze behaviors. In M. Lewis & L. Rosenblum (Eds.), *The effect of the infant on its caregiver.* New York: Wiley-Interscience.

Stevenson, H. W., & Lee, S. (1990). Contexts of achievement. *Monograph of the Society for Research in Child Development, 55,* 1–2.

Stevenson, H. W., Chen, C., & Uttal, D. H. (1990). Beliefs and achievement: A study of black, white and Hispanic children. *Child Development, 61,* 508–523.

Stien, P. T., & Kendall, J. C. (2003). *Psychological trauma and the developing brain: Neurologically based interventions for troubled children.* Binghamton, NY: Haworth Press.

Stott, L. H., & Ball, R. S. (1957). Consistency and change in ascendance-submission in the social interaction of children. *Child Development, 28,* 259–272.

Straus, M. A. (2001). *Beating the devil out of them: Corporal punishment in American families and its effects on children.* (2nd ed.). New Brunswick, NJ: Transaction Publishers.

Straus, M. A., & Mathur, A. (1996). Social change and change in approval of corporal punishment by parents from 1968 to 1994. In D. Frehsee, W. Horn, & K. D. Bussman (Eds.), *Family violence against children.* Berlin: Walter deGruyter.

Stray-Gundersen, K. (1995). *Babies with Down syndrome: A new parent's guide* (2nd ed.). Bethesda, MD: Woodbine House.

Streissguth, A. P. (1997). *Fetal alcohol syndrome: A guide for families and communities.* Baltimore, MD: Brookes.

Stringer-Seibold, T., Stanberry, A. M., Stanberry, J. P., & Seibold, J. M. (1996, Fall). Strengths and needs of divided families. Research highlights. *Dimensions of Early Childhood, 24*(4), 22–29.

Swanson J., Lerner, M., March, J., & Gresham, F. M. (1999). Assessment and intervention for attention-deficit/hyperactivity disorder in the schools: Lessons from the MTA study. *Pediatric Clinics of North America, 46*(5), 993–1009.

Tannen, D. (1990). *You just don't understand.* New York: William Morrow.

Tannen, D. (2002). *I only say this because I love you.* New York: Ballentine Books.

Tanner-Halverson, K. (1996). A demonstration classroom for young children with FAS. In A. P. Streissguth and J. Kanter (Eds.), *The challenge of fetal alcohol: Overcoming secondary disabilities.* Seattle: University of Washington Press.

Taylor, M. C. (2000). Social contextual strategies for reducing racial discrimination. In S. Oskamp (Ed.), *Reducing prejudice and discrimination.* Mahwah, NJ: Erlbaum.

Teaching Tolerance Project. (1997). *Starting small: Teaching tolerance in preschool and the early grades.* Montgomery, AL: Southern Poverty Law Center.

Thomas, A., & Chess, S. (1977). *Temperament and development.* New York: Brunner/Mazel.

Thomas, A., Chess, S., & Birch, H. G. (1970). The origin of personality. *Scientific American, 233,* 102–109.

Thompson, M., Grace, C., & Cohen, L. (2001). *Best friends, worst enemies: Understanding the social lives of children.* New York: Ballantine.

Thorne, B. (1997). Girls and boys together but mostly apart. In E. N. Junn & C. Boyatzis (Eds.), *Annual editions: Child growth and development 97/98* (4th ed.). New York: McGraw-Hill. (Original work published in *GenderPlay: Girls and Boys in School*, Rutgers University Press, 1993).

Thorpe, K., & Daly, K. (1999). Children, parents and time. The dialectics of control. In C. L. Shehan (Ed.), *Through the eyes of the child: Revisioning children as active agents of family life.* New York: JAI Press.

Tjaden, P., & Thoennes, N. (2000). *Full report of the prevalence, incidence, and consequences of violence against women: Findings from the National Violence Against Women Survey.* Washington, DC: National Institute of Justice (Report No. NCJ 183721).

Tomasello, M., Kruger, A., & Ratner, H. H. (1993). Cultural learning. *Behavioral and Brain Sciences, 16,* 495–552.

Toner, I. J., Parke, R. D., & Yussen, S. R. (1978). The effect of observation of model behavior on the establishment and stability of resistance to deviation in children. *Journal of Genetic Psychology, 132,* 283–290.

Toner, I. J., & Potts, R. (1981). Effect of modeled rationales on moral behavior, moral choice, and level of moral judgment in children. *Journal of Psychology, 107,* 153–162.

Torrey, E. F. (2001). *Surviving schizophrenia: A manual for families, consumers, and providers* (4th ed.). Burlington, MA: Quill Pen Press.

Tower, C. (1996). *Child abuse and neglect.* Boston, MA: Allyn & Bacon.

Trad, P. V. (1986). *Infant depression: Paradigms and paradoxes.* Berlin: Axel Springer Verlag.

Trad, P. V. (1987). *Infant and childhood depression: Developmental factors* (Wiley Series in Child and Adolescent Mental Health). Hoboken, NJ: Wiley.

Trad, P. V. (1991). *Interventions with infants and parents: The theory and practice of previewing.* Hoboken, NJ: Wiley.

Trad, P. V. (1994). *Infant depression.* St. Northvale, NJ: Jason Aronson.

Trawick-Smith, J. (1997). *Early childhood development in multicultural perspective.* Upper Saddle River, NJ: Merrill Education/Prentice Hall.

Trehub, S. (1973). Infants' sensitivity to vowel and tonal contrasts. *Developmental Psychology, 9,* 81–96.

U.S. Department of Health and Human Services (US DHHS), Administration on Children, Youth, and Families (ACF). (2001). *In focus: Understanding the effects of maltreatment on early brain development.* Washington, DC: Government Printing Office.

U.S. Department of Health and Human Services (US DHHS), Administration on Children, Youth, and Families (ACF). (2003b). *Child maltreatment.* Washington, DC: Government Printing Office. Retrieved November 19, 2005, from http://www.acf.hhs.gov/.

U.S. Department of Health and Human Services (US DHHS), Administration for Children and Families, Puma, M., Bell, S., Cook, R., Heid, C., & Lopez, M. (2005). *Head Start impact study: First year findings.* Washington, DC: Government Printing Office.

U.S. Department of Health and Human Services, Administration on Children, Youth, and Families. (2007). *Child maltreatment 2005.* Washington, DC: Government Printing Office.

Ulich, R. (1954). *Three thousand years of educational wisdom.* Cambridge, MA: Harvard University Press.

Van Ausdale, D., & Feagin, J. R. (2001). *The first R: How children learn race and racism.* Lanham, MD: Rowman & Littlefield.

Vance, E., & Weaver, P. (2002). *Class meetings: Young children solving problems together.* Washington, DC: NAEYC.

Vardin, P. A. (2003, Winter). Montessori and Gardner's theory of multiple intelligences. *Montessori Life, 15*(1), 40–43.

Verderber, R. F., & Verderber, K. S. (1998). *Interact: Using interpersonal communication skills.* Belmont, CA: Wadsworth.

von Frisch, K. (1974). Decoding the language of the bee. *Science, 185,* 663–668.

von Goethe, W. (1995). Conversations of German refugees: Wilhelm Meister's journeyman years, or the renunciants (J. Van Heurck, Trans.). In J. K. Brown (Ed.), *Goethe's collected works* (reprint ed.; Vol. 10). Princeton, NJ: Princeton University Press.

von Mutius, E. (2000). The burden of childhood asthma. *Archives of Disease in Childhood,* June, *82,* ii2–ii5.

Wailoo, K. (2001). *Dying in the city of the blues: Sickle cell anemia and the politics of race and health.* Chapel Hill: University of North Carolina Press.

Wakschlag, L. S., Pickett, K. E., Cook, E., Benowitz, N. L., & Leventhal, B. L. (2002). Maternal smoking during pregnancy and severe antisocial behavior in offspring: A review. *American Journal of Public Health, 92,* 966–974.

Wakschlag, L. S., Pickett, K. E., Kasza, K. E., & Loeber, R. (2006). Is prenatal smoking associated with a developmental pattern of conduct problems in young boys? *Journal of the American Academy of Child and Adolescent Psychiatry,* April, *45*(4), 461–467.

Walker, L. J., & Taylor, J. H. (1991). Family interactions and the development of moral reasoning. *Child Development, 62,* 264–283.

Wallach, L. B. (1997). Breaking the cycle of violence. In K. M. Paciorek & J. H. Munro (Eds.), *Annual editions: Early childhood education 97/98* (18th ed.). New York:

McGraw-Hill. (Original work published in *Children Today, 23*[3], 1994–1995).

Waltz, M. (2001). *Tourette's syndrome: Finding answers and getting help.* Sebastopol, CA: O'Reilly.

Wang, C. T., & Daro, D. (1998). *Current trends in child abuse reporting and fatalities: The results of the 1997 annual fifty state survey.* Chicago: National Committee to Prevent Child Abuse.

Warren, S. L., Emde, R. N., & Sroufe, L. A. (2000). Internal representations: Predicting anxiety from children's play narratives. *Journal of American Academy of Child & Adolescent Psychiatry, 39*(1), 100–107.

Watson, J. (1930). *Behaviorism* (2nd ed.). Chicago: University of Chicago Press.

Watson, J. (1973). Smiling, cooing and "the game." *Merrill-Palmer Quarterly, 18,* 323–339.

Watson, M., Ecken, L., & Kohn, A. (2003). *Learning to trust: Transforming difficult elementary classrooms through developmental discipline.* San Francisco, CA: Jossey-Bass.

Webster-Stratton, C. (2000). *How to promote children's social and emotional competence.* London: Paul Chapman.

Wechsler, D. (1958). *The measurement and appraisal of adult intelligence* (4th ed.). Baltimore, MD: Williams & Wilkins.

Weiser, M. (1982). *Group care and education of infants and toddlers.* St. Louis, MO: Mosby.

Weiss, C. D., & Lillywhite, H. S. (1976). *Communicative disorders: A handbook for prevention and early intervention.* St. Louis, MO: Mosby.

Weitzman, M., Byrd, R. S., Aligne, C. A., & Moss, M. (2002). The effects of tobacco exposure on children's behavioral and cognitive functioning: Implications for clinical and public health policy and future research. *Neurotoxicology and Teratology, 24,* 397–406.

Welsh, B. C., & Farrington, D. P. (2007). Key challenges and prospects in peer-based delinquency prevention programs: Comment on van Lier, Vitaro, and Eisner. *European Journal on Criminal Policy and Research.* Published online, June. Retrieved September 19, 2007, from http://www.springerlink.com/content/t164618n6243403p/.

Werner, E. E. (1987). Vulnerability and resiliency in children at risk for delinquency: A longitudinal study from birth to adulthood. In J. D. Burchard & S. N.

Burchard (Eds.), *Primary prevention of psychopathology: Prevention of delinquent behavior* (Vol. 10, 16–43). Newbury Park, CA: Sage.

Werner, N. E., & Evans, I. M. (1971). Perception of prejudice in Mexican-American preschool children. In N. N. Wagner & M. J. Haug (Eds.), *Chicano: Social and psychological perspectives.* St. Louis, MO: Mosby.

White, B., & Watts, J. (1973). *Experience and environment: Major influences on the development of the young child* (Vol. 2). Upper Saddle River, NJ: Prentice Hall.

White, B., Kaban, B., & Attanucci, J. (1979). *The origins of human competence: The final report of the Harvard preschool project.* Lanham, MD: Lexington Books.

White, B. L. (1975). *The first three years of life.* New York: Avon.

White, B. L. (1995). *The new first three years of life* (rev. ed.). New York: Simon & Shuster.

Wilcox-Herzog, A., & Ward, S. L. (2004, Fall). Measuring teachers' perceived interactions with children: A tool for assessing beliefs and intentions. *Early Childhood Research and Practice, 6*(2). Retrieved March 4, 2006, from http://ecrp.uiuc.edu/.

Williams, R. (2001). Culture is ordinary. In J. Higgins (Ed.), *The Raymond Williams reader* (10–24). Oxford, UK: Blackwell.

Williams, G. M., O'Callaghan, M., Najman, J. M., Bor, W., Andersen, M. J., & Richards, D. (1998). Maternal cigarette smoking and child psychiatric morbidity: A longitudinal study. *Pediatrics, 102,* e11.

Winslade, J., & Monk, G. (2000). *Narrative mediation: A new approach to conflict resolution.* San Francisco, CA: Jossey-Bass.

Wittmer, D. S., & Honig, A. S. (1997). Encouraging positive social development in young children. In K. M. Paciorek & J. H. Munro (Eds.), *Annual editions: Early childhood education 97/98* (18th ed.). New York: McGraw-Hill. (Original work published in *Young Children,* July 1994).

Wolff, P. (1963). Observations on the early development of smiling. In B. M. Foss (Ed.), *Determinants of infant behavior* (Vol. 2). London: Methuen.

Wong, B. Y. L. (2004). *Learning about learning disabilities* (3rd ed.). Burlington, MA: Academic Press.

Woolfolk, A. (2004). *Educational psychology* (9th ed.). Boston, MA: Allyn & Bacon.

Worth, K., & Grollman, S. (2003). *Worms, shadows, and whirlpools: Science in the early childhood classroom.* Washington, DC: NAEYC.

Yarrow, A. (1991). *Latecomers: Children of parents over 35.* New York: Free Press.

Yoshinaga-Itano, C. (2004). Levels of evidence: universal newborn hearing screening (UNHS) and early hearing detection and intervention systems (EHDI). *Journal of Communication Disorders, 37*(5), 451–465.

Zahn-Waxler, C., Radke-Yarrow, M., & King, R. A. (1979). Child rearing and children's prosocial initiations towards victims of distress. *Child Development, 50,* 319–330.

Zeanah, C. H., Ed. (2000). *Handbook of infant mental health* (2nd ed.). New York: Guilford.

Zeanah, C. H., Boris, N. W., & Larrieu, J. A. (1997). Infant development and developmental risk: A review of the past 10 years. *Journal of the American Academy of Child & Adolescent Psychiatry, 36*(2), 165–178.

Zeidner, M., Matthews, G., & Roberts, R. D. (2001). Slow down, you move too fast: Emotional intelligence remains an "elusive" intelligence. *Emotion, 1*(3), 265–275.

Zigler, E., Singer, D., & Bishop-Josef, S. (2004). *Children's play: The roots of reading.* Washington, DC: Zero to Three.

Index